Macmillan/McGraw-Hill Edition

McGRAW-HILL READING

McGraw-Hill
School Division

New York   Farmington

Contributors

The Princeton Review, Time Magazine, Accelerated Reader

The Princeton Review is not
affiliated with Princeton
University or ETS.

McGraw-Hill School Division

A Division of The McGraw·Hill Companies

McGraw-Hill School Division
Two Penn Plaza
New York, New York 10121

Printed in the United States of America

ISBN 0-02-184776-2/5, U.6
1 2 3 4 5 6 7 8 9 073 04 03 02 01 00 99

McGRAW-HILL READING

**McGraw-Hill
School Division**

New York   Farmington

Selected Quizzes Prepared by **Accelerated Reader**

McGraw-Hill Reading
Authors
Make the Difference...

Dr. James Flood

Ms. Angela Shelf Medearis

Dr. Jan E. Hasbrouck

Dr. Scott Paris

Dr. James V. Hoffman

Dr. Steven Stahl

Dr. Diane Lapp

Dr. Josefina Villamil Tinajero

Dr. Karen D. Wood

Contributing
Authors

Dr. Barbara Coulter

Ms. Frankie Dungan

Dr. Joseph B. Rubin

Dr. Carl B. Smith

Dr. Shirley Wright

Part 1
START TOGETHER

Focus on Reading and Skills

All students start with the SAME:
- Read Aloud
- Pretaught Skills
  Phonics
  Comprehension
- Build Background
- Selection Vocabulary

...Never hold a child back. Never leave a child behind.

Part 2
MEET INDIVIDUAL NEEDS

Read the Literature

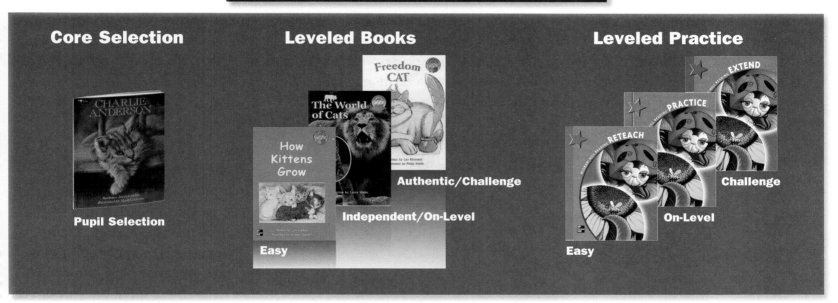

Core Selection

Pupil Selection

Leveled Books

Easy

Independent/On-Level

Authentic/Challenge

Leveled Practice

Easy

On-Level

Challenge

Examples Taken From Grade 2

Part 3
FINISH TOGETHER

Build Skills

All students finish with the SAME:
- Phonics
- Comprehension
- Vocabulary
- Study Skills
- Assessment

McGraw-Hill Reading
Applying the Research

Phonological Awareness

Phonological awareness is the ability to hear the sounds in spoken language. It includes the ability to separate spoken words into discrete sounds as well as the ability to blend sounds together to make words. A child with good phonological awareness can identify rhyming words, hear the separate syllables in a word, separate the first sound in a word (onset) from the rest of the word (rime), and blend sounds together to make words.

Recent research findings have strongly concluded that children with good phonological awareness skills are more likely to learn to read well. These skills can be improved through systematic, explicit instruction involving auditory practice. McGraw-Hill Reading develops these key skills by providing an explicit Phonological Awareness lesson in every selection at grades K-2. Motivating activities such as blending, segmenting, and rhyming help to develop children's awareness of the sounds in our language.

Guided Instruction/ Guided Reading

Research on reading shows that guided instruction enables students to develop as independent, strategic readers. *The reciprocal-teaching model* of Anne-Marie Palincsar encourages teachers to model strategic-thinking, questioning, clarifying, and problem-solving strategies for students as students read together with the teacher. In McGraw-Hill Reading, guided instruction for all Pupil Edition selections incorporates the Palincsar model by providing interactive questioning prompts. *The guided-reading model* of Gay Su Pinnell is also incorporated into the McGraw-Hill Reading program. Through the guided-reading lessons provided for the leveled books offered with the program, teachers can work with small groups of students of different ability levels, closely observing them as they read and providing support specific to their needs.

By adapting instruction to include successful models of teaching and the appropriate materials to deliver instruction, McGraw-Hill Reading enables teachers to offer the appropriate type of instruction for all students in the classroom.

Phonics

Our language system uses an alphabetic code to communicate meaning from writing. Phonics involves learning the phonemes or sounds that letters make and the symbols or letters that represent those sounds. Children learn to blend the sounds of letters to decode unknown or unfamiliar words. The goal of good phonics instruction is to enable students to read words accurately and automatically.

Research has clearly identified the critical role of phonics in the ability of readers to read fluently and with good understanding, as well as to write and spell. Effective phonics instruction requires carefully sequenced lessons that teach the sounds of letters and how to use these sounds to read words. The McGraw-Hill program provides daily explicit and systematic phonics instruction to teach the letter sounds and blending. There are three explicit Phonics and Decoding lessons for every selection. Daily Phonics Routines are provided for quick reinforcement, in addition to activities in the Phonics Workbook and technology components. This combination of direct skills instruction and applied practice leads to reading success.

Curriculum Connections

As in the child's real-world environment, boundaries between disciplines must be dissolved. Recent research emphasizes the need to make connections between and across subject areas. McGraw-Hill Reading is committed to this approach. Each reading selection offers activities that tie in with social studies, language arts, geography, science, mathematics, art, music, health, and physical education. The program threads numerous research and inquiry activities that encourage the child to use the library and the Internet to seek out information. Reading and language skills are applied to a variety of genres, balancing fiction and nonfiction.

Integrated Language Arts

Success in developing communication skills is greatly enhanced by integrating the language arts in connected and purposeful ways. This allows students to understand the need for proper writing, grammar, and spelling. McGraw-Hill Reading sets the stage for meaningful learning. Each week a full writing-process lesson is provided. This lesson is supported by a 5-day spelling plan, emphasizing spelling patterns and spelling rules, and a 5-day grammar plan, focusing on proper grammar, mechanics, and usage.

Meeting Individual Needs

Every classroom is a microcosm of a world composed of diverse individuals with unique needs and abilities. Research points out that such needs must be addressed with frequent intensive opportunities to learn with engaging materials. McGraw-Hill Reading makes reading a successful experience for every child by providing a rich collection of leveled books for easy, independent, and challenging reading. Leveled practice is provided in Reteach, Practice, and Extend skills books. To address various learning styles and language needs, the program offers alternative teaching strategies, prevention/intervention techniques, language support activities, and ESL teaching suggestions.

Assessment

Frequent assessment in the classroom makes it easier for teachers to identify problems and to find remedies for them. McGraw-Hill Reading makes assessment an important component of instruction. Formal and informal opportunities are a part of each lesson. Minilessons, prevention/intervention strategies, and informal checklists, as well as student self-assessments, provide many informal assessment opportunities. Formal assessments, such as weekly selection tests and criterion-referenced unit tests, help to monitor students' knowledge of important skills and concepts. McGraw-Hill Reading also addresses how to adapt instruction based on student performance with resources such as the Alternate Teaching Strategies. Weekly lessons on test preparation, including test preparation practice books, help students to transfer skills to new contexts and to become better test takers.

McGraw-Hill School
TECHNOLOGY

*inter*NET CONNECTION For information on research that supports this program, visit **www.mhschool.com/reading**

McGraw-Hill Reading

Theme Chart

MULTI-AGE Classroom

Using the same global themes at each grade level facilitates the use of materials in multi-age classrooms.

GRADE LEVEL	Experience Experiences can tell us about ourselves and our world.	Connections Making connections develops new understandings.
Kindergarten	**My World** We learn a lot from all the things we see and do at home and in school.	**All Kinds of Friends** When we work and play together, we learn more about ourselves.
Subtheme 1	At Home	Working Together
Subtheme 2	School Days	Playing Together
1	**Day by Day** Each day brings new experiences.	**Together Is Better** We like to share ideas and experiences with others.
2	**What's New?** With each day, we learn something new.	**Just Between Us** Family and friends help us see the world in new ways.
3	**Great Adventures** Life is made up of big and small experiences.	**Nature Links** Nature can give us new ideas.
4	**Reflections** Stories let us share the experiences of others.	**Something in Common** Sharing ideas can lead to meaningful cooperation.
5	**Time of My Life** We sometimes find memorable experiences in unexpected places.	**Building Bridges** Knowing what we have in common helps us appreciate our differences.
6	**Pathways** Reflecting on life's experiences can lead to new understandings.	**A Common Thread** A look beneath the surface may uncover hidden connections.

Themes: Kindergarten – Grade 6

Six Units
IN EVERY GRADE

Expression	Inquiry	Problem-Solving	Making Decisions
There are many styles and forms for expressing ourselves.	By exploring and asking questions, we make discoveries.	Analyzing information can help us solve problems.	Using what we know helps us evaluate situations.
Time to Shine We can use our ideas and our imagination to do many wonderful things.	**I Wonder** We can make discoveries about the wonders of nature in our own backyard.	**Let's Work It Out** Working as part of a team can help me find a way to solve problems.	**Choices** We can make many good choices and decisions every day
Great Ideas	In My Backyard	Try and Try Again	Good Choices
Let's Pretend	Wonders of Nature	Teamwork	Let's Decide
Stories to Tell Each one of us has a different story to tell.	**Let's Find Out!** Looking for answers is an adventure.	**Think About It!** It takes time to solve problems.	**Many Paths** Each decision opens the door to a new path.
Express Yourself We share our ideas in many ways.	**Look Around** There are surprises all around us.	**Figure It Out** We can solve problems by working together.	**Starting Now** Unexpected events can lead to new decisions.
Be Creative! We can all express ourselves in creative, wonderful ways.	**Tell Me More** Looking and listening closely will help us find out the facts.	**Think It Through** Solutions come in many shapes and sizes.	**Turning Points** We make new judgments based on our experiences.
Our Voices We can each use our talents to communicate ideas.	**Just Curious** We can find answers in surprising places.	**Make a Plan** Often we have to think carefully about a problem in order to solve it.	**Sorting It Out** We make decisions that can lead to new ideas and discoveries.
Imagine That The way we express our thoughts and feelings can take different forms.	**Investigate!** We never know where the search for answers might lead us.	**Bright Ideas** Some problems require unusual approaches.	**Crossroads** Decisions cause changes that can enrich our lives.
With Flying Colors Creative people help us see the world from different perspectives.	**Seek and Discover** To make new discoveries, we must observe and explore.	**Brainstorms** We can meet any challenge with determination and ingenuity.	**All Things Considered** Encountering new places and people can help us make decisions.

Our Voices

Creative people express themselves in many ways.

written by **Veronica Chambers**
illustrated by **Paul Lee**

SKILLS			
Comprehension	**Vocabulary**	**Study Skill**	**Phonics**
• **Review** Judgments and Decisions • **Review** Draw Conclusions	• **Review** Context Clues	• Using the Library/ Media Center: Read a Map	• **Review** /ù/ and /yù/

HISTORICAL FICTION

written by **Washington Irving**
dramatized by **Adele Thane**
illustrated by **Gary Kelley**

SKILLS			
Comprehension	**Vocabulary**	**Study Skill**	**Phonics**
• **Review** Cause and Effect • **Review** Draw Conclusions	• **Review** Antonyms and Synonyms	• Using the Library/ Media Center: Conduct an Interview	• **Review** /z/, /j/, and /f/

A PLAY

Unit Planner

	WEEK 1 Amistad Rising: A Story of Freedom	**WEEK 2** Rip Van Winkle
▌▌ Leveled Books	**Easy:** *Flight of the Trumpeters* **Independent:** *Home Across the Ice* **Challenge:** *Maggie Comes Home*	**Easy:** *A Matter of Time* **Independent:** *H.G. Wells, Man of the Future* **Challenge:** *A Knight's Journey*
☑ **Tested Skills**	☑ **Comprehension** Review Judgments and Decisions, 618A–618B, 647E–647F, Review Draw Conclusions, 647G–647H ☑ **Vocabulary** Review Using Context Clues to Build Vocabulary, 647I–647J ☑ **Study Skills** Read a Map, 646	☑ **Comprehension** Review Cause and Effect, 650A–650B, 673E–673F, Review Draw Conclusions, 673G–673H ☑ **Vocabulary** Review Synonyms and Antonyms, 673I–673J ☑ **Study Skills** Conduct an Interview, 672
Minilessons	**Phonics and Decoding:** /u/ and /yu/, 629 **Review Setting,** 625 **Review Suffixes,** 635 **Review Fact and Fiction,** 627 **Review Summarize,** 631 **Review Analyze Character,** 641	**Phonics and Decoding:** Hard *g*, Soft *g*, 657 **Character,** 659 **Prefixes,** 661 **Summarize,** 665 **Fact and Fiction,** 667
Language Arts	**Writing:** Write a Story Sequel, 647K **Grammar:** Adverbs, 647M–647N **Spelling:** Homophones and Homographs, 647O–647P	**Writing:** Write a Dialogue, 673K **Grammar:** Adverbs that Compare, 673M–673N **Spelling:** Words with Prefixes, 673O–673P

Activities

Curriculum Connections		**WEEK 1**	**WEEK 2**
	Social Studies	**Read Aloud:** "Harriet Tubman," 616E	**Read Aloud:** "The Princess on the Pea," 648E
	Mathematics	**Stories in Art:** *Village Voices,* 616/617	**Stories in Art:** *View of the Hudson River from Fort Knyphansen,* 648/649
	Science	**Math:** Tight Fit, 622	**Social Studies:** The Stamp Act, 652, Explorers, 654, Revolutionary War, 662
	Music	**Social Studies:** Africa, 626	**Science:** Thunder, 658, Inventions, 664
	Art	**Science:** Sea Food, 630	**Math:** What is the Year? 660
CULTURAL PERSPECTIVES		Views on Slavery, 634	Words from the Dutch, 656

WEEK 3 — Sea Maidens of Japan

Easy: *Unusual Occupations*
Independent: *The Beekeepers' Story*
Challenge: *The Flight of Kites*

☑ **Comprehension**
Review Sequence of Events, 676A–676B, 697E–697F, Review Cause and Effect, 697G–697H

☑ **Vocabulary**
Review Context Clues, 697I–697J

☑ **Study Skills**
Choose Reference Sources, 696

Phonics and Decoding: /ou/ spelled ou and ow, 683
Review Main Idea, 685
Review Draw Conclusions, 687
Review Context Clues, 691

Writing: Write a Two–Character Scene, 697K
Grammar: Avoiding Double Negatives, 697M–697N
Spelling: Words with Suffixes, 697O–697P

Read Aloud: "Turtle's Race with Beaver," 674E

Stories in Art: *The Workplace,* 674/675

Social Studies: Map Skills, 678

Science: Staying Under, 680

Science: Sea Turtles, 686

Social Studies: Japanese Tea Ceremony, 690

Haiku and Tanka Poetry, 684

WEEK 4 — The Silent Lobby

Easy: *The Day My Grandpa Voted*
Independent: *Vote for Me!*
Challenge: *Voting in America*

☑ **Comprehension**
Review Judgments and Decisions, 700A–700B, 717E–717F, Review Draw Conclusions, 717G–717H

☑ **Vocabulary**
Review Synonyms and Antonyms, 717I–717J

☑ **Study Skills**
Use an Outline, 716

Phonics and Decoding: Unstressed Syllables, 711
Review Context Clues, 703
Review Main Idea, 705
Review Make Inferences, 707

Writing: Write a Character Description, 717K
Grammar: Prepositions, 717M–717N
Spelling: Words with Suffixes, 717O–717P

Read Aloud: "Martin Luther King," 698E

Stories in Art: *Martin Luther King,* 698/699

Science: Learning About the Weather, 706

Math: Counting the Votes, 708

Social Studies: Voting Rights, 710

Get Out the Vote, 704

WEEK 5 — Amazon Alert!

Self–Selected Reading of Leveled Books

☑ **Comprehension**
Review Sequence of Events, 720A–720B, Review Cause and Effect, 727E–727F, Review Synonyms and Antonyms, 727G–727H

☑ **Vocabulary**
Review Context Clues, 727I–727J

☑ **Study Skills**
Use an Encyclopedia, 726

Writing: Write a Story, 727K
Grammar: Combining with Adjectives and Adverbs, 727M–727N
Spelling: Words from Math, 727O–727P

Read Aloud: "For Old Time's Sake: A Tree Speaks," 718E

Stories in Art: *Rock and Flower,* 718/719

WEEK 6 — Review, Writing Process, Assessment

Self–Selected Reading

☑ **Assess Skills**
Judgments and Decisions
Draw Conclusions
Cause and Effect
Sequence of Events
Synonyms and Antonyms
Context Clues
Read a Map
Conduct an Interview
Choose Reference Sources
Use an Outline
Use an Encyclopedia

☑ **Assess Grammar and Spelling**

☑ **Unit Progress Assessment**

☑ **Standardized Test Preparation**

Unit Writing Process: Write a Story, 729A–729F

Cooperative Theme Project Research and Inquiry: Protecting Our Environment, 615

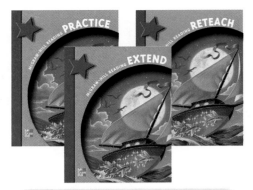

LITERATURE

LEVELED BOOKS

Easy
- *Flight of the Trumpeters*
- *A Matter of Time*
- *Making Pipes Is His Bag*
- *The Day My Grandpa Voted*

On-Level
- *Home Across the Ice*
- *H.G. Wells, Man of the Future*
- *The Beekeeper's Story*
- *Vote for Me!*

Challenge
- *Maggie Comes Home*
- *A Knight's Journey*
- *The Flight of Kites*
- *Voting in America*

STUDENT LISTENING LIBRARY AUDIOCASSETTES
Recordings of the student book selections and poetry.

SKILLS

LEVELED PRACTICE

Practice Book: Student practice for phonics, comprehension, vocabulary, and study skills plus practice for instructional vocabulary and story comprehension. Take-Home Story included for each lesson.

Reteach: Reteaching opportunities for students who need more help with assessed skills.

Extend: Extension activities for vocabulary, comprehension, story, and study skills.

TEACHING CHARTS
Instructional charts for modeling vocabulary and tested skills. Also available as transparencies.

WORD BUILDING MANIPULATIVE CARDS
Cards with words and structural elements for word building and practicing vocabulary.

LANGUAGE SUPPORT BOOK
ESL Parallel teaching lessons and appropriate practice activities for students needing language support.

PHONICS AND PHONEMIC AWARENESS PRACTICE BOOK
Additional practice focusing on vowel sounds, phonograms, blends, digraphs, and key phonetic elements.

LANGUAGE ARTS

GRAMMAR PRACTICE BOOK
Provides practice for grammar and mechanics lessons.

SPELLING PRACTICE BOOK
Provides practice with the word list and spelling patterns. Includes home involvement activities.

DAILY LANGUAGE ACTIVITIES
Provides daily and regular practice of grammar, mechanics, and usage. Available as blackline masters and transparencies.

McGraw-Hill School
TECHNOLOGY

*inter*NET **CONNECTION** Extend lesson activities through Research and Inquiry ideas.

Visit
www.mhschool.com/reading

Resources for Meeting Individual Needs

	EASY	ON-LEVEL	CHALLENGE	LANGUAGE SUPPORT

UNIT 6

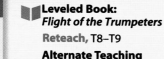

Amistad Rising: A Story of Freedom

EASY	ON-LEVEL	CHALLENGE	LANGUAGE SUPPORT
Leveled Book: *Flight of the Trumpeters* **Reteach,** T8–T9 **Alternate Teaching Strategies,** T60–T66 **Writing:** 647K–647L	**Leveled Book:** *Home Across the Ice* **Practice,** T6–T7 **Alternate Teaching Strategies,** T60–T66 **Writing:** 647K–647L	**Leveled Book:** *Maggie Comes Home* **Extend,** T10–T11 **Writing:** 647K–647L	**Teaching Strategies** **Language Support** **Alternate Teaching Strategies,** T60–T66 **Writing:** 647K–647L

Rip Van Winkle

EASY	ON-LEVEL	CHALLENGE	LANGUAGE SUPPORT
Leveled Book: *A Matter of Time* **Reteach,** T18–T19 **Alternate Teaching Strategies,** T60–T66 **Writing:** 673K–673L	**Leveled Book:** *H.G. Wells, Man of the Future* **Practice,** T16–T17 **Alternate Teaching Strategies,** T60–T66 **Writing:** 673K–673L	**Leveled Book:** *A Knight's Journey* **Extend,** T20–T21 **Writing:** 673K–673L	**Teaching Strategies** **Language Support** **Alternate Teaching Strategies,** T60–T66 **Writing:** 673K–673L

Sea Maidens of Japan

EASY	ON-LEVEL	CHALLENGE	LANGUAGE SUPPORT
Leveled Book: *Making Pipes Is His Bag* **Reteach,** T28–T29 **Alternate Teaching Strategies,** T60–T66 **Writing:** 697K–697L	**Leveled Book:** *The Beekeeper's Story* **Practice,** T26–T27 **Alternate Teaching Strategies,** T60–T66 **Writing:** 697K–697L	**Leveled Book:** *The Flight of Kites* **Extend,** T30–T31 **Writing:** 697K–697L	**Teaching Strategies** **Language Support** **Alternate Teaching Strategies,** T60–T66 **Writing:** 697K–697L

The Silent Lobby

EASY	ON-LEVEL	CHALLENGE	LANGUAGE SUPPORT
Leveled Book: *The Day My Grandpa Voted* **Reteach,** T38–T39 **Alternate Teaching Strategies,** T60–T66 **Writing:** 717K–717L	**Leveled Book:** *Vote for Me!* **Practice,** T36–T37 **Alternate Teaching Strategies,** T60–T66 **Writing:** 717K–717L	**Leveled Book:** *Voting in America* **Extend,** T40–T41 **Writing:** 717K–717L	**Teaching Strategies** **Language Support** **Alternate Teaching Strategies,** T60–T66 **Writing:** 717K–717L

Amazon Alert!

EASY	ON-LEVEL	CHALLENGE	LANGUAGE SUPPORT
Review **Reteach,** T48–T49 **Alternate Teaching Strategies,** T60–T66 **Writing:** 727K–727L	**Review** **Practice,** T46–T47 **Alternate Teaching Strategies,** T60–T66 **Writing:** 727K–727L	**Review** **Extend,** T50–T51 **Writing:** 727K–727L	**Teaching Strategies** **Language Support** **Alternate Teaching Strategies,** T60–T66 **Writing:** 727K–727L

INFORMAL

Informal Assessment

- Comprehension 618B, 647F, 650B, 673F, 673H, 676B, 697F, 697H, 700B, 717F, 717H, 720B, 727F
- Vocabulary 647J, 673J, 697J, 717J, 727J

Performance Assessment

- Scoring Rubrics 647L, 673L, 697L, 717L, 727L, 729B, 729D, 729F
- Research and Inquiry 615, 727
- Writing Process 647K, 673K, 697K, 717K, 727K, 729A, 729C, 729E
- Listening, Speaking Viewing Activities 616–617, 616E, 628, 647K–L, 648–49, 648E, 673K–L, 674–675, 674E, 697K–L, 698–699, 718–719, 718E, 727K–L
- Cross-Curricular Activities

Leveled Practice

Practice, Reteach, Extend

- **Comprehension**
  Judgments and Decisions, T60
  Cause and Effect, T64
  Sequence of Events, T66
  Draw Conclusions, T62
- **Vocabulary Strategies**
  Context Clues: Content Area Specialized Vocabulary
  Antonyms and Synonyms, T65
- **Study Skills**
  Read a Map, 646
  Conduct an Interview, 672
  Chose Reference Sources, 696
  Use an Outline, 716
  Use an Encyclopedia, 726

FORMAL

Selection Tests

- Skills and Vocabulary Words
  Amistad Rising: A Story of Freedom
  Rip Van Winkle
  Sea Maidens of Japan
  The Silent Lobby
  Amazon Alert!

Unit 6 Assessment

- **Comprehension**
  Judgments and Decisions
  Cause and Effect
  Sequence of Events
  Draw Conclusions
  Synonyms & Antonyms
- **Vocabulary Strategies**
  Context Clues: Content Area
    Specialized Vocabulary
  Synonyms and Antonyms

Grammar and Spelling Assessment

- **Grammar**
  Adverbs
- **Spelling**
  Homophones and Homographs
  Words with Prefixes
  Words with Suffixes
  Words with Suffixes

Diagnostic/Placement Evaluation

Test Preparation

- See Test Power in Teacher's Edition

Assessment Checklist

Student .... Grade ....

Teacher ....

	Amistad Rising: A Story of Freedom	Rip Van Winkle	Sea Maidens of Japan	The Silent Lobby	Amazon Alert!	Assessment Summary
LISTENING/SPEAKING						
Participates in oral language experiences.						
Listens and speaks to gain knowledge of culture.						
Speaks appropriately to audiences for different purposes.						
Communicates clearly.						
READING						
Uses a variety of word identification strategies, including						
• Context Clues						
• Synonyms & Antonyms						
Reads with fluency and understanding.						
Reads widely for different purposes in varied sources.						
Develops an extensive vocabulary.						
Uses a variety of strategies to comprehend selections.						
• Judgments and Decisions						
• Cause and Effect						
• Sequence of Events						
• Draw Conclusions						
Responds to various texts.						
Analyzes the characteristics of various types of texts, including						
• Story Elements (Character, Setting, Plot)						
Conducts research using various sources, including						
• Read a Map						
• Conduct an Interview						
• Choose Reference Sources						
• Use an Outline						
• Use an Encyclopedia						
Reads to increase knowledge.						
WRITING						
Writes for a variety of audiences and purposes.						
Composes original texts using the conventions of written language such as capitalization and penmanship.						
Spells proficiently.						
Composes texts applying knowledge of grammar and usage.						
Uses writing processes.						
Evaluates own writing and writing of others.						

+ Observed   − Not Observed

614H

Introducing the Theme

Crossroads

Decisions cause changes that can enrich our lives.

PRESENT THE THEME Read the theme statement to students. Invite them to share experiences they've had making important decisions. What happened as a result of the decision? Do you wish you had made different decision?

READ THE POEM Explain that people make decisions every day. Some are routine. (What should I wear to school?) Others are important and can change a life. (We're moving.) Read aloud "Paper I" by Carl Sandburg. What decision is the author asking you to make?

STUDENT LISTENING LIBRARY AUDIOCASSETTES

MAKE CONNECTIONS Have students preview the unit, reading the selection titles and looking at the illustrations. Have them work in small groups to brainstorm a list of ways that the stories, poems, and the Time for Kids magazine article relate to the theme Crossroads.

Groups can then compare their lists as they share them with the class.

614

THEME SUMMARY

Each of the five selections relates to the unit theme Crossroads as well as the global theme Expression. These thematic links will help students to make connections across texts.

Amistad Rising People make decisions about slavery.

Rip Van Winkle Rip decides to go hunting and returns 20 years later.

Sea Maidens of Japan A Japanese girl decides to conquer her fear.

The Silent Lobby A group of African Americans decides to make their votes count.

Amazon Alert! Decisions to clear land devastates the Amazon rain forest.

CROSSROADS

Paper I

Paper is two kinds, to write on, to wrap with.

If you like to write, you write.

If you like to wrap, you wrap.

Some papers like writers, some like wrappers.

Are you a writer or a wrapper?

by Carl Sandburg

615

LEARNING ABOUT POETRY

Literary Devices: Free Verse
Read the poem aloud. Have students listen for rhyme and rhythm. Does the poem have a definite rhythm? Rhyme? The poem is written in free verse, a style of poetry made free of restrictions on rhythm and rhyme Point out the importance of punctuation and line breaks in poetry. A comma signals a short pause; a period and line break signals a long

pause. Have students read the poem aloud with pauses.

Poetry Activity Have students decide if they are writers or wrappers. Invite them to write a brief poem in free verse on the what it's like to be a writer or a wrapper.

Research and *Inquiry*

 Theme Project: Protecting Our Environment Ask teams of students to discuss how people pollute, protect, and cleanup the environment. Students should focus on one of those broad topics to create a board game, including game cards with questions and multiple-choice answers. Each correct and incorrect answer should have consequences for players.

List What They Know Have students list what they know about how people pollute, protect, and clean up the environment.

Ask Questions and Identify Resources Ask students to brainstorm and list questions they would need to answer to prepare their board games.

QUESTIONS	POSSIBLE RESOURCES
• What harms the environment?	• Interview officials at the EPA.
• How can we reduce pollution?	• Look in the encyclopedia
• How can we clean up the environment?	• Search the Internet

Remind students to record important details.

 Have students visit *www.mhschool.com/reading*

Create a Prototype When their research is complete, direct students to present a prototype of their game, including the board, cards, name and logo, chips, and playing instructions.

615

Amistad Rising: A Story of Freedom

Selection Summary   This well-known story, based on historical events, tells of the trial of Joseph Cinqué, a captive who led a revolt aboard a slave ship.

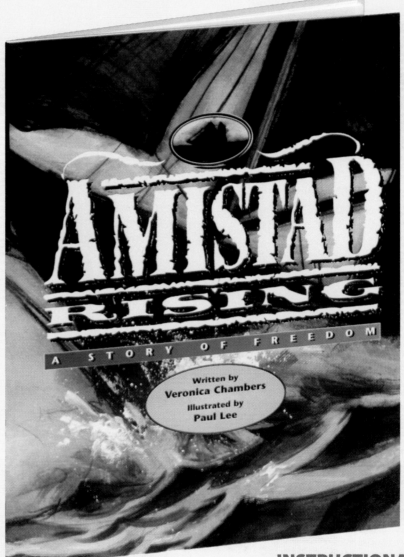

Written by
Veronica Chambers

Illustrated by
Paul Lee

**Student
Listening
Library
Audiocassette**

INSTRUCTIONAL
Pages 618–643

About the Author   Researching the story of Joseph Cinqué allowed Veronica Chambers to make discoveries about her own African heritage. It also enabled her to communicate an important message about freedom.

About the Illustrator   A graduate of the Art Center College of Design in Pasadena, California, Paul Lee has worked for several years as a freelance illustrator. Lee is proud that *Amistad Rising* is his first book for young people.

Resources for Meeting Individual Needs

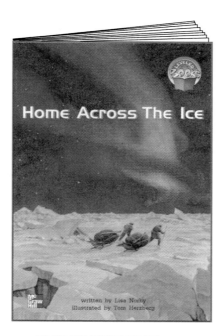

EASY
Pages 647A, 647D

INDEPENDENT
Pages 647B, 647D

CHALLENGE
Pages 647C, 647D

LEVELED PRACTICE

Reteach, 186–192
blackline masters with reteaching opportunities for each essential skill

Practice, 186–192
workbook with Take-Home stories and practice opportunities for each assessed skill and story comprehension

Extend, 186–192
blackline masters that offer challenge activities for each assessed skill

ADDITIONAL RESOURCES

- **Language Support Book** 201–208
- **Take-Home Story, Practice** p. 187a
- **Alternate Teaching Strategies** T60–T66

McGraw-Hill School
TECHNOLOGY

interNET CONNECTION Research and Inquiry Ideas. Visit **www.mhschool.com/reading**

Suggested **Lesson Planner**

 Available on CD-ROM

READING AND LANGUAGE ARTS	**DAY 1** *Focus on Reading and Skills*	**DAY 2** *Read the Literature*
● **Comprehension** ● **Vocabulary** ● **Phonics/Decoding** ● **Study Skills** ● **Listening, Speaking, Viewing, Representing**	**Read Aloud and Motivate,** 616E *Harriet Tubman* **Develop Visual Literacy,** 616/617 ☑ **Review Judgments and Decisions,** 618A–618B **Teaching Chart 151** Reteach, Practice, Extend, 186	**Build Background,** 618C Develop Oral Language **Vocabulary,** 618D *coax navigate perished* *escorted nightfall ushered* **Teaching Chart 152** **Vocabulary Cards** Reteach, Practice, Extend, 187 **Read the Selection,** 618–643 ☑ Review Judgments and Decisions **Minilessons,** 625, 627, 631, 635, 641 **Cultural Perspectives,** 634

● **Curriculum Connections**	**Works of Art,** 616/617	**Social Studies,** 618C
● **Writing**	**Writing Prompt:** Write a description of life on the *Amistad* during the storm. Use details to tell how it felt to be on the ship.	**Writing Prompt:** Imagine you are a slave on the *Amistad*. Write a letter to your parents in Sierra Leone telling in chronological order where you have sailed. **Journal Writing,** 643 Quick-Write
● **Grammar**	**Introduce the Concept: Adverbs,** 647M Daily Language Activity 1. The chains creaked. eerily 2. Cinqué thought he would be free. never 3. He planned his escape. carefully **Grammar Practice Book,** 161	**Teach the Concept: Adverbs,** 647M Daily Language Activity 1. Cinqué freed the others. quickly 2. They tried to steer the ship. even 3. People sat in the courtroom. nervously **Grammar Practice Book,** 162
● **Spelling**	**Pretest: Homophones and Homographs,** 647O Spelling Practice Book, 161–162	**Explore the Pattern: Homophones and Homographs,** 647O Spelling Practice Book, 163

DAY 3 — Read the Literature

Rereading for Fluency, 642

Story Questions, 644
Reteach, Practice, Extend, 188

Story Activities, 645

Study Skill, 646
 Read a Map
Teaching Chart 153
Reteach, Practice, Extend, 189

Test Power, 647

 Read the Leveled Books
Guided Reading
/ù/ and yù/
Review Judgments and Decisions
Instructional Vocabulary

 Link Math, 622

Writing Prompt: Write a diary entry from the point of view of Cinqué telling the events of the night he broke free from his shackles.

Writing Process: Write a Story Sequel, 647K Prewrite, Draft

Review and Practice: Adverbs, 647N
Daily Language Activity
1. Cinqué tossed up a line to him.
   eagerly
2. It was hard to sit in court every day.
   quietly
3. John Quincy Adams carried a small book with him. always

Grammar Practice Book, 163

Practice and Extend: Homophones and Homographs, 647P
Spelling Practice Book, 164

DAY 4 — Build and Review Skills

 **Read the Leveled Books and Self-Selected Books**

 Review Judgments and Decisions, 647E–647F
Teaching Chart 154
Reteach, Practice, Extend, 190
Language Support, 206

 Review Draw Conclusions, 647G–647H
Teaching Chart 155
Reteach, Practice, Extend, 191
Language Support, 207

 Link Social Studies, 625

Writing Prompt: Write a persuasive paragraph telling why John Quincy Adams was a good man.

Writing Process: Write a Story Sequel, 647K Revise

Meeting Individual Needs for Writing, 647L

Review and Practice: Adverbs, 647N
Daily Language Activity
1. Cinqué tried to smile, but he was feeling ill. occasionally
2. Cinqué would be home. never
3. He was captured a year ago. almost

Grammar Practice Book, 164

Proofread and Write: Homophones and Homographs, 647P
Spelling Practice Book, 165

DAY 5 — Build and Review Skills

Read Self-Selected Books

Review Context Clues, 647I–648J
Teaching Chart 156
Reteach, Practice, Extend, 192
Language Support, 208

Listening, Speaking, Viewing, Representing, 647L
Analyze the Sequel
Create a Trilogy

Minilessons, 625, 627, 631, 635, 641,

Phonics Review /ù/ and yù/

Link Science, 630

Writing Prompt: Imagine you are a character in the selection. Describe how you are dressed, walk and talk, and how you feel as you board the ship for home.

Writing Process: Write a Story Sequel, 647K Edit/Proofread, Publish
Phonics Workbook,

Assess and Reteach: Adverbs, 647N
Daily Language Activity
1. The Court had made such a ruling.
   never
2. The prisoners walked in the dark.
   quickly
3. He slept during the mutiny. soundly

Grammar Practice Book, 165–166

Assess and Reteach: Homophones and Homographs, 647P
Spelling Practice Book, 166

Read Aloud and Motivate

Harriet Tubman
a poem by Eloise Greenfield

Harriet Tubman didn't take no stuff

Wasn't scared of nothing neither

Didn't come in this world to be no slave

And wasn't going to stay one either

"Farewell!" she sang to her friends one night

She was mighty sad to leave 'em

But she ran away that dark, hot night

Ran looking for her freedom

She ran to the woods and she ran through the woods

With the slave catchers right behind her

And she kept on going till she got to the North

Where those mean men couldn't find her

Nineteen times she went back South

To get three hundred others

Continued on pages T2–T5

Oral Comprehension

LISTENING AND SPEAKING Motivate students to review what they know about making judgments and decisions by reading aloud this poem. Ask students to listen for the decisions that Harriet Tubman made. When you have finished reading, ask: "What did Harriet Tubman decide to do to help enslaved people? Would you have acted in the same way? Why or why not?"

Activity Have students write and then read their own poems about making decisions. If they want to write poems that rhyme, suggest that they compile a list of rhyming words related to the topic of their poem. Students may wish to generate this list with a partner.

▶ **Linguistic**

Develop Visual Literacy

Link
Works of Art

Stories in Art

Like writers and musicians, artists communicate through their art. Some express their ideas about culture. Others use their art to get their values and "message" across.

Look at the painting. What do you see? Notice the use of repeated colors, lines, and shapes. How does it balance the painting? Does it give you the feeling of harmony? How?

Look at the painting again. Which people are singing? Do they seem to be in harmony with nature? With each other? What might the artist be saying about the need to lift our voices together? Could that be his message? What do you think?

Village Voices
by Ashley Bryan, 1992

616

617

Objective: Review Judgments and Decisions

VIEWING *Village Voices,* by Ashley Bryan, captures the feeling of friendship and harmony in simple colors and shapes. Have students close their eyes and describe the painting. Afterward, ask them if the painting's use of repeated colors, lines, and shapes helped them remember the picture. Discuss what students remember about the way the artist has grouped the figures and interwoven the human faces with natural objects.

Read the page with students, encouraging individual interpretations of the painting.

Ask students to identify the judgments that the artist is making about people and nature. For example:

- The flowers have faces, suggesting that people need to be nurtured like flowers.
- The people are singing together, indicating that they are in harmony with each other and with nature.

REPRESENTING Have students write a poem based on the painting. Direct them to choose the "message" of their poem first.

OBJECTIVES

Students will identify and evaluate judgments and decisions in a text.

TEACHING TIP

INSTRUCTIONAL

Students may have difficulty understanding the difference between a judgment and a decision. Remind them that a judgment is an opinion or choice that is used to make a decision. For example, a person would make a judgment about whether a bridge is safe to cross and then use this information to make a decision whether to cross the bridge or not.

Review Judgments and Decisions

PREPARE

Identify Judgments and Decisions
Have students think of a time when they had to make a difficult decision. Ask: Did you make the right or wrong decision? Can a decision be right and wrong at the same time?

TEACH

Define Judgments and Decisions
Tell students: Strategic readers look for the judgments and decisions characters in a story make. They think about **all** the information given by the author when identifying judgments and decisions.

Waiting and Wondering

Mindy grew tired of waiting. Mindy's mother was supposed to pick her up at school 3 P.M., and it was nearly 3:30. Mindy's favorite television show came on at 4 and she now worried that she would miss it.

Mindy's mother would not be happy if Mindy took the bus home. But that's what Mindy was thinking of doing. She and her mother had taken the bus from school to home many times, so Mindy knew what to do. But if mother arrived and couldn't find Mindy she would worry. Mindy didn't want to make her mother worry. Mindy decided to wait for her mother to pick her up.

Teaching Chart 151

Read the Story and Model the Skill
Display **Teaching Chart 151.** Have students pay attention to clues about judgments and decisions as you read the passage.

MODEL As I read, I learn that Mindy has a difficult decision to make. She is thinking about leaving school without her mother. She knows the way home by bus. But Mindy begins to see the negative side of making the decision to take the bus, and she decides to wait for her mother. I thought about Mindy's choice and decided she made the right decision.

Evaluate Judgments and Decisions
Encourage students to discuss whether or not Mindy made the right decision. Have them draw a circle around words or phrases in the text that give clues to Mindy's judgments and decisions.

PRACTICE

Create a Decision Chart

Using a Decision chart, have students record the event and the decision mentioned in the teaching chart. ▶ **Linguistic/Logical**

WHAT HAPPENED	DECISION
Mindy's mother is late picking her up.	Mindy decides to wait until her mother arrives.

ASSESS/CLOSE

Make Judgments and Decisions

Ask students to think about what Mindy would do if a friend's mother offered to drive her home. In what ways would her judgments be similar to the ones she made when thinking about riding the bus? (Mindy knew that her mother would not be happy and she did not want to make her mother worry.) What decision would Mindy probably make about accepting a ride from her friend's mother? (She would decline the offer and continue to wait for her mother to arrive.)

.

SELECTION Connection

Students will identify judgments and decisions when they read *Amistad Rising* and the Leveled Books.

ALTERNATE TEACHING STRATEGY

JUDGMENTS AND DECISIONS

For a different approach to teaching this skill, see page T60.

Meeting Individual Needs for Comprehension

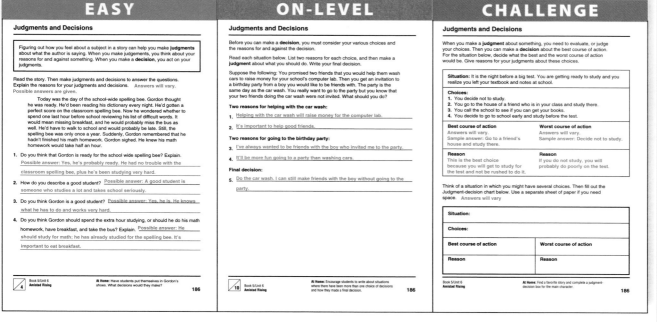

EASY

Judgments and Decisions

Figuring out how you feel about a subject in a story can help you make **judgments** about what the author is saying. When you make judgements, you think about your reasons for and against something. When you make a **decision**, you act on your judgments.

Read the story. Then make judgments and decisions to answer the questions. Explain the reasons for your judgments and decisions. Answers will vary. Possible answers are given.

Today was the day of the school-wide spelling bee. Gordon thought he was ready. He'd been reading his dictionary every night. He'd gotten a perfect score on the classroom spelling bee. Now he wondered whether to spend one last hour before school reviewing his list of difficult words. It would mean missing breakfast, and he would probably miss the bus as well. He'd have to walk to school and would probably be late. Still, the spelling bee was only once a year. Suddenly, Gordon remembered that he hadn't finished his math homework. Gordon sighed. He knew his math homework would take half an hour.

1. Do you think that Gordon is ready for the school wide spelling bee? Explain. Possible answer: Yes, he's probably ready. He had no trouble with the classroom spelling bee, plus he's been studying very hard.

2. How do you describe a good student? Possible answer: A good student is someone who studies a lot and takes school seriously.

3. Do you think Gordon is a good student? Possible answer: Yes, he is. He knows what he has to do and works very hard.

4. Do you think Gordon should spend the extra hour studying, or should he do his math homework, have breakfast, and take the bus? Explain. Possible answer: He should study for math; he has already studied for the spelling bee. It's important to eat breakfast.

Book 5/Unit 6
4 Amistad Rising

At Home: Have students put themselves in Gordon's shoes. What decisions would they make?

186

ON-LEVEL

Judgments and Decisions

Before you can make a **decision**, you must consider your various choices and the reasons for and against the decision.

Read each situation below. List two reasons for each choice, and then make a **judgment** about what you should do. Write your final decision.

Suppose the following: You promised two friends that you would help them wash cars to raise money for your school's computer lab. Then you get an invitation to a birthday party from a boy you would like to be friends with. The party is the same day as the car wash. You really want to go to the party but you know that your two friends doing the car wash were not invited. What should you do?

Two reasons for helping with the car wash:

1. Helping with the car wash will raise money for the computer lab.

2. It's important to help good friends.

Two reasons for going to the birthday party:

3. I've always wanted to be friends with the boy who invited me to the party.

4. It'll be more fun going to a party than washing cars.

Final decision:

5. Do the car wash. I can still make friends with the boy without going to the party.

Book 5/Unit 6
10 Amistad Rising

At Home: Encourage students to write about situations where there have been more than one choice of decisions and how they made a final decision.

186

CHALLENGE

Judgments and Decisions

When you make a **judgment** about something, you need to evaluate, or judge your choices. Then you can make a **decision** about the best course of action. For the situation below, decide what the best and the worst course of action would be. Give reasons for your judgments about these choices.

Situation: It is the night before a big test. You are getting ready to study and you realize you left your textbook and notes at school.

Choices:
1. You decide not to study.
2. You go to the house of a friend who is in your class and study there.
3. You call the school to see if you can get your books.
4. You decide to go to school early and study before the test.

Best course of action	Worst course of action
Answers will vary. Sample answer: Go to a friend's house and study there.	Answers will vary. Sample answer: Decide not to study.
Reason This is the best choice because you will get to study for the test and not be rushed to do it.	**Reason** If you do not study, you will probably do poorly on the test.

Think of a situation in which you might have several choices. Then fill out the Judgment-decision chart below. Use a separate sheet of paper if you need space. Answers will vary

Situation:	
Choices:	
Best course of action	**Worst course of action**
Reason	**Reason**

Book 5/Unit 6
Amistad Rising

At Home: Find a favorite story and complete a judgment-decision box for the main character.

186

Reteach, 186   Practice, 186   Extend, 186

618B

Build Background

Social Studies

Anthology and Leveled Books

Evaluate Prior Knowledge

CONCEPT: RETURNING HOME Ask students to share their experiences being away from home and wanting to return. How long were they away? Who and what did they miss? To whom did they turn for help?

GETTING THERE Work with students to create a cluster chart. Have students write the words "Going Home" in the center. Then have them list various places they visit often. Next to each place name, students should write the one or more ways to return home from that point.

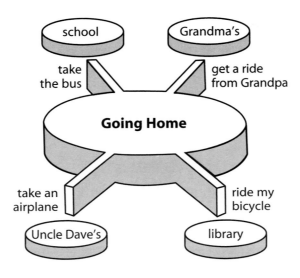

Graphic Organizer 29

TRAVEL TIPS Encourage students to work in pairs to create travel plans for a three-day trip to visit a family member. Have students write a schedule of what they would do each day, how they would get from place to place, and how much each activity would cost.

Develop Oral Language

DISCUSS WAYS TO TRAVEL Encourage

ESL students to brainstorm a list of ways they could travel by water and by land. If possible, bring in magazine pictures or photos of different types of land and water transportation.

Draw a two-column chart on the chalkboard. Label one side *Land* and the other side *Water*. List student responses in the chart. Discuss the responses and have students identify where each mode of travel is found. For example, a subway (or metro) is a type of land transportation usually found in a large city.

Ask students to expand the chart with additional information, such as the advantages and disadvantages of each kind of transportation.

Vocabulary

Key Words

1. At (nightfall) Joseph Cinqué watched the last rays of the sun disappear. 2. He was worried; he knew that he couldn't (navigate) this ship in the right direction—toward Africa. 3. (Escorted) by a friend, Cinqué went to speak to the Spanish sailors. 4. He tried to (coax) them with gentle gestures and soothing tones to steer the ship to Africa. 5. But the sailors weren't eager to help. Their fellow sailors had already (perished) and they were afraid of dying at Joseph Cinqué's hands. 6. In disgust, Cinqué had the sailors (ushered) from the deck of the ship to a small cabin by four of the largest African mutineers.

Teaching Chart 152

Definitions

nightfall (p. 622) the beginning of night

navigate (p. 632) to steer a ship

escorted (p. 634) accompanied

coax (p. 628) to persuade gently

perished (p. 622) died

ushered (p. 628) led to a place by another person

SPELLING/VOCABULARY CONNECTIONS

See Spelling Challenge Words, pages 6470–647P.

Vocabulary in Context

IDENTIFY VOCABULARY WORDS
Display **Teaching Chart 152** and read the passage with students. Have volunteers circle each vocabulary word and underline other words that are clues to its meaning.

DISCUSS MEANINGS Ask questions like these to help clarify word meanings:

• Is nightfall closer to dinner or breakfast?

• Is it possible to navigate a large ship without a map?

• Is it better to go alone to a party or to be escorted by a friend?

• How would you coax a kitten to come down from the branch of a tree?

• Did many people perish when the *Titanic* sank?

• Have you ever been ushered to your seat in a theater or church?

Practice

DEMONSTRATE WORD MEANING Have partners choose vocabulary cards from a pile and demonstrate each word meaning with pantomime, drawing, or verbal clues.

▶ **Kinesthetic/Linguistic**

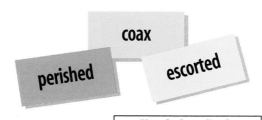

Vocabulary Cards

WRITE A SHORT STORY Have students write a short story using as many of the vocabulary words as possible.

▶ **Linguistic**

Take-Home Story 187a
Reteach 187
Practice 187 • Extend 187

Guided Instruction

Preview and Predict

Have students preview the selection. Using words from the story, talk about the details of the illustrations.

- Does this story take place in the present day, or in the past? How can you tell?
- Where does this story take place?
- What do you think this story will most likely be about?
- Is this going to be fiction or nonfiction? How can you tell? (Explain that this selection is historical fiction, combining fictional elements with factual historical events.) *Genre*

Next, have students record their predictions.

PREDICTIONS	WHAT HAPPENED
The Africans will take over the slave ship.	
The Africans will be freed in the end.	

Set Purposes

What do students want to learn by reading the story? For example:

- Where is the ship going?
- Why do the Africans take over the ship?

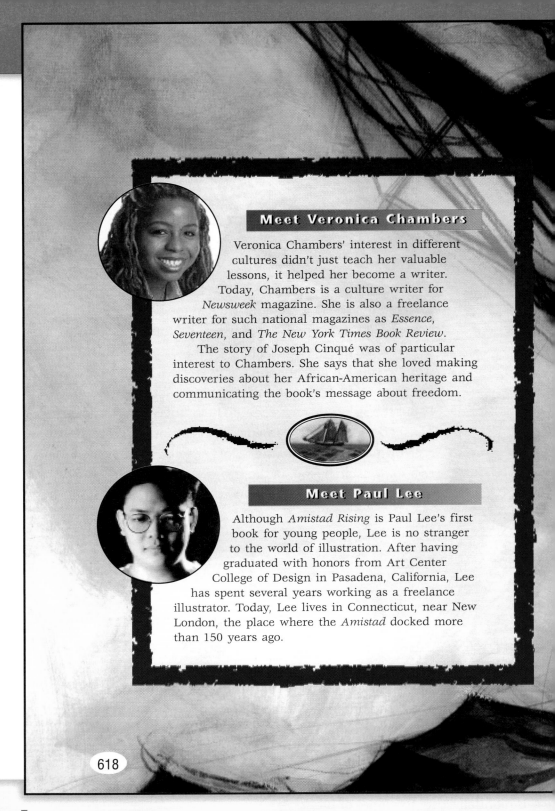

Meet Veronica Chambers

Veronica Chambers' interest in different cultures didn't just teach her valuable lessons, it helped her become a writer. Today, Chambers is a culture writer for *Newsweek* magazine. She is also a freelance writer for such national magazines as *Essence*, *Seventeen*, and *The New York Times Book Review*.

The story of Joseph Cinqué was of particular interest to Chambers. She says that she loved making discoveries about her African-American heritage and communicating the book's message about freedom.

Meet Paul Lee

Although *Amistad Rising* is Paul Lee's first book for young people, Lee is no stranger to the world of illustration. After having graduated with honors from Art Center College of Design in Pasadena, California, Lee has spent several years working as a freelance illustrator. Today, Lee lives in Connecticut, near New London, the place where the *Amistad* docked more than 150 years ago.

618

Meeting Individual Needs • Grouping Suggestions for Strategic Reading

EASY

ESL **Read Together** Read the story together or invite students to use the **Listening Library Audiocassettes.** Pause and model the strategy of making judgments and decisions with the students as you read. Guided Instruction and Intervention prompts offer additional help with vocabulary and comprehension.

ON-LEVEL

Guided Reading Read the selection with students, using the Guided Instruction prompts. Encourage volunteers to read passages from the story out loud and to discuss the judgments and decisions made by the characters in the story. Have students use the chart to record judgments and decisions as they read.

CHALLENGE

Read Independently Have students set purposes before they read. Remind students that identifying the judgments and decisions made by the characters can help them understand the story better. After reading, have students retell the story, read passages from the story out loud, or use their charts to record information.

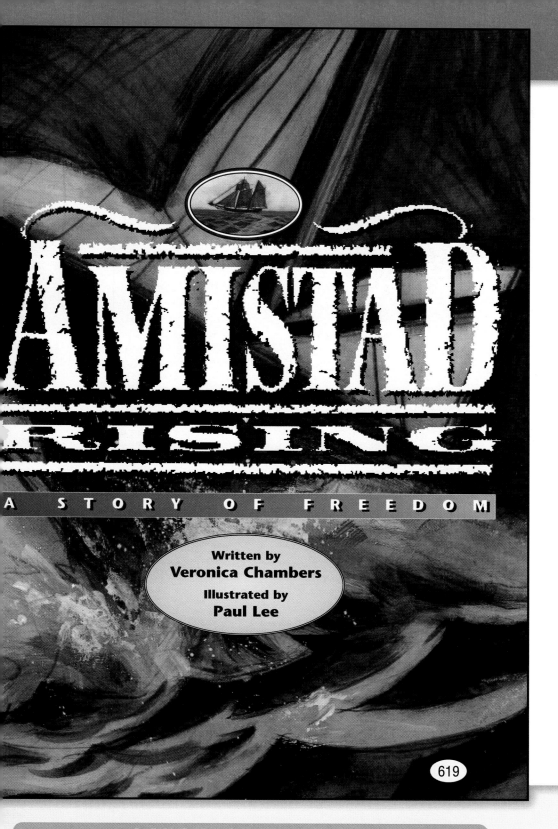

619

Guided Instruction

☑ **Judgments and Decisions**

Strategic Reading Explain to the students that identifying judgments and decisions will help them understand the meaning of the story they are going to read.

Before we begin reading, let's prepare a Decision chart to record decision-making in the story.

WHAT HAPPENED	DECISION

① **JUDGMENTS AND DECISIONS** The subtitle of this selection is "A Story of Freedom." I wonder what kind of decisions will have to be made in this story. Does anyone want to make a prediction? (Students might think one decision will involve whether the Africans should be made slaves or set free.)

Story Words

The words below may be unfamiliar to students. Have them check their meaning and pronunciation in the Glossary beginning on page 730.

- tempestuous, p. 622
- provisions, p. 624
- boon, p. 630
- abolitionists, p. 634
- mutiny, p. 636
- provoking, p. 639

LANGUAGE SUPPORT

A blackline master of the Decision chart can be found in the **Language Support Book.**

619

Guided Instruction

(2) **What is the setting of this story?** (the ocean many years ago) **Who is the main character?** (Joseph Cinqué) **How do you know?** (The author writes: "Ask the ocean about the legend of Joseph Cinqué, and this is what you might hear.") *Character/Setting*

 CONTEXT CLUES **Do you know what the word** *renegade* **means? Can you figure it out from the words or sentences around it?**

620

 PREVENTION/INTERVENTION

CONTEXT CLUES Remind students that one way to learn the meaning of a word they do not know is to study the context, or surroundings, in which the word appears. Sometimes context clues point to the exact meaning of a word. More often, they simply give an overall sense of what the word may mean.

Have students read the entire sentence in which the word *renegade* appears. What words can help them understand the meaning? (*slaves, leaving his mark on history*)

Then have students read the next paragraph. Which phrase is a clue to the meaning of *renegade*? (*battled nations to be free again*)

Ask: Do these clues give an exact meaning of *renegade* or just an overall sense of its meaning? Name a word that may have a meaning similar to *renegade*. (*rebellious*)

Guided Instruction

3 This passage about the ocean sounds strange. In the second paragraph, the author says that this is a true story. But is it strictly true to say that rivers and lakes whisper names? What conclusion can you draw about the author's purpose in writing about the event? (Sample answer: She is using poetic language to make the story more mythical than historical—to make it larger and more important than a simple event.) *Draw Conclusions*

S tand here with me on the shores of New London, Connecticut. Feel the cool breeze of the Atlantic Ocean on your face. Feel the dirt beneath your feet; this land is far from ordinary. It was here, upon this very spot, that Joseph Cinqué set foot in America, bringing with him a group of renegade slaves and leaving his mark on history.

This is a story about the changing winds of fortune, about a man who was born free, was made a slave, and battled nations to be free again. It is a true story. And like so many stories, it begins not on land but at sea.

Have you ever wondered why the ocean is so wide? It's because it holds so much history. There's not a drop of seawater that doesn't have a secret; not a river or a lake that doesn't whisper someone's name. Ask the ocean about the legend of Joseph Cinqué, and this is what you might hear.

2 **3**

621

LANGUAGE SUPPORT

ESL Some students might be confused by the figurative language in this selection. Read the last paragraph on page 621 with students. Ask: What might the author mean by saying the "ocean holds history"? (Sample answer: She might say this to suggest to the reader that history is like the ocean—much of it lies beneath the surface—or that the ocean is very old and has witnessed much history.)

Guided Instruction

4 **JUDGMENTS AND DECISIONS**
Why did the slave traders do such horrible things? Was it right for people to treat others so harshly?

MODEL The author tells us that slave traders grew rich from trading in human beings. These slave traders probably felt that having a lot of money was more important than treating all people equally. Therefore they decided to force Africans into slavery so that they could get lots of money. It is clearly wrong for the slave traders to treat people so brutally.

The year was 1839. Owning slaves was still legal, although the stealing of slaves from Africa was not. Slavery was a huge business. Many slave traders had grown rich from selling human beings, and they were reluctant to give it up.

It was nightfall when the slave ship *Teçora* set sail from Sierra Leone, a small country on the coast of West Africa. The water rippled like quicksilver in the moonlight as the ship voyaged toward Cuba. But in the ship's hold, more than five hundred Africans were held prisoner. There was no toilet, there was no bath, and the stench was unbearable. The Africans were chained together in pairs. Heavy iron shackles bound their hands and their feet. Movement was difficult. Escape was impossible. Disease and malnutrition claimed the lives of many; others perished under the murderous beatings of the slave traders. The dead were tossed overboard without a thought.

After two tempestuous months at sea, the *Teçora* arrived in Cuba. There, fifty-three of the prisoners—including four children—were sold to two Spanish slave traders and forced to board yet another ship to take them to a Cuban plantation.

4 This ship was called *Amistad*, the Spanish word for "friendship."

622

Activity

Cross Curricular: Math

TRANSATLANTIC JOURNEY The *Teçora* took two months to sail from Africa across the Atlantic Ocean to Cuba. Discuss with students why this journey might have taken so long. Explain that the journey from west to east took even longer, because of the way the winds blew.

RESEARCH AND INQUIRY Have students research different types of ships from history and how quickly they could travel across the Atlantic. Have them make a graph of their results. Students might also research how long this journey takes today by airplane.

▶ **Mathematical/Spatial**

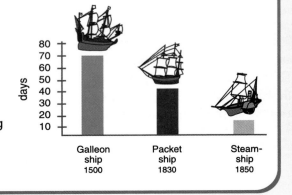

Guided Instruction

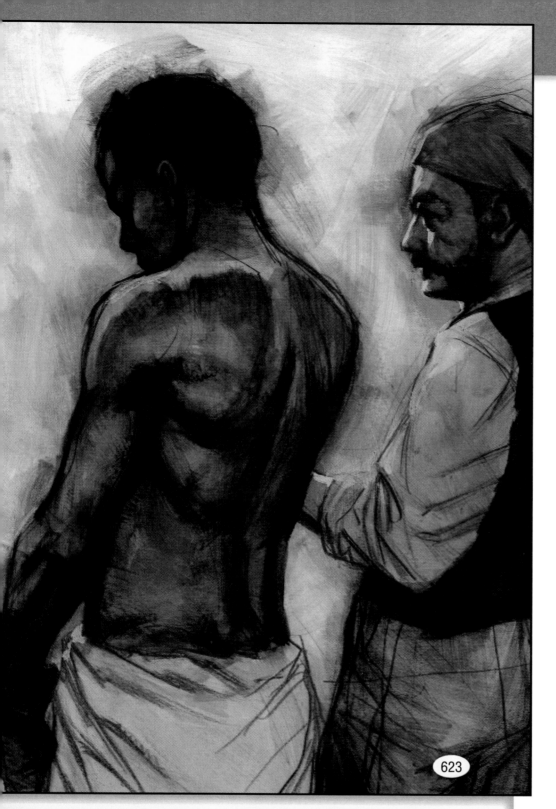

623

WORD STRUCTURE Do you know the meaning of the word *malnutrition* in the second paragraph on page 622? What smaller word do you see in *malnutrition*?

PREVENTION/INTERVENTION

WORD STRUCTURE Write the word *malnutrition* on the chalkboard. Explain that dividing a word into its parts can help in understanding the word. Draw a line between the prefix *mal-* and the base word *nutrition*. Ask students if they know the meaning of the word *nutrition*. (nourishment or the way food is taken in and used by a living thing) Ask students if they know the meaning of the prefix *mal-*. (badly or inadequate) Ask: What does the combined word mean? (bad or inadequate nourishment)

Have students look in a dictionary to find other words with the *mal-* prefix. (malcontent, malfunction, malpractice)

623

Guided Instruction

 Have you ever been in a situation where you didn't know where you were or where you were going? How did it make you feel? (Students might remember waking up in a strange house when on a visit, or in a car after dozing off, and wondering where they were.) **What did you do in that situation?** (Sample answers: I called for my parents, I looked around until I recognized my surroundings.) *Critical Thinking*

624

Three days into the journey, the *Amistad* sailed through an unexpected storm. The ship was battered by roaring rain and wind. The trip took longer than the crew expected and provisions were low. Each slave survived on a daily meal of two potatoes, a banana, and just a little water.

In the hold of the ship, a young man tried to quell his unsettled stomach. Fear gripped him as he watched his fellow Africans suffer and starve. He was young and afraid, but destiny had a plan for him. His name was Singbe, although the slavers had given him the Spanish name Joseph Cinqué, and he belonged to a group of people called Mende who lived near Sierra Leone. He had been working on a village road when he was seized and sold to the slavers of the *Teçora*.

625

Guided Instruction

6 **JUDGMENTS AND DECISIONS**
Why did the crew provide little food for the slaves? Do you think the crew had the same amount to eat as the slaves? (There were few provisions on the ship and the slaves were harshly treated. The slave traders probably decided to give the Africans as little food as possible and save as much as possible for themselves.)

Minilesson

REVIEW

Setting

Remind students that understanding the setting of a story is important to understanding the story itself. Discuss the setting of the slave ship *Teçora* with students. How does the author describe it? What could Cinqué see, hear, smell, touch, or taste while he was in the hold with the other prisoners? Encourage students to close their eyes and imagine what it would be like to be in such a place.

Activity Have students write a description about being in the hold of a slave ship. Encourage them to focus on sensations in their description—sight, sounds, smells, tastes, and textures.

Guided Instruction

7 **JUDGMENTS AND DECISIONS** Are the Africans making judgments about their future? (They aren't making judgments, but they are guessing about what might happen to them.) **Can you make a judgment without any information?** (no)

8 **JUDGMENTS AND DECISIONS** Has Joseph Cinqué made a decision here? **What decision has he made?** (He decided to find out what was going to happen to him and the other Africans.) **What caused Joseph Cinqué to make his decision?** (Possible answer: He made his decision out of fear about the future, or his longing to return home.) **Let's add this information to our Decision chart.**

WHAT HAPPENED	DECISION
Joseph Cinqué is kidnapped and imprisoned on a ship.	He decides to find out what is going to happen to him and his fellow prisoners.

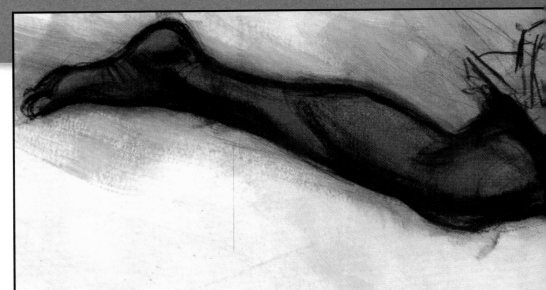

During the first two months of his captivity, Cinqué was disturbed to find that he had begun to forget little things about Africa—the smell of freshly harvested rice, the color of the sunsets, the feel of wet grass beneath his running feet. When he closed his eyes, he could see these things only as distant and blurry as a dream. But he could never forget the people he had left behind. His wife. His three children. His mother and father.

Every day Cinqué grew more restless, wondering what the Spaniards intended to do with him and the other Africans. Though **7** they were forbidden to speak, his companions whispered questions: What lay ahead? What would slavery mean? Would they simply be **8** transported from ship to ship indefinitely?

Cinqué had to find out.

9

626

Cross Curricular: Social Studies

JOURNEY FROM AFRICA Joseph Cinqué was kidnapped near what is now the country Sierra Leone.

RESEARCH AND INQUIRY Have students research information about Sierra Leone, particularly as it was in 1839, when Cinqué was captured.

Encourage students to use various resources to aid their search, including historical atlases and travel books.

▶ **Intrapersonal/Linguistic**

interNET CONNECTION Students can learn more about Sierra Leone by visiting **www.mhschool.com/reading**

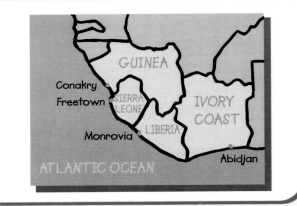

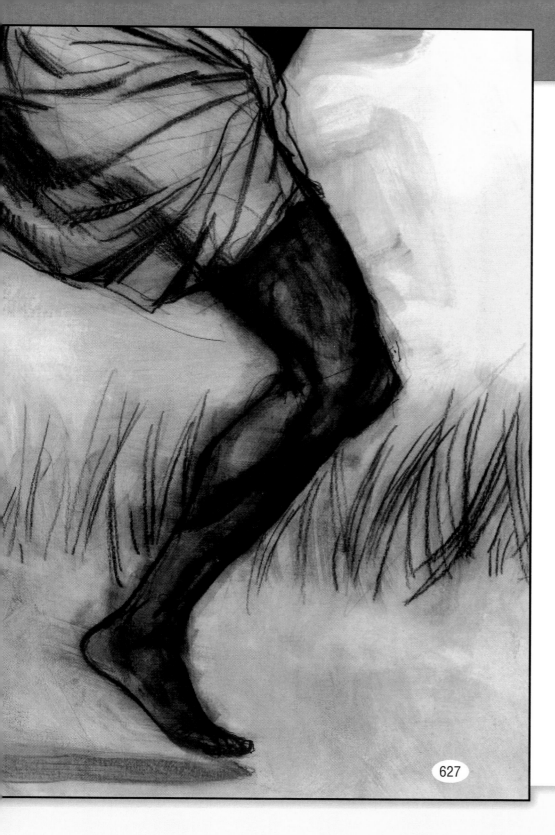

627

Guided Instruction

9 Cinqué and the other captives were forbidden to speak. How do you think they communicated with one another? (gestures, whispers, facial expressions) *Make Inferences*

Guided Instruction

10 It says here that Joseph Cinqué concluded that the Africans were going to be eaten. Do you think he got the right idea? (no) **Why not?** (Celestino was playing a joke on him.) *Draw Conclusions*

11 **JUDGMENTS AND DECISIONS**
What has Joseph Cinqué decided? (that he won't let the slave traders eat him) **What do you think he will do now?** (Possible answer: Joseph Cinqué will try to escape.) Let's add this information to our Decision chart.

WHAT HAPPENED	DECISION
Joseph Cinqué is kidnapped and imprisoned on a ship.	He decides to find out what is going to happen to him and his fellow prisoners.
Cinqué thinks the slave traders plan to kill him and the other Africans.	Cinqué decides to escape.

Visual Literacy

VIEWING AND REPRESENTING

Discuss the illustration on page 629. What do the two men seem to be feeling? How can you tell? (The man in the background seems to feel powerful. He is standing tall with his arms crossed. The other man seems to feel uncertain or afraid. His eyes are open wide.)

Occasionally, a few captives were allowed on deck for some air. Cinqué waited for his turn, and when he was finally ushered above, he attempted to coax some answers from Celestino, the cook. The two men communicated with hand gestures, for neither spoke the other's language.

Cinqué demanded to know what would happen to them.

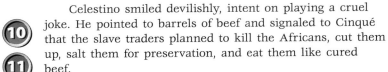

Celestino smiled devilishly, intent on playing a cruel **10** joke. He pointed to barrels of beef and signaled to Cinqué that the slave traders planned to kill the Africans, cut them up, salt them for preservation, and eat them like cured **11** beef.

Fear and anger filled Cinqué. He would not be eaten by the white men who held him captive. He would not.

628

629

Minilesson

REVIEW

/ù/ and /yù/

Have students pronounce the words *cook* and *would* on page 628.

- Ask students what vowel sound these words have in common. (/ù/)

- Explain that this sound can also be spelled *u* and give *pull* as an example.

Have students pronounce the word *cured* on page 628.

- Ask students what vowel sound is in this word. (/yù/)

Activity Have students brainstorm other words with /ù/ spelled *u, oo, ou* and /yù/ spelled *u*. Create a wall chart and list the words under each spelling.

LANGUAGE SUPPORT

ESL Some students who are primarily non-English speaking might relate to the trouble Joseph Cinqué has communicating with Celestino. Encourage students to form pairs and role-play a situation in which neither student speaks the other's language. Have them use gibberish to communicate. Students might role-play trying to buy something, or learning directions to some place. Encourage the students to discuss their efforts to communicate. Were they able to get their point across? What clues did they use to understand the other person?

629

Guided Instruction

12 Why was it so important that the Africans found a box of sugarcane knives? What do you think they will do next? (Sample answer: They will fight or kill the slave traders.) *Make Predictions*

TEACHING TIP

INSTRUCTIONAL As students read, point out that one way to understand what Cinqué and the other captives are going through is to visualize the setting, characters, and events in the story. What do they think the *Amistad* looked like? How did everyone fit onto such a crowded ship? What sounds did they hear? What did they smell?

630

Cross Curricular: Science

SHIP'S PROVISIONS Point out to students that the author mentions bananas, bread, and cured beef as foods that were eaten aboard the ship. Discuss with students the special demands on food that was stored and eaten on a ship. (It had to be preserved, and not attract insects or other pests.)

Activity Have students work in small groups to prepare a list of provisions for an ocean voyage in the nineteenth century. Remind them to choose foods that could stay edible after weeks of storage.

▶ **Interpersonal/Logical**

potatoes | hard tack

pickled limes | cured beef

He decided to strike that night. With a loose nail he had found earlier in a deck board, he picked the lock on his shackles, freeing himself and then the other prisoners. Once free, they quieted the four children and searched the cargo hold. A box of sugarcane knives was discovered a boon!

631

Guided Instruction

Guided Instruction

13 **JUDGMENTS AND DECISIONS**
What has Joseph Cinqué decided to do now? (force the sailors to take him and the others back to Africa) Let's add this information to the chart.

WHAT HAPPENED	DECISION
Joseph Cinqué is kidnapped and imprisoned on a ship.	He decides to find out what is going to happen to him and his fellow prisoners.
Cinqué thinks the slave traders plan to kill him and the other Africans.	Cinqué decides to escape.
The Africans fight the sailors and take control of the ship.	Cinqué decides to force the sailors to sail back to Africa.

14 **JUDGMENTS AND DECISIONS**
Was it right or wrong for the Africans to kill the sailors on board the *Amistad?* Did they have any other choices? (Sample answer: It was wrong for the Africans to kill the sailors, but they had to in order to escape.)

SELF-MONITORING

STRATEGY

REREAD Rereading a part of the story can help a reader to understand why characters make certain judgments and decisions. Pause and allow students to look back and reread a passage they found difficult.

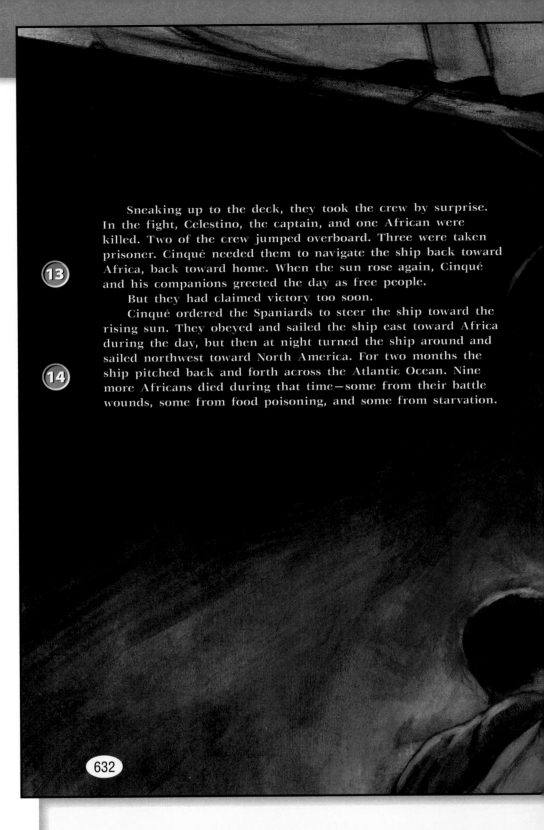

13   Sneaking up to the deck, they took the crew by surprise. In the fight, Celestino, the captain, and one African were killed. Two of the crew jumped overboard. Three were taken prisoner. Cinqué needed them to navigate the ship back toward Africa, back toward home. When the sun rose again, Cinqué and his companions greeted the day as free people.

But they had claimed victory too soon.

14   Cinqué ordered the Spaniards to steer the ship toward the rising sun. They obeyed and sailed the ship east toward Africa during the day, but then at night turned the ship around and sailed northwest toward North America. For two months the ship pitched back and forth across the Atlantic Ocean. Nine more Africans died during that time—some from their battle wounds, some from food poisoning, and some from starvation.

632

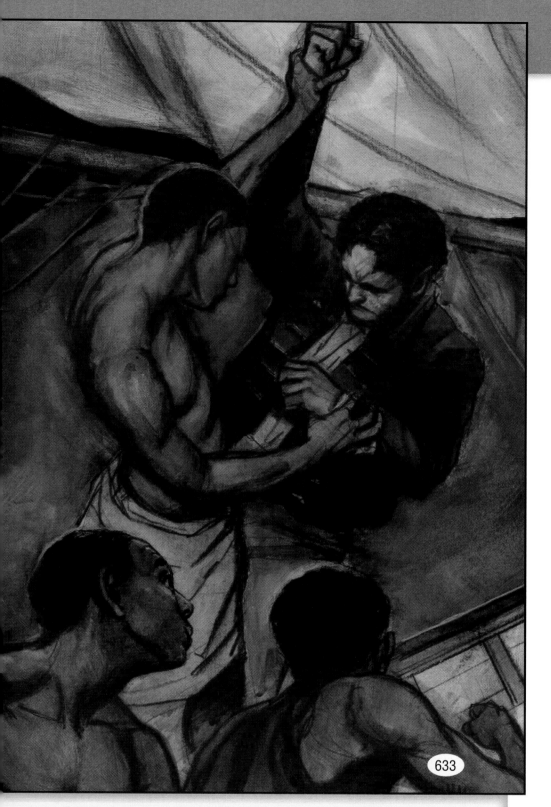

633

Guided Instruction

COMPOUND WORDS Read the first paragraph on page 632 again. What does the word *overboard* mean?

PREVENTION/INTERVENTION

COMPOUND WORDS Explain that the word *overboard* is a compound word. Ask students to name the two base words that combine to make this compound word. (*over* and *board*) Explain that this word means "over the side of a ship."

Challenge students to find another compound word on page 632. (*north-west*) Ask students to explain the meaning of this word. (the direction between north and west on a compass) Explain that *northwest* is called an "intermediate direction." Ask students to name the other three intermediate directions. (northeast, southwest, southeast)

Guided Instruction

15 **JUDGMENTS AND DECISIONS** Read the second paragraph carefully. How did people in the United States feel about slavery? Did they all feel the same way? (No. The lieutenant thought it would be a good idea to sell the Africans as slaves. The abolitionists were fighting against slavery.)

Then, on August 27, 1839, the *Amistad* was escorted by an American ship into the harbor of New London, Connecticut. Weary, hungry, and hopelessly lost, Cinqué and the others were forced to come ashore.

15 An American naval lieutenant saw the possibility for quick profits in the Africans. But this was the North, and a group of whites and free blacks campaigning against the institution of slavery was gaining popularity. They called themselves abolitionists, and they took on Cinqué and the other Africans as their most important case.

The Africans were sent to prison in New Haven, Connecticut, until a decision could be made.

The abolitionists managed to find a translator, and Cinqué told his story in a U.S. court. He was only twenty-five years old, but his experience on the *Amistad* had given him the confidence of a much older man.

The courtroom was crowded, and many were moved by Cinqué's impassioned words.

"I am not here to argue the case against slavery," Cinqué said, "though I will say it is a sin against man and God. I am here to argue the facts. The indisputable, international law is that the stealing of slaves from Africa is now illegal."

634

635

Guided Instruction

MULTIPLE-MEANING WORDS
Read the sentence that contains the word *institution* in the second paragraph. What do you think the word *institution* means in this sentence?

Minilesson

REVIEW

Suffixes

Point out to students the words *abolitionist* and *translator* on page 634. Remind students that the suffixes *-ist* and *-or* refer to types of people. The suffix *-ist* is often used to mean a person who believes in a point of view. The suffix *-or* means someone who does something as a profession.

Activity Have students write a list of root words they know that can be changed by adding the suffix *-ist* or *-or*. (Some examples are *environmental* [environmentalist], *science* [scientist], *navigate* [navigator], *act* [actor], *educate* [educator].)

PREVENTION/INTERVENTION

MULTIPLE-MEANING WORDS
Have students reread the sentence that contains *institution*. Explain that this word can have different meanings in different contexts. This sentence tells us that the *institution* is one of slavery, and that it is being campaigned against by whites and free blacks. Ask students if this

meaning of *institution* is an idea or an object.

Have students look at the pictures throughout the story. Lead them to see that the practice, or idea, of slavery was an institution. Contrast this meaning of *institution* with that of a building, such as a church or a school.

635

Guided Instruction

 JUDGMENTS AND DECISIONS
What decision did the judge make about Cinqué and the others? (The judge decided they should be freed.) What do you think caused the judge to make that decision? (Sample answer: Cinqué's speech may have convinced the judge to free the Africans.) Remember to record these events and decisions on the Decision chart.

WHAT HAPPENED	DECISION
Joseph Cinqué is kidnapped and imprisoned on a ship.	He decides to find out what is going to happen to him and his fellow prisoners.
Cinqué thinks the slave traders plan to kill him and the other Africans.	Cinqué decides to escape.
The Africans fight the sailors and take control of the ship.	Cinqué decides to force the sailors to sail back to Africa.
The Africans are captured and put on trial.	The judge decides to free Cinqué and his countrymen.

 How do you think you would feel about the judge's decision if you were Cinqué? How would you express that in your face and body? *Critical Thinking/ Kinesthetic*

"The men who kidnapped us, who beat and tortured us, were—and are—guilty of this crime," Cinqué continued.

"We are a peaceful people. We regret the loss of life caused by our mutiny. But we are not savages. We took over the ship to save our lives. We have done no wrong. Allow us to go home."

The weekend before the judge made his decision, Cinqué and his companions waited in the New Haven jail, their hearts filled with fear and hope. The judge held the power to make the Africans slaves or to set them free. On Monday morning, January 13, 1840, they worried no longer. He had decided they should be returned home.

They were free.

636

Cross Curricular: Music

FOLK HERO Discuss Joseph Cinqué with students in terms of folk heroes, such as John Henry, Daniel Boone, or Davey Crockett. All three were folk heroes, and the songs written about them help us remember. If possible, sing or play the songs that have been written about these people.

Encourage students to work alone or in pairs to create a folk song about Joseph Cinqué. Suggest they make up a tune, or else use one of the tunes they are familiar with for the music. Have students write new words telling the story of Joseph Cinqué.

▶ **Musical/Linguistic**

637

Guided
Instruction

TEACHING TIP

INSTRUCTIONAL The language in this selection is particularly rhythmic and evocative. Encourage students to enjoy the selection by reading parts or all of it out loud.

Guided Instruction

18 Look at the picture on pages 638 and 639. Who do you think the two people are? (Joseph Cinqué and John Quincy Adams) **Where are they and what are they doing?** (They are in the courthouse; Adams is speaking, Cinqué is listening.) **What are Cinqué and Adams looking at?** (Sample answer: They are looking at a Justice of the Supreme Court.) *Character/Setting*

638

CULTURAL PERSPECTIVES

VIEWS ON SLAVERY In 1839, slavery was a controversial issue in the United States. In other countries, such as Great Britain, slavery had been abolished. However, in many countries and colonies in the Americas, such as Cuba, slavery was still legal.

Activity Have students work in small groups to research when slavery was outlawed in different countries. Have each group create a time line from 1800–1900 listing the years different countries abolished slavery.

▶ **Interpersonal/Linguistic**

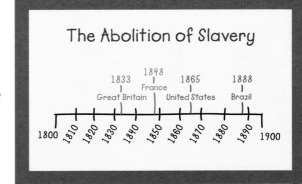

The Abolition of Slavery

1833 Great Britain | 1848 France | 1865 United States | 1888 Brazil

1800 1810 1820 1830 1840 1850 1860 1870 1880 1890 1900

But as Cinqué was soon to learn, the passage to freedom was as winding as the *Amistad*'s journey across the sea. President Martin Van Buren, concerned that freeing the Mende would enrage southern slave holders, ordered the district attorney to file an appeal so the case would be heard in the U.S. Supreme Court. And because of this, Cinqué gained his greatest American ally: former president John Quincy Adams.

Having heard about the mutineers, Adams came out of retirement to argue Cinqué's case. He was seventy-two years old. It had been more than thirty years since he had argued a case in a courtroom, and the thought of bearing the responsibility for this one worried the elderly statesman deeply.

But inspired by Cinqué, whom many of the abolitionists had begun to refer to as the Black Prince, Adams tirelessly prepared his defense. In court he spoke on behalf of the Mende for seven and a half hours. Sweat poured from his brow, and his voice filled the packed courtroom as he presented his case. There were many factors at play: Were the Africans the rightful property of the Spaniards? Were they brutal murderers? Or were they freedom fighters, no different than the men and women who had rebelled against England and founded the United States of America? There was also international pressure. Spain wanted the slaves and the *Amistad* returned to Cuba; could the United States risk provoking European ire over the lives of the thirty-five surviving Africans?

After Adams made his closing arguments, the Supreme Court retired to deliberate. For Cinqué and the others, the fearful process of waiting and praying began again.

A week later, on March 9, 1841, the Supreme Court announced that Adams had prevailed.

The Africans were truly free.

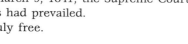
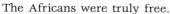

639

Guided Instruction

19 **JUDGMENTS AND DECISIONS** Why do you think President Van Buren decided to appeal the case against Cinqué? (Sample answer: He was afraid of enraging Southern slaveholders. Remind students to support their conclusions with clues from the text.)

20 **JUDGMENTS AND DECISIONS** Many decisions are mentioned on this page. What are some of them? (The President decides to appeal the case. John Quincy Adams decides to argue for Cinqué and the others. The court decides to free the Africans.)

LANGUAGE SUPPORT

ESL Some students might be confused by the third paragraph on page 639. The author lists many questions. Discuss with students why the author would write these thoughts as questions, rather than statements. What answer was Adams expecting the court to make to his questions? Encourage students to work in pairs to practice turning statements into questions that imply an answer. (For example: "I am a good student" to "Am I not a good student?")

Guided Instruction

(21) JUDGMENTS AND DECISIONS
Was it right for the Supreme Court to free Cinqué and the others? (yes) Who should have paid to send the Africans home? (Possible answer: The slave traders should pay for their voyage.)

(22) The author writes about the people tasting the sweetness of freedom in their mouths. Can you really taste freedom? Maybe feeling free is like tasting something sweet. How do you think the author would describe the taste of anger? *Make Inferences/Kinesthetic*

(21) It took eight months for the abolitionists to raise the money for the Africans' long journey back to West Africa. But at last the ship sailed, and when the African coast was finally in sight, Cinqué gathered everyone together.

"Let us give praise and thanks," Cinqué called out, his voice booming across the deck. "By the strength of our spirit and with the assistance of our ancestors, we are not slaves today. Our children will not be slaves. And their children will not be slaves. We are exactly as God willed us to be. My brothers, my sisters, we are free." Savoring the word, he let it melt like sugar on his tongue. He paused and then tasted the word again. "Free," he said, more softly now.

(22) Each person aboard the ship felt the word coming up from their hearts, tasted the sweetness of it in their mouths, then released it into the salty sea air. "Free," they said in unison. "We are free."

640

641

Guided Instruction

Guided Instruction

(23) JUDGMENTS AND DECISIONS Let's complete our Decision chart. How did the events of this story affect the decisions made by the characters?

WHAT HAPPENED	DECISION
Joseph Cinqué is kidnapped and imprisoned on a ship.	He decides to find out what is going to happen to him and his fellow prisoners.
Cinqué thinks the slave traders plan to kill him and the other Africans.	Cinqué decides to escape.
The Africans fight the sailors and take control of the ship.	Cinqué decides to force the sailors to sail back to Africa.
The Africans are captured and put on trial.	The judge decides to free Cinqué and his countrymen.
President Van Buren appeals the decision and the case goes to the Supreme Court.	The Supreme Court decides in the Africans' favor and they sail home.

RETELL THE STORY Ask volunteers to tell the major events of the story by referring to their charts. Then have partners write two sentences that summarize the story.
Summarize

STUDENT SELF-ASSESSMENT

- How did using the strategy of identifying judgments and decisions help me to understand the story?

  TRANSFERRING THE STRATEGY

- When might I try using this strategy again? In what other reading could the Decision chart help me?

If you stand right here on the New London shore, you can hear the words of the great Joseph Cinqué. His voice is so powerful that it travels across both space and time. If you bend down to the Atlantic, you can hear it in the beating of the waves. The wind whispers it as it blows around your head. And when the rain falls, it's like tears of happiness.

You can hear his words almost anywhere you listen for them: "We are free. Free. Free. Free."

642

REREADING FOR *Fluency*

GROUP Have students read this story out loud in small groups, each person reading a page.

READING RATE You may want to evaluate a student's reading rate. Have the student read aloud from *Amistad Rising* for one minute. Place a self-stick note after the last word read. Then count the number of words he or she has read.

Alternatively, you could assess small groups or the whole class together by having students count words and record their own scores.

Use the Reading Rate form in the **Diagnostic/Placement Evaluations** booklet to evaluate students' performance.

643

Guided Instruction

Return to Predictions and Purposes

Review with students their story predictions and reasons for reading the story. Were their predictions correct? Did they discover what they wanted to know?

PREDICTIONS	WHAT HAPPENED
The Africans will take over the slave ship.	The Africans did take over the slave ship. They were caught and put on trial.
The Africans will be freed in the end.	The Africans won their freedom because of Joseph Cinqué's speech and John Quincy Adams' help.

INFORMAL ASSESSMENT

JUDGMENTS AND DECISIONS

HOW TO ASSESS

- Encourage students to point out places in this story where Joseph Cinqué makes decisions or judgments.

Students should identify an important judgment or decision made by Joseph Cinqué, such as his decision to escape.

FOLLOW UP Work with students who are having difficulty identifying judgments and decisions by pointing out the places in the story where characters take action. Have them read the passage immediately before the one in which the character takes action.

LITERARY RESPONSE

QUICK-WRITE Have students write their thoughts about this story in their journals. Use these questions to help students get started:

JOURNAL

- Would the courts have decided this case differently if importing slaves from Africa had still been legal in 1839?

- Do you think the language that the author uses makes the story stronger or weaker? Why?

ORAL RESPONSE Have students use their journal entries to discuss the story and the way it is written.

Story Questions

Amistad Rising

Have students discuss or write answers to the questions on page 644.

Answers:

1. The Africans were chained together with shackles. They were beaten and given little food. *Literal/Plot*

2. Cinqué decides to take over the ship to keep from being sold as a slave. *Inferential/Judgments and Decisions*

3. The *Amistad* case helped convince people that slavery was wrong. *Inferential/Draw Conclusions*

4. Cinqué and other Africans are kidnapped by slave traders. They take over the *Amistad* and are put on trial. They are finally freed and return home. *Critical/Summarize*

5. Cinqué might tell them to follow their goals without letting anything stand in their way. *Critical/Reading Across Texts*

Write a story sequel For a full writing process lesson, see pages 647K–647L.

Story Questions & Activities

1. How were the Africans treated on the slave ship *Amistad*?

2. Why does Joseph Cinqué decide to take over the ship? Do you think his decision was a good one? Explain.

3. How did Joseph Cinqué leave his mark on American history?

4. What happens in this true story?

5. Imagine that Joseph Cinqué became part of the painting on pages 616–617. What do you think he would say to the people who are singing in the picture?

Write a Story Sequel

What do you think happened after Cinqué went home to his village in West Africa? Choose events that could have happened, and write a story sequel. Include a beginning, a middle, and an end. Write character dialogue, and make sure there is a strong setting and plenty of action.

Meeting Individual Needs

EASY	ON-LEVEL	CHALLENGE

EASY

Vocabulary

Write the best words from the box to complete the paragraph.

escorted	navigate	perished	ushered	nightfall	coax

Carolina worked carefully to _navigate_ the ship safely to shore through the storm. She knew she had to reach land before _nightfall_ blinded her. Once she sailed the boat into the harbor, a pilot boat _escorted_ it to the dock. At the dock, the harbor master _ushered_ in a Coast Guard officer to ask Carolina some questions. She struggled to _coax_ explanations through her chattering lips. The officer praised Carolina, saying that without her sailing skills, she might have _perished_ in the storm.

Story Comprehension

Circle the answer to each question about "Amistad Rising."

1. Why are Joseph and the other Africans taken from their home?
   (a.) to be sold as slaves   b. to build a village road   c. to be killed
2. What do the captive Africans do on board the *Amistad*?
   a. buy their freedom   (b.) take over the ship   c. sink the ship
3. What were the rules about slavery at this time?
   a. Slave trading was legal.   b. Slave owning was not legal.
   (c.) Slave trading was not legal.
4. In what country are the Africans jailed after landing on the *Amistad*?
   a. Africa   (b.) United States   c. Cuba
5. What happens to the Africans in the United States after the trial?
   (a.) They are set free to return to Africa.   b. They are tried and jailed for life.
   c. They are freed to live in New London.

At Home: Think of another sentence that tells something about "Amistad Rising."
187–188   Book 5/Unit 6 *Amistad Rising* 5

Reteach, 188

ON-LEVEL

Story Comprehension

Review "Amistad Rising." Then answer the questions below.
Answers will vary. Sample answers shown.

1. Who is the main character of "Amistad Rising"? Where was this person from?
   His original name was Singbe, but he was given the name Joseph Cinqué by the slave traders; Sierra Leone, which is located in West Africa.

2. When does this story take place? Is it a true story or not? How do you know?
   1839–1840; It is true; the author says that it is a true story at the beginning.

3. What was Joseph Cinqué doing when he was captured and sold as a slave? Whom did he leave behind when he was forced into slavery? He was working on a village road in Africa; he left behind his wife, his three children, and his parents.

4. What were conditions like on the slave ship? Give an example. Conditions were awful: It was overcrowded; there was no bathroom, no fresh air; the people were put in chains so they could not move; there wasn't enough food or water.

5. What happened to many of the enslaved Africans while they were on the slave ship? Explain. Many died (perished) of disease, starvation, and beatings.

6. What was the one event that made Joseph Cinqué decide to lead the rebellion on the *Amistad*? The ship's cook, Celestino, led Joseph Cinqué to believe that the slave traders were going to kill the Africans and eat them.

At Home: Encourage students to write a summary for "Amistad Rising" and to share it with a family member. Students may create a visual retelling with a storyboard.
188   Book 5/Unit 6 *Amistad Rising* 6

Practice, 188

CHALLENGE

Vocabulary

coax	escorted	navigate	nightfall	perished	ushered

Sometimes it is difficult to remember the meaning of vocabulary words. You can use synonyms to help you memorize the meaning of words. For example, *escorted* means to "accompany," or "to go with." Find synonyms that can help you memorize the meaning of each word.

coax _urge, influence_
navigate _steer_
nightfall _dusk, evening_
perished _die, pass away_
ushered _escorted, guided_

Story Comprehension

In "Amistad Rising," Joseph Cinqué makes the very important decision to rebel against the slave traders that hold him captive. Write down the reasons for his decision. Then write down the possible choices he had. Do you think he made the best choice? Explain why.

Answers will vary. Possible response: Cinqué had the choice to either remain in slavery or to rebel against his captors. He made the right choice because he eventually won his freedom.

At Home: Create a flow chart that shows Joseph Cinqué's decision-making process.
187–188   Book 5/Unit 6 *Amistad Rising*

Extend, 188

Freewrite

Choose one of the many beautiful illustrations from "Amistad Rising." Look carefully at the picture and visualize the setting, characters, and events. Freewrite for three minutes. Put down everything that you see and your feelings about the picture.

Charlestown, July 24th, 1769.

TO BE SOLD,

On THURSDAY the third Day of AUGUST next,

A CARGO
OF
NINETY-FOUR
PRIME, HEALTHY

NEGROES,

CONSISTING OF
Thirty-nine MEN, Fifteen Boys, Twenty-four WOMEN, and Sixteen GIRLS.
JUST ARRIVED,
In the Brigantine DEMBIA, Francis Bare, Master, from SIERRA-LEON, by
DAVID & JOHN DEAS.

Find a Primary Source

"Amistad Rising" is a secondary source. Secondary sources are written by people who were not there themselves when the events were taking place. Yet they are usually based on primary sources. Find a primary source that sheds light on "Amistad Rising." Letters, diaries, news articles, speeches, and court records are all primary sources. Paintings, portraits, and posters of the period are, too. Compare and share sources with classmates.

Find Out More

John Quincy Adams defended Joseph Cinqué in court. What do you know about Adams, the sixth President of the United States? What were some of his greatest achievements? Start by checking in an encyclopedia or in a book about Presidents. Use what you learn to write a brief biography. Place your work in your portfolio. Refer to it when reading about John Quincy Adams in your social studies textbook.

645

Story Activities

Freewrite

Have each student freewrite for three minutes after they have spent a few minutes looking carefully at one of the illustrations. Encourage students to imagine the different sights and sounds and smells that exist in the picture. Invite students to share their writing with the class.

Find a Primary Source

Encourage groups of students to work together to find a primary source that gives additional information on *Amistad Rising*. Remind students that a primary source is written by someone who was actually at the event when it was taking place. Have students compare and share sources with their classmates.

Find Out More

RESEARCH AND INQUIRY Have students work with partners to find out more about John Quincy Adams. Suggest that they create a time line to organize some important events of his life. Students might also focus on interesting facts about Adams, such as the fact that his father was also President of the United States.

*inter***NET** **CONNECTION** For more information on John Quincy Adams, students can visit *www.mhschool.com/reading*

FORMAL ASSESSMENT

After page 645, see the Selection Assessment.

Study Skills

GRAPHIC AIDS

OBJECTIVES Students will read and interpret a map.

PREPARE Read the passage with students. Display **Teaching Chart 153.**

TEACH Have students look at the map. Encourage them to look for the places mentioned in *Amistad Rising*.

PRACTICE Have students answer questions 1–5. Review the answers with them.

1. North America to West Africa; Africa to Cuba/West Indies; and Cuba/West Indies to North America. **2.** Rum and manufactured goods. **3.** Cuba/West Indies. **4.** The trade routes form a triangle. **5.** It shows where the Africans came from, where they were supposed to go, and where they came to shore.

ASSESS/CLOSE Encourage students to use the map to locate other places.

Study Skills

Read a Map

What do you know about the triangular trade route? In the story, Joseph Cinqué and many other Africans were taken captive by slave traders. Thousands of Africans died on the voyage to the Americas. Look at the map of the triangular trade route. The first leg of the triangle started at ports such as Boston or New York. Traders sailed from these ports to the coast of West Africa. There they traded rum and iron goods for gold, ivory, and Africans. The second leg of the triangle began in Africa. From there, thousands of Africans were taken to the West Indies, where they were traded for molasses. In the last leg of the triangle, the ships returned to New England.

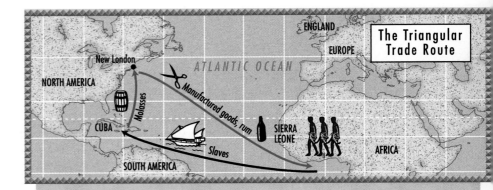

Use the map to answer these questions.

1 What were the three legs of the triangular trade route?

2 What products were shipped from New England to Africa?

3 What was the destination of most of the enslaved Africans?

4 Why was this called the triangular trade route?

5 How does using this map help you understand the events in "Amistad Rising"?

Meeting Individual Needs

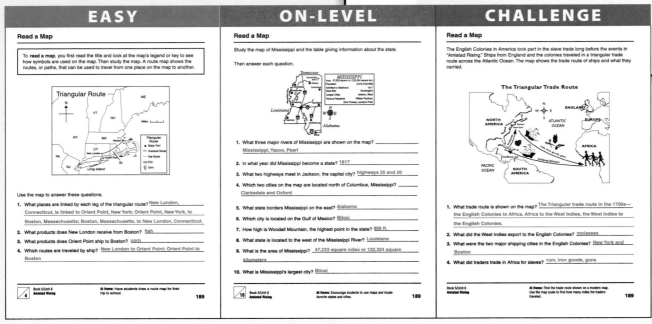

| Reteach, 189 | Practice, 189 | Extend, 189 |

TAAS TEST POWER

Test

Power

Test Tip

Rule out wrong answer choices.

DIRECTIONS

Read the sample story. Then read each question about the story.

SAMPLE

The Krispies Contest

Trisha saw an advertisement for a contest on the back of her favorite box of cereal. Trisha decided to enter as soon as she could. This is what she saw:

Krispies!

Krispies cereal is having an essay contest!
Write a fifty-word essay that tells why you love to eat Krispies cereal. The deadline is November 1—so don't delay!

1st Place: A lifetime supply of Krispies cereal!
2nd Place: Krispies cereal jeans jacket.
3rd Place: A Krispies cereal T-shirt and a <u>coordinating</u> baseball cap— both with our logo on them!

1 In this story the word <u>coordinating</u> means —

- ● matching
- ○ colorful
- ○ important
- ○ different

2 According to the contest advertisement, to enter the contest you need to —

- ○ give your friends Krispies cereal
- ● write an essay
- ○ order a jeans jacket
- ○ wear a Krispies cereal T-shirt

Did you rule out wrong answers? Tell how.

647

Test Power

THE PRINCETON REVIEW

Read the Page

Have students read *all* the information in the ad. Remind students to read through each answer choice before choosing the best one.

Discuss the Questions

Question 1: This question asks students to define a word in context. The clue, "both with our logo on them!" will help students eliminate answers that don't make sense.

Question 2: This question requires students to locate information in the advertisement. Have students look at the ad. Ask them to tell you where they can find the information about what one needs to do to enter the contest. The first sentences of the ad say, "Krispies cereal is having an essay contest! Write a fifty-word essay...." Eliminate answers that aren't supported by the passage.

For The Princeton Review test preparation practice for **TerraNova, ITBS,** and **SAT-9,** visit the McGraw-Hill School Division Web site. See also McGraw-Hill's *Standardized Test Preparation Book.*

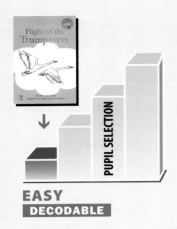

PUPIL SELECTION

EASY
DECODABLE

Leveled Books

Flight of the Trumpeters

retold by Lisa Norby
illustrated by Susan Kathleen Hartung

EASY

Flight of the Trumpeters

/ủ/ and /yủ/

☑ **Judgments and Decisions**

☑ **Instructional Vocabulary:** *coax, escorted, navigate, nightfall, perished, ushered*

Guided Reading

PREVIEW AND PREDICT Discuss each illustration up to page 11 and predict what the story is about.

SET PURPOSES Have students write what they intend to find out by reading *Flight of the Trumpeters*.

READ THE BOOK Use questions like the following to guide students' reading or after they have read the story independently.

Page 4: Look at the word *mute* on this page. What vowel sound is in this word? /ủ/ What other words have this same sound? (Sample answers: *use, yule, huge*) *Phonics and Decoding*

Page 4: What judgment does the author make about mute swans? (They are not good for the environment) What does the author base this judgment on? (They drive away ducks and destroy underwater plants) *Judgments and Decisions*

Page 8: What would you do if you were going to *coax* an animal to follow you? Use your body to show what you would do. *Instructional Vocabulary*

Page 11: What judgment did the baby swans make about Gavin Shire and why? (That he was their mother, because he was the first thing they saw when they hatched) *Judgments and Decisions*

Page 16: Why does the author call the first migration a success? (Because the swans followed the plane, arrived at their winter home, and made a good effort at returning) *Drawing Conclusions*

RETURN TO PREDICTIONS AND PURPOSES Have students review their purposes for reading. Did they find out what they wanted? Encourage students to discuss their responses to the story, and how close they came to their predictions about it.

LITERARY RESPONSE Discuss these questions:

- What is your favorite part of this story?
- Would you like to see the trumpeter swans in flight? Why?

Also see the story questions and activity in *Flight of the Trumpeters*.

Answers to Story Questions

1. Hunters killed them for their feathers; some swans ate old lead pellets.
2. Because of a natural phenomenon called imprinting, the swans followed the first thing they saw after they hatched.
3. They do not want the birds to become extinct.
4. The author wants to inform readers about the trumpeters and what is being done to help them migrate so that year after year they will be able to return to their winter and summer homes.
5. Answers will vary, but should generally relate to the theme of returning home.

Story Questions and Activity

1. How did trumpeter swans almost become extinct?
2. Why did Isabelle, Sidney, and Yo-Yo follow the ultralight plane?
3. Why do you think scientists and bird lovers are working so hard to bring back trumpeter swans?
4. What is the main idea of the book?
5. What about this story relates to *Amistad Rising*? Explain your answer.

More Research

At your school or local library, find the book *The Trumpet of the Swan* by E.B. White. Read it and write a one-page book report about it.

from Flight of the Trumpeters

Leveled Books

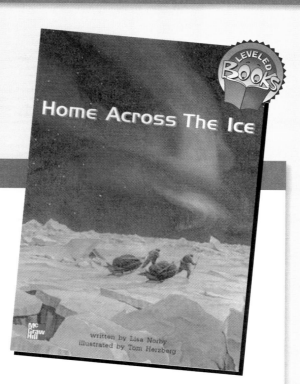

INDEPENDENT

Home Across the Ice

☑ **Judgments and Decisions**

☑ **Instructional Vocabulary:**
coax, escorted, navigate, nightfall, perished, ushered

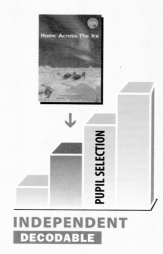

INDEPENDENT
DECODABLE

Guided Reading

PREVIEW AND PREDICT Discuss each illustration up to page 8 and predict what the story is about.

SET PURPOSES Discuss with students what purpose they might have for reading *Home Across the Ice*. Have them write their purposes in their journals.

READ THE BOOK Use questions such as the following to guide students as they read or after they have read the story independently.

Page 3: What judgment did Fritjof Nansen make about ice? (That it could be a friend, rather than an enemy.) *Judgments and Decisions*

Page 4: Did Fritjof Nansen prepare well or poorly for the journey? Use words from the story to support your answer. (Answers will vary: most students would answer that he prepared well.) *Drawing Conclusions*

Page 5: What did Fritjof Nansen decide to do when he realized his dogsled team wouldn't reach the North Pole? (To turn back) *Judgments and Decisions*

Page 8: What does it mean when the author says "Nightfall came earlier every day"? (That the sun was setting earlier and earlier) *Instructional Vocabulary*

Page 11: Did Fritjof make the right decision when he jumped in the water? Explain. (Sample answer: he did, since he managed to save their kayaks.) *Judgments and Decisions*

Page 16: How would you describe Fritjof Nansen? (Sample answer: he is brave, or resourceful.) *Judgments and Decisions*

RETURN TO PREDICTIONS AND PURPOSES Have students return the predictions they made about this story. How close were they to what actually happened in the book? Encourage students to discuss their purposes for reading the book and whether those purposes were fulfilled.

LITERARY RESPONSE Discuss these questions:

• What was your favorite part of this story?

• What sort of expedition would you like to go on? Why?

Also see the story questions and activity in *Home Across the Ice*.

Answers to Story Questions

1. It had a rounded bottom so that ice would slide underneath it.
2. It was good because he was courageous and used his resources to conquer any problems that came his way. He also was moving "forward" and onward to arrive home safely.
3. Answers will vary but may include: the men made wise choices in their use of the resources around them, such as making a den of walrus skin, and using other parts of the animal to survive. Nansen was quick thinking when dealing with the threatening polar bear and the bears attacking the den.
4. A true account of how two men survived a long trek and returned home safely.
5. Answers will vary.

Story Questions and Activity

1. What was special about the Fram's construction?
2. The word *fram* means "forward." Why was this a good motto for Nansen?
3. Did Nansen and Johansen make good judgments about how to survive on the ice?
4. What is the main idea of the book?
5. What about this story is similar to the story of Joseph Cinqué in *Amistad Rising?* What do Cinqué and Fridtjof Nansen share in common?

Make a Ship

Make a ship that looks similar to the *Fram*. You might use molding materials, wood or cut cardboard. Think about how you will form the ship's round bottom. Add a name to your ship that makes a good motto for you. Share your ship and your motto with classmates.

from Home Across the Ice

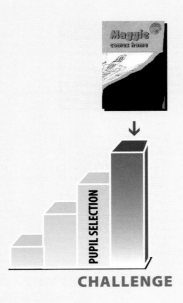

PUPIL SELECTION

CHALLENGE

Leveled Books

Maggie comes home

CHALLENGE

Maggie Comes Home

☑ **Judgments and Decisions**

☑ **Instructional Vocabulary:** *coax, escorted, navigate, night-fall, perished, ushered*

Guided Reading

PREVIEW AND PREDICT Have students look at the illustrations up to page 7 and predict what the story is about.

SET PURPOSES Have students write why they want to read *Maggie Comes Home*.

READ THE BOOK Use questions like the following to guide students as they read.

Page 3: What judgments has Maggie made about Waynesville so far? (Sample answer: it doesn't feel like home.) *Judgments and Decisions*

Page 8: Look at the word *navigate* on this page. What synonyms can you think of for *navigate*? (steer, maneuver) *Instructional Vocabulary*

Page 11: Why does Maggie decide she must put the red boots away in a box? (Because her aunt tells her they are old and valuable.) *Judgments and Decisions*

Page 13: Why is Maggie so frightened? (Sample answer: Maggie thinks she's seen a ghost.) *Drawing Conclusions*

Page 16: What caused Maggie to change her mind about Waynesville? (Sample answer: some students might mention the story her aunt tells) *Judgments and Decisions*

RETURN TO PREDICTIONS AND PURPOSES Have students discuss the book and their purposes in reading it. Did they learn what they hoped to from the book? Remind students to check their predictions to see how close they were predicting what information the book would contain.

LITERARY RESPONSE Discuss these questions:

• What do you think happened next in the story?

• What are some things you might like to find in an attic?

Also see the story questions and activity in *Maggie Comes Home*.

Answers to Story Questions

1. She was five years old, in kindergarten.
2. They both had the same name and they both had to adjust to moving from one place to another.
3. After she heard that her great-grandmother eventually adjusted to her move; also the phone call from Rachel helped convince her that she would be making new friends.
4. It is about a young girl's adjustment to her move to a new town and new school far away from her old ones.
5. Answers will vary.

Story Questions and Activity

1. How old was Maggie when she left Waynesville?
2. Why did Maggie feel close to her great grandmother, even though she had never met her?
3. At what point in the story did Maggie decide that Waynesville might not be a bad place to live after all?
4. What is the story mostly about?
5. What are some things about this story that remind you of *Amistad Rising*? Explain why.

Write a Story

Imagine you are exploring an attic in an old house. Write a story about what you find and explain what it means to you.

from Maggie Comes Home

Activities
Anthology and Leveled Books

Connecting Texts

OBSTACLES Have students make charts showing what obstacles each character had to overcome before they could get home, or felt that they were at home.

Amistad Rising	Flight of the Trumpeters	Home Across the Ice	Maggie Comes Home
• Joseph Cinqué had to convince the Supreme Court to let him go home.	• The swans had to learn how to migrate in order to reach their winter homes.	• Fritjof Nansen had to survive for months on an ice floe in the Arctic before he could return home.	• Maggie has to overcome her own negative feelings about her new home.

Viewing/Representing

HOME DISPLAYS Divide students into four groups, one for each story. Have each group research information about the homes described in the different selections. Encourage the groups to create dioramas, attaching labels or short passages to help describe each home.

AUDIENCE RESPONSE Allow students to view the dioramas, and to write a sentence or two about the most interesting aspect of each diorama.

Research and Inquiry

HOME HISTORIES Encourage students to find out information about the houses or buildings they live in. When were they built? What style were they built in? Encourage students to check local history books, books on architecture, as well as the Internet, and write a short report about their homes, or the home of a relative or neighbor.

interNET CONNECTION Students can learn more about building styles by visiting **www.mhschool.com/reading** on the Internet.

TESTED

OBJECTIVES

Students will identify judgments and decisions.

TEACHING TIP

INSTRUCTIONAL

Encourage students to list reasons "pro" and "con" when trying to make a difficult decision.

Review Judgments and Decisions

PREPARE

Discuss Judgments and Decisions in Amistad Rising

Review: Discuss with students the decisions and judgments that were made by the characters in *Amistad Rising*. Ask students if they agreed with all the decisions and judgments made in the story. Which ones did they agree/disagree with? Why? Remind students that it is important to look at the events leading up to a character's decision in order to understand their actions.

TEACH

Read the Passage

Ask students to pay attention to judgments and decisions as you read the passage with them.

"Come Help Us"

John Quincy Adams opened the letter from his friend in Washington, D.C. "Come help us," said the letter. "We are trying to defend a group of African slaves. They have broken the law by mutinying aboard a ship and killing some of the crew. We might lose the case, but our arguments could convince people that slavery is wrong. I know you are busy fighting against slavery in Massachusetts, but I wish you would make the time to come and help out." Adams folded the letter and thought to himself, "If I don't go, these Africans might be enslaved."

Teaching Chart 154

Model the Skill

Display **Teaching Chart 154.** Discuss clues in the passage that help readers identify judgments and decisions.

MODEL John Quincy Adams has to decide whether to stay in Massachusetts or go to Washington, D.C. to help argue the *Amistad* case. The letter says that John Quincy Adams is busy fighting against slavery in Massachusetts. If he was fighting against slavery, I think he must have thought that slavery was wrong. He will probably decide to go to Washington, D.C.

PRACTICE

Make Decisions

GROUP

Encourage students to underline the words on the Teaching Chart that give information about decisions and judgments.

Then have students pretend that they are John Quincy Adams and they have received the letter. Encourage groups to make a list of the "pros" and "cons" of going to Washington, D.C. to help with the *Amistad* case. ▶ **Interpersonal/Visual**

PRO	CON
Help a friend.	It is a long trip.
Persuade people that slavery is wrong.	There is work to do in Massachusetts to fight against slavery.
Help the Africans become free.	Might lose the case.

ASSESS/CLOSE

Make a Judgement

Have students show by raising hands whether they would choose to go to Washington, D.C. or stay in Massachusetts. Encourage students to share which reason they found most compelling in making their decision.

Meeting Individual Needs for Comprehension

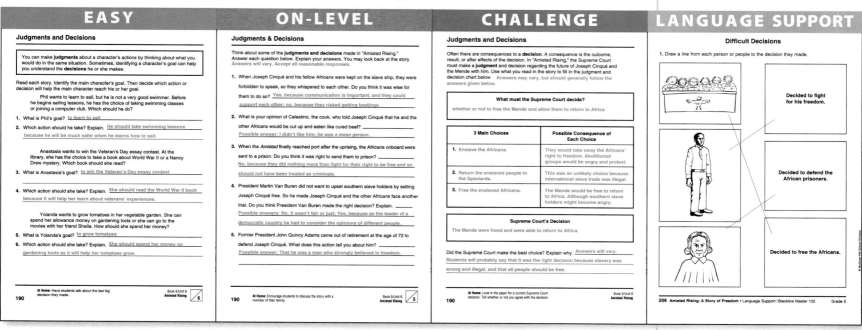

EASY	ON-LEVEL	CHALLENGE	LANGUAGE SUPPORT
Reteach, 190	Practice, 190	Extend, 190	Language Support, 206

OBJECTIVES

Students will review how to draw conclusions.

Review Draw Conclusions

PREPARE

Discuss Drawing Conclusions
Remind students that drawing conclusions means using information in the story and what they know from experience to reach a final opinion about a person, place, event, or situation. Encourage students to discuss their conclusions about Joseph Cinqué's abilities as a leader.

TEACH

Read the Passage and Model the Skill
Read the passage on **Teaching Chart 155** to students.

A Strange Room

The room was one of the strangest places Joseph Cinqué had ever seen. At one end was a <u>tall bench.</u> One man sat behind the bench. He was <u>wearing a black robe.</u> The man <u>held a hammer</u>, but he wasn't building anything. There were other tables, each with one or more men sitting behind them. Every so often, one of the men would stand up and talk for a long time. There were many people in the room, but they never laughed or smiled.

Teaching Chart 155

Discuss clues in the passage that help readers to draw conclusions about Joseph Cinqué's whereabouts.

MODEL The writer describes a room with a man sitting behind a tall bench. The man sitting behind the bench is wearing a black robe and holding a hammer. I know that a judge sits behind a tall bench, wears a black robe, and might use a tool, called a gavel, that looks like a hammer. I can draw the conclusion that Cinqué is in a courtroom.

PRACTICE

Draw Conclusions

PARTNERS

Have students underline clues that support the conclusion that Cinqué is in a courtroom. Then have them reread "A Strange Room." Ask them to draw conclusions about the character Cinqué from what they read. Have partners create charts that list some conclusions they have made about the character and reasons that support their conclusions.

▶ **Interpersonal/Visual**

ASSESS/CLOSE

Use Clues to Draw Conclusions

GROUP

Have students work in small groups to play a variation of the game "Twenty Questions." Explain the rules to students: One student should think of a famous person or place and write the name on a sheet of paper. The other students can then ask up to 20 questions about the person/place. The questions receive yes or no answers. Have students keep track of how many questions they ask before being able to guess the answer.

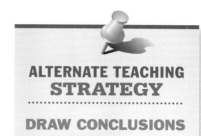

ALTERNATE TEACHING
STRATEGY
· ·
DRAW CONCLUSIONS
For a different approach to teaching this skill, see page T62.

Meeting Individual Needs for Comprehension

EASY	ON-LEVEL	CHALLENGE	LANGUAGE SUPPORT

EASY

Draw Conclusions

You can use clues from your reading to **draw conclusions**, or figure out things about story characters and events. Often, you need to use clues from your own experience as well. Try to draw your conclusions by using the clues in each sentence.

Read the sentences. Circle the letter next to each correct conclusion. Then explain your answer. Use the clue from the sentences.

1. Andie plays basketball on Mondays, tennis on Tuesdays, volleyball on Thursdays, and soccer on Saturday mornings.
   a. Andie is the best athlete in school.
   (b.) Andie enjoys playing sports.
   c. Andie doesn't like schoolwork.
2. Clue: Andie plays many sports.

3. Chandra uses her books on the American West and her collection of historical movies about cowboys to write her "Ride the Range" column for the school newspaper.
   (a.) Chandra has studied the American West carefully.
   b. Chandra knows nothing about the American West.
   c. Chandra doesn't like to write.
4. Clue: Chandra owns both books and movies about the American West.

5. Ming spoke only Chinese when she entered our school last month.
   a. Ming was born in England.
   b. Ming doesn't want to speak English.
   (c.) Ming's family speaks Chinese at home.
6. Clue: Ming speaks only Chinese at school.

Book 5/Unit 6
Amistad Rising   At Home: Have students think about the last story they read. Have them talk about a conclusion that they were able to draw from it.   191

ON-LEVEL

Draw Conclusions

When you **draw conclusions**, you use facts from a story as well as your own knowledge and experience. Drawing conclusions as you read can help you better understand a story. Answers will vary. Accept all well-reasoned responses.

Read the selection below, and then answer each question. Describe the clues that helped you draw each conclusion. Answers will vary.

Every weekday Inga and her father walked into town together. She often had to rush to keep up with him. Inga noticed that her father always slowed down just as they got to the watchmaker's shop. There, in the front window, was a beautiful, marble chess set. Her father never said anything about it, but Inga could tell he admired it. She had seen her father's collection of faded newspaper pictures of him playing chess years ago. In them, he looked very serious as he played. Inga checked the price of the set and decided she would start saving her allowance.

Two days before her father's birthday, Inga watched closely as her father slowed down in front of the watchmaker's shop. This time he actually stopped and she heard him say, "It's gone." Inga had to hide her smile.

1. What sort of chess player was Inga's father when he was young? Probably a very good player.

2. Story clue: There were pictures in the newspaper of him playing chess.

3. Experience clue: If you are really good at something, your picture might be in the newspaper. Since there were many pictures of him, he must have won a lot of chess games.

4. What happened to the marble chess set in the watchmaker's window? Inga bought the chess set for her father's birthday.

5. Story clue: Inga had started saving her allowance, and she smiled when her father mentions the chess set is gone.

6. Experience clue: I have saved my allowance for special presents.

Book 5/Unit 6
Amistad Rising   At Home: Encourage students to draw conclusions about an article in the newspaper.   191

CHALLENGE

Draw Conclusions

When you read a historical story, you can often **draw conclusions** about the ideas the author is presenting. You may draw conclusions from what is written on the page and from what you already know.

1. The prisoners aboard the *Amistad* were held in the ship's hold. They had no baths, no toilets, and were chained together. Many died of disease, malnutrition, and from beatings.
   • What conclusion can you draw about the way the Africans' captors felt about their prisoners?
   Answers will vary. Possible response: The captors had no respect or regard for the Africans' health or welfare. They were only interested in the money they could get by selling them as slaves.

2. Celestino, the cook, tells Joseph Cinqué that the slave traders were going to kill the Africans, cut them up, and prepare them to be eaten, like cured beef.
   • What conclusion can you draw about the type of man Celestino is?
   Answers will vary. Possible response: Celestino is most likely a cruel person who has no regard for others.

3. After the uprising, the Spaniards sail the ship back towards Africa by day, but then turn the ship around and sail in the opposite direction by night. The *Amistad*, therefore, sails in circles for two months.
   • What conclusions can you draw about the Africans' knowledge of navigating ships on the Ocean?
   Answers will vary. Possible response: They were not familiar with ship navigation or they would have been able to tell they were going in circles. They did not know how to use the stars in the night sky as guides.

4. John Adams comes out of retirement to defend Cinqué and the Mende. He is worried about the responsibility he has taken on.
   • What conclusions can you draw about the way Adams felt about slavery?
   Answers will vary. Possible answer: He believed very strongly that slavery was wrong, or he probably would not have come out of retirement and taken the case.

Book 5/Unit 6
Amistad Rising   At Home: Discuss how drawing conclusions can help you better understand what you read.   191

LANGUAGE SUPPORT

What Was Joseph Like?

strong   proud

brave   homesick

Grade 5   Language Support/Blackline Master 103 • Amistad Rising: A Story of Freedom   207

Reteach, 191   Practice, 191   Extend, 191   Language Support, 207

647H

OBJECTIVES

Students will use context clues to determine the meaning of specialized vocabulary.

Review Context Clues

PREPARE

Discuss Context Clues Remind students that many stories contain special vocabulary words that are not used in everyday speech. Context clues can help them to understand the special vocabulary in a story. Ask students to think about stories they know of that contain special vocabulary.

TEACH

Read the Passage In *Amistad Rising,* context clues can help students understand difficult words that are related to the slave trade and colonialism. Read the passage to students and display **Teaching Chart 156.** Ask students to pay attention to context clues that will help them understand difficult words.

Slavery in the United States

The slave traders forced the captives out of the locked room and into the street. Because their legs were shackled, the captives could walk only with great difficulty. These men and women had been taken from freedom in Africa and forced into captivity in America. They would be sold at the slave auction to work in the cotton fields of plantations. As this scene occurred over and over in the South, abolitionists in the North made speeches and wrote pamphlets to bring an end to slavery.

Teaching Chart 156

Identify Special Vocabulary and Model the Skill Have students circle different vocabulary words that relate to slavery. Then model finding context clues that can help them understand these words.

MODEL I can tell from the first sentence that the word *captives* must mean "prisoners" because they were kept in a locked room. *Shackled* must mean "chained together" since this made it difficult for the people to walk. The words *cotton fields* are context clues for the vocabulary word *plantation:* this must be a kind of farm.

PRACTICE

Identify and Use Context Clues

PARTNERS

Have students underline words on the Teaching Chart that serve as context clues for the circled words. Remind students that context clues can be single words or entire phrases and that they can appear before or after the vocabulary word. Have partners try writing definitions for the circled words. Have pairs exchange and compare their definitions.

▶ **Linguistic/Interpersonal**

ASSESS/CLOSE

Create Context Clues

GROUP

Have students work in small groups to create sentences with context clues. First, students should choose three difficult words from *Amistad Rising* or from another source. Then have them write sentences that contain each word as well as context clues that hint at its meaning. They should circle the difficult word. Groups should then exchange sentences and see if they can figure out the meaning of the circled words from the context clues provided.

Meeting Individual Needs for Vocabulary

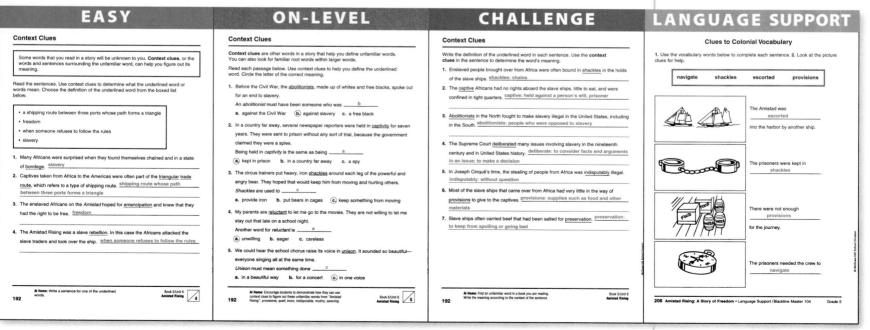

Reteach, 192   Practice, 192   Extend, 192   Language Support, 208

Writing a Story

TECHNOLOGY TIP

Have students review their drafts for logical order. Do the ideas flow smoothly? If not, encourage them to try moving paragraphs or sentences around by cutting and pasting the text.

Prewrite

WRITE A STORY SEQUEL Present this writing assignment: A story sequel begins where the first story stops. It continues the first story, telling what happened after it ended. You are going to write a sequel to *Amistad Rising: A Story Of Freedom.*

Strategy: Visualize Suggest that students let their minds wander to "see" what happens to Joseph Cinqué and his shipmates next. Have them list events and feelings on a flow chart. Have them consider:

- What happens when Joseph Cinqué and his shipmates return to their homes in Africa?
- How are they greeted by the people in their village?
- How do they feel about being back in Africa?
- What happens next in their lives?

Draft

USE CHART Students should use ideas from their visualization exercise and chart to write their sequels. Remind students that the sequel should be based on the first story. But, it should also be able to stand on its own as a separate story.

Revise

SELF-QUESTIONING Ask students to assess their drafts.

- Does my sequel continue the first story?
- Is there a clear beginning, middle and end to the story?
- Does my sequel read as a separate story?

Edit/Proofread

CHECK FOR ERRORS Students should reread their sequels for content, grammar, spelling, and punctuation.

Publish

SHARE THE SEQUELS Have volunteers read their sequels to the class, and discuss each sequel. Is it a continuation of the first story? Is it a satisfying story? Can it stand alone as a separate story?

A Changed Man

Joseph Cinqué finally returned to his village. There was a celebration to welcome him home.

At first Joseph was glad to be home. He wanted to resume his old life. But he was a changed man. He had seen other parts of the world. He had seen other languages and customs. Now the village felt small to him. He was no longer content with his old life.

After a while, Joseph left the village and brought his family to the capital. He decided to study law. He became a lawyer and devoted his life to helping other people who were in trouble.

Years passed. Joseph never went back to his village. He had a successful new life in the city. But every morning, when he greeted the sun and inhaled the city air, he always felt an ache in his heart. He would always miss the simple life of his village and his people.

Presentation Ideas

Have students create a book jacket for their sequel. Have students display book jacket while presenting their sequel to the class.

▶ **Viewing/Representing**

CREATE A TRILOGY Have students suggest a follow-up to each other's sequels. After each sequel is presented, ask students to suggest ideas for a story that continues this one. ▶ **Speaking/Listening**

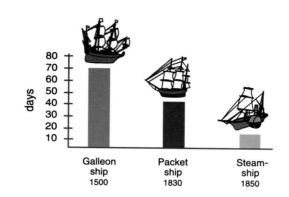

Consider students' creative efforts, possibly adding a plus (+) for originality, wit, and imagination.

Scoring Rubric

Excellent	Good	Fair	Unsatisfactory
4: The writer	**3:** The writer	**2:** The writer	**1:** The writer
• shows a clear understanding of sequel form.	• shows an understanding of sequel form.	• shows a limited understanding of sequel form.	• does not show an understanding of sequel form.
• makes sophisticated use of characters and events.	• makes imaginative use of characters and events.	• may not delve into characters and events.	• may not use characters and events.
• has a lively progression of new story events.	• has a progression of new story events.	• may lose grasp of the story line.	• may present disconnected images and ideas.
• presents a fresh, well-crafted story that holds a reader's interest.	• creates a story that holds the reader's interest.	• creates a sequel with some references to the original.	• may have severe trouble with basic storytelling and writing skills.

0: The writer leaves the page blank or fails to respond to the writing task. The student does not address the topic or simply paraphrases the prompt. The response is illegible or incoherent.

For a 6-point or an 8-point scale, see pages T105–T106.

Meeting Individual Needs for Writing

EASY	ON-LEVEL	CHALLENGE
Poster Have the students create posters announcing Joseph Cinqué's return to his village and inviting villagers to a celebration.	**Speech** Have the students write a speech given by the head of Joseph Cinqué's village, welcoming Joseph back to the village.	**Letter** Have the students write a from Joseph to his wife. The letter is written after Joseph has been away from his village for one year. Describe what Joseph is feeling after being away from his home, what his life consists of now, and his hopes for the future.

COMMUNICATION TIPS

REPRESENTING Suggest that students think about their creative process. Ask them to discuss why they have made particular choices in their writing.

LISTENING Suggest that students focus on their immediate response to the sequel. Do they like how this story begins or not? Does their attitude change as they hear the rest of the story? Why or why not?

LANGUAGE SUPPORT

 ESL Have students write four simple sentences or about what happened to Joseph Cinqué after he returned to his village. Have them work with a partner to help them with words they may not be familiar with.

PORTFOLIO Invite students to include their story sequels or another writing project in their portfolios.

LANGUAGE SUPPORT

Have students complete the following sentence: *John walks _____.* Have volunteers pantomime the adverbs used in the sentence.

DAILY LANGUAGE ACTIVITIES

Write each day's Daily Language Activities on the board or use **Transparency 26.** Have students orally revise the sentences by adding adverbs. Sample answers given for Day 1.

Day 1

1. The chains creaked. *eerily*
2. Cinqué thought he would be free. *never*
3. He planned his escape. *carefully*

Day 2

1. Cinqué freed the others.
2. They tried to steer the ship.
3. People sat in the courtroom.

Day 3

1. Cinqué tossed a line to him.
2. It was hard to sit in court every day.
3. John Quincy Adams carried a small book with him.

Day 4

1. Cinqué tried to smile, but he was feeling ill.
2. Cinqué would be home.
3. He was captured a year ago.

Day 5

1. The court had made such a ruling.
2. The prisoners walked in the dark.
3. He slept during the mutiny.

Daily Language Transparency 26

DAY 1 Introduce the Concept

Oral Warm-Up Read this sentence: *Cinqué moved quickly.* Ask students to identify the word that describes how Cinqué moved.

Introduce Adverbs Explain that sometimes adverbs are used to make descriptions clearer. Discuss:

> ### Adverbs
>
> - An adverb is a word that tells more about a verb, an adjective, or another adverb.
> - An adverb can tell how, when, or where an action takes place.

Present the Daily Language Activity and have students revise the sentences orally. Then ask them to write the sentences, using different adverbs.

 Assign the daily Writing Prompt on page 616C.

Adverbs

- An **adverb** is a word that tells more about a verb, an adjective, or another adverb.
- An adverb can tell *how, when,* or *where* an action takes place.

Underline the adverb in each sentence. On the line, write whether the adverb describes *how, when,* or *where.*

1. The slave ship <u>slowly</u> left the harbor. _____ how
2. The ship stank <u>inside</u>. _____ where
3. Spanish traders treated the slaves <u>roughly</u>. _____ how
4. Dead slaves were thrown <u>overboard</u>. _____ where
5. Stormy winds tossed the ship <u>mercilessly</u>. _____ how
6. Cinqué <u>always</u> thought about his wife and children. _____ when
7. He looked <u>downand</u> started planning. _____ where
8. Cinqué freed himself and <u>then</u> freed other slaves. _____ when
9. The men fought <u>hard</u>. _____ how
10. <u>Later</u> a judge sat and listened to their case. _____ when
11. The Africans waited <u>nervously</u> for his decision. _____ how
12. Because they were free, they <u>gladly</u> gave thanks. _____ how

Grade 5/Unit 6
Amistad Rising

Extension: Have students write three sentences about a historical event. Ask them to tell where, when, and how the event happened.

161

GRAMMAR PRACTICE BOOK, PAGE 161

DAY 2 Teach the Concept

Review Adverbs Have students identify the adverbs in the following sentence: *The crew sailed yesterday.*

More About Adverbs Ask students to explain what an adverb does and to give examples. Then present the following:

> - An adverb can describe an adjective or another adverb.

List the following adverbs: *almost, fairly, quite, slightly, terribly, too, completely, hardly, really, so, very.* Have volunteers use them in sentences.

Present the Daily Language Activity. Have students orally add an adverb to each sentence.

 Assign the daily Writing Prompt on page 616C.

Adverbs

- An adverb can describe an adjective or another adverb.

In these sentences, the adverbs describe verbs, adverbs, or adjectives. Underline each adverb

1. The anchor sank <u>slowly</u>.
2. Cinqué decided <u>very quickly</u>.
3. The sails were <u>almost</u> full.
4. I think that Cinqué acted <u>quite bravely</u>.
5. He and the other enslaved Africans were <u>finally</u> free.

Complete each sentence with an adverb that describes the underlined word. You can choose from the adverbs in the box. Answers will vary.

| almost | very | completely | terribly | quite | rather | too |

6. Slave traders acted _____ very _____ selfishly.
7. The ships fought _____ quite _____ hard.
8. The skies were _____ terribly _____ black.
9. The stars were _____ completely _____ amazing.
10. The judge will decide _____ rather _____ quickly.

162

Extension: Ask partners to write three sentences with at least one adverb in them. Have partners try to add another adverb to each other's sentences.

Grade 5/Unit 6
Amistad Rising

GRAMMAR PRACTICE BOOK, PAGE 162

Adverbs

DAY 3 — Review and Practice

Learn from the Literature Review adverbs. Read the first sentence in the second paragraph on page 626.

> **Every day Cinqué grew more restless, wondering what the Spaniards intended to do with him and the other Africans.**

Ask students to identify the adverb in the sentence. Invite students to suggest other adverbs that might be added to the sentence.

Work with Adverbs Present the Daily Language Activity and have students suggest adverbs to add to each sentence.

Have students pick sentences from *Amistad Rising*, write them down, and then add adverbs. Encourage students to illustrate their sentences.

 Assign the daily Writing Prompt on page 616D.

DAY 4 — Review and Practice

Review Adverbs Present the sentences from the Daily Language Activity for Days 1 through 3. Ask students to tell whether the adverbs answer *how, when,* or *where*. Then present the Daily Language Activity for Day 4.

Mechanics and Usage Before students begin the daily Writing Prompt on page 616D, review the usage of the words *good* and *well*. Discuss:

Using *Good* and *Well*

- *Good* is an adjective and is used to describe nouns.

- *Well* is an adverb that tells *how* about a verb.

- Do not confuse the adjective *good* with the adverb *well*.

Give students these examples: Janie is a *good* dog. Janie behaves *well*.

 Assign the daily Writing Prompt on page 616D.

DAY 5 — Assess and Reteach

Assess Use the Daily Language Activity and page 165 of the **Grammar Practice Book** for assessment.

Reteach Have students create lists of adverbs, or use the list of adverbs from the Daily Language Activities. Have students write and illustrate a sentence containing an adverb from their list. Have volunteers identify the adverb in the sentence and tell whether the adverb answers *how, when,* or *where*.

Have students create a word wall with lists of adverbs that describe the *how,* the *when,* and the *where* of verbs, adjectives, or other adverbs.

Use page 166 of the **Grammar Practice Book** for additional reteaching.

 Assign the daily Writing Prompt on page 616D.

Writing with Adverbs

- An **adverb** is a word that tells more about a verb, an adjective, or another adverb.
- An adverb can tell *how, when,* or *where* an action takes place.

Read the following story once. Then write adverbs in the spaces. Make sure that each adverb makes sense. Answers will vary.

Another Fight for Freedom

Abd al-Rahman Ibrahima was _____very_____ courageous. He was the son of a West African chieftain. Because he was a prince, Ibrahima was educated _____carefully_____. He _____quickly_____ learned how to read and write. He studied _____quite_____ hard to learn history, mathematics, and Moslem traditions. One day, Dr. Cox, a white man, became _____terribly_____ lost in the jungle. He _____earnestly_____ begged Ibrahima's people for help. They _____immediately_____ saved his life, and Ibrahima became _____rather_____ good friends with him.

When Ibrahima was in his twenties, he _____suddenly_____ was captured in a war. He was sold as a slave and _____later_____ taken to America. One day, Ibrahima was traveling _____wearily_____ along a dirt road in Mississippi. _____Then_____ he saw Dr. Cox. The doctor was glad to see Ibrahima. He frowned _____angrily_____, though, when he learned that the African prince was enslaved. Dr. Cox wrote to friends, and they _____quickly_____ tried to help. They _____finally_____ gained Ibrahima his liberty, and he died a free man in Africa.

15 Grade 5/Unit 6
Amistad Rising

Extension: Have small groups of students discuss the characteristics of heroism. Ask them to identify and comment upon adverbs that come up during the discussion. 163

Using *Good* and *Well*

- *Good* is an adjective and is used to describe nouns.
- *Well* is an adverb that tells *how* about a verb.
- Do not confuse the adjective *good* with the adverb *well*.

Read both sentences in each pair. Circle the letter of the sentence that uses *good* or *well* correctly.

1. a. The crew did not treat the captives good.
   (b.) The crew did not treat the captives well.
2. **(a.)** People on the Amistad did not eat well.
   b. People on the Amistad did not eat good.
3. **(a.)** The slaves fought well for their freedom.
   b. The slaves fought good for their freedom.
4. a. Cinqué fought for a well cause.
   (b.) Cinqué fought for a good cause.
5. **(a.)** Many good people helped abolish slavery.
   b. Many well people helped abolish slavery.

Write *well* or *good* to complete each sentence correctly. Then underline the word that *well* or *good* describes.

6. Would John Quincy Adams be a _____good_____ lawyer for the Africans?
7. The former President wondered if he would do _____well_____.
8. When the time came, he spoke _____well_____ for the Mende.
9. Adams was a _____good_____ judge of character.
10. Like the American patriots, he explained, they had fought _____well_____ for freedom.

164

Extension: Challenge students to write a poem about Cinqué's voyage home. Ask them to use the descriptive words *good* and *well* in their poems.

Grade 5/Unit 6
Amistad Rising **10**

Adverbs

Rewrite each sentence twice. Each time, add an adverb that tells when, where, or how. Answers will vary.

1. The ship sails.
   The ship sails soon.
   The ship sails quickly.
2. Cinqué fought.
   Cinqué fought courageously.
   Then Cinqué fought.
3. Slave owners worked.
   Slave owners worked quickly.
   Slave owners worked there.
4. The waves are rising.
   Now the waves are rising.
   The waves are rising angrily.
5. The judge spoke.
   The judge spoke softly.
   Later, the judge spoke.

B. Write *well* or *good* to complete each sentence correctly.

6. During the storm, the ship did not travel _____well_____.
7. A courageous leader is a _____good_____ role model.
8. The ship's food did not taste _____good_____.
9. John Quincy Adams argued _____well_____ for the defense.
10. He was a _____good_____ lawyer.

10 Grade 5/Unit 6
Amistad Rising

165

5 Day Spelling Plan

LANGUAGE SUPPORT

Say and write the words pain and pane. Ask students whether the words sound the same or different. (same) Ask students how they can tell which spelling to use. (by the meaning of the word)

DICTATION SENTENCES

Spelling Words

1. The plant turned brown and died.
2. The calf sleeps in the stable.
3. After my fall, I had a pain in my knee.
4. The medicine heals the cat's wound.
5. Please put waste in this can.
6. The ropes bound the poles together.
7. Rocks broke one pane in the window.
8. My shirt is below my waist.
9. He locked jewels in the bank vault.
10. He dyed the shoes blue.
11. My class is in the main building.
12. I was the sole person left in the room.
13. Let's haul this boat out of the water.
14. The current in this river is too strong.
15. People who are idle don't work.
16. Go down a short hall to the library.
17. The currant is a raisin used in bread.
18. There wasn't a soul in the locked store.
19. The lion shook his mane.
20. The rock idol is performing.

Challenge Words

21. I had to coax the cat from the tree.
22. We escorted the children to the park.
23. Can I navigate the boat on this trip?
24. Many perished in the hurricane.
25. The driver ushered us to our seats.

DAY 1 Pretest

Assess Prior Knowledge Use the Dictation Sentences at the left and **Spelling Practice Book** page 161 for the pretest. Allow students to correct their own papers. Students who require a modified list may be tested on the first ten words.

Spelling Words		Challenge Words
1. **died**	11. main	21. **coax**
2. stable	12. sole	22. **escorted**
3. pain	13. haul	23. **navigate**
4. wound	14. current	24. **perished**
5. waste	15. idle	25. **ushered**
6. **bound**	16. hall	
7. pane	17. currant	
8. waist	18. soul	
9. vault	19. mane	
10. **dyed**	20. idol	

*Note: Words in **dark type** are from the story.*

Word Study On page 162 of the **Spelling Practice Book** are word study steps and an at-home activity.

SPELLING PRACTICE BOOK, PAGE 161

WORD STUDY STEPS AND ACTIVITY, PAGE 162

DAY 2 Explore the Pattern

Sort and Spell Words Remind students that homophones are words that sound the same but have different spellings and meanings; homographs are words that are spelled the same but have different origins and meanings, and sometimes different pronunciations. Have students read the Spelling Words aloud and sort them as below.

Homophones			
died	waste	sole	current
dyed	waist	soul	currant
pain	main	haul	idle
pane	mane	hall	idol

Homographs			
stable	wound	bound	vault

Word Wall Have students create a word wall based on the word sort and add more words from their reading.

SPELLING PRACTICE BOOK, PAGE 163

Homophones and Homographs

| DAY 3 | Practice and Extend | DAY 4 | Proofread and Write | DAY 5 | Assess and Reteach |

Word Meaning: Synonyms Remind students that a synonym is a word that has the same or almost the same meaning as another word. Ask students to think of synonyms for as many of the Spelling Words as they can (Examples: dyed/colored, pain/hurt). Write sentences using the words.

If students need extra practice, have partners give each other a midweek test.

Glossary Review word histories in the Glossary. Have students:

- write the Challenge Word *navigate* and look up its word history in the Glossary.

- write the Latin words that *navigate* comes from and their meanings. (*navis*, "ship"; *agere*, "to drive")

Proofread Sentences Write these sentences on the chalkboard, including the misspelled words. Ask students to proofread, circling incorrect spellings and writing the correct spellings. There are two spelling errors in each sentence.

> We (died) the dress from the (waste) down. **(dyed, waist)**
>
> The (mane) (pain) of glass should be cleaned. **(main, pane)**

Have students create additional sentences with errors for partners to correct.

Have students use as many Spelling Words as possible in the daily Writing Prompt on page 616D. Remind students to proofread their writing for errors in spelling, grammar, and punctuation.

Assess Students' Knowledge Use page 166 of the **Spelling Practice Book** or the Dictation Sentences on page 647O for the posttest.

Personal Word List If students have trouble with any lesson words, they should add them to their personal lists of troublesome words in their journals. Have students write a context sentence or definition for each word.

Students should refer to their word lists during later writing activities.

SPELLING PRACTICE BOOK, PAGE 164

Homophones and Homographs

died	waste	vault	haul	currant
stable	bound	dyed	current	soul
pain	pane	main	idle	mane
wound	waist	sole	hall	idol

Complete each sentence below with a spelling word.
1. Wear the belt around your ___waist___ to hold the pants up.
2. My sister ___dyed___ her hair red.
3. The male lion has a ___mane___.
4. The river's ___current___ carried the boat downstream.
5. The old dog ___died___ after becoming very sick.
6. I had a ___currant___ muffin for breakfast.
7. When I hurt my arm, the ___pain___ was very bad.
8. The coat closet is in the ___hall___ next to the door.

Similar Meanings
Write the spelling word which comes closest to the word or phrase below.
9. firm ___stable___
10. injury ___wound___
11. useless ___waste___
12. tied ___bound___
13. glass ___pane___
14. safe ___vault___
15. chief ___main___
16. only ___sole___
17. inactive ___idle___
18. spirit ___soul___
19. carry ___haul___
20. image ___idol___

Challenge Extension: Imagine you went on a boat trip during your vacation. Write sentences for each of the Challenge Words describing what happened on the trip.
164   Grade 5/Unit 6 Amistad Rising   20

SPELLING PRACTICE BOOK, PAGE 165

Homophones and Homographs

Proofreading Activity
There are six spelling mistakes in the letter below. Circle the misspelled words. Write the words correctly on the lines below.

To my dear wife,

My (sool) has longed for you and for Africa. The ship is ready, and I will be (bowned) for home tomorrow. Do not worry or think about the (pane) I have suffered. Every (woond) is healed. The chains that were on my ankles and around my (wayst) are gone forever. The fair wind and ocean (currnt) will bring me back to you soon.

With love,
Singbe

1. ___soul___ 3. ___pain___ 5. ___waist___
2. ___bound___ 4. ___wound___ 6. ___current___

Writing Activity
In the story "Amistad Rising," the author wrote, "there is not a drop of sea water that doesn't have a secret; not a river or lake that doesn't whisper someone's name." Supposing that the water was alive, what secret might it have? Use four spelling words in your writing.

10   Grade 5/Unit 6 Amistad Rising
165

SPELLING PRACTICE BOOK, PAGE 166

Homophones and Homographs

Look at the words in each set below. One word in each set is spelled correctly. Use a pencil to fill in the circle next to the correct word. Before you begin, look at the sample sets of words. Sample A has been done for you. Do Sample B by yourself. When you are sure you know what to do, you may go on with the rest of the page.

Sample A:
- (A) fownd
- (B) faund
- (C) found
- (D) fount

Sample B:
- (A) whind
- (B) wynde
- (C) winde
- (D) wind

1. (A) died (B) dyd (C) dide (D) deid
2. (E) stabul (F) stabell (G) stayble (H) stable
3. (A) pian (B) pain (C) payne (D) paine
4. (E) wound (F) wunde (G) wownd (H) wouwened
5. (A) wayste (B) waiste (C) waste (D) wast

6. (E) bownd (F) bounde (G) baund (H) bound
7. (A) paine (B) pane (C) payen (D) payn
8. (E) wayst (F) wast (G) waist (H) wayest
9. (A) vault (B) vawlt (C) vaulet (D) vawld
10. (E) diyed (F) deyed (G) dyed (H) dieed

11. (A) maine (B) mayne (C) maiyn (D) main
12. (E) sool (F) sole (G) soel (H) sol
13. (A) haul (B) haile (C) hawl (D) hawle
14. (E) curint (F) currint (G) current (H) currunt
15. (A) iddle (B) idle (C) idel (D) iddel

16. (E) hawle (F) hawl (G) halle (H) hall
17. (A) curant (B) cureant (C) currant (D) currante
18. (E) soole (F) sool (G) coul (H) soll
19. (A) mane (B) mayn (C) maine (D) meane
20. (E) idyl (F) iddel (G) idol (H) iddol

166   Grade 5/Unit 6 Amistad Rising   20

647P

Rip Van Winkle

Selection Summary Students will delight in reading this play, based on Washington Irving's "timeless" tale, "Rip Van Winkle." Adapted from a European folk tale and reset nearly two centuries ago in the Catskill Mountains, students will come face-to-face with "Hendrik Hudson and his merry crew," as well as with Rip Van Winkle, the man who slept for twenty years.

RIP VAN WINKLE

BY WASHINGTON IRVING   DRAMATIZED BY ADELE THANE
ILLUSTRATED BY GARY KELLEY

Student Listening Library Audiocassette

INSTRUCTIONAL
Pages 650–669

About the Author The famous author of the *Sketch Book,* which contains the classic stories, "Rip Van Winkle" and "The Legend of Sleepy Hollow," Washington Irving often wrote under the pen names of Geoffrey Crayon and Diedrich Knickerbocker. So famous was Irving that the name of Knickerbocker came to be used to identify the first American school of writers, the *Knickerbocker Group.* Born in 1783 in New York City, Irving is considered by some critics to be the first great American writer.

Resources for
Meeting Individual Needs

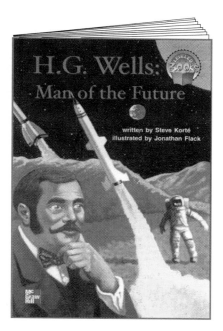

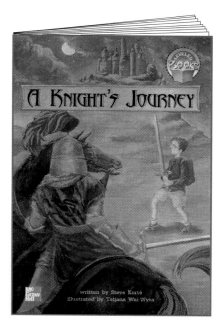

EASY
Pages 673A, 673D

INDEPENDENT
Pages 673B, 673D

CHALLENGE
Pages 673C, 673D

LEVELED PRACTICE

Reteach, 193–199
blackline masters with reteaching opportunities for each assessed skill

Practice, 193–199
workbook with Take-Home stories and practice opportunities for each assessed skill and story comprehension

Extend, 193–199
blackline masters that offer challenge activities for each assessed skill

ADDITIONAL RESOURCES

- **Language Support Book,** 209–216
- **Take-Home Story, Practice,** p. 194a
- **Alternative Teaching Strategies,** T60–T66

McGraw-Hill School
TECHNOLOGY

interNET CONNECTION Research and Inquiry Ideas. Visit **www.mhschool.com/reading**

Suggested
Lesson Planner

 Available on CD-ROM

READING AND LANGUAGE ARTS	**DAY 1** *Focus on Reading and Skills*	 **DAY 2** *Read the Literature*
● **Comprehension** ● **Vocabulary** ● **Phonics/Decoding** ● **Study Skills** ● **Listening, Speaking, Viewing, Representing**	**Read Aloud and Motivate,** 648E *The Princess on the Pea* **Develop Visual Literacy,** 648/649 ☑ **Review Cause and Effect,** 650A–650B **Teaching Chart 157** Reteach, Practice, Extend, 193	**Build Background,** 650C Develop Oral Language **Vocabulary,** 650D *husking landlord rascals* *keg oblige sprawled* **Teaching Chart 158** **Vocabulary Cards** Reteach, Practice, Extend, 194 **Read the Selection,** 650–669 ☑ Review Cause and Effect ☑ Review Judgments and Decisions **Minilessons,** 657, 659, 661, 665 **Cultural Perspectives,** 656
● **Curriculum Connections**	 **Works of Art,** 648/649	**Link** **Social Studies,** 650C
● **Writing**	**Writing Prompt:** Imagine that Dame Van Winkle convinces Rip to do his household chores. Write a brief description telling how Rip performs one of his chores.	**Writing Prompt:** Write a dialogue between Rip Van Winkle and Hendrik Hudson. Imagine that each is trying to impress the other by boasting about past accomplishments. **Journal Writing,** 669 Quick-Write
● **Grammar**	**Introduce the Concept: Adverbs that Compare,** 673M Daily Language Activity 1. Judy ran fastest than Luke. faster 2. Of all the girls, Katchen worked harder. hardest 3. Rip slept longest than I did. longer **Grammar Practice Book,** 167	**Teach the Concept: Adverbs that Compare,** 673M Daily Language Activity 1. Hendrik acted more bravely of all. most 2. You dance gracefullier than a bird. more gracefully 3. I nap more soundly than Rip does. more soundly **Grammar Practice Book,** 168
● **Spelling**	**Pretest: Words with Prefixes,** 673O Spelling Practice Book, 167–168	**Explore the Pattern: Words with Prefixes,** 673O Spelling Practice Book, 169

Meeting Individual Needs

 = **Skill Assessed in Unit Test**

Read EVERY DAY

DAY 3 — Read the Literature

Rereading for Fluency, 668

Story Questions, 670
> Reteach, Practice, Extend, 195

Story Activities, 671

Study Skill, 672
> ✓ Conduct an Interview
> **Teaching Chart 159**
> Reteach, Practice, Extend, 196

Test Power, 673

Read the Leveled Books
Guided Reading
Hard *g*, soft *g*
> ✓ Review Cause and Effect
> ✓ Instructional Vocabulary

DAY 4 — Build Skills

 Read the Leveled Books and Self-Selected Books

✓ **Review Cause and Effect,** 673E–673F
> **Teaching Chart 160**
> Reteach, Practice, Extend, 197
> Language Support, 214

✓ **Review Draw Conclusions,** 673G–673H
> **Teaching Chart 161**
> Reteach, Practice, Extend, 198
> Language Support, 215

DAY 5 — Build Skills

 Read Self-Selected Books

✓ **Review Synonyms and Antonyms,** 673I–673J
> **Teaching Chart 162**
> Reteach, Practice, Extend, 199
> Language Support, 216

Listening, Speaking, Viewing, Representing, 673L
> Act Out the Dialogue
> Make a Video

Minilessons, 657, 659, 661, 665

Phonics Review
> Hard *g*, soft *g*, 657
> **Phonics Workbook**

Activity Social Studies, 652

Writing Prompt: Write a diary entry from Judy Van Winkle's point of view about her father, Rip. Include details describing how her father speaks when he tells stories.

Writing Process: Write a Dialogue, 673K
> Prewrite, Draft

Review and Practice: Adverbs that Compare, 673N
Daily Language Activity
1. We ate more faster than Rip. faster
2. Judy sings sweetlier than a wren. more sweetly
3. She yells louder of all. loudest

Grammar Practice Book, 169

Practice and Extend: Words with Prefixes, 673P
Spelling Practice Book, 170

Activity Science, 658

Writing Prompt: You are a sports reporter at Hudson's ninepins game. Write your script for the evening news.

Writing Process: Write a Dialogue, 673K
> Revise

Meeting Individual Needs for Writing, 673L

Review and Practice: Adverbs that Compare, 673N
Daily Language Activity
1. It rains hardest now than ever. harder
2. She spent money most wisely than he did. more wisely
3. Wolf barked more loudly of all. most loudly

Grammar Practice Book, 170

Proofread and Write: Words with Prefixes, 673P
Spelling Practice Book, 171

Activity Math, 660

Writing Prompt: Imagine you have been resting for 20 years. Describe how your body moves as you walk down the mountain after a 20-year rest.

Writing Process: Write a Dialogue, 673K
> Edit/Proofread, Publish

Assess and Reteach: Adverbs that Compare, 673N
Daily Language Activity
1. Rip acted nicer of all. nicest
2. He looks oldest now than before. older
3. Of all the men in town, Rip worked most slowest. most slowly

Grammar Practice Book, 171–172

Assess and Reteach: Words with Prefixes, 673P
Spelling Practice Book, 172

Link

Language Arts

Read Aloud and Motivate

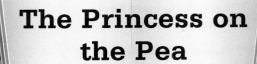

The Princess on the Pea

a story by
Hans Christian Andersen

Once upon a time there was a prince; he wanted a princess, but it had to be a real princess. So he traveled all over the world to find one, but everywhere he went something was wrong. There were princesses enough, but were they real princesses? That was the problem. There was always something not quite right. So he came home again, feeling very sad; he would so much have liked to find a real princess.

One night there was a terrible storm. There was thunder and lightning, and the rain came pouring down—it was quite dreadful! Someone was heard knocking on the city gate, and the old king went to open it.

Outside stood a princess, but goodness, what a sight she was from the rain and the cruel weather. Water was running from her hair and down her clothes. It ran in at the toes of her shoes and out at the heels, and still she said she was a real princess.

Well, we shall soon see about that! thought the old queen. She didn't say anything but went to the bed-

Continued on pages T2–T5

Oral Comprehension

LISTENING AND SPEAKING Encourage students to review what they know about cause and effect as you read them this tongue-in-cheek fairy tale about the qualities of a real princess. When you have finished reading, ask: "Why was the prince having trouble finding a wife? What kind of wife did he want? Why? How did the princess react to the pea?" As students respond, ask them to compare this princess to the princess in "Touch the Moon," from Unit 5.

Activity Have students work in small groups to create an interpretive dance that shows the story of "The Princess on the Pea" through movement. Invite each group to choose appropriate music and to perform their dance for the class. ▶ **Interpersonal/Musical**

Develop Visual Literacy

Works of Art

Stories in Art

Landscapes often create a peaceful scene. What does the artist want you to see in this painting? A quiet day along the Hudson River? A day long ago?

Look at this picture. Notice the details. What colors does the artist use? How do they help create a quiet mood? What is the effect of the setting on the painting? How do the setting and the mood affect you?

Suppose that you had a time machine. Would you want to go back to the time in the painting? How would you feel in that setting? What things would you want to know? Why?

View of the Hudson River from Fort Knyphansen
by Thomas Davies
Royal Ontario Museum, Toronto, Canada

648

649

Objective: Review Cause and Effect

VIEWING In his view of the Hudson River, Thomas Davies has captured light and shadow to create a quiet mood in a country setting. Discuss other ways that the artist has created this peaceful affect. Help students to see the affect of the weather, the river, the rolling hills, and the strolling people on the scene.

Read the page with students, encouraging individual interpretations of the painting.

Ask students to support the cause-and-effect relationships in the painting. For example:

• The dull tones of blue, green, and gray create a peaceful effect.
• The rolling hills and flat river are very relaxing.

REPRESENTING Much like a painting, music can have a strong effect. Have students select two kinds of music, and listen to one kind as they rest and the other as they exercise. Have them play the music in class and explain how each piece causes them to feel a certain way.

Students will relate what happens in a story to why it happens.

LANGUAGE SUPPORT

ESL Have students preview the first four pages of the selection. If necessary, build background on the play format.

Review Cause and Effect

PREPARE

Discuss Reasons for Events

Have students think about something they did the day before. Then ask: What caused you to do it?

TEACH

Define Cause and Effect

Tell students: When something happens, you can usually figure out why it happened. For example, you do very well on a test because you listened in class and you studied. In other words, your study habits *caused* you to do well.

Tell students that they can follow a story more closely by analyzing the events in terms of cause and effect.

It's Easy to Forget

Rip Van Winkle's daughter, Judy, had to prepare an oral report for school. So she rushed home after school and started to think about her report. When she heard some friends playing nearby, she went out to ask them to quiet down. Then she saw that they were playing her favorite game, so Judy decided to join in the game. She was having so much fun, she forgot all about the report. The next day, Judy's oral report got a poor grade because she was not prepared.

Teaching Chart 157

Read the Story and Model the Skill

Display **Teaching Chart 157.** Ask students to listen closely to events that take place. Then have them tell why each event happened.

MODEL Judy went outside *because* she heard some friends playing. Judy joined in the game *because* it was her favorite. Judy did poorly on her report *because* she played instead of doing her homework.

PRACTICE

Create a Cause and Effect Chart

ONE

Have students circle the causes of events in the story and underline the results, or effects. Then, using a Cause and Effect chart, have students record notes from "It's Easy to Forget." Help them begin filling in the chart and have students complete it. ▶ **Linguistic/Logical**

CAUSE	EFFECT
Judy hears her friends outside.	Judy goes outside, leaving her homework behind.
Judy is not prepared.	She gets a poor grade.

ASSESS/CLOSE

Write Causes and Effects

Ask students: Will a cause always result in the same effect? Use your Cause and Effect chart to write different effects for each cause. (Sample answer: Judy has to prepare a report and she meets with a friend to share ideas.) Can what happens have more than one reason? Use your Cause and Effect chart to write different causes for each effect. (Sample answer: Judy got a bad grade because she could not find the information she needed.)

SELECTION
Connection

Students will identify cause and effect when they read *Rip Van Winkle* and the Leveled Books.

ALTERNATE TEACHING STRATEGY

CAUSE AND EFFECT

For a different approach to teaching this skill, see page T64.

Meeting Individual Needs for Comprehension

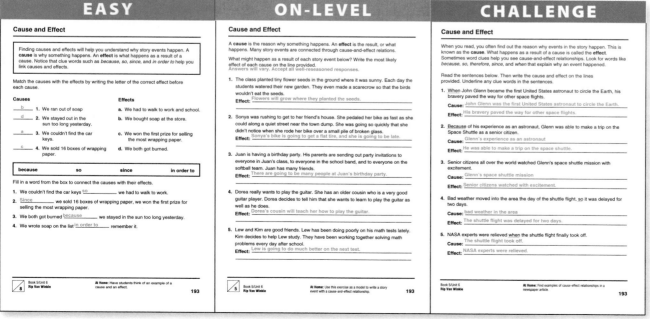

EASY	ON-LEVEL	CHALLENGE
Reteach, 193	Practice, 193	Extend, 193

Build Background

Social Studies

Anthology and Leveled Books

Evaluate Prior Knowledge

CONCEPT: ANOTHER TIME AND PLACE
Rip Van Winkle is a story that happens in the past, during the Revolutionary War. Each event in the story causes another. Have students share their knowledge of important historical events. Ask them to identify causes of these events.

IDENTIFY CHAIN OF EVENTS
Sometimes, one event leads to another, which in turn leads to another, and so on. In other words, each effect becomes the cause of another effect. Have students fill in a Chain of Related Events diagram using an example from experience or by making one up. ▶ **Logical/Visual**

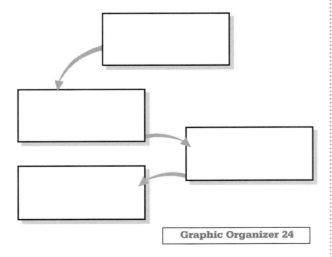

Graphic Organizer 24

REWRITE A STORY Have students choose and summarize a familiar story from a book, a television show, or the local newspaper. Then have them change one or more details in the story and rewrite the story to show how the changes affect everything else in the story.

PARTNERS   WRITING

Develop Oral Language

DISCUSS WHY THINGS HAPPEN Have
ESL students keep a journal for one full day. At the end of the day, students should choose five events and write a sentence describing the cause of each.

Provide students with interesting photos from magazines or newspapers. Without giving them any context for the photos, have volunteers explain what is happening in the images and speculate on why. List responses on the chalkboard.

Ask students to imagine that they could go back in time. What events in their lives might they change? How would they cause this change?

Vocabulary

Key Words

1. Rip Van Winkle was on his way to the local (husking) bee to prepare his neighbor's corn. 2. The (landlord) who ran the tavern stopped to ask Rip a favor. 3. He wanted Rip to help him lift a large, wooden (keg) into his cart. 4. Rip was happy to (oblige,) and he hoisted the keg over his head for his friend. 5. The landlord said the merchant who sold him the keg was a (rascal) because he disappeared, leaving the landlord to carry it to the tavern. 6. Rip climbed up into the landlord's horse-drawn cart and (sprawled) out comfortably in the seat as they headed into town.

Teaching Chart 158

Vocabulary in Context

IDENTIFY VOCABULARY WORDS
Display **Teaching Chart 158** and read the passage with students. Have volunteers circle each vocabulary word and underline other words that are clues to its meaning.

DISCUSS MEANINGS Ask questions like these to help clarify word meanings:

- Have you ever husked corn in preparation for dinner?

- Does anyone you know pay rent to a landlord?

- How is the word *obligation* related to *oblige*?

- In what situation might you have heard the word *rascal*?

- When is it appropriate to be sprawled on the floor and when is it inappropriate?

Practice

DEMONSTRATE WORD MEANING Have partners choose vocabulary cards from a pile and demonstrate each word meaning with pantomime, drawings, or verbal clues.

▶ **Kinesthetic/Linguistic**

Vocabulary Cards

WRITE CONTEXT SENTENCES Have partners write context sentences, leaving a blank for each vocabulary word. Have them exchange papers to fill in the blanks or use vocabulary cards to show answers.

▶ **Linguistic/Interpersonal**

SPELLING/VOCABULARY CONNECTIONS

See Spelling Challenge Words, pages 6730–673P.

ON-LEVEL

Husking Bee

Rosa and Hank each sat on a *keg* as they worked. It was Saturday afternoon, and they were busily shredding husks from ears of corn. There was a huge pile of corn in front of them. They did this work for their *landlord*, Mr. Simpson, who owned the farm. Their work helped pay their rent on the farm.

"Those rascals never do their share of the work," complained Hank. He was referring to the laughing children *sprawled* on a haystack. They were the sons of Mr. Simpson.

"That's because they don't have to *oblige* anyone," commented Rosa. "They can spend their time doing as they please."

"Well, one thing's for sure," said Hank, "when I'm older, I'm going to own my own farm."

1. What is another word for *rascal*? troublemaker; lazy or dishonest

2. What is a word from the story that means "a small barrel"? keg

3. What does the word *husking* mean, as it is used in this story? removing the dry, leaf-like outer covering (husk) from an ear of corn

4. What does it mean to be "*sprawled* on a haystack"? sitting or lying on a haystack with arms and legs spread out

5. Why do you think Hank says what he does at the end? How do you think he feels about having to *oblige* the *landlord*? He is probably feeling angry that he has to work while other kids play; he doesn't want to be obliged to any landlord again.

Book 5/Unit 6
Rip Van Winkle   **At Home:** Use the vocabulary words to write a short story about having to oblige someone.   **194a**

Take-Home Story 194a
Reteach 194
Practice 194 • Extend 194

Guided Instruction

Preview and Predict

Have students read the title and preview the selection, looking for clues about what happens to the main character.

- What clues do the pictures give about the events of the story?
- When and where might the story take place?
- What will the selection most likely be about?
- In what format will the story be told? How can you tell? (A play begins by listing the cast of characters. It is written in dialogue and provides stage directions.) *Genre*

Have students record their predictions.

PREDICTIONS	WHAT HAPPENED
The main character, Rip Van Winkle, goes off to war.	
Rip Van Winkle meets a woman and a child.	

Set Purposes

What do students want to find out by reading the story? For example:

- Who is Rip Van Winkle?
- What problems does Rip experience?

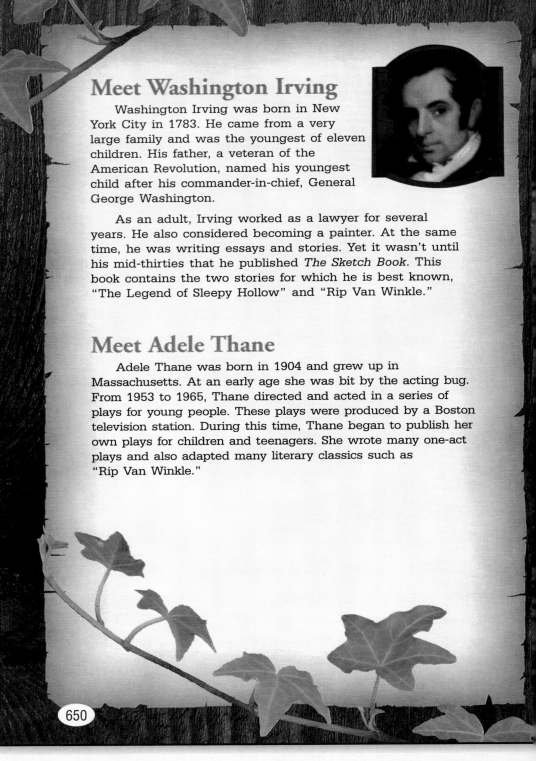

Meet Washington Irving

Washington Irving was born in New York City in 1783. He came from a very large family and was the youngest of eleven children. His father, a veteran of the American Revolution, named his youngest child after his commander-in-chief, General George Washington.

As an adult, Irving worked as a lawyer for several years. He also considered becoming a painter. At the same time, he was writing essays and stories. Yet it wasn't until his mid-thirties that he published *The Sketch Book*. This book contains the two stories for which he is best known, "The Legend of Sleepy Hollow" and "Rip Van Winkle."

Meet Adele Thane

Adele Thane was born in 1904 and grew up in Massachusetts. At an early age she was bit by the acting bug. From 1953 to 1965, Thane directed and acted in a series of plays for young people. These plays were produced by a Boston television station. During this time, Thane began to publish her own plays for children and teenagers. She wrote many one-act plays and also adapted many literary classics such as "Rip Van Winkle."

650

Meeting Individual Needs • Grouping Suggestions for Strategic Reading

EASY	ON-LEVEL	CHALLENGE
Read Together Read the story with students or have them use the **Listening Library Audiocassette.** Have students use the Cause and Effect chart to record important information from the story. Guided Instruction and Prevention/Intervention prompts offer additional help with vocabulary and comprehension.	**Guided Reading** Have students read the story first on their own. Review the story words on page 651, making sure students are comfortable with the terms. Then have students reread the story with you, choosing from the Guided Instruction questions and directing students to chart cause-and-effect relationships.	**Read Independently** Remind students that relating cause and effect for actions and events within the story can help them understand the story. Have students set up a Cause and Effect chart as on page 651. After reading, they should be able to use their charts to summarize the story.

RIP VAN WINKLE

BY WASHINGTON IRVING   DRAMATIZED BY ADELE THANE
ILLUSTRATED BY GARY KELLEY

651

LANGUAGE SUPPORT

The Cause and Effect chart is available as a blackline master in the **Language Support Book.**

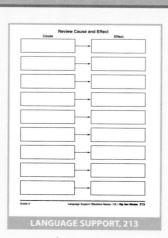

LANGUAGE SUPPORT, 213

Guided Instruction

☑ **Cause and Effect**
☑ **Draw Conclusions**

Strategic Reading Before we begin reading, let's prepare a Cause and Effect chart so we can analyze the events in the story.

CAUSE	EFFECT

① **DRAW CONCLUSIONS** Are you familiar with the story of Rip Van Winkle? Why do you think this image of a sleeping man is used to begin this story? (Many students may know that the story is about a man who falls asleep for a long time, even if they do not know the details of the story. The sleeping man is the most familiar image of this story.)

Story Words

The words below may be unfamiliar. Have students check their meanings and pronunciations in the Glossary beginning on page 730.

- enlist, p. 655
- masthead, p. 661
- revolt, p. 653
- tavern, p. 652

651

Guided Instruction

2 How would you describe the setting of the story? (The story takes place in a small village in what is now New England prior to the American Revolution, when this country was under British rule. King George III was the King of England at the time. The fact that America consists of colonies indicates a very different political situation than exists today.) **Setting**

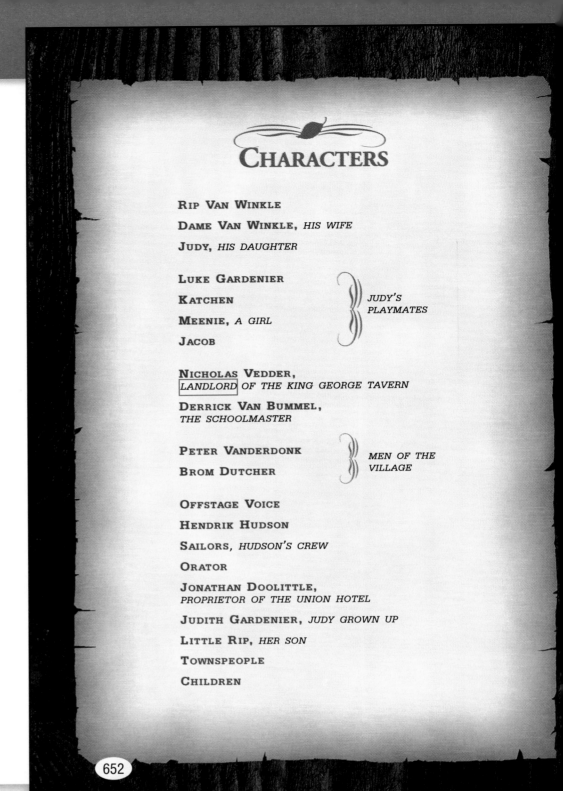

CHARACTERS

RIP VAN WINKLE

DAME VAN WINKLE, *HIS WIFE*

JUDY, *HIS DAUGHTER*

LUKE GARDENIER

KATCHEN   } *JUDY'S PLAYMATES*

MEENIE, *A GIRL*

JACOB

NICHOLAS VEDDER, LANDLORD *OF THE KING GEORGE TAVERN*

DERRICK VAN BUMMEL, *THE SCHOOLMASTER*

PETER VANDERDONK

BROM DUTCHER   } *MEN OF THE VILLAGE*

OFFSTAGE VOICE

HENDRIK HUDSON

SAILORS, *HUDSON'S CREW*

ORATOR

JONATHAN DOOLITTLE, *PROPRIETOR OF THE UNION HOTEL*

JUDITH GARDENIER, *JUDY GROWN UP*

LITTLE RIP, *HER SON*

TOWNSPEOPLE

CHILDREN

652

Cross Curricular: Social Studies

THE STAMP ACT Van Bummel is angry about the Stamp Act, passed by King George, which taxed colonists for issuing legal documents and newspapers.

RESEARCH AND INQUIRY Have students research events leading to the American Revolution. Groups of students should prepare posters showing how several causes combined, resulting in the war of independence.

 interNET CONNECTION Students can learn more about the American Revolution by visiting **www.mhschool.com/reading**

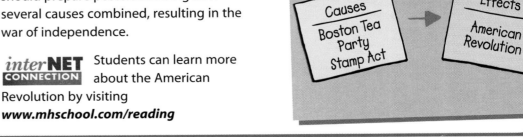

Causes
Boston Tea Party
Stamp Act
→
Effects
American Revolution

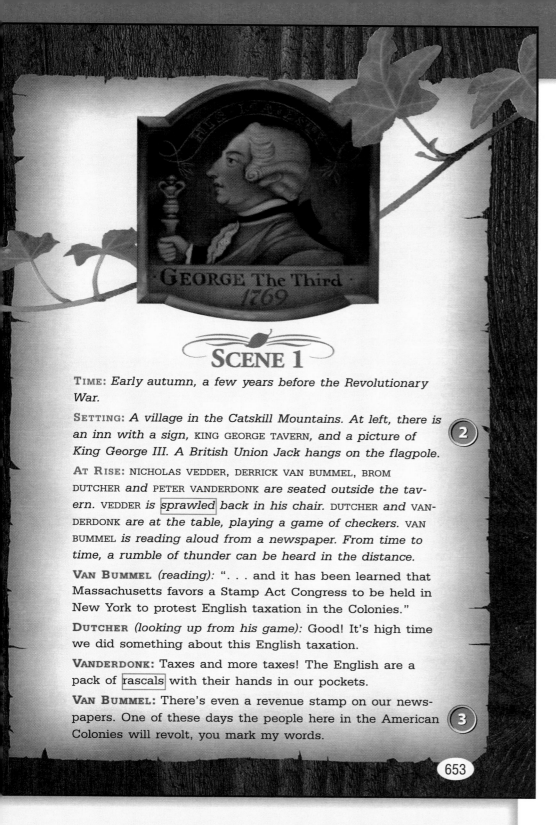

SCENE 1

TIME: *Early autumn, a few years before the Revolutionary War.*

SETTING: *A village in the Catskill Mountains. At left, there is an inn with a sign,* KING GEORGE TAVERN, *and a picture of King George III. A British Union Jack hangs on the flagpole.*

AT RISE: NICHOLAS VEDDER, DERRICK VAN BUMMEL, BROM DUTCHER *and* PETER VANDERDONK *are seated outside the tavern.* VEDDER *is* sprawled *back in his chair.* DUTCHER *and* VANDERDONK *are at the table, playing a game of checkers.* VAN BUMMEL *is reading aloud from a newspaper. From time to time, a rumble of thunder can be heard in the distance.*

VAN BUMMEL *(reading):* ". . . and it has been learned that Massachusetts favors a Stamp Act Congress to be held in New York to protest English taxation in the Colonies."

DUTCHER *(looking up from his game):* Good! It's high time we did something about this English taxation.

VANDERDONK: Taxes and more taxes! The English are a pack of rascals with their hands in our pockets.

VAN BUMMEL: There's even a revenue stamp on our newspapers. One of these days the people here in the American Colonies will revolt, you mark my words.

653

(3) **CAUSE AND EFFECT** Why did Van Bummel predict that the American colonies would revolt against England? Have students act out the roles of the men having a discussion at the beginning of the play. *Role-Play*

MODEL I think Van Bummel and the other men are upset that England has imposed so many taxes on them. England even taxed the newspaper the men were reading. Van Bummel predicted that the colonists would soon become so angry with England's treatment they would revolt.

653

Guided Instruction

4 **DRAW CONCLUSIONS** What can you conclude about Rip Van Winkle's personality from what the other men say about him? (Rip Van Winkle must have an easygoing personality because Vedder describes Rip as a person not troubled by political issues.)

5 **CAUSE AND EFFECT** Why was Dame Van Winkle angry at Rip? Record your notes in your Cause and Effect chart.

CAUSE	EFFECT
Rip Van Winkle is playing checkers instead of fetching water.	Dame Van Winkle pushes Rip with a broom and nags him to get water.

TEACHING TIP

INSTRUCTIONAL Students will probably be confused when they read the term *galligaskins.* Explain that the term refers to loosely-fitting breeches worn in the 16th and 17th centuries. Breeches are pants reaching just below the knees.

VEDDER (*pointing off right as a merry whistle is heard*): Well, here comes one man who is not troubled by these problems—Rip Van Winkle. (RIP VAN WINKLE *enters, a wooden bucket in one hand, his gun in the other. He props his gun against the tree trunk, then crosses to the group of men.*)

RIP: Good afternoon, Nick Vedder—Brom—Peter. (*to* VAN BUMMEL) Good afternoon, Mr. Schoolmaster. (*They return his greeting. There is a loud rumble of thunder and* RIP *cocks his head.*) Just listen to that, will you!

DUTCHER: We're probably in for a storm after this heat all day.

VEDDER: Sit down, Rip. Derrick is reading us the news.

VANDERDONK: How about a game of checkers, Rip?

RIP (*hesitating*): I don't know. Dame Van Winkle sent me for a bucket of water, but—maybe *one* game. (*He sets down the bucket and draws a stool up to the table, as* VANDERDONK *rises.*)

DUTCHER: Your move, Rip. (*Suddenly* DAME VAN WINKLE'S *voice is heard from off right.*)

DAME VAN WINKLE (*calling from off right*): Rip! R-i-p! *Rip Van Winkle!*

RIP: Oh, my galligaskins! It's my wife! (*Before he can get to his feet,* DAME VAN WINKLE *enters with a broom. She looks at the men, then crosses directly to* RIP.)

DAME VAN WINKLE: So this is how you draw water from the well! Sitting around with a lot of lazy good-for-nothing loafers. (*She tries to hit* RIP *with the broom.*) Pick up that bucket, you dawdling Dutchman, and fill it with water!

RIP (*snatching up the bucket and dodging out of the way*): Hey there, Dame, I'm not an old rug to be beaten with a broomstick.

DAME VAN WINKLE: Well, you might better be. An old rug is more use than you. At least it would keep our feet warm in winter, which is more than you can do. Little you care that your family is starving and the cow is gone.

654

Cross Curricular: Social Studies

EXPLORERS Henry Hudson (Hendrik Hudson in Dutch) is usually credited with discovering the Hudson River in 1609. However, it was actually stumbled upon by an Italian, Giovanni da Verrazano, in 1524.

RESEARCH AND INQUIRY Have students research North America's early explorers. Encourage them to report findings.

 Students can learn more about early American explorers by visiting **www.mhschool.com/reading**

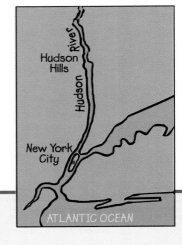

RIP: The cow gone?

DAME VAN WINKLE: Aye, the cow is gone and the cabbage trampled down. When are you going to mend the fence?

RIP: It rained yesterday—

DAME VAN WINKLE: If excuses were shillings, we'd be rich!

RIP: I'll mend the fence—tomorrow.

DAME VAN WINKLE: Tomorrow, tomorrow! All your work is going to be done tomorrow! (*RIP goes to the well as she starts off right, still talking.*) You show enough energy when there's a husking bee or an errand to run for the neighbors, but here at home . . . (*She exits. RIP lowers his bucket into the well. The other men rise to go into the tavern.*)

VEDDER: Poor Rip! His wife has the scoldingest tongue in the Hudson Valley.

VAN BUMMEL: A sharp tongue is the only tool that grows keener with use.

DUTCHER: What would you do, Derrick, if you had a wife like Van Winkle's?

VAN BUMMEL: War could be no worse. I would enlist. (*They all laugh and exit through the door of the tavern. RIP turns to leave, then stops and smiles, as children's voices are heard off left. JUDY, LUKE, KATCHEN, MEENIE, holding a kite, and JACOB, carrying a bow, run in, left, and shout with delight when they see RIP.*)

CHILDREN (*ad lib*): There he is! There's Rip Van Winkle! (*etc. They surround him, chattering excitedly.*)

JUDY: Hello, Father, I've brought some of my friends.

RIP: Glad to see you, children.

JACOB (*holding out bow*): Oh, Rip, there's something wrong with my bow. Every time I go to shoot, the cord slips. (*RIP takes the bow, draws his knife from his pocket and cuts the notch deeper for the cord.*)

RIP: There, Jacob, try that, and see if it doesn't work.

655

Guided Instruction

6 CAUSE AND EFFECT How did Rip Van Winkle's cow get away? (Rip had not fixed his broken fence.) How did the cow's escape affect the Van Winkles' garden? (When the cow escaped, it trampled the cabbage.)

7 DRAW CONCLUSIONS Why might you conclude that Rip Van Winkle is a procrastinator, or puts off his chores?

MODEL I can draw this conclusion based on Rip's actions. For example, when Dame Van Winkle yells at Rip to fix the fence, he makes excuses for why he has not fixed it. Then, instead of jumping up to fix it right away, he says that he'll do it tomorrow.

 MULTIPLE-MEANING WORDS Read the sentence in which Dame Van Winkle calls Rip a *loafer*. See the third speech from bottom on page 654. What are two meanings for the word *loafer*? How is the word used in this story?

 PREVENTION/INTERVENTION

MULTIPLE-MEANING WORDS
Have students reread the sentence that contains the word *loafers*. Explain that the term can be used to describe either a person who spends time lounging about or an informal shoe. Point out that the term is further described here by the saying *good-for-nothing*, which indicates a lazy person.

Ask students to relate the two uses of the term *loafer*. For example, people might wear loafers when they are relaxing, or not working.

Guided Instruction

8 Do you think that Rip Van Winkle is a kind man? Support your answer with examples. (Rip is a kind man because he helps the neighbors and children whenever they are in need.) *Character*

9 **CAUSE AND EFFECT** Why does Rip tell his daughter Judy about Hendrik Hudson? Add your answer to your Cause and Effect chart.

CAUSE	EFFECT
Rip Van Winkle is playing checkers instead of fetching water.	Dame Van Winkle pushes Rip with a broom and nags him to get water.
Judy is afraid of the thunder she hears.	Rip explains that it is only Hendrik Hudson playing ninepins.

JACOB *(pretending to shoot):* Yes, it's all right now.

MEENIE *(holding out kite):* My kite won't stay up, Rip.

RIP *(taking off part of the tail):* Now it will, Meenie—and this breeze is just right for it. *(He hands kite to MEENIE.)*

KATCHEN: My mother wants you to plug up her rain barrel, so she'll be able to wash next week.

RIP: Tell her I'll fix it tonight, Katchen.

LUKE: Rip, will you see what's the matter with my whistle? I made it just the way you showed me, but it isn't any good. *(He hands RIP a whistle.)*

8

RIP *(examining it):* You haven't whittled it right there, Luke. Here, I'll fix it for you. *(He sits on the bench under the tree and begins to whittle.)*

JUDY: Tell us a story, Father!

LUKE: Yes, you tell better stories than anybody in the Catskills. *(The children all gather around RIP, sitting on the ground.)*

RIP: What shall it be about?

JACOB: Indians!

KATCHEN: I like witches and goblins best. *(A long roll of thunder is heard.)*

JUDY: Oh, Father, hear that! Hear the thunder!

RIP: Why, don't you know what that is, Judy? That's Hendrik Hudson and his famous crew, playing ninepins up in the mountains. *(More thunder is heard.)*

MEENIE: Oh, what a noise they make!

RIP: Yes, they are jolly fellows. They sail the wide sea over in their ship, the *Half-Moon,* then every twenty years they come back to the Catskills.

JACOB: What do they do that for?

RIP: Oh, old Hendrik Hudson likes to revisit the country he discovered and keep a watchful eye over his river, the Hudson.

9

656

CULTURAL PERSPECTIVES

DUTCH TREATS Many foods, devices, and words were handed down from Dutch settlers. For example, cookies and waffles were brought here from the Netherlands. H-frame barns and open hearths are Dutch inventions. Some names of locations in New York, such as Fishkill (Vis Kill) and the Catskill (Kaatskills) Mountains, were derived from the Dutch language.

Activity Research and write a pamphlet about one item associated with Dutch culture and its significance in your life.

JACOB: I wish I could see Hendrik Hudson and his crew.

RIP: Peter Vanderdonk says his father saw them once in their funny breeches, playing at ninepins up in the hills. *(A loud peal of thunder is heard.)* Listen to the balls rolling! That must be Hendrik Hudson himself, the Flying Dutchman! *(DAME VAN WINKLE enters with broom as RIP is speaking.)*

DAME VAN WINKLE: So! Here you are, telling stories without a word of truth in 'em! Oh, *I* could tell a story or two myself—about a shiftless husband who does nothing but whittle and whistle. Whittle and whistle! What a job for a grown man! *(She snatches the whistle from RIP.)*

LUKE *(pleadingly):* It's my whistle! Please don't break it, Dame Van Winkle.

DAME VAN WINKLE: Take it and begone! *(She gives LUKE the whistle and he runs off.)* Judy, you go and ask Dame Vedder for an armful of wood. Your father is too busy spinning yarns to split wood for *our* fire. *(JUDY goes off behind the tavern.)* As for the rest of you, go home if you have any homes, and don't keep hanging around here like stray dogs looking for bones. *(She sweeps the children off the stage with her broom.)* Get along! Begone, all of you! Go home now! *(With arms akimbo, she faces RIP.)* Well, what do you have to say for yourself? *(RIP shrugs, shakes his head and says nothing.)* Nothing as usual. *(RIP goes to the tree for his gun.)* What are you getting your gun for? Going off to the mountains, no doubt. Anything to keep you out of the house.

RIP *(good-naturedly):* Well, wife, you have often told me—*my* side of the house is the *outside*. Where's my dog? Where's Wolf?

DAME VAN WINKLE: Wolf is tied up in the cellar.

RIP: You didn't tie up Wolf?

DAME VAN WINKLE: I certainly did. That dog tracked up my kitchen floor right after I'd finished scrubbing it.

(657)

⑩

Guided Instruction

⑩ **CAUSE AND EFFECT** Why does Judy have to get firewood from Dame Vedder? (because Dame Van Winkle feels that Rip is too lazy to split wood for his own family) Would volunteers please pantomime the part of the story in which Dame Van Winkle sends Luke away, orders Judy to get wood, and scolds Rip. *Pantomime*

Minilesson

REVIEW

/z/, /j/, /f/

Explain to students that some consonant sounds have more than one spelling.

- Have students say the words *revisit* and *busy* on pages 656 and 657, and *rheumatism* on page 662. Pronounce the words again emphasizing the /z/ sound in each word. Then ask students how /z/ is spelled in each word *(s)* and what other spellings there are for this sound. *(z, zz)*

- Have students say *oblige* and *passage* on pages 661 and 662. Ask how the /j/ sound is spelled in these words. *(ge)*

- Remind students the /f/ sound is sometimes spelled with *ph,* as in *phone.*

Activity Have small groups look through the selection and other reading for more words with one of these sounds.

LANGUAGE SUPPORT

ESL Because of its historical setting, this play features vocabulary and idioms that may challenge students. For example, some students may be unfamiliar with these expressions: *if excuses were shillings* (p. 655), *sharp tongue* (p. 655), *witches and goblins* (p. 656), and *playing ninepins* (p. 657). Model using these in sentences, then replacing them with words or expressions that students know. Add context by using gestures and facial expressions to illustrate meanings.

657

Guided Instruction

11 Do you think Rip had good intentions of doing his chores? (Yes. He understands why his wife is angry and he promises to take care of all the work that needs to be done. He just does not get to it.) *Character*

Well, if you're going hunting, go, and don't come back until you bring us something for supper. And if you can't bring any supper, don't bring yourself.

JUDY (*re-entering from up left, her arms full of logs*): But, Mother, it's going to rain.

DAME VAN WINKLE (*taking the wood*): Pooh! Your father won't get as wet as we will in the house, with the roof leaking and the windows broken. You hurry home now. And bring that bucket of water your father managed to get this far. (DAME VAN WINKLE *starts right, but* JUDY *stays behind with* RIP.)

RIP (*calling after his wife*): Wife, turn Wolf loose when you get home. (DAME VAN WINKLE *looks back at him angrily, tosses her head, and exits right.*)

JUDY (*starting to cry as she puts her hand in* RIP's): Father, where will you go if it rains?

RIP: I'll find a place. Don't cry, Judy. Remember your little song? Come, we'll sing it together. (*They sing an appropriate folk song, such as "Rosa, Will We Go Dancing?"*)

JUDY (*hugging* RIP): Oh, Father, I hope you have wonderful luck. Then Mother won't be so cross.

RIP: I don't blame her for being cross with me sometimes. I guess I don't do much work around here. But I'm going to do better, Judy. I'm going to do all the jobs your mother has been after me about.

DAME VAN WINKLE (*calling from off*): Ju-dee! Ju-dee!

RIP: There's your mother. I'd better be off. Goodbye, Judy dear. (*He walks left, whistling for his dog*) Come, Wolf! Come, boy! (*A dog's bark is heard off left, as* RIP *turns, waves to* JUDY, *and exits.*)

JUDY (*waving*): Goodbye, Father. (LUKE *enters from right and joins* JUDY *as loud crash of thunder is heard. Startled,* JUDY *clings to* LUKE.) Oh, Luke, listen to that thunder!

LUKE: It's only Hendrik Hudson's men playing ninepins. Don't be scared, Judy.

658

Cross Curricular: Science

THUNDER When there is thunder, there must be lightning. Lightning causes the air it travels through to expand explosively. The sound of that expansion is thunder.

Lightning and thunder occur at the same time; but because light travels almost a million times faster than sound we see lightning before we hear thunder. Count the seconds between a flash of lightning and a clap of thunder and divide by 5, to estimate the number of miles between where you are and where the lightning flash hit.

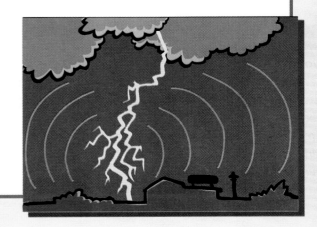

659

Guided Instruction

Minilesson

REVIEW

Character

Tell students: You can understand why a character acts in a certain way by analyzing him or her. One way to do this is to search for information in the story that tells you what a character thinks and does. Then make inferences based on the information.

Activity Tell students: Pay attention to Rip Van Winkle's thoughts and actions. Jot down words describing his behavior and personality. (Descriptions may include *kind, lazy, helpful, thoughtful, curious, confused, happy, content.*)

Guided Instruction

 CAUSE AND EFFECT Why is Luke carrying this pail of water? (Rip was supposed to fetch the water, but he didn't. When he headed off for the mountains, his daughter Judy began to carry the bucket. But her friend Luke wanted to help her, so he carried the bucket.)

13 How do you know where Rip is at the beginning of Scene 2? (The play includes an explanation of the time, setting, and activity at the beginning of each scene. Here, Rip is in the Catskill Mountains.) *Setting*

JUDY: I'm not—that is, not very.

DAME VAN WINKLE *(calling from off):* Judy! Ju-dee!

LUKE: You'd better go in or you'll catch it. Your mother is getting awfully free with her broomstick lately. Here, I'll carry your bucket for you. *(He exits right with the bucket of water.* JUDY *lingers behind to look off in direction her father has taken as the thunder gets louder. Then humming softly to herself, she exits right.)*

CURTAIN

SCENE 2

TIME: *Later the same afternoon.*

SETTING: *A forest glade, high in the Catskill Mountains. There is a tree stump at right center, and a large bush at far left. This scene may be played before the curtain.*

AT RISE: RIP, *carrying his gun, enters left, dragging his feet wearily. He sinks down on the stump.*

RIP: Whew! That was a climb! All the way up the mountain. How peaceful it is up here. No one to scold me, no one to wave a broomstick. Ah, me! *(He gives a big sigh of contentment.)* I wonder where Wolf is. Wolf! Here, boy! *(He whistles and a dog barks off left.)* That's it, Wolf, sick 'em! I hope we get something this time. We can't go home until we do. *(A loud crash of thunder is heard.)* That thunder sounds much louder up here in the mountains than down in the valley. Maybe it's going to rain after all.

VOICE *(calling from off, high-pitched, like a bird-call):* Rip Van Winkle! *(*RIP *looks around wonderingly.)* Rip Van Winkle!

RIP *(rising):* That's my name. Somebody is calling me.

VOICE *(off):* Rip Van Winkle!

RIP: Is it Dame Van Winkle? No—she would never follow me up here. *(Sound of a ship's bell is heard from off right.)* What was that? *(Bell rings again.)* A ship's bell! But how

660

Cross Curricular: Math

WHAT IS THE YEAR? Henry Hudson and his crew explored the Hudson River in 1609. Legend says that the explorer returns every 20 years. In what year did Rip Van Winkle go to sleep (1769, based on progression 1609-1629-1649-1669-1689-1709-1729-1749-1769-1789) and in what year did he awaken? (1789) Suppose you wanted to look for Henry Hudson in the Catskill Mountains. What is the next year he and his crew are scheduled to appear? (2009)

1609–1629–1649–1669–1689–1709–1729–1749–1769–1789–

can that be? A ship? Up here in the mountains? *(He gazes off right, in astonishment.)* It *is* a ship! Look at it! Sails all set—a Dutch flag at the masthead. *(Ship's bell is heard again, fainter.)* There, it's gone. I must have imagined it. *(1ST SAILOR with a* keg *on his back, enters from right and goes to center, as* RIP *watches him in amazement.)* By my galligaskins, what a funny little man! And how strangely he's dressed. Such old-fashioned clothes! *(1ST SAILOR stops at center.* RIP *goes to meet him.)* Hello, old Dutchman. That keg looks heavy. Let me carry it for you. *(He relieves* 1ST SAILOR *of the keg.)* By golly, it is heavy! Why did you bring this keg all the way up here to the top of the mountain? And who are you, anyhow?

1ST SAILOR *(gruffly):* Don't ask questions. Set it down over there. *(He points left to a spot beside the bush.)*

RIP *(obeying cheerfully):* Anything to oblige. *(There is a commotion off right, and* HENDRIK HUDSON *and his crew enter, capering and shouting. They carry bowling balls and ninepins and a drum.* 2ND SAILOR *has a burlap bag containing drinking mugs thrown over his shoulder.* RIP *turns to* 1ST SAILOR.*)* Why, bless my soul! Here are a lot of little fellows just like yourself. *(to* SAILORS, *as they gather at center)* Who are you?

SAILORS *(shouting):* Hendrik Hudson and his merry crew!

HUDSON *(stepping forward):* Set up the ninepins, men, and we'll have a game. *(Two or three sailors set up the ninepins at extreme right.* HUDSON *speaks to the* 1ST SAILOR.)* You there, fill up the flagons! *(2ND SAILOR opens sack and passes out the mugs.* HUDSON *turns to* RIP.)* Now then, Rip Van Winkle, will you drink with us?

RIP: Why, yes, thank you, Captain Hudson. I'm quite thirsty after my long climb up the mountain. *(The mugs are filled from keg.)*

2ND SAILOR *(raising his mug in toast):* To Hendrik Hudson, the *Half-Moon,* and its merry crew!

661

Guided Instruction

(14) DRAW CONCLUSIONS What modern game do you think is related to ninepins? (bowling)

(15) Do you think Rip is dreaming or does he really see Hendrik Hudson? (Answers will vary. The author describes Rip as being awake at this point, but the events are open to interpretation.) **Make Inferences**

Minilesson

REVIEW

Prefixes

Remind students that a prefix is a group of letters added to the beginning of a word to change its meaning. Common prefixes include *un-, re-, mis-, de-, anti-,* and *trans-.*

Have students:

- read the stage direction explaining that Rip's character goes offstage to change his costume.

- identify the prefixes in *unseen* and *return.*

Activity Have each student select a prefix and check a dictionary for example words. Then ask them to write a paragraph with at least five words with the prefix.

Guided Instruction

 **CAUSE AND EFFECT** What made Rip Van Winkle fall asleep? (the drink that Hendrik Hudson gave him) Add this information to your Cause and Effect chart.

CAUSE	EFFECT
Rip Van Winkle is playing checkers instead of fetching water.	Dame Van Winkle pushes Rip with a broom and nags him to get water.
Judy is afraid of the thunder she hears.	Rip explains that it is only Hendrik Hudson playing ninepins.
Hendrik Hudson gives Rip Van Winkle a drink.	Rip falls asleep for twenty years.

ALL (*as they raise their mugs*): To Hendrik Hudson, the *Half-Moon*, and its merry crew!

RIP (*lifting his mug*): Well, gentlemen, here's to your good health. May you live long and prosper. (*RIP drinks and smacks his lips.*) Ah! This is the best drink I ever tasted, but it makes me feel very sleepy. (*HUDSON and his men begin to bowl. As they roll th balls, the thunder increases. RIP yawns.*) Ho, hum! I can't keep my eyes open. I guess I'll lie down—(*Carrying his gun, he goes behind bush at left, and lies down out of sight. NOTE: Unseen by audience, RIP may go offstage for necessary costume changes and return in time for his awakening.*)

HUDSON (*to SAILORS*): Now, men, let's stop our game of ninepins, and have a merry dance. Then we'll be off, to return again in twenty years. (*One of the men beats the drum, and SAILORS dance. At the end of the dance, 1ST SAILOR points to bush where RIP is sleeping.*)

1ST SAILOR: Look! Rip Van Winkle is asleep.

HUDSON: Peace be with the poor fellow. He needs to take a good long rest from his nagging wife. Sh-h-h-h! (*He places his finger to his lips and they all go about quietly gathering up the ninepins, balls, mugs, keg, etc., then they tiptoe off the stage, their voices dying away to a whisper. The lights may dim briefly to indicate the passage of twenty years, and recorded music may be played. When the lights come up, RIP is heard yawning behind the bush, then he stands up with great difficulty. He limps to center, carrying a rusty gun. His clothes are shabby, and he has a long white beard.*)

RIP (*groaning*): Ouch, my back! It's so stiff. And my legs— just like pokers. My, my, but I'm shaky! I feel as if I'd grown to be an old man overnight. It must be rheumatism coming on. Oh, won't I have a blessed time with Dame Van Winkle if I'm laid up with rheumatism. Well, I'd better get along home to Dame Van Winkle. (*He looks at the gun he is carrying.*) Why, this rusty old thing is not my gun! Somebody has

662

Cross Curricular: Social Studies

REVOLUTIONARY WAR The main event of this story, even though it is not described, is the American Revolution.

RESEARCH AND INQUIRY Have students research the effect the American Revolution had on the 13 colonies. Ask them to write a newspaper article describ- ing how the new country set up its government.

*inter***NET** **CONNECTION** Students can learn more about the Declaration of Independence by visiting **www.mhschool.com/reading**

Guided Instruction

SELF-MONITORING

STRATEGY

ASK FOR HELP Remind students that asking good questions shows that students are thinking with a critical eye. Ask students to identify any questions they may have or anything they do not understand in the story to this point. Point out the story may not provide answers to all questions. Authors often leave interpretations up to their readers.

MODEL I don't understand where the mountain is in relation to the village. Are they far away from each other? How and why did Rip get to the mountaintop? Where is his house?

LANGUAGE SUPPORT

ESL Pair a native speaker of English with a second-language learner. Have partners rewrite the first several lines of dialogue in Scene 3. Then have them read lines from their version of the scene.

Guided Instruction

17 **DRAW CONCLUSIONS** The towns-people are singing the praises of George Washington. What must have happened while Rip Van Winkle was asleep? (The American Revolution occurred while Rip was asleep.)

18 **DRAW CONCLUSIONS** Although many things changed as Rip slept, some stayed the same. Explain. (The town, the tavern, and the people standing about make a familiar picture even though the names and faces have changed.) What might this tell you about the author's view of the war? (For some people, such as Rip, not much changed as a result of the American Revolution.)

played a trick on me. *(suddenly recollecting)* It's that Hendrik Hudson and his men! They've stolen my gun, and left this rusty one for me! *(He puts his hand to his head.)* Another scolding in store from the Dame. *(He whistles.)* Wolf! Here, Wolf! Have those scamps stolen my dog, too? He'd never leave me. *(He whistles again.)* Come on, old boy! Maybe he found it too cold and went home to be warmed by his mistress' broomstick. Well, I will follow after and get my hot welcome, too. *(He shoulders the rusty gun and totters off.)*

CURTAIN

SCENE 3

TIME: *Twenty years after Scene 1.*

SETTING: *Same as Scene 1, except that the sign above the tavern door reads:* UNION HOTEL—PROPRIETOR, JONATHAN DOOLITTLE. *A picture of George Washington has replaced that of King George III. Washington's name is printed below the picture and an American flag flutters on a pole above it.*

AT RISE: *An* ORATOR *is standing on a bench, haranguing a crowd of* TOWNSPEOPLE.

ORATOR: Remember the Boston Tea Party! Remember Bunker Hill! Who saved this country? Who is the father of this country?

TOWNSPEOPLE: George Washington! Washington for President! *(etc. They sing "Yankee Doodle.")*

> Father and I went down to camp
> Along with Captain Good'in,
> There we saw the men and boys
> As thick as hasty puddin'.
>
> Yankee Doodle keep it up.
> Yankee Doodle Dandy.
> Mind the music and the step
> And with the girls be handy.

17

18 *(*RIP *enters with a troop of children, who laugh and jeer at him.)*

664

Cross Curricular: Science

INVENTIONS Tell students: Discuss discoveries or an invention of today that you think would be most impressive to someone awaking from a twenty-year sleep. Create a brochure describing the invention and why it is important. You may choose to have the person wake up today, or you can imagine and describe new inventions for a person waking up twenty years from today.

COMPUTER

CHILDREN *(ad lib):* Look at him! He looks like a scarecrow! Where did you come from, Daddy Long-legs? Where did you get that gun? *(etc.* RIP *and* CHILDREN *go to center.* 1ST CHILD *stands in front of* RIP, *and crouches down, pulling on an imaginary beard.)*

1ST MAN: Billy goat, billy goat! *(*CHILDREN *begin stroking imaginary beards until* RIP *does the same. He is amazed to find he has a beard.)*

RIP: By my galligaskins, what's this?

2ND CHILD: It's a beard, old Father Time. Didn't you know you had a beard?

RIP: But I didn't have one last night. *(*CHILDREN *laugh and mock him.)*

ORATOR *(to* RIP*):* What do you mean by coming here at election time with a gun on your shoulder and a mob at your heels? Do you want to cause a riot?

RIP: Oh, no, sir! I am a quiet man and a loyal subject of King George!

CHILDREN AND TOWNSPEOPLE *(shouting, ad lib):* A spy! Away with him! Lock him up. *(etc.)*

JONATHAN DOOLITTLE *(stepping forward from crowd):* Hold

19

665

Guided Instruction

19 **CAUSE AND EFFECT** Why did the children make fun of Rip? (He had grown a long beard during his sleep.)

Minilesson

REVIEW

Summarize

Remind students that summarizing is telling the main events of a story. It can help keep the plot of a story clear. Ask students to summarize the events of the story up to the end of page 665.

Activity Have students:

- work in groups to create a series of storyboards to describe the important events. Each storyboard should have a drawing on it along with a simple caption.

- display and discuss their finished work.

Guided Instruction

(20) DRAW CONCLUSIONS How can you tell what happened to the country while Rip was asleep? (When Rip went to sleep, the King of England led the colonies. When he woke up, he was considered a spy for supporting the King. The political leadership had changed.)

(21) CAUSE AND EFFECT What effect does Rip's tale have on the townspeople? (They think he is crazy, which they indicate by glancing at each other and tapping their heads.)

(p/i) DECODING/CONTEXT CLUES Read the last line on page 667. Sound out the word in parentheses. (incredulously) What does this word mean?

Fluency

READ WITH EXPRESSION Have students practice oral reading skills using pages 665–666, which contain stage directions and dialogue. Advise students their intonation should vary to reflect the mood of the passage.

Model fluent reading by

- reading exclamations to convey urgency.
- pausing for a moment when each speaker finishes a line of dialogue.
- spacing out the descriptive stage directions for dramatic effect.

Encourage students to use gestures and facial expressions as they read.

---

on a minute! We must get to the bottom of this. *(to RIP)* Aren't you a supporter of Washington for President?

RIP *(puzzled):* Eh? Supporter of Washington? *(shaking his head, wholly bewildered)* I don't understand. I mean no harm. I only want to find my friends. They were here at the tavern yesterday.

DOOLITTLE: Who are these friends of yours? Name them.

RIP *(hesitantly):* Well, one is the landlord—

(20) DOOLITTLE: *I* am the landlord of this hotel—Jonathan Doolittle.

RIP: Why, what happened to Nicholas Vedder?

1ST WOMAN *(pushing her way out of the crowd):* Nicholas Vedder? Why, he's dead and gone these eighteen years.

RIP: No, no, that's impossible! Where's Brom Dutcher? And the schoolmaster, Van Bummel—?

1ST MAN: Brom Dutcher was killed in the war at Stony Point.

2ND MAN: And Van Bummel went off to the war, too. He became a great general, and now he's in Congress.

RIP: War? What war?

2ND MAN: Why, the war we fought against England, and won, of course.

RIP: I don't understand. Am I dreaming? Congress? Generals? What's happened to me?

DOOLITTLE *(impatiently):* Now, we've had enough of this nonsense. Who are you, anyway? What is your name?

RIP *(utterly confused):* I don't know. I mean, I was Rip Van Winkle yesterday, but today—

DOOLITTLE: Don't try to make sport of us, my man!

RIP: Oh, indeed, I'm not, sir. I was myself last night, but I fell asleep on the mountain, and Hendrik Hudson and his crew changed my gun, and everything's changed, and I'm changed, and I can't tell what my name is, or who I am! **(21)** *(TOWNSPEOPLE exchange significant glances, nod knowingly, and tap their foreheads.)*

666

(p/i) PREVENTION/INTERVENTION

DECODING/CONTEXT CLUES
Have students reread the last six lines of page 667. Help them sound out *incredulously*. Ask:

- How would you describe Rip's emotions?
- How would you describe Judith's emotions?

Lead students to recognize that Rip is happy he has found someone he knows in this strange world he has awoken to. Judith believes her father dead or missing. She is skeptical about believing him. Explain *incredulous* means unwilling or unable to believe something. The suffix *-ly* indicates that she responds to Rip in a disbelieving manner.

2ND MAN *(shaking his head)*: Hendrik Hudson, he says! Poor chap. He's mad. Let's leave him alone.

RIP *(in great distress)*: Isn't there anybody here who knows who I am?

WOMAN *(soothingly)*: Why, you're just yourself, old man. Who else do you think you could be? *(JUDITH GARDENIER enters from left, leading* LITTLE RIP *by the hand. He hangs back, whimpering.)*

JUDITH: Hush, Rip! The old man won't hurt you. **22** **23**

RIP *(turning in surprise)*: Rip? Who said Rip?

JUDITH: Why, I did. I was just telling my little boy not to be frightened.

RIP *(scanning her face)*: And what is your name, my good woman?

JUDITH: My name is Judith, sir.

RIP: Judith? Did you say Judith? *(in great excitement)* And your father—what was his name?

JUDITH: Ah, poor man, his name was Rip Van Winkle. It's twenty years since he went away from home. We never heard of him again.

RIP *(staggered)*: Twenty years!

JUDITH: Yes, it must be all of that. His dog came back without him. I was a little girl then.

RIP: And your mother—where is she?

JUDITH: My mother is dead, sir.

RIP *(sighing)*: Ah, but that woman had a tongue! Well, peace be with her soul. Did you love your father, Judith?

JUDITH: With all my heart. All the children in the village loved him, too.

RIP: Then look at me. Look closely, my dear Judy. I am your father.

JUDITH *(incredulously)*: You? My father?

667

Guided Instruction

22 **CAUSE AND EFFECT** What made Rip notice his daughter?

MODEL Let me think. First, Rip heard a woman call his own name, referring to a boy. He then asked the woman her name and realized that it was his daughter.

23 **CAUSE AND EFFECT** Compare how the child in the illustration responded to Rip with how children responded to him before he fell asleep.

Minilesson

REVIEW

Fact and Nonfact

Although the story of Rip Van Winkle is fictional, it contains references to events that occurred and places that exist. Recognizing which statements or ideas can be proved true (facts) and which can be proved false (nonfacts) will help readers better understand the story.

Activity Tell students: Along with other members of your group, find references to both factual and nonfactual events in the story. Explain what sources you used to check the factual events such as encyclopedias, history books, and maps.

Guided Instruction

(24) CAUSE AND EFFECT Let's use the Cause and Effect chart to record a few events in Scene 3 and to summarize the play.

CAUSE	EFFECT
Rip Van Winkle is playing checkers instead of fetching water.	Dame Van Winkle pushes Rip with a broom and nags him to get water.
Judy is afraid of the thunder she hears.	Rip explains that it is only Hendrik Hudson playing ninepins.
Hendrik Hudson gives Rip Van Winkle a drink.	Rip falls asleep for 20 years.
Rip falls asleep and awakens 20 years later.	Rip finds many things in town have changed—and learns of the American Revolution.
Rip's daughter Judith had named her son Rip.	Rip Van Winkle hears someone calling his name and recognizes his grown daughter.

RETELL THE STORY Ask volunteers to retell the story, referring to their charts. Then have partners summarize the story. Have them focus on cause-and-effect relationships. *Summarize*

STUDENT SELF-ASSESSMENT

- How did using the strategy of relating causes to their effects help me understand the story?
- How did the Cause and Effect chart help?

TRANSFERRING THE STRATEGY

- When might I try using this strategy again?

668

REREADING FOR *Fluency*

PARTNERS Have students choose a favorite section of the story to read to a partner. Encourage students to read with feeling and expression.

READING RATE You may want to evaluate a student's reading rate. Have the student read aloud from *Rip Van Winkle* for one minute. Ask the student to place a self-stick note after the last word read. Then count the number of words he or she has read.

Alternatively, you may assess small groups or the whole class together by having students count words and record their own scores.

Use the Reading Rate form in the **Diagnostic/Placement Evaluations** booklet to evaluate students' performance.

RIP: We used to sing a little song together, remember? *(He sings a few lines from the folk song sung in Scene 1.)*

JUDITH *(slowly):* Yes, my father used to sing that song with me, but many people know it.

RIP: Do you remember, Judy, that I told you the story of how Hendrik Hudson and his crew played ninepins in the mountains just before I went off hunting with Wolf?

JUDITH *(excitedly):* Yes! And Wolf *was* our dog's name! Oh, Father, it's really *you!*

RIP *(taking her in his arms):* Yes, my little Judy—young Rip Van Winkle once, old Rip Van Winkle now. *(TOWNSPEOPLE talk excitedly among themselves as they watch RIP and JUDITH.)*

JUDITH: Dearest Father, come home with me. Luke and I will take good care of you.

RIP: Luke?

JUDITH: Luke Gardenier, my old playmate. You used to make whistles for him and take him fishing. We were married when he came back from the war.

RIP: Ah, the war. There is so much I have to catch up with.

JUDITH: You will have plenty of time to do that—and you must tell us what happened to you.

RIP: Maybe you won't believe what happened to me, Judy—it was all so strange. *(RIP reaches out a hand to LITTLE RIP, who shyly takes it, and they start off left, JUDITH following. A loud clap of thunder stops them. RIP turns front and shakes his fist toward the mountains.)* Oh, no you don't, Hendrik Hudson! You don't get me back up there again. *(There is an answering roll of thunder that sounds like a deep rumble of laughter as the curtain falls.)*

THE END

669

LITERARY RESPONSE

QUICK-WRITE Invite students to record their thoughts about the story. These questions may help them get started:

- How would you describe Rip Van Winkle?
- What do you think of how Rip dealt with his responsibilities?

ORAL RESPONSE Have students share their journal writings and discuss what part of the story they enjoyed most.

Guided Instruction

Return to Predictions and Purposes

Review with students their story predictions and reasons for reading the story. Were their predictions correct? Did they find out what they wanted to know?

PREDICTIONS	WHAT HAPPENED
The main character, Rip Van Winkle, goes off to war.	Rip Van Winkle falls asleep and misses the entire war.
Rip Van Winkle meets a woman and a child.	After being gone for 20 years, Rip is reunited with his daughter, and he meets his grandson.

INFORMAL ASSESSMENT

CAUSE AND EFFECT

HOW TO ASSESS

- Can students identify cause-and-effect relationships in the story?
- Can students recognize how historical events affected Rip?

Students should recognize that Rip lived shortly before and after the American Revolution. They should also be able to analyze the events of the story by identifying why they happened.

FOLLOW UP If students have trouble recognizing cause-and-effect relationships in the story, review the Cause and Effect charts.

If students have trouble seeing that each event can be explained, ask them to change an action in the story and imagine its effect.

Story Questions

Have students discuss or write answers to the questions on page 670.

1. The story takes place in New York's Catskill Mountains in the 1700s. *Literal/Setting*

2. Sample answer: Hudson and his crew give Rip a special drink, which causes Rip to sleep. Rip's sleep causes him to miss the American Revolution. *Cause and Effect*

3. Sample answer: He has an active imagination and he also actually falls asleep and dreams. *Inferential/Character*

4. Sample answer: The story is about a man who sleeps for 20 years, through the American Revolution of the late 1700s. *Critical/Summarize*

5. Sample answers: Rip might ask "Where am I?" People might ask Rip "Who are you?" *Critical/Reading Across Texts*

Write a Dialogue For a full writing process lesson related to this writing suggestion, see the lesson on pages 673K–673L.

Story Questions & Activities

1. When and where does the story take place?

2. What causes Rip to sleep for 20 years? What happens to him as a result?

3. Why is Rip a "dreamer" in more ways than one? Explain.

4. What is this famous story about?

5. Imagine that Rip Van Winkle awoke to find himself inside the painting on pages 648–649. What might he ask the people in the picture? What might they ask him?

Write a Dialogue

Suppose that Rip Van Winkle had not slept for 20 years, but for 250 years! Imagine that he had awakened in your hometown! Write a dialogue between Rip Van Winkle and you. What questions might he ask you? What would you want to know about his life in the past? Use dialogue form. Explain any modern inventions you mention, such as cars, airplanes, and computers.

Meeting Individual Needs

EASY

Vocabulary

Read each clue. Find the correct vocabulary word in the box and write it on the line in the right-hand column next to its clue.

| landlord | oblige | rascals | sprawled | husking | keg |

Clues — **Vocabulary Words**

1. jar or barrel — keg
2. building owner — landlord
3. spread out — sprawled
4. to please — oblige
5. a way of taking the husk off corn — husking
6. mischievous people or cheaters — rascals

Story Comprehension

Write a ✔ next to every sentence that tells something true about "Rip Van Winkle."

✔ 1. "Rip Van Winkle" takes place just before the time of the Revolutionary War.

___ 2. Rip Van Winkle thinks children are too noisy.

✔ 3. Rip Van Winkle would rather spend time with his friends than work.

___ 4. Rip Van Winkle meets no one on his journey into the mountains.

✔ 5. Rip Van Winkle sleeps in the mountains for over 20 years.

✔ 6. While Rip Van Winkle is gone, the Revolutionary War is fought.

At Home: Have students write sentences using two of the vocabulary words.

194–195 Book 5/Unit 6 Rip Van Winkle

Reteach, 195

ON-LEVEL

Story Comprehension

Review the play "Rip Van Winkle." Then complete the story chart below. For each scene in the play, describe the time and place of the setting. Then list the characters. Lastly, write a short summary of each scene. Answers will vary. Sample answers are shown.

Scene 1

1. **Setting:** Time: early autumn, a few years before the Revolutionary War
   Place: a village in the Catskill Mountains, outside of the King George tavern

2. **Characters:** Van Bummel, Vanderdonk, Vedder, Dutcher, Rip Van Winkle, Dame Van Winkle, Judy, Jacob, Luke, Meenie, Katchen

3. **Summary:** Rip is playing checkers with other village men in front of the tavern, when his wife, Dame Van Winkle, enters and scolds him for not doing doing his chores. She sends him off into the forest to hunt for their supper.

Scene 2

4. **Setting:** Time: same day as scene 1, later in the afternoon
   Place: in a forest glade in the Catskill Mountains

5. **Characters:** Rip Van Winkle, Henrik Hudson and his crew of sailors

6. **Summary:** While in the mountains, Rip Van Winkle meets the legendary Henrik Hudson and his crew of sailors. They give Rip a drink from their keg. Then they set up a game of ninepins. Rip falls asleep from the drink and sleeps for 20 years.

At Home: Encourage students to act out a scene from "Rip Van Winkle" for or with family members.

195 Book 5/Unit 6 Rip Van Winkle

Practice, 195

CHALLENGE

Vocabulary

| husking | keg | landlord | oblige | rascals | sprawled |

At the end of "Rip Van Winkle," Rip goes back to his daughter's home. Write a scene between Rip and his daughter telling what might have happened after they arrived home. Use as many vocabulary words as possible.
Answers will vary, but should include at least four vocabulary words used in the correct context and parts of speech.

Extend 195

Story Comprehension

At the end of the story, Judith finally believes that Rip is her father. Tell how she is able to come to this conclusion.
Rip tells her about a song he used to sing when she was a little girl. He tells her that he had a dog named Wolf. He reminds her of the story he used to tell her about Hendrik Hudson.

At Home: Find 5 unfamiliar words in a magazine. After looking up their definition in a dictionary, discuss how you can remember the meanings of these words.

194–195 Book 5/Unit 6 Rip Van Winkle

Extend, 195

Create a Time Line

Legend has it that Hendrik Hudson and his crew sailed up and down the Hudson River looking for a passage to the north. But they never found it. Who was the real Hendrik (or Henry) Hudson? What did he do or fail to do? What happened to him? Read about Henry Hudson in an encyclopedia, or in a social studies textbook. Draw a time line of his journeys. List the dates of his expeditions in order, and write a brief description of each.

1600 1610 1620 1630 1640

Draw a Costume

"By my galligaskins," says Rip, when he discovers that he has a long beard. Galligaskins are the loose trousers that Rip may have worn. Use an encyclopedia or a book about the history of fashion to find out how people in the 13 colonies dressed in the 1700s. Make a drawing and label the different articles of clothing.

Find Out More

The story of Rip Van Winkle takes place in the Catskill Mountains. Where are these mountains located? Who settled there? Find the Catskills on a map of New York State. Research five interesting facts about them and the surrounding area. Compare your information with your partner's.

671

Story Activities

Create a Time Line

Materials: resource materials (encyclopedia, social studies text, or book of American legends) and chart paper

PARTNERS Have students work in pairs and use the reference materials to create a time line of Henry Hudson's expeditions. Be sure to have them write a short description of each journey.

Draw a Costume

Materials: books about style of dress during colonial times

Have students research the type of clothing that was worn in the 1700s. Then have them draw a person wearing clothing from that period.

Find Out More

RESEARCH/INQUIRY Have students use reference materials to learn more **PARTNERS** about the setting of the story, the Catskill Mountains. If available, have students use the Internet. With a partner, have them list five facts about the mountains and the area.

 For more information on the Catskill Mountains, students can visit **www.mhschool.com/reading**

FORMAL ASSESSMENT

After page 671, see the Selection Assessment.

Study Skills

LIBRARY/MEDIA CENTER

OBJECTIVES Students will recognize the importance of interviewing.

PREPARE Read the passage with students. Display **Teaching Chart 159.**

TEACH Explain to students the importance of writing questions before they interview. Have students write 3–5 questions they would like to ask Rip Van Winkle.

PRACTICE Have students answer questions 1–5. Discuss the answers.
1. helps spark questions; **2.** to ensure the right questions are asked; **3.** to have a record of what the person said; **4.** to avoid mistakes in recording and reporting what was said; **5.** personal facts and feelings.

ASSESS/CLOSE Have students plan an interview with an important person from history.

Study SKILLS

Conduct an Interview

One way to get information about someone is to interview them. Suppose you were going to interview Rip Van Winkle. What questions would you ask? Like a letter or a dialogue, an **interview** follows a pattern of questions and answers. Here are some ways you can prepare for an interview.
- Decide the questions you will ask beforehand.
- Make note cards of the main questions.
Then follow these speaking and listening guidelines.

SPEAKING AND LISTENING GUIDELINES:
An Interview
- State the purpose of the interview clearly.
- Be polite. Ask questions simply and directly.
- Listen closely to the answers and take notes about them.
- Ask questions to get more information about an answer.

Use the information about interviewing to answer these questions.

1 Why is it important to know something about the person you are interviewing before the interview?

2 Why should you write down the questions you will ask?

3 Why do you need to take notes during the interview?

4 Why are good speaking and listening skills important during an interview?

5 What kind of information can you get from an interview that you cannot get from a book or another source?

Meeting Individual Needs

EASY	ON-LEVEL	CHALLENGE

EASY — Conduct an Interview

Conducting an interview is a useful way of getting information about other people's experiences. To prepare for an interview, ask yourself what you want to learn from your subject. Then think about questions to ask.

Town Crier

Memo: To All Reporters
From: Jillian Kroll

Please remember these tips when you start interviewing:
• Prepare questions in advance. Remember to use the question words: who! what! when! why! and how!
• Explain why you want the interview and how it will be used.
• During the interview, listen carefully to the person's answers.
• Take notes so that you will not forget what the person has said.
• Thank the person for the interview

Use the information about interviewing to answer the questions.

1. What should you do before an interview? prepare and list questions

2. What should you do during an interview? listen carefully to the person's answers

3. What should you do after an interview? Thank the person for the interview and neatly rewrite the information you have gathered.

4. Why is it important to listen carefully at an interview? so you can write down the correct answers

Book 5/Unit 6
Rip Van Winkle
At Home: Have students prepare for an interview with Rip Van Winkle.
196

ON-LEVEL — Conduct an Interview

An **interview** is a way to gain information from someone. An interview follows a pattern of questions and answers. To prepare yourself to interview somebody, you need to figure out what questions you should ask.

Think about how you would conduct an interview with someone. Then answer the questions below.

Answers may vary.

1. Why is it important to know something about the person you are going to interview before you conduct the interview? It will help me to know the person's background and personality. Then I can ask more exact questions.

2. Why should you write down the questions you want to ask? So that I don't forget what I want to ask.

3. Why do you need to take notes during the interview? So that I don't forget what I hear.

4. Why is it important to be polite during the interview? I do not want to offend the person I am interviewing, because then he or she might not want to answer all my questions.

5. What sort of information does an interview give that you might not find in a book or another reference source? I might find out more personal information or anecdotes (individual stories) that would not be in a book or reference source.

Book 5/Unit 6
Rip Van Winkle
At Home: Write five questions you would ask if you were interviewing a reporter about what his or her job is like.
196

CHALLENGE — Conduct an Interview

In "Rip Van Winkle," Rip awakens to a world that has changed drastically during his 20-year sleep. For young people, such as his grandson, Rip Van Winkle could be an important source of information from the past.

Conduct an interview with an older person who could tell you what life was like 20 years ago, before you were born. First, create a list of at least eight questions you will ask. Write your questions below.
Answers will vary.

After you have finished your list, conduct your interview. Take notes as you go along. Then use your notes and what you have learned to write an article on a separate sheet of paper about the person you interviewed.
Answers will vary.

Book 5/Unit 6
Rip Van Winkle
At Home: Find an example of an interview in a newspaper or magazine. What are some of the questions that were asked?
196

Reteach, 196   Practice, 196   Extend, 196

TEST POWER

DIRECTIONS

Read the sample story. Then read each question about the story.

SAMPLE

Caterina Tries Something New

Caterina was frustrated with drawing. She could never seem to get her pen to draw what she saw in her mind. Whenever she completed a drawing on paper, it never looked the way that she wanted it to look.

One day, Caterina's art teacher invited her to try something new—computer art. Caterina sat down in front of the computer and held the special pen in her hand. As she traced the pen along the pad, lines simultaneously appeared on the computer screen.

Caterina carefully thought about what she wanted to draw. Slowly, she began to draw the lines on the screen. When she was finished, she looked at what she'd created. It was amazing! Her drawing was similar to what she had pictured before she started.

Caterina smiled at her new discovery.

1 Why did Caterina try computer art?

   ○ She was interested in computers.

   ● Her teacher offered her the opportunity.

   ○ Caterina didn't enjoy her art class any more.

   ○ She was taking a computer art class.

2 You can tell that Caterina's computer art picture —

   ● satisfied her

   ○ disappointed her

   ○ was crooked

   ○ was of a flower

673

Test Power

THE PRINCETON REVIEW

Read the Page

Have students read the passage, the questions, and the answer choices. Tell students to choose the best answer.

Discuss the Questions

Question 1: This question requires students to draw a conclusion about the character's behavior. Direct students back to the passage. Remind them not to rely on their memory. Ask, "Who invited Caterina to try something new? What happened just before she sat down at the computer?"

Question 2: This question requires students to infer how Caterina feels about her computer art picture. There are two clues in the passage that provide information about her feelings: "It was amazing!" and "Caterina smiled at her new discovery." Have students read the answer choices and eliminate those that do not make sense.

For The Princeton Review test preparation practice for **TerraNova, ITBS,** and **SAT-9,** visit the McGraw-Hill School Division Web site. See also McGraw-Hill's *Standardized Test Preparation Book.*

PUPIL SELECTION

↓

EASY
DECODABLE

Leveled Books

LEVELED BOOKS

A Matter of Time

written by Steve Korté
illustrated by John Hovell

EASY

A Matter of Time

/z/, /j/, and /f/

☑ **Cause and Effect**

☑ **Instructional Vocabulary:**
husking bee, keg, landlord,
oblige, rascals, sprawled

Guided Reading

PREVIEW AND PREDICT Discuss each illustration up to page 5. Have students predict what the story will be about and how it will end.

SET PURPOSES Have students write about why they want to read *A Matter of Time*.

READ THE BOOK Use questions like the following to guide students as they read or after they have read the story independently.

Page 2: Why is Maria in an office when the story begins? (She volunteered to help her mother.) *Cause and Effect*

Page 3: Why did Maria want to start the copying by herself? (Maria wanted to show her mother that she was responsible.) *Cause and Effect*

Page 4: What is the vocabulary word on this page? (landlord) Can you use the word in a sentence? (Sample answers: My uncle rents his apartment from a landlord.) *Instructional Vocabulary*

Pages 6-7: What happened to Maria? (Instead of traveling to the fifteenth floor, Maria traveled through time to the forty-first century.) *Draw Conclusions*

Page 10: Look at the words *eject* and *emerged* on this page. How are the /j/ sounds different in each word? (Hard j sound in eject, soft j sound in emerged) *Phonics and Decoding*

Page 16: Why did Maria decide to have her mother come along the next time she needed to make photocopies? (If anything unusual were to happen, she would have her mother to protect her.) *Cause and Effect*

RETURN TO PREDICTIONS AND PURPOSES Have students look back at their predictions. Ask which predictions were close to the story and why. Have students review their purposes for reading. Did they find out what they wanted to know?

LITERARY RESPONSE Discuss these questions:

* What do you think Maria thought the "New" room would be like before she got there?

* What was your favorite part of the story?

Also see the story questions and activity in *A Matter of Time*.

Answers to Story Questions

1. She had been thinking about the future a few minutes earlier.
2. She volunteered to test the rocket, and she took a chance on using the "eject" button.
3. Answers will vary.
4. The past and the future may not always be what you expected them to be.
5. Answers will vary.

Story Questions and Activity

1. Why did Maria decide to explore the "new" room first?
2. How was Maria brave in the room of the future?
3. If you had to choose between a room of the future and a room of the past, which would you choose?
4. What is the story mostly about?
5. If Rip Van Winkle had to choose between the two signs marked "Old" and "New," which do you think he would choose? Explain your answer.

Design a Robot

Draw a picture of robot or construct one using materials you have on hand. Write a paragraph about your robot, telling what it can do. Tell whether the robot can be used best in the 21st Century or the 41st Century.

from A Matter of Time

Leveled Books

PUPIL SELECTION

INDEPENDENT
DECODABLE

INDEPENDENT

H.G. Wells: Man Of The Future

☑ **Cause and Effect**

☑ **Instructional Vocabulary:**
husking bee, keg, landlord, oblige, rascals, sprawled

Guided Reading

PREVIEW AND PREDICT Have students look at the illustrations up to page 5 and discuss each one. Ask students to predict what the story will be about. Have them record their predictions in a journal.

SET PURPOSES Have students write about why they want to read *H.G. Wells: Man Of The Future*. For example, *I will find out what type of machine this man invents.*

READ THE BOOK Use questions like the following to guide students as they read or after they have read the story independently.

Page 2: What caused H.G. Wells to take an interest in reading at a young age? (Wells was poor and led a modest lifestyle. Reading took him beyond his own world.) *Cause and Effect*

Page 5: Why didn't Wells have to worry about having enough money to pay his landlord? (Wells' book, *The Time Machine*, was a success and brought him wealth.) *Cause and Effect*

Page 6: Ask a volunteer to read the sentence containing the vocabulary word *obliged*. Can you think of another word

related to this word? (obligated) *Instructional Vocabulary*

Page 11: How did Earth die in Wells' book *The Time Machine*? (The sun grew into a huge dome that covered a tenth of the dark sky. With the sun so huge, animals died both on land and in the ocean.) *Cause and Effect*

Page 12-13: Why hasn't an actual time machine become a reality? (Sample answer: it is not possible to travel back or forward in time.) *Drawing Conclusions*

RETURN TO PREDICTIONS AND PURPOSES Have students look back at their predictions. Ask if any predictions were close to the story and why. Have students review their purposes for reading. Did they find out what they wanted to know?

LITERARY RESPONSE Discuss these questions:

- What was your favorite part of the story?

- Where would you like to go in a time machine if you could?

Also see the story questions and activity in *H.G. Wells: Man of the Future.*

Answers to Story Questions

1. The Earth being attacked by Martians, and the time machine.
2. His creative mind combined with his scientific training.
3. Answers will vary.
4. In many of his books, H.G. Wells was able to predict certain things that would happen in the future.
5. Answers will vary.

Story Questions and Activity

1. Which predictions and stories of H. G. Wells have not come true?
2. How do you think H. G. Wells was able to predict so many inventions and events?
3. If you could journey in a time traveling machine, would you do it? If your answer is yes, would you travel to the past or future? If your answer is no, why not?
4. What is the main idea of this story?
5. If *Rip Van Winkle* had woken up in the land of the Elois and the Morlocks, which group do you think he would fit in better with? Why?

Travel Back in Time

Reread page 7. Think about what would have happened if the time traveler had gone back in time instead of journeying into the future. Choose a destination in the past for the time traveler, and describe what he would see in the place you choose.

from H.G. Wells: Man of the Future

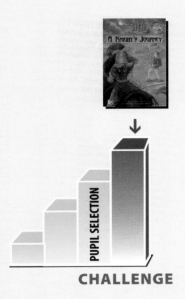

PUPIL SELECTION

CHALLENGE

Leveled Books

CHALLENGE

A Knight's Journey

☑ **Cause and Effect**

☑ **Instructional Vocabulary:**
husking bee, keg, landlord, oblige, rascals, sprawled

Guided Reading

PREVIEW AND PREDICT Have students look at the illustrations up to page 14 and discuss them. Ask students to predict how the story will end. Have them record their predictions in their journals.

SET PURPOSES Have students write about why they want to read *A Knight's Journey*. For example, *I will find out how the boy gets out of jail.*

READ THE BOOK Use questions like the following to guide students as they read or after they have read the story independently.

Page 3: What caused Jason to fall to the ground? (He backed up into a suit of armor, which bumped him on the head.) *Cause and Effect*

Page 7: Why was the knight taking Jason to Camelot? (Sample answer: the knight wasn't sure where Jason came from and he thought the king would know what to do with him.) *Drawing Conclusions*

Page 9: Read the sentence containing the vocabulary word. What is a keg? (Sample answer: A keg is a large container used for holding liquids.) *Instructional Vocabulary*

Page 10: What caused King Arthur to have Jason arrested? (Jason told Arthur about the future, which frightened and confused the king.) *Cause and Effect*

Page 16: How did Jason find himself back in the present? (His friends shouted at him to wake up and he woke up on the floor of the museum.) *Cause and Effect*

RETURN TO PREDICTIONS AND PURPOSES Have students look back at their predictions. Ask if anyone predicted the ending. Have students review their purposes for reading. Did they find out what they wanted to know?

LITERARY RESPONSE Discuss these questions:

• What are some things you would like to ask someone from the past if you could?

• Do you think Jason will ever end up in King Arthur's court again?

Also see the story questions and activity in *A Knight's Journey*.

Answers to Story Questions

1. He thought Jason was attacking him with the sword.
2. He did not understand how Jason was able to predict the future and he was scared of Jason's cellular phone.
3. Jason loved the stories of King Arthur and knew the legend of Arthur very well.
4. It is about a boy who is knocked in the head who dreams that he is in King Arthur's Court.
5. Answers will vary.

Story Questions and Activity

1. Why was the knight so angry with Jason when he first encountered him in the field?
2. Why did King Arthur put Jason in a prison cell?
3. How did Jason know what the future would hold for King Arthur?
4. What is the story mostly about?
5. What if Jason had met Rip Van Winkle when he traveled back in time? How do you think this story would have been different?

Back in Time

Choose a time in the past that you would like to visit. If you could bring only three items back with you, what would you bring and why? Be sure to explain how these items would be useful to you in the past.

from A Knight's Journey

Activities
Anthology and Leveled Books

Connecting Texts

TIME LINES Write the story titles on a time line. Discuss with students how time is involved in each story. Point out that some stories involve going back in time, while others involve moving forward. Call on volunteers from each reading level. Use the time line to indicate the direction the story moves. Then write a brief description of what happened.

Past	Present	Future	
	Rip Van Winkle	→	Rip falls asleep and wakes up 20 years later
Maria walks into a room that is in the past.	A Matter of Time	→	Maria takes an elevator to the forty-first century.
	H.G. Wells: Man Of The Future	→	H.G. Wells imagines inventions in the future.
	A Knight's Journey		Jason falls asleep and dreams that he is in King Arthur's court in the fifth century

Viewing/Representing

GROUP PRESENTATIONS Divide the class into groups, one for each of the four books read in the lesson. Have each group identify something that caused the main character to travel to a different time. Then ask them to orally summarize the book, using pictures they have drawn. Have each group present its pictures and summary.

AUDIENCE RESPONSE Ask students to analyze each group's presentation. Allow time for questions after each presentation. Make sure that everyone can recognize the cause and effect in each story.

Research and Inquiry

MORE ABOUT TIME Have students think about how things change over time. Then have them

- choose a topic they find interesting, such as technology, dancing, or even a sport

- use books to find out how the topic has changed over the last one hundred years

- talk to an adult to find out how they may have been affected by such changes

- draw a time line showing what they have found. Add to the time line by making predictions for the future.

*inter***NET** **CONNECTION** Students can visit *www.mhschool.com/reading* for more information.

Review Cause and Effect

PREPARE

Discuss Cause and Effect

Review: You can follow a story more closely by trying to figure out what might happen as a result of each event.

TEACH

Read "Rip and the Roof" and Model the Skill

Read "Rip and the Roof." Focus students' attention on the causes for and effects of each action described.

Rip and the Roof

Rip Van Winkle's roof had a hole in it <u>because</u> a tree branch fell during a winter storm. <u>Since</u> it was so cold, Rip decided to wait until spring to fix it.

<u>Due to</u> Dame Van Winkle's nagging, Rip climbed up to the roof to take a look. To Rip's surprise, he found being on the roof <u>so</u> relaxing <u>that</u> he leaned back and fell asleep.

Rip woke up <u>when</u> he got hungry. Then his wife told him that he had better fix the roof <u>if he wanted to</u> eat dinner.

Teaching Chart 160

Discuss clues in the passage that help readers recognize cause-and-effect relationships.

MODEL The first sentence tells me that Rip Van Winkle's roof had a hole. The hole was caused by a tree branch falling during a winter storm. What was the effect of the cold weather on Rip's actions? He decided to wait until spring to fix the roof.

PRACTICE

Identify the Cause for Each Effect

GROUP

Cause-and-effect relationships can often be determined by the writer's use of clue words such as *because, since, if,* and *in order to.* Have students underline clues such as these in **Teaching Chart 160.**

▶ **Logical**

ASSESS/CLOSE

Relate Causes and Effects

PARTNERS

Divide students into pairs. Have one student in each pair draw a cartoon showing a scene. Then have the second student draw what happens as a result. For example, the first frame might show a young child climbing up on a pile of books to reach a cookie jar. The next frame might show cookies all over the floor. Then have one student in the pair draw what happened and challenge the other student to draw the cause.

ALTERNATE TEACHING STRATEGY

CAUSE AND EFFECT

For a different approach to teaching this skill, see page T64.

SELF-SELECTED Reading

Students may choose from the following titles.

ANTHOLOGY

- *Rip Van Winkle*

LEVELED BOOKS

- *A Matter of Time*
- *H.G. Wells, Man of the Future*
- *A Knight's Journey*

Bibliography, pages T76–T77

Meeting Individual Needs for Comprehension

EASY	ON-LEVEL	CHALLENGE	LANGUAGE SUPPORT

EASY — Cause and Effect

A **cause** is the why something happens. An **effect** is the event, feeling, or situation that results from the cause. Clue words can help you understand the relationship between cause and effect.

Read each cause. Then circle the letter next to the effect that could most likely result from the cause.

1. Ned ate three hot dogs, two hamburgers, a plate of potato salad, and a huge slice of watermelon.
   a. Ned is still hungry.
   b. Ned might have a stomachache from being too full.
   c. Ned doesn't like picnic food.

2. Ginger left her bike out in the snow all night.
   a. She cannot use it for school today.
   b. It is bright red.
   c. Ginger's bike will stay in the garage all year.

3. Liam slammed the phone down without even saying good-bye to Sean.
   a. Liam is glad Sean called.
   b. Liam is excited about talking to Sean.
   c. Liam is angry with Sean.

4. Andrea has no money to buy a snack today.
   a. Andrea had lunch today.
   b. Andrea will not have a snack today.
   c. Andrea's friend, Hunter, will share his snack with Andrea.

5. Max broke his leg playing baseball the week before the big game.
   a. Max will hit a home run to win the big game.
   b. Max will play badly in the big game.
   c. Max will have to miss the big game.

At Home: Have students think about something that happened in school. Have them talk about why it happened and the effects of what happened.

197   Book 5/Unit 6 Rip Van Winkle 5

ON-LEVEL — Cause and Effect

A **cause** is the reason why something happens. An **effect** is a result of the cause of what happens. Story events are often connected by a cause-and-effect relationship.

Complete the chart below to show the cause-and-effect links between events in "Rip Van Winkle." Supply the missing cause or effect in the correct column.

Cause	Effect
1. Vedder and Vanderdonk invite Rip to sit down and join them for a game of checkers.	1. Rip stops doing his chores to play a game of checkers with the men.
2. Rip stops doing his chores to play a game of checkers with the men.	2. Dame Van Winkle is angry with her husband Rip.
3. Rip forgets to mend the fence as his wife told him.	3. The cow escapes.
4. Henrick Hudson and his crew play ninepin up in the mountains.	4. Rip says the result is thunder.
5. Henrik Hudson and his sailors give Rip Van Winkle a drink from their keg.	5. Rip Van Winkle falls asleep for 20 years.
6. Rip Van Winkle has a beard and is 20 years older.	6. Judith does not recognize her father at first.

At Home: Encourage students to share their knowledge of cause-and-effect relationships with a member of their family.

197   Book 5/Unit 6 Rip Van Winkle 6

CHALLENGE — Cause and Effect

A **cause** is the reason why something happens. An **effect** is the result. Below are some examples of effects from the story "Rip Van Winkle." Write the cause for each effect.

1. In the beginning of the story, Van Brummel is reading that a Stamp Act Congress is being held in New York.
   Cause: You may have to remind students that this Congress, or meeting, was held to protest English taxation in the colonies.

2. When Rip is talking to the children, they think they hear thunder coming from the mountains. What does Rip tell them is the cause?
   Cause: Hendrik Hudson and his men are playing ninepins.

3. Dame Van Winkle is angry when she catches Rip telling stories to the children.
   Cause: Rip is supposed to be gathering wood and doing his chores.

4. Rip goes off to the mountain with his dog and his gun.
   Cause: To go hunting; maybe avoid doing chores.

5. Rip falls asleep in the mountains after visiting with Hendrik Hudson and the sailors.
   Cause: He drinks from the sailor's keg, and the drink makes him sleepy.

6. When Rip awakens, his back is stiff, his clothes are shabby, and he has grown a long white beard.
   Cause: He has been asleep for 20 years.

7. When Rip walks into town after his 20-year sleep, the townspeople think he is a spy and want to put him in jail.
   Cause: Rip says that he is loyal to King George at a time when people are preparing to elect the new country's first President; he does not know that the Revolutionary War has taken place.

At Home: Find an example of cause and effect in a favorite story.

197   Book 5/Unit 6 Rip Van Winkle

LANGUAGE SUPPORT — Ninepin Cause and Effect

1. Draw a line connecting each effect to its cause.

...because he slept for twenty years.

Dame Van Winkle is angry.

...because Rip didn't do his chores.

Rip takes a nap.

...because the drink made him sleepy.

Rip wakes looking old and frail.

214 Rip Van Winkle • Language Support/Blackline Master 106   Grade 5

Reteach, 197   Practice, 197   Extend, 197   Language Support, 214

OBJECTIVES

Students will draw conclusions from information in a story.

TEACHING TIP

INSTRUCTIONAL Help students realize that conclusions are not explicitly stated in the story. However, different pieces of information may point to a single conclusion. If some information opposes the conclusion, the conclusion is incorrect and must be replaced by one that is consistent with all of the information provided.

Review Draw Conclusions

PREPARE

Discuss the Evidence for Conclusions

Review: You can draw conclusions from two or more ideas or pieces of information in a reading selection. A conclusion may be specific to a character or a more general statement that applies to the entire story. Ask students how paying attention to the details in a story can help them draw conclusions about the characters and the plot.

TEACH

Read "Peace and Tranquillity" and Model the Skill

Ask students to pay attention to the details as you read the **Teaching Chart** passage.

Peace and Tranquillity

While his wife shouted out a list of chores for Rip Van Winkle to do, he headed off in the other direction. As Dame Van Winkle's voice became faint in the distance, Rip Van Winkle stopped to smell his favorite flowers. He took a deep breath as he sat upon the rock he knew so well. Then he called his faithful companion, his dog Wolf. Rip handed Wolf a chicken bone he had hidden in his pocket. Then he leaned back and began to whittle a small whistle. Rip could not imagine doing anything else today.

Teaching Chart 161

Discuss details that help readers draw conclusions.

MODEL I can tell that Dame Van Winkle probably nags Rip frequently since he simply walked away without becoming upset. I also think that Rip has been to this spot before because he knows the flowers and rocks. He has probably come here before with his dog. I also think that Rip secretly took the chicken bone out of the house so that his wife did not notice when he gave it to the dog.

PRACTICE

Draw Conclusions

ONE

Have students underline details in "Peace and Tranquillity" that help them draw conclusions about Rip Van Winkle.

Then ask questions based on those conclusions. Ask: Do you think Rip

- has a wife who is quiet and shy?
- has found this spot for the first time?
- loves animals?
- is a nervous man who must always keep busy?
- enjoys the beauty of nature?

Have students write a sentence using details from the reading to explain their answers to each question.

ASSESS/CLOSE

Analyze the Details of a Mystery

PARTNERS

Detectives use bits of information to draw conclusions about a case. Have students write a paragraph describing a series of clues relating to some topic. For example, they might write a description of the weather, providing clues to the season of the year. Or they might write a mystery about an apple missing from the kitchen. On a separate sheet of paper, they should write the topic. Then have each student trade paragraphs with a partner so that each student can draw conclusions from the clues. If students are unable to draw expected conclusions, tell students to revise their information.

LOOKING AHEAD

Students will apply this skill as they read the next selection, *Sea Maidens of Japan.*

ALTERNATE TEACHING STRATEGY

. . . .

DRAW CONCLUSIONS

For a different approach to teaching this skill, see page T62.

Meeting Individual Needs for Comprehension

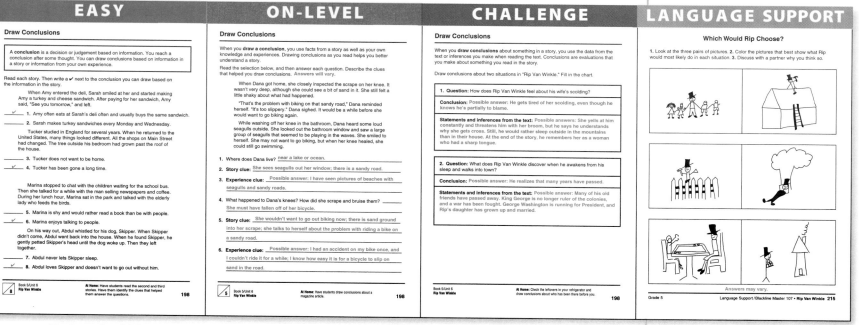

EASY	ON-LEVEL	CHALLENGE	LANGUAGE SUPPORT
Reteach, 198	Practice, 198	Extend, 198	Language Support, 215

673H

OBJECTIVES

Students will identify and compare synonyms and antonyms.

Review Antonyms and Synonyms

PREPARE

Discuss Meaning of Synonyms and Antonyms   Remind students that synonyms are words that have the same meaning. Antonyms are words that have opposite meanings.

TEACH

Read the Passage and Model the Skill   Have students read the passage on **Teaching Chart 162.**

Upon the Mountain

As Dame Van Winkle <u>entered</u> the town square, Rip Van Winkle <u>exited</u> to go up the mountain. When he got to the top he felt <u>cold</u>, although it was <u>hot</u> down in the village. The thunder that he heard in the village as a <u>soft</u> rumble was now <u>loud</u>. Rip was a bit (frightened) even though he was not usually (scared.) After all, Rip was a (jolly) fellow, who was (merry) wherever he was. But he was also a (lazy) sort, (shiftless) in everything he did. While <u>up</u> on the mountain, he took a nap and did not go <u>down</u> until 20 years later.

Teaching Chart 162

Have volunteers circle the synonyms in the passage and underline the antonyms. Challenge students to make a list of the words they identified in the passage. Model identifying synonyms and antonyms.

MODEL   I see the words *entered* and *exited* in the first sentence. They have opposite meanings. I should underline them because they are antonyms. In the fourth sentence, the words *frightened* and *scared* have the same meaning. I should circle these synonyms.

ALTERNATE TEACHING **STRATEGY**

ANTONYMS AND SYNONYMS

For a different approach to teaching this skill, see page T65.

PRACTICE

Identify Synonyms and Antonyms

GROUP

Divide the class into groups. Ask one student in each group to draw a picture to represent a synonym or antonym. For example, he or she might draw a person climbing a ladder to represent the word *up*. Then challenge the rest of the group to come up with a drawing that represents the same word and a second drawing that represents the word's opposite. ▶ **Visual/Linguistic**

ASSESS/CLOSE

Use Synonyms and Antonyms

PARTNERS

Have students write each of the words listed below. Ask them to work with a partner to write a paragraph using all the words. Then have them find antonyms for the words on the left and synonyms for the words on the right. Ask them to write a new paragraph using these new words.

summer	**seek**
large	**round**
cheerful	**thrilling**

Meeting Individual Needs for Vocabulary

EASY	ON-LEVEL	CHALLENGE	LANGUAGE SUPPORT
Reteach, 199	Practice, 199	Extend, 199	Language Support, 216

Writing a Story

GRAMMAR/SPELLING
CONNECTIONS

See the 5-Day Grammar and Usage Plan on adverbs that compare, pages 673M–673N.

See the 5-Day Spelling Plan on words with prefixes, pages 673O–673P.

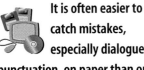

TECHNOLOGY TIP

It is often easier to catch mistakes, especially dialogue punctuation, on paper than on screen. For proofreading, encourage students to print out their work, mark the corrections on paper, and then enter the corrections to the document.

Prewrite

WRITE A DIALOGUE Present this writing assignment: As a play, Rip Van Winkle depends on dialogue to tell its story. Writing good dialogue is a skill all fiction writers must learn. Write dialogue that might have been spoken between Rip and his wife if she had been alive when he returned.

Strategy: Visualize Suggest that students let their minds wander and "see" Rip and his wife talking to each other.

- Where does the conversation take place?
- How is Rip feeling?
- How does Dame Van Winkle feel?

CHART TALK Have students work in small groups to brainstorm topics for a dialogue between Rip and his wife. Then have students create a two-column chart that tells who is talking on one side and what they are saying in the other column.

Draft

DEVELOP IDEAS Students should use ideas from their brainstormed topics to write their dialogue. Remind students to imagine the kinds of things that these characters would say to each other. Encourage them to use the dialogue to move the story along.

Revise

SELF-QUESTIONING Ask students to assess their drafts.

- Is my dialogue realistic?
- Are these people talking to each other and listening to each other?
- Does any of the conversation need to be elaborated upon?

Edit/Proofread

CHECK FOR ERRORS Students should reread their dialogue for content, grammar, spelling, and punctuation.

Publish

SHARE THE DIALOGUE Have students read their dialogue aloud, and discuss it. Is it realistic? Is it logical? Does it tell a story? Is it interesting to listen to?

A Reunion

Dame Van Winkle: Where have you been all these years?
Rip: I was playing ninepins with Hendrik Hudson and his crew, and I fell...
Dame Van Winkle: Don't tell those lies to me!
Rip: But it isn't a lie. It's the truth. I was...I fell asleep.
Dame Van Winkle: You fell asleep for 20 years? That I believe!
Rip: But I'm back now.
Dame Van Winkle: And I'm glad to see you.
Rip: Are you? I thought you'd be angry.
Dame Van Winkle: No, I'm glad you're back. The fence still needs mending! The cows need to be milked! The house needs a new roof!

Presentation Ideas

ACT OUT THE DIALOGUE Have students act out their dialogue in front of the class. Discuss the differences in impact dialogue can have when it is read and when it is performed.
▶ **Speaking/Listening**

MAKE A TAPE Record students acting out the dialogue, then play it back and analyze the scene. Have students suggest ways to give the dialogue more impact, then try the scene again. ▶ **Viewing/Representing**

Consider students' creative efforts, possibly adding a plus (+) for originality, wit, and imagination.

For a 6-point or an 8-point scale, see pages T105–T106.

Meeting Individual Needs for Writing

EASY	ON-LEVEL	CHALLENGE
Flyer Have students create flyers made during Rip's absence, announcing that he is missing. In addition to a picture of Rip, the flyers should include information about Rip.	**Essay** Have students create a magazine article written by Rip, describing his feelings about being asleep for 20 years. What does he regret? What is he happy about?	**Interview** Have students pretend they are newscasters. Have them write an interview that may have been conducted with Rip after he returned home. Then have them role-play the interview.

5 Day Grammar and Usage Plan

Select three volunteers to jump. Have the class use words such as *higher* and *highest* in sentences that compare how they jumped.

DAILY LANGUAGE ACTIVITIES

Have students correct the sentences orally. Sample answers given for Days 1 and 2.

Day 1

1. Judy ran fastest than Luke. faster
2. Of all the girls, Katchen worked harder. hardest
3. Rip slept longest than I did. longer

Day 2

1. Hendrik acted more bravely of all. most bravely
2. You dance gracefullier than a bird. more gracefully
3. I nap most soundly than Rip does. more soundly

Day 3

1. We ate more faster than Rip.
2. Judy sings sweetlier than a wren.
3. She yells louder of all.

Day 4

1. It rains hardest now than ever.
2. She spent money most wisely than he did.
3. Wolf barked more loudly of all.

Day 5

1. Rip acted nicer of all.
2. He looks oldest now than before.
3. Of all the men in town, Rip worked most slowest.

Daily Language Transparency 27

673M   *Rip Van Winkle*

DAY 1   Introduce the Concept

Oral Warm-Up Read this sentence aloud: *Sarah walked faster than Josh.* Ask students to tell how many people are being compared. Point out the adverb ending with *-er.*

Adverbs Adverbs tell how, when, or where an action happened. Present the following:

> ### Adverbs That Compare
>
> - An adverb can compare two or more actions.
> - Add *-er* to most short adverbs to compare two actions.
> - Add *-est* to most short adverbs to compare more than two actions.

Present the Daily Language Activity and have students correct orally. Then have students use the correct forms of *fast* to compare two things, and then three things.

 Assign the daily Writing Prompt on page 648C.

Adverbs That Compare

- An adverb can compare two or more actions.
- Add *-er* to most short adverbs to compare two actions.
- Add *-est* to most short adverbs to compare more than two actions.

Read the sentences. Write the correct form of the adverb in parentheses.

1. (long) Of the many storms this season, this storm raged _____longest_____ of all.
2. (hard) Lightning hit _____harder_____ on the hill than in the valley.
3. (high) The mountains rose _____higher_____ than the mesa.
4. (long) Rip slept _____longer_____ than he ever had before.
5. (long) In fact, Rip slept _____longest_____ of all.
6. (hard) Dame Van Winkle worked _____harder_____ than Rip.
7. (fast) Rip ran _____faster_____ than he walked.
8. (early) The ship's bell rang _____earlier_____ the second time.
9. (early) Wolf left the mountain _____earlier_____ than Rip did.
10. (late) Rip left the mountain _____latest_____ of all.
11. (near) The thunder boomed _____nearer_____ than a few minutes ago.
12. (soon) Rip wished that he had gotten up _____sooner_____ than he did.

Grade 5/Unit 6
Rip Van Winkle

Extension: Ask students to compare two actions with the following adverbs: *hard, short, fast.* Then ask them to compare three or more actions with the same adverbs.

167

GRAMMAR PRACTICE BOOK, PAGE 167

DAY 2   Teach the Concept

Review Adverbs That Compare Ask students how adverbs can be used to compare two things or three things.

Introduce Comparative Adverbs Present the following:

> ### Adverbs That Compare
>
> - Use *more* or *most* to form comparisons with adverbs that end in *-ly* or most other adverbs with two or more syllables.
> - Use *more* to compare two actions; use *most* to compare more than two.
> - When you use *more* or *most*, do not use the ending *-er* or *-est.*

Present the Daily Language Activity. Then have students write sentences using the correct forms of *slowly* and *carefully* to compare two things, and then three things.

 Assign the daily Writing Prompt on page 648C.

Adverbs That Compare

- Use *more* or *most* to form comparisons with adverbs that end in *-ly* or most other adverbs with two or more syllables.
- Use *more* to compare two actions; use *most* to compare more than two.
- When you use *more* or *most*, do not use the ending *-er* or *-est.*

Read the sentences. Write the correct form of the adverb in parentheses.

1. (slowly) Rip walked _____more slowly_____ than Wolf.
2. (quietly) Rip spoke _____more quietly_____ to children than his wife did.
3. (impatiently) Dame Van Winkle speaks the _____most impatiently_____ of all.
4. (closely) Rip looked _____more closely_____ around him than he had looked a minute ago.
5. (shyly) Of all the villagers, Little Rip greeted Rip _____most shyly_____.

Read each sentence. If the adverb is correct, write Correct on the line. If it is not correct, rewrite the sentence so that the adverb will be correct.

6. The people shouted angrilier at Rip than they did at Wolf.
   The people shouted more angrily at Rip than they did at Wolf.
7. The whistle played more beautifully than the last one played.
   Correct
8. That man sleeps more quietly of all.
   That man sleeps most quietly of all.
9. Rip answered most soonest of all the husbands.
   Rip answered soonest of all the husbands.
10. The thunder clapped more violenter than it had the last time.
    The thunder clapped more violently than it had the last time.

168

Extension: Have students write descriptions of a character in the play. Ask them to compare his or her actions to those of other villagers. Students should exchange descriptions and proofread for correct use of adverbs that compare.

Grade 5/Unit 6
Rip Van Winkle

GRAMMAR PRACTICE BOOK, PAGE 168

Adverbs That Compare

DAY 3 — Review and Practice

Learn from the Literature Review how to make comparisons using adverbs. Read the stage direction when the children appear on page 654 of *Rip Van Winkle.*

> **They surround him, chattering excitedly.**

Ask students to identify the adverb in the sentence. Then ask them to rewrite the sentence to compare the chatter of one child with that of the rest. (most)

Compare Using Adverbs Present the Daily Language Activity and have students correct the sentences orally.

Have students make a two-column chart. Then ask them to go through the story and write at least five stage directions in the first column. In the second column, they should rewrite the direction to make it into a comparison.

 Assign the daily Writing Prompt on page 648D.

DAY 4 — Review and Practice

Review Adverbs That Compare Write the adverbs from the Daily Language Activities for Days 1 through 3 on the chalkboard. Ask students to use the adverbs in sentences that compare two actions and three or more actions. Then present the Daily Language Activity for Day 4.

Mechanics and Usage Before students use the daily Writing Prompt on page 648D, review the use of *more* and *most.*

More and Most

- Never add *-er* and *more* to the same adverb.
- Never add *-est* and *most* to the same adverb.

 Assign the daily Writing Prompt on page 648D.

DAY 5 — Assess and Reteach

Assess Use the Daily Language Activity and page 171 of the **Grammar Practice Book** for assessment.

Reteach Have students write each rule about adverbs that compare from the lesson grammar concepts on an index card.

Ask students to select from the Daily Language Activity sentences to find an example that matches each rule. They should write the sentence on the appropriate index card and note how the rule tells them to correct the sentence.

Have students create a word wall with a list of adverbs and the forms that can be used to compare.

Use page 172 of the **Grammar Practice Book** for additional reteaching.

 Assign the daily Writing Prompt on page 648D.

Grammar Practice Book, Page 169

Adverbs That Compare

- An adverb can compare two or more actions.
- Add *-er* to most short adverbs to compare two actions. Add *-est* to most short adverbs to compare more than two actions.
- Add *more* or *most* to form comparisons with adverbs that end in *-ly* or most other adverbs with two or more syllables. Use *more* to compare two actions; use *most* to compare more than two. When you use *more* or *most*, do not use the ending *-er* or *-est.*

Circle the adverbs in these paragraphs. Then write the paragraph correctly.

Rip Van Winkle lived near the Catskill Mountains. These mountains rise highest than the land around them, and the storms rage fiercer as you climb more higher on the slope. In the summer, thunderstorms arrive frequenter and lightning strikes most violentest than in the winter.

Today, The Hudson River passes through much of New York State. It runs slowlier as it falls lowly to flat land. As it passes New York City, the river runs slower of all.

Many years ago, people worked more harder than today to ship goods upstate. Ships from New York Harbor carried cargo more efficienter than mules did. Today, trucks and trains travel more speedier and most cheaply than ships do. In the years ahead, the river will continue to be importanter to people.

Rip Van Winkle lived near the Catskill Mountains. These mountains rise higher than the land around them, and the storms rage more fiercely as you climb higher on the slope. In the summer, thunderstorms arrive more frequently and lightning strikes more violently than in the winter.

Today, The Hudson River passes through much of New York State. It runs more slowly as it falls lower to flat land. As it passes New York City, the river runs slowest of all.

Many years ago, people worked harder than today to ship goods upstate. Ships from New York Harbor carried cargo more efficiently than mules did. Today, trucks and trains travel more speedily and more cheaply than ships do. In the years ahead, the river will be more important to people.

10 Grade 5/Unit 6 Rip Van Winkle **Extension:** Invite pairs or groups of students to create and present a story about a local storm. Suggest that they include a local historical figure in their stories. Ask students to include at least five adverbs that compare. 169

GRAMMAR PRACTICE BOOK, PAGE 169

Grammar Practice Book, Page 170

Using More and Most

- Never add *-er* and *more* to the same adverb.
- Never add *-est* and *most* to the same adverb.

Read each sentence. If the sentence uses *more* and *most* correctly, write **Correct.** Otherwise, rewrite the sentence to make the use of *more* and *most* correct. Answers may vary.

1. The thunder pealed more loudlier every minute.
   The thunder pealed more loudly every minute.

2. The wind blew more fiercer than it had before.
   The wind blew more fiercely than it had before.

3. The river rose more fitfullier than it fell.
   The river rose more fitfully than it fell.

4. Rip Van Winkle slept most soundest of all.
   Rip Van Winkle slept most soundly of all.

5. Dame Van Winkle talked more loudly than other people.
   Correct

6. Rip's wife died more earlier than he did.
   Rip's wife died earlier than he did.

7. Hendrik Hudson played ninepins most loudest of all.
   Hendrik Hudson played ninepins loudest of all.

8. Is this the story told most frequently of New York's local legends?
   Correct

9. The high school group performed the play more professionaller than our class did.
   The high school group performed the play more professionally than our class did.

10. Rip climbed more higher and more quicker than he expected.
    Rip climbed higher and more quickly than he expected.

170 *Grade 5/Unit6 Rip Van Winkle 10*

GRAMMAR PRACTICE BOOK, PAGE 170

Grammar Practice Book, Page 171

Adverbs That Compare

Choose the sentence in each group that is written incorrectly. Circle the letter of the incorrect sentence.

1. a. The children work more diligently than their father does.
   b. The children work most diligently than their father does.
   c. The children work most diligently of all.

2. a. Wolf comes more readily to Rip than he does to Dame.
   b. Wolf comes more readily to Rip than to Dame.
   c. Wolf comes more readily to Rip than even the children do.

3. a. Rip works more lovingly with children than he does with his wife.
   b. Of all the men in the village, Rip works most lovingly with the children.
   c. Rip works most lovingly with children than he does with his wife.

4. a. Rip slept longest than he worked.
   b. Rip slept longer than he worked.
   c. Rip slept longest of all.

5. a. Judith stared hardest at Rip than Doolittle did.
   b. Of all the villagers, Judith stared hardest at Rip.
   c. Judith stared harder at Rip than Doolittle did.

B. Choose the comparing adverb that best completes the sentence. Circle the letter of your answer.

6. Hendrik Hudson plays ninepins _____ than he sings.
   a. loudest
   b. louder
   c. more louder

7. Hendrik Hudson dances _____ today than yesterday.
   a. most merrily
   b. more merrier
   c. more merrily

8. The Hudson River flows _____ in the spring than in the summer.
   a. rapidest
   b. most rapidly
   c. more rapidly

8 Grade 5/Unit 6 Rip Van Winkle 171

GRAMMAR PRACTICE BOOK, PAGE 171

GRAMMAR PRACTICE BOOK, PAGE 172

673N

5 Day Spelling Plan

LANGUAGE SUPPORT

Remind students that when a prefix is added to a word, the word changes in meaning. Write the following on the chalkboard: *replaced, unseen, precook, disobey, incorrect*. Have volunteers draw a line between the prefix and the base word.

DICTATION SENTENCES

Spelling Words

1. Her little sister goes to preschool.
2. They replaced the ruined rug.
3. The author is unknown.
4. Try not to disobey your parents.
5. The trail is invisible in the dark.
6. We saw a preview of the show.
7. Rest to regain your health.
8. The cloudy sky hid unseen stars.
9. A hurt arm will cause discomfort.
10. She wrote an incorrect answer.
11. Precook meat before baking it in a dish.
12. I recall what happened a year ago.
13. A child is unable to drive a bus.
14. Don't trust dishonest leaders.
15. Sell me the inexpensive hat.
16. Let's prearrange her birthday party.
17. We can revisit the farm in the spring.
18. He slept late and was unaware of time.
19. We disapprove of unkind words.
20. No one believed the incredible story.

Challenge Words

21. The farmer is husking corn.
22. The landlord wants his money.
23. He will oblige us with his help.
24. Those rascals will get in trouble.
25. She sprawled in her large chair.

DAY 1 — Pretest

Assess Prior Knowledge Use the Dictation Sentences at the left and **Spelling Practice Book** page 167 for the pretest. Allow students to correct their own papers. Students who require a modified list may be tested on the first ten words.

Spelling Words		Challenge Words
1. preschool	11. precook	21. **husking**
2. **replaced**	12. recall	22. **landlord**
3. unknown	13. unable	23. **oblige**
4. disobey	14. dishonest	24. **rascals**
5. invisible	15. inexpensive	25. **sprawled**
6. preview	16. prearrange	
7. regain	17. **revisit**	
8. **unseen**	18. unaware	
9. discomfort	19. disapprove	
10. incorrect	20. incredible	

*Note: Words in **dark type** are from the story.*

Word Study On page 168 of the **Spelling Practice Book** are word study steps and an at-home activity.

DAY 2 — Explore the Pattern

Sort and Spell Words List the prefixes *re-, un-, pre-, dis-, in-*. Ask students where a prefix goes. (at the beginning of a word) Have them read the Spelling Words aloud and sort them as below.

Words with prefixes

re-	*pre-*	*in-*
replaced	preschool	invisible
regain	preview	incorrect
recall	precook	inexpensive
revisit	prearrange	incredible

un-	*dis-*
unknown	disobey
unseen	discomfort
unable	dishonest
unaware	disapprove

Word Wall Have students create a word wall based on the word sort and add more words from their reading.

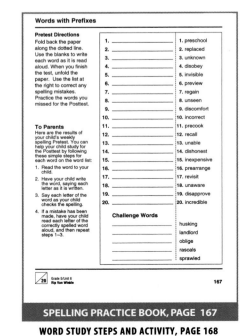

SPELLING PRACTICE BOOK, PAGE 167

WORD STUDY STEPS AND ACTIVITY, PAGE 168

SPELLING PRACTICE BOOK, PAGE 169

Words with Prefixes

Word Meaning: Prefixes Remind students that a prefix is a syllable or group of syllables added to the beginning of a word to change its meaning. Write prefix definitions on the chalkboard: *re-* means "again" or "back"; *un-, dis-, in-* mean "the opposite of" or "not"; *pre-* means "before." Have students use this information to define the Spelling Words.

If students need extra practice, have partners give each other a midweek test.

Glossary Review how word definitions appear in the Glossary. Have partners:

• write each Challenge Word.

• look up the definition in the Glossary.

• write a sentence using each word.

Proofread Sentences Write these sentences on the chalkboard, including the misspelled words. Ask students to proofread, circling incorrect spellings and writing the correct spellings. There are two spelling errors in each sentence.

The store ⟨riplaced⟩ the ⟨inexpensave⟩ toy. (replaced, inexpensive)

They were ⟨unawear⟩ of the ⟨incorect⟩ answer. (unaware, incorrect)

Have students create additional sentences with errors for partners to correct.

WRITING Have students use as many Spelling Words as possible in the daily Writing Prompt on page 648D. Remind students to proofread their writing for errors in spelling, grammar, and punctuation.

Assess Students' Knowledge Use page 172 of the **Spelling Practice Book** or the Dictation Sentences on page 673O for the posttest.

Personal Word List Encourage students to add troublesome JOURNAL lesson words to their personal lists of troublesome words in their journals. Have students circle the prefix in each word and write the meaning of the prefix.

Students should refer to their word lists during later writing activities.

Words with Prefixes (Page 170)

preschool	invisible	discomfort	unable	revisit
replaced	preview	incorrect	dishonest	unaware
unknown	regain	precook	inexpensive	disapprove
disobey	unseen	recall	prearrange	incredible

Complete each sentence below with a spelling word.

1. My dog ran so fast, I was __unable__ to catch up to him.
2. I __replaced__ my blue shirt with a white one.
3. The location of her lost glove is __unknown__.
4. The three-year-old boy spends each morning at __preschool__.
5. Do not __disobey__ your parents.
6. The insect was so tiny it was nearly __invisible__.
7. If we score this goal, we will __regain__ the lead in the game.
8. I don't __recall__ your name, although I met you last night.

Write the spelling word that matches each meaning below.

9. to cook beforehand __precook__
10. lack of comfort __discomfort__
11. not correct __incorrect__
12. to visit again __revisit__
13. not seen __unseen__
14. to view in advance __preview__
15. not honest __dishonest__
16. to arrange before __prearrange__
17. not expensive __inexpensive__
18. not aware __unaware__
19. to not approve __disapprove__
20. not credible __incredible__

Challenge Extension: Write one fill-in sentence for each Challenge Word. Exchange your sentences with a partner and fill in the blank in each sentence.

170   Grade 5/Unit 6 Rip Van Winkle / 20

SPELLING PRACTICE BOOK, PAGE 170

Words with Prefixes (Page 171)

Proofreading Activity

There are six spelling mistakes in the paragraph below. Circle the misspelled words. Write the words correctly on the lines below.

Rip Van Winkle didn't mean to ⟨disobay⟩ his wife, but he continued to ⟨disaprove⟩ of his behavior. Dame Van Winkle wanted the wood to be fetched and the roof to be ⟨replaiced⟩. When Rip goes to the mountains to get wood, he hears an ⟨unsceen⟩ person calling his name. He meets Henrik Hudson and his crew and plays a game of ninepins and then falls asleep. When Rip Van Winkle wakes up, he is ⟨unawear⟩ that twenty years have passed. His daughter Judith finds it ⟨incredeble⟩ that he has finally returned!

1. __disobey__   3. __replaced__   5. __unaware__
2. __disapprove__ 4. __unseen__   6. __incredible__

Writing Activity

Make believe that you have fallen asleep for twenty years. Write about what you find when you wake up. Use four spelling words in your writing.

10 Grade 5/Unit 6 Rip Van Winkle

171

SPELLING PRACTICE BOOK, PAGE 171

Word with Prefixes (Page 172)

Look at the words in each set below. One word in each set is spelled correctly. Use a pencil to fill in the circle next to the correct word. Before you begin, look at the sample sets of words. Sample A has been done for you. Do Sample B by yourself. When you are sure you know what to do, you may go on with the rest of the page.

Sample A:
- (A) retirn
- (B) retern
- (C) raturn
- (D) return ●

Sample B:
- (A) untye
- (B) unntie
- (C) untie
- (D) untai

1. (A) preskul (B) preschool ● (C) prischool (D) preeschool
2. (E) replad (F) replaced ● (G) ryplaced (H) replaced
3. (A) unknown ● (B) unnown (C) unnknowne (D) unknowen
4. (E) desobey (F) disobey ● (G) disoay (H) desobay
5. (A) unvisable (B) invisble (C) invisible ● (D) infissable
6. (E) preevew (F) preview ● (G) prevewe (H) priview
7. (A) reegane (B) regane (C) regain ● (D) rigain
8. (E) unseen ● (F) unsene (G) enseen (H) umseen
9. (A) descomfit (B) discomfit (C) descomfort (D) discomfort ●
10. (E) encorrekt (F) inexpensive ● (G) incorrect (H) incorrict
11. (A) precook ● (B) preecook (C) pricook (D) precuk
12. (E) recaul (F) recall ● (G) recal (H) ricall
13. (A) inable (B) unible (C) unble (D) unable ●
14. (E) deshonist (F) dishonst (G) dishonest ● (H) deshonest
15. (A) inekspensive (B) inexpensive ● (C) inexpinsive (D) unexpensive
16. (E) prearrange ● (F) preeaarange (G) priarrange (H) preirange
17. (A) reevisit (B) revisit ● (C) revisit (D) rivisit
18. (E) unaware ● (F) inaware (G) uneware (H) unawers
19. (A) disapprove ● (B) desapprove (C) disaprove (D) disapprov
20. (E) incratable (F) incredible ● (G) incredible (H) encredible

172   Grade 5/Unit 6 Rip Van Winkle / 20

SPELLING PRACTICE BOOK, PAGE 172

Sea Maidens of Japan

Selection Summary Students will read about a Japanese girl who struggles to follow in her mother's footsteps and become an *ama,* a deep-sea diver of Japan.

**Student
Listening
Library
Audiocassette**

INSTRUCTIONAL
Pages 676–693

About the Author A resident of Colorado, Lili Bell showed talent as an athlete at an early age. She excelled at ski racing and was a top-ranking tennis player. Bell's involvement in sports allowed her to travel all over the world. *Sea Maidens of Japan* is her first book for children.

About the Illustrator Erin McGonigle Brammer is a freelance illustrator and graphic designer. Erin says that she enjoyed illustrating *Sea Maidens of Japan,* her first book for children.

Resources for Meeting Individual Needs

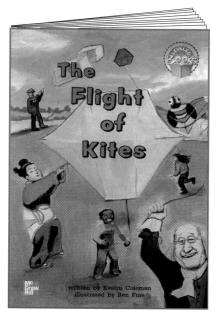

EASY
Pages 697A, 697D

INDEPENDENT
Pages 697B, 697D

CHALLENGE
Pages 697C, 697D

LEVELED PRACTICE

Reteach, 200–206
blackline masters with reteaching opportunities for each assessed skill

Practice, 200–206
workbook with Take-Home stories and practice opportunities for each assessed skill and story comprehension

Extend, 200–206
blackline masters that offer challenge activities for each assessed skill

ADDITIONAL RESOURCES

- **Language Support Book,** 217–224
- **Take-Home Story, Practice,** p. 201a
- **Alternative Teaching Strategies,** T60–T66

McGraw-Hill School
TECHNOLOGY

interNET CONNECTION Research and Inquiry Ideas.
Visit **www.mhschool.com/reading**

Suggested Lesson Planner

READING AND LANGUAGE ARTS	DAY 1 *Focus on Reading and Skills*	DAY 2 *Read the Literature*
● **Comprehension** ● **Vocabulary** ● **Phonics/Decoding** ● **Study Skills** ● **Listening, Speaking, Viewing, Representing**	**Read Aloud and Motivate,** 674E *Turtle's Race with Beaver* **Develop Visual Literacy,** 674/675 ☑ **Review Sequence of Events,** 676A–676B **Teaching Chart 163** Reteach, Practice, Extend, 200	**Build Background,** 676C Develop Oral Language **Vocabulary,** 676D | cove	driftwood	host
disgrace	flail	sizzle | **Teaching Chart 164** **Vocabulary Cards** Reteach, Practice, Extend, 201 **Read the Selection,** 676–693 ☑ Review Sequence of Events ☑ Review Draw Conclusions **Minilessons,** 683, 685, 687, 691 **Cultural Perspectives,** 684
● **Curriculum Connections**	**Link** Works of Art, 674/675	**Link** Social Studies, 676C
● **Writing**	**Writing Prompt:** Imagine you are Kiyomi's older sister. Write a paragraph explaining why you don't want to become an ama, like Okaasan.	**Writing Prompt:** Write a persuasive paragraph from the point of view of the star turtle convincing Kiyomi to dive off the deck of the ama boat. **Journal Writing,** 693 Quick-Write
● **Grammar**	**Introduce the Concept: Negatives,** 697M Daily Language Activity **Sea Maidens of Japan** 1. Kiyomi wasn't no swimmer. any 2. She couldn't go in no deep water. any 3. She didn't want to be no ama. an **Grammar Practice Book,** 173	**Teach the Concept: Negatives,** 697M Daily Language Activity 1. Kiyomi didn't want to go nowhere without the rope. anywhere 2. Kiyomi didn't see nobody. anybody 3. There weren't really no mermaids. any **Grammar Practice Book,** 174
● **Spelling**	**Pretest: Words with Suffixes,** 697O **Spelling Practice Book,** 173–174	**Explore the Pattern: Words with Suffixes,** 697O **Spelling Practice Book,** 175

Meeting Individual Needs

 = **Skill Assessed in Unit Test**

Read EVERY DAY

DAY **3** Read the Literature	DAY **4** Build Skills	DAY **5** Build Skills

DAY 3 — Read the Literature

Rereading for Fluency, 692

Story Questions, 694
  Reteach, Practice, Extend, 202

Story Activities, 695

Study Skill, 696
   Choose Reference Sources
  Teaching Chart 165
  Reteach, Practice, Extend, 203

Test Power, 697

 Read the Leveled Books
  Guided Reading
  /ou/ spelled *ou* and *ow*
  ☑ Review Sequence of Events
  ☑ Instructional Vocabulary

DAY 4 — Build Skills

 Read the Leveled Books and Self-Selected Books

☑ **Review Sequence of Events,** 697E–697F
  Teaching Chart 166
  Reteach, Practice, Extend, 204
  Language Support, 222

☑ **Review Cause and Effect,** 697G–697H
  Teaching Chart 167
  Reteach, Practice, Extend, 205
  Language Support, 223

DAY 5 — Build Skills

Read Self-Selected Books

☑ **Review Context Clues,** 697I–697J
  Teaching Chart 168
  Reteach, Practice, Extend, 206
  Language Support, 224

Listening, Speaking, Viewing, Representing, 697L
  Act Out the Scene
  Make a Video

Minilessons, 685, 687, 691

Phonics Review,
  /ou/ spelled *ou* and *ow*, 683
  Phonics Workbook

 **Activity** Science, 680

Activity Science, 686

Activity Social Studies, 690

 Writing Prompt: Write an informative paragraph telling what an ama can and cannot do.

Writing Process: Write a Two-Character Scene, 697K
  Prewrite, Draft

 Writing Prompt: Write a speech from Okaasan to her daughter telling what she will miss by not being an ama.

Writing Process: Write a Two-Character Scene, 697K
  Revise

Meeting Individual Needs for Writing, 697L

 Writing Prompt: Write a list of rules for behavior when watching the sea turtles lay their eggs.

Writing Process: Write a Two-Character Scene, 697K
  Edit/Proofread, Publish

Review and Practice: Negatives, 697N
Daily Language Activity
1. She didn't see the turtles nowhere. anywhere
2. No turtles would never come. ever
3. She can't harm no turtles. any

Grammar Practice Book, 175

Review and Practice: Negatives, 697N
Daily Language Activity
1. The star turtle hadn't been in no water before. any
2. She wasn't no swimming champ. any
3. She didn't want no one to make her mom feel bad. anyone

Grammar Practice Book, 176

Assess and Reteach: Negatives, 697N
Daily Language Activity
1. Kiyomi wasn't scared no more. any
2. She'd never be scared of no water again. any
3. The ama never use no breathing apparatus. any

Grammar Practice Book, 177–178

Practice and Extend: Words with Suffixes, 697P
Spelling Practice Book, 176

Proofread and Write: Words with Suffixes, 697P
Spelling Practice Book, 177

Assess and Reteach: Words with Suffixes, 697P
Spelling Practice Book, 178

Link

Language Arts

Read Aloud and Motivate

Turtle's Race With Beaver

a story told by Joseph Bruchac

Turtle lived in a quiet pool in the big Swamp. There were plenty of fish for him to catch and trees lined the edges of his fishing hole. One day the sun was very hot and Turtle grew sleepy. He crawled onto the mud bank at the edge of his pool, made himself comfortable and soon was fast asleep. He must have slept much longer than he intended, for when he woke up something was definitely wrong. There was water all around him and even over his head! He had to swim and swim to reach the surface and, as he poked his head up into the air, he heard a loud, earsplitting WHAP!

Turtle looked around and soon saw another animal swimming toward him. The animal had big front teeth and a large wide tail. "What are you doing in my pond?" Turtle called out to the animal.

"Your pond? This is my pond and I am Beaver! I built that dam over there and made this place."

Turtle looked. It was true, there was a big dam across the stream, and it

Continued on pages T2–T5

Oral Comprehension

LISTENING AND SPEAKING As you read aloud this folk tale about a turtle who outwits a beaver, encourage students to think about the sequence of the events in the story. When you have finished reading, ask: "What happens in this story? Is there more than one kind of race in this story? What is it?" Discuss how this story is like "Fox Fools Eagle," in Unit 5. Lead students to see that both stories involve a "race of wits."

Activity Have pairs of students perform a pantomime of "Turtle's Race with Beaver" in front of the class, as other students take turns narrating the story. Some students might wish to rehearse before their performance, others might prefer to improvise in front of the class. ▶ **Kinesthetic/Interpersonal**

Develop Visual Literacy

Anthology pages 674–675

Stories in Art

Like dialogue in a play, a picture can speak to you. It can tell you many things.

Look at this Japanese woodcut. The artist printed it from a block of wood into which he carved many details. What details do you see? What events do they show you? Can you tell that the women are working with silkworms? How? What do you think they do in a workday? What might they do first? Next? Last?

Look at the picture again. Notice the Japanese scroll at the top. Do you think it describes the events in the picture? Why or why not? Would you like to do this kind of work? Explain your reasons.

The Workplace, 19th Century Japanese
David David Gallery, Philadelphia

674

675

Objective: Sequence of Events

VIEWING In this nineteenth-century woodcut, the artist captures the activities taking place in a Japanese workplace. Have students notice the rich detail, revealing the many activities that must be done in a work day. Ask students to look closely at the detail and imagine what the workers are doing. Then encourage them to discuss with a partner what they see.

Read the page with students, reminding them that a work of art must be looked at with a "fresh" eye each time it is viewed.

Ask students to make inferences about the sequence of events taking place in this picture. For example:

- What might the workers do first?
- What might they do at the end of each day?

REPRESENTING Have students draw a storyboard that illustrates what they do before, during, and after school each day. Encourage them to include rich detail in, and a caption for, each picture.

OBJECTIVES

Students will recognize the sequence of events.

LANGUAGE SUPPORT

ESL Students will benefit from acting out and dramatizing new vocabulary, concepts, and events. Have students act out the meaning of transitional words such as *while* or *during* (two students doing different things at the same time), *before, after, first,* and *last.*

Review Sequence of Events

PREPARE

Discuss Sequences You Know
Have students tell the order of the events on a typical school day. Ask: What do you do when you first get to school? What happens next? What happens after you eat lunch?

TEACH

Define Sequence of Events
Tell students: Every story contains events that happen in a certain order. Sequence can often be identified by the author's use of time-order or transitional words such as *first, then, next, before, after, finally,* and *last.* Paying attention to the sequence of events can help you understand what happens in the story.

The Start of a Winning Season

Thomas and the other boys sat on the bleachers <u>while</u> waiting for their coach to arrive. Today was the first practice of the season, and Thomas wasn't sure he would be good enough. <u>As</u> the coach walked up, he said, "Welcome back! I want five laps." The boys took off running. <u>Next</u>, the boys did some drills and played a practice game. <u>Finally</u>, the practice was over. "Thomas," the coach called, "you did great. We're lucky to have you." Thomas smiled <u>as</u> he headed home.

Teaching Chart 163

Read the Story and Model the Skill
Display **Teaching Chart 163.** Have students look for transition words that signal the sequence of events.

MODEL I know from the word *while* in the first sentence that two things are happening at the same time. The boys are sitting on the bleachers at the same time that they are waiting.

Identify Sequence Words
Have students underline the words that help them identify the sequence of events in the story.

PRACTICE

Create a Sequence of Events Chart

GROUP

Have students use a Sequence of Events chart to record the story events in the correct sequence. Remind them to use transitional words. ▶ **Visual/Logical**

> While waiting for the coach, Thomas is feeling unsure about whether he will make the team.

▼

> Then the coach arrives, welcomes the team, and starts practice.

▼

> Next, the boys run laps, do some drills, and play a game.

▼

> Finally, practice is over, and the coach praises Thomas.

▼

> As he heads home, Thomas feels happy.

ASSESS/CLOSE

Identify the Sequence of Events

Have partners work together to chart the sequence of events of a familiar story or movie. Have volunteers scramble the order of the events on their charts and challenge the class to put them in the correct order.

SELECTION Connection

Students will identify sequence of events when they read *Sea Maidens of Japan* and the Leveled Books.

ALTERNATE TEACHING STRATEGY

SEQUENCE OF EVENTS

For a different approach to teaching this skill, see page T66.

Meeting Individual Needs for Comprehension

EASY

Sequence of Events

Determining the **sequence of events**, or the order in which events happen, will help you understand stories. Clue words such as *before, first, then, after, next, last,* and *finally* can help you understand the order in which events happen in a story.

Read the story. Underline the clue words that help you understand the sequence of events. Below the story are a number of the stories' events listed out of order. Number the listed events in the correct sequence in which they happen.

When Kenzo awoke in the morning, he first put on several layers of clothing. Before Kenzo left the house he had a bowl of sticky rice for breakfast. When he finished eating, he started biking on his mail route. He grabbed his mailbag. Then he stopped to drop off a letter at Mrs. Murasaki's house and then climbed the mountain road where he made his next stop to deliver a box to the Uchido family. After biking farther up the road, Kenzo made his last stop of the morning at Tamiko's. Finally, he returned home.

4 Kenzo delivered a box to the Uchido family.
3 Kenzo started biking along his mail route.
6 Kenzo returned home.
2 Kenzo had sticky rice for breakfast.
1 Kenzo dressed in several layers of clothing.
5 Kenzo stopped at Tamiko's.

Book 5/Unit 6
Sea Maidens of Japan 6

At Home: Have students think about what they did yesterday. Have them put those events in sequence.

200

ON-LEVEL

Sequence of Events

Events in a story happen in a certain **sequence** or order. By recognizing that sequence you can make better sense of a story.

Read the short story. The story chart below lists the story events out of order. Number each event in the correct sequence.

One sunny day, Tanika and Jamal rode their bikes to the State Fair. When they got to the fairgrounds, they discovered that there was a long line for tickets.

First they locked their bikes. Then they waited in line. While they were waiting they talked about the rides they would take. They had enough money to buy tickets for two rides and popcorn. Jamal really wanted to ride on the ponies. Since it was almost his birthday, they rode the ponies first. Tanika really wanted to go on the Ferris wheel, so that was their second ride.

While they were riding the Ferris wheel, Jamal and Tanika saw dark clouds approaching. As soon as they got off the Ferris wheel, it got windy, and started to rain. They ran for the nearest telephone booth where they called their uncle to come pick them up.

Sequence	Event
3	Tanika and Jamal wait in line to buy tickets.
6	They see dark clouds approaching.
2	Tanika and Jamal lock up their bikes.
5	They go on the Ferris wheel.
4	They ride the ponies.
8	They call their uncle to come pick them up.
1	Tanika and Jamal ride their bikes to the State Fair.
7	The wind and rain start.

Book 5/Unit 6
Sea Maidens of Japan 8

At Home: Have students identify the sequence of events of a book or movie.

200

CHALLENGE

Sequence of Events

Writers often tell about the events in a story in a certain order. This is called **sequence of events**. Words such as *first, next, finally, after, later, during,* and *while* often signal a transition from one event to another and can help you figure out the sequence of a story.

Read each of the events below. Put them in the correct sequence. Underline any signal words that help you keep the events in order.

6 At the check-out counter, Jan discovered she had no money.
1 Jan decided to make a pie for her dinner guests.
4 While she was shopping for the ingredients, Jan decided to get some ice cream to go with the pie.
8 When Jan arrived home, she was finally ready to bake the pie.
2 First, she chose a recipe that was her grandmother's.
5 Jan decided on vanilla and chocolate.
3 Next, Jan made a list of ingredients she would need.
7 The store had a cash machine, so Jan used her cash card to pay for the groceries.

Think of your favorite story. What do you remember about the sequence of the story? Write a sequence of the main events of the story from beginning to end.

Answers will vary.

_____
_____
_____
_____
_____
_____
_____

Book 5/Unit 6
Sea Maidens of Japan

At Home: Cut out a cartoon strip in a newspaper. Cut apart the separate squares of the cartoon. Have a friend put the cartoon in the correct sequence.

200

Reteach, 200   Practice, 200   Extend, 200

Build Background

Social Studies

Anthology and Leveled Books

Evaluate Prior Knowledge

CONCEPT: UNUSUAL OCCUPATIONS
The characters in this story have what many people might consider an unusual occupation. Have students give examples of occupations that are specific to a particular time or place. For example, lobster fishers work only in certain coastal areas.

BRAINSTORM OCCUPATIONS Have students brainstorm a list of unusual occupations. Discuss what makes each job unusual. Help them create a web. ▶ **Logical/Visual**

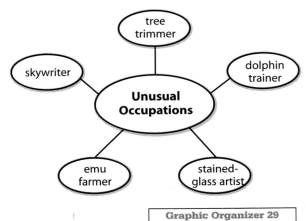

Graphic Organizer 29

EXPLORE AN OCCUPATION Give
  students an occupational area such as agriculture,
PARTNERS **WRITING**
business, or fine arts. Have partners explore their occupational area and list the types of occupations that it includes. Have students share their findings with the class.

Develop Oral Language

OCCUPATION CHARADES Using a variety of magazines or books, show students pictures that represent different jobs or careers. Have students tell what they see in each picture and what they think the person does.

Next, write the names of several different occupations on strips of paper and place them in a small box. Have volunteers choose a strip from the box and pantomime the occupation they chose in front of the class. Have other students guess the occupation being pantomimed.

Vocabulary

Key Words

1. Kiyomi worries that she might disgrace her mother when she tries to dive and that others will think badly of her if she fails. 2. To keep herself from worrying, she walks to the shore of her favorite cove. 3. She pretends to host a party in which her guests are mermaids. 4. She imagines she uses driftwood that has been washed ashore from the water to make a fire. 5. She places shellfish over the flames, which begin to sizzle as they cook. 6. Soon, Kiyomi has forgotten about her fear that her arms and legs will flail wildly when she dives.

Teaching Chart 164

Vocabulary in Context

IDENTIFY VOCABULARY WORDS
Display **Teaching Chart 164** and read the passage with students. Have volunteers circle each vocabulary word and underline other words that are clues to its meaning.

DISCUSS MEANINGS Ask questions like these to help clarify word meanings:

- What might someone do that would disgrace a parent?
- Where might you find a cove?
- Have you ever hosted a party?
- What two words make up the compound word *driftwood*? How do these words help you understand the meaning of *driftwood*?
- What types of things have you heard sizzle?
- Why might a baby flail its arms and legs?

Practice

DEMONSTRATE WORD MEANING Have partners choose vocabulary cards from a pile and use each word in a sentence that demonstrates its meaning.

▶ Linguistic/Oral

Vocabulary Cards

CREATE A CROSSWORD PUZZLE Have students create a crossword puzzle using the vocabulary words. They can create their own grid or use large graph paper. Have them exchange their puzzles with partners and complete their partners' puzzles. ▶ Linguistic/Logical

efinitions

disgrace (p. 679) to cause loss of honor or respect

cove (p. 680) a small sheltered bay or inlet

host (p. 680) to invite people to visit as guests

driftwood (p. 682) wood that floats on water or is brought to the shore by water

flail (p. 687) to wave or move about wildly

sizzle (p. 691) to make a hissing or sputtering sound

SPELLING/VOCABULARY CONNECTIONS
See Spelling Challenge Words, pages 697O–697P.

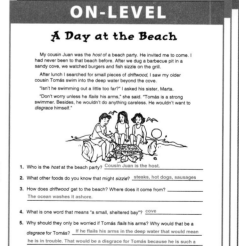

ON-LEVEL

A Day at the Beach

My cousin Juan was the *host* of a beach party. He invited me to come. I had never been to that beach before. After we dug a barbecue pit in a sandy cove, we watched burgers and fish sizzle on the grill.

After lunch I searched for small pieces of *driftwood*, I saw my older cousin Tomás swim into the deep water beyond the cove.

"Isn't he swimming out a little too far?" I asked his sister, Marta.

"Don't worry unless he *flails* his arms," she said. "Tomás is a strong swimmer. Besides, he wouldn't do anything careless. He wouldn't want to *disgrace* himself."

1. Who is the *host* at the beach party? Cousin Juan is the host.
2. What other foods do you know that might *sizzle*? steaks, hot dogs, sausages
3. How does *driftwood* get to the beach? Where does it come from? The ocean washes it ashore.
4. What is one word that means "a small, sheltered bay"? cove
5. Why should they only be worried if Tomás *flails* his arms? Why would that be a *disgrace* for Tomás? If he flails his arms in the deep water that would mean he is in trouble. That would be a disgrace for Tomás because he is such a strong swimmer.

Book 5/Unit 6
Sea Maidens of Japan

At Home: Have students make a collage using pictures or symbols to represent the vocabulary words as used in this story.

201a

Take-Home Story 201a
Reteach 201
Practice 201 • Extend 201

676D

Guided Instruction

Preview and Predict

Have students read the title and preview the story, looking for pictures that give strong clues about the events in the story and the order in which they take place.

- What clues do the title and illustrations give about where the story might take place?
- What do the illustrations tell you about story events?
- What will the story most likely be about?
- Will the story be a realistic one or a fantasy? How can you tell? (The setting looks real and the characters' actions seem real.) *Genre*

Have students record their predictions.

PREDICTIONS	WHAT HAPPENED
The young girl will learn to dive.	
The young girl takes care of a turtle.	

Set Purposes

What do students want to find out by reading the story? For example:

- What are sea maidens?
- What is the girl doing with the young turtle?

Meet
Lili Bell

Sports led Lili Bell to travel all over the world at an early age. She was a very good ski racer who later went on to become a top-ranked tennis player. One tennis competition in which she participated was held in Japan. It was on a Japanese beach filled with star sand that she was inspired to write *The Sea Maidens of Japan*. The story of young Kiyomi is Bell's first book for young people. Today, the writer lives in Colorado with her husband and two children.

Meet
Erin McGonigle Brammer

The Sea Maidens of Japan is Erin McGonigle Brammer's first book for young readers. Her stunning earth-tone illustrations capture the Asian style of the book and the traditions of the Japanese *ama*. Brammer is a freelance illustrator and graphic designer. About working on books for young people, Brammer says that she really enjoys the challenge.

676

Meeting Individual Needs • Grouping Suggestions for Strategic Reading

EASY

Read Together Read the story with students or have them read along with the **Listening Library Audiocassettes.** Have students use the Sequence of Events chart to record the order of events in the story. Guided Instruction and Intervention prompts offer additional help with vocabulary and comprehension.

ON-LEVEL

Guided Reading Preview the story words listed on page 677. Have students read the selection together, choosing from the Guided Instruction questions as you go. Have them use the Sequence of Events chart to record the order of important events in the story. You may want to have students read the story first on their own.

CHALLENGE

Read Independently Remind students that identifying the sequence of events will help them comprehend the story. Have students set up a Sequence of Events chart. After reading, they can use their chart to summarize the story.

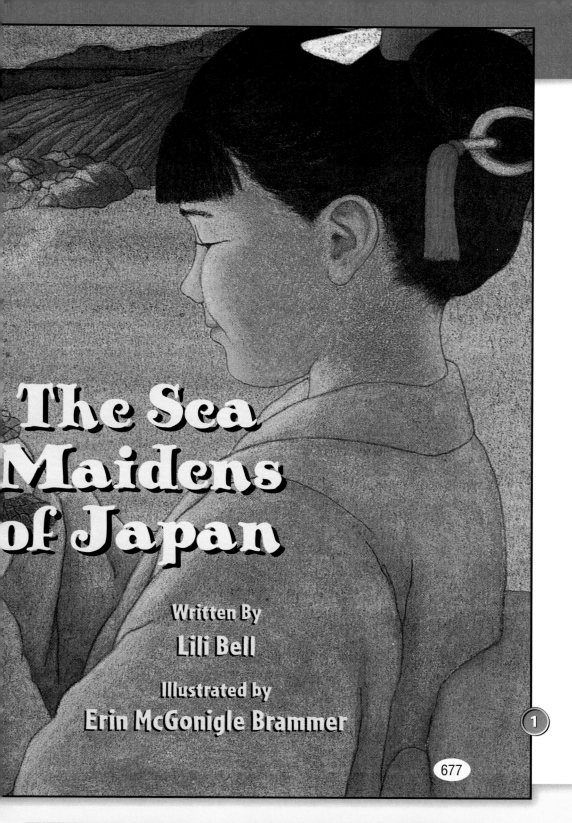

The Sea Maidens of Japan

Written By
Lili Bell

Illustrated by
Erin McGonigle Brammer

677

Guided Instruction

☑ **Sequence of Events**

☑ **Draw Conclusions**

Strategic Reading Before we begin reading, let's prepare a Sequence of Events chart to record the important events in the story and the order in which they occur.

```
┌────────────────────────────┐
│                            │
└────────────────────────────┘
              ↓
┌────────────────────────────┐
│                            │
└────────────────────────────┘
              ↓
┌────────────────────────────┐
│                            │
└────────────────────────────┘
```

(1) SEQUENCE OF EVENTS What is happening in the picture? (A girl is standing near the water holding a young turtle.) Do you think this happened before or after the girl picked up the turtle? (after)

Story Words

The words below may be unfamiliar. Have students check their meaning and pronunciation in the Glossary beginning on page 730.

- abalone, p. 678
- incoming, p. 683
- maidens, p. 678

LANGUAGE SUPPORT

The Sequence of Events chart is available as a blackline master in the **Language Support Book.**

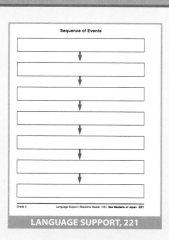

Guided Instruction

2 When readers begin a story, they try to find out who the characters are and what the setting of the story is. Who is the main character in this story? (Kiyomi) What have you learned about her? (She is a young girl who will grow up to be an ama like her mother. She is learning to dive.) Where does this story take place? (in Japan, near and in the sea) *Character/Setting*

3 SEQUENCE OF EVENTS What important event is described on this page? Let's add this detail to our chart.

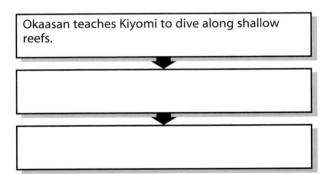

Okaasan teaches Kiyomi to dive along shallow reefs.

↓

↓

We are called the *ama,* the sea maidens of Japan. My mother's mother and even her great-grandmother's mother were fisherwomen who dove to the ocean floor to harvest seafood for the great emperors of Japan.

When I'm older, I'll learn to hold my breath under water for over a minute and gather abalone and seaweed for my family and our village. Okaasan, that is what I call my mama, teaches me to dive and fish along the shallow reefs.

678

Activity

Cross Curricular: Social Studies

MAP SKILLS Display a world map. Have students

- locate Japan.
- name the nearest countries.
- name the bodies of water that surround Japan.

- estimate how far away Japan is from the United States.

Discuss with students why they think the sea would be an important influence on the lives of people in Japan.

▶ **Mathematical/Spatial/Linguistic**

"Kiyomi, when you're older and follow our tradition," she tells me, "you will not have the rope attached to your waist. You must find your own way without me."

Hearing this, my stomach flutters. I must not disgrace Okaasan and fail because I am afraid of the deep waters. I long to be a brave ama diver, but I don't want to be swallowed up by the dark, deep waters.

My two older sisters chose the modern way of life and work in the city at the fish canneries. They will not become ama, like Okaasan and me.

679

Guided Instruction

4 **SEQUENCE OF EVENTS** What does Kiyomi's mother do first to teach her how to dive? (Her mother ties a rope to her.) How will Kiyomi dive when she gets older? (She will dive without a rope.)

5 Who is telling the story, and how can you tell? (Kiyomi. The narrator uses the pronoun *I*.) *Narrative Point of View*

ANTONYMS Which word in the second paragraph means the opposite of *afraid?*

6 **DRAW CONCLUSIONS** How does Kiyomi feel about diving alone? (She is afraid.) What clues in the story tell you she is afraid? (When she hears that she will dive alone, her stomach flutters and she says she doesn't want to be swallowed up by the dark, deep waters.)

PREVENTION/INTERVENTION

ANTONYMS Ask students to look for the word *afraid* in the second paragraph. Then have them look for the word that means the opposite. (brave) Challenge them to name two other antonyms for *afraid*, such as *bold* and *courageous*.

Have students find the antonyms of the following words in the passage:

- *younger* (older)
- *succeed* (fail)
- *ancient* (modern)
- *shallow* (deep)

Guided Instruction

7 **SEQUENCE OF EVENTS** How does Kiyomi keep herself busy while her mother dives? List the things she does in the order that she does them.

MODEL First, Kiyomi pretends to host a tea ceremony for mermaids, and she chases away schools of fish. Then the author uses the phrase *at the end of the day*. This helps me know that Kiyomi counts stars *after* she chases fish. The phrase *in the middle of the night* is another clue that helps me put the events in the correct sequence. Okaasan wakes Kiyomi up to watch the sea turtles lay their eggs *after* she counts stars. Though the author doesn't say so, this must have happened after Kiyomi has been sleeping for some time.

While my mother dives, I wait alone for long hours on the shore of a special cove. On this coral beach, every grain of sand is shaped like a star. Sitting in a shallow pool, I pretend to host tea ceremonies for mermaids. I chase schools of fish away from my treasure chest. At the end of the day, I wait for Okaasan and count the stars on the beach and in the sky.

7 In the middle of the night, Okaasan wakes me. "Come, Kiyomi, the sea turtles will lay their eggs on the beach tonight," she whispers.

680

Cross Curricular: Science

STAYING UNDER As an ama, Kiyomi will dive for over a minute before coming to the surface. Sea mammals also come to the surface to breathe. Ask students to give examples of these animals.

RESEARCH AND INQUIRY Have students choose a sea mammal and find out how long it can stay underwater. Have the class create a bulletin-board display showing a bar graph of breathing times. ▶ **Logical/Mathematical**

inter**NET** **CONNECTION** Students can learn more about sea mammals by visiting **www.mhschool.com/reading**

Whale: underwater time 2 hours

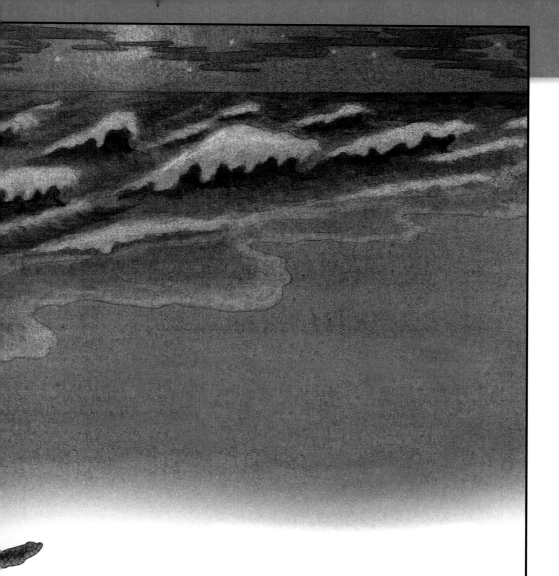

It is hard for me to open my eyes. Gently shaking my shoulder, she says, "Wake up, little one, the sea turtles come only once a year."

The moon is bright and the sky sparkles with stars. Gusts of wind sting my cheeks, leaving a strong, salty taste in my mouth. As each wave pounds at the shore, the ocean roars and foams like a terrible dragon. We wait a long time. I poke a stick at a pile of strong-smelling sea kelp circled with flies. I feel like a tiny fly next to the great power of the ocean.

681

Guided Instruction

8 **SEQUENCE OF EVENTS** Let's fill in our chart with the important events of the story that have occurred so far.

Okaasan teaches Kiyomi to dive along shallow reefs.

↓

Kiyomi waits on the shore while Okaasan dives in the deep water.

↓

LANGUAGE SUPPORT

ESL Read the second paragraph on page 681 aloud. Tell students that writers often describe things by telling how they sound, smell, feel, and taste as well as by how they look. Point out the words the author uses in this paragraph that appeal to the sense of touch (sting), taste (salty), hearing (pounds, roars like a terrible dragon), smell (strong-smelling sea kelp), and sight (bright, sparkles).

Encourage students to illustrate with gestures or with pictures some words that describe sights, sounds, smells, tastes, and touches.

Guided Instruction

9 **SEQUENCE OF EVENTS** What transitional words does the author use on these two pages to help the reader identify the sequence of events? (as, just then, begin)

 erhaps the ocean is too rough for the turtles to come. As we head home, rain clouds veil the starlight. The sky is so dark that I trip over pieces of driftwood. Okaasan waits for me and places her warm hand in mine.

9

682

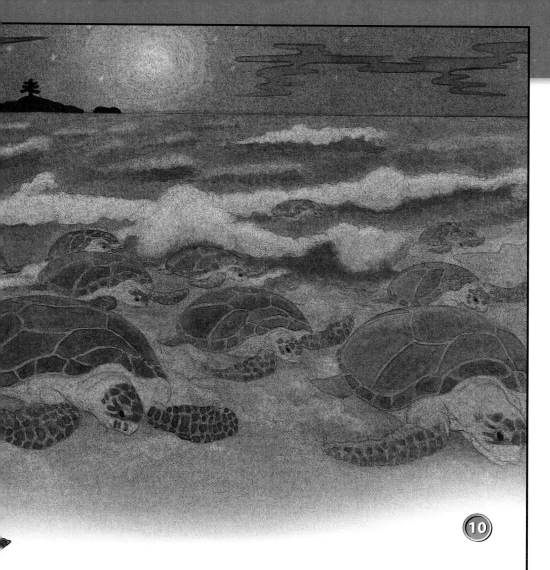

Just then, with each incoming wave, the sea turtles begin to appear. They are graceful and smooth in the water. On land they struggle, slow and awkward, onto the beach to select a nesting spot. I cup my hand over my mouth to hush my giggling as they dig a hole with their hind flippers and spray sand in each other's faces.

683

Guided Instruction

10 **DRAW CONCLUSIONS** Look at the illustration on these two pages. What does it tell you about this part of Japan?

MODEL I can see that there are islands off the coast. The land is hilly and mountainous. The weather is warm during this time of year.

WORD STRUCTURE Read the second sentence on this page. Do you know what the word *graceful* means?

Minilesson

REVIEW

/ou/ and /oi/

Remind students that both the /ou/ and /oi/ sounds can be spelled more than one way.

- Read aloud the second sentence on page 682. Ask students how *clouds* is spelled and write it on the board. Underline the *ou*, and ask students what sound these letters make. (/ou/)

- Ask students if they know another spelling for the /ou/ sound. (ow)

Activity Divide the class into teams. Have one team list words that have the /ou/ sound spelled *ou* or *ow*. Have the other list words that have the /oi/ sound spelled *oi* or *oy*. Give one point for each word that contains the /ou/ or /oi/ sound.

PREVENTION/INTERVENTION

WORD STRUCTURE Remind students that they can divide words into parts to help them understand their meanings.

- Write the word *graceful* on the chalkboard.

- Ask students to define the base word *grace* and the suffix *-ful*.

Have students think of other words that end with the suffix *-ful*.

Guided Instruction

11 What do you think the baby turtles will do after they hatch from the eggs? Pantomime what they will do. *(They will dig their way out of the nest and crawl to the water without their mother's help.)* *Make Predictions/Pantomime*

TEACHING TIP

MANAGEMENT As students read aloud, make observations about fluency and decoding skills to determine where help may be needed. Classify problems by type, such as:

- reading rate
- accuracy
- fluidity or rhythm
- inappropriate phrasing
- expressiveness

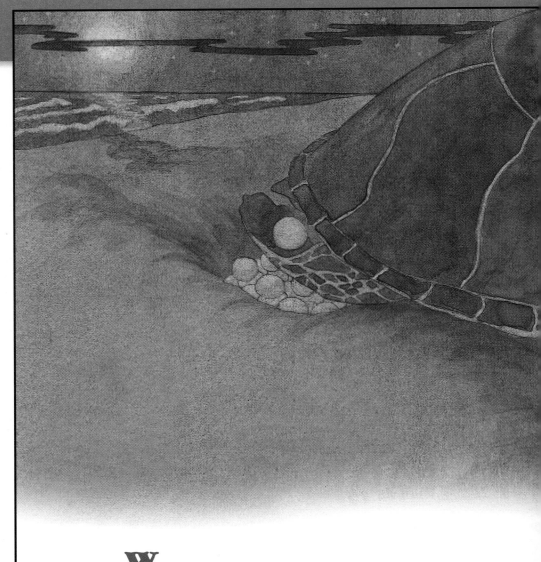

We hear one turtle moan and strain, tears running from her eyes, as she lays dozens of eggs that look like soft, shiny balls. She brushes sand over her nest and begins the slow trip back to the ocean, leaving her babies to find their own way. A wave sweeps her into the sea and she disappears.

11

684

CULTURAL PERSPECTIVES

HAIKU AND TANKA This tale uses language rich in sensory images like those found in poetry. Japanese poetry includes haiku and tanka. A haiku is a short, non-rhyming poem with this pattern:

- First line: setting (five syllables)
- Second line: action (seven syllables)

- Third line: conclusion (five syllables).

A tanka is a five-line poem with the syllabic pattern of 5, 7, 5, 7, 7.

Activity Have students create their own haiku or tanka poems.
▶ **Linguistic**

Cold waves tumbling in

A sea turtle lays her eggs

Then she disappears

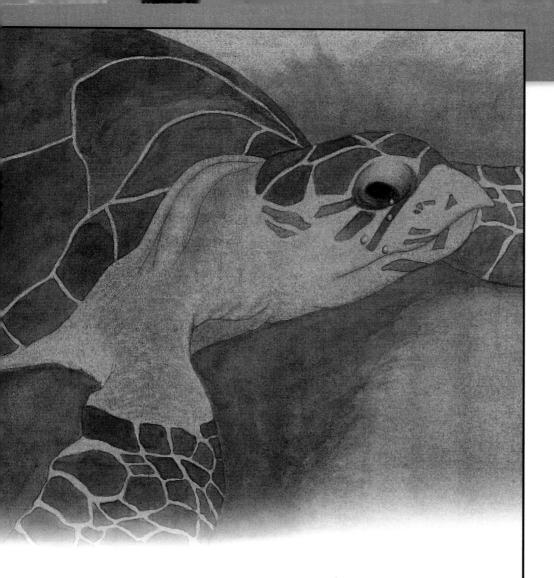

Every day I visit the beach to check the nests. The sun soaks the sand with warmth for the eggs to grow. Some eggs are scooped up in the fishermen's buckets. Others are eaten by hungry birds and crabs, but I try to chase them away.

685

Guided Instruction

12 How does the author show us that Kiyomi is concerned about the sea turtle eggs? (She returns every day to check the nests and tries to chase away animals that eat eggs.) *Character*

Minilesson

REVIEW

Main Idea

Remind students that paragraphs are often organized around main ideas with supporting details.

- Have students find the main idea of the paragraph on page 685. (Kiyomi checks on the nests of turtle eggs.)

- Have students list the supporting details in this paragraph as you place them in a Main Idea chart.

Activity Have students choose other paragraphs from the story and complete a Main Idea chart for them.

LANGUAGE SUPPORT

ESL Read the first sentence on page 685 aloud. Point out that the verb in this sentence, *visit*, is in the present tense. Explain that when we describe something that happens on a regular basis, such as every day or every month, we use the present tense of a verb. For example, you say, "Every morning, I *brush* my teeth." If, on the other hand, you were to say, "Every morning, I *brushed* my teeth," this would mean that you used to brush your teeth every morning, but you don't do it any more.

Have students give examples of sentences that use the present tense to describe actions they do every day. Then have them give examples of sentences that use the past tense to describe actions they no longer do.

685

Guided Instruction

(13) About how long did it take for the turtles to hatch? (two months) *Draw Conclusions*

(14) **SEQUENCE OF EVENTS** What happens after the baby turtle runs the wrong way and before the wave washes him out to sea? (Kiyomi picks him up. She notices a star shape on his shell. She guides the turtle to the shore.)

(15) **SEQUENCE OF EVENTS** Let's add a new event to the Sequence of Events chart.

> Okaasan teaches Kiyomi to dive along shallow reefs.

⬇

> Kiyomi waits on the shore while Okaasan dives in the deep water.

⬇

> Kiyomi helps the star turtle into the sea.

 (13) After two full moons pass, I see a nest hatch on the star cove. Out of the sand pops a tiny flipper, a head, and then an entire body. Ten, twelve, fifteen little turtles emerge from the depths of the star sand and scurry toward the ocean.

One confused baby turtle runs in the wrong direction—away from the water! He scrambles toward the soft orange light that glows from

686

Activity

Cross Curricular: Science

SEA TURTLES Kiyomi watches sea turtles come to shore to lay their eggs. Ask students what they know about sea turtles. Create a K-W-L chart to record their information. Fill in the first two columns.

RESEARCH AND INQUIRY Have students look for information about sea turtles in books about marine life. Have them give brief oral reports of their findings. As students give their reports, fill in the third column of the chart.

▶ **Linguistic/Interpersonal**

What I Know	What I Want to Know	What I Learned
Sea turtles live in water.	Which bodies of water do sea turtles live in?	
Sea turtles are very big.	How big do sea turtles grow?	

the paper lanterns in the village. I run after the little turtle and pick him up. On his shell is the shape of a grain of star sand. He flails his neck and flippers. Gently, I guide the frightened turtle to the shoreline. A huge wave swallows him and carries him out to the deep sea.

   I wonder if the star turtle is strong enough to survive. I wonder, too, if I am strong enough to be an ama diver.

687

Guided Instruction

16 What does Kiyomi compare herself to in the last paragraph on page 687? (She compares herself to the little sea turtle.) **How are they alike?** (They are both young and frightened. They both must dive into the ocean.) *Compare and Contrast*

SELF-MONITORING

STRATEGY

SEARCH FOR CLUES Searching for clues can help a reader draw conclusions. Ask students to look for clues that suggest how Kiyomi feels about the star turtle.

Minilesson

REVIEW

Draw Conclusions

Remind students that good readers can draw conclusions about what might happen as the result of a certain event in a story.

- Ask students to conclude what would have happened to the turtle if Kiyomi had not taken it to the water.

- Ask students what evidence led them to their conclusion.

Activity Have students write a conclusion about why the sea turtles dig holes in which to lay their eggs. Remind students to give evidence from the story that supports their conclusions.

Guided Instruction

(17) SEQUENCE OF EVENTS How many years have passed since Kiyomi has helped the young sea turtle? (several) What is Kiyomi expected to do now? (She must make her first deep water dive with the ama.) What happens when it is time for her to dive? (She is too afraid to jump into the water.)

(18) DRAW CONCLUSIONS Why does Kiyomi's mother sigh and look away from her? (She is disappointed in her daughter and embarrassed in front of the other divers.) Why does Kiyomi toss and turn in bed? (She feels terrible about being afraid to dive. She is also worried about embarrassing her mother.)

(p/i) CONTEXT CLUES Read the first paragraph on this page. What does *despair* mean?

Several fishing seasons come and go. The time arrives for me to make a deep water dive with the ama. I try, but I cannot peel my feet off the boat deck to jump into the dark, murky water. Okaasan sighs and looks down, away from me. To my despair, I hear muffled giggles.

At night I toss and turn in bed like a fish caught in a net. I get up, look out the window, and see the faint glow of the city lights. My mind is set. I will run to the city and find my sisters rather than embarrass Okaasan any further.

688

Fluency

REPEATED READINGS The text on pages 688 and 689 provides an excellent opportunity for students to practice fluent reading. To guide them, you may wish to model fluent reading of the passage by

- pausing briefly at commas.
- dropping intonation and pausing at the ends of sentences.
- reading the dramatic parts of the narrative with expression.
- slowing the reading rate during the more dramatic material.

Students should practice reading the passage in pairs until their reading is fluent.

(p/i) PREVENTION/INTERVENTION

CONTEXT CLUES Tell students that sometimes a reader must use the context of the paragraph, not just a single sentence, to determine the meaning of an unknown word.

Ask students what events in this paragraph help determine the meaning of *despair*. (Kiyomi cannot jump into the water. Her mother is ashamed. The others watch her and giggle.)

Okaasan is quiet as she serves our breakfast. Finally she says, "Kiyomi, you will come with me to the ama boats today."

Cupping my soup bowl in both hands, I take a sip but can barely taste or swallow.

"Kiyomi-chan, you must keep trying," she says.

At the dock, the ama prepare for a day of work. We put white cream on my face to protect it from the cold, salty water. Moments later, the boats creep through a thick fog, farther from the village than I've ever been. Almost ready to dive, I look at the black water and begin to shake. **19** **20**

689

Guided Instruction

19 **SEQUENCE OF EVENTS** Let's add another event to our charts.

Okaasan teaches Kiyomi to dive along shallow reefs.

▼

Kiyomi waits on the shore while Okaasan dives in the deep water.

▼

Kiyomi helps the star turtle into the sea.

▼

Kiyomi is too afraid to make her first deep water dive.

20 Do you think Kiyomi will jump into the water? Explain your answer. (Sample answer: I think she will jump. She will remember the tiny turtle that she helped into the ocean. It will make her feel braver to know that she is not the only small thing swimming in the deep water.) *Make Predictions*

LANGUAGE SUPPORT

ESL On the chalkboard, write the sentence that contains the word *cream*. Tell students that sometimes an English word like *cream* has more than one meaning. How the word is used in a sentence can help a reader determine its meaning.

Have students look up the word *cream* in a dictionary. Ask them which of the dictionary meanings of the word is used in the passage.

Guided Instruction

21 What made Kiyomi finally jump into the sea? (She saw the star turtle.) **Why would seeing the star turtle give Kiyomi the courage to dive?** (She saw that even though the turtle was once small and afraid, he was surviving in the sea. She compared herself to the turtle and saw herself as brave.) *Make Inferences*

22 **SEQUENCE OF EVENTS** **What events on this page happen more than once?** (Kiyomi sees something moving in the water twice. She takes two breaths before she dives. She keeps diving all morning.)

Something moves in the water, but I cannot see what it is. A drum pounds in my chest. I look at Okaasan and she nods at me firmly. Again, I see something move in the water. This time, I see the outline of a turtle. My heart leaps. Could it be the star turtle?

21 I take a deep breath and blow through pursed lips, sounding like the distant cry of a gull on a wind-swept beach. I hold in another breath, force my feet off the deck, and dive.

22 Stroking the water furiously, I try to keep up with the sea turtle. As he swoops deeper to the ocean floor, I recognize the star on his shell. Grabbing his shell, we rise together to the surface for air. I turn loose, tread water, and watch the turtle gracefully swim away.

690

Activity

Cross Curricular: Social Studies

JAPANESE TEA CEREMONY As a girl, Kiyomi pretended to host tea ceremonies. The Japanese tea ceremony is a custom that goes back hundreds of years. This ceremony is a time for concentrating on harmony, respect, and tranquillity.

Bring in several teas, including those from Japan, for students to sample. Have students taste and describe the different flavors. Invite students to find out more about Japanese tea ceremonies.

Guided Instruction

23 How is Kiyomi changed in this story?
(She has become older and braver. She has become an ama.) *Character*

All morning I dive deep, hunt for abalone, and pry them off the rocks with my knife. When I return to the boats, all the ama are pleased.

"Today, Kiyomi, you have become an ama," Okaasan says proudly.

On a small island beach we collect firewood and dry leaves. Women, wrapped in thin, white clothing, huddle around the fire as shellfish sizzle in the embers. I cannot tell if I tremble from the cold or excitement. My skin is swollen and pale. An older ama places a blanket on my shoulders. With chopsticks, we pick the flavorful fish from the shells.

In the surf, I see the star turtle bobbing in the water, watching me. I smile at my friend as a huge wave sweeps him into the deep waters. On this island beach I sit for the first time among the brave ama, the sea maidens of Japan.

23

691

Minilesson

REVIEW

Context Clues

Remind students that they can use familiar words to determine the meaning of an unknown word.

- Read the fourth sentence on page 691 aloud. Ask students to name familiar words in this sentence that give clues to the meaning of *embers*. (fire, sizzle)

- What can you infer from these clues? (Embers are hot; they are part of a fire.)

Activity Read aloud the following sentence: *The frigid air made Marco shiver as he walked through the snowfall.* Have students write a definition of *frigid*.

Guided Instruction

24 Is Kiyomi a *kachido* or *funado*? How do you know? (She is a funado because she dove from a boat in deep water.) *Draw Conclusions*

25 **SEQUENCE OF EVENTS** Let's complete the Sequence of Events chart.

Okaasan teaches Kiyomi to dive along shallow reefs.

↓

Kiyomi waits on the shore while Okaasan dives in the deep water.

↓

Kiyomi helps the star turtle into the sea.

↓

Kiyomi is too afraid to make her first deep water dive.

↓

Kiyomi sees the star turtle and dives into the deep water.

RETELL THE STORY Ask volunteers to use the chart to retell the story. Have them focus on Kiyomi's problem and how it is solved. *Summarize*

STUDENT SELF-ASSESSMENT

- How did using the strategy of identifying the sequence of events help me to understand the story?

- How did using the Sequence of Events chart help me?

TRANSFERRING THE STRATEGY

- When might I try using this strategy again? In what other reading could the chart help me?

Author's Note

The *ama* are Japanese sea divers who hunt for fish, shellfish, and seaweed without the aid of underwater breathing apparatus. Most of the ama are women, particularly in the fishing communities of central Japan. The *kachido*, "walking people," dive in shallow water from the shore and toss their catch into floating wooden tubs. The *funado*, "ship people," are older and more experienced and dive in deeper waters from an anchored **24** boat. The ama hunt mostly for *awabi* (abalone), *sazae* (wreath shell snail), *tengusa* (agaragar), and *eganori* (a kind of edible seaweed). The ama's method of diving was first recorded by Chinese **25** observers in Japan during the third century.

Pronunciation Guide

abalone	*ab-a-lo-nee*
ama	*a-ma*
awabi	*a-wa-bee*
eganori	*e-ga-no-ree*
funado	*fu-na-do*
kachido	*ka-chee-do*
Kiyomi	*Kee-yo-mee*
Okaasan	*O-ka-a-san*
sazae	*sa-za-e*
tengusa	*ten-gu-sa*

692

REREADING FOR *Fluency*

PARTNERS Have students choose a favorite section of the story to read to a partner. Encourage students to read with feeling and expression.

READING RATE To evaluate a student's reading rate, have the student read aloud from *Sea Maidens of Japan* for one minute. Ask the student to place a self-stick note after the last word read. Then count the number of words he or she has read.

Alternatively, you could assess small groups or the whole class together by having students count the words and record their own scores.

Use the Reading Rate form in the **Diagnostic/Placement Evaluations** booklet to evaluate students' performance.

Guided Instruction

Return to Predictions and Purposes

Review with students their story predictions and reasons for reading the story. Were their predictions correct? Did they find out what they wanted to know?

PREDICTIONS	WHAT HAPPENED
The young girl will learn to dive.	At first Kiyomi is afraid to dive alone into the deep, dark water. Later she becomes an ama.
The young girl takes care of a turtle.	Kiyomi takes care of a turtle that later helps her overcome her fear of diving.

SEQUENCE OF EVENTS

HOW TO ASSESS

- Can students identify time words that signal the order of events to the reader?
- Can they make a time line of the main events of the story?

Students' time lines should show that the day on which Kiyomi sees the turtles lay their eggs is about two months before the day the turtle eggs hatch. Kiyomi makes her first deep water dive several years after she sees the turtles hatch.

FOLLOW UP If students have trouble identifying time words in the story, ask questions such as: How do you know that time passed between the hatching of the turtle eggs and Kiyomi's first deep water dive?

If students have trouble making a time line, draw a sample on the chalkboard showing a typical school year. Include such events as the first day of school, holidays, and the last day of school.

LITERARY RESPONSE

QUICK-WRITE Invite students to record their thoughts about the story. These questions may help them get started:

- How would you describe Kiyomi's relationship with her mother?
- What do you think happened to Kiyomi and the turtle after the end of the story?

ORAL RESPONSE Have students share their journal writings and discuss the parts of the story they enjoyed most. Which illustrations did they find most interesting?

693

Story Questions

Have students discuss or write answers to the questions on page 694.

Answers:

1. She teaches her to dive in shallow water with a rope. *Literal/Sequence of Events*

2. Sample answer: She does not dive. She is still too afraid. *Inferential/Character*

3. Sample answer: She does not want to disgrace her mother. *Inferential/Conclusions*

4. Sample answer: 1) Okaasan teaches Kiyomi to dive in shallow water. 2) Kiyomi helps the star turtle. 3) Kiyomi is afraid to make a deep-water dive. 4) The star turtle gives Kiyomi courage to dive. *Summarize/Sequence of Events*

5. Sample answer: Both women are strong and wise, and both show respect for traditions and for their families. *Critical/Reading Across Texts*

Write a Two-character Scene For a full writing process lesson, see pages 697K–697L.

Story Questions & Activities

1. What does Kiyomi's mother do to prepare her to become an *ama*?

2. What happens the first time Kiyomi tries to dive alone? What does this tell you about her?

3. Why does Kiyomi want to be a brave *ama*?

4. What are the events in this story? List them in order.

5. How is Kiyomi's mother like the mother in "The Wise Old Woman"?

Write a Two-character Scene

Create a scene for a play based on "The Sea Maidens of Japan." Write a conversation between Kiyomi and her mother that could have taken place as Kiyomi prepares for her first deep-water dive. Begin by making a story map. Outline the setting, the characters, the problem, the events, and the solution. Then write your scene. Be sure to use the correct form for your dialogue.

Meeting Individual Needs

EASY

Vocabulary

Choose the word that fits the clue. Then fill in the crossword puzzle.

| disgrace | flails | host | sizzle | cove | driftwood |

Across
3. shame, embarrass
5. flops about
6. person who invites you to a party

Down
1. bubble while cooking
2. wood brought on shore by the ocean
4. protected area along the seashore

Story Comprehension

Write the answer to each question about "Sea Maidens of Japan."

1. What does Kiyomi want to learn from her mother? She wants to learn how to become an ama, a fisherwoman who dives for seafood.

2. What problem faces Kiyomi and her mother? Kiyomi is afraid of swimming in the deep water.

3. How does Kiyomi feel about the work she does with her mother? She wants to succeed. She is afraid of disgracing the family.

4. How does the sea turtle help Kiyomi on her first dive? She sees the grown sea turtle as a friend. It gives her a ride up from the sea floor for air and makes her feel less alone.

Reteach 202

At Home: Have students think of something they could say to Kiyomi to calm her fears.

201–202

Book 5/Unit 6
Sea Maidens of Japan 4

Reteach, 202

ON-LEVEL

Story Comprehension

Answer the questions about "Sea Maidens of Japan." You may want to look back at the story for help. Answers will vary. Sample responses shown.

1. Whose voice is the narrator of "Sea Maidens of Japan"? Kiyomi, a little girl

2. Who is Okaasan? What does she do for a living? Okaasan is Kiyomi's mother; she is a fisherwoman, or ama, who holds her breath to dive for seafood.

3. What is Okaasan trying to teach Kiyomi? Why does Okaasan tie a rope around Kiyomi's waist? She is trying to teach Kiyomi to dive and fish along the coral reefs. She uses the rope for safety, in case she has to pull Kiyomi up to the surface quickly.

4. What do Kiyomi's two older sisters do for work? Did they choose to follow the ama tradition, too? No; they chose the modern life and work in a fish cannery in the city.

5. What does Kiyomi do while waiting alone on the shore as her mother dives for seafood? She pretends to host tea ceremonies (tea parties) for mermaids; she chases schools of fish from their treasure chest.

6. What does Okaasan take Kiyomi to see in the middle of one night? sea turtles laying their eggs.

7. What happens when Kiyomi has to make her first deep water dive with the ama? She is too scared to dive into the water. She is afraid she will disgrace her mother.

8. What is so special about the sea turtle that swims with Kiyomi when she finally makes a deep water dive with the ama? It has the same star on the back of its shell as the baby turtle she had helped rescue.

At Home: Let students act out a scene from "Sea Maidens of Japan."

202

Book 5/Unit 6
Sea Maidens of Japan 8

Practice, 202

CHALLENGE

Vocabulary

| cove | disgrace | driftwood | flails | host | sizzle |

Crossword puzzles are popular games that help you remember words. Below make up a crossword puzzle using the vocabulary words above and some words of your own choice. Give the puzzle to a friend to solve.

Puzzles will vary, but should include all six vocab words.

Extend 202

Story Comprehension

Signal, or clue words often help tell the sequence of events. Look through the story, "Sea Maidens of Japan" and find sentences with clue words that show the passage of time, or that indicate sequence. Write them in the correct order.

Answers should include sentences that indicate the passage of time.

At Home: Newspaper articles often tell news events in sequence. Find a news article and write down the main events in the correct sequence.

201–202

Book 5/Unit 6
Sea Maidens of Japan

Extend, 202

Make a Shadow Box

What is abalone? Why do the *amas* have to dive for it? How is it used? Use an encyclopedia to learn more about this sea creature. Then bring to class a button or a piece of jewelry that is made from abalone shell. With a group, paste your abalone objects in a shadow box or a shoebox. Display your works.

Create a Japanese Cookbook

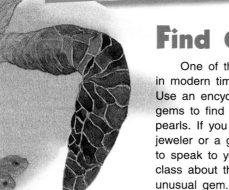

The people of the village eat the abalone and seaweed that the *ama* bring out of the sea. In fact, Japan relies on the sea for much of its food. In your library or at home, find a Japanese cookbook. Work with a group to choose some interesting Japanese seafood recipes. Copy these recipes, and place them in a Japanese cookbook of your own design.

Find Out More

One of the major uses for *amas* in modern times is as pearl divers. Use an encyclopedia or a book about gems to find out about pearls. If you can, invite a jeweler or a gemologist to speak to your class about this unusual gem.

695

Story Activities

Make a Shadow Box

Materials: encyclopedia, buttons or pieces of jewelry that are made from abalone shells, a shoe box, glue

GROUP Have groups of three or four students work together to research abalone. Groups can present their information to the class. Suggest that each student present a part of his or her group's research.

You may want to have students bring a variety of objects from the sea to put in their shadow boxes. Possible objects include shells, sand dollars, pieces of natural sponges, or small sticks of driftwood.

Create a Japanese Cookbook

Materials: Japanese cookbook or cookbook with Japanese recipes, paper

GROUP Have students illustrate their recipes with Japanese-style art and compile them into a class cookbook. You may want to have a day when students can bring in a sample of food from the cookbook to share with the class.

Find Out More

RESEARCH AND INQUIRY If you plan to have a speaker visit your classroom, **ONE** have students find out basic information about pearls beforehand so that they might prepare questions to ask the visitor.

FORMAL ASSESSMENT

After page 695, see Selection Assessment.

Study Skills

LIBRARY/MEDIA CENTER

OBJECTIVES Students will

- identify a variety of reference sources.
- choose appropriate reference sources.

PREPARE Read the passage with students. Display **Teaching Chart 165.**

TEACH Invite volunteers to read the description of each reference source aloud and give examples of when each might be used.

PRACTICE Have students answer questions 1–5. Review the answers with them. **1.** a dictionary **2.** an encyclopedia **3.** an atlas **4.** a thesaurus **5.** You can find the information you need faster if you know where to look for it.

ASSESS/CLOSE Have students choose a reference source and create small posters that begin, "Use a(n) _____ if you're looking for _____." (For example: Use an encyclopedia if you're looking for information about Albert Einstein.) Have them list at least three examples on their posters.

Study SKILLS

Choose Reference Sources

When you want information, you can choose from a number of different reference sources.

Almanac: a book of information about important people, places, and events. An almanac is published each year so that it has up-to-date facts and figures.

Atlas: a book of maps that gives information about different places.

Dictionary: a book that lists words in alphabetical order, their meanings, pronunciations, parts of speech, and other information.

Encyclopedia: a set of books containing articles about people, places, things, events, and ideas. The articles are arranged in alphabetical order in volumes. When you use an encyclopedia to find facts about a topic, you need to have a **key word** in mind.

Thesaurus: a book of synonyms. **Synonyms** are words with the same or almost the same meaning. A thesaurus may be arranged like a dictionary, with the entry words shown in alphabetical order.

Use the information about different reference sources to answer these questions.

1 In which reference book would you look to find out how to pronounce *abalone*?

2 Where would you look to find out about deep-sea diving?

3 In which book would you find maps of Japan?

4 Where would you look to find synonyms of the word *strong*?

5 How can you save time if you know which reference book to use?

Meeting Individual Needs

EASY	ON-LEVEL	CHALLENGE

Read a News Article

A newspaper carries stories and articles of current interest. A **news article** begins with a headline that tries to catch your attention. It is usually in large, bold letters. The dateline tells where and when the story was written. The article will answer the questions: *who? what? when? where? why?* and *how?*

Read the newspaper article. Then answer the questions below.

An Eagle Interested in Education

by MARISSA MOLINE

CLEVELAND, MAY 1, 2000—Bald Eagles are known for building nests along the shore and keeping an eye on the water for prey. They have never been known for their interest in schooling.

Today, however, on the first day of May, an eagle was spotted high atop a tree next to a fifth-grade classroom at Middletown Elementary School.

The eagle appears to be staying in Cleveland for a while. It has begun to build a nest, while apparently keeping an eye on the fifth grade. Many students have found themselves being watched through the window by their new feathered friend.

They have decided to begin a study of eagles and their habits. It is hard to know who is learning more, the eagle or the fifth graders!

1. What is the headline of this news story? *An Eagle Interested in Education*
2. Where was the story written? *Cleveland*
3. Who is this story about? *fifth graders and an eagle*
4. What is the main idea of the story? *An eagle is building a nest beside a classroom.*
5. Where did this take place? *at the Middletown Elementary School*
6. When did the story happen? *May 1, 2000*

Book 5/Unit 5
Tonweya and the Eagles
At Home: Ask students to cut out three newspaper articles, label its parts, and underline the most important ideas.
166

Read a News Article

A **news article** is a newspaper story about an important news event based on facts. It always begins with a **headline** that is meant to catch the reader's attention. It also has a **dateline** that tells where and when the story was written.

Look at the news article below, then answer the questions.

Kids News Network

Tornado Strikes Worcester

By ALACHA McREA

BOSTON, March 28, 2001 – It looked like just another warm spring day in Worcester, Massachusetts, and Nancy Lopes had just stepped outside with her dog, Snoozer, to take a walk when she noticed a huge dark cloud approaching. Moments later James Lopes, her father, called out to her from the kitchen window and told her to hurry back inside. Mr. Lopes had just heard a tornado warning on the radio. The family quickly headed to the basement for safety.

The tornado soon touched down in their neighborhood. It tore the roof off of the Lopes' house as well as six others on their street. Their refrigerator landed in a tree a half mile away. Their car was destroyed when a giant oak tree crashed down on it. Power and telephone lines are still down. The family said they were glad no one was hurt and thankful that they heard the advance warning system on the radio.

1. What is the headline of the news article? *Tornado Strikes Worcester*
2. Where and when was the news story written? *Boston; May 28*
3. Who is the news story about? *Nancy Lopes and her family.*
4. What city did the tornado hit? *Worcester, Massachusetts.*
5. What is the story about? *A tornado touched down in the Lopes' neighborhood causing a lot of damage.*
6. What was the family's reaction to the tornado? *They were thankful that no one was hurt and that there was an advance warning system.*

Book 5/Unit 5
Tonweya and the Eagles
At Home: Have students read a newspaper article and summarize it to a family member.
166

Read a News Article

News articles give factual accounts of current events. Each news article has several parts.

Headline: the title of the article
By-line: the name of the reporter who wrote the news article
Dateline: place where the story originated
Lead paragraph: a short summary of the most important ideas in the news article; answers the questions *who* was involved, *what* happened, *when* it happened, *where* it happened, and *how* it was resolved.

Find a news article of interest to you in a local paper. Read the article, then fill in the chart below.

Headline: Answers will vary.

By-line: Answers will vary.
Dateline:

Who: Answers will vary. Accept all reasonable answers.
What:
When:
Where:
Why:
How:

Book 5/Unit 5
Tonweya and the Eagles
At Home: Write a news article that tells about an interesting event in your community.
166

Reteach, 203   Practice, 203   Extend, 203

TEST POWER

Test
Power
THE
PRINCETON
REVIEW

Test Tip

Tell yourself the story again in your own words.

DIRECTIONS

Read the sample story. Then read each question about the story.

SAMPLE

Billy's Introduction to the News

Billy's father purchased a newspaper subscription for him for his eleventh birthday. Billy wasn't too sure about the gift, but he was polite when his father handed him the subscription notice.

"I think you'll enjoy the newspaper if you give it a chance. This will help you keep up with what's going on in town," his father said.

When Billy's first newspaper came the following week, he carefully spread it out and began to read it.

When his father got home that night, Billy said, "Dad, did you see the front page of the newspaper today? The town is thinking about building a new high school. And the art guild is looking for more funding for the exhibit."

Billy's father chuckled and said, "It sounds to me as if the newspaper is a hit after all!"

1   At the beginning of the passage, how does Billy feel about reading the newspaper?

   ○ Delighted

   ○ Fortunate

   ○ Excited

   ● Doubtful

2   When Billy gets the newspaper in the future, he will probably —

   ○ give it to his father to read

   ● read it right away

   ○ put it in the recycling bin

   ○ send money to the art guild

Read the Page

Direct students to read *all* the answer choices for each question.

Discuss the Questions

Question 1: This question requires that students understand Billy's feelings at the beginning of the passage—the clue: "Billy wasn't too sure about the gift."

Question 2: This question requires students to determine what Billy will *probably* do when he receives the newspaper in the future. Given the information in the passage, is it likely that Billy will "give it to his father to read"? There is nothing in the passage to support that answer. Will he "read it right away"? Yes, he probably will, because he seemed excited about the paper. Will he "put it in the recycling bin"? Will he "send money to the art guild"? Neither of these is supported by the passage.

For The Princeton Review test preparation practice for **TerraNova, ITBS,** and **SAT-9,** visit the McGraw-Hill School Division Web site. See also McGraw-Hill's *Standardized Test Preparation Book.*

EASY
DECODABLE

Leveled Books

LEVELED BOOKS

Making Pipes are His Bag

written by Janet Cassidy

McGraw Hill

EASY

Making Pipes Is His Bag

Words with /ou/
☑ **Sequence of Events**
☑ **Instructional Vocabulary:** *cove, disgrace, driftwood, flails, host, sizzle*

Guided Reading

PREVIEW AND PREDICT Have students examine the illustrations up to page 10. Point out that they are photographs. Ask students what they think the title means, then predict what the book is about.

SET PURPOSES Have students write two questions about bagpipes they would like to have answered. For example, What do you make a bagpipe with? Who plays bagpipes?

READ THE BOOK Use questions like the following to guide students' reading or after they have read the story independently.

Page 3: How did Charley Kron's experience playing the clarinet and bassoon prepare to play the bagpipes? (They are also reed instruments that you blow air thought to produce sound.) *Drawing Conclusions*

Page 4: Notice the word hours in the third line. What sound does ou make in this word? (/ou/) What other spelling makes /ou/? (ow) Find other words on this page that make the /ou/ sound spelled ou and ow. (how, out) *Phonics and Decoding*

Page 4: What did Charley do before returning to Scotland the second time?

(He finished college.) What words help you know the order in which the events on this page happened? (next, at the same time, after) *Sequence of Events*

Page 6: What does it mean that New York City is "host" to a large parade? (The city is the site of the parade or welcomes it.) *Vocabulary*

Page 11: What must be done to the wood before it can be used? (It must be aged for several years to dry it.) *Sequence of Events*

RETURN TO PREDICTIONS AND PURPOSES Discuss students' predictions. Have students review their purposes for reading. Did they find out what they wanted to know?

LITERARY RESPONSE Invite students to discuss these questions:

- What about the bagpipe appealed to Charley Kron?

- What instrument would you like to play? What about it appeals to you? Why do people pick one instrument over another?

Also see the story questions and activity in *Making Pipes Is His Bag.*

Answers to Story Questions

1. It is made of wood-usually African blackwood-attached to a leather bag.
2. He loved the sound of the instrument and was fascinated by the machines used to make them.
3. Answers will vary, but may include: love of the instrument itself, sense of satisfaction from making something well.
4. The book is about a man who makes bagpipes, and the process of making pipes.
5. Answers will vary.

Story Questions and Activity

1. What is a bagpipe made of?
2. What attracted Charley Kron to the craft of making bagpipes?
3. Why do you think someone would enjoy making musical instruments for a living?
4. What is the main idea of this book?
5. Being a bagpipe maker is an unusual occupation. In what ways does it compare to the women who dive for abalone in *Sea Maidens of Japan?*

Drawn to Music

Listen to a recording of bagpipe music. Then write a paragraph to express how the music makes you feel.

from Making Pipes Is His Bag

Leveled Books

PUPIL SELECTION

INDEPENDENT
DECODABLE

INDEPENDENT

The Beekeepers' Story

☑ **Sequence of Events**

☑ **Instructional Vocabulary:**
cove, disgrace, driftwood, host, flail, sizzle

Guided Reading

PREVIEW AND PREDICT Examine the illustrations through page 5 and predict what it is about.

SET PURPOSES Have students write what they want to find out about honey and the people who grow it.

READ THE BOOK Use questions like the following to guide students' reading, or to emphasize reading strategies after they have read the story independently.

Page 4: What happens after the pollen is transformed into honey? (The honey is stored in the six-sided cells of the honeycomb.) What word helps signal order in this paragraph? (then) *Sequence of Events*

Page 8: What three things do the Solbergs do with the honey after they filter it? (They bottle it, label it, and place it in the storeroom) *Sequence of Events*

Page 11: This article mentions four types of honey that the Solberg's harvest. Which is produced first, second, third, and last? (spring wildflower, mesquite, salt cedar, and summer wildflower honey) *Sequence of Events*

Page 12: Why do you suppose the hives grow quickly in spring? (The bee population increases in spring and more honey is being produced.) *Drawing Conclusions*

Page 15: What does the word *flail* mean? (To move or swing as if with a flail.) **Name two synonyms for flail.** (thrash, wave, flutter) *Vocabulary*

RETURN TO PREDICTIONS AND PURPOSES Discuss students' predictions. Ask if students learned what they wanted to know about beekeeping. Have students review their purposes for reading. Were their predictions accurate?

LITERARY RESPONSE Discuss these questions:

• Name a few traits you see in the Solbergs that you think other beekeepers might have. Why are these traits important for beekeeping.

• Would you find beekeeping a rewarding profession? What about it appeals to you?

Also see the story questions and activity in *The Beekeepers' Story.*

Answers to Story Questions

1. Add more supers to give the bees more room, divide the hive in two, or destroy the new queen cells.
2. If part of the hive has no new queen to regroup around, the hive is more likely to stay together.
3. Answers will vary but can include: It teaches him about the lifecycles of flowers and bees in relation to this.
4. It is about beekeepers and what they do to raise bees and gather and package their honey to sell.
5. Answers will vary.

Story Questions and Activity

1. What does a beekeeper do to try to prevent a bee hive from swarming?
2. Why might destroying the new queen cells stop a hive from swarming?
3. Gordon says beekeeping helps keep him curious about the world, because he must pay close attention to the weather. What else do you think his job teaches him about the world?
4. What is the main idea of the book?
5. Beekeeping is an unusual occupation. In what ways does it compare to the women who dive for abalone in *Sea Maidens of Japan*?

Make a Crossword Puzzle

Make up a crossword puzzle using the words: beekeeper, super, and hives. Find at least five other words in the story to use in your puzzle. Use a dictionary to help you define each word. When your puzzle is completed, make copies, and distribute it to your classmates.

from The Beekeepers' Story

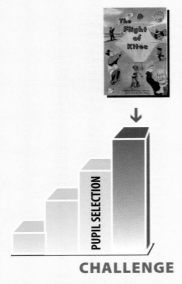

PUPIL SELECTION

CHALLENGE

Answers to Story Questions

1. A bird in flight or possibly a person's desire to fly like a bird.
2. First he flew (directed) his kite toward Canada. Then he tied a clothesline to the kite line. Finally, he guided the kite to the Canadian shore.
3. Any of the following: Art, craft skills, engineering, science, physics, aeronautics, history, language arts, poetry, writing, drama, mathematics, music, dance, choreography, weather, coordination, graceful movements, hand-eye-coordination.
4. Kites have played an important role in history. Some people make a decision to work at something they love to do, even if they don't make a lot of money.
5. Answers will vary.

Story Questions and Activity

1. What might have inspired the first kite to be made in the United States?
2. Explain, step by step, how Homan Walsh got his kite to Canada.
3. If a teacher wanted to use kites to help students learn, what subjects or skills might be included?
4. What is the main idea of the book?
5. In what ways are kite makers and flyers similar to the Japanese women who dive for abalone in the story, *Sea Maidens of Japan*?

A Kite for You

You will need:

8" x 11" sheet of paper, straw, stapler, scissors, string and drawing paper

Draw a dove on your sheet of paper. Then fold the paper as instructed, attach the straw with a stapler, and punch out your holes. Now attach a string and you're ready to fly your kite.

from The Flight of the Kites

Leveled Books

CHALLENGE

The Flight of Kites

☑ **Sequence of Events**
☑ **Instructional Vocabulary:** *cove, disgrace, driftwood, flails, host, sizzle*

Guided Reading

PREVIEW AND PREDICT Ask the students to look at the cover and table of contents and tell what this selection is about. Have students predict what information they might learn from this text.

SET PURPOSES Have students write what they want to find out about kites. For example, When was the first kite made? How do they fly?

READ THE BOOK Use questions like the following to guide students' reading before or after they have read the story independently.

Page 4: What did Homan do after he let out enough line? (He tied a clothesline to it.) What signal words does the author use on this page to help the reader keep track of the order the events took place? (after, on that day, later) *Sequence of Events*

Page 5: What is a cove? (a sheltered bay or inlet) Why would people fish in them? (Fish might stay there to keep out of the waves.) *Vocabulary*

Page 6: How does this author help the reader know in what order events took place on this page? (She uses dates and the word today.) *Sequence of Events*

Page 13: How do you think flying kites might keep a person young? (Possible answer: Kite flying is an enjoyable activity many people start when they are children.) *Drawing Conclusions*

Page 15: How do you think kiting built Captain Pamela Kirk's self-confidence? (Possible answer: Kiting requires many difficult flight skills such as navigation and precision.) *Drawing Conclusions*

RETURN TO PREDICTIONS AND PURPOSES Discuss students' predictions. Ask which were close to the information presented in the selection. Have students review their purposes for reading. Did they find out what they wanted to know?

LITERARY RESPONSE Discuss these questions:

• Have you ever flown a kite? What about it did you enjoy?

• What other activities might help "keep people young"?

Also see the story questions and activity in *The Flight of Kites*.

Activities
Anthology and Leveled Books

Connecting Texts

CONNECTING TEXTS Track the sequence of events. Write the selection titles on a four-column chart. Discuss with students the unusual occupations presented in each selection. Have students discuss the organization and the scope of the story. Call on volunteers from each reading level and write their comments on the chart.

Sea Maidens of Japan	Making Pipes are His Bag	The Bee-keepers' Story	The Flight of Kites
• Kiyomi is an ama. • The story is written in chronological order. • It tells of Kiyomi from the time she is a young girl to when she becomes a successful ama.	• Charley Kron makes and sells bagpipes • His lifelong interest in bagpipes is described in chronological order. • The article tells how to make bagpipes.	• The Solbergs are beekeepers. • The book describes one honey-gathering season. • It tells how honey is collected and made ready for sale.	• Kite making has a long tradition. • The book describes kites from past to present. • The book mentions kite enthusiasts today.

Viewing/Representing

GROUP PRESENTATIONS Divide the class into groups, one for each of the four books read in the lesson. (For *Sea Maidens of Japan*, combine students of different reading levels.) Have each group research and create a model of one of the items that are discussed in the selections, such as a beehive, a bagpipe, or a kite. Have eavch group present their project to the class.

AUDIENCE RESPONSE Ask students to pay attention to each group's model. Allow time for questions after each group presentation.

Research and Inquiry

MORE ABOUT OCCUPATIONS Have students think of an occupation that is of interest. Have them:

- find out what training or education is needed.
- find out what the job entails—its duties and responsibilities.
- locate biographies of people who have been successful in the occupation
- interview someone in the occupation

interNET CONNECTION Have students log on to **www.mhschool.com/reading** to find out more about careers.

Review Sequence of Events

Students will identify the sequence of events in a passage.

TEACHING TIP

MANAGEMENT You may want to assign a page of the story to each student during the Practice Activity. Remind students that they should use transitional words such as *first, then,* and *finally* to make the sequence of events easy to follow when the sentences are out of order.

PREPARE

Discuss Sequence of Events and Transitional Words

Review: The sequence of events is the order in which the action of a story takes place. Authors sometimes use transitional words to help readers identify the sequence. Ask students to give examples of some of the transitional words in the selection they just read.

TEACH

Read "The Star Turtle" and Model the Skill

Ask students to pay close attention to the sequence of events and the transitional words as you read **Teaching Chart 166** with them.

The Star Turtle

Each day, Kiyomi checked the eggs to make sure they were safe. Then, after two months, she saw the nest hatch. First, tiny flippers popped out of the shells. Then the heads and bodies emerged. Kiyomi watched as the tiny turtles headed toward the sea. One turtle, however, headed in the wrong direction. When Kiyomi saw this, she rushed to the turtle's aid. As she carried the turtle toward the water, she noticed a star shape on its back. She placed the star turtle near the water's edge. Soon, the turtle was carried out to sea. As she watched the waves, Kiyomi wondered if the turtle would survive.

Teaching Chart 166

Discuss the sequence of events and how the transitional words help signal the order of the story events.

MODEL The transitional words in this passage make the sequence of events easy to follow. For example, the word *then* in the fourth sentence tells me that the head and body of the turtles came out of the eggs after the flippers. I know not all stories will have so many transitional words. Then I'll have to look for other sequence clues.

PRACTICE

Identify Sequence of Events

PARTNERS

Have students circle the transitional words and list the sequence of events in "The Star Turtle." Then have students write the events from a page of *Sea Maidens of Japan* on sentence strips. Tell students to include transitional words in their sentences to signal the order of the action. Have them mix up their sentence strips and exchange them with partners. Partners must use the transitional words to put the strips in order. Have students discuss whether the transitional words helped them determine the order more easily. ▶ **Logical**

ASSESS/CLOSE

Arrange Events in Order

GROUP

Divide the class into small groups. Have each group write a paragraph that uses time words (such as *later that day* or *after the sun set*) to indicate the sequence of events. Have students copy each sentence of their paragraphs onto sentence strips and exchange them with another group. Students must try to put the strips in order using only context and clues from the time words.

ALTERNATE TEACHING STRATEGY

SEQUENCE OF EVENTS

For a different approach to teaching this skill, see page T66.

SELF-SELECTED Reading

Students may choose from the following titles.

ANTHOLOGY

• Sea Maidens of Japan

LEVELED BOOKS

• Making Pipes Is His Bag

• The Beekeeper's Story

• The Flight of Kites

Bibliography, pages T76–T77

Meeting Individual Needs for Comprehension

EASY	ON-LEVEL	CHALLENGE	LANGUAGE SUPPORT

EASY — Sequence of Events

Sequence of events is the order in which events happen. Recognizing the order of events will help you understand stories.

Read the list of what Kiyomi does in "Sea Maidens of Japan." Then put the list in the correct order. You may look back at the story for help.

Events
• She helps the baby sea turtle find the water.
• She celebrates her success around the fire with the other ama.
• Kiyomi dives wearing a rope.
• Kiyomi watches the sea turtles make nests and lay eggs.
• She dives bravely with the help of the sea turtle.
• She stays on the boat out of fear of deep water diving.

1. Kiyomi dives wearing a rope.
2. Kiyomi watches the sea turtles make nests and lay eggs.
3. She helps the baby sea turtle find the water.
4. She stays out of fear of deep water diving.
5. She dives bravely with the help of the sea turtle.
6. She celebrates her success around the fire with the other ama.

At Home: Have students write the sequence of events of their favorite story.

204 • Book 5/Unit 6 • Sea Maidens of Japan • 6

Reteach, 204

ON-LEVEL — Sequence of Events

Events in a story happen in a certain **sequence** or order. Below is a story chart listing events from "Sea Maidens of Japan." Number each event in the order in which it happened in the story.

Sequence	Event
10	Kiyomi smiles as a wave sweeps the grown sea turtle back to deeper waters.
1	Okaasan starts teaching Kiyomi to dive and fish along the coral reef.
4	Kiyomi cannot make herself jump from the boat on her first deep water dive with the ama.
8	Kiyomi finishes her first successful deep water dive with the ama.
2	Okaasan takes Kiyomi out at night to watch the sea turtles lay their eggs.
5	Kiyomi puts white cream on her face to protect it from the cold, salty water.
9	Kiyomi eats shellfish on an island beach with the other ama.
3	Kiyomi guides the confused baby sea turtle to the water.
7	Kiyomi recognizes the star on the grown sea turtle's back.
6	Kiyomi is afraid to jump into the deep water.

At Home: Have students explain where they would include the scene of Kiyomi pretending to host a tea ceremony for mermaids in this chart.

204 • Book 5/Unit 6 • Sea Maidens of Japan • 10

Practice, 204

CHALLENGE — Sequence of Events

Below are events from "Sea Maidens of Japan" that are listed out of order. Figure out the correct **sequence of events**. Then write the correct order of each event on the lines.

2 Kiyomi waits on the beach while her mother dives.
12 All day Kiyomi dives for abalone, then she sits with the sea maidens of Japan.
4 As Kiyomi watches, the sea turtles come out of the ocean and lay their eggs on the beach.
7 One baby turtle runs in the wrong direction, and Kiyomi guides it gently back to the sea.
9 Kiyomi is afraid to jump off the boat.
1 Kiyomi's mother tells her she will someday become an ama, a sea maiden of Japan.
5 Every day Kiyomi visits the nests of the sea turtles.
3 Okaasan wakes Kiyomi in the middle of the night to take her to the sea turtles.
8 After several fishing seasons pass, it is time for Kiyomi to make her first dive.
10 Kiyomi finally dives into the ocean.
6 After two full moons pass, the sea turtles hatch from their nests.
11 Kiyomi sees the star turtle, and it guides her back to the top of the water for air.

At Home: Write instructions on how to do something in the proper sequence such as making a sandwich or cooking spaghetti.

204 • Book 5/Unit 6 • Sea Maidens of Japan

Extend, 204

LANGUAGE SUPPORT — Learning to Dive

1. Write a word or words to describe each picture below. 2. Cut out the pictures. 3. Put them in order to show what happened.

brave — too young

learning — scared

222 Sea Maidens of Japan • Language Support/Blackline Master 00 • Grade 5

Language Support, 222

Students will determine cause and effect.

TEACHING TIP

INSTRUCTIONAL

Remind students that cause-and-effect relationships can often be determined by the author's use of clue words such as *because, since,* and *in order to.*

Review Cause and Effect

PREPARE

Discuss Cause and Effect

Explain: Looking for cause-and-effect relationships can help you to understand why things happen or to determine what might happen as the result of an event.

TEACH

Read the Passage and Model the Skill

Read **Teaching Chart 167** with students. Focus their attention on the cause-and-effect relationships as you read this passage.

Kiyomi Becomes an Ama

Kiyomi wants to be an ama, but she is afraid of the water. She worries that she will disgrace her mother. One summer, Kiyomi watches a nest of sea turtles hatch. She helps one turtle get to the water after it becomes confused by the light on the shore. After several years, it is time for Kiyomi to dive alone. During her first try, she becomes so frightened she cannot move. During the next day's dive, however, Kiyomi sees the sea turtle swimming. The turtle gives her the courage to jump into the water. She swims with the turtle and is no longer afraid. She has become an ama.

Teaching Chart 167

Ask volunteers to identify the cause-and-effect relationships in this passage. Have students underline the cause once and the effect twice.

MODEL Kiyomi helps the turtle into the ocean. What will be the effect of this action? As I read on, I find that Kiyomi sees the turtle again years later. The turtle has survived as a result of Kiyomi's action.

PRACTICE

Create a Cause and Effect Chart

GROUP

Have students create a Cause and Effect chart based on "Kiyomi Becomes an Ama." Give them one or two examples to help them get started. ▶ **Linguistic/Visual**

CAUSE	EFFECT
Kiyomi is afraid of the water.	She worries she may disgrace her mother.
A light is shining on shore.	The turtle becomes confused.
Kiyomi is afraid to dive.	She cannot move.
Kiyomi sees the turtle.	She jumps in the water.

ASSESS/CLOSE

Use a Chart to Show Cause-and-Effect Relationships

ONE

Have students create a Cause and Effect chart to show at least five cause-and-effect relationships from their own lives.

CAUSE	EFFECT
I study for tests.	I get good grades.
I practice my soccer skills.	I make the team.

ALTERNATE TEACHING STRATEGY

CAUSE AND EFFECT

For a different approach to teaching cause and effect, see page T64.

LOOKING AHEAD

Students will apply this skill as they read the next selection, *The Silent Lobby*.

Meeting Individual Needs for Comprehension

EASY

Context Clues

Some stories have unfamiliar words that are important to understanding the topic of the story. You can use **context clues**—the words and sentences near an unfamiliar word—to help you understand the unfamiliar word. Look for these types of context clues:

• Antonyms (words with opposite meanings) that tell what a word *doesn't* mean.
• Comparisons with words or ideas that are familiar to you, such as using synonyms (words with similar meanings).

Look at the box of definitions below. Then read the sentences using context clues to help you define the underlined word.

• a machine that can do human tasks
• equipment that can go under the water's surface
• air tanks carried on the back of a deep sea diver
• breathing tube for underwater swimming

1. Like a large straw, a <u>snorkel</u> brings air to a swimmer whose face is just under the water. breathing tube for underwater swimming

2. Do you use <u>submersibles</u> or only equipment that stays on the water's surface? equipment that can go under the waters surface

3. The <u>robot</u> in the factory was designed to help build new cars. a machine that can do human tasks

4. Divers carry scuba equipment to bring them air while diving underwater. air tanks carried on the back of a deep sea diver

At Home: Have students read sentences 1 and 2. Have them tell which clues helped them define the underlined word.

206   Book 5/Unit 6 Sea Maidens of Japan   4

Reteach, 205

ON-LEVEL

Cause and Effect

A **cause** is the reason why something happens. An **effect** is the result, or what happens. Many story events are connected through cause-and-effect relations.

What might happen as a result of each story event below? Write down the most likely effect of each cause. Answers will vary. Accept all well-reasoned responses. Possible answers are shown.

1. Sea turtles planted their eggs in the sand where the sun would keep the eggs warm. Volunteers then guarded the beach where the eggs were laid. They made sure no harm could come to the eggs.
   Effect: Sea turtles will hatch from the eggs.

2. Andrea would become forgetful after she played too many computer games. One night she decided to make a cake after she finished playing her favorite game. When she put the cake in the oven to bake, she forgot to set the timer.
   Effect: Andrea is going to forget about the cake baking in the oven; it's going to burn.

3. Julio has to quickly get to the school bus stop or he will miss the bus. On his way, he decides to stop at the newsstand for a quick look at one of his favorite magazines. He reads an entire article before he leaves.
   Effect: Julio is going to miss the school bus.

4. Jim is getting ready to run in a big race. Naturally, he is a little nervous. He even forgot to tie a double knot in his laces, the way his coach told him to. In the middle of the race, Jim suddenly feels the laces on one of his sneakers come free.
   Effect: Jim might trip over on his sneaker laces if he doesn't stop to tie his shoes.

5. It is the day before the last big spelling test of the year. Amanda decides that she would much rather fly her new kite than study for a test.
   Effect: Amanda is going to do poorly on the last big spelling test.

5   Book 5/Unit 6 Sea Maidens of Japan   At Home: Ask students to write several story events that show a cause-and-effect relationship.   205

Practice, 205

CHALLENGE

Context Clues

Read the paragraph. Write the meanings of the underlined words, using only the **context clues** from the paragraph to help you write your definitions.

There are seven <u>species</u> of sea turtles. They are similar in that the females lay their eggs on the beach, then return to the ocean. Most sea turtles are found in tropical and subtropical seas. An exception is the Atlantic ridley turtle, which is <u>restricted</u> to the Gulf of Mexico. Over thousands of years, sea turtles have <u>evolved</u> a streamlined <u>carapace</u>, or shell. They have <u>adapted</u> to their <u>aquatic</u> environments by developing special glands that remove salt from their bodies. Some sea turtles are <u>endangered</u> by being over-hunted by humans for their tortoise shells, hide, and oil. One sea turtle, the Indo-Pacific ridley, has been <u>exploited</u> for its leather and oil in such areas as the Pacific coast of Mexico.

Answers will vary, but should include an appropriate definition.

1. **species** class, breed, kind, category of animals
2. **restricted** confined to a certain area
3. **evolved** change over time
4. **carapace** the shell of a sea turtle
5. **adapting** become better suited to an environment
6. **aquatic** water, marine
7. **endangered** at risk, in danger
8. **exploited** used, taken advantage of

At Home: Choose three of the above words and use them in a sentence that shows their meaning.

206   Book 5/Unit 6 Sea Maidens of Japan

Extend, 205

LANGUAGE SUPPORT

Cause and Effect Match

1. Look at each picture below. 2. Read the sentence in each picture. 3. Find the cause of each, cut it out, and paste it in the box below the picture.

Kiyomi puts the baby turtle into the water	Kiyomi sits on the edge of the boat while the others are in the water
...because the baby turtle was lost.	...because Kiyomi is afraid of the deep water.

Kiyomi is underwater holding on to the sea turtle	Kiyomi sits around the fire with the other ama's
...because the sea turtle comes to Kiyomi's boat.	...because Kiyomi is now a brave ama.

...because the baby turtle was lost.   ...because Kiyomi is now a brave ama.

...because the sea turtle comes to Kiyomi's boat.   ...because Kiyomi is afraid of the deep water.

Grade 5   Language Support/Blackline Master 00 • Sea Maidens of Japan   223

Language Support, 223

697H

OBJECTIVES

Students will use context to determine the meaning of content-area and specialized vocabulary.

TEACHING TIP

INSTRUCTIONAL Give students the following tips for determining the meaning of an unfamiliar word: use context clues; use the meaning of a root word to infer the word's meaning; use illustrations or photos to confirm word meanings.

Review Context Clues

PREPARE

Discuss Using Context to Determine the Meanings

Remind students that they can often determine the meaning of an unfamiliar word by paying attention to nearby words, or the context in which it appears.

TEACH

Read the Passage and Model the Skill

Have students read the passage on **Teaching Chart 168.**

The Ama

The ama, Japanese fisherwomen who dive into deep water to collect shellfish such as abalone, do not use diving equipment. They learn to dive deep and hold their breath as they search the sea bottom for edible plants and animals such as awabi, sazae, and eganori. Many ama are taught to dive by their mothers, just as Kiyomi was taught by Okaasan. The tradition is often passed down for many generations.

Teaching Chart 168

Model using context clues to figure out the meaning of an unfamiliar word.

MODEL There are unfamiliar words related to Japanese culture in this passage. I can determine their meanings by paying attention to the context. The word *ama* is defined immediately after it is used. It means a Japanese woman who dives for shellfish.

Have students define *abalone* by using the context of the sentence in which it appears. Ask what they can infer from the words *such as* in this sentence. (Abalone is a type of shellfish.)

PRACTICE

Determine Meanings of Unfamiliar Words

PARTNERS

Have volunteers circle unfamiliar words in the passage and then underline the context clues that helps them determine the words' meanings. Have partners write definitions of the words based on the clues. Have pairs exchange, compare, and discuss the definitions. ▶ **Linguistic/Interpersonal**

ASSESS/CLOSE

Create and Use Context Clues

Have each student choose one of the words from the Pronunciation Guide included at the end of the story on page 692. Have students use the words in paragraphs including context clues that will help the reader determine the words' meanings. They may also want to draw pictures to go with their paragraphs.

Have students exchange paragraphs and write definitions of their partners' chosen words.

ALTERNATE TEACHING STRATEGY

CONTEXT CLUES

For a different approach to teaching context clues, see page T63.

Meeting Individual Needs for Vocabulary

EASY	ON-LEVEL	CHALLENGE	LANGUAGE SUPPORT

EASY

Context Clues

Some stories have unfamiliar words that are important to understanding the topic of the story. You can use **context clues**—the words and sentences near an unfamiliar word—to help you understand the unfamiliar word. Look for these types of context clues:

- Antonyms (words with opposite meanings) that tell what a word *doesn't* mean.
- Comparisons with words or ideas that are familiar to you, such as using synonyms (words with similar meanings).

Look at the box of definitions below. Then read the sentences using context clues to help you define the underlined word.

- a machine that can do human tasks
- equipment that can go under the water's surface
- air tanks carried on the back of a deep sea diver
- breathing tube for underwater swimming

1. Like a large straw, a snorkel brings air to a swimmer whose face is just under the water. _breathing tube for underwater swimming_

2. Do you use submersibles or only equipment that stays on the water's surface? _equipment that can go under the waters surface_

3. The robot in the factory was designed to help build new cars. _a machine that can do human tasks_

4. Divers carry scuba equipment to bring them air while diving underwater. _air tanks carried on the back of a deep sea diver_

At Home: Have students read sentences 1 and 2. Have them tell which clues helped them define the underlined word.

206 Book 5/Unit 6 Sea Maidens of Japan 4

ON-LEVEL

Context Clues

Context clues are words or sentences in a story that help you define unfamiliar words.

Read each passage below. Use context clues to help define the underlined word. Circle the letter of the correct meaning.

1. Many people eat abalone. Abalone live in shells. Some people call them shellfish, but abalone aren't any type fish.
An *abalone* must be similar to a ___b___
a. small plant   (b.) snail   c. sea shell

2. After high school, Sonny found a job at the local cannery. He ran one of the big noisy machines that fill cans with all sorts of food.
A *cannery* must be like a ___a___
(a.) factory   b. can of food   c. big loud, machine

3. My great-grandparents used to harvest seaweed along the shore. They used the plant for soup. Nowadays, kelp is used to make all sorts of things.
Kelp must be a kind of ___c___
a. shell   b. fish   (c.) seaweed

4. We had to use a crowbar to pry open the heavy metal door.
To *pry* something is to ___b___
a. hammer it into place   (b.) use force to open it   c. make a good try

5. Even though the rest of the class tried to muffle their laughter by putting their hands over their mouths, Suki could hear them laughing.
When people *muffle* their laughter they are trying to ___c___
a. make it sound louder   b. make it sound silly   (c.) hide the sound of it

At Home: Encourage students to demonstrate how they used context clues to figure out these unfamiliar words from "Sea Maidens of Japan."

206 Book 5/Unit 6 Sea Maidens of Japan 5

CHALLENGE

Context Clues

Read the paragraph. Write the meanings of the underlined words, using only the **context clues** from the paragraph to help you write your definitions.

There are seven species of sea turtles. They are similar in that the females lay their eggs on the beach, then return to the ocean. Most sea turtles are found in tropical and subtropical seas. An exception is the Atlantic ridley turtle, which is restricted to the Gulf of Mexico. Over thousands of years, sea turtles have evolved a streamlined carapace, or shell. They have adapted to their aquatic environments by developing special glands that remove salt from their bodies. Some sea turtles are endangered by being over-hunted by humans for their tortoise shells, hide, and oil. One sea turtle, the Indo-Pacific ridley, has been exploited for its leather and oil in such areas as the Pacific coast of Mexico.

Answers will vary, but should include an appropriate definition.

1. **species** _class, breed, kind, category of animals_
2. **restricted** _confined to a certain area_
3. **evolved** _change over time_
4. **carapace** _the shell of a sea turtle_
5. **adapting** _become better suited to an environment_
6. **aquatic** _water, marine_
7. **endangered** _at risk, in danger_
8. **exploited** _used, taken advantage of_

At Home: Choose three of the above words and use them in a sentence that shows their meaning.

206 Book 5/Unit 6 Sea Maidens of Japan

LANGUAGE SUPPORT

Kiyami's Letter

1. Use the words above to fill in the blanks in Kiyami's letter.

abalone	driftwood	cove	disgrace	turtles	ama

Dear Sisters,

I am learning to dive with the ___ama___. I work hard and do not want to ___disgrace___ Mother. I watch Mother dive from the shore of the special ___cove___. Soon I will hunt for ___abalone___ with the others. Today I found a piece of ___driftwood___ in the sand. Tonight, Mother and I are going to watch for sea ___turtles___. I hope you are well.

Love,
Kiyami

224 See Maidens of Japan • Language Support/Blackline Master 112 Grade 5

Reteach, 206   **Practice, 206**   **Extend, 206**   **Language Support, 224**

Writing a Story

**GRAMMAR/SPELLING
CONNECTIONS**

See the 5-Day Grammar and
Usage Plan on negatives, pages
697M–697N.

See the 5-Day Spelling Plan on
words with suffixes, pages
6970–697P.

TECHNOLOGY TIP

Have students create
a file just for first
drafts. Have them
save each first draft in this file
before they start editing and
revising. Students may want to
revisit their draft at a later date.

Prewrite

WRITE A SCENE   Present this writing
assignment: In *Sea Maidens of Japan,* most of
the action takes place between Kiyomi and
her mother. What happens between them
moves the story forward. Write a new scene
for these two characters.

FOCUSING QUESTIONS   Have students
use a Sequence of Events chart to organize
their ideas and answer the following questions:

- What do I know about Kiyomi and her
mother?
- What is going to happen in my scene?
- How will the scene end?

Kiyomi and her mother are close.

↓

My scene will show Kiyomi sharing her feelings with her mother.

↓

Graphic Organizer 17

Strategy: Dramatize Have students work in
pairs to improvise scenes between Kiyomi and
her mother. Students should take turns suggesting a situation. Have students improvise
at least two scenes before they begin writing.

Draft

USE THE DRAMATIZATION   Students
should use ideas from their graphic organizers
and dramatizations to write their scenes.
Remind students that the scene should unfold
logically, with one event leading to another,
and should have a beginning, middle, and end.

Revise

SELF-QUESTIONING   Ask students to assess
their drafts.

- Is my scene logical?
- Does one event lead to another?
- Are my characters realistic, based on what I
know about them from the story?
- Do I need to elaborate by adding details to
any of the events?

Edit/Proofread

CHECK FOR ERRORS   Students should
reread their scenes for content, logic, dialogue,
content, grammar, spelling, and punctuation.

Publish

SHARE THE SCENES   Have students perform their scenes for the class, and discuss
each one. Is it realistic? Is it logical? Is it based
on the characters and situations in the story?
Does it have a beginning, middle, and end?

A Scene from "Sea Maidens of Japan"

(A fishing boat. Kiyomi sits, staring into the water,
   frightened. Mama sits down next to her.)
Kiyomi: Mama, I'm scared. How can I be an "ama" if I'm
   afraid to jump into the water?
Mama: Everyone is afraid of the water at first. And I was
   frightened, just as you are.
Kiyomi: But you're not frightened anymore?
Mama: No. After you dive a few times you stop being
   frightened.
Kiyomi: Will I ever stop being frightened?
Mama: Would I make you do something that always
   frightened you?
Kiyomi: No, mama. You wouldn't. That makes me feel better.

Presentation Ideas

ACT OUT THE SCENE Have students act out their scenes in front of the class. Then have them suggest other ways to play the scene. Repeat the scene using the suggestions, and discuss the differences in each version. ▶ **Speaking/Listening**

MAKE PROPS Have students make props or scenery to enhance the production of their scenes. ▶ **Viewing/Representing**

Consider students' creative efforts, possibly adding a plus (+) for originality, wit, and imagination.

For a 6-point or an 8-point scale, see pages T105–T106.

Meeting Individual Needs for Writing

EASY	ON-LEVEL	CHALLENGE
Photographs Have students find pictures in magazines that depict unusual ways in which people find or capture food. Have the students write their own captions for the pictures.	**Letter** Have students write a letter from Kiyomi to one of her older sisters, describing her experiences on the night she became an ama.	**Dialogue** Have students write dialogue that takes place between Kiyomi and one or both of her sisters when they return to the village for a visit.

5 Day Grammar and Usage Plan

Write the following sentence on the board and read it aloud: *She didn't bring no paper.* Ask students why the sentence sounds awkward.

DAILY LANGUAGE ACTIVITIES

Have students correct the sentences orally, eliminating the double negative.

Day 1

1. Kiyomi wasn't no swimmer.
   (Kiyomi wasn't a swimmer.)
2. She couldn't go in no deep water.
   (She couldn't go in deep water.)
3. She didn't want to be no ama.
   (She didn't want to be an ama.)

Day 2

1. Kiyomi didn't want to go nowhere without the rope.
2. Kiyomi didn't see nobody.
3. There weren't really no mermaids.

Day 3

1. She didn't see turtles nowhere.
2. No turtles would never come.
3. She can't harm no turtles.

Day 4

1. The star turtle hadn't been in no water before.
2. She wasn't no swimming champ.
3. She didn't want no one to make her mom feel bad.

Day 5

1. Kiyomi wasn't scared no more.
2. She'd never be scared of no water again.
3. The ama never use no breathing apparatus.

Daily Language Transparency 28

697M *Sea Maidens of Japan*

DAY 1 Introduce the Concept

Oral Warm-Up Ask students which of these sentences sounds better: *I don't see nothing. I see nothing.*

Introduce Negatives Using more than one negative in a sentence is usually incorrect. Present:

> ### Avoiding Double Negatives
>
> - A negative is a word that means "no," such as *not, never, nobody, nowhere,* and contractions with *n't.*
> - Do not use two negatives in the same sentence.
> - You can fix a sentence with two negatives by removing one.

Ask students which sentence is correct: *I don't have no money. I have no money.* Then present the Daily Language Activity and have students correct orally.

 Assign the daily Writing Prompt on page 674C.

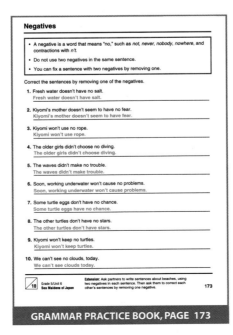

Negatives

- A negative is a word that means "no," such as *not, never, nobody, nowhere,* and contractions with *n't.*
- Do not use two negatives in the same sentence.
- You can fix a sentence with two negatives by removing one.

Correct the sentences by removing one of the negatives.

1. Fresh water doesn't have no salt.
   Fresh water doesn't have salt.
2. Kiyomi's mother doesn't seem to have no fear.
   Kiyomi's mother doesn't seem to have fear.
3. Kiyomi won't use no rope.
   Kiyomi won't use rope.
4. The older girls didn't choose no diving.
   The older girls didn't choose diving.
5. The waves didn't make no trouble.
   The waves didn't make trouble.
6. Soon, working underwater won't cause no problems.
   Soon, working underwater won't cause problems.
7. Some turtle eggs don't have no chance.
   Some turtle eggs have no chance.
8. The other turtles don't have no stars.
   The other turtles don't have stars.
9. Kiyomi won't keep no turtles.
   Kiyomi won't keep turtles.
10. We can't see no clouds, today.
    We can't see clouds today.

Extension: Ask partners to write sentences about beaches, using two negatives in each sentence. Then ask them to correct each other's sentences by removing one negative.

Grade 5/Unit 6
Sea Maidens of Japan   173

GRAMMAR PRACTICE BOOK, PAGE 173

DAY 2 Teach the Concept

Review Negatives Ask students to give examples of negatives.

More About Negatives Tell students that when a sentence has two negatives, they should correct it.

> - You can correct a sentence with two negatives by changing one negative to a positive word.

List on the board the following negatives and their corresponding positive words: *no/any; never/ever; nothing/anything; nobody/anybody; no one/anyone; nowhere/anywhere.*

Give this example: *Kiyomi didn't want no one to laugh at her. Kiyomi didn't want anyone to laugh at her.*

Use Negatives Present the Daily Language Activity. Then have the students use negatives in sentences.

 Assign the daily Writing Prompt on page 674C.

Negatives

- You can correct a sentence with two negatives by changing one negative to a positive word.

Negative	Positive
no	any
never	ever
nothing	anything
nobody	anybody
no one	anyone
nowhere	anywhere

Rewrite the sentences. Look for sentences with two negatives. Use a positive word in place of one of the negatives.

1. We never have no sea turtles where we live.
   We never have any sea turtles where we live.
2. Fish don't have lungs nowhere.
   Fish don't have lungs anywhere.
3. Flounders don't have no eyes on one side.
   Flounders don't have any eyes on one side.
4. The baby turtles didn't never hesitate.
   The baby turtles didn't ever hesitate.
5. Sharks won't eat none of these turtles.
   Sharks won't eat any of these turtles.
6. We didn't see whales nowhere.
   We didn't see whales anywhere.
7. The girl has never found no pearls.
   The girl has never found any pearls.
8. Kiyomi didn't have no problems diving.
   Kiyomi didn't have any probems diving.

Extension: Ask students to proofread recent writing assignments, looking for double negatives.

174   Grade 5/Unit 6
Sea Maidens of Japan   6

GRAMMAR PRACTICE BOOK, PAGE 174

Negatives

Learn from the Literature Review negatives. Read the last sentence on page 679 of *Sea Maidens of Japan*:

> They will **not** become ama, like Okaasan and me.

Ask students to identify the negative word. Ask students if more than one negative appears in this sentence.

Correct Double Negatives Present the Daily Language Activity and have students correct the sentences orally. Ask students to write sentences about themselves using two negatives. Have them exchange their papers and correct the sentences.

 WRITING Assign the daily Writing Prompt on page 674D.

Review Negatives Have students explain how double negatives should be corrected. Then present the Daily Language Activity for Day 4.

Mechanics and Usage Review:

Contractions and Apostrophes

- A contraction is a shortened form of two words.

- A contraction may be formed by combining a verb with the word *not*.

- An apostrophe (') shows where one or more letters have been left out.

List these on the board: *can't/cannot; don't/do not; doesn't/does not; didn't/did not; couldn't/could not; wouldn't/would not; shouldn't/should not.* Discuss which letters are replaced by apostrophes. Note the two letters left out in *can't*.

 WRITING Assign the daily Writing Prompt on page 674D.

Assess Use the Daily Language Activity and page 177 of the **Grammar Practice Book** for assessment.

Reteach Have one partner sketch a person engaged in an activity. Then have the other partner sketch the same person unable or not allowed to perform the activity. Have them exchange papers and write captions for the sketches. Tell them to use negative words and positive words where needed.

Have students create a word wall with the negative and positive words. Use page 178 of the **Grammar Practice Book** for additional reteaching.

 WRITING Assign the daily Writing Prompt on page 674D.

Negatives (Grammar Practice Book, page 175)

- A negative is a word that means "no," such as *not, never, nobody, nowhere,* and contractions with *n't*.
- Do not use two negatives in the same sentence.
- You can fix a sentence with two negatives by removing one.
- You can correct a sentence with two negatives by changing one negative to a positive word.

Read each group of sentences. Cross out the sentence that is incorrect.

1. The sea is never calm in this bay.
   The sea is not ever calm in this bay.
   ~~The sea is not never calm in this bay.~~
2. ~~The girl never dove for abalone with nobody.~~
   The girl never dove for abalone with anybody.
   The girl dove for abalone with nobody.
3. ~~There weren't never so many turtles before.~~
   There were never so many turtles here before.
   There weren't ever so many turtles before.
4. I don't see any good places to dive today.
   ~~I don't see no good places to dive today.~~
   I see no good places to dive today.

Read the sentences. Rewrite each one two different ways.

5. The sun don't never shine in these caves.
   The sun doesn't ever shine in these caves.
   The sun never shines in these caves.
6. There aren't no octopuses or abalone in the bay.
   There aren't any octopuses or abalone in the bay.
   There are no octopuses or abalone in the bay.
7. We didn't catch nothing today.
   We caught nothing today.
   We didn't catch anything today.
8. The turtles aren't nowhere near here today.
   The turtles aren't anywhere near here today.
   The turtles are nowhere near here today.

Extension: Ask students to write a poem about the sea turtle. Ask them to use three of the above contractions in their poems. Invite four negative sentences, using negatives correctly.

Grade 5/Unit 6
Sea Maidens of Japan 175

GRAMMAR PRACTICE BOOK, PAGE 175

Contractions and Apostrophes (Grammar Practice Book, page 176)

- A contraction is a shortened form of two words.
- A contraction may be formed by combining a verb with the word not.
- An apostrophe (') shows where one or more letters have been left out.

isn't	is not	doesn't	does not
aren't	are not	didn't	did not
wasn't	was not	couldn't	could not
can't	cannot	wouldn't	would not
don't	do not	shouldn't	should not

Rewrite each sentence correctly. Use a contraction for every underlined pair of words. Correct any double negatives.

1. I <u>do not</u> travel to Japan no more.
   I don't travel to Japan anymore.
2. There <u>are not</u> no turtle nests under those trees.
   There aren't any turtle nests under those trees.
3. Sea turtles <u>were not</u> protected until recently.
   Sea turtles weren't protected until recently.
4. You <u>should not</u> bother no turtles on the beach.
   You shouldn't bother any turtles on the beach.
5. We <u>could not</u> never swim the length of this bay.
   We couldn't ever swim the length of this bay.
6. The ama <u>is not</u> coming up for air yet.
   The ama isn't coming up for air yet.
7. <u>Does not</u> no one want to practice diving?
   Doesn't anyone want to practice diving?
8. My ancestors <u>did not</u> come from nowhere near Tokyo.
   My ancestors didn't come from anywhere near Tokyo.

Extension: Ask students to write a poem about the sea turtle. Ask them to use three of the above contractions in their poems. Invite students to read their poems aloud for the class.

176 Grade 5/Unit 6
Sea Maidens of Japan

GRAMMAR PRACTICE BOOK, PAGE 176

Negatives and Contractions (Grammar Practice Book, page 177)

A. If the sentence is correct, write correct on the line. If it is not correct, rewrite it correctly. Answers may vary.

1. Please don't bother no wild sea creatures.
   Please don't bother any wild sea creatures.

2. The sea isn't never so stormy as it was yesterday.
   The sea isn't ever so stormy as it was yesterday.

3. The job of an ama is not easy.
   correct

4. The ama must not do nothing but look for abalone.
   The ama must do nothing but look for abalone.

5. My sister isn't going to work as no ama no more.
   My sister isn't going to work as an ama anymore.

B. Write contractions for the following pairs of words.

6. can not   can't
7. does not   doesn't
8. should not   shouldn't
9. are not   aren't
10. could not   couldn't
11. would not   wouldn't
12. did not   didn't

Grade 5/Unit 6
Sea Maidens of Japan 177

GRAMMAR PRACTICE BOOK, PAGE 177

GRAMMAR PRACTICE BOOK, PAGE 178

5Day Spelling Plan

LANGUAGE SUPPORT

ESL To help students distinguish between the Spanish adverb suffix *-mente* and the English noun suffix *-ment*, write and read aloud sentences using the nouns *amusement, announcement*.

DICTATION SENTENCES

Spelling Words

1. She read a remarkable book.
2. Dawn at the lake was peaceful.
3. I waited countless hours.
4. Her foolishness got her in trouble.
5. We love the excitement of the parade.
6. He gave a reasonable answer.
7. Seals are graceful in the water.
8. He said the cut was painless.
9. I have a weakness for sweets.
10. Let's go to the amusement park.
11. Look respectable for your job interview.
12. The sun is harmful to skin.
13. I didn't follow his meaningless advice.
14. I like the softness of pure cotton.
15. Get treatment for your hurt knee.
16. It is honorable to tell the truth.
17. I tasted the flavorful soup.
18. The tiny mouse was defenseless.
19. Coffee can cause nervousness.
20. I read the announcement to the class.

Challenge Words

21. Unfair work practices are a disgrace.
22. She found driftwood on the beach.
23. The fish flails its tail.
24. They will host a party for her friends.
25. Listen to the oil sizzle in the pan.

DAY 1 Pretest

Assess Prior Knowledge Use the Dictation Sentences at the left and **Spelling Practice Book** page 173 for the pretest. Allow students to correct their own papers. Students who require a modified list may be tested on the first ten words.

Spelling Words		Challenge Words
1. remarkable	11. respectable	21. **disgrace**
2. peaceful	12. harmful	22. **driftwood**
3. countless	13. meaningless	23. **flails**
4. foolishness	14. softness	24. **host**
5. **excitement**	15. treatment	25. **sizzle**
6. reasonable	16. honorable	
7. **graceful**	17. **flavorful**	
8. painless	18. defenseless	
9. weakness	19. nervousness	
10. amusement	20. announcement	

*Note: Words in **dark type** are from the story.*

Word Study On page 174 of the **Spelling Practice Book** are word study steps and an at-home activity.

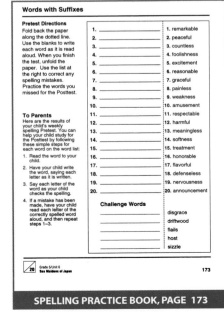

SPELLING PRACTICE BOOK, PAGE 173

WORD STUDY STEPS AND ACTIVITY, PAGE 174

DAY 2 Explore the Pattern

Sort and Spell Words Write the suffixes *-less, -ness, -able, -ful,* and *-ment* on the board. Ask students which suffixes create nouns and which create adjectives. Have them read the Spelling Words aloud and sort them as below.

Words with suffixes

-less	-able	-ment
countless	remarkable	excitement
painless	reasonable	amusement
meaningless	respectable	treatment
defenseless	honorable	announce-ment

-ness	-ful
foolishness	peaceful
weakness	graceful
softness	harmful
nervousness	flavorful

Word Wall Have students create a word wall based on the word sort and add more words from their reading.

SPELLING PRACTICE BOOK, PAGE 175

Words with Suffixes

Word Meaning: Suffixes Remind students that knowing the meanings of suffixes can help them define words. List the following: *-less* means "without"; *-ness* means "the state of being"; *-able* means "able to be" or "worthy of"; *-ful* means "full of"; *-ment* means "the act of" or "the state of being." Have students use the suffix definitions to define the Spelling Words.

If students need extra practice, have partners give each other a midweek test.

Glossary Remind students that a synonym is a word with the same or almost the same meaning as another word. Review where synonyms can be found in the Glossary. Have partners:

- look up each Challenge Word and find any synonyms.

- write the Challenge Word and its synonym. (flail/thrash)

Proofread Sentences Write these sentences on the chalkboard, including the misspelled words. Ask students to proofread, circling incorrect spellings and writing the correct spellings. There are two spelling errors in each sentence.

> Her nervessnous didn't show when she delivered her remarkible speech. (nervousness, remarkable)

> Scientists have spent countlass hours exploring a new treatment for the common cold. (countless, treatment)

Have students create additional sentences with errors for partners to correct.

 Have students use as many Spelling Words as possible in the daily Writing Prompt on page 674D. Remind students to proofread their writing for errors in spelling, grammar, and punctuation.

Assess Students' Knowledge Use page 178 of the **Spelling Practice Book** or the Dictation Sentences on page 697O for the posttest.

Personal Word List Encourage students to add troublesome lesson words to their personal lists of troublesome words in their journals. Have students note the meaning of the suffix and write a context sentence for each word.

Students should refer to their word lists during later writing activities.

Worksheet (left, page 176)

Words with Suffixes

remarkable	excitement	weakness	meaningless	flavorful
peaceful	reasonable	amusement	softness	defenseless
countless	graceful	respectable	treatment	nervousness
foolishness	painless	harmful	honorable	announcement

Complete each sentence below with a spelling word.

1. The president's visit caused ___excitement___ among the townspeople.
2. The soldier received an ___honorable___ discharge.
3. The captain will make an important ___announcement___ tonight.
4. Her determination to win the medal was ___remarkable___.
5. The car accident caused a ___weakness___ in her leg.
6. I felt quiet and ___peaceful___ sitting alone by the lake.
7. The poor mouse was ___defenseless___ against the hungry owl.
8. Overeating is ___harmful___ to your health.

Word Meanings: Suffixes
Write the spelling word for each meaning given below.

9. the state of being foolish ___foolishness___
10. something that amuses ___amusement___
11. full of flavor ___flavorful___
12. the state of being nervous ___nervousness___
13. without pain ___painless___
14. the act of treating ___treatment___
15. without meaning ___meaningless___
16. full of grace ___graceful___
17. worthy of respect ___respectable___
18. the state of being soft ___softness___
19. too many to be counted ___countless___
20. showing reason ___reasonable___

176 Challenge Extension: Write one sentence for each Challenge Word. Grade 5/Unit 6 Sea Maidens of Japan 20

SPELLING PRACTICE BOOK, PAGE 176

Worksheet (middle, page 177)

Words with Suffixes

Proofreading Activity
There are six spelling mistakes in the letter below. Circle the misspelled words. Write the words correctly on the lines below.

Dear Sister,

As I write this to you, I am filled with excitement. Mother took me to see the turtles hatch. It was night, and the beach was very peaceful. Then a remarkible thing happened. The countliss turtle babies hatched! Hundreds of tiny, defenceless turtles crawled awkwardly across the sand. Once they started to swim in the ocean, they were very graceful. I made friends with one turtle. I hope to see her again next year.

See you soon,

Kiyomi

1. ___excitement___   3. ___remarkable___   5. ___defenseless___
2. ___peaceful___   4. ___countless___   6. ___graceful___

Writing Activity
Have you ever had to overcome your fear of something? Write a brief paragraph about your experience, using four spelling words.

_____
_____
_____
_____

10 Grade 5/Unit 6 Sea Maidens of Japan 177

SPELLING PRACTICE BOOK, PAGE 177

Worksheet (right, page 178)

Words with Suffixes

Look at the words in each set below. One word in each set is spelled correctly. Use a pencil to fill in the circle next to the correct word. Before you begin, look at the sample sets of words. Sample A has been done for you. Do Sample B by yourself. When you are sure you know what to do, you may go on with the rest of the page.

Sample A:
- (A) pointess
- (B) poyntless
- (C) pointiss
- (D) pointless ●

Sample B:
- (A) usefull
- (B) usefule
- (C) useful
- (D) usseful

1.
- (A) remarcible
- (B) remarkable
- (C) remarkible
- (D) remarcable

2.
- (E) peceful
- (F) peacful
- (G) peacefull
- (H) peaceful

3.
- (A) countis
- (B) countiss
- (C) countless
- (D) countells

4.
- (E) foolishness
- (F) fulishness
- (G) foolishniss
- (H) foolishnes

5.
- (A) eksitement
- (B) exitment
- (C) exsitemint
- (D) excitement

6.
- (E) resonable
- (F) reasonable
- (G) reasinible
- (H) reasonible

7.
- (A) graceful
- (B) graceful
- (C) gracful
- (D) graseful

8.
- (E) paneless
- (F) painiss
- (G) painless
- (H) painles

9.
- (A) weakness
- (B) weakness
- (C) weakniss
- (D) wekeness

10.
- (E) amusement
- (F) amuzement
- (G) amusemint
- (H) amusemunt

11.
- (A) respectible
- (B) respectibble
- (C) respectable
- (D) respectuble

12.
- (E) harmful
- (F) humful
- (G) harmfell
- (H) harmful

13.
- (A) meaningliss
- (B) meaningless
- (C) meaningles
- (D) meaningliss

14.
- (E) sawfness
- (F) sofness
- (G) softness
- (H) softniss

15.
- (A) treatment
- (B) tretement
- (C) treatment
- (D) treatmant

16.
- (E) honorable
- (F) honirable
- (G) honarible
- (H) honerable

17.
- (A) flavrful
- (B) flavorfull
- (C) falvorful
- (D) flavurfull

18.
- (E) defensliss
- (F) defenseless
- (G) defencelss
- (H) defenseluss

19.
- (A) nervusniss
- (B) nervisness
- (C) nervousness
- (D) nervousnous

20.
- (E) annownment
- (F) announcement
- (G) announcemint
- (H) announcement

178 Grade 5/Unit 6 Sea Maidens of Japan 20

SPELLING PRACTICE BOOK, PAGE 178

The Silent Lobby

Selection Summary In this story, a boy and his father travel from Mississippi to Washington, D.C., to lobby Congress before it votes on an important civil rights issue.

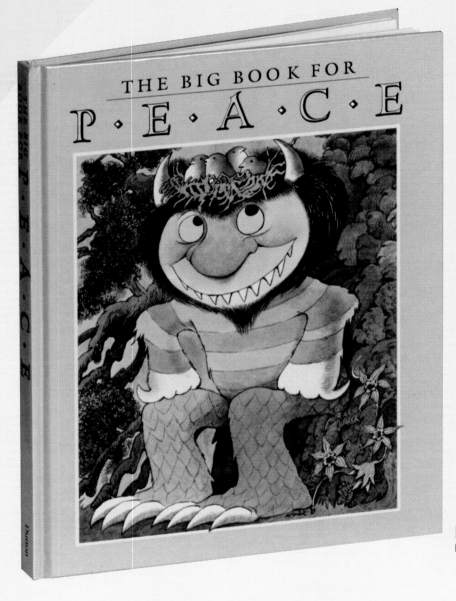

**Student
Listening
Library
Audiocassette**

INSTRUCTIONAL
Pages 700–713

About the Author A woman of many talents, Mildred Pitts Walter has been a teacher, a civil rights activist, and an award-winning children's author. These roles influence her story *The Silent Lobby*. Pitts Walter also travels for inspiration. Perhaps her most important journey was a trip to Africa, where she discovered that she wasn't simply "African" or "American," but a special blend of the two.

Resources for Meeting Individual Needs

LEVELED BOOKS

EASY
Pages 717A, 717D

INDEPENDENT
Pages 717B, 717D

CHALLENGE
Pages 717C, 717D

LEVELED PRACTICE

Reteach, 207–213

blackline masters with reteaching opportunities for each assessed skill

Practice, 207–213

workbook with Take-Home stories and practice opportunities for each assessed skill and story comprehension

Extend, 207–213

blackline masters that offer challenge activities for each assessed skill

ADDITIONAL RESOURCES

- **Language Support Book,** 225–232
- **Take-Home Story, Practice,** p. 208a
- **Alternative Teaching Strategies,** T60–T66

McGraw-Hill School
TECHNOLOGY

interNET CONNECTION Research and Inquiry Ideas. Visit *www.mhschool.com/reading*

Suggested Lesson Planner

 Available on CD-ROM

READING AND LANGUAGE ARTS	**DAY 1** *Focus on Reading and Skills*	**DAY 2** *Read the Literature*
● **Comprehension** ● **Vocabulary** ● **Phonics/Decoding** ● **Study Skills** ● **Listening, Speaking, Viewing, Representing**	**Read Aloud and Motivate,** 698E *Martin Luther King* **Develop Visual Literacy,** 698/699 ☑ **Review Judgments and Decisions,** 700A–700B 　**Teaching Chart 169** 　Reteach, Practice, Extend, 207	**Build Background,** 700C Develop Oral Language **Vocabulary,** 700D *interpret　　persuade　　shabby* *pelted　　　register　　soothing* **Teaching Chart 170** **Vocabulary Cards** Reteach, Practice, Extend, 208 **Read the Selection,** 700–713 　☑ Review Judgments and Decisions 　☑ Review Cause and Effect **Minilessons,** 703, 705, 707, 711 **Cultural Perspectives,** 704
● **Curriculum Connections**	**Link** Works of Art, 698/699	**Link** Social Studies, 700C
● **Writing**	**Writing Prompt:** Write a letter from Craig to his mother telling about the bus ride from Mississippi to Washington.	**Writing Prompt:** Write a newspaper account of observing the bus stalled in front of the Capitol. **Journal Writing,** 713 　Quick-Write
● **Grammar**	**Introduce the Concept: Prepositions,** 717M 　Daily Language Activity 　1. The bus drove _____ the bridge. over 　2. We waited _____ the street. across 　3. Papa looked _____ the engine. at **Grammar Practice Book,** 179	**Teach the Concept: Prepositions,** 717M 　Daily Language Activity 　1. Icy rain poured _____ a dark cloud. from 　2. Craig waited _____ the bus as Papa spoke _____ the man. for, to 　3. It arrived _____ the city _____ noon. in, at **Grammar Practice Book,** 180
● **Spelling**	**Pretest: Words with Suffixes,** 717O Spelling Practice Book, 179–180	**Explore the Patterns: Words with Suffixes,** 717O Spelling Practice Book, 181

Meeting Individual Needs

 = **Skill Assessed in Unit Test**

Read EVERY DAY

DAY 3 — Read the Literature

Rereading for Fluency, 712

Story Questions, 714
Reteach, Practice, Extend, 209

Story Activities, 715

Study Skill, 716
☑ Use an Outline
Teaching Chart 171
Reteach, Practice, Extend, 210

Test Power, 717

Read the Leveled Books
Guided Reading
Unstressed Syllables
☑ Review Judgments and Decisions
☑ Instructional Vocabulary

 Science, 706

Writing Prompt: Imagine that it has been one day since the bus left with your husband and son on it. Write a story describing what you did all day.

Writing Process: Write a Character Description, 717K
Prewrite, Draft

Review and Practice: Prepositions, 717N
Daily Language Activity
1. The doorman stood _____ the door.
   by
2. We wanted to get _____ the Capitol.
   near
3. He told us to go _____ the tunnel _____ the building. into, behind

Grammar Practice Book, 181

Practice and Extend: Words with Suffixes, 717P
Spelling Practice Book, 182

DAY 4 — Build Skills

Read **Read the Leveled Books and Self-Selected Books**

☑ **Review Judgments and Decisions,** 717E–717F
Teaching Chart 172
Reteach, Practice, Extend, 211
Language Support, 230

☑ **Review Drawing Conclusions,** 717G–717H
Teaching Chart 173
Reteach, Practice, Extend, 212
Language Support, 231

Math, 708

Writing Prompt: Write a poem about wanting to vote in 1965 in Mississippi.

Writing Process: Write a Character Description, 717K
Revise

Meeting Individual Needs for Writing, 717L
Grammar Practice Book, 182

Review and Practice: Prepositions, 717N
Daily Language Activity
1. We couldn't enter _____ passes.
   without
2. I sat _____ Papa _____ the gallery.
   with, at
3. Papa sat _____ the edge _____ his seat and looked _____ all the people. on, of, at

Proofread and Write: Words with Suffixes, 717P
Spelling Practice Book, 183

DAY 5 — Build Skills

Read **Read Self-Selected Books**

Vocabulary Strategy

☑ **Review Synonyms and Antonyms,** 717I–717J
Teaching Chart 00
Reteach, Practice, Extend, 213
Language Support, 232

Listening, Speaking, Viewing, Representing, 717L
Create a Metaphor
Illustrate Character

Minilessons, 703, 705, 707

Phonics Review
Unstressed Syllables, 711
Phonics Workbook

Social Studies, 710

Writing Prompt: Write a description of the bus ride home from Washington, D.C. Include descriptions of where the bus stopped and what the people did.

Writing Process: Write a Character Description, 717K
Edit/Proofread, Publish

Assess and Reteach: Prepositions, 717N
Daily Language Activity
1. This story was told _____ my father.
   by
2. He believed _____ freedom _____ all.
   in, for
3. Winning the right to vote was difficult _____ all _____ us. for, of

Grammar Practice Book, 183–184

Assess and Reteach: Words with Suffixes, 717P
Spelling Practice Book, 184

Read Aloud and Motivate

Martin Luther King
a poem by Aileen Fisher

Because he took a stand for
peace

and dreamed that he would
find

a way to spread equality

to all of humankind,

Because he hated violence

and fought with words, not
guns,

he won a timely victory

as one of freedom's sons;

Because he died for liberty,

the bells of history ring

to honor the accomplishments

of Martin Luther King.

Oral Comprehension

LISTENING AND SPEAKING Before you read aloud this poem that pays tribute to Martin Luther King, Jr., remind students to consider what they know about making judgments and decisions. When you have finished reading, ask: "What judgments did Martin Luther King make? What courses of action did he decide to take?"

 Ask students to select phrases from the poem that describe judgments and decisions, such as "took a stand for peace" or "fought with words, not guns." Supply magazines for students to use to create collages that depict the meanings expressed by these phrases. Have students paste the pictures together in creative ways, and title each collage with a phrase from the poem. ▶ **Visual/Spatial/Interpersonal**

Develop **Visual Literacy**

Anthology pages 698–699

Objective: Review Judgment and Decisions

VIEWING In his portrait of Martin Luther King, Jr., Thomas Blackshear has painted his subject in a very distinguished pose. Ask students if they think this is a realistic portrait. Encourage them to explain their reasons. Discuss the details that the artist chose to include in his picture. Ask students if they would have included other details from Dr. King's life if they had created this artwork.

Read the page with students, encouraging individual interpretations of the painting.

Ask students to make judgments and decisions about the portrait. For example:

• The people across the bottom of picture probably represent those millions who marched for Civil Rights in the 1950s and 1960s.

• The church window and Dr. King's hands suggest an attitude of thoughtfulness and prayer.

REPRESENTING Have students make a list of their heroes. Ask them to paint a portrait of one hero. Encourage students to include details that show why the person is heroic.

OBJECTIVES

Students will identify and analyze judgments and decisions made by story characters.

TEACHING TIP

INSTRUCTIONAL

Encourage students to list reasons for and against a particular decision.

Review Judgments and Decisions

PREPARE

Use Familiar Context

Invite students to recall stories in which the main characters had to make difficult decisions. How did they reach their decisions? What judgments led to these decisions?

TEACH

Define Judgments and Decisions

Tell students: Making judgments and decisions means thinking about all the possible choices to find the best one. Before you make a decision, you need to evaluate all the information.

The Dilemma

Elizabeth and her friend Becky were having a serious argument. Their parents had said that they could spend the whole summer together, either with Becky's father in Montana, or with Elizabeth's family at the beach. Elizabeth thought that the beach would be great. They could swim every day. But Becky wanted to go to Montana and see her father. There, they could ride horses every day. What should the girls do?

Teaching Chart 169

Read the Story and Model the Skill

Display **Teaching Chart 169.** Have students pay attention to clues about judgments and decisions.

MODEL Let's look at the words that show the judgments Elizabeth and Becky are making about their situation. Elizabeth thinks going to the beach would be great, because they could swim every day. So she decides that the beach would be better than Montana.

Identify Judgments and Decisions

Have student volunteers underline words on this chart that show judgments that Elizabeth and Becky make, and circle the words that show the decision that they face.

PRACTICE

Analyze the Choices

Using a Judgments and Decisions chart, have students record how the girls feel about the situation and what they might choose to do. Help students begin filling in the chart. ▶ **Logical/Intrapersonal**

JUDGMENTS	DECISIONS
If they go to the beach, the girls can swim in the ocean every day.	The beach is a better place to spend the summer.
In Montana Becky can see her father, and the girls can go horseback riding.	Montana is a better place to spend the summer.
They would rather be together in the summer than do what they each want apart.	Maybe they should spend part of the summer at the beach and part of it in Montana.

ASSESS/CLOSE

Make a Decision

Have students work in pairs, pretending to be Elizabeth and Becky. Have them discuss the situation, present their judgments about the summer, and see if they can come to a decision that will satisfy both of them. Encourage them to continue using the chart to record each student's argument.

Students will evaluate judgments and decisions when they read *The Silent Lobby* and the Leveled Books.

ALTERNATE TEACHING STRATEGY

JUDGMENTS AND DECISIONS

For a different approach to teaching this skill, see page 60.

Meeting Individual Needs for Comprehension

EASY	ON-LEVEL	CHALLENGE

EASY

Judgments and Decisions

Making **judgments** is the process of determining how you think and feel about ideas, actions, characters, or events. After you determine how you feel, you can make a **decision** as to whether you agree with the reasons behind the ideas, actions, character or events.

Read the paragraph. Then read the choices below the paragraph and write your decision as to which is the best choice. Explain your judgment by giving the reasons for your decisions.   Answers will vary but should be supported with reasons.

   Suppose you were on a school committee that decides what programs the school should have. When there isn't enough money to pay for every program your group decides which program to keep, and which to leave out.

• after-school classes in pottery, painting, and basket-making
• extra buses to bring students to school

1. **Decision:** Sample answer: Cut the after-school classes because they are
   extra. Keep the buses because students need to get to school.

• add additional desserts in the school cafeteria
• a training program to teach students how to use the Internet

2. **Decision:** Sample answer: Keep the training program for learning the Internet.
   Desserts aren't as important as learning how to use the Internet.

• more gym space so students can have room for other sports
• a teacher's aide so that students can have more playground time

3. **Decision:** Sample answer: Cut the additional gym space. Keep the teacher's
   aide so that students can get exercise both in and out of gym class.

• science program for students who like to make inventions
• program teaching students safety tips

4. **Decision:** Sample answer: Cut the safety program because kids can invent
   on their own time. Keep the science program because safety is important.

Book 5/Unit 6
The Silent Lobby
4

At Home: Have students think of two sets of choices and then make a judgment about which is more important.
207

ON-LEVEL

Judgments & Decisions

Before you make a **decision**, you consider the reasons for and against the decision. Read each situation below. List two reasons for or against each choice, and then make a **judgment** about what you should do. Write your final decision. Answers will vary. Possible answers are shown.

Suppose the following: You have a small collection of favorite books. One of your friends asks to borrow a book from your collection. When you notice your friend is holding a tattered magazine, you remember that last year this same friend borrowed a book, and it came back battered and worn. Although your friend apologized and even offered to replace the book, you said not to bother. Your friend has lent you his things in the past. Do you think you should lend this same friend a book this time?

Two reasons for lending your friend another book:

1. My friend has lent me things, so I will lend the book.

2. It's good to give friends second chances.

Two reasons against lending your friend another book:

3. The book my friend wants to borrow is one of my favorites.

4. My friend does not take good care of his things. The book might be ruined.

Final decision:

5. I lend my friend the book but explain that it is important to take care of the
   book.

Book 5/Unit 6
The Silent Lobby
5

At Home: Encourage students to discuss how they made their final decisions.
207

CHALLENGE

Judgments and Decisions

When you make a **judgment** about something, you need to evaluate, or judge, your choices. Then you can decide on the best course of action. Many of our lawmakers use judgments and **decisions** everyday as they consider which bills, or laws, they want to create and enact.

Suppose that the members of your local community have gotten together and proposed some new bills for your town. Read each situation below. Make a judgment as to the best decision for each one.

1. Your local library is open from Monday through Thursday from 9 A.M. to 9 P.M. and on Fridays and Saturdays from 9 A.M. to 5 P.M. A bill has been proposed to keep the local public library open on Fridays and Saturdays until 9 P.M. and on Sundays from 9 A.M. to 4 P.M. during the school year from September through June. The reason is to allow more time for students to use the library for their school work. Some local townspeople do not want to pay for the extra cost of running the library during these additional hours.

How would you vote on this bill? Give reasons for your decision.
Answers will vary. Students should back up their judgments with reasons for
their decisions.

2. A bill has been proposed to turn the old school field into a shopping center. Some people feel that the new shopping center will bring more business into town. Others feel that the field should be used for sports events and that the new shopping center will only increase traffic problems.

How would you vote on this bill? Give reasons for your decision.
Answers will vary. Students should explain the judgments they used to arrive at
their decisions.

Book 5/Unit 6
The Silent Lobby

At Home: Look in your local paper to find an example of a bill that was passed in your community. Do you agree with the decision?
207

Reteach, 207   Practice, 207   Extend, 207

Build Background

Social Studies

Anthology and Leveled Books

Evaluate Prior Knowledge

CONCEPT: VOTING Ask students to share their experiences with voting. Perhaps they have voted for class officers in the past. Or perhaps they voted in their families about family decisions.

GO VOTE Ask students what steps are involved when voting for a candidate or on an issue. Help them make a Sequence of Events chart to record the process.

▶ **Logical/Visual**

VOTING: SEQUENCE OF EVENTS

Register to vote.

⬇

Familiarize yourself with the candidates and the issues.

⬇

Find out what day to vote.

⬇

Find out where to vote.

⬇

Find out what time the polls open and close.

⬇

Bring your registration card to the polls and vote.

BEING HEARD Have each student pick an   issue or candidate he or she feels strongly about, such as who is the best singer or musical group or the best athlete. Have students write to persuade others to vote for their candidates or issues.

Develop Oral Language

CAMPAIGN POSTER Ask students to
ESL brainstorm a list of candidates and issues about which they feel strongly.

Write the list on the chalkboard. Encourage students to tell why the candidates or issues are so important.

Have each student pick one issue or candidate he or she feels strongly about. Using pasteboard and markers, have students create posters with words and pictures describing why people should vote for their candidates or issues.

Vocabulary

Key Words

1. Papa walked to the bus station as the heavy rain (pelted) him. 2. He wanted to (register) to vote. 3. While standing at the terminal, he noticed a woman in a thin, (shabby) coat. 4. She recognized him from the rally and wanted to (persuade) him against giving up. 5. The woman walked over to Papa and quietly spoke to him in a (soothing) voice. 6. "It can be difficult to (interpret) the meaning of the state constitution, but just do your best today," she said.

Teaching Chart 00

Definitions

pelted (p. 706) struck over and over with small hard things

register (p. 702) to have one's name placed on a list or record

shabby (p. 705) worn-out and faded

persuade (p. 706) to cause to do or believe something by pleading or giving reasons; convince

interpret (p. 703) to explain the meaning of

soothing (p. 700) quiet or calming

Vocabulary in Context

IDENTIFY VOCABULARY WORDS
Display **Teaching Chart 00** and read the passage with students. Have volunteers circle each vocabulary word and underline other words that are clues to its meaning.

DISCUSS MEANINGS
Ask questions like these to help clarify word meanings:

- How would it feel to get pelted by hail?
- Can you think of a time when a family member needed to register, other than to vote?
- Does an old and worn shirt look new or shabby?
- How do you persuade your parents to agree with you?
- Which is more soothing, a harp solo or a drum solo?
- Have you ever tried to interpret someone else's gestures?

Practice

DEMONSTRATE WORD MEANING
Have partners choose vocabulary cards from a pile and demonstrate each word meaning with pantomime, drawing, or verbal clues.

▶ **Kinesthetic/Linguistic**

Vocabulary Cards

USE WORDS IN CONTEXT

WRITING Have students write context sentences for each of the vocabulary words.

▶ **Linguistic**

SPELLING/VOCABULARY CONNECTIONS
See Spelling Challenge Words, pages 717O–717P.

ON-LEVEL

Judgments & Decisions

Before you make a **decision**, you consider the reasons for and against the decision. Read each situation below. List two reasons for or against each choice, and then make a **judgment** about what you should do. Write your final decision.
Answers will vary. Possible answers shown.
Suppose the following: You have a small collection of favorite books. One of your friends asks to borrow a book from your collection. When you notice your friend is holding a tattered magazine, you remember that last year this same friend borrowed a book, and it came back battered and worn. Although your friend apologized and even offered to replace the book, you said not to bother. Your friend has lent you his things in the past. Do you think you should lend this same friend a book this time?

Two reasons for lending your friend another book:

1. My friend has lent me things, so I will lend the book.
2. It's good to give friends second chances.

Two reasons against lending your friend another book:

3. The book my friend wants to borrow is one of my favorites.
4. My friend does not take good care of his things. The book might be ruined.

Final decision:

5. I lend my friend the book but explain that it is important to take care of the book.

Book 5/Unit 6
The Silent Lobby   At Home: Encourage students to discuss how they made their final decisions.   207

Take-Home Story 207a
Reteach 207
Practice 207 • Extend 207

Guided Instruction

Preview and Predict

Have students read the title and preview the story, looking for pictures that give strong clues about the setting and characters.

- Who will be the main character in this story?

- What is this story probably about?

- Will the story be a realistic one or a fantasy? How can you tell? (Realistic, perhaps even historical, because the people in the illustrations seem to be doing things that real people might do.) *Genre*

Have students make a Predictions chart to record their predictions about the story.

PREDICTIONS	WHAT HAPPENED
I think this story will be about a trip.	
I think the boy will play an important part in the story.	

Set Purposes

What do students want to find out by reading the story? For example:

- Where are these people going?

- What part does the boy play in the story?

The old bus chugged along the Mississippi highway toward Washington, D.C. I shivered from icy winds and from excitement and fear. Excitement about going to Washington and fear that the old bus would stall again on the dark, lonely, icy road and we'd never make it.

Oh, just to sleep. The chug-chug-chugging of the old motor was not smooth enough to make soothing sounds, and I could not forget the words Mama and Papa had said just before me and Papa left to pick up twenty other people who filled the bus.

"It's too dangerous," Mama had said. "They just might bomb that bus."

"They could bomb this house for that matter," Papa said.

700

Meeting Individual Needs · Grouping Suggestions for Strategic Reading

EASY	ON-LEVEL	CHALLENGE
Read Together Read the story with students or have them use the **Listening Library Audiocassette.** Have students use the Judgments and Decisions chart to record important information about judgments and decisions. Guided Instruction and Intervention prompts offer additional help with vocabulary and comprehension.	**Guided Reading** Read the story words listed on page 701. You may wish to have the students read or listen to the audiocassette on their own first. Then read the selection with students, using the Guided Instruction prompts. Notice any difficulties students have when reading and emphasize those parts of the Guided Instruction.	**Read Independently** Have students set purposes before they read. Remind them that identifying the judgments and decisions characters face will help them understand the story. Have students set up a Judgments and Decisions chart as on page 706. After reading, they can use their charts to summarize the story.

"I know," Mama went on. "That's why I don't want you to go. Why can't you just forget about this voting business and let us live in peace?"

"There can be no peace without freedom," Papa said. **(2)**

"And you think someone is going to give you freedom?" Mama asked with heat in her voice. "Instead of going to Washington, you should be getting a gun to protect us."

"There are ways to win a struggle without bombs and guns. I'm going to Washington and Craig is going with me."

"Craig is too young."

"He's eleven. That's old enough to know what this is all about," Papa insisted.

701

Guided Instruction

☑ **Judgments and Decisions**
☑ **Cause and Effect**

Strategic Reading Before we begin reading, let's prepare Judgments and Decisions charts. We can write story notes in our charts to help us understand the story.

(1) **CAUSE AND EFFECT** What keeps the main character awake on the bus? (The motor of the bus is not smooth enough to lull him to sleep, and he cannot forget his mother's concerns.)

(2) **JUDGMENTS AND DECISIONS** Craig's mother and father have made different judgments about the bus trip. How does Mama feel about it? What does Papa think?

MODEL I think Craig's mother is afraid of the risks because she says the trip is dangerous. I think Craig's father is putting his fears aside so he can focus on how important it is to have the freedom to vote.

Story Words

The words below may be unfamiliar. Have students check their meanings and pronunciations in the Glossary beginning on page 73.

- petitions, p. 703
- legislators, p. 706
- credentials, p. 709

LANGUAGE SUPPORT

A blackline master of the chart used in this story can be found in the **Language Support Book.**

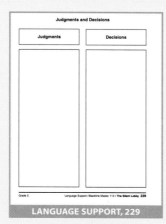

Judgments and Decisions

Judgments	Decisions

Grade 5   Language Support / Blackline Master 113 • **The Silent Lobby 229**

Guided Instruction

③ JUDGMENTS AND DECISIONS We need two volunteers to role-play Mama and Papa as they discuss the bus trip to Washington. Talk about the reasons why Papa and Craig should or should not go on the bus trip. Show us how you came to your final decision. *Role-Play*

HOMOPHONES Find the word *poll* on page 703. What other words sound like *poll*?

TEACHING TIP

INSTRUCTIONAL Refer to a classroom map to remind students of the distance from Mississippi to Washington, D.C. Have students use a distance key to determine the mileage between the two regions and estimate driving time.

Fluency

READ DIALOGUE Encourage students to think about the difference between reading dialogue and the rest of the text in a story. Suggest that students read page 703 in pairs, one reading just the dialogue and the other reading the rest of the text. Remind students to focus on

- speaking with feeling.
- pausing slightly at each comma.
- pausing longer at periods.

For more practice, have students reread the passage, switching parts.

---

 knew. It had all started two years ago, in 1963. Papa was getting ready to go into town to register to vote. Just as he was leaving, Mr. Clem, Papa's boss, came and warned Papa that he should not try to register.

"I intend to register," Papa said.

"If you do, I'll have to fire you." Mr. Clem drove away in a cloud of dust.

"You ought not go," Mama said, alarmed. "You know that people have been arrested and beaten for going down there." ③

"I'm going," Papa insisted.

"Let me go with you, Papa." I was scared, too, and wanted to be with him if he needed help.

"No, you stay and look after your mama and the house till I get back."

Day turned to night, and Papa had not returned. Mama paced the floor. Was Papa in jail? Had he been beaten?

702

PREVENTION/INTERVENTION

HOMOPHONES Write the word *poll* from page 703 on the chalkboard. Ask students if they can think of another word that sounds the same as *poll* but is spelled differently. (pole) What is the meaning of *pole*? (a long, thin piece of metal or wood such as a flagpole; opposite ends such as the North Pole and the South Pole) Point out that these are not the same meanings as *poll* on page 703. Have students use a dictionary and context clues to define *poll* as it is used in the sentence. (a place where people go to vote in an election)

We waited, afraid. Finally, I said, "Mama, I'll go find him."

"Oh, no!" she cried. Her fear scared me more, and I felt angry because I couldn't do anything.

At last we heard Papa's footsteps. The look on his face let us know right away that something was mighty wrong.

"What happened, Sylvester?" Mama asked.

"I paid the poll tax, passed the literacy test, but I didn't interpret the state constitution the way they wanted. So they wouldn't register me."

Feeling a sense of sad relief, I said, "Now you won't lose your job."

"Oh, but I will. I tried to register."

Even losing his job didn't stop Papa from wanting to vote. One day he heard about Mrs. Fannie Lou Hamer and the Mississippi Freedom Democratic Party. The Freedom Party registered people without charging a poll tax, without a literacy test, and without people having to tell what the Mississippi Constitution was about.

On election day in 1964, Papa proudly voted for Mrs. Hamer, Mrs. Victoria Grey, and Mrs. Annie Devine to represent the people of the Second Congressional District of Mississippi. Eighty-three thousand other black men and women voted that day, too. Great victory celebrations were held in homes and churches. But the Governor of Mississippi, Paul B. Johnson, declared all of those eighty-three thousand votes of black people illegal. He gave certificates of election to three white men—William Colmer, John Williams, and a Mr. Whittier—to represent the mostly black Second Congressional District.

Members of the Freedom Party were like Papa—they didn't give up. They got busy when the governor threw out their votes. Lawyers from all over the country came to help. People signed affidavits saying that when they tried to register they lost their jobs, they were beaten, and their homes were burned and churches bombed. More than ten thousand people signed petitions to the governor asking him to count their votes. There was never a word from the governor.

703

Guided Instruction

4 **JUDGMENTS AND DECISIONS** Papa lost his job because he tried to register. Do you think this event supports Mama's judgment about registering? (Sample answers: Yes; without Papa's job, the family could suffer. No; freedom is more important than a job.)

5 **CAUSE AND EFFECT** Why do you think the people at the polls wouldn't let Papa register to vote?

MODEL I think the reason Papa wasn't allowed to vote was because he was African American. When he joined the Freedom Party, he voted with eighty-three thousand other African American men and women who had never voted before. I think that at that time African Americans weren't allowed to vote.

Minilesson
REVIEW
Context Clues

Remind students that readers often look at the words around an unfamiliar word to try and understand its meaning. Sometimes there are clues in the text that help students learn new words. Point out the word *affidavits* on page 703 and ask students if they can determine its meaning.

Activity Encourage students to write down unfamiliar words in the story. Have them use context clues to determine meanings. Let students look up the words in the dictionary to see if their definitions were correct.

LANGUAGE SUPPORT

ESL Some students might be confused by the phrase "mighty wrong." Although pairing the words "mighty" and "wrong" might seem strange, it's a colorful way to say "very wrong." Explain that in American English we sometimes use phrases like this for emphasis. Have partners list similar expressions. (*pretty ugly* and *super dull*)

Guided Instruction

6 The policeman is impatient and yells at Papa. Keeping in mind the setting, especially the time of the story, can you tell why this is? (The story takes place during the mid-1960s when racial tension was common.) *Character, Setting*

My mind returned to the sound of the old bus slowly grinding along. Suddenly the bus stopped. Not again! We'd never make it now. Papa got out in the cold wind and icy drizzling rain and raised the hood. While he worked, we sang and clapped our hands to keep warm. I could hear Sister Phyllis praying with all her might for our safety. After a while we were moving along again.

I must have finally fallen asleep, for a policeman's voice woke me. "You can't stop here near the Capitol," he shouted.

"Our bus won't go," Papa said.

"If you made it from Mississippi all the way to D.C., you'll make it from here," the policeman barked.

At first the loud voice frightened me. Then, wide awake, sensing the policeman's impatience, I wondered why Papa didn't let him know that we would go as soon as the motor started. But Papa, knowing that old bus, said nothing. He stepped on the starter. The old motor growled and died. Again the policeman shouted, "I said get out of here."

704

CULTURAL PERSPECTIVES

GET OUT THE VOTE In 1963, it was difficult for African Americans to vote. What voting difficulties do people in other countries face? Encourage students to discuss what they know about how people in other countries vote.

RESEARCH AND INQUIRY Have students work in pairs to research how registration and voting take place in other countries. Have each pair choose a different country to report on.

*inter*NET **CONNECTION** Students can learn about voting in other nations by visiting **www.mhschool.com/reading**

"We'll have to push it," Papa said.

Everyone got off the bus and pushed. Passersby stopped and stared. Finally we were safe on a side street, away from the Capitol with a crowd gathered around us.

"You mean they came all the way from Mississippi in that?" someone in the crowd asked.

Suddenly the old bus looked shabby. I lowered my head and became aware of my clothes: my faded coat too small; my cotton pants too thin. With a feeling of shame, I wished those people would go away.

"What brings you all to the District?" a man called to us.

"We've come to see about seating the people we voted for and elected," Papa answered. "Down home they say our votes don't count, and up here they've gone ahead and seated men who don't represent us. We've come to talk about that."

"So you've come to lobby," a woman shouted. The crowd laughed.

Why were they laughing? I knew that to lobby meant to try to get someone to decide for or against something. Yes, that was

705

Guided Instruction

7 How does Craig feel about himself and the people he's with? (He is ashamed because they looked poor and shabby.) **What caused Craig to feel this way?** (Someone in the crowd made a negative remark about the bus.) *Draw Conclusions*

8 **CAUSE AND EFFECT** What caused the crowd to laugh? (They didn't feel Papa and the others were worthy enough to make a difference.)

CONTEXT CLUES Sometimes when there are unfamiliar words in a story the author will give a definition in the text. Let's see how the author helps us understand the meaning of the word *lobby*.

PREVENTION/INTERVENTION

CONTEXT CLUES Remind students that writers often give clues to the meaning of unfamiliar words in the text. Have a volunteer read the last two paragraphs on page 705. Ask students to identify the phrase which defines the word *lobby*.

Minilesson

REVIEW

Main Idea

Remind students that the main idea is what a passage or story is about. Details in the story support or explain that idea. Ask students to identify the main idea of page 705.

Activity Have each student write a short paragraph. Working in pairs, have the students switch paragraphs and see if their partners can identify the main idea.

Guided Instruction

⑨ JUDGMENTS AND DECISIONS
Should Papa and the others stay in the cold and keep trying even though they're too late to lobby, or should they turn around and go home? What decision do you think they will make? Let's add our answers to our chart.

JUDGMENTS	DECISIONS
Mama thinks it's too dangerous for Papa to register to vote.	She tells Papa not to go.
Papa thinks that the freedom to vote is very important.	Papa registers to vote.
Craig, Papa, and the people on the bus are too late to lobby.	They will decide to stay and keep trying.

⑩ CAUSE AND EFFECT What caused the crowd to leave? (Rain began to fall.)

why we had come. I wished I could have said to those people who stood gawking at us that the suffering that brought us here was surely nothing to laugh about.

The laughter from the crowd quieted when another woman shouted, "You're too late to lobby. The House of Representatives will vote on that issue this morning."

⑨ Too late. That's what had worried me when the old bus kept breaking down. Had we come so far in this cold for nothing? Was it really too late to talk to members of the House of Representatives to persuade them to seat our representatives elected by the Freedom Party, *not* the ones chosen by the governor?

⑩ Just then rain began to fall. The crowd quickly left, and we climbed onto our bus. Papa and the others started to talk. What would we do now? Finally, Papa said, "We can't turn back now. We've done too much and come too far."

After more talk we all agreed that we must try to do what we had come to do. Icy rain pelted us as we rushed against cold wind back to the Capitol.

A doorman stopped us on the steps. "May I have your passes?"

"We don't have any," Papa replied.

"Sorry, you have to have passes for seats in the gallery." The doorman blocked the way.

"We're cold in this rain. Let us in," Sister Phyllis cried.

"Maybe we should just go on back home," someone suggested.

"Yes. We can't talk to the legislators now, anyway," another woman said impatiently.

"No," Papa said. "We must stay if we do no more than let them see that we have come all this way."

"But we're getting soaking wet. We can't stand out here much longer," another protested.

"Can't you just let us in out of this cold?" Papa pleaded with the doorman.

706

Activity

Cross Curricular: Science

CLIMATE Did the people from Mississippi expect the rain they encountered in Washington, D.C.? Encourage students to discuss the differences in climate in different parts of the country.

RESEARCH AND INQUIRY Have students research and chart the differences in the climates of four states.

▶ **Interpersonal/Logical**

 Students can learn more about weather patterns by visiting **www.mhschool.com/reading**

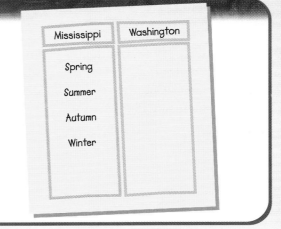

Mississippi	Washington
Spring	
Summer	
Autumn	
Winter	

"Not without passes." The doorman still blocked the way. Then he said, "There's a tunnel underneath this building. You can go there to get out of the rain."

We crowded into the tunnel and lined up along the sides. My chilled body and hands came to life pressed against the warm walls. Then footsteps and voices echoed through the tunnel. Police. This tunnel . . . a trap! Would they do something to us for trying to get in without passes? I wanted to cry out to Papa, but I could not speak.

The footsteps came closer. Then many people began to walk by. When they came upon us, they suddenly stopped talking. Only the sound of their feet echoed in the tunnel. Where had they come from? What did they do? "Who are they, Papa?" I whispered.

"Congressmen and women." Papa spoke so softly, I hardly heard him, even in the silence.

They wore warm coats, some trimmed with fur. Their shoes gleamed. Some of them frowned at us. Others glared. Some sighed quickly as they walked by. Others looked at us, then turned their eyes to their shoes. I could tell by a sudden lift of the head and a certain look that some were surprised and scared. And there were a few whose friendly smiles seemed to say, Right on!

I glanced at Papa. How poor he and our friends looked beside those well-dressed people. Their clothes were damp, threadbare, and wrinkled; their shoes were worn and mud stained. But they all stood straight and tall.

My heart pounded. I wanted to call out to those men and women, "Count my papa's vote! Let my people help make laws, too." But I didn't dare speak in that silence.

Could they hear my heart beating? Did they know what was on my mind? "Lord," I prayed, "let them hear us in this silence."

707

Guided Instruction

11 What conclusion does Craig make about the tunnel? (The tunnel is a trap to punish them for trying to enter the building without passes.) *Draw Conclusions*

12 **JUDGMENTS AND DECISIONS** Look at how the author describes the people walking by in the tunnel. Let's have three volunteers act out the attitudes of some of the people who walk by. *Pantomime*

Minilesson

REVIEW

Make Inferences

Remind students that when the author does not state something directly, the reader must make inferences. Point out that the author does not explain why the doorman tells the group about the tunnel on page 707. Encourage students to infer the doorman's reason for telling them.

Activity Have students write a few sentences about an inference they made while reading this story and explain why they made it.

Guided Instruction

13 **CAUSE AND EFFECT** Why do you suppose Congressman Ryan and the others worked late into the night? (They needed to get as many votes as possible, especially since Papa and the others were late and could not help them lobby.)

TEACHING TIP

INSTRUCTIONAL Make sure students understand the process of lobbying. Explain that lobbyists try to persuade public officials to agree with their ideas. Tell students that lobbying does not have to happen at a particular place or time of day.

Then two congressmen stopped in front of Papa. I was frightened until I saw smiles on their faces.

"I'm Congressman Ryan from New York," one of them said. Then he introduced a black man: "This is Congressman Hawkins from California."

"I'm Sylvester Saunders. We are here from Mississippi," Papa said.

"We expected you much earlier," Congressman Ryan said.

"Our old bus and bad weather delayed us," Papa explained.

"That's unfortunate. You could've helped us a lot. We worked late into the night lobbying to get votes on your side. But maybe I should say on *our* side." Mr. Ryan smiled.

"And we didn't do very well," Congressman Hawkins said.

"We'll be lucky if we get fifty votes on our side today," Congressman Ryan informed us. "Maybe you would like to come in and see us at work."

"We don't have passes," I said, surprised at my voice.

"We'll see about getting all of you in," Congressman Hawkins promised.

708

Cross Curricular: Math

COUNTING THE VOTES There are 435 representatives and 100 senators in the United States Congress. Have students figure out how many votes are needed to make a majority in each house. Then have them calculate how many votes are needed for a two-thirds majority to override a presidential veto.

Have students make one circle graph for each chamber in Congress, showing the number of votes needed to make a simple majority and the number needed for a two-thirds majority.

▶ **Mathematical/Visual**

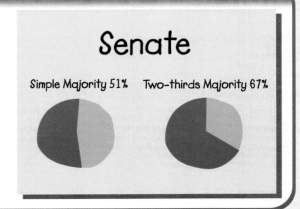

Senate

Simple Majority 51%   Two-thirds Majority 67%

Alittle later, as we found seats in the gallery, Congressman Gerald Ford from the state of Michigan was speaking. He did not want Mrs. Hamer and other fairly elected members of the Freedom Party seated in the House. He asked his fellow congressmen to stick to the rule of letting only those with credentials from their states be seated in Congress. The new civil rights act would, in time, undo wrongs done to black Americans. But for now, Congress should let the men chosen by Governor Johnson keep their seats and get on with other business.

Then Congressman Ryan rose to speak. How could Congress stick to rules that denied blacks their right to vote in the state of Mississippi? The rule of letting only those with credentials from a segregated state have seats in the House could not *justly* apply here. **(14)**

I looked down on those men and few women and wondered if they were listening. Did they know about the petitions? I remembered what Congressman Ryan had said: "We'll be lucky if we get fifty. . . ." Only 50 out of 435 elected to the House.

Finally the time came for Congress to vote. Those who wanted to seat Mrs. Hamer and members of the Freedom Democratic Party were to say, yes. Those who didn't want to seat Mrs. Hamer were to say, no.

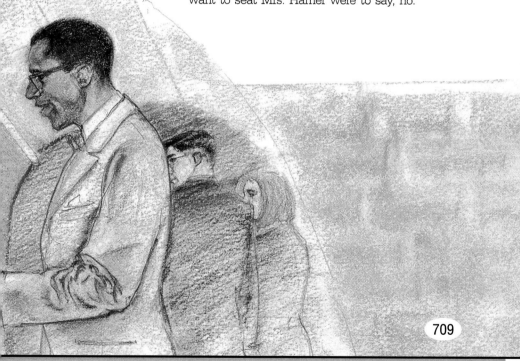

709

Guided Instruction

(14) **JUDGMENTS AND DECISIONS** What decision does Congressman Ryan hope the House will make? Let's add this information to our charts.

JUDGMENTS	DECISIONS
Mama thinks it's too dangerous for Papa to register to vote.	She tells Papa not to go.
Papa thinks that the freedom to vote is very important.	Papa registers to vote.
Craig, Papa, and the people on the bus are too late to lobby.	They will decide to stay and keep trying.
The rules that denied representation to blacks are unfair.	The people who were elected by the majority of voters should be seated in Congress.

(p/i) **WORD STRUCTURE/MULTIPLE-MEANING WORDS** Look at the word *justly* in the second paragraph. What do you think it means?

Ⓢ ELF-MONITORING

STRATEGY

REREAD Rereading a part of the story can help you understand what judgments and decisions a character faces.

(p/i) PREVENTION/INTERVENTION

WORD STRUCTURE/MULTIPLE-MEANING WORDS Write *justly* on the chalkboard. Ask a volunteer to circle the suffix and then tell what part of speech the word is. (adverb) Point out that the word *justly* has been italicized for emphasis. Many students may not be aware that the base word *just* has a meaning other than *only*. Discuss how *just* can also mean *fair*. Explain that the word *justice* is related to this meaning of *just*. Then guide students to see that *justly* means *in a fair way*.

Guided Instruction

(15) **CAUSE AND EFFECT** Why do you think so many congressmen and congresswomen voted for Democratic Freedom Party representatives? (Sample answer: Members of Congress were moved by seeing the people in the tunnel.)

At every yes vote I could hardly keep from clapping my hands and shouting, "Yea! Yea!" But I kept quiet, counting: thirty, then forty, forty-eight . . . only two more. We would lose badly.

Then something strange happened. Congressmen and congresswomen kept saying "Yes. Yes. Yes." On and on, "Yes." My heart pounded. Could we win? I sat on my hands to keep from clapping. I looked at Papa and the others who had come with us. They all sat on the edge of their seats. They looked as if they could hardly keep from shouting out, too, as more yes votes rang from the floor.

When the voting was over, 148 votes had been cast in our favor. What had happened? Why had so many changed their minds?

(15)

710

Cross Curricular: Social Studies

VOTING RIGHTS Registering to vote today is different from Papa's experience.

- Have students find out the requirements for voting in the United States.
- Help them compare registering to vote today with Papa's experience when he tried to register.

RESEARCH AND INQUIRY Have students work in groups to write a report about voter registration requirements in two different states. ▶ **Linguistic**

interNET CONNECTION Students can learn more about voter registration by visiting **www.mhschool.com/reading**

Voter Registration Application

Name _____
Address _____
City ____ State ___
Birthdate _____
Place of Birth _____

Later, Papa introduced me to Congressman Hawkins. The congressman asked me, "How did you all know that some of us walk through that tunnel from our offices?"

"We didn't know," I answered. "We were sent there out of the rain."

"That's strange," the congressman said. "Your standing there silently made a difference in the vote. Even though we lost this time, some of them now know that we'll keep on lobbying until we win."

I felt proud. Papa had been right when he said to Mama, **16** "There are ways to win a struggle without bombs and guns." We had lobbied in silence and we had been *heard*.

711

711

Guided Instruction

(17) JUDGMENTS AND DECISIONS
Let's complete our charts.

JUDGMENTS	DECISIONS
Mama thinks it's too dangerous for Papa to register to vote.	She tells Papa not to go.
Papa thinks that the freedom to vote is very important.	Papa registers to vote.
Craig, Papa, and the people on the bus are too late to lobby.	They will decide to stay and keep trying.
The rules that denied representation to blacks are unfair.	The people who were elected by the majority of voters should be seated in Congress.
Craig believes Papa was correct about the importance of freedom to vote.	He and the others will probably keep lobbying until they win.

RETELL THE STORY Ask volunteers to tell the major events of the story. Then have partners write sentences that summarize the story. *Summarize*

STUDENT SELF-ASSESSMENT

- How did identifying judgments and decisions help me understand the story?
- How did the chart help me?

TRANSFERRING THE STRATEGY

- When might I try using this strategy again?

President Lyndon B. Johnson shakes hands with Dr. Martin Luther King, Jr., after signing the Omnibus Civil Rights Act on June 29, 1964.

Note: *This story is a fictional account of one demonstration by African Americans during the decade of the 1960s. Many nonviolent demonstrations were held for voting rights, for jobs, and for freedom to use restaurants, libraries, schools, and public restrooms. This one took place on January 4, 1965.*

On June 29, 1964, President Lyndon Baines Johnson signed the Omnibus Civil Rights Act banning discrimination in voting, jobs, public facilities, and in housing. On August 6, 1965, President Johnson signed the Voting Rights Act, which guarantees the right to vote without penalties or poll taxes. **(17)**

712

REREADING FOR *Fluency*

GROUP Have students choose a favorite section of the story to read aloud to others. Encourage students to read with feeling and expression.

READING RATE You may want to evaluate a student's reading rate. Have the student read aloud from *The Silent Lobby* for one minute. Place a self-stick note after the last word read.

Then count the number of words he or she has read.

Alternatively, you could assess small groups or the whole class together by having students count words and record their own scores.

Use the Reading Rate form in the **Diagnostic/Placement Evaluations** booklet to evaluate students' performances.

Meet Mildred Pitts Walter

Mildred Pitts Walter had never thought of writing books. Then she met a book salesperson. She told him that there were not enough stories about African American children. He suggested that Walter try writing one. She did, and his company published her first book, *Lillie of Watts*.

Writing "The Silent Lobby" was important to Walter. She herself was deeply involved in the civil rights movement. During the 1950s and 1960s, Walter worked hard for equal rights in Los Angeles, California, her home. She struggled to make sure that people of every color could live wherever they wanted.

Many of Mildred Pitts Walter's characters show the same courage she did. "My characters must make choices," Walter observed, "and once they have made those choices, they have to work them through. That's what life is—making a series of choices—and people who cannot choose for themselves don't grow."

713

LITERARY RESPONSE

QUICK-WRITE Invite students to record their thoughts about the story. These questions may help them get started:

• Why was it so important for the people from Mississippi to speak to the representatives in Washington, D.C.?

• What would you have done if you had lived in Mississippi at that time?

ORAL RESPONSE Have students share their journal writings and discuss what part of the story they enjoyed most.

Guided Instruction

Return to Predictions and Purposes

Review with students their story predictions and reasons for reading the story. Were their predictions correct? Did they find out what they wanted to know?

PREDICTIONS	WHAT HAPPENED
I think this story will be about a trip.	The story was about a trip to Washington, D.C. to lobby for voting rights.
I think the boy will play an important part in the story.	Craig was more of an observer than someone who played an important part in the story.

INFORMAL **ASSESSMENT**

JUDGMENTS AND DECISIONS

HOW TO ASSESS Encourage students to point out places in this story where characters make judgments. Ask how these judgments helped the characters make decisions.

FOLLOW UP Work with students who are having difficulty identifying judgments and decisions by pointing out the places in the story where something surprising takes place. Explain that there were probably judgments and decisions that led to the surprising development. Encourage students to search for these judgments and decisions.

Story Questions

Have students discuss or write answers to the questions on page 714.

Answers:

1. They want to persuade Congress to seat the candidates who were elected by African American voters. *Literal/Details*

2. Sample answer: Unless they are free, people cannot feel secure, happy, or peaceful. *Inferential/Judgments and Decisions*

3. Sample answer: It shows the representatives how much the demonstrators are willing to go through. *Make Inferences*

4. a boy witnesses a demonstration that helps persuade Congress to support civil rights for African Americans *Summarize*

5. Craig respects his father's judgments in *The Silent Lobby*. In *Sea Maidens of Japan*, Kiyomi shows respect when she obeys her mother. *Critical/Reading Across Texts*

Write a Character Description For a full writing process lesson, see pages 717K–717L.

Story Questions & Activities

1. Why are Craig and his father going to Washington, D.C.?

2. What do you think Craig's father means when he says, "There can be no peace without freedom"?

3. What makes the silent lobby so effective?

4. Do you think this selection has an important message? Explain.

5. Compare Craig's relationship with his father with Kyomi's attitude toward her mother in "The Sea Maidens of Japan." How are their relationships built on respect?

Write a Character Description

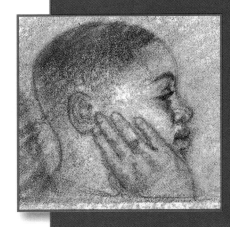

The events in this story are told through Craig's eyes. Write a character description of Craig. First, make a chart that tells *What He Does, What He Says, How He Feels,* and *How People Feel About Him.* Then use the information on the chart to give your readers a clear picture of Craig.

Meeting Individual Needs

EASY

Vocabulary

Read each clue. Then find and circle the vocabulary word in the row of letters.

interpret	pelted	persuade	register	shabby	soothing

1. convince   j i k n w q (p e r s u a d e) x v d f g
2. sign up   z w i r t g s d j (r e g i s t e r) o u
3. worn out   q (s h a b b y) e i t v g s d o k j w o
4. hit hard   x z v i w o k n (p e l t e d) a e n b d
5. understand   q o i j k m d s r e (i n t e r p r e t)
6. calming   e i d s c (s o o t h i n g) m z s o k e

☐ 6

Story Comprehension

Reteach 209

Write the answer to each question about "The Silent Lobby."

1. Who is telling the story in "The Silent Lobby"? Craig, a young African American boy is telling the story.

2. When and where does the story take place? the first half of 1960s; it takes place in Mississippi and Washington, D.C.

3. What right does Craig's father think is important? He believes his right to vote is important.

4. Why is Congressman Ryan sorry that the members of the Freedom Party arrive late? He feels that they could have helped the lobby to get more votes.

5. Why is Craig surprised by his vote in Congress? There are many more votes cast in the Freedom Party's favor than he thought there would be.

At Home: Have students write and answer two questions about "The Silent Lobby."

208–209   Book 5/Unit 6 The Silent Lobby 5

ON-LEVEL

Story Comprehension

Review or reread "The Silent Lobby." Then answer the questions below.
Answers will vary. Sample answers are shown.

1. Who is telling the story of "The Silent Lobby"? Explain. Craig Saunders, an 11-year-old boy from Mississippi whose father is leading a group of citizens from The Freedom Party to lobby for voting rights in Washington, D.C.

2. Why didn't Craig's mother want him to go to Washington, D.C.? She thought he was too young, and that the trip would be too dangerous.

3. What did they make Craig's father do when he tried to register to vote? Explain what happened. They made him pay a poll tax; pass a literacy test; and interpret the state constitution. They decided he didn't interpret the same state constitution correctly, so they wouldn't let him register to vote.

4. Who is Mrs. Fannie Lou Hamer? What did she do? She started the Mississippi Freedom Party and registered people to vote without charging a poll tax or making them take tests. She was also elected to be a representative to Congress, but was barred from taking office by the governor of Mississippi.

5. What happened to the 83,000 votes that the African Americans cast during Mississippi's 1964 election? What about the people they voted for? The governor of Mississippi declared the votes illegal and threw them out. Then he put the men he wanted into office instead of those the voters of the Second District wanted.

6. How would this story have been different if the doorman hadn't let the people from Mississippi take shelter from the rain in the tunnel? Explain. The ending would have been completely different because then the members of congress would not have had to face the people from Mississippi. By at least seeing the group, many members of Congress actually changed their minds.

At Home: Encourage students to make a storyboard to retell "The Silent Lobby."

209   Book 5/Unit 6 The Silent Lobby 6

CHALLENGE

Vocabulary

interpret	pelted	persuade	register	shabby	soothing

Suppose that you are Craig in the story, "The Silent Lobby." Write a letter home describing the events of the day in Washington, D.C. Use as many vocabulary words in your letter as possible.
Answers will vary, but should include at least four vocabulary words used in correct context and parts of speech.

Extend 209

Story Comprehension

Suppose you are a newspaper reporter who is covering the story of the Mississippi Freedom Democratic Party's trip to Washington, D.C. Tell in your story the events that led to the vote of 148 votes cast in favor of the party. Remember, a news story tells who was involved, what happened, when it happened, where it happened, and how the events happened.
Answers will vary, but should include the italicized details from instructions

At Home: Talk about different ways that you remember how to spell difficult words.

208–209   Book 5/Unit 6 The Silent Lobby

Reteach, 209   Practice, 209   Extend, 209

Make a Pamphlet

"The Silent Lobby" is about the struggle for civil rights in the United States in the 1950s and 1960s. Use your social studies textbook, an encyclopedia, or another book to learn about the civil rights movement. Focus on the leaders, the Civil Rights Act of 1964, and the Voting Rights Act of 1965. Share what you learn in a group pamphlet.

★ Plan a Lobby ★

Members of organizations and corporations are always lobbying Congress for or against something. Look up the word *lobby* in a dictionary. Be sure that you understand its meaning. Then choose something in your school or community that you would lobby for or against. Plan how you would go about lobbying for your idea. What will you need? How will you get support? Set up a roundtable discussion to talk about ideas.

Find Out More

How does a bill become a law? Use your social studies textbook, an encyclopedia, or a book about government to find out how laws are made. Write down the steps a bill goes through before it is signed into law. Use your notes to draw a diagram of the law-making process.

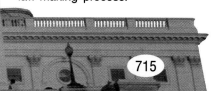

715

Story Activities

Make a Pamphlet

Materials: paper, pens or pencils, scissors, paste, photographs or illustrations from the Civil Rights movement

GROUP Encourage students to work in small groups to create pamphlets about the Civil Rights movement. Have students research the movement using textbooks, history books, or encyclopedias. If possible, have students illustrate their pamphlets with illustrations or photocopies of photographs.

Plan a Lobby

GROUP Encourage students to plan a lobbying effort for a cause that interests them. Have students brainstorm in small groups, with one student writing down ideas. Then have each group present their ideas to the entire class and discuss the feasibility and effectiveness of the various ideas.

Find Out More

RESEARCH AND INQUIRY Have students find information about how bills become laws. Encourage them to use books about government, textbooks, or encyclopedias, as well as the Internet, to research the topic.

FORMAL ASSESSMENT

After page 715, see Selection Assessment.

Study Skills

GRAPHIC AIDS

OBJECTIVES Students will use an out line to identify main ideas and supporting facts.

PREPARE Display **Teaching Chart 171.**

TEACH Review the concept of an outline with students.

PRACTICE Have students answer questions 1–5. **1.** An outline shows main ideas. **2.** Dr. King's Early Life, The Montgomery Years, The Strong Civil Rights Years; they are next to the large Roman numerals **3.** The Roman numerals denote main ideas, while the capital letters show details. **4.** under main idea III **5.** Using an outline enables you to visualize and to organize information in a selection.

ASSESS/CLOSE Have students create an outline, showing two or three main ideas and supporting facts about a topic.

Study Skills

Use an Outline

In the story, you learned some important information about the history of the civil rights movement. If you were asked to write a report about this movement, how would you begin? Making an **outline** would help you group facts and organize your information.

Suppose that you decided to narrow your topic to the life of Dr. Martin Luther King, Jr. You could begin your outline with three main ideas: "Dr. King's Early Life," "The Montgomery Years," "The Strong Civil Rights Years." As you collected facts, you would place each one under the appropriate main idea. By using roman numerals and capital letters, you could organize your outline to look like this:

I. Dr. King's Early Life
  A. Born in Atlanta in 1929
  B. Graduated from Morehouse Col
  C. Became a minister and earned a doctor's degree
II. The Montgomery Years
  A. Became pastor of the Dexter Baptist Church in Montgomery, Alabama, in 1954
  B. Led Montgomery bus boycott
  C. Elected president of the Souther Christian Leadership Conference
III. The Strong Civil Rights Years
  A. Jailed for disobeying unjust laws
  B. Strong voice for civil rights and nonviolence
  C. Led March on Washington in 1963
  D. Killed in Memphis in 1968

Use the outline to answer these questions.

1. How does an outline help you group facts?

2. What are the three main ideas in the outline? How do you know?

3. How do roman numerals and capital letters help you organize your outline?

4. Where would you place this fact in your outline? *Gave "I have a dream" speech on the steps of Lincoln Memorial on August 28, 1963.*

5. How can using an outline help you organize and understand information?

Meeting Individual Needs

EASY	ON-LEVEL	CHALLENGE

EASY

Use an Outline

An **outline** helps you organize information and plan your writing. You can use an outline for writing stories, opinion essays, or information reports. When you write an outline, make main headings for the main ideas you want to include. Then list related facts under each main heading. Label main headings with roman numerals and related facts with capital letters.

Papa loses job for trying to register.
Governor declares votes illegal.
Silent Lobby turned away at Capitol.
Silent Lobby watches Congress vote.

Silent Lobby meets Congressmen in tunnel.
148 votes are cast for the Silent Lobby cause.
Papa finds Freedom Party and votes.
Papa is not allowed to register to vote.

Organize the entries in the columns above in the outline format below. You may use information from either column for each main idea.

1. Main Idea #1   I. History of Papa's fight to vote
2. Related Fact: A. Papa not allowed to register to vote.
3. Related Fact: B. Papa loses job for trying to register.
4. Related Fact: C. Papa finds Freedom Party and votes.
5. Related Fact: D. Governor declares votes illegal.

6. Main Idea #2:   II. Events of Silent Lobby trip
7. Related Fact: A. Silent Lobby turned away at Capitol
8. Related Fact: B. Silent Lobby meets Congressmen in tunnel
9. Related Fact: C. Silent Lobby watches Congress vote
10. Related Fact: D. 148 votes are cast for the Silent Lobby cause

Book 5/Unit 6
The Silent Lobby   8   At Home: Have students add one more related fact to the history of the Silent Lobby or the events of the Silent Lobby.   210

ON-LEVEL

Use an Outline

Using an **outline** can help you to group facts and organize information. In an outline, a Roman numeral is placed before each main idea. Beneath that, capital letters organize the important facts that support the main idea. Study this section of an outline. Then answer the questions below. *Answers may vary.*

III. Women Pilots in the Thirties
  A. Beryl Markham survives crash on Cape Breton.
  B. Jean Batten sets second for South Atlantic flight.
  C. Louise Thaden wins Bendix trophy in 1936.
  D. Amelia Earhart makes last flight, 1937.

1. Which section of the outline is presented here? the third section
2. What is the main idea of this section? How do you know what it is about?
The main idea is about women pilots in the 1930s. I can tell because it is written next to a Roman numeral.
3. What sort of information follows the capital letters? facts that support the main idea
4. If you found out about another woman pilot in the 1930s, how would you include her in the outline? Explain. I would add another capital letter (E) to this section and put the information about her there or if she was in the early 1930s, put her in the correct place chronologically and reorder the entries.
5. How could you use an outline to help you study a textbook to prepare for a test? I could make an outline of each chapter in the textbook to find the main ideas and supporting facts.

Book 5/Unit 6
The Silent Lobby   5   At Home: Encourage students to explain how they would use an outline for their next research report.   210

CHALLENGE

Use an Outline

In "The Silent Lobby" you got an idea of how Congress works to pass bills. If you were asked to write a report on the three branches of our government, how would you organize your information? An outline such as the one below would help you get started.

The Government of the United States
I. Executive Branch
  A. Carries out laws
  B. Conducts public and foreign affairs
  C. Headed by the President
II. Legislative Branch
  A. Makes laws
  B. House of Representatives
    1. Elected every 2 years
    2. Number of house members based on a state's population
  C. Senate
    1. Elected every 6 years
    2. Two Senators for each state
III. Judiciary Branch
  A. Supreme Court
  B. District Courts

1. What are the main ideas of this outline? How do you know?
The main ideas are the three branches of our national government. They are shown by roman numerals I, II, and III.
2. Where would you place this fact on the outline? One chief justice and eight justices make up the Supreme Court.
You would put in under Supreme Court and label it 1.
3. How are outlines organized?
Outlines use roman numerals and letters to show topics and subtopics.
4. Where would you place facts about the President's foreign affairs issues.
Under 1, letter B

Book 5/Unit 6
The Silent Lobby   At Home: Discuss how an outline helps you organize information.   210

Reteach, 210   Practice, 210   Extend, 210

TEST POWER

Test Tip

If you are spending too much time on a question, see if there are any answer choices you can rule out.

DIRECTIONS

Read the sample story. Then read each question about the story.

SAMPLE

The Cactus

A cactus is a plant specially developed to live in a hot, dry area. There are more than 2000 different species of cacti on earth, and about 200 different kinds in the United States.

Cacti come in many different shapes and sizes. One kind is only a few inches across and grows very low to the ground. Another kind, the giant elephant cactus, can grow to be more than 60 feet tall and more than ten feet around. It would take you and two friends to encircle an elephant cactus with your arms. But you don't want to do it. With the sharp barbs on the plant, it's never worth hugging a cactus!

1   The word species in this story means —

   ● types
   ○ weeds
   ○ deserts
   ○ animals

2   Which of these is a FACT presented in this story?

   ○ Cacti grow in warm, moist areas of the United States.
   ○ There are more than 2000 different kinds of cactus in the United States.
   ● The elephant cactus can grow to be 60 feet tall.
   ○ Only one type of cactus has sharp barbs.

Which answer choices did you rule out right away? Tell why.

717

Test Power

THE PRINCETON REVIEW

Read the Page

Remind students to pay attention to the sentence with an underlined word.

Discuss the Questions

Question 1: This question asks students to define a word in context. Remind students to look for clues. Point out: The passage says that while there are "more than 2000 different species of cacti on earth," there are "about 200 different kinds in the United States." The 200 different kinds in the United States is a subset of the 2000 different species. It can therefore be assumed that species also means "kinds" or "types."

Question 2: This question requires students to determine which of the answer choices is a FACT in the passage. The incorrect answer choices are not FACTS in the passage. Guide students to eliminate answers that are *not* FACTS.

For The Princeton Review test preparation practice for **TerraNova, ITBS,** and **SAT-9,** visit the McGraw-Hill School Division Web site. See also McGraw-Hill's *Standardized Test Preparation Book.*

EASY
DECODABLE

Leveled Books

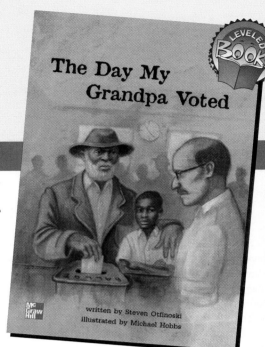

EASY

The Day My Grandpa Voted

Unstressed Syllables

☑ **Judgments and Decisions**

☑ **Instructional Vocabulary:**
interpret, pelted, persuade, register, shabby, soothing

Guided Reading

PREVIEW AND PREDICT Preview the illustrations up to page 11. As you guide students through the illustrations, have them predict what the story is about and have them write their ideas in their journals.

SET PURPOSES Have students write questions they would like to have answered by reading *The Day My Grandpa Voted*. For instance, Why was this day memorable?

READ THE BOOK Use questions like the following to guide students' reading before or after they have read the story independently.

Page 2: Point out to students the word *traveling* in the third paragraph of this page. Of the three syllables in this word, which is unstressed? (the middle) How is it spelled, and how is it pronounced? (el; /əl/) *Phonics*

Page 5: Why is Grandpa so determined to vote this year? (because white people kept him from voting before) *Cause and Effect*

Page 7: The author describes Grandpa's coat as *shabby*. What does that tell us about Grandpa? (Possible answer: He is poor and has had a hard life.) *Vocabulary*

Page 8: What judgment does Freddie make at this point in the story about voting? (that it isn't worth the effort) *Making Judgments and Decisions*

Page 16: Have the people in Grandpa's family changed their minds about voting? (Pa did; the author doesn't say if Mama did or not.) How does the boy feel about voting now? (He's proud of Grandpa for voting.) *Making Judgments and Decisions*

RETURN TO PREDICTIONS AND PURPOSES Have students review and discuss their predictions. Which were accurate? Which questions were answered? Which were not?

LITERARY RESPONSES Discusses the questions:

- What is it about Grandpa that makes him willing to expend the great effort to vote?

- What effect will this day have on Freddie's life?

- Have you ever witnessed a person exhibit great courage, as Grandpa does?

Also see the story questions and activity in *The Day My Grandpa Voted*.

Answers to Story Questions

1. It is told by Freddie, Amos's grandson.
2. He didn't go because he felt the white people in town would give him a very hard time when he tried to vote.
3. The authorities took it out of service so black people couldn't cross the river to get to the polling place.
4. It is about one black man's courage in standing up for his rights and the effect his actions had on his grandson.
5. Answers will vary.

Story Questions and Activity

1. Who is the person telling this story?
2. Why didn't Amos' son John go with him to vote?
3. What is the likely reason that the ferry was out of order when Grandpa and Freddie got there?
4. What is the story mostly about?
5. In what ways is this story similar to *The Silent Lobby*? In what ways is it different?

Made for the Movies

Imagine that this story was turned into a movie. Create an ad for the movie. Illustrate it with a dramatic scene from the story. Include the title, leading actors, and other important information.

from The Day My Grandpa Voted

Leveled Books

INDEPENDENT

Vote for Me!

☑ Judgments and Decisions

☑ Instructional Vocabulary:
interpret, pelted, persuade, register, shabby, soothing

Guided Reading

PREVIEW AND PREDICT Preview the illustrations through page 6 and predict what the story is about.

SET PURPOSES Discuss with students what purpose they might have for reading *Vote for Me!* Have them write two questions they would like to have answered.

READ THE BOOK Use questions like the following to guide students' reading, or after they have read the story independently to emphasize reading strategies.

Page 6: The author uses the word *soothing* in the last paragraph to describe words. What others things can be soothing? (Possible answers: music, hot chocolate, people's voices, cool hands) *Vocabulary*

Page 10: Do you think Cindy made the right decision? Why? (Possible answer: Cindy should have voted for herself.) *Making Judgments and Decisions*

Page 11: What effect did Cindy's voting for Hector have on the election? (Since she lost by one vote, voting for Hector caused her to lose the election.) *Cause and Effect*

Page 15: What do you think Cindy meant when she said "some things are more important than winning"? (Possible answer: Being a friend is better than being president.) *Making Judgments and Decisions*

Page 16: What decisions or judgments do Cindy and Hector make on this page? (Cindy decides to run for class president; Hector decides to be her speech writer. Hector judges the cafeteria food.) *Making Judgments and Decisions*

RETURN TO PREDICTIONS AND PURPOSES How close were students' predictions to what actually happened in the book? Did they find out what they wanted to know?

LITERARY RESPONSE Discuss these questions with students:

• Who did you want to win the election?

• Have you ever had to pick between two conflicting values (as Cindy does in deciding whether to vote for herself of Hector)? What helped you make your decision?

Also see the story questions and activity in *Vote for Me!*

INDEPENDENT
DECODABLE

PUPIL SELECTION

Answers to Story Questions

1. She is running for fifth-grade class president.
2. She is afraid she will lose her friendship with Hector, who is also running.
3. Answers will vary but may include: He will probably not make a good president because he makes promises he cannot keep.
4. It is about two friends who are divided when both decide to run for class president, and who become friends again after they both lose.)
5. Answers will vary.

Story Questions and Activity

1. What political job is Cindy Wu running for?
2. Why does Cindy have mixed feelings about winning the election?
3. Do you think that Ron Baker will make a good class president. Why or why not?
4. What is the story mostly about?
5. What kind of advice would Craig from *The Silent Lobby* have for each of the three candidates running for office? Explain.

A Campaign Speech

Imagine you are running for class president at your school. Write a campaign speech for yourself. State what your qualifications are and what you will do to try to improve the school. Read your speech to a friend.

from Vote for Me!

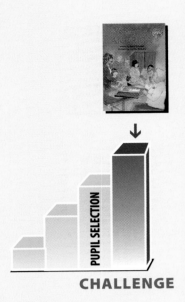

PUPIL SELECTION

CHALLENGE

Leveled Books

CHALLENGE

Voting in America

- ☑ **Judgments and Decisions**
- ☑ **Instructional Vocabulary:** *interpret, pelted, persuade, register, shabby, soothing*

Guided Reading

PREVIEW AND PREDICT Read the title and have students preview the illustrations through page 8 and predict what the story is about.

SET PURPOSES Have students write why they plan to read *Voting in America,* noting questions they would like to have answered by the text.

READ THE BOOK Use questions like the following to guide students' reading.

Page 5: What effect did preventing men without money from voting before the 1820s have on election results? (It kept all the elected representatives acting in the interests of wealthier citizens.) *Cause and Effect*

Page 10: What do you think about the arguments against women voting? (Possible answer: The arguments don't make much sense today.) *Making Judgments and Decisions*

Page 10: In the final paragraph, the author uses the word *shabby*. What does the word mean in this context? (poor) What other meaning does the word have? (It means ragged or unkempt when it describes clothing.) *Vocabulary*

Page 13: Why do you think Congress waited so long to grant voting rights to Native Americans? (Possible answer: Native Americans originally outnumbered the colonists in the United States.) *Making Judgments and Decisions*

Page 16: Do you think we are better or worse off now that more adults are able to vote? (Possible answer: It is better to have more voters.) *Making Judgments and Decisions*

RETURN TO PREDICTIONS AND PURPOSES Did students learn what they hoped to from the book? Did their predictions match the story?

LITERARY RESPONSE Discuss these questions with students:

- Why do you think many people do not vote?

- What qualities would you look for in a representative? What issues would you want to see addressed?

Also see the story questions and activity in *Voting in America.*

Answers to Story Questions

1. White men who owned property or other wealth could vote.
2. Much of the country supported the civil rights movement and wanted new laws.
3. This was the year that African American men gained the right to vote, which inspired women to act similarly in order to gain their own rights.
4. Different groups of people struggled for many years to win the right to vote in our nation.
5. Answers will vary.

Story Questions and Activity

1. Who could vote in colonial America?
2. Why did Congress finally pass laws to end discrimination against black voters in the South?
3. Why do you think women began to organize themselves nationally to fight for the vote specifically in the year 1870?
4. What is the main idea of the book?
5. How do you think Craig's experience in *The Silent Lobby* might have been different if the 24th Amendment had not yet been passed?

Winning the Vote

Research the life of one famous person who helped win voting rights for their group, such as Susan B. Anthony or Martin Luther King, Jr. Then write a short report on their efforts and what they accomplished.

from Voting in America

Activities
Anthology and Leveled Books

Connecting Texts

JUDGMENTS AND DECISIONS Write each story title on a four-column chart. Have students discuss the judgments and decisions made in each story. Have students record responses on their charts.

Silent Lobby	The Day My Grandpa Voted	Vote for Me!	Voting in America
Papa and the others decided to lobby in Washington, D.C.	Grandpa decided to vote in the election.	Cindy decided to vote for Hector instead of voting for herself.	Congress decided to grant voting rights to Native Americans.

Viewing/Representing

GROUP PRESENTATIONS Divide students into four groups, one for each story. (For *Silent Lobby* combine students of different reading levels.) Encourage each group to find an event from the book to dramatize. The group should add dialogue and characters to flesh out the event and make sets if possible. Have each group perform their dramatization for the rest of the class.

AUDIENCE RESPONSE Allow time for students to ask questions or comment on what they enjoyed about each group's presentation. Can they imagine any ways in which events might have worked out differently?

Research and Inquiry

LOCAL ELECTIONS Have students research their local election district. Challenge them to create a graphic map showing their local election district, with a breakdown of precinct, city, county, state, and federal districts.

interNET CONNECTION Students can learn more about voting by visiting
www.mhschool.com/reading

Students will identify and analyze judgments and decisions.

Review Judgments and Decisions

PREPARE

Discuss Judgments and Decisions

Remind students that identifying judgments and decisions that characters make can help them understand the story. Encourage students to discuss some of the judgments and decisions made in the story.

TEACH

Read the Passage and Model the Skill

Ask students to pay attention to judgments and decisions as you read "Bus Trouble" with them.

Bus Trouble

Even with the whole group pushing the broken-down bus, it was slow going.

Mr. Smith sighed and said, "<u>Let's just leave the bus here. We can't waste our time pushing this old thing!</u>"

"<u>But if we leave it here, the police will tow it away</u>," said Mrs. Franklin.

"<u>You know, we ought to push it to a garage and have it fixed</u>," said Papa. "<u>We borrowed it, so it's our responsibility now.</u>"

Mr. Smith scowled and snapped, "<u>Why should we pay for it? It's not our bus!</u>"

Teaching Chart 172

Have a volunteer find and underline clues in the passage that help them identify each character's judgment and decision about what to do with the bus.

MODEL *Everyone has his or her own opinion about what to do with the broken bus. How does Mr. Smith feel about pushing the bus? He says it's a waste of time. He decides that they should leave the bus where it is. What does Mrs. Franklin have to say about that?*

PRACTICE

Review Judgments and Decisions

ONE

Have students fill out the chart to show the judgments and decisions made in "Bus Trouble." ▶ **Visual/Linguistic**

JUDGMENTS	DECISIONS
Mr. Smith thinks that pushing the bus is a waste of time.	Leave the bus where it is.
Mrs. Franklin believes that if they leave the bus, it will be towed.	Continue pushing the bus.
Papa says it is their responsibility to have the bus fixed.	Push the bus to the nearest garage and have it fixed.
Mr. Smith thinks that since it's not their bus, they should not be responsible.	Don't pay for it.

ASSESS/CLOSE

Share Judgments and Decisions

GROUP

Have students write an imaginary dialogue that might have taken place between Mr. Smith, Mrs. Franklin, and Papa when they learned that they could not go into the Capitol.

ALTERNATE TEACHING STRATEGY

JUDGMENTS AND DECISIONS

For a different approach to teaching this skill, see page T60.

SELF-SELECTED Reading

Students may choose from the following titles.

ANTHOLOGY
• The Silent Lobby

LEVELED BOOKS
• The Day My Grandpa Voted
• Vote for Me!
• Voting in America

Bibliography, pages T76–T77

Meeting Individual Needs for Comprehension

EASY	ON-LEVEL	CHALLENGE	LANGUAGE SUPPORT
Judgments and Decisions	**Judgments & Decisions**	**Judgments and Decisions**	**Decide Your Vote**

EASY

Judgments and Decisions

To make **judgments**, you look at how you think and feel about something. To make **decisions**, you often compare two or more possibilities and choose the one that agrees with how you think or feel about the topic.

In "The Silent Lobby" many characters made judgments and decisions. Read each sentence below. Decide how you feel or think about it and write your response on the line that reads: **Judgment**. Then, write what you think should be done on the line labeled: **Decision.** Answers will vary but should be explained.

1. Eleven years of age is too young to be involved in political protests.
   a. **Judgment:** Possible answer: I agree.
   b. **Decision:** Possible answer: Kids can have strong beliefs, just like adults. However they are too young to be placed in dangerous situations.

2. Keeping Papa from registering to vote was wrong.
   a. **Judgment:** Possible answer: I agree.
   b. **Decision:** Possible answer: Papa had the right to vote, just like any other United States citizen.

3. The Silent Lobby should have gone home after their bus broke down.
   a. **Judgment:** Possible answer: I disagree.
   b. **Decision:** Possible answer: They should have stayed, because their presence was important to the outcome of the vote.

4. People can never change other people's ideas.
   a. **Judgment:** Possible answer: I disagree.
   b. **Decision:** Possible answer: I would try to talk to people and get them to understand my ideas.

At Home: Have students tell what they might do in Craig's shoes. Would they choose the same actions that he did?

211   Book 5/Unit 6 The Silent Lobby **8**

ON-LEVEL

Judgments & Decisions

Think about some of the **judgments and decisions** that people made in "The Silent Lobby." Answer each question below. Explain your answers. You may want to look back at the story for help.
Answers will vary. Accept all well-reasoned responses.

1. Mr. Clem told Craig's father that he would fire him if he tried to register to vote. Craig's father decided to register to vote. Did Craig's dad do the right thing? Explain. Possible answers: Yes, because Craig's dad had a right to vote, and he needed to fight for those rights. No, because then he wouldn't be able to support his family.

2. Do you think the Governor of Mississippi made the right decision when he threw out all the votes that African Americans had cast in 1964? Explain. Possible answer: No, he didn't respect the choices that the voters had made.

3. What is your opinion of Mrs. Fannie Lou Hamer, who decided to set up the Mississippi Freedom Democratic Party? Explain. Possible answer: She did a great thing, because she helped people to register to vote; she showed true leadership.

4. Do you think the doorman at the Capitol who refused to let in the people from Mississippi was making a fair decision to block them from entering? Explain. No, I don't think he was being fair. He wasn't very kind to them, so I thought he was against their cause. I doubt he knew the effect they'd have by standing in the tunnel. Yes, as long as he kept every person out who didn't have a pass, then he was just doing his job.

5. During the vote in Congress, Craig decided to sit on his hands as he watched. Do you think this was wise of him? Possible answer: yes, because he was so happy to see everyone changing their minds and voting yes that he wanted to clap his hands, and that might have gotten him—and the group he was with—in trouble.

At Home: Encourage students to discuss their answers here with a member of their family.

211   Book 5/Unit 6 The Silent Lobby **5**

CHALLENGE

Judgments and Decisions

In the story "The Silent Lobby" the members of the House of Representatives must make a decision as to whether or not to seat the representatives elected by the Freedom Party. Suppose you are a member of the House. As a congressperson, it is your responsibility to **judge** all sides of an issue. Then, you must make a **decision** to vote yes or no. Decide how you would vote on the issue raised by the Freedom Party. Give reasons as they are presented in the story to back up your decision. Write your argument in the space provided.

Answers will vary but should include important details form the story.

At Home: People often debate an issue. Look up the word debate. Write a sentence to show its meaning.

211   Book 5/Unit 6 The Silent Lobby

LANGUAGE SUPPORT

Decide Your Vote

1. Write an X in the box for the answer you agree with. 2. Tally the class votes.

Answers will vary.

Question 1: Should students be allowed to bring pets to this school?

☐ Yes   ☐ No

Question 2: Should students in school have recess?

☐ Yes   ☐ No

Question 3: Should students have ice cream for lunch?

☐ Yes   ☐ No

Question 4: Should students have homework?

☐ Yes   ☐ No

230 The Silent Lobby • Language Support/Blackline Master 114   Grade 5

Reteach, 211   **Practice, 211**   **Extend, 211**   Language Support, 230

717F

Students will use story clues to draw conclusions.

TEACHING TIP

Remind students to use information in the text, as well as their own knowledge, to draw conclusions.

Review Draw Conclusions

PREPARE

Discuss Drawing Conclusions

Remind students that drawing conclusions requires logical reasoning —putting together two or more ideas or pieces of information to reach a conclusion.

TEACH

Draw Conclusions

Read "Registration." Have students listen for clues that tell them what the man behind the desk is like.

Registration

Papa <u>nervously</u> approached the man behind the desk. "<u>G - good</u> day, sir," Papa began. Then he <u>squared his shoulders</u> and said in a <u>steady voice</u>, "I'd like to register to vote."

"Why, sure. No problem," the man replied. His <u>lips curled</u> back in a smile, but his <u>eyes were cold</u>. "You can register, just like everybody else—if you can pass this little test on our state constitution," he said with a <u>snicker</u>.

Teaching Chart 173

Ask a volunteer to find and underline clues that tell how Papa felt and clues that tell about the man's attitude towards Papa.

MODEL Papa was nervous at first, but then he squared his shoulders and spoke in a steady voice. I think that means that he felt braver. The man behind the desk smiled, but his eyes were cold. I think that means that he didn't like Papa.

Find Clues

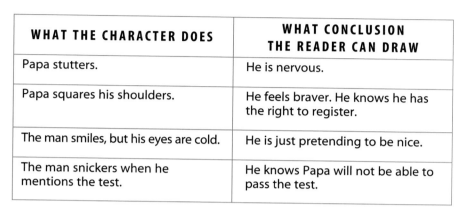

Have students use what they learned in the story and clues in "Registration" to fill out the chart. ▶ **Visual/Intrapersonal**

WHAT THE CHARACTER DOES	WHAT CONCLUSION THE READER CAN DRAW
Papa stutters.	He is nervous.
Papa squares his shoulders.	He feels braver. He knows he has the right to register.
The man smiles, but his eyes are cold.	He is just pretending to be nice.
The man snickers when he mentions the test.	He knows Papa will not be able to pass the test.

ASSESS/CLOSE

Determine Clues and Draw Conclusions

Have students look for clues in *The Silent Lobby* that helped them draw conclusions about characters or events. Have them write them in the chart.

CLUES	CONCLUSIONS

ALTERNATE TEACHING STRATEGY

DRAW CONCLUSIONS

For a different approach to teaching this skill, see page T62.

LOOKING AHEAD

Students will apply this skill as they read the next selection, *Amazon Alert!*

Meeting Individual Needs for Comprehension

EASY

Draw Conclusions

To **draw conclusions**, first think about clues in the story and what you know from your own experiences. Then try to figure out what may happen with characters and events in a story.

Read each story. Circle the conclusion you can draw for each story.

Twana's mind kept wandering from her reading. She could picture a fresh, crispy apple. Then she thought about a warm piece of toast. Her stomach started to growl. She had to read the page over again to understand it.

1. Twana is probably
   a. bored   **b.** hungry   c. tired

Craig wants to go with Papa to try to register to vote. When Papa doesn't come home, Craig wants to search for him. When the Silent Lobby goes to Washington, Craig wants to go too.

2. Craig probably
   a. wants to support Papa.
   b. wants to be alone.
   c. does not care about voting.

Jamie could hear birds chirping. The sky was bright even at breakfast time. She saw buds growing on the trees and each day was a little warmer. The ground was getting softer and water from melting snow was filling the streams.

3. Jamie can see that
   a. breakfast is great.   b. the sky is often dark.   **c.** spring is near.

Stefan wrote to the school board asking them to change the rules about skateboards. He listed facts to tell them why skateboards are safe. Stefan put up posters all around school asking other students to write the school board too.

4. It seems that
   a. Stefan loves to write letters.
   b. Stefan is not interested in skateboards.
   c. Stefan thinks students should be allowed to skateboard.

Book 5/Unit 6
The Silent Lobby   **At Home:** Have students identify the clues they used to help them draw the conclusion in each paragraph.   212

Reteach, 212

ON-LEVEL

Draw Conclusions

To **draw a conclusion** when reading a story, you use facts from a story as well as your own knowledge and experience. Drawing conclusions as you read can help you better understand a story.

Read the selection below, and then answer each question. Describe the clues that helped you draw conclusions for question 1. Answers will vary.

Naseem rested his head on one arm. On the kitchen table before him was a blank sheet of paper. Crumpled papers were all over the floor under the table. Fatima pushed aside a mound of library books and sat down.

"Listen, Naseem, you just have to tell yourself, 'You can do it!' Fatima said. "Look, you've done all the research."

Naseem lifted his head and stared outside the kitchen window.

"You have until tomorrow morning," she reminded him. "If you just pick up the pen and start writing now, you'll be OK—as long as you just stop tossing away everything you write." Fatima uncrumpled one of the papers. "And I'd use this, if I were you," she suggested as she handed him the outline.

1. What is it that Naseem has to do? How can you tell? Write the clues that helped you below. He has to write a research report.

2. **Story clues:** The library books, the blank sheet of paper, the crumpled papers, the outline; Fatima refers to research and to writing.

3. **Experience clues:** When I work on a research report, I usually have a pile of library books and papers.

4. How is Naseem feeling? How can you tell? He is feeling frustrated and hopeless. I can tell by the way he has his head down on his arm, how he stares out the window, how he keeps crumpling up what he writes.

5. What kind of person is Fatima? How can you tell? She is helpful and kind. She cheers Naseem on. She gives him good advice.

Book 5/Unit 6
The Silent Lobby   **At Home:** Encourage students to share how they used drawing conclusions to answer these questions.   212

Practice, 212

CHALLENGE

Draw Conclusions

You can **draw conclusions** about a character in a story by the way the character acts, thinks, and feels. Use what you have read in "The Silent Lobby" to draw conclusions about each character below.

1. How do you think Mama feels about the bus trip Papa and Craig are going to take? Explain the reasons for your conclusion.
   Possible answer: Mama does not want Papa and Craig to go on the bus trip. She feels that it is too dangerous. She is afraid the bus will be bombed.

2. How do you think that Papa feels about violence?
   Possible answer: Papa does not believe that violence is the way to solve problems. He is opposed to violence and continues to pursue his goals by using peaceful ways of getting something done, such as lobbying.

3. How do you think Congressmen Ryan and Hawkins feel about the cause of the Freedom Party? Explain why you think so.
   Possible answer: They support the cause of the Freedom Party. They work late into the night lobbying to get votes on the side of the Freedom Party.

4. Do you think that Craig will continue to fight for causes in the same manner as his father? Explain why you think so.
   Possible answer: Craig will most likely lobby for causes rather than resort to violence. He has seen how lobbying can get results, and he is proud of his father and the Freedom Party.

Book 5/Unit 6
The Silent Lobby   **At Home:** Discuss how drawing conclusions can help you better understand what you read.   212

Extend, 212

LANGUAGE SUPPORT

What Do You See?

1. Look at the pictures. 2. Write one or two words to describe each picture.
Answers will vary.

	lost / lonely / dog
	broken / glass / window
	flat / mad / bike
	happy / dad / hug

Grade 5   Language Support/Blackline Master 00 • The Silent Lobby 231

Language Support, 231

OBJECTIVES

Students will identify and use antonyms and synonyms .

TEACHING TIP

INSTRUCTIONAL You may wish to bring in a thesaurus and discuss how students can use it to find synonyms and sometimes antonyms. Encourage students to use a thesaurus when they revise their writing.

Review Antonyms and Synonyms

> **PREPARE**

Define Synonyms and Antonyms

Remind students that synonyms are words that have similar meanings. Antonyms are words that have opposite meanings.

> **TEACH**

Read the Passage and Model the Skill

Have students read "Waiting in the Rain." Tell them to look for synonyms and antonyms as they read.

Waiting in the Rain

Craig looked at the well-dressed congressmen and -women, and felt <u>ashamed</u> of his (shabby) clothes. But when he thought of his (brave) Papa and the good work he was trying to do, he felt <u>proud</u>. He decided it didn't matter that their shoes were <u>shiny</u>, while his own were <u>dull</u> and scuffed.

(Icy) wind whipped the (ragged) hem of Craig's coat. (Freezing) rain ran down his neck. But Craig put his hand in Papa's and felt warm and (unafraid.)

Teaching Chart 174

Help students identify antonyms and synonyms.

MODEL This paragraph has a lot of adjectives in it. Let's see if any of them are antonyms or synonyms. Craig feels ashamed of his clothes. But then he feels proud when he thinks of his father. Ashamed is the opposite of proud, so I'll underline those words on the chart.

Identify Synonyms and Antonyms

Have students find all the synonym and antonym pairs in "Waiting in the Rain." They should circle synonyms and underline antonyms. Then have partners create charts of synonyms and antonyms. Tell them to fill the rest of the blank boxes in the chart. ▶ **Linguistic/Spatial**

SYNONYM PAIRS	ANTONYM PAIRS
brave/unafraid	ashamed/proud
icy/freezing	shiny/dull
ragged/shabby	

ASSESS/CLOSE

Find More Synonyms and Antonyms

Have students make a similar chart for antonyms and synonyms they find in the story. Have them try to write a paragraph that uses the words they write in their chart.

ALTERNATE TEACHING STRATEGY

ANTONYMS AND SYNONYMS

For a different approach to teaching this skill, see page T65.

Meeting Individual Needs for Vocabulary

EASY	ON-LEVEL	CHALLENGE	LANGUAGE SUPPORT
Synonyms and Antonyms	**Synonyms and Antonyms**	**Synonyms and Antonyms**	**Synonyms and Antonyms**

EASY

Synonyms and Antonyms

Synonyms are words with the same or similar meanings. **Antonyms** are words with opposite or nearly opposite meanings.

Read each sentence. Then use the clue provided to help you complete the sentence with the correct word from the box.

| dangerous | gawking | complaints | active |
| courage | alarmed | wrinkled | unfortunate |

1. The people in the Silent Lobby must have had a lot of _courage_
   Clue: antonym for *fear*
2. During the 1960's, people sometimes got hurt during _dangerous_ protests.
   Clue: antonym for *safe*
3. Mama was _alarmed_ by the risks Papa was taking in registering to vote.
   Clue: synonym for *frightened*
4. The Freedom Party was very _active_ in working for voting rights.
   Clue: synonym for *busy*
5. Craig felt badly when a crowd of people stood _gawking_ at his bus.
   Clue: synonym for *staring*
6. The members of the Freedom Party wanted to be sure its _complaints_ were heard somehow.
   Clue: synonym for *protests*
7. After standing in the rain, all our clothes were _wrinkled_ and wet.
   Clue: antonym for *smooth*
8. The delay in reaching Washington was _unfortunate_ as The Freedom Party missed its chance to lobby for votes.
   Clue: antonym for *lucky*

At Home: Have students write sentences for one antonym and one synonym.

213   Book 5/Unit 6 The Silent Lobby   8

ON-LEVEL

Synonyms and Antonyms

Synonyms are words with the same, or nearly the same, meanings and are used for different situations.
Antonyms are words with opposite, or nearly opposite, meanings and are used for contrast or to show differences.
Divide the words in the box into pairs of synonyms and antonyms and then write each pair under the correct column below.

shabby	soothing	elect	beaten
gawked	returned	alarming	pelted
left	right	stalling	threadbare
wrong	moving	lobby	vote
awake	asleep	stared	persuade

Synonyms
1. shabby, threadbare
2. gawked, stared
3. beaten, pelted
4. elect, vote
5. lobby, persuade

Antonyms
6. soothing, alarming
7. asleep, awake
8. stalling, moving
9. wrong, right
10. left, returned OR left, right

Compare the underlined words in each sentence. Are they antonyms or synonyms?

11. While the traffic was <u>moving</u> quickly all around us, our car kept <u>stalling</u>.
   antonyms
12. My favorite sweater began to look <u>shabby</u>. Even the patches on the elbows were <u>threadbare</u>.   synonyms

At Home: Encourage students to use a thesaurus to decide if the words protested and pleaded are synonyms or antonyms. Have them explain.

213   Book 5/Unit 6 The Silent Lobby   12

CHALLENGE

Synonyms and Antonyms

Tell whether the pair of underlined words in the following sentences are **synonyms** or **antonyms**.

1. Some members of the House were <u>for</u> the bill to be passed, and some members were <u>against</u>.
   antonyms
2. Craig's Mama was <u>afraid</u> for her son and her husband, but Craig and his Dad did not seem to be that <u>scared</u>.
   synonyms
3. The people of the Freedom party stood <u>calmly</u> and <u>quietly</u> in the tunnel as the members of the House of Representatives walked by.
   synonyms
4. To Craig, the men and women of the House seem <u>tall</u> and <u>towering</u> as they passed by him in the tunnel.
   synonyms
5. The house member to the <u>right</u> of Congressman Ryan voted yes, but the house member on his <u>left</u> voted no.
   antonyms
6. Each day, the <u>men</u> and <u>women</u> of Congress must make important decisions about laws and issues that affect people in our country.
   antonyms
7. As the Freedom Party waited outside the Capitol building, it <u>rained</u> and <u>poured</u> on them.
   synonyms
8. The people of the Freedom Party were <u>happy</u> and <u>thrilled</u> to have gotten so many votes in their favor.
   synonyms

At Home: Make a list of words that are synonyms. Then find an antonym for each.

213   Book 5/Unit 6 The Silent Lobby

LANGUAGE SUPPORT

Synonyms and Antonyms

1. Read each bold word in the left column of the chart below. 2. Draw a circle around the word in the column on the right that is its synonym (same). 3. Underline the word in the column on the right that is its antonym (opposite).

scared	(afraid)	<u>calm</u>
for	(against)	with
shabby	(worn)	<u>fancy</u>
soothing	(calming)	<u>exciting</u>
persuade	(encourage)	discourage
silent	(quiet)	loud

232 The Silent Lobby • Language Support / Blackline Master 116   Grade 5

Reteach, 213   Practice, 213   Extend, 213   Language Support, 232

Writing a Story

GRAMMAR/SPELLING CONNECTIONS

See the 5-Day Grammar and Usage Plan on prepositions, pages 717M–717N.

See the 5-Day Spelling Plan on words with suffixes, pages 717O–717P.

TECHNOLOGY TIP

Some students may try to make their work perfect when writing a first draft on the computer. Remind them to focus on getting their ideas down, and use their computer editing tools later.

Prewrite

WRITE A CHARACTER DESCRIPTION
The Silent Lobby doesn't use words to describe the characters in the story, but we get a sense of them from how they behave and the things they do. A character description contains all the information about a character that a writer needs. Write a description for one character in *The Silent Lobby*.

Strategy: Character Web Have students choose a character from the story, and make a Character Traits Web to organize their ideas. Students may answer the following questions:

- How does this character look and behave?
- What words would best describe this person?
- What examples from the story help portray this person?

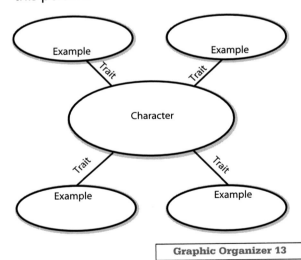

Graphic Organizer 13

Draft

USE THE WEB Have students elaborate upon ideas from their graphic organizers to craft their character descriptions. Encourage them to use vivid sensory details that bring the character to life.

Revise

SELF-QUESTIONING Ask students to assess their drafts.

- Is my character description based on information in the story?
- Is my character description thorough?
- Does it have everything necessary to write a story with this character in it?

Edit/Proofread

CHECK FOR ERRORS Students should reread their character descriptions checking for details, accuracy, grammar, spelling, and punctuation.

Publish

SHARE THE DESCRIPTIONS Have students perform their scenes for the class, and discuss each one. Is it realistic? Is it logical? Is it based on the characters and situations in the story? Does it have a beginning, middle, and end?

Character Description of Congressman Ryan

Congressman Ryan is a great representative. He proved he is a hard worker because he worked late into the night to gather votes.

Mr. Ryan is a friendly man because he stopped to talk to the people in the tunnel. He is humble because he was willing to let the people in the tunnel help him. He proved he was sensitive by inviting people to come to Congress to watch the vote.

Ryan showed that he is dedicated by arguing on the floor of Congress for what he believed. He is brave because he fought for what he believed in.

Presentation Ideas

PANTOMIME A CHARACTER Have a student pantomime the character description, using body language and facial expressions, while someone else reads the description aloud to the class. ▶ **Speaking/Listening**

ILLUSTRATE CHARACTER DESCRIPTIONS Have students listen to the character descriptions and respond by drawing a picture that comes to mind.
▶ **Viewing/Representing**

Friendly

Consider students' creative efforts, possibly adding a plus (+) for originality, wit, and imagination.

Scoring Rubric

Excellent	Good	Fair	Unsatisfactory
4: The writer	**3:** The writer	**2:** The writer	**1:** The writer
• uses detailed clues from the story to craft a well-rounded character description.	• builds a character description from a range of story details.	• may use story details to describe a character.	• may not present details from the story.
• uses vivid sensory language to create a unique image of the character.	• includes sensory imagery to paint a picture of the character.	• may describe the character, but may omit distinguishing details.	• may not describe a specific character.
• gives a strong sense of the character's personality and feelings.	• provides a solid sense of the character's personality.	• may touch on personality, but not in any detailed depth.	• may not grasp the task to describe a person.

0: The writer leaves the page blank or fails to respond to the writing task. The student does not address the topic or simply paraphrases the prompt. The response is illegible or incoherent.

For a 6-point or an 8-point scale, see pages T105–T106.

Meeting Individual Needs for Writing

EASY

Newspaper Stories Have students find newspaper stories or pictures that show ways in which the struggle depicted in *The Silent Lobby* is still going on today. Have them bring in the stories, write a one-sentence summary, and present them to the class.

ON-LEVEL

Letter Have students write a letter from Craig to his father, saying how he feels about him and expressing his feelings and thoughts about their trip to Washington.

CHALLENGE

Letter Have students write a letter from Craig to his father, written when Craig is a grown man, with a son of his own. What would Craig say to his father years after their trip to Washington, and now that he is a father?

LANGUAGE SUPPORT

ESL English learners will benefit from using gestures to help them remember prepositions, such as *in, over, under, down,* or *up.*

DAILY LANGUAGE ACTIVITIES

Have students orally complete the sentences by filling in the missing prepositions. Sample answers given for Days 1–3.

Day 1

1. The bus drove _____ the bridge. over
2. We waited _____ the street. across
3. Papa looked _____ the engine. at

Day 2

1. Icy rain poured _____ a dark cloud. from
2. Craig waited _____ the bus as Papa spoke _____ the man. for, to
3. It arrived _____ the city _____ noon. in, at

Day 3

1. The doorman stood _____ the door. by
2. We wanted to get _____ the capitol. near
3. He told us to go _____ the tunnel _____ the building. into, under

Day 4

1. We couldn't enter _____ passes.
2. I sat _____ Papa _____ the gallery.
3. Papa sat _____ the edge _____ his seat and looked _____ all the people.

Day 5

1. This story was told _____ my father.
2. He believed _____ freedom _____ all.
3. Winning the right to vote was difficult _____ all _____ us.

Daily Language Transparency 29

DAY 1 Introduce the Concept

Oral Warm-Up Say: *They went to the Capitol and talked to members of Congress.* Note how the word *to* in the sentence links the ideas together.

Introduce Prepositions Present the following:

Prepositions

- A **preposition** comes before a noun or pronoun and relates that noun or pronoun to another word in a sentence.

- Common prepositions are *about, above, across, after, at, behind, down, for, from, in, near, of, on, over, to,* and *with.*

Present the Daily Language Activity. Then have students identify prepositions in sentences such as: *We ran down the street. They arrived in Chicago at noon.*

 WRITING Assign the daily Writing Prompt on page 698C.

Prepositions

- A **preposition** comes before a noun or pronoun and relates that noun or pronoun to another word in the sentence.
- Common prepositions are *about, above, across, after, at, behind, down, for, from, in, near, of, on, over, to, with.*

Read each sentence. Underline the prepositions. There may be more than one in each sentence.

1. Craig walked behind his father.
2. The bus traveled slowly on the highway.
3. The tired bus stalled near the Capitol.
4. Papa knew that peace came only with freedom.
5. On election day, Papa voted in town.
6. Craig waited in the hallway with his father.
7. Everyone climbed off the bus.
8. Papa stayed out late at night.
9. At least, we received a lot of votes.
10. Craig's family was worried about bombs.
11. Across the room, a congressman spoke about justice.
12. The gallery is there, above the main floor.
13. After awhile, we had seats in the gallery.
14. The congressperson spoke over the loudspeaker.

Grade 5/Unit 5 14
The Silent Lobby

Extension: Invite students to write and deliver speeches on civil rights. Ask them to circle prepositions in their written copies.

179

GRAMMAR PRACTICE BOOK, PAGE 179

DAY 2 Teach the Concept

Review Prepositions Ask students to give examples of prepositions.

Introduce Prepositional Phrases Present and discuss the following:

Prepositional Phrases

- A **prepositional phrase** is a group of words that begins with a preposition and ends with a noun or pronoun.

- The object of a preposition is the noun or pronoun that follows the preposition.

Display sentences such as: *The ball landed on the grass.* Have students identify the preposition and the object of the preposition.

Present the Daily Language Activity. Have students write three sentences containing prepositional phrases.

 WRITING Assign the daily Writing Prompt on page 698C.

Prepositional Phrases

- A prepositional phrase is a group of words that begins with a preposition and ends with a noun or pronoun.
- The object of a preposition is the noun or pronoun that follows the preposition.

Underline the preposition in each sentence. Circle the object of the preposition.

1. We wonder who is seated in Congress.
2. A congressperson spoke to us.
3. Mama said good-bye from the door.
4. The old bus made it all the way with all its problems.
5. Congresspeople walked through the tunnel.
6. Equality means one vote for every adult.
7. Craig spoke up above the noise.
8. Some congresspeople were on our side.

Complete each sentence with a prepositional phrase. Answers will vary.

9. _____On the road_____, it was cold and rainy.
10. Craig's family wanted to talk _____with the congresspeople_____.
11. No one would let them sit _____in the gallery_____.
12. Civil rights are important _____for everyone_____.
13. Craig was proud _____of his father_____.
14. They were sent to wait _____in the tunnel_____.
15. Craig stood _____up for freedom_____.

180

Extension: Ask students to rewrite sentences 9 through 15, adding at least one more prepositional phrase to each sentence.

Grade 5/Unit 5 15
The Silent Lobby

GRAMMAR PRACTICE BOOK, PAGE 180

Prepositions

Review Prepositions Read this sentence from page 706 of *The Silent Lobby*.

> **Icy rain pelted us as we rushed against cold wind back to the Capitol.**

Ask students to identify the prepositions in the sentence. Encourage students to explain how they identified the words as prepositions.

Identifying Prepositions Present the Daily Language Activity and have students complete the sentences orally.

Have students read a page from *The Silent Lobby*. Have them list all the prepositions they can find on the page.

 Assign the daily Writing Prompt on page 698D.

Review Prepositions Write some of the prepositions used to complete the sentences from the Daily Language Activity, Days 1 through 3. Invite students to create new sentences using the prepositions listed. Then present the Daily Language Activity for Day 4.

Mechanics and Usage A prepositional phrase may come at the beginning of a sentence. Display and discuss:

- Put a comma after a prepositional phrase composed of four or more words that comes at the beginning of a sentence.

Provide examples such as: *After the long test, we were very tired*.

 Assign the daily Writing Prompt on page 698D.

Assess Use the Daily Language Activity and page 183 of the **Grammar Practice Book** for assessment.

Reteach Have students write prepositions on index cards. Then have each student pick a card. Whichever preposition they pick, they must create a sentence containing the preposition.

Have each student illustrate a different preposition, then display them all together in a mosaic.

Use page 184 of the **Grammar Practice Book** for additional reteaching.

 Assign the daily Writing Prompt on page 698D.

Prepositions and Prepositional Phrases

- **A preposition** comes before a noun or pronoun and relates that noun or pronoun to another word in the sentence.
- **Common prepositions** are *about, above, across, after, at, behind, down, for, from, in, near, of, on, over, to, with.*
- **A prepositional phrase** is a group of words that begins with a preposition and ends with a noun or pronoun.
- The object of a preposition is the noun or pronoun that follows the preposition.

Underline the prepositional phrase in each sentence. Write the object of the preposition on the line.

1. Craig fought the good fight <u>for freedom</u>. _____ freedom
2. An old bus might never make it <u>to the city</u>. _____ city
3. Papa put his arm <u>around Craig's shoulders</u>. _____ Craig's shoulders
4. The civil rights movement was a struggle <u>in the South</u>. _____ south
5. Today every American can vote <u>on election day</u>. _____ election day
6. <u>Across the road</u>, Craig saw the Capitol. _____ road
7. <u>Near the Capitol</u>, a crowd gathered. _____ Capitol

Complete the sentences with prepositional phrases. Answers will vary.

8. <u>After the demonstration</u> some Congresspeople changed their minds.
9. Craig learned a valuable lesson <u>on that day</u>.
10. <u>On the way to Washington,</u> the bus had engine trouble.
11. <u>Before the vote,</u> there seemed to be no hope.
12. Craig sat <u>in the gallery</u>.

Grade 5/Unit 6
The Silent Lobby

Extension: Have students write ten sentences, each with at least one prepositional phrase. Have them underline the prepositional phrases.   181

GRAMMAR PRACTICE BOOK, PAGE 181

Commas and Prepositional Phrases

- A prepositional phrase may come at the beginning of a sentence.
- Put a comma after a prepositional phrase composed of four or more words that comes at the beginning of a sentence.

Read the essay. Place commas where they are needed.

Before the civil rights movement, life was hard in many black communities. In the southern states, African-Americans were turned away from many restaurants and stores. On city buses, African-Americans had to sit in the back. At many voting polls, African-Americans were forced to take unfair tests. Even in the public schools, African American students were treated unfairly.

Martin Luther King was a champion of civil rights. He knew every American should have the chance to vote. He believed all people should attend decent schools and be able to use public transportation, restrooms, and restaurants. Soon many people were marching. Over the entire United States, people spoke up for equality. With such a strong public protest, changes were bound to take place. After a long hard struggle, the Civil Rights Act was passed.

182   Grade 5/Unit 6
The Silent Lobby   6

GRAMMAR PRACTICE BOOK, PAGE 182

Prepositions

Circle the letter of the preposition that fits best in each sentence.

1. Craig's community fought _____ civil rights.
   a. near
   b. for
   c. at
2. The Capitol is _____ Washington, D.C.
   a. in
   b. over
   c. under
3. The struggle against prejudice continues _____ America.
   a. of
   b. before
   c. across
4. People everywhere fought _____ violence.
   a. to
   b. without
   c. of
5. Please give this letter _____ the congressperson.
   a. after
   b. near
   c. to
6. Craig was a young boy _____ the south.
   a. from
   b. after
   c. with
7. Papa knew a lot _____ prejudice.
   a. across
   b. with
   c. about
8. We trust our congressperson will vote _____ our cause.
   a. over
   b. of
   c. for

Grade 5/Unit 6
The Silent Lobby   183

GRAMMAR PRACTICE BOOK, PAGE 183

5 Day Spelling Plan

DICTATION SENTENCES

Spelling Words

1. The teacher gives us instruction.
2. Do you have a suggestion for the plan?
3. I read the newspaper for information.
4. I go to school to get an education.
5. Use your imagination to create a story.
6. Make a selection from these books.
7. Mistakes can cause confusion.
8. Did you get the invitation to my party?
9. What is the main attraction of the show?
10. We made a reservation for dinner.
11. My sister will vote in this election.
12. The goal of perfection is just a dream.
13. We had a phone conversation.
14. The store is moving to a new location.
15. The population of the city is growing.
16. Noise makes me lose my concentration.
17. Give this matter your consideration.
18. The human rights demonstration is now.
19. A constitution guides a government.
20. I want to make a correction to my paper.

Challenge Words

21. Help me interpret these rules.
22. Persuade me to change my mind.
23. All visitors must register in the book.
24. My old dress looks shabby.
25. The soft music is very soothing.

DAY 1 — Pretest

Assess Prior Knowledge Use the Dictation Sentences at the left and **Spelling Practice Book** page 179 for the pretest. Allow students to correct their own papers. Students who require a modified list may be tested on the first ten words.

Spelling Words		Challenge Words
1. instruction	11. **election**	21. **interpret**
2. suggestion	12. perfection	22. **persuade**
3. information	13. conversation	23. **register**
4. education	14. location	24. **shabby**
5. imagination	15. population	25. **soothing**
6. selection	16. concentration	
7. confusion	17. consideration	
8. invitation	18. **demonstration**	
9. attraction	19. **constitution**	
10. reservation	20. correction	

*Note: Words in **dark type** are from the story.*

Word Study On page 180 of the **Spelling Practice Book** are word study steps and an at-home activity.

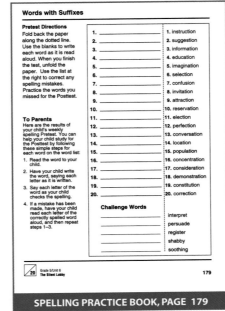

SPELLING PRACTICE BOOK, PAGE 179

WORD STUDY STEPS AND ACTIVITY, PAGE 180

DAY 2 — Explore the Pattern

Words with Suffixes Write *education* on the chalkboard and underline the suffix *-ion.* Ask students what the base word is and how its spelling changes when the suffix is added. (*educate;* final *e* is dropped.) Have students read the Spelling Words aloud and sort them as below.

Words with suffixes

-ion

instruction	perfection
suggestion	location
education	population
selection	concentration
confusion	demonstration
attraction	constitution
election	correction

-ation

information	reservation
imagination	conversation
invitation	consideration

Spelling Patterns Have students identify which base words change their spelling when the suffix is added and which do not.

Words with Suffixes

instruction	imagination	attraction	conversation	consideration
suggestion	selection	reservation	location	demonstration
information	confusion	election	population	constitution
education	invitation	perfection	concentration	correction

Sort each spelling word according to the suffix which it contains. Write the words which contain the following suffixes:

-ion		**-ation**	
1. instruction		15. information	
2. suggestion		16. imagination	
3. education		17. invitation	
4. selection		18. reservation	
5. confusion		19. conversation	
6. attraction		20. consideration	
7. election			
8. perfection			
9. location			
10. population			
11. concentration			
12. demonstration			
13. constitution			
14. correction			

SPELLING PRACTICE BOOK, PAGE 181

Words with Suffixes

DAY 3 — Practice and Extend

Word Meaning: Suffixes Remind students that adding *-ion* or *-ation* to a word changes it from a verb to a noun. Tell students that the suffixes *-ion* and *-ation* mean "the act of" or "the state of being." Have students use the suffix definitions to figure out the meanings of the Spelling Words.

If students need extra practice, have partners give each other a midweek test.

Glossary Review the illustrative sentences in the Glossary. Have partners:

- write each Challenge Word.
- look up each word in the Glossary and find the illustrative sentence.
- write the illustrative sentence for each word.

DAY 4 — Proofread and Write

Proofread Sentences Write these sentences on the chalkboard, including the misspelled words. Ask students to proofread, circling incorrect spellings and writing the correct spellings. There are two spelling errors in each sentence.

> We should have a conversasion about the elektion. (conversation, election)
>
> Did you use my sugestion about printing the invitasion? (suggestion, invitation)

Have students create additional sentences with errors for partners to correct.

WRITING Have students use as many spelling words as possible in the daily Writing Prompt on page 698D. Remind students to proofread their writing for errors in spelling, grammar, and punctuation.

DAY 5 — Assess and Reteach

Assess Students' Knowledge Use page 184 of the **Spelling Practice Book** or the Dictation Sentences on page 717O for the posttest.

Personal Word List Have students add any troublesome words in the lesson to their personal lists of troublesome words in their journals. Have students write a definition for each word using the suffix and base (root) word. Students can refer to their word lists during later writing activities.

Spelling Practice Book, Page 182

Words with Suffixes

instruction	imagination	attraction	conversation	consideration
suggestion	selection	reservation	location	demonstration
information	confusion	election	population	constitution
education	invitation	perfection	concentration	correction

Complete each sentence below with a spelling word.

1. Getting a good ___education___ will help you get a good job.
2. The clothing store had a large ___selection___ of suits.
3. I sent my best friend the first ___invitation___ to my party.
4. I called the restaurant and made a ___reservation___ for dinner.
5. He ran for mayor during the November ___election___.
6. Cities have a larger ___population___ than towns.

Similar Words

Write the spelling word which is closest in meaning to each word or phrase.

7. teaching ___instruction___
8. idea ___suggestion___
9. chaos ___confusion___
10. appeal ___attraction___
11. excellence ___perfection___
12. place ___location___
13. close attention ___concentration___
14. display ___demonstration___
15. body of laws ___constitution___
16. revision ___correction___
17. data ___information___
18. fantasy ___imagination___
19. talk ___conversation___
20. careful thought ___consideration___

182 | Challenge Extension: Write one sentence for each Challenge Word. | Grade 5/Unit 6 The Silent Lobby | 20

SPELLING PRACTICE BOOK, PAGE 182

Spelling Practice Book, Page 183

Words with Suffixes

Proofreading Activity

There are six spelling mistakes in the letter below. Circle the misspelled words. Write the words correctly on the lines below.

Dear Congressman Hawkins,

I want to thank you for supporting our cause during our visit to Washington. There was so much confusin in that tunnel before you stopped and had a converzashun with my father. My mother thought this kind of demonstrator wouldn't do any good. But thanks to you and other members of Congress, the whole American adult population can vote. I hope you win your next elektion. Thank you again for your help and your considderation.

Sincerely,
Craig

1. ___confusion___ 3. ___demonstration___ 5. ___election___
2. ___conversation___ 4. ___population___ 6. ___consideration___

Writing Activity

Think of something you would like to see the government do for you or for your community. Write a letter to your representative in Congress describing what you would like done. Use four spelling words in your writing.

18 | Grade 5/Unit 6 The Silent Lobby | 183

SPELLING PRACTICE BOOK, PAGE 183

Spelling Practice Book, Page 184

Words with Suffixes

Look at the words in each set below. One word in each set is spelled correctly. Use a pencil to fill in the circle next to the correct word. Before you begin, look at the sample sets of words. Sample A has been done for you. Do Sample B by yourself. When you are sure you know what to do, you may go on with the rest of the page.

Sample A:
- (A) stashion
- (B) stashun
- (C) staytion
- (D) station

Sample B:
- (A) invenshion
- (B) invention
- (C) invendion
- (D) invenntion

1. (A) instiction (B) instruction (C) instruction (D) instrection
2. (E) sujestion (F) sugestion (G) suggestion (H) sudjestion
3. (A) information (B) infirmation (C) infomation (D) imformation
4. (E) edoocation (F) edyucation (G) educatin (H) education
5. (A) imajination (B) imadjination (C) imagination (D) imaginaton

6. (E) seelection (F) selection (G) silection (H) selection
7. (A) confusion (B) confusion (C) confoson (D) confyusin
8. (E) invitashun (F) invitation (G) invetation (H) invitaton
9. (A) attraction (B) atraction (C) attractin (D) attrction
10. (E) reservation (F) riservation (G) resivation (H) reservation

11. (A) election (B) eliction (C) elektion (D) electon
12. (E) prefection (F) perfection (G) pirfection (H) perfektion
13. (A) conversion (B) confersation (C) conversation (D) convisation
14. (E) lokation (F) location (G) locatin (H) locashun
15. (A) population (B) popyulation (C) popultion (D) populaton

16. (E) consentation (F) concintraton (G) concentration (H) consintration
17. (A) considuration (B) consideration (C) consideraton (D) consideration
18. (E) demonstration (F) demonstration (G) deminstraytin (H) deminstraton
19. (A) constitultion (B) constitution (C) constitution (D) constitution
20. (E) correction (F) correcton (G) corection (H) correcton

184 | Grade 5/Unit 6 The Silent Lobby | 20

SPELLING PRACTICE BOOK, PAGE 184

Amazon Alert!

Selection Summary In this article, students will read about the loss of large areas of the Amazon rain forest, a valuable and largely unexplored ecosystem. The article explores ways to protect the rain forest against further destruction.

TIME
FOR KIDS
SPECIAL REPORT

Amazon
ALERT!

People in Brazil burn down trees in the Amazon rain forest to make way for homes.

Student Listening Library Audiocassette

INSTRUCTIONAL
Pages 720–723

Resources for Meeting Individual Needs

EASY
Pages 727A, 727D

INDEPENDENT
Pages 727B, 727D

CHALLENGE
Pages 727C, 727D

LEVELED PRACTICE

Reteach, 214–
blackline masters with reteaching opportunities for each assessed skill

Practice, 214–
workbook with Take-Home stories and practice opportunities for each assessed skill and story comprehension

Extend, 214–
blackline masters that offer challenge activities for each assessed skill

ADDITIONAL RESOURCES

- **Language Support Book,** 233–
- **Take-Home Story, Practice,** p.
- **Alternative Teaching Strategies,** T60–T66

McGraw-Hill School
TECHNOLOGY

inter**NET** Research and Inquiry Ideas. Visit
CONNECTION *www.mhschool.com/reading*

Suggested Lesson Planner

READING AND LANGUAGE ARTS	**DAY 1** *Focus on Reading and Skills*	**DAY 2** *Read the Literature*
• **Comprehension** • **Vocabulary** • **Phonics/Decoding** • **Study Skills** • **Listening, Speaking, Viewing, Representing**	**Read Aloud and Motivate,** 718E *For Old Time Sake: A Tree Speaks* **Develop Visual Literacy,** 718/719 ☑ **Review Sequence of Events,** 720A–720B **Teaching Chart 175** Reteach, Practice, Extend, 214	**Build Background,** 720C Develop Oral Language **Vocabulary,** 720D *confirmed lush variety* *isolated tropical wonderland* **Teaching Chart 176** **Vocabulary Cards** Reteach, Practice, Extend, 215 **Read the Selection,** 720–723 ☑ Review Sequence of Events ☑ Review Draw Conclusions
• **Curriculum Connections**	 **Works of Art,** 718/719	Science, 720C
• **Writing**	**Writing Prompt:** Imagine you are a monkey living in the Amazon rain forest. Write a letter to a logger explaining how your home is being affected by logging.	**Writing Prompt:** You are on vacation in the Amazon rain forest. Write a diary entry describing your two favorite activities you did that day. **Journal Writing,** 723 Quick-Write
• **Grammar**	**Introduce the Concept: Sentence Combining,** 727M Daily Language Activity 1. Parrots live in the rain forest. The parrots are brightly colored. 2. The piranha is fierce. The piranha lives in the Amazon River. 3. Monkeys swing on vines. They swing wildly. **Grammar Practice Book,** 185	**Teach the Concept: Sentence Combining,** 727M Daily Language Activity 1. Indian tribes are isolated. They are in the rain forest. 2. The Indian cobra is deadly. The Indian cobra lives in the rain forest. **Grammar Practice Book,** 186
• **Spelling**	**Pretest: Words from Math,** 727O Spelling Practice Book, 185–186	**Explore the Patterns: Words from Math,** 727O Spelling Practice Book, 187

Read EVERY DAY

✓ = **Skill Assessed in Unit Test**

DAY 3 — Read the Literature

Rereading for Fluency, 722

Story Questions, 724
Reteach, Practice, Extend, 216
Story Activities, 725

Study Skill, 726
✓ Use an Encyclopedia
Teaching Chart 177
Reteach, Practice, Extend, 217

Test Power, 727

Read the Leveled Books
Guided Reading
✓ Review Sequence of Events
✓ Instructional Vocabulary

Writing Prompt: Write a letter from the point of view of an Indian in Brazil to Possuelo thanking him for the work he is doing.

Writing Process: Write a Story, 727K
Prewrite, Draft

Review and Practice: Sentence Combining, 727N
Daily Language Activity
1. The Amazon rain forest is very large. This forest is lush.
2. The flying dragon lizard glides swiftly. It glides from tree to tree.

Grammar Practice Book, 187

Practice and Extend: Words from Math, 727P
Spelling Practice Book, 188

DAY 4 — Build and Review Skills

Read the Leveled Books and Self-Selected Books

✓ **Review Cause and Effect,** 727E–727F
Teaching Chart 178
Reteach, Practice, Extend, 218
Language Support, 238

✓ **Review Synonyms and Antonyms,** 727G–727H
Teaching Chart 179
Reteach, Practice, Extend, 219
Language Support, 239

Writing Prompt: Write a monologue by a construction supervisor who is building roads in the rain forest.

Writing Process: Write a Story, 727K
Revise

Meeting Individual Needs for Writing, 727L

Review and Practice: Sentence Combining, 727N
Daily Language Activity
1. The rain forest is being destroyed. It is being destroyed quickly.
2. Space satellites take pictures. They take pictures of the Amazon.

Grammar Practice Book, 188

Proofread and Write: Words from Math, 727P
Spelling Practice Book, 189

DAY 5 — Build and Review Skills

Read Self-Selected Books

✓ **Review Context Clues**
Teaching Chart 140
Reteach, Practice, Extend, 220
Language Support, 240

Listening, Speaking, Viewing, Representing, 727L
Publish Your Book
Make a Speech

Writing Prompt: You and your best friend are sailing down the Amazon River. Write a story telling about two events that happened on one day of your trip.

Writing Process: Write a Story, 727K
Edit/Proofread, Publish

Assess and Reteach: Sentence Combining, 727N
Daily Language Activity
1. Many houseplants came from the rain forest. The plants are popular.
2. Possuelo is working to protect Indians. He is working tirelessly.

Grammar Practice Book, 189–190

Assess and Reteach: Words from Math, 727P
Spelling Practice Book, 190

Link

Language Arts

Read Aloud and Motivate

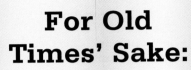

For Old Times' Sake:

a poem by James Kirkup

I live out my life

in these widening rings

like a thrown stone's ripples

from the centre of things.

I grew with each year

in sunshine and dark;

each ripple expanded

my long coat of bark.

How small my beginnings,

the seed of my heart—

but growing and flowing

with life from the start.

So many bird songs

are caught in my grooves,

and voices, and laughter,

and wild horses' hooves!

Continued on pages T2–T5

Oral Comprehension

LISTENING AND SPEAKING As you read aloud this poem in which an old tree tells about its life, encourage students to think about the sequence of the events in the tree's life. When you have finished reading, ask: "What do the rings of the tree have to do with the order of events in the tree's life? How does the poet let you know that time has passed?"

Activity Provide water color or tempera paints and paper for students to use to paint the tree at each season or stage of its life. Students can label their paintings with phrases or verses from the poem. Display their artwork in class. ▶ **Visual/Spatial**

Develop Visual Literacy

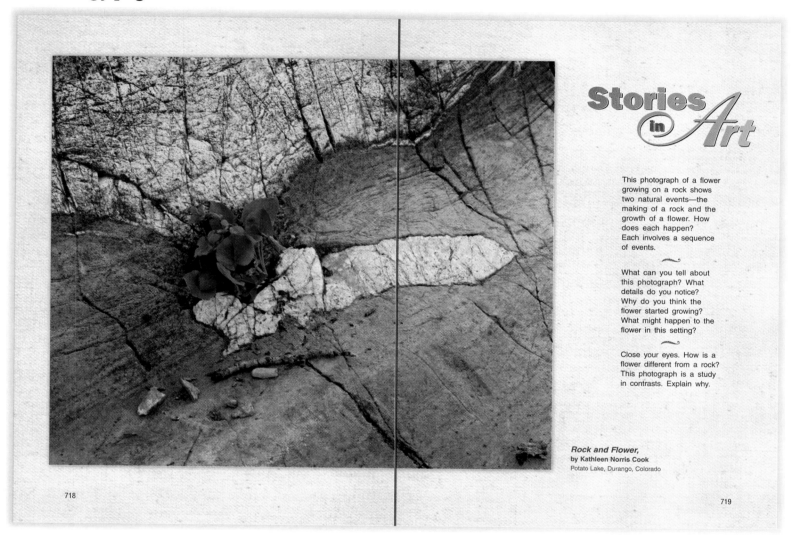

Stories in Art

This photograph of a flower growing on a rock shows two natural events—the making of a rock and the growth of a flower. How does each happen? Each involves a sequence of events.

~

What can you tell about this photograph? What details do you notice? Why do you think the flower started growing? What might happen to the flower in this setting?

~

Close your eyes. How is a flower different from a rock? This photograph is a study in contrasts. Explain why.

Rock and Flower,
by Kathleen Norris Cook
Potato Lake, Durango, Colorado

718

719

Objective: Review Sequence of Events

VIEWING Have students look carefully at the photograph. Ask if this image would have been as spectacular if it had been drawn or painted instead. Lead students to describe the sequence of events that occurs during the formation of a rock and during the growth of a flower. Discuss how the photographer used the composition of his work to get across the idea of strength in the beauty of nature.

Read the page with students, encouraging individual interpretations of the photograph.

Ask students to support inferences they make about the sequence of events in the photograph. For example:

• The rock must have cracked to allow the flower to grow through it.

• A seed must have reached the soil beneath the rock in order for the flower to grow.

REPRESENTING Have students write a story that begins with a flashback. They should begin with the final scene, much like the flower in the rock, and use the plot of the story to discuss the events that led up to the final scene.

Review **Sequence of Events**

Students will arrange events in sequence.

TEACHING TIP

INSTRUCTIONAL A time line can be useful in organizing events in sequence. It can be used for short as well as long spans of time. Have students

- prepare a time line to show the steps they might follow in preparing for an activity. Have them include art showing each step.
- display their time lines.

PREPARE

Discuss Sequence of Events
Have students brainstorm a sequence of events related to one aspect of their lives. For example, students are educated sequentially (preschool, kindergarten, elementary school, middle school, high school, college, graduate school).

TEACH

Define Sequence of Events
Tell students: To understand a story fully it is important to identify the time order in which the events in the story occur, or the sequence of events. Point out that clue words such as *first*, *next*, and *finally* can help them recognize a sequence of events.

Remembering a Tree

(Last week,) Rafael visited the home in which he grew up. He was amazed at how tall the tree in his old front yard had grown. Rafael and his father had planted the tree when Rafael was five years old. He and his father bought the tree at a plant nursery and brought it home to plant. The tree was about the length of a shoe box. (First) they dug a large hole and placed the tree in it. Next they covered the roots with dirt and patted it down. Finally they watered the tree. (Throughout the years,) the tree had grown and grown. (Now) it is about the length of a fire truck.

Teaching Chart 175

Read the Story and Model the Skill
Display **Teaching Chart 175.** Tell students to read "Remembering a Tree," focusing on the sequence of events.

MODEL As I read, I see the clue words *first, next,* and *finally,* which give me information about the sequence of events in the story.

Identify Sequence of Events in the Text
Have students list Rafael's actions in the order in which they are presented in the story. Are the events presented in chronological order? Tell students to circle the clue words or phrases that indicate sequence of events.

PRACTICE

Create a Sequence of Events Chart

Using a Sequence of Events chart, have students record notes on the planting of the tree from the passage. Help them begin filling in the chart and have volunteers complete it. ▶ **Linguistic/Logical**

When Rafael was five, he and his father bought a small tree.

▼

They brought the tree home.

▼

ASSESS/CLOSE

Judge the Importance of Sequence

In life, the sequence in which events occur can be important or unimportant. For example, it is important to put on your socks before putting on your shoes, but sequence is unimportant when it comes to the order in which you brush your teeth and wash your face.

Have groups of students think of at least four examples in which sequence is important or unimportant. Ask groups to share their examples with the class.

SELECTION
Connection

Students will apply sequence of events when they read *Amazon Alert!*

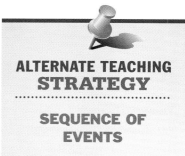

ALTERNATE TEACHING
STRATEGY

SEQUENCE OF EVENTS

For a different approach to teaching this skill, see page T66.

Meeting Individual Needs for Comprehension

EASY

Sequence of Events

When reading a short story following the **sequence of events**, or the order in which things occur, will help you better understand the story. Clue words such as *before, first, then, next, after, last,* and *finally* help to show a stories' sequence.

Read the story. Circle the sequence clue words. Afterwards, remember the sequence so that you can answer questions 1 to 4.

Omar had to write a report about Brazil. First, he located Brazil on a world map. He discovered that it is in South America. Then he identified three important cities in Brazil—Rio de Janeiro, São Paulo, and Brasília. Next, he looked at many books for ideas about natural wonders in Brazil. His favorite area of Brazil was the Amazon River Basin and its rain forest. After outlining his report, he neatly wrote it out in long hand and handed it into his teacher. Then he recited his report for his class. Finally, Omar said, "Now I'd really love to visit Brazil."

1. Did Omar identify the cities in Brazil before or after he located Brazil on the map?
   a. before   **b. after**

2. Did Omar locate key cities in Brazil before or after reading books about Brazil's natural wonders?
   a. before   b. after

3. Did Omar outline his report before or after he wrote it in long hand?
   a. before   b. after

4. Did Omar decide he wanted to visit Brazil before or after he wrote his report?
   a. before   **b. after**

Book 5/Unit 6
Amazon Alert!   **10**

At Home: Have students write the sequence of events for the last trip they took, neighbor without being paid.   214

Reteach, 214

ON-LEVEL

Sequence of Events

Events in a story happen in a certain **sequence** or order. By recognizing that sequence you can make better sense of a story.

Read the short story. The story chart below lists story events that are out of order. Number each event in the correct sequence.

Arnie has a job delivering newspapers to his neighbors in the morning. He gets up before sunrise to start his work. It is still dark when he rides five blocks to the newspaper truck. There, Mr. Popkin loads 50 newspapers onto the red wagon attached to the back of Arnie's bike. Then Arnie spends almost two hours riding his bike up and down the streets in his neighborhood.

When he gets to Mr. Hanson's house, he finds a blueberry muffin waiting for him in the newspaper basket. Mr. Santiago greets Arnie at his fence, because he knows Arnie is scared of the Santiago's big barking dogs. Mr. Santiago hopes someday Arnie will not be afraid of the dogs. Poor Arnie always hands him the paper and rushes off.

When he arrives home, Arnie's dad has breakfast waiting for him. Arnie puts the blueberry muffin in the cupboard, deciding he'll eat it later.

Sequence	Event
8	Arnie decides to keep the muffin in the cupboard and to eat it later.
6	Arnie is scared of the Santiago's dogs, so he hands the paper to Mr. Santiago and rushes off.
3	Mr. Popkin loads Arnie's wagon with newspapers.
2	Arnie rides his bike five blocks to the newspaper truck.
4	Mr. Santiago greets Arnie at his fence.
5	Arnie finds a blueberry muffin waiting for him at Mr. Hanson's.
7	Arnie arrives home and eats breakfast.
1	Arnie gets up before sunrise.

Book 5/Unit 6
Amazon Alert!   **8**

At Home: Have students identify the sequence of events of a favorite book or movie.   214

Practice, 214

CHALLENGE

Sequence of Events

In nonfiction articles, writers often use visual aides to show the **sequence of events**. Time lines show the order of events by using dates along a vertical or horizontal line. Flow charts show the order of events by using arrows and boxes to show what happened first, next, and last.

Below are examples of a time line and a flow chart. Follow the directions for each.

1. Fill in the time line below to show the sequence of the major events in your school day. Fill in the times and the events of the day as you go along.
   Answers will vary, but events should follow logical steps in a student's school day.

7:00 A.M.	Time:	Time:	Time:	Time:
Get up. Eat breakfast.				

2. Use the boxes in the flow chart to show the sequence of events on a Saturday that was special for you. Answers will vary but should include events in logical sequence.

Event 1 [   ]

▼

Event 2 [   ]

▼

Event 3 [   ]

▼

Event 4 [   ]

Book 5/Unit 6
Amazon Alert!

At Home: Look for examples of time lines and flow charts in magazines and newspapers.   214

Extend, 214

Build Background

Science

Evaluate Prior Knowledge

CONCEPT: SEQUENCE OF EVENTS
Many natural events take place slowly, over long periods of time. For example, it could take many years for a mountain to form. Other natural events, such as earthquakes and tornadoes, take place quickly. Have students discuss natural processes that occur quickly and slowly.

ANALYZE CYCLES Explain that sometimes a sequence of events ends where it began, and starts all over again. Such a sequence is called a *cycle*. Water follows a cycle. It falls to Earth as rain, evaporates, forms clouds, and falls again as rain. Have students think of cycles they complete repeatedly, such as washing dishes. Ask them to record the cycle on a circular story map. ▶ **Logical/Visual**

Develop Oral Language

DISCUSS EVENTS IN THE NEWS Bring **ESL** in several action photos from top news stories in magazines or newspapers. Ask students to imagine the events leading up to the event shown in the photo.

Ask students to think of words that indicate the order in which events have occurred; for example, *first, then, next, before, after, finally, last,* and so on. Write the words on the chalkboard. Have a volunteer write a sentence for each word.

Divide students into small groups. Assign one sentence on the chalkboard to each group. Challenge students to create stories sandwiching each sentence between before-and-after events. Have each group recite its story to the rest of the class.

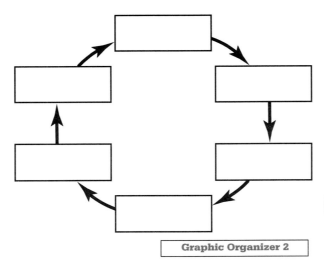

Graphic Organizer 2

ORGANIZE A MORNING Have students record what they do in the morning before school. Stress the importance of describing the events as they occur.

PARTNERS   WRITING

TEACHING TIP

MANAGEMENT Once you assign the Circular Story Map exercise, explain the Organize a Morning activity. Have students continue working on these activities.

As students work, present the Develop Oral Language activity to students who need help with oral language facility.

LANGUAGE SUPPORT

See the **Language Support Book**, pages 233–236, for teaching suggestions for Build Background and Vocabulary.

Vocabulary

Key Words

1. The (tropical) rain forest of South America is home to plant and animal species that thrive in warm, humid climates. 2. It may have the greatest (variety) of plants and animals on Earth, too numerous to count. 3. The (lush) forest is so thick with plants and trees you could swing from tree to tree for miles. 4. An amazing collection of animals, such as monkeys, parrots, and jaguars, roams in this magical (wonderland) 5. But there is trouble in paradise. Satellite photographs have (confirmed) environmentalists' fears, proving the rain forest is shrinking due to human activity. 6. This means many species of animals and plants face extinction, and the once-(isolated) tribes of Indians living there might be forced to move to crowded cities.

Teaching Chart 176

tropical (p. 721) hot and humid

variety (p. 721) an assortment or collection of different things

lush (p. 721) abundant and plentiful, especially in terms of plant life

wonderland (p. 721) an enchanted place; a land of surprises or marvels

confirmed (p. 721) having been settled as true

isolated (p. 723) separated from others

SPELLING/VOCABULARY CONNECTIONS

See Spelling Challenge Words, pages 7270–727P.

Vocabulary in Context

IDENTIFY VOCABULARY WORDS
Display **Teaching Chart 176** and read the passage with students. Have volunteers circle each vocabulary word and underline other words that are clues to its meaning.

DISCUSS MEANINGS Ask questions such as these to help clarify word meanings:

* How would you describe the weather on a tropical island?

* Do you enjoy visiting a variety of gardens and zoos? Give some examples.

* Where might you find a lush landscape?

* What two words make up the word *wonderland*? Use the word in a sentence.

* Should you believe a rumor if it has not been confirmed?

* Where might you go if your teacher tells you to find an isolated place to study?

Practice

DEMONSTRATE WORD MEANING Have partners choose vocabulary cards from a pile and demonstrate each word meaning with pantomime, drawings, or verbal clues.

▶ **Kinesthetic/Linguistic**

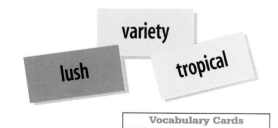

Vocabulary Cards

WRITE CONTEXT SENTENCES Have

partners write context sentences, leaving a blank for each vocabulary word. Have them exchange papers to fill in the blanks or use vocabulary cards to show answers. ▶ **Linguistic**

ON-LEVEL

Secret Garden

Reporters *confirmed* today that there is indeed a secret garden in the desert. Traveling to an isolated cottage on the outskirts of a small desert town, they discovered what one reporter called a *wonderland*.

"In the back of the abandoned cottage is a high stone wall that is clearly falling apart," claimed one reporter. "We were surprised to find what we did behind it."

"When we walked out of the cottage's back door and into the garden, it was like walking into a *tropical* forest," said the reporter. "I have never, in all my life, seen such a *variety* of plants and flowers. There were several kinds of palm trees and brightly colored birds flew among the trees. How could such a *lush* place survive in a desert?" Then, at the edge of the garden we saw a large well.

1. What does it mean if something is *confirmed*? It is proven true.

2. What sort of cottage is an *isolated* one? It is one set apart from the others.

3. What does the word *variety* mean as it is used in this story? a number of different kinds

4. What is one word that means "typical of the warmer regions of Earth"? tropical

5. What makes this "secret garden" a *lush wonderland*? It is lush because it has so many plants. It is a wonderland because it seems magical that such a garden could be possible in a desert.

Book 5/Unit 6
Amazon Alert!   At Home: Make a collage depicting a tropical wonderland.   215a

Take-Home Story 215a
Reteach 215
Practice 215 • Extend 215

720D

Guided Instruction

Preview and Predict

Have students read the title and preview the selection, looking for photos, section headings, and graphic aids that give strong clues about sequence of events and drawing conclusions.

- What clues do the pictures give about the story? How are the pictures related?
- What will the story most likely be about?
- Will the story be realistic or fictional? How can you tell? (The images are of real places, animals, and people. The story is nonfiction, based on fact.) *Genre*

Set Purposes

What do students want to find out by reading the story? For example:

- What is a rain forest?
- Where is the Amazon rain forest?
- Why is the rain forest being destroyed?
- Why is the rain forest important?

TIME FOR KIDS

SPECIAL REPORT

Amazon ALERT!

People in Brazil burn down trees in the Amazon rain forest to make way for homes.

720

Meeting Individual Needs • Grouping Suggestions for Strategic Reading

EASY

Read Together Read the story with students or have them use the **Listening Library Audiocassette.** Have students use the Sequence of Events chart to record the events in the story. Guided Instruction and Intervention prompts offer additional help with decoding, vocabulary, and comprehension.

ON-LEVEL

Guided Reading Review the story words listed on page 721. Have students read the story or listen to the **Listening Library Audiocassette.** Choose from the Guided Instruction questions as you read the story with students, directing them to record information on their Sequence of Events charts.

CHALLENGE

Read Independently Have students read independently. Remind them that paying attention to the sequence of events will help them understand the story. Have students set up Sequence of Events charts. After reading, they can use their charts to summarize the article.

Brazil Acts to Save the Rain Forest

The lush Amazon rain forest stretches about 2.7 million square miles. Brightly colored parrots, swift jaguars, and fierce piranhas make their home in the tropical forest and its many rivers. Monkeys swing among high branches and vines. The Amazon holds one-fifth of the planet's fresh water supply and the world's widest variety of wildlife.

For decades, this wildlife wonderland has been shrinking as farmers and others clear the land. Brazil's government has confirmed what environmentalists have feared: the 1990s was a terrible decade for the rain forest. According to information from Brazil's government, the destruction of the forest there reached record levels in 1995. In that year alone, 11,200 square miles were burned or cleared. That's nearly twice what was lost in 1994. Overall, one-eighth of the giant rain forest has been destroyed.

The bad news from Brazil was followed by a ray of hope. Brazil has promised to do a better job enforcing laws that protect its natural treasure.

GUYANA
SURINAME
FRENCH GUIANA
VENEZUELA
COLOMBIA
ECUADOR
Amazon River
Amazon Rain Forest
PERU
BOLIVIA
BRAZIL
PARAGUAY
ARGENTINA
URUGUAY
SOUTH AMERICA
Pacific Ocean
Atlantic Ocean
CHILE

TIME FOR KIDS Map

This fierce piranha lives in the Amazon River.

721

Guided Instruction

☑ **Sequence of Events**
☑ **Draw Conclusions**

(1) **SEQUENCE OF EVENTS** Describe what might be the sequence of events in building a house in the rain forest.

MODEL I see the lush growth of plants in the photograph. I read that people burn the forest to make room for their homes. The sequence of events: **1.** People decide where to put their homes; **2.** They burn the forest down to clear a space; **3.** They build their homes.

(2) **SEQUENCE OF EVENTS** What changes occurred in the Amazon rain forest during the first half of the 1990s?

MODEL The 1990s was a terrible decade for the rain forest according to the story. The destruction of the rain forest reached record levels in 1995. So the changes happened over time and deforestation is still occurring.

Story Words

The words below may be unfamiliar. Have students check their meanings and pronunciations in the Glossary beginning on page 730.

- wildlife, p. 721
- loggers, p. 722

LANGUAGE SUPPORT

The Sequence of Events chart is available as a blackline master in the **Language Support Book.**

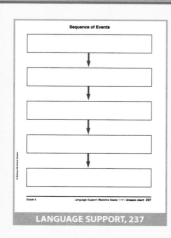

Sequence of Events

Grade 5   Language Support/Blackline Master 117 • Amazon Alert! **237**

LANGUAGE SUPPORT, 237

721

Guided Instruction

③ DRAW CONCLUSIONS Do you feel people who destroy the rain forest should be fined? Give reasons for your answer. (Sample answer: Yes, because they are harming a very precious resource.)

④ SEQUENCE OF EVENTS Use a Sequence of Events chart to record events in the story.

SEQUENCE OF EVENTS

Loggers, miners, and farmers cut down rain forest trees and plants.

⬇

People and animals living in the rain forest lose their homes and sources of food, and the world loses a valuable resource.

⬇

Brazil places limits on clearing land in the rain forest.

⬇

People ignore the laws protecting the rain forest.

⬇

Brazil punishes people who break the law with heavy fines.

ORGANIZE INFORMATION Tell students to summarize the article. Ask them how organizing the sequence of events helps them summarize the story. *Summarize*

WHO'S KILLING THE FOREST?

Loggers, miners, and farmers from Brazil and nearby countries have been rapidly moving into the Amazon since the 1960s. Some cut down trees for wood and paper. The loss of trees is called deforestation. Others simply burn the forest to clear the land. Construction of roads and airplane runways has also damaged the region.

Space satellites regularly take pictures of the Amazon. The information that got Brazil to help save the rain forest was based on these pictures. Deforestation slowed down in 1996 and 1997. But that's not necessarily because people were protecting the forest. It's because heavy rainfall made it harder to burn trees.

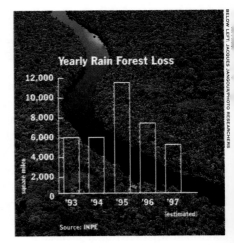

Yearly Rain Forest Loss

Source: INPE

Brazil's rain forest is filled with winding rivers like the one above.

Stephan Schwartzman of the Environmental Defense Fund calls the pace of destruction "alarming." He and other scientists are worried that they will run out of time to study the plants and animals of the rich forest. "The great tragedy is how much isn't known," he says.

CRACKING DOWN ON CRIMINALS

To slow down deforestation, Brazil decided to get tougher on people who abuse the Amazon. In 1996 Brazil placed limits on clearing land in the region. But officials did not always enforce the laws. Now those who damage the rain forest will be punished with big fines and ordered to repair the damage. "This can make a big difference," says Schwartzman. "There is hope."

722

Two macaws preen for the camera.

REREADING FOR *Fluency*

PARTNERS Have students choose favorite sections of the article to read to a partner. Encourage them to read with feeling and expression.

READING RATE To evaluate a student's reading rate, have him or her read aloud from *Amazon Alert!* for one minute. Ask the student to place a self-stick note after the last word read. Then count the number of words read.

Alternatively, you could assess small groups or the whole class together by having students count words and record their own scores.

Use the Reading Rate form in the **Diagnostic/Placement Evaluations** booklet to evaluate students' performance.

HELPING INDIANS

As the Amazon rain forest disappears, so may the way of life of native people who live there—that is, unless Sydney Possuelo has his way. Possuelo is the head of Brazil's Department of Isolated Indians, and an expert on the native tribes of the Amazon. He is helping to preserve not only the natives' ways of life but also their rain forest habitat.

Dozens of tribes make their home in unexplored areas of the Amazon. They hunt for food and make their own simple tools, clothing, and shelter. But this life is endangered by gold miners, farmers, and others pressing into new areas of the rain forest.

In the past, the Brazilian government responded by trying to prepare the tribes to live in modern society outside the forest.

Possuelo thought that the Indians and the rain forest deserved a better solution. Over time, he convinced the government that instead of trying to modernize isolated tribes, it should shield Indian land and traditions from the modern world. That way, says Possuelo, the Indians "can live their traditional life-style."

Today Possuelo has seven teams working full time to track down isolated tribes and protect them. The work is sometimes dangerous. Says Possuelo, "It involves months of being in the jungle." But finally the Indians are thankful they can again roam free through their lands. Environmentalists praise Possuelo for the protection he provides for the rich rain forest and all its species, human and nonhuman. But Possuelo insists that he is not a hero: "I like the jungle and Indians. It is not a sacrifice for me."

FIND OUT MORE
Visit our website:
www.mhschool.com/tfk

This Indian woman is a member of the Yanomami tribe. Her way of life is in danger of disappearing.

Based on an article in *TIME FOR KIDS*.

723

Guided Instruction

Return to Predictions and Purposes

Review with students their predictions and reasons for reading the story. Were their predictions correct? Did they find out what they wanted to know?

INFORMAL ASSESSMENT

SEQUENCE OF EVENTS

HOW TO ASSESS
- Can students describe and chart the sequence of events leading to the destruction of the rain forest?
- Can students predict and chart a sequence of events that would restore rain forest land?

Students should realize that the events in a story can often be organized sequentially. They should also realize that developing this skill will help them gain a deeper understanding of the text.

FOLLOW UP If students have trouble understanding sequence of events, have them think of the sequence of events leading to the completion of a simple task, such as planting a tree. Ask volunteers to write their sequence of events on the chalkboard.

LITERARY RESPONSE

QUICK-WRITE Invite students to record their thoughts about the article. These questions help them get started:

Why are people destroying the rain forest? Why is losing the rain forest a tragedy?

ORAL RESPONSE Have students share their journal writing and discuss what part of the story they enjoyed most and why.

*inter*NET CONNECTION For more information or activities on the rain forest, have students go to *www.mhschool.com/tfk*

Activity Have students create a series of maps showing the deforestation of the Amazon rain forest over the years.

723

Story Questions

Have students discuss or write answers to the questions on page 724.

Answers:

1. People are destroying the forest.
   Literal/Summarize

2. Brazil will allow only a limited amount of rain forest land to be cleared.
   Literal/Summarize

3. The rain forest is home to a diverse population of plants and animals.
   Inferential/Judgment and Decisions

4. People are trying to save the rain forest and its resources from destruction.
   Critical/Main Idea

5. Sample answer: Parts of my rain forest have been destroyed, but there is hope. If people do not interfere with nature, it will renew itself. *Critical/Reading Across Texts*

Write A Story For a full writing process lesson, see pages 727K–727L.

Story Questions & Activities

1. What is happening to the Amazon rain forest?

2. What is Brazil doing to save the rain forest?

3. What makes the Amazon rain forest important to everyone?

4. What is the main idea of this selection?

5. Imagine that one of the animals from the Amazon rain forest stepped into the painting on pages 718–719. How could it use its own experience to describe the message of the picture?

Write a Story

Many stories have been written about the rain forest. Some have been told from the animals' point of view. Choose a narrator for a story about the rain forest. Your story might be told by the loggers who are cutting down the trees or by the people or animals whose homes are being destroyed. Use one point of view throughout. Create a plot with a problem that is solved at the end.

Meeting Individual Needs

EASY	ON-LEVEL	CHALLENGE

EASY

Vocabulary

Use the correct word from the list to complete the sentences.

variety	lush	wonderland	tropical	confirmed	isolated

1. All around our home in Florida was a ___lush___ garden of plants.
2. There were bushes, trees, and a ___variety___ of different flowers.
3. The garden felt like my own ___tropical___ rain forest, complete with a small stream running through it.
4. What a ___wonderland___ for birds and small animals to live in.
5. The animals felt safe because the garden seemed ___isolated___ and protected.
6. People ___confirmed___ that our garden was the biggest in the city.

Story Comprehension

Reteach 216

Write a ✔ next to each true sentence about "Amazon Alert."

✔ 1. The Amazon rain forest holds the world's widest variety of wildlife.
✔ 2. The government of Brazil wants to protect the Amazon's rain forest.
✔ 3. Logging, mining, and farming are dangers to the rain forest.
✔ 4. Brazil has begun to punish people who hurt the rain forest.
___ 5. There are no people living in the Amazon rain forest.
✔ 6. The government in Brazil is now working to protect rain forest peoples and their traditional ways of life.
___ 7. Building more roads and airports has helped protect the rain forest.
✔ 8. Heavy rains in some years have protected the rain forest by making it harder to burn trees.

At Home: Have students write one more sentence that tells about "Amazon Alert."

215–216

Book 5/Unit 6
Amazon Alert! 8

ON-LEVEL

Story Comprehension

Answer the questions below about "Amazon Alert!" You may refer back to the story. Answers will vary. Sample responses are shown.

1. How big is the Amazon rain forest? Give the area in square miles. _____ 2.7 million square miles.

2. How much of our planet's fresh water supply does the Amazon hold? _____ one-fifth of the planet's fresh water supply.

3. What is deforestation? Who is responsible for it in the Amazon region? Deforestation is the loss of trees; loggers, miners, and farmers are responsible.

4. Why do people in Brazil burn down trees in the Amazon rain forest? to clear the land to make way for homes and farms

5. How much of the rain forest has been destroyed so far? one-eighth

6. What is the government of Brazil doing about the destruction of the Amazon rain forest? They are trying to do a better job of enforcing laws to protect the Amazon and stop people from abusing the natural resources there.

7. Why did deforestation slow down in 1996 and 1997? Heavy rainfall made it harder to burn down the trees.

8. Whose way of life in the Amazon is in danger of disappearing? the way of life of Indian groups, like the Yanomami

At Home: Share what you have learned about the Amazon rain forest with a member of your family.

216

Book 5/Unit 6
Amazon Alert! 8

CHALLENGE

Vocabulary

confirmed	isolated	lush	tropical	variety	wonderland

Write an article that describes why it is important to protect the world's rain forests. Use as many vocabulary words as you can in your article.
Answers may vary, but should include at least four vocabulary words used in correct context and parts of speech.

_____

_____

_____

_____

Extend 216

Story Comprehension

Work in a small group of three or four students. Turn the article "Amazon Alert!" into short informative skit. Find lines in the article that you can use in your skit, and assign each student in the group a role or character that deals with an issue discussed in "Amazon Alert." Present your skits to the class. Then have class members answer the following questions based on the information in the skit.

1. What conclusions can you draw about the need to protect our rain forests?
   Answers will vary.

2. Why do you think the Yanomami and the other Indians of the rain forest would prefer to live in their traditional life style?
   Answers will vary. Possible answers might include: modern ways are unknown to them; they are comfortable living on their own land and following ways and customs that are meaningful to them.

At Home: Choose two of the vocabulary words shown above. Find a synonym and antonym for each.

215–216

Book 5/Unit 6
Amazon Alert!

Reteach, 216   Practice, 216   Extend, 216

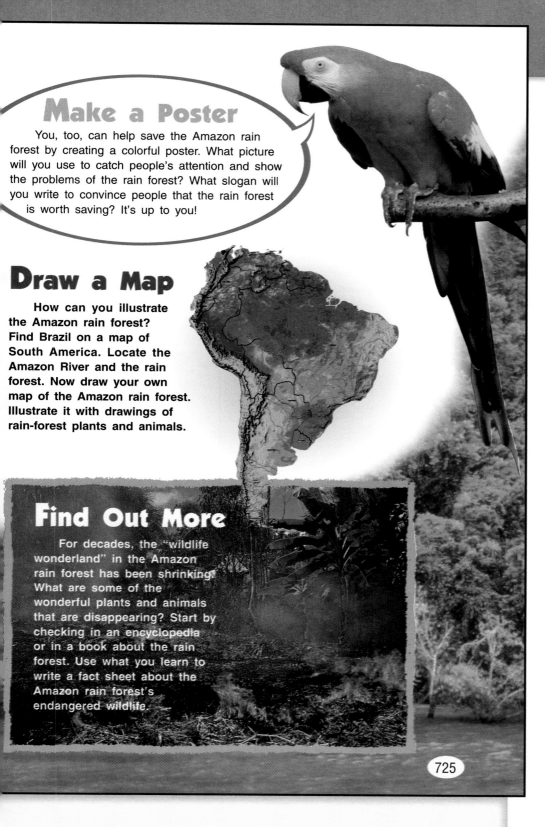

Make a Poster

You, too, can help save the Amazon rain forest by creating a colorful poster. What picture will you use to catch people's attention and show the problems of the rain forest? What slogan will you write to convince people that the rain forest is worth saving? It's up to you!

Draw a Map

How can you illustrate the Amazon rain forest? Find Brazil on a map of South America. Locate the Amazon River and the rain forest. Now draw your own map of the Amazon rain forest. Illustrate it with drawings of rain-forest plants and animals.

Find Out More

For decades, the "wildlife wonderland" in the Amazon rain forest has been shrinking. What are some of the wonderful plants and animals that are disappearing? Start by checking in an encyclopedia or in a book about the rain forest. Use what you learn to write a fact sheet about the Amazon rain forest's endangered wildlife.

725

Story Activities

Make a Poster

Materials: posterboard or large sheet of paper, markers, crayons, or paints

PARTNERS Have partners create a mural of the rain forest, saving space for a slogan. Ask students to use their posters and slogans to script a television commercial to teach people about the rain forest. Have them present their commercials to the class.

Draw a Map

Materials: world map, paper, colored pencils

GROUP Students can gain perspective of land mass by locating where they live on a world map. Have them discuss features of their own region, such as animals, plants, and buildings. How are these features similar to/different from the rain forest?

Find Out More

RESEARCH AND INQUIRY Ask students to research the difference between tropical and temperate rain forests. **GROUP** Have them create a world map showing each type of rain forest. Encourage them to use photographs or drawings to show how the rain forests are alike and different.

 Students can learn more about the rain forest by visiting *www/mhschool.com/reading*

FORMAL ASSESSMENT

After page 727, see the Selection and Unit Assessments.

725

Study Skills

LIBRARY/MEDIA CENTER

OBJECTIVES Students will:

- recognize the usefulness of an encyclopedia.
- use key words to research topics.

PREPARE Read the information with students. Display **Teaching Chart 177.**

TEACH Information in the encyclopedia is arranged alphabetically in volumes. Name several subjects, and have students tell you in which volume to look.

PRACTICE Have students answer questions 1–5. Review the answers with them.
1. information about people, places, things, events, and ideas; **2.** the volume labeled *P*; **3.** Yes. A lot of information about jaguars exists; **4.** macaw, birds, rain forest; **5.** I would look up my topic in the encyclopedia, which will also state where to look for more information.

ASSESS/CLOSE Have students tell how they would use the encyclopedia to write a report on parrots in the Amazon rain forest.

Study SKILLS

Use an Encyclopedia

Suppose that you were asked to write a research report about the Amazon rain forest. How would you begin? You could start by looking in an encyclopedia. An **encyclopedia** is a set of books that has articles about people, places, things, events, and ideas. The articles are arranged in alphabetical order in volumes.

When you use an encyclopedia to find facts about a topic, you must have a **key word** in mind. For example, for a research paper on the Amazon rain forest, you would look under the key word *Amazon* or *rain forest*.

Use the encyclopedia to answer these questions.

1 What kind of information does an encyclopedia have?

2 In which volume would you look for information on piranhas?

3 Do you think that you would find a separate article on jaguars? Why or why not?

4 What key word would you use to find information about Macaws in the rain forest?

5 How would you use an encyclopedia to write a research report?

Meeting Individual Needs

EASY	ON-LEVEL	CHALLENGE

Use an Encyclopedia

You can use an **encyclopedia** to find information for research reports and other writing assignments. Encyclopedias contain articles and facts about people, places, things, events, and ideas. The articles are arranged alphabetically. Usually encyclopedias are arranged in a series of volumes.

Use the information above to answer the questions.

1. How is an encyclopedia organized? _Information is arranged alphabetically in one or more volumes._

2. Which volume has information about Brazil? _volume 2_

3. In which volume would you find an article titled Macaws? _volume 6_

4. Which volume has information about Rio de Janeiro? _volume 9_

5. In which volume would you look for information about the environment? _volume 4_

Book 5/Unit 6
Amazon Alert!   At Home: Have students think of a topic that interests them and look it up in an encyclopedia.   217

Use an Encyclopedia

An **encyclopedia** is a research tool. It is a set of books containing articles about important people, places, things, events, and ideas. The articles are arranged by alphabetical order in volumes. When you use an encyclopedia to find facts about a topic, you must have a "key word" in mind. Look at the illustration to answer the questions.

1. Why would you want to use an encyclopedia to write a report about something? Possible answer: _An encyclopedia is a research tool that can help me quickly find out basic facts._

2. If you wanted to research information on the history of kites, what key word would you use to find your subject? _kites_

3. In which volume would you look for information about *costumes*? _volume 3, C–D_

4. In which volume would you look for information about the history of the United States? _volume 11, T – U - V, maybe A for a general overview of the Americas._

5. Which volumes do you think might have articles about French painters and artists? Explain. _volumes 1, 4, and 8; vol. 1 might have an article about artists, vol. 4 F about France and French painting, and vol. 8 P–Q might list painters. Also any of the volumes in which you would find the individual French artists you read about._

Book 5/Unit 6
Amazon Alert!   At Home: Encourage students to use a key word to research information in an encyclopedia and share their findings with a family member.   217

Use an Encyclopedia

Encyclopedias include articles on a great many subjects. They are useful when you need to find basic information about a topic. Suppose you were going to write an article about rain forests. You would need to narrow down your topic. Look at the list of possible topics below, then answer the questions.

The Amazon Rain Forest	Rain Forest Animals
People of the Rain Forest	Rain Forests of Africa
Plants of the Rain Forest	Rain Forests of New Guinea

1. Suppose you wanted to write a report about rain forest animals. In which encyclopedia volumes would you look? _You could look under R for rain; F for forests; A for animals, Africa, and Amazon; N for New Guinea. You could also look under the names of specific rain forest animals._

2. Suppose you wanted to write a report on the rain forests of New Guinea. In which encyclopedia volumes would you look? _You could look under R for rain forests or under N for New Guinea._

3. Choose one of the above topics. Use encyclopedias to write an outline a short report. Look under subcategories of your topic for subject areas you could include in your report.
Answers will vary.

Book 5/Unit 6
Amazon Alert!   At Home: Research the kinds of encyclopedias that are available in your local library. Which encyclopedias would you most likely to use in a report?   217

Reteach, 217   Practice, 217   Extend, 217

TEST POWER

Test Tip
Always read the answer choices carefully.

DIRECTIONS
Read the sample story. Then read each question about the story.

SAMPLE

Frida Kahlo

Many people consider Frida Kahlo to be one of the best Mexican artists of the twentieth century. Born in Mexico City in 1907, Frida was an active and beautiful child. At age 18, however, she had a terrible accident. Afterward, she spent many months recovering in bed.

In order to pass the time, Frida began painting. What started as a hobby soon became her life's work.

Frida married artist Diego Rivera in 1929. Rivera encouraged Frida's painting. He also thought that she should wear traditional, colorful Mexican clothing and silver jewelry. Frida became known for always dressing in this unusual style.

In 1953, a year before her death, Frida had her only art show. It was a great success. Today, Frida Kahlo's art is collected by art collectors around the world and is shown in many art museums.

1 In 1929, Frida —
- ○ was born in Mexico
- ● married Diego Rivera
- ○ had her first art show
- ○ turned 18 years old

2 Which is a FACT stated in the story?
- ○ Kahlo's jewelry is in art museums.
- ○ Rivera was Kahlo's art instructor.
- ○ Kahlo was Mexico's best artist.
- ● Kahlo's art is now in museums.

Test Power

THE PRINCETON REVIEW

Read the Page

Ask students to pay careful attention to underlined words and to *when* events happen in the passage.

Discuss the Questions

Question 1: This question requires students to recall a fact from the passage. Refer back to the passage to double-check *all* facts. Students should *not* rely on memory. Ask, "Where is the date 1929 mentioned in the passage?" Answer: paragraph 3. Ask, "What happened in 1929?" Remind students to eliminate wrong answers.

Question 2: This question requires students to determine which of the answer choices is a FACT stated in the passage. The incorrect answers in this question are not FACTS stated in the story. Remind students to use process of elimination to work through choices.

727

For The Princeton Review test preparation practice for **TerraNova, ITBS,** and **SAT-9,** visit the McGraw-Hill School Division Web site. See also McGraw-Hill's *Standardized Test Preparation Book.*

EASY
DECODABLE

☑ **Phonics**

- /ü/ and /yü/, /z/, /j/, and /f/
- /ou/ and /oi/
- unstressed syllables

☑ **Comprehension**

- Judgments and Decisions
- Draw Conclusions
- Cause and Effecct
- Sequence of Events

Answers to Story Questions
Answers will vary.

EASY

Story Questions for Selected Reading

1. What is the main problem or issue in this selection?
2. What event stands out?
3. How does chapter one set the stage for what follows?
4. Why do you think the author chose this topic?
5. What crossroads does each character come to?

Draw a Book Cover

Draw a new cover for the selection that shows a sequence of events from the story.

Self-Selected Reading
Leveled Books

EASY

UNIT SKILLS REVIEW

☑ **Comprehension**

Help students self-select an Easy Book to read and apply phonics and comprehension skills.

Guided Reading

PREVIEW AND PREDICT Discuss the illustrations in the beginning of the book. Have students predict what the story is about. Point out to students any chapter headings for additional clues to what the story is about. Have students write their predictions in their journals.

SET PURPOSES Have students write why they selected the book and what they want to find out by reading it. You may also want to ask students to pay attention to the sequence of events.

READ THE BOOK Use questions like the following to guide students' reading or after they have read the story independently.

- Identify a conclusion that one character in the story draws. *Draw Conclusions*
- Which sequence words does the author use to help you determine the sequence of events in the story? *Sequence of Events*
- Which events cause the problem encountered by characters in the story? *Cause and Effect*

- When confronted with a problem, what decision does a character make about how to solve it? *Judgments and Decisions*

RETURN TO PREDICTIONS AND PURPOSES Discuss students' predictions. Have students review their purposes for reading. Did they find out what they wanted to know? Did they have any questions left unanswered?

LITERARY RESPONSE Have students discuss questions like the following:

- What part of the book was most interesting? Why?
- If you had found yourself in the situation of the main character, what would you have done?
- If you could change one thing about the story, what would it be?

Self-Selected Reading
Leveled Books

INDEPENDENT

☑ UNIT SKILLS REVIEW

☑ Comprehension

Help students self-select an Independent Book to read and apply comprehension skills.

Guided Reading

PREVIEW AND PREDICT Discuss the illustrations in the beginning of the book. Have students predict what the story is about and list their ideas. If the book has chapter headings, point them out to students as additional clues that tell what the story is about. Have students write their predictions in their journals.

SET PURPOSES Have students write why they selected the book and what they want to find out about the book. You may also want to ask students to pay attention to the sequence of events.

READ THE BOOK Use questions like the following to guide students' as they read or after they have read the book independently.

- Which event is the most critical in the story? Where in the sequence of events does it fall? *Sequence of Events*

- If the story had happened in a different time or place, what effect would it have on the characters? *Cause and Effect*

- What conclusion can you draw about the main character in the book? *Draw Conclusions*

- How does a character solve the problem he or she is faced with? *Judgments and Decisions*

RETURN TO PREDICTIONS AND PURPOSES Discuss students' predictions. Have students review their purposes for reading. Did they find out what they wanted to know? Did they have any questions left unanswered?

LITERARY RESPONSE The following questions will help focus students' responses.

- If you could give advice to the characters in the story, what would it be?

- What did you learn in the book that might be useful to you in your own life?

INDEPENDENT
DECODABLE

☑ Comprehension

- Judgments and Decisions
- Draw Conclusions
- Cause and Effect
- Sequence of Events

Answers to Story Questions

Answers will vary and should include examples and details from stories students have read.

INDEPENDENT

Story Questions for Selected Reading

1. Why did the author choose to write this selection?

2. What event stands out most?

3. What details helped you better understand the story?

4. How do you think the characters in the selection felt about each other? Explain.

5. What crossroads does a character in the story come to?

Write a Letter

Write a letter to one of the characters describing how the events in one of the chapters affected you.

PUPIL SELECTION

CHALLENGE

☑ Comprehension

- **Judgments and Decisions**
- **Draw Conclusions**
- **Cause and Effect**
- **Sequence of Events**

Answers to Story Questions
Answers will vary.

CHALLENGE

Story Questions for Selected Reading

1. How might this selection have been different if it were written in a different genre?

2. What questions would you like to ask a person in the story?

3. How do you feel about the solution to the problem?

4. Which problem reminded you of a judgment or decision you had to make?

5. How does this selection fit in with the unit theme "Crossroads"?

Write An Interview

Write interview questions about the story to the author and answer them from the author's point of view.

Self-Selected Reading
Leveled Books

CHALLENGE

UNIT SKILLS REVIEW

☑ Comprehension

Help students self-select a Challenge Book to read and apply comprehension skills.

Guided Reading

PREVIEW AND PREDICT Discuss the illustrations in the beginning of the book. If the book has chapter headings, point them out to students for additional clues to what the story is about. Have students write their predictions in their journals.

SET PURPOSES Have students write why they selected the book and what they want to find out about the book. Ask them to share their purposes. You may also want to ask students to pay attention to the sequence of events.

READ THE BOOK Use questions like the following to guide students' reading or after they have read the story independently.

- How could a change in the sequence of events have altered the story? Would the change have made the selection more enjoyable or less enjoyable? *Sequence of Events*

- What actions taken by the main character affect the outcome of the story? *Cause and Effect*

- What events led up to the problem? Could the characters have made other decisions that would have resolved things more easily? *Judgments and Decisions*

- Which can you conclude about the main character? *Draw Conclusions*

RETURN TO PREDICTIONS AND PURPOSES Discuss students' predictions. Have students review their purposes for reading. Did they find out what they wanted to know? Were any questions left unanswered?

LITERARY RESPONSE Have students discuss questions like the following:

- What part of the story did you like most?

- How would the book have been different if the characters were you and your friends?

- What piece of advice would you want to give the main character?

Activities

Anthology and Leveled Books

Connecting Texts

CLASS DISCUSSION Write the theme "Crossroads" in the center of the semantic map. Write the story titles from four to six selections in the balloons connected to the center. Discuss with students what crossroads is encountered by characters in each selection. Chart their ideas in the semantic map as in the example at right.

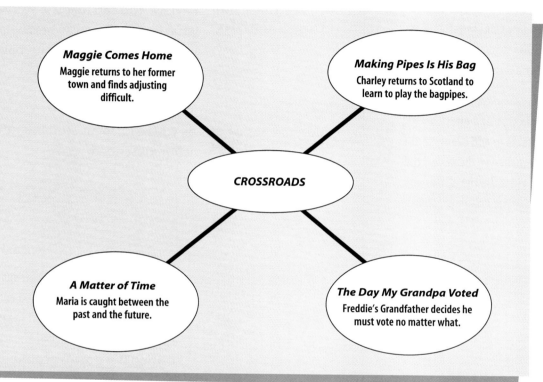

Maggie Comes Home
Maggie returns to her former town and finds adjusting difficult.

Making Pipes Is His Bag
Charley returns to Scotland to learn to play the bagpipes.

CROSSROADS

A Matter of Time
Maria is caught between the past and the future.

The Day My Grandpa Voted
Freddie's Grandfather decides he must vote no matter what.

Viewing/Representing

GROUP PRESENTATIONS Have students break into groups in which students have all read the same title. Have each group pick an important scene from a story to reenact and explain why the scene is important.

AUDIENCE RESPONSE Ask students to listen quietly to each group's presentation. After viewing the reenactments, have each student turn to a partner and summarize for him or her the importance of the scene they have watched.

Research and Inquiry

CHOOSE A TOPIC Have students choose a topic to research. Invite them to:

- list a few questions about their topics

- talk to teachers and librarians about ways to find information

- take notes as they gather information.

 INTERNET CONNECTION Have students log on to **www.mhschool.com/reading** for links to Web pages.

727D

Students will identify cause-and-effect relationships.

LANGUAGE SUPPORT

ESL Invite volunteers to pantomime key events from the story. Ask the other students to write a sentence describing each event.

Continue working with the concept of cause and effect, asking volunteers to add events to the story. Challenge the rest of the class to identify the causes and effects of the imagined events.

Review Cause and Effect

PREPARE

Discuss Cause and Effect

Review: You can follow a story more precisely by paying attention to what happens (cause) and what results (effect). Ask: How might the weather be the cause for what you wore to school this morning?

TEACH

Read "A Basket of Berries" and Model the Skill

As you read, focus students' attention on the cause and effect of each action described.

A Basket of Berries

An Indian girl went deep into the tropical rain forest to pick berries. She spotted a bush laden with berries near the edge of a river. The girl leaned over to reach the bush. As a result, she lost her balance and fell into the river. The river carried her downstream because the water was moving quickly. Luckily, the water slowed making it possible for her to grab a branch and pull herself out.

Teaching Chart 178

Discuss clues (words like *as a result* and *because*, for example) in the passage that can help readers see cause-and-effect relationships.

MODEL The girl wanted to pick berries. That is a cause for an action or event. She went deep into the forest, which is the effect created by her desire to pick berries.

PRACTICE

Identify Cause and Effect

GROUP

Ask students to circle the events in the story that are causes. Then have them underline their effect.

▶ Logical/Linguistic

ASSESS/CLOSE

Relate Causes and Effects

GROUP

Remind students that identifying what happens and why in a story will increase their skill as readers. Have students use a Cause and Effect chart to organize information in the story "Trouble in Paradise" (**Teaching Chart 179,** page 727G).

CAUSE	EFFECT

ALTERNATE TEACHING STRATEGY

· ·

CAUSE AND EFFECT

For a different approach to teaching this skill, see page T64.

SELF-SELECTED Reading

· ·

Students may choose from the following titles.

ANTHOLOGY

• Amazon Alert!

LEVELED BOOKS

All titles for the unit Bibliography, pages T76–T77

Meeting Individual Needs for Comprehension

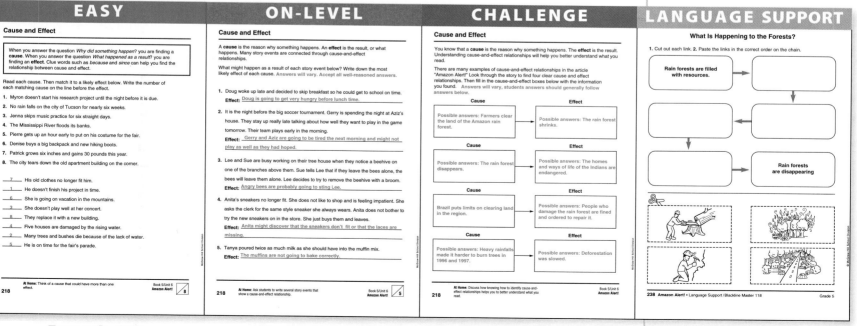

Reteach, 218   Practice, 218   Extend, 218   Language Support, 238

Students will identify and compare synonyms and antonyms.

Review Antonyms and Synonyms

PREPARE

Discuss Synonyms and Antonyms

Remind students that synonyms are words having the same meaning. Antonyms are words having opposite meanings. Challenge each student to come up with a pair of synonyms or antonyms.

TEACH

Read "Trouble in Paradise" and Model the Skill

Ask students to pay attention to the details as you read **Teaching Chart 179** with them.

Trouble in Paradise

The Amazon rain forest faces serious <u>problems</u>, with few <u>solutions</u> in sight. In the past 20 years, interest in rain forest land has <u>grown</u>. As a result, the forest has <u>shrunk</u>.

<u>Destruction</u> of the trees and plants by land developers and farmers is the major (reason) for such shrinkage. The (motive) behind the destruction is money. Special-interest groups have planned the <u>construction</u> of buildings and farms on rain forest land. But is this plan sound economically?

Without trees, swift-moving water, from frequent rainfalls will wash (away) earth, thereby endangering a building's foundation. What's more, (rain) forest soil isn't rich enough to support crops.

Teaching Chart 179

Ask students to circle pairs of synonyms in the passage and underline pairs of antonyms. Have them list the words.

MODEL I know a problem is *a condition or fact that causes trouble*. A solution is *the answer to a problem*. Therefore the words *problem* and *solution* must be antonyms.

PRACTICE

Judge the Effects of Using Synonyms

ONE

Explain that some synonyms convey different feelings or moods. Using a synonym that's right on target can make a story more interesting. Ask students to make the following story more interesting by substituting synonyms for the underlined words. Point out that in doing this students should try to capture the flavor of a class picnic. ▶ **Linguistic**

The day of the fifth-grade picnic was <u>hot</u>, but <u>nice</u>. The students were <u>happy</u> to be outside. There were <u>a lot of</u> <u>games</u> to play and races to run. Students <u>ate</u> <u>good</u> food. At the end of the day, everyone was <u>tired</u>.

ASSESS/CLOSE

Matching Synonyms and Antonyms

GROUP

Create sets of index cards with the following words: *funny, amusing, comical, entertaining, good, skillful, proficient, qualified, capable, loud, noisy, deafening, happy, glad, cheerful, delighted.*

Have students work in groups of four, sorting the index cards into related sets of synonyms. Students may need to define some words before they can complete the exercise.

When finished, ask each group to make up its own set of index cards using antonyms. Direct groups to switch and sort cards.

ALTERNATE TEACHING STRATEGY

ANTONYMS AND SYNONYMS

For a different approach to teaching this skill, see page T65.

Meeting Individual Needs for Comprehension

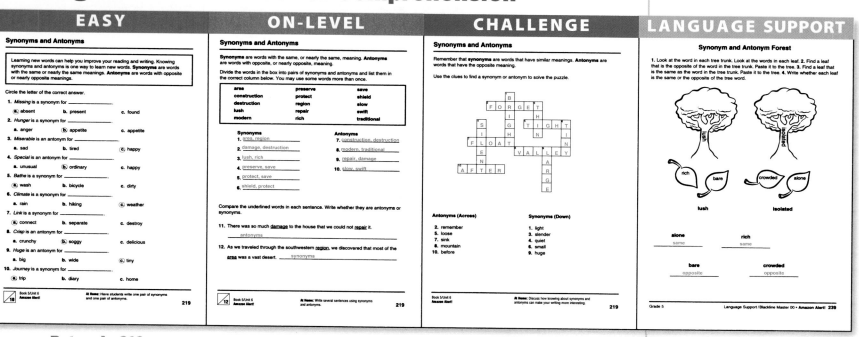

Reteach, 219   Practice, 219   Extend, 219   Language Support, 239

727H

OBJECTIVES

Students will figure out the meaning of unfamiliar words by using clues from the context in which the word appears.

TEACHING TIP

INSTRUCTIONAL Remind students that not all sentences have context clues. In such cases, they can gather clues about the meaning of a word from the passage in which the word occurs.

• Select a newspaper or magazine article. Ask students to make inferences about the meaning of an unfamiliar term based on the passage in which the word is used.

• Help students identify clues related to word meaning.

Review Context Clues

PREPARE

Discuss Context Clues   Remind students that words, sentences, and phrases surrounding an unfamiliar word can often provide clues to the word's meaning.

TEACH

Read "Home, Sweet Home" and Model the Skill   Have students read **Teaching Chart 180** and circle the unfamiliar words.

Home, Sweet Home

Scientists estimate that the rain forest is home to half the different animal species on Earth, with birds that migrate to the warm forests in the winter.

Many of those animals may not exist in the future because they might become extinct. Some are already on the EPA's endangered species list which means they exist in very low numbers.

Deforestation, the cutting down of trees and plants, is destroying the animals' homes and food sources. The only way to preserve these animals is to work toward protecting the rain forest.

Teaching Chart 180

Assist students in finding context clues to unfamiliar words.

MODEL   The word *species* in the first sentence is unfamiliar. I search for context clues in trying to discover its meaning. First I look at the words immediately preceding and see the phrase *different animal*. I know this is an adverbial phrase modifying the word *species*. Therefore, a *species* must be a kind of animal.

PRACTICE

Identifying Context Clues

GROUP

Have volunteers underline context clues for the circled words in **Teaching Chart 180.** Then challenge students to define each term in their own words.

ASSESS/CLOSE

Use Context Clues

PARTNERS

Have students select a word from the dictionary. Then tell them to write a sentence using the word, providing a context clue to its meaning. Have partners exchange sentences and try to define each other's words based on context. If students have difficulty guessing word meaning, have writers revise their sentences and give a better context clue.

ALTERNATE TEACHING STRATEGY

CONTEXT CLUES

For a different approach to teaching this skill, see page T63.

Meeting Individual Needs for Vocabulary

EASY	ON-LEVEL	CHALLENGE	LANGUAGE SUPPORT

EASY

Context Clues

When you are reading information it is important to pay attention to **context clues**. Context clues will help you figure out the meanings of words you don't know. Context clues include words near the unfamiliar word as well as the general topic of the selection.

Use context clues to help you figure out the meaning of the underlined word in each sentence. Then write each underlined word on the line next to the correct context clue below.

1. Forests are very important for the environment. Forests protect or <u>conserve</u> the environment in many ways.
2. For example, the <u>soil</u>, or top part of the ground in the forest, soaks up the rain.
3. Healthy soil helps prevent flooding and the wearing down, or <u>erosion</u>, of the land.
4. Also, when rain water passes through layers of soil and rock, it becomes clean <u>ground water</u>—a fresh source of water for lakes and streams.
5. Forests also have many layers, or <u>strata</u>, of plants that help the environment.
6. The plants give off a gas that all living things need to live. If plants did not give off <u>oxygen</u>, living things could not survive.

<u>soil</u> _____ a. top layer of the ground
<u>oxygen</u> _____ b. a gas that all living things need
<u>ground water</u> _____ c. rain water that passes through the ground
<u>conserve</u> _____ d. protect or keep from harm
<u>erosion</u> _____ e. the wearing down of the land
<u>strata</u> _____ f. layers of plants or soil

At Home: Have students tell what context clues they used to figure out the meanings of unfamiliar words in "Amazon Alert!"

220   Book 5/Unit 6 Amazon Alert! /6

ON-LEVEL

Context Clues

You can use **context clues** to help you define unfamiliar words.

Read each passage below. Use context clues to help you define the underlined word. Circle the letter of the correct meaning.

1. Many <u>ecologists</u> went to study the effects of pollution on wildlife.
   An <u>ecologist</u> must be a kind of _____ b
   a. firefighter   **b.** scientist   c. lawyer
2. During the 1980s, many rock bands made music videos. There was a huge growth in video sales during that <u>decade</u>.
   A <u>decade</u> must last _____ b
   a. a couple of years   **b.** ten years   c. 100 years
3. We entered the giant cave. The guide explained that this was a <u>habitat</u> where many bats lived.
   A <u>habitat</u> must be a kind of _____ c
   a. animal behavior   b. plant   **c.** community where animals live
4. The problem in the Amazon rain forest is that people <u>abuse</u> the resources there. That is what is destroying the region.
   To <u>abuse</u> is to _____ a
   a. use wrongly   b. treat fairly   c. be resourceful
5. The people in the village want to <u>modernize</u> the local water supply by putting in an electric water pump.
   To <u>modernize</u> must mean to _____ c
   a. keep supplying water   b. make things better   **c.** make things up-to-date
6. Sometime you have to <u>sacrifice</u> what you really want for the sake of something or someone else.
   To <u>sacrifice</u> must mean to _____ a
   a. give something up   b. want something   c. understand

At Home: Make a list of context clues you used to define any unfamiliar words you found while reading "Amazon Alert!"

220   Book 5/Unit 6 Amazon Alert! /6

CHALLENGE

Context Clues

Read the paragraph. Use the **context clues** to write a definition of the underlined words. Answers will vary.

   Today many scientists are discussing the <u>ecology</u> of the rain forests. Knowing about the <u>relationships</u> between living things and their environment has helped scientists understand more about the <u>delicate</u> balance of nature that exists in our world's rain forests. Even the slightest change can affect the <u>population</u> of an animal or plant species. To understand the rain forest, a person needs to know a little about its <u>environment</u>. The soil, <u>climate</u>, and animal life of rain forests are like no other place on Earth. Rain forests generally get a tremendous amount of rainfall each year. Large amounts of rainfall increase the growth of <u>vegetation</u>, causing treetops to form large <u>canopies</u> covering the forest floors. An <u>abundance</u> of plant and animal life exists in the rain forest canopies. Scientists believe there are still thousands of unknown and undiscovered <u>species</u> of life in the rain forests.

1. ecology   the relationship between living things and their environment
2. relationships   connections between different things.
3. delicate   fragile; easily unsettled or upset
4. population   a certain number; a group of animals or plants
5. environment   surroundings, soil, climate, vegetation, and animal life
6. climate   general weather patterns
7. vegetation   plant life
8. canopies   coverings; a tree covering
9. abundance   a large amount
10. species   a group of similar animals or plants

At Home: Identify the clues in the paragraph that helped you with the words.

220   Book 5/Unit 6 Amazon Alert!

LANGUAGE SUPPORT

Dictionary Search

1. Read the dictionary words and definitions. 2. Fill in the blanks with the correct words.

1. The Amazon is a wildlife _____wonderland_____

2. The _____tropical_____ forest is a warm place where many animals live.

3. The rain forest is filled with _____lush_____ vegetation.

4. Sydney Possuelo helps find _____isolated_____ tribes and protect them.

5. It was _____confirmed_____ that the 1990s were a terrible decade for the rain forests.

6. The Amazon holds the world's widest _____variety_____ of wildlife.

confirmed - proven to be true
isolated - alone
lush - filled with growth
tropical - relating to a warm region
variety - many different types
wonderland - a place of beauty and charm

240 Amazon Alert! • Language Support/Blackline Master 00   Grade 5

Reteach, 220	Practice, 220	Extend, 220	Language Support, 240

GRAMMAR/SPELLING CONNECTIONS

See the 5-Day Grammar and Usage Plan on sentence combining, pages 727M–727N.

See the 5-Day Spelling Plan on words from math, pages 727O–727P.

TECHNOLOGY TIP

Advise students to name their files so they are easy to remember and find. If students use difficult names for their files, it may take longer to find them, or they may not be able to find them at all.

Writing a Story

Prewrite

WRITE A STORY Present this writing assignment: *Amazon Alert!* is a non-fiction story. It contains real, factual information. Write an original fictional story that may or may not be based on real, or factual information.

Strategy: Sequence Guide students to visualize the story they want to write. Have them use a Sequence of Events chart to plan their stories. Students should answer the following questions:

- What is the story about, and who are the characters?
- When and where does the story take place?
- What will happen? How will it end?

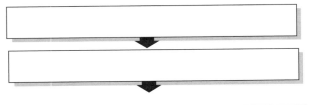

Graphic Organizer 17

Draft

USE THE SEQUENCE Students should allow their imaginations to flow freely. Encourage them to create unique characters and plot events. Have students build their stories with a beginning, middle, and end by using their ideas from the sequence chart.

Revise

SELF-QUESTIONING Ask students to assess their drafts.

- Is my story line complete?
- Do my characters seem alive?
- Did I create a beginning, middle, and end?
- Do I need to develop more expressive details?

Edit/Proofread

CHECK FOR ERRORS Have students read their stories for content, logic, structure, grammar, spelling, and punctuation.

Publish

SHARE THE STORIES Have students write final versions of their stories, and read each other's work. Make the stories available for everyone to see, and schedule a class reading.

Kim's Dream

Kim wanted more than anything to be on the school basketball team. But Kim wasn't very tall. So she practiced every day.

"You'll never make the team," her sister told her. "You're not tall enough."

"Yes, I will," Kim answered. "If I practice hard enough." And she went up for another rebound.

Finally, it was time to go out for the team. "You'll never make the team," the girl standing next to her said. "You're not tall enough."

Kim answered, "We'll see what happens."

Soon it was Kim's turn on the court. Her hook shot went in. Her lay-up went in. Her shot from the foul line swooshed through the basket. She jumped for a rebound and tapped the ball in.

A week later, the names of the new basketball team were posted at the school. And there was Kim's name! She had made the team!

Presentation Ideas

PUBLISH YOUR BOOK Have students illustrate their stories. Then have them make a book cover and bind them. Display the published stories in the classroom.

▶ Viewing/Representing

MAKE A SPEECH Have students give an author's talk explaining why they wrote their story, what inspired it, and how they worked out the characters, plot, and ending.

▶ Speaking/Listening

Consider students' creative efforts, possibly adding a plus (+) for originality, wit, and imagination.

Scoring Rubric

Excellent	Good	Fair	Unsatisfactory
4: The writer	**3:** The writer	**2:** The writer	**1:** The writer
• creates highly-developed characters, setting and plot. • creates dialogue that pushes the story ahead, and shows characters. • has a clear progression of story	• has met the criteria for a story. • uses dialogue to move events ahead. • has a progression of story events with a beginning, middle and end.	• has attempted to write a story with a setting and plot. • may create characters with limited detail. • does not show a clear progression of story events.	• has not met the criteria for a story. • may have a very limited grasp of storytelling and conventions. • may present disconnected events and details.

0: The writer leaves the page blank or fails to respond to the writing task. The student does not address the topic or simply paraphrases the prompt. The response is illegible or incoherent.

For a 6-point or an 8-point scale, see pages T105–T106.

Meeting Individual Needs for Writing

[Below-Level]

Button Have the students create a button that encourages people to do something to preserve the rain forest. The button should have an image and a slogan.

ON-LEVEL

Expedition Have the students use what they learned in *Amazon Alert!* to write a fictional account of an expedition to the rain forest to help a native tribe.

CHALLENGE

Fantasy Have students imagine they are a creature of the rain forest such as a native, a bird, a fish, an animal, an insect, a tree, or a flower. Have them write about what life is like in the rain forest and what will happen if the rain forest is destroyed.

COMMUNICATION TIPS

REPRESENTING The cover of a book creates people's first impressions of it. Keep this in mind when you design the cover for your story.

SPEAKING When you speak, speak to everyone in the room. Don't look down at the floor, look around the room, and make eye contact with people.

LANGUAGE SUPPORT

ESL Students may want to draw several sequential pictures that tell a story. Then have them write sentences to go with the picture.

PORTFOLIO Invite students to include their stories or another writing project in their portfolios.

5 Day Grammar and Usage Plan

LANGUAGE SUPPORT

ESL Sentence combining with adjectives and adverbs may be difficult for new learners of English. Pair them with native speakers.

DAILY LANGUAGE ACTIVITIES

Have students combine the sentences orally.

Day 1

1. Parrots live in the rain forest. The parrots are brightly colored.
2. The piranha is fierce. The piranha lives in the Amazon River.
3. Monkeys swing on vines. They swing wildly.

Day 2

1. Indian tribes are isolated. They are in the rain forest.
2. The Indian cobra is deadly. The Indian cobra lives in the rain forest.

Day 3

1. The Amazon rain forest is very large. This forest is lush.
2. The flying dragon lizard glides swiftly. It glides from tree to tree.

Day 4

1. The rain forest is being destroyed. It is being destroyed quickly.
2. Space satellites take pictures. They take pictures of the Amazon.

Day 5

1. Many houseplants came from the rain forest. The plants are popular.
2. Possuelo is working to protect Indians. He is working tirelessly.

Daily Language Transparency 30

DAY 1 Introduce the Concept

Oral Warm-Up *The tall man walked quickly down the street.* Ask students to identify an adjective, an adverb, and a prepositional phrase.

Combine Sentences with Adjectives and Adverbs When you write two sentences that tell about the same person, place, or thing, or about the same action, you can sometimes combine them. Leave out the words that repeat. Discuss:

- Two sentences can be combined by adding an adjective or adverb to one sentence.

Give examples such as: *Felix has a cat. The cat is white.* (Felix has a white cat.) *A baby cried. It cried loudly.* (A baby cried loudly.)

Present the Daily Language Activity. Have students combine sentences orally.

 WRITING Assign the daily Writing Prompt on page 718C.

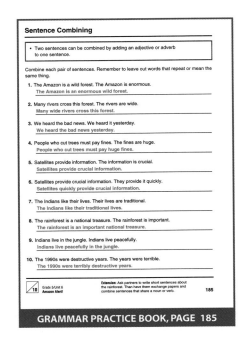

Sentence Combining

- Two sentences can be combined by adding an adjective or adverb to one sentence.

Combine each pair of sentences. Remember to leave out words that repeat or mean the same thing.

1. The Amazon is a wild forest. The Amazon is enormous.
   The Amazon is an enormous wild forest.

2. Many rivers cross this forest. The rivers are wide.
   Many wide rivers cross this forest.

3. We heard the bad news. We heard it yesterday.
   We heard the bad news yesterday.

4. People who cut trees must pay fines. The fines are huge.
   People who cut trees must pay huge fines.

5. Satellites provide information. The information is crucial.
   Satellites provide crucial information.

6. Satellites provide crucial information. They provide it quickly.
   Satellites quickly provide crucial information.

7. The Indians like their lives. Their lives are traditional.
   The Indians like their traditional lives.

8. The rainforest is a national treasure. The rainforest is important.
   The rainforest is an important national treasure.

9. Indians live in the jungle. Indians live peacefully.
   Indians live peacefully in the jungle.

10. The 1990s were destructive years. The years were terrible.
    The 1990s were terribly destructive years.

Extension: Ask partners to write short sentences about the rainforest. Then have them exchange papers and combine sentences that share a noun or verb.

Grade 5/Unit 6
Amazon Alert! 185

GRAMMAR PRACTICE BOOK, PAGE 185

DAY 2 Teach the Concept

Review Adjectives and Adverbs Ask students how to use adjectives and adverbs to combine sentences.

Combining with Prepositional Phrases Review the definition of a prepositional phrase. Discuss:

- Two sentences can be combined by adding a prepositional phrase to one sentence.

Give examples such as: *The train left the station. The train left at noon.* (The train left the station at noon.)

Present the Daily Language Activity and have students combine sentences orally. Then have students write sentences that a partner can combine by adding a prepositional phrase to one sentence.

WRITING Assign the daily Writing Prompt on page 718C.

Sentence Combining

- Two sentences can be combined by adding a prepositional phrase to one sentence.

Read the pair of sentences. Combine each pair, using a prepositional phrase. Answers may vary.

1. The Yanomami live traditionally. The Yanomami live in the Amazon.
   The Yanomami live traditionally in the Amazon.

2. People cut trees. The trees are cut for fuel and lumber.
   People cut trees for fuel and lumber.

3. The rain hits the ground. The rain hits during the night.
   The rain hits the ground during the night.

4. Piranha eat other fish. Piranha eat in the Amazon River.
   Piranha eat other fish in the Amazon River.

5. Deforestation threatens life. Deforestation threatens around the world.
   Deforestation threatens life around the world.

6. Environmentalists protect the rainforest. They work in Brazil.
   Environmentalists in Brazil protect the rainforest.

7. Parrots live nearby. Parrots live in the canopy.
   Parrots live nearby in the canopy.

8. Farmers plant crops. Farmers plant near the rainforest.
   Farmers plant crops near the rainforest.

9. Environmentalists appreciate Possuelo. They appreciate his hard work.
   Environmentalists appreciate Possuelo for his hard work.

10. The rivers run full. The rivers run across the jungle.
    The rivers run full across the jungle.

Extension: Ask partners to give each other topics related to the rainforest. Have each student write four sentences about the topic. Then challenge partners to write as many combinations of the sentences as they can.

186

Grade 5/Unit 6
Amazon Alert!

GRAMMAR PRACTICE BOOK, PAGE 186

Sentence-Combining

DAY 3 — Review and Practice

Learn from the Literature Read the second sentence on page 721 of *Amazon Alert!*:

> **Brightly colored parrots, swift jaguars, and fierce piranhas make their home in the tropical forest and its many rivers.**

Ask students to identify the adjectives, adverb, and prepositional phrase in this sentence.

Combine Sentences Present the Daily Language Activity and have students combine sentences orally.

Have students read the first paragraph on page 722, looking for prepositional phrases. Have them write down each phrase. Then have students use the phrases to write short sentences that a partner can combine.

 Assign the daily Writing Prompt on page 718D.

DAY 4 — Review and Practice

Review Combining Sentences Have students give examples of sentences that combine two ideas using adjectives, adverbs, or prepositional phrases. Then present the Daily Language Activity for Day 4.

Mechanics and Usage Before students begin the daily Writing Prompt on page 718D, display and discuss:

- Begin every sentence with a capital letter.
- Use the correct end mark for each sentence.
- Use a comma to set off a person's name when the person is spoken to directly.
- Use a comma after introductory words such as *yes*, *no*, and *well*.

 Assign the daily Writing Prompt on page 718D.

DAY 5 — Assess and Reteach

Assess Use the Daily Language Activity and page 189 of the **Grammar Practice Book** for assessment.

Reteach Have students write on index cards three rules for combining sentences with adjectives, adverbs, and prepositional phrases.

For each set of sentences in the Daily Language Activities for Days 1 through 5, have students indicate which part of speech allows them to combine the sentences—adjective, adverb, or prepositional phrase. Then have them write each example on the appropriate index card.

Have students create a word wall with a list of adjectives, adverbs, and prepositional phrases and examples of how they can be used to combine sentences.

Use page 190 of the **Grammar Practice Book** for additional reteaching.

 Assign the daily Writing Prompt on page 718D.

Sentence Combining

- Two sentences can be combined by adding an adjective or adverb to one sentence.
- Two sentences can be combined by adding a prepositional phrase to one sentence.

Read each paragraph. Look for sentences that can be combined. Choose the best way to combine the sentences as you rewrite the paragraphs. Answers may vary.

The jungle has many animals and plants. The animals and plants are diverse. Scientists have not counted even half of their numbers. People study the rainforest. They study it continually. Some plants can be used for medicines. These plants are in the rainforest. Some plants can cure diseases. The diseases are serious.

The jungle has many diverse animals and plants. Scientists have not counted even half of their numbers. People study the rainforest continually. Some plants in the rainforest can be used for medicines. Some plants can cure serious diseases.

People can protect the rainforest. The rainforest is fragile. You can recycle paper and wood. You can recycle in your home. Architects can build with steel. They can build often. If you care a lot, you can also call an environmental group. You can call soon. You can save the trees. The trees are in the rainforest.

People can protect the fragile rainforest. You can recycle paper and wood in your home. Architects can often build with steel. If you care a lot, you can also call an environmental group soon. You can save the trees in the rainforest.

Extension: Ask students to write two versions of a poem about forests. Have them write one version that contains small choppy sentences and stanzas. Have them write another version by combining shorter sentences.

Grade 5/Unit 6 — Amazon Alert! — 10 — 187

GRAMMAR PRACTICE BOOK, PAGE 187

Using Punctuation Marks

- Begin every sentence with a capital letter.
- Use the correct end mark for each sentence.
- Use a comma to set off a person's name when the person is spoken to directly.

Rewrite the sentences. Add capitalization, end punctuation, and commas where they are needed.

1. martin have you ever been to the rainforest
   Martin, have you ever been to the rainforest?

2. our plane landed in Sao Paulo
   Our plane landed in Sao Paulo.

3. there are so many beautiful flowers
   There are so many beautiful flowers there!

4. this jungle is incredible
   This jungle is incredible!

5. anita can you tell me the name of that bird
   Anita, can you tell me the name of that bird?

6. the canopy is full of light
   The canopy is full of light.

7. jennifer look at the monkeys
   Jennifer, look at the monkeys.

8. kito what are you photographing
   Kito, what are you photographing?

9. dad I can't see where you are pointing
   Dad, I can't see where you are pointing.

10. i want to visit the Amazon rainforest
    I want to visit the Amazon rainforest.

Extension: Have partners write funny statements, exclamations, and questions about monkeys. Ask them to omit capitalization, end punctuation, and commas. Then have partners correct each other's writing.

188 — Grade 5/Unit 6 — Amazon Alert! — 10

GRAMMAR PRACTICE BOOK, PAGE 188

Sentence Combining and Using Punctuation Marks

A. Combine each pair of sentences. Write the new sentence on the line.

1. Monkeys eat bananas. Monkeys eat in the treetops.
   Monkeys eat bananas in the treetops.

2. Monkeys play tricks. The tricks are funny.
   Monkeys play funny tricks.

3. People build houses. People build with wood.
   People build houses with wood.

4. The Amazon has trees. The trees are incredible.
   The Amazon has incredible trees.

5. Indians gather plants. Indians gather in the rainforest.
   Indians gather plants in the rainforest.

6. The Yanomami have hunted animals. The Yanomami have hunted for centuries.
   The Yanomami have hunted animals for centuries.

7. People breathe oxygen. People breathe into their lungs.
   People breathe oxygen into their lungs.

B. Rewrite each sentence. Add punctuation and capitals.

8. Fernando will you write about the rainforest
   Fernando, will you write about the rainforest?

9. these birds are amazing
   These birds are amazing!

10. amy there are orchids in this forest
    Amy, there are orchids in this forest.

11. what do the birds eat
    What do the birds eat?

12. Delia watch out for that snake
    Delia, watch out for that snake!

Grade 5/Unit 6 — Amazon Alert! — 12

189

GRAMMAR PRACTICE BOOK, PAGE 189

5Day Spelling Plan

LANGUAGE SUPPORT

To help students distinguish between short and long vowel sounds, read aloud these words: *man, mane; mill, mile; bet, beet; rod, rode.* Have students repeat each word and say the vowel sound.

DICTATION SENTENCES

Spelling Words

1. The numbers are ordered from first to fourth.
2. A penny is equal to one cent.
3. The years range from two to ten.
4. The difference between six and two is four.
5. The volume of the bottle is one gallon.
6. I have to multiply two times four.
7. How often it happens is the frequency.
8. Mathematics is the study of numbers.
9. A centimeter is a small measurement.
10. The formula is a useful rule.
11. The product of two times three is six.
12. The bottle holds one liter of water.
13. Find the ratio of boys to girls in the class.
14. Show the information on a bar graph.
15. A millimeter is very small.
16. The estimated amount is not exact.
17. Measure the angle of the square.
18. I spend a portion of the day in school.
19. Add one-eighth of a pint.
20. Divide to find the quotient.

Challenge Words

21. Newspapers confirmed the rumor.
22. Someone alone on an island is isolated.
23. The rain forests are lush and green.
24. The tropical weather is very hot.
25. The zoo has a variety of animals.

DAY 1 Pretest

Assess Prior Knowledge Use the Dictation Sentences at the left and **Spelling Practice Book** Page 185 for the pretest. Allow students to correct their own papers. Students who require a modified list may be tested on the first ten words.

Spelling Words		Challenge Words
1. **ordered**	11. product	21. **confirmed**
2. equal	12. liter	22. **isolated**
3. range	13. ratio	23. **lush**
4. **difference**	14. bar graph	24. **tropical**
5. volume	15. millimeter	25. **variety**
6. multiply	16. **estimated**	
7. frequency	17. angle	
8. mathematics	18. portion	
9. centimeter	19. **one-eighth**	
10. formula	20. quotient	

*Note: Words in **dark type** are from the story.*

Word Study On page 186 of the **Spelling Practice Book** are word study steps and an at-home activity.

Words from Math

Pretest Directions
Fold back the paper along the dotted line. Use the blanks to write each word as it is read aloud. When you finish the test, unfold the paper. Use the list at the right to correct any spelling mistakes. Practice the words you missed for the Posttest.

1. _____	1. ordered
2. _____	2. equal
3. _____	3. range
4. _____	4. difference
5. _____	5. volume
6. _____	6. multiply
7. _____	7. frequency
8. _____	8. mathematics
9. _____	9. centimeter
10. _____	10. formula
11. _____	11. product
12. _____	12. liter
13. _____	13. ratio
14. _____	14. bar graph
15. _____	15. millimeter
16. _____	16. estimated
17. _____	17. angle
18. _____	18. portion
19. _____	19. one-eighth
20. _____	20. quotient

To Parents
Here are the results of your child's weekly spelling Pretest. You can help your child study for the Posttest by following these simple steps for each word on the word list:
1. Read the word to your child.
2. Have your child write the word, saying each letter as it is written.
3. Say each letter of the word as your child checks the spelling.
4. If a mistake has been made, have your child read each letter of the correctly spelled word aloud, and then repeat steps 1–3.

Challenge Words
_____ confirmed
_____ isolated
_____ lush
_____ tropical
_____ variety

Grade 5/Unit 6
Amazon Alert!
185

SPELLING PRACTICE BOOK, PAGE 185

WORD STUDY STEPS AND ACTIVITY, PAGE 186

DAY 2 Explore the Pattern

Sort and Spell Words Say *estimate* and *equal*. Ask students if they hear a short or long vowel sound in the first syllable of each word. (short *e*, long *e*) Have students read the Spelling Words aloud and sort them as below, according to the vowel sound in the first syllable.

Short Vowel Sound

difference	centimeter	angle
volume	product	one-eighth
multiply	millimeter	
mathematics	estimated	

Long Vowel Sound

equal	frequency	ratio
range	liter	quotient

R-Controlled Vowel Sound

ordered	bar graph
formula	portion

Word Wall Have students create a word wall based on the word sort and add more words from their reading.

Words from Math

ordered	volume	centimeter	ratio	angle
equal	multiply	formula	bar graph	portion
range	frequency	product	millimeter	one-eighth
difference	mathematics	liter	estimated	quotient

Say the spelling word to yourself. Then sort the word according to the vowel sound you hear in its first syllable. Write the words on the lines below.

Long vowel sound		**Short vowel sound**	
1. equal		11. difference	
2. range		12. volume	
3. frequency		13. multiply	
4. liter		14. mathematics	
5. ratio		15. centimeter	
6. quotient		16. product	
R-controlled vowel sound		17. millimeter	
7. ordered		18. estimated	
8. formula		19. angle	
9. bar graph		20. one-eighth	
10. portion			

Grade 5/Unit 6
Amazon Alert!
187

SPELLING PRACTICE BOOK, PAGE 187

Words from Math

<table>
<tr><td>DAY 3</td><td>Practice and Extend</td></tr>
</table>

Word Meaning: Multiple Meaning

Remind students that some words can have more than one meaning. Ask students to read the Spelling Words, looking for words that have a meaning not related to math. Have them write sentences for these words.

If students need extra practice, have partners give each other a midweek test.

Glossary
Review the syllable division key in the Glossary. Have partners:

- write each Challenge Word.

- use the Glossary to find out the number of syllables in each word.

- find the symbol that shows which syllable should be stressed.

- divide each word into syllables and underline the stressed syllable.

<table>
<tr><td>DAY 4</td><td>Proofread and Write</td></tr>
</table>

Proofread Sentences
Write these sentences on the chalkboard, including the misspelled words. Ask students to proofread, circling incorrect spellings and writing the correct spellings. There are two spelling errors in each sentence.

The diffrence between 5 and 3 is 2, but the prodect of the two numbers is 15. (difference, product)

She estamated the length to be one centameter. (estimated, centimeter)

Have students create additional sentences with errors for partners to correct.

WRITING Have students use as many Spelling Words as possible in the daily Writing Prompt on page 718D. Remind students to proofread their writing for errors in spelling, grammar, and punctuation.

<table>
<tr><td>DAY 5</td><td>Assess and Reteach</td></tr>
</table>

Assess Students' Knowledge
Use page 190 of the **Spelling Practice Book** or the Dictation Sentences on page 727O for the posttest.

Personal Word List
JOURNAL If students have trouble with any lesson words, they should add them to their personal lists of troublesome words in their journals. Have students write a phrase defining each word.

Students should refer to their word lists during later writing activities.

SPELLING PRACTICE BOOK, PAGE 188

Words from Math

ordered	volume	centimeter	ratio	angle
equal	multiply	formula	bar graph	portion
range	frequency	product	millimeter	one-eighth
difference	mathematics	liter	estimated	quotient

Definitions
Write the spelling word that matches the definition.

1. the same as — equal
2. how often something happens — frequency
3. a chart that shows math results — bar graph
4. arithmetic — mathematics
5. 1/100 meter — centimeter
6. 1/1,000 meter — millimeter
7. proportion — ratio
8. scope — range
9. fixed rule or method — formula
10. arranged — ordered
11. remainder after subtracting — difference
12. amount of space occupied — volume
13. result of multiplication — product
14. roughly calculated — estimated
15. segment of something — portion

Challenge Extension: Write one fill-in sentence for each Challenge Word. Exchange papers with a partner and complete each fill-in sentence.

188   Grade 5/Unit 6 Amazon Alert! | 15

SPELLING PRACTICE BOOK, PAGE 189

Words from Math

Proofreading Activity
There are six spelling mistakes in the sentences below. Circle the misspelled words. Write the words correctly on the lines below.

In mathematicks, it helps to remember each formula you learn in order to solve new problems. For example, in order to find the volume of a cube, one must multiply the length, width, and height. The resulting produckt represents the space occupied by the cube. When dealing with large numbers, an answer can be estimayted in order to first find the ranje to which the number belongs, and then locate the exact answer.

1. mathematics   3. mulitply   5. estimated
2. formula   4. product   6. range

Writing Activity
Pretend you take a trip to the Amazon rain forest. Write about what you might see or do there. Use four spelling words in your writing.

_____

_____

_____

18   Grade 5/Unit 6 Amazon Alert!   189

SPELLING PRACTICE BOOK, PAGE 190

Words from Math

Look at the words in each set below. One word in each set is spelled correctly. Use a pencil to fill in the circle next to the correct word. Before you begin, look at the sample sets of words. Sample A has been done for you. Do Sample B by yourself. When you are sure you know what to do, you may go on with the rest of the page.

Sample A:
(A) diveide
(B) diveyde
(C) devide
(D) divide

Sample B:
(A) numer
(B) nomber
(G) number
(H) numler

1. (A) ordured (B) ordered (C) ordred (D) orderd
2. (E) eequal (F) ekwal (G) equal (H) equal
3. (A) range (B) raing (C) reang (D) ranghe
4. (E) diference (F) diffurence (G) difference (H) difrence
5. (A) volume (B) valume (C) voloome (D) volyume
6. (E) multipli (F) multiply (G) mulitply (H) multiplie
7. (A) freequensy (B) freequency (C) frequency (D) frequensy
8. (E) mathematics (F) mathamatics (G) mathamathics (H) mathmathics
9. (A) centumetre (B) centimeter (C) centemeeter (D) centimetr
10. (E) formoola (F) fourmula (G) formula (H) formyula
11. (A) produckt (B) produck (C) prodakt (D) product
12. (E) liter (F) leeter (G) leter (H) litur
13. (A) rateo (B) ratio (C) ratioh (D) rashio
14. (E) barr graf (F) bar graf (G) bar graph (H) barr graph
15. (A) milimeeter (B) millimeter (C) milimeter (D) millimiter
16. (E) estimeted (F) ectimated (G) estimeated (H) estimated
17. (A) angele (B) angle (C) angul (D) angil
18. (E) porshun (F) portun (G) portion (H) porton
19. (A) one-eighth (B) one-eigth (C) one-eithgh (D) one-eaghth
20. (E) qwotient (F) quotent (G) quotient (H) qotient

190   Grade 5/Unit 6 Amazon Alert! | 20

727P

Wrap Up the Theme

Crossroads

Decisions cause changes that can enrich our lives.

REVIEW THE THEME Remind students that all the selections in this unit relate to the theme Crossroads. Were students surprised at any of the decisions made by the characters? Ask students to name other stories or movies they know that also fit the theme Crossroads.

READ THE POEM Read aloud the lyrics for "Frederick Douglass" by Langston Hughes. As students listen, ask them to think about how Frederick Douglass lived his life, and how his life would have changed if his decisions had been different.

STUDENT LISTENING LIBRARY AUDIOCASSETTES

MAKE CONNECTIONS Have students work in small groups to brainstorm a list of ways that the stories, poems, and the Time for Kids magazine article relate to the theme Crossroads.

Groups can then compare their lists as they share them with the class.

Frederick Douglass
— 1817-1895 —

Douglass was someone who,
Had he walked with wary foot
And frightened tread,
From very indecision
Might be dead,
Might have lost his soul,
But instead decided to be bold
And capture every street
On which he set his feet,
To route each path
Toward freedom's goal,
To make each highway
Choose *his* compass' choice,
To all the world he cried,
Hear my voice! . . .
Oh, to be a beast, a bird,
Anything but a slave! he said.

Who would be free
Themselves must strike
The first blow, he said.

He died in 1895.
He is not dead.

by Langston Hughes

728

LOOKING AT GENRE

Have students review *Amistad Rising,* historical fiction, and *Rip Van Winkle,* a play.

Help students list the key characteristics of each literary form or genre. Can they name other historical fiction and plays?

HISTORICAL FICTION: *AMISTAD RISING*	PLAY: *RIP VAN WINKLE*
• Based on real characters and events	• Story told in dialogue on a stage, with actors playing the characters
• Setting is real	• Characters and events may be realistic or not.
• Story mostly descriptive, little dialogue	• Setting involves scenery and props

Research and Inquiry

Complete the Theme Project Have students work in teams to complete their group project. Encourage students to create game cards that have several acceptable answers with different point values assigned. Encourage them to share tasks of designing and coloring the game board and game cards or writing the questions to the game cards, so that each team member can contribute.

Make a Classroom Presentation Have teams take turns presenting their board games and game cards. Be sure to allow time for questions from the audience.

Draw Conclusions Have students draw conclusions about what they learned from researching and preparing their projects. Was the resource chart they made helpful? What other resources did they use? What conclusions have students made about the different ways that they can help save the environment? Finally, ask students if doing the research will now change the way they view the environment. What will they do next to help protect the environment?

Ask More Questions What additional questions do students now have about the environment? What else would students like to find out? You might encourage students to play each others' games and see what new things about the environment they can learn.

LEARNING ABOUT POETRY

LITERARY DEVICES: NARRATIVE VERSE A narrative poem tells a story, often in very few words. In the poem *Frederick Douglass,* Langston Hughes tells the story of Douglass' life, focusing on the most essential part, his fight to abolish slavery. Ask students what clue in the title suggests the poem is a narrative.

POETRY ACTIVITY Assign each group either the word Frederick or the word Douglass, and have students write an acrostic poem, using words that describe Frederick Douglass. They may wish to use encyclopedias or other resources for additional information on Douglass' life. Display the poems in the classroom.

Writing a Story

CONNECT TO LITERATURE In *Amistad Rising*, a young African slave struggles to achieve freedom for himself and his fellow captives. Review with children the obstacles which Joseph Cinqué faced and discuss what personal qualities helped him reach his goal.

GROUP

A little girl named Joanie wanted to play basketball. She'd watch children at the ball court every day and cheer every time someone made a basket. Joanie dreamed of making baskets, too.

Joanie couldn't play ball with her friends because she was a wheelchair user. But she had very strong arms and a very good aim.

One day, Uncle Joe came by and said, "Joanie, let's go to a basketball game."

Joanie looked away and said, "What's the use? I'll never play anyway."

Uncle Joe just smiled and helped Joanie get into the car. They came to a ball court Joanie had never seen. She saw a fast game going on with kids her own age. And all of them were using wheelchairs! Looking up at her uncle, Joanie broke into a huge smile and wheeled eagerly onto the court, ready to play ball.

Prewrite

PURPOSE AND AUDIENCE Students will write a story in which a child must overcome a big obstacle to achieve a goal. They can pretend to write for a book of stories about courage.

STRATEGY: MAKE A STORY CHART Help students explore ideas for characters and story lines. Have them jot down traits they want to create for their main character. Have them discuss ideas for the characters' appearance, attitude, and ways of moving and speaking. Then show them how to use a story chart to sketch out a plot.

Use **Writing Process Transparency 6A** as a model.

FEATURES OF STORY WRITING

- unfolds a sequence of original narrative events
- has a beginning, middle, and end
- can explore character, plot, dialogue, setting

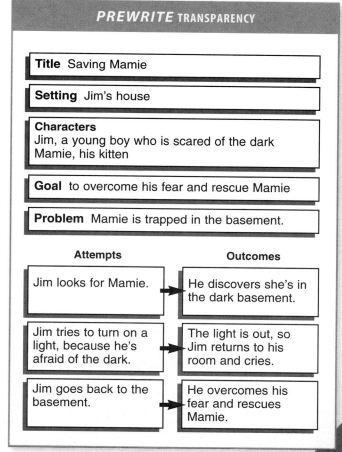

PREWRITE TRANSPARENCY

Title Saving Mamie

Setting Jim's house

Characters
Jim, a young boy who is scared of the dark
Mamie, his kitten

Goal to overcome his fear and rescue Mamie

Problem Mamie is trapped in the basement.

Attempts	Outcomes
Jim looks for Mamie.	He discovers she's in the dark basement.
Jim tries to turn on a light, because he's afraid of the dark.	The light is out, so Jim returns to his room and cries.
Jim goes back to the basement.	He overcomes his fear and rescues Mamie.

Writing a Story

Draft

STRATEGY: FREEWRITING Have students write freely from their imaginations. Guide them to create a unique personality for their main character. Encourage students to explore humor and emotions in their writing and to have fun experimenting with unexpected plot turns. They can refer back to their charts for theme ideas and plot structure, but invite them to add imaginative events and rich sensory elements.

Use **Writing Process Transparency 6B** to model a first draft.

LANGUAGE CONTROL Have students jot down action verbs from their story charts. Have them consult a thesaurus to expand their adjective lists. Then have them make a list of adverbs for each verb. Encourage them to use some of these new words in their stories.

LANGUAGE SUPPORT

Some students may need help developing an original main character. Suggest they use someone they know as a jumping-off point. Guide them to write a list of new physical and personality details to change the character.

DRAFT TRANSPARENCY

Saving Mamie

Jim heard it all the way upstairs in his room. It was my kitten, Mamie crying out loud. Jim followed the sound, and it took him down to the basement stairs. He pulled the string to turn on the light but nothing happened. Jim didnt move one inch more.

Mamie was in the basement. He stood and listened to the cat's sad meows and felt terrible. "She must be even most scared than I am," Jim thought.

He got so upset that he ran back to his room. Then Jim cried as sad as Mamie. He sat there for a long time. The cat could still be heard crying. Then suddenly, was it quiet.

That's when Jim stood up, and went back to the basement stairs. "Mamie?" he said in a shaky voice.

The cat replied with a single long meow. Taking a deep breath the boy went down the stairs and finds his best friend hiding under his old wagon. Seconds later, he were upstairs in the bright kitchen, cuddling like long-lost friends. And that's how Jim overcame his feare of the dark. For the love of Mamie.

Revise

Have students work in teams to share revision ideas. Coach them in offering concrete suggestions for character and plot possibilities. Each team can make comment sheets noting what they liked best about each other's work, as well as their suggested revisions.

Use **Writing Process Transparency 6C** for classroom discussion on the revision process. Ask students to comment on how revisions may have improved this writing example.

STRATEGY: ELABORATION Discuss with students various ways to elaborate on their drafts. Encourage them to look at their stories with a fresh eye. Write these questions on the board for students to think about as they revise:

- How do each of my characters help move the story forward?

- Can a reader follow the events easily?

- Did I show how the main character overcomes an obstacle?

TEACHING TIP

TEACHER CONFERENCE
While students are revising, circulate and conference with each team. You can use these questions as a basis for your conferencing:

- Do your characters feel real to you? Why?
- What is special about your main character?
- What is interesting or important about the obstacle they face?
- Do your descriptions bring the story to life?

REVISE TRANSPARENCY

Overcoming Fear
~~Saving Mamie~~

                    the sound
Jim heard it all the way upstairs in his room. It was my
                    for help
kitten, Mamie crying ~~out loud.~~ Jim followed the sound,

and it took him down to the basement stairs. He pulled
                                          The small boy
the string to turn on the light but nothing happened. ~~Jim~~
        another
didnt move one inch ~~more.~~   but it was dark down there.

       Mamie was in the basement. ~~He stood and~~
ing   , Jim
listened to the cat's sad meows ~~and~~ felt terrible. "She

must be even most scared than I am," Jim thought.
                    and sat on his bed with his hands over his ears
       He got so upset that he ran back to his room.

Then Jim cried as sad as Mamie. He sat there for a

long time. The cat could still be heard crying. Then

suddenly, was it quiet.
                                                    dark
       That's when Jim stood up, and went back to the

basement stairs. "Mamie?" he said in a shaky voice.

       The cat replied with a single long meow. Taking a

deep breath the boy went down the stairs and finds his

best friend hiding under his old wagon. Seconds later,

he were upstairs in the bright kitchen, cuddling like

long-lost friends. ~~And that's how~~ Jim overcame his

feare of the dark. For the love of Mamie.

729D

Writing a Story

Edit/Proofread

After students finish revising their stories, have them proofread for final corrections and additions.

GRAMMAR/SPELLING CONNECTIONS

See the 5-Day Grammar and Usage Plans, pages 647M–647N, 673M–673N, 697M–697N, 717M–717N, and 727M–727N.

See the 5-Day Spelling Plans, pages 6470–647P, 6730–673P, 6970–697P, 7170–717P, and 7270–727P.

GRAMMAR, MECHANICS, USAGE

- Use possessive pronouns correctly.
- Be sure pronouns and verbs agree.
- Use adverbs correctly.
- Use quotation marks at the beginning and end of a person's exact words.

Publish

SHARE THE STORIES Students can read their work aloud to the class. You can bind their stories in a class anthology and put a copy in the school library.

Use **Writing Process Transparency 6D** as a proofreading model, and **Writing Process Transparency 6E** to discuss presentation ideas.

PROOFREAD TRANSPARENCY

Overcoming Fear

Saving Mamie

¶Jim heard it all the way upstairs in his room. It was my kitten, Mamie, crying out loud. Jim followed the sound, and it took him down to the basement stairs. He pulled the string to turn on the light but nothing happened. Jim didnt move one inch more.

Mamie was in the basement. He stood and listened to the cat's sad meows and felt terrible. "She must be even most scared than I am," Jim thought.

He got so upset that he ran back to his room. Then Jim cried as sad as Mamie. He sat there for a long time. The cat could still be heard crying. Then suddenly, was it quiet.

That's when Jim stood up and went back to the basement stairs. "Mamie?" he said in a shaky voice.

The cat replied with a single long meow. Taking a deep breath the boy went down the stairs and finds his best friend hiding under his old wagon. Seconds later, he were upstairs in the bright kitchen, cuddling like long-lost friends. And that's how Jim overcame his feare of the dark. For the love of Mamie

PUBLISH TRANSPARENCY

Overcoming Fear

Jim heard the sound all the way upstairs in his room. It was his kitten, Mamie, crying for help. Jim followed the sound, and it took him down to the basement stairs. He pulled the string to turn on the light, but nothing happened. The small boy didn't move another inch.

Mamie was in the basement, but it was dark down there. Listening to the cat's sad meows, Jim felt terrible. "She must be even more scared than I am," Jim thought.

He got so upset that he ran back to his room and sat on his bed with his hands over his ears. Then Jim cried as sadly as Mamie. He sat there for a long time. The cat could still be heard crying. Then suddenly, it was quiet.

That's when Jim stood up and went back to the dark basement stairs. "Mamie?" he said in a shaky voice.

The cat replied with a single long meow. Taking a deep breath, the boy went down the stairs and found his best friend hiding under his old wagon. Seconds later, they were upstairs in the bright kitchen, cuddling like long-lost friends. For the love of Mamie, Jim overcame his fear of the dark.

Presentation Ideas

ACT OUT THE STORY Volunteers can act out their stories alone or with a partner. Invite students from other classes to attend the performance. ▶ **Speaking/Listening/Viewing**

MAKE A COVER Have students make story covers showing their main characters in an important scene. Have volunteers display their covers on a class or hall bulletin board. ▶ **Representing/Viewing**

Scoring Rubric: 6-Trait Writing

4 Excellent	3 Good	2 Fair	1 Unsatisfactory
• **Ideas & Content** creates an entertaining, richly detailed story about overcoming an obstacle; characters, setting, and events are skillfully developed.	• **Ideas & Content** presents a focused, interesting story with distinct characters, setting, and events.	• **Ideas & Content** attempts to write a story; may not elaborate adequately; may lose control of the narrative after a good beginning.	• **Ideas & Content** may not understand how to tell a story; narrative may go off in several directions, without a sense of purpose.
• **Organization** unfolds a consistent, carefully planned narrative; sequence moves the reader smoothly through events; inviting beginning and satisfying ending.	• **Organization** has a carefully planned narrative strategy; story is easy to follow, through beginning, middle, and end; ideas are evenly connected.	• **Organization** may not craft a clear story structure, or may have trouble tying ideas and events together; story line may be vague or incomplete.	• **Organization** shows extreme lack of organization that interferes with understanding the text; sequence of events may be disorganized or incomplete.
• **Voice** shows originality, liveliness, and a strong personal message that speaks directly to the reader; explores a wide range of emotions.	• **Voice** makes a strong effort to share an authentic personal message that reaches out to an audience.	• **Voice** may get the basic story across, without a sense of involvement of reaching out to an audience; writing is flat and lifeless.	• **Voice** does not attempt to make sense, share ideas, or connect with a reader.
• **Word Choice** imaginative use of figurative and everyday words brings the story to life; sophisticated vocabulary creates a striking picture of individual characters who overcome an obstacle.	• **Word Choice** has overall clarity of expression; effective control of both new and everyday words; vocabulary is used to enliven the idea of overcoming an obstacle.	• **Word Choice** does not explore words that express clear ideas or feelings; may not choose words that create memorable pictures for the reader.	• **Word Choice** does not choose words that convey clear feelings or images; some word choices may detract from the meaning of the story.
• **Sentence Fluency** crafts creative, effective sentences that flow in a smooth rhythm; dialogue, if used, sounds natural and animates the story.	• **Sentence Fluency** crafts careful, easy-to-follow sentences; may effectively use fragments and/or dialogue to strengthen and enhance the story.	• **Sentence Fluency** may have trouble with complex sentences; sentences are understandable, but may be choppy, rambling, or awkward.	• **Sentence Fluency** constructs incomplete, rambling, or confusing sentences; may have trouble understanding how words, ideas, and sentences fit together.
• **Conventions** shows strong skills in a wide range of writing conventions; proper use of the rules of English enhances clarity and narrative style.	• **Conventions** makes some errors in spelling, capitalization, punctuation or usage, but these do not interfere with understanding the story; some editing may be needed.	• **Conventions** makes enough noticeable mistakes which may interfere with a smooth reading of the story.	• **Conventions** makes repeated errors in spelling, word choice, punctuation and usage; errors prevent an even reading of the text.

This piece is blank or fails to respond to the writing task. The topic is not addressed, or the student simply paraphrases the prompt. The response may be illegible or incoherent.

VOCABULARY

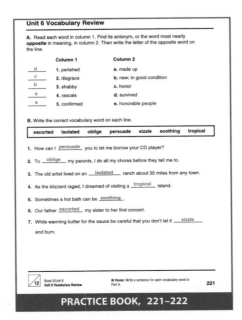

ONE Have each student pick one place mentioned in one of the stories. Then have the students write a postcard to the class using five of the vocabulary words. Share the postcards with the group.

Unit Review

Amistad Rising: A Story of Freedom

coaxed	navigate	perished
escorted	nightfall	ushered

Rip Van Winkle

husking	landlord	rascals
keg	oblige	sprawled

The Sea Maidens of Japan

cove	driftwood	host
disgrace	flails	sizzle

The Silent Lobby

interpret	persuade	shabby
pelted	register	soothing

Amazon Alert!

confirmed	lush	variety
isolated	tropical	wonderland

Unit 6 Vocabulary Review

A. Read each word in column 1. Find its antonym, or the word most nearly **opposite** in meaning, in column 2. Then write the letter of the opposite word on the line.

	Column 1	Column 2
d	1. perished	a. made up
c	2. disgrace	b. new; in good condition
b	3. shabby	c. honor
e	4. rascals	d. survived
a	5. confirmed	e. honorable people

B. Write the correct vocabulary word on each line.

escorted	isolated	oblige	persuade	sizzle	soothing	tropical

1. How can I _persuade_ you to let me borrow your CD player?

2. To _oblige_ my parents, I do all my chores before they tell me to.

3. The old artist lived on an _isolated_ ranch about 35 miles from any town.

4. As the blizzard raged, I dreamed of visiting a _tropical_ island.

5. Sometimes a hot bath can be _soothing_.

6. Our father _escorted_ my sister to her first concert.

7. While warming butter for the sauce be careful that you don't let it _sizzle_ and burn.

Book 5/Unit 6
Unit 6 Vocabulary Review 12

At Home: Write a sentence for each vocabulary word in Part A.

221

PRACTICE BOOK, 221–222

GRAMMAR

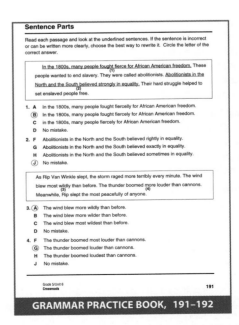

PARTNERS Have students play "Where, When, How." Write the names of the story characters on index cards. Write a variety of action verbs on index cards. Have pairs of students draw a character and a verb card. Then have them write a short story about the character and the action answering the questions *Where? When?* and *How?*

Unit Review

Amistad Rising: A Story of Freedom
Adverbs

Rip Van Winkle
Adverbs that Compare

The Sea Maidens of Japan
Negatives

The Silent Lobby
Prepositions

Amazon Alert!
Sentence Combining

Sentence Parts

Read each passage and look at the underlined sentences. If the sentence is incorrect or can be written more clearly, choose the best way to rewrite it. Circle the letter of the correct answer.

In the 1800s, many people fought fierce for African American freedom. These (1) people wanted to end slavery. They were called abolitionists. Abolitionists in the North and the South believed strongly in equality. Their hard struggle helped to (2) set enslaved people free.

1. **A** In the 1800s, many people fought fiercely for African American freedom.
   (B) In the 1800s, many people fought fiercely for African American freedom.
   C in the 1800s, many people fiercely for African American freedom.
   D No mistake.

2. **F** Abolitionists in the North and the South believed rightly in equality.
   G Abolitionists in the North and the South believed exactly in equality.
   H Abolitionists in the North and the South believed sometimes in equality.
   (J) No mistake.

As Rip Van Winkle slept, the storm raged more terribly every minute. The wind blew most wildly than before. The thunder boomed more louder than cannons. (3) (4) Meanwhile, Rip slept the most peacefully of anyone.

3. **(A)** The wind blew more wildly than before.
   B The wind blew more wilder than before.
   C The wind blew most wildest than before.
   D No mistake.

4. **F** The thunder boomed most louder than cannons.
   (G) The thunder boomed louder than cannons.
   H The thunder boomed loudest than cannons.
   J No mistake.

Grade 5/Unit 6
Crossroads

191

GRAMMAR PRACTICE BOOK, 191–192

SPELLING

ONE

Let each student choose one spelling word. Have them draw a crossword puzzle box on grid paper and write two clues for the word. The clues can suggest the spelling, the meaning, or the sound of the word. In groups of four, have students combine their boxes to make crossword puzzles for independent work.

Unit Review

Homophones and Homographs
died
dyed
current
currant
wound

Words with Prefixes
recall
unaware
preschool
dishonest
invisible

Words with Suffixes
meaningless
foolishness
honorable
graceful
amusement

Words with Suffixes
attraction
perfection
constitution
imagination
consideration

Words
difference
millimeter
frequency
liter
formula

Grade 5/Unit 6 Review Test

Read each sentence. If an underlined word is spelled wrong, fill in the circle that goes with that word. If no word is spelled wrong, fill in the circle below NONE.
Read Sample A and do Sample B.

A. The loud soond came from a high tower.
   A   B   C

A. Ⓐ ● Ⓒ Ⓓ NONE

B. The grate balloon burst with a bang.
   A   B   C

B. ● Ⓑ Ⓒ Ⓓ NONE

1. I was unaware that he dyid from his wound.
   A   B   C

1. Ⓐ Ⓑ ● Ⓓ NONE

2. Do you recall with what frequensy the child goes to school?
       E   F   G

2. Ⓔ ● Ⓖ Ⓗ NONE

3. The graceful and honorable lawyer referred to the constitution.
       A   B   C

3. Ⓐ Ⓑ Ⓒ ● NONE

4. The current preschool program is meeningless.
       E   F   G

4. Ⓔ Ⓕ ● Ⓗ NONE

5. The atraction of the constitution was that it was honorable.
       A   B   C

5. ● Ⓑ Ⓒ Ⓓ NONE

6. I can recall the perfection of the math formula.
          E   F   G

6. Ⓔ Ⓕ Ⓖ ● NONE

7. I was unaware that the currint was in the liter container.
       A   B   C

7. Ⓐ Ⓑ ● Ⓓ NONE

8. The formula shows the difference between a quart and a liter.
       E   F   G

8. Ⓔ Ⓕ Ⓖ ● NONE

9. I recall that the invisible man ate a corrant.
     A   B   C

9. Ⓐ Ⓑ Ⓒ ● NONE

10. She learned the difference between a liter and a milimeter.
                    E   F   G

10. Ⓔ Ⓕ ● Ⓗ NONE

24 | Grade 5/Unit 6 Review Test   191

SPELLING PRACTICE BOOK, 191–192

☑ SKILLS & STRATEGIES

Comprehension
☑ Judgments and Decisions

Cause & Effect
☑ Draw Conclusions
☑ Sequence of Events
☑ Context Clues

Vocabulary Strategies
☑ Context Clues
☑ Synonyms & Antonyms

Study Skills
☑ Read a Map
☑ Conduct an Interview
☑ Choose Reference Sources
☑ Use an Outline
☑ Use an Encyclopedia

Writing
☑ Write a Story

Assessment
Follow-Up

Use the results of the informal and formal assessment opportunities in the unit to help you make decisions about future instruction.

SKILLS AND STRATEGIES	Reteaching Blackline Masters	Alternate Teaching Strategies
Comprehension		
Judgments and Decisions	186, 190, 207, 211	T60
Cause and Effect	193, 197, 205, 218	T64
Draw Conclusions	191, 198, 212	T62
Sequence of Events	200, 214	T66
Context Clues	192, 206, 220	T63
Vocabulary Strategy		
Context Clues	192, 206, 220	T63
Antonyms and Synonyms	199, 213, 219	T65
Study Skills		
Reference Sources	189, 196, 203, 210, 217	T61

Writing	Alternate Writing Project— Easy	Unit Writing Process Lessons
Write a Story	647L, 673L, 697L, 717L, 727L	729A–F

McGraw-Hill School
TECHNOLOGY

*inter***NET** CONNECTION · Research & Inquiry Ideas. Visit
www.mhschool.com/reading

Glossary

Introduce students to the Glossary by reading through the introduction and looking over the pages with them. Encourage the class to talk about what they see.

Words in a glossary, like words in a dictionary, are listed in **alphabetical order.** Point out the **guide words** at the top of each page that tell the first and last words appearing on that page.

Point out examples of **entries** and **main entries.** Read through a simple entry with the class, identifying each part. Have students note the order in which information is given: entry words(s), definition(s), example sentence, syllable division, pronunciation respelling, part of speech, plural/verb/adjective forms.

Note that if more than one definition is given for a word, the definitions are numbered. Note also the format used for a word that is more than one part of speech.

Review the parts of speech by identifying each in a sentence:

inter.	*adj.*	*n.*	*conj.*	*adj.*	*n.*
Wow!	A	dictionary	and	a	glossary
v.	*adv.*	*pron.*	*prep.*	*n.*	
tell	almost	everything	about	words!	

Explain the use of the **pronunciation key** (either the **short key,** at the bottom of every other page, or the **long key,** at the beginning of the glossary). Demonstrate the difference between **primary** stress and **secondary** stress by pronouncing a word with both.

Point out an example of the small triangle signaling a homophone. **Homophones** are words with different spellings and meanings but with the same pronunciation. Explain that a pair of words with the superscripts **1** and **2** are **homographs**—words that have the same spelling, but different origins and meanings, and in some cases, different pronunciations.

The **Word History** feature tells what language a word comes from and what changes have occurred in its spelling and/or meaning. Many everyday words have interesting and surprising stories behind them. Note that word histories can help us remember the meanings of difficult words.

Allow time for students to further explore the Glossary and make their own discoveries.

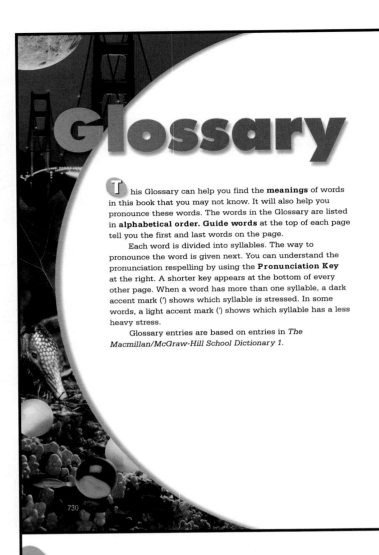

Glossary

This Glossary can help you find the **meanings** of words in this book that you may not know. It will also help you pronounce these words. The words in the Glossary are listed in **alphabetical order. Guide words** at the top of each page tell you the first and last words on the page.

Each word is divided into syllables. The way to pronounce the word is given next. You can understand the pronunciation respelling by using the **Pronunciation Key** at the right. A shorter key appears at the bottom of every other page. When a word has more than one syllable, a dark accent mark (´) shows which syllable is stressed. In some words, a light accent mark (´) shows which syllable has a less heavy stress.

Glossary entries are based on entries in *The Macmillan/McGraw-Hill School Dictionary 1.*

Guide Words

adobe/banner

First word on the page

Last word on the page

Sample Entry

Main entry → **adobe** A sandy kind of clay used to make bricks. Bits of straw are sometimes mixed with the clay, and the bricks are dried in the sun. Many buildings in Mexico and the southwestern United States are made of *adobe.* ← Example sentence

← Definition

Syllable division → **a•do•be** (ə dō´ bē) *noun,* *plural* **adobes.** ← Part of speech

Plural form   Pronunciation

a	at, bad	d	dear, soda, bad
ā	ape, pain, day, break	f	five, defend, leaf, off, cough, elephant.
ä	father, car, heart		
âr	care, pair, bear, their, where	g	game, ago, fog, egg
e	end, pet, said, heaven, friend	h	hat, ahead
ē	equal, me, feet, team, piece, key	hw	white, whether, which
i	it, big, English, hymn	j	joke, enjoy, gem, page, edge
ī	ice, fine, lie, my	k	kite, bakery, seek, tack, cat
îr	ear, deer, here, pierce	l	lid, sailor, feel, ball, allow
o	odd, hot, watch	m	man, family, dream
ō	old, oat, toe, low	n	not, final, pan, knife
ô	coffee, all, taught, law, fought	ng	long, singer, pink
ôr	order, fork, horse, story, pour	p	pail, repair, soap, happy
oi	oil, toy	r	ride, parent, wear, more, marry
ou	out, now	s	sit, aside, pets, cent, pass
u	up, mud, love, double	sh	shoe, washer, fish, mission, nation
ū	use, mule, cue, feud, few	t	tag, pretend, fat, button, dressed
ü	rule, true, food	th	thin, panther, both,
u̇	put, wood, should	th	this, mother, smooth
ûr	burn, hurry, term, bird, word, courage	v	very, favor, wave
		w	wet, weather, reward
ə	about, taken, pencil, lemon, circus	y	yes, onion
b	bat, above, job	z	zoo, lazy, jazz, rose, dogs, houses
ch	chin, such, match	zh	vision, treasure, seizure

Aa

abalone A large sea snail that has a flat, pearly shell; its meat is used for food. For dinner we ordered *abalone* at the restaurant.
ab•a•lo•ne (ab´ə lō´nē) *noun, plural* **abalones.**

abolitionist A person who was in favor of ending slavery in the United States before the Civil War. The *abolitionists* wanted to set the slaves free.
a•bo•li•tion•ist (ab´ə lish´ə nist) *noun, plural* **abolitionists.**

accurate Correct, exact, or precise. The newspaper stories about the accident were not *accurate.*
▲ **Synonym:** precise
ac•cu•rate (ak´yər it) *adjective.*

Language Note

A **synonym** is a word that has the same meaning as another word. A synonym for *accurate* is *precise.*

acre A measure of land equal to 43,560 square feet. An acre is slightly smaller in size than a football field. The farmer planted one *acre* of corn.
a•cre (ā´kər) *noun, plural* **acres.**

adobe 1. A brick made of clay, sometimes mixed with straw, and dried in the sun. They built the house entirely of *adobe* bricks. 2. A building made with adobe bricks, popular in Mexico and the southwestern United States. On our drive through New Mexico, many of the houses we saw were *adobes.*
a•do•be (ə dō´bē) *noun, plural* **adobes.**

afford 1. To have enough money to pay for. Can you *afford* a new car? 2. To be able to give or do. They couldn't *afford* the time to help us.
af•ford (ə fôrd´) *verb,* **afforded, affording.**

amplify 1. To make louder or stronger. The microphone will *amplify* the speaker's voice so that everyone can hear. 2. To give more details about; explain more. The teacher asked me to *amplify* my report by giving more details.
am•pli•fy (am´plə fī´) *verb,* **amplified, amplifying.**

---

anchor A heavy metal device that is attached to a ship by a chain or cable. When an *anchor* is dropped overboard, it digs into the ground below the water and keeps the ship from drifting. *Noun.*—To hold something in place with an anchor. We will *anchor* the boat while we fish. *Verb.*
an•chor (ang´kər) *noun, plural* **anchors;** *verb,* **anchored, anchoring.**

Word History

Anchor comes from the Greek word *ankyra.* It was first used in the English language in the 12th century.

apologize To say one is sorry or embarrassed; make an apology. I *apologized* to my parents for being rude.
a•pol•o•gize (ə pol´ə jīz´) *verb,* **apologized, apologizing.**

approve 1. To have or give a favorable opinion. My parents don't *approve* of my staying up very late. 2. To consent or agree to officially; authorize. The town *approved* the construction of a public swimming pool.
ap•prove (ə prüv´) *verb,* **approved, approving.**

arrowhead The pointed tip or head of an arrow. The scientists found *arrowheads* on the site of ancient hunting grounds.
ar•row•head (ar´ō hed´) *noun, plural* **arrowheads.**

arrowhead

arroyo A ditch with steep sides that has been cut in the ground by the force of running water; gully. Arroyos are dry most of the year. During the rainy season, the rains cut *arroyos* into the ground.
ar•roy•o (ə roi´ō) *noun, plural* **arroyos.**

assignment 1. Something that is assigned. My arithmetic *assignment* is to do ten multiplication problems. 2. The act of assigning. The company's president is responsible for the *assignment* of tasks to employees.
as•sign•ment (ə sīn´mənt) *noun, plural* **assignments.**

astound To surprise very much; amaze; astonish. The first flight into outer space *astounded* the whole world.
▲ **Synonym:** surprise
as•tound (ə stound´) *verb,* **astounded, astounding.**

at; āpe; fär; câre; end; mē; it; īce; pîerce; hot; ōld; sông; fôrk; oil; out; up; ūse; rüle; pu̇ll; tûrn; chin; sing; shop; thin; this; hw in white; zh in treasure. The symbol ə stands for the unstressed vowel sound in about, taken, pencil, lemon, and circus.

athletic 1. Of or having to do with an athlete or athletics. Our school has just bought new *athletic* equipment. 2. Active and strong. My grandparents are very *athletic*; they love to swim and ice-skate.
ath•let•ic (ath let′ik) *adjective.*

atmosphere 1. The layer of gases that surrounds the Earth. The atmosphere is made up of oxygen, nitrogen, carbon dioxide, and other gases. Outer space lies beyond the Earth's *atmosphere.* 2. The layer of gases that surrounds any heavenly body. Scientists do not think people could live in the *atmosphere* of Mars.
at•mos•phere (at′məs fîr′) *noun, plural* **atmospheres.**

auction A public sale at which things are sold to the person who offers the most money. My cousin bid five dollars for a rocking chair at the village *auction. Noun.*—To sell at an auction. We *auctioned* off our old furniture. *Verb.*
auc•tion (ôk′shən) *noun, plural* **auctions;** *verb,* **auctioned, auctioning.**

automatically Done in a manner without a person's control. I breathe *automatically* when I'm asleep.
au•to•mat•i•cal•ly (ô′tə mat′i kəl lē) *adverb.*

avalanche The swift, sudden fall of a mass of snow, ice, earth, or rocks down a mountain slope. The *avalanche* completely covered the village with mud.
av•a•lanche (av′ə lanch′) *noun, plural* **avalanches.**

awesome Causing wonder or fear. The huge whale was an *awesome* sight.
awe•some (ô′səm) *adjective.*

banner A piece of cloth that has a design and some writing on it. *Noun.* —Important; outstanding. With the hedges and roadsides full of raspberries, it was a *banner* season for raspberry pickers. *Adjective.*
ban•ner (ban′ər) *noun, plural* **banners;** *adjective.*

Word History

The word *banner* appeared in the English language during the 13ᵗʰ century and is thought to have come from the language of the Goths. Their word *bandwo* meant "sign."

---

barrier Something that blocks the way. The fallen tree was a *barrier* to traffic on the road.
bar•ri•er (bar′ē ər) *noun, plural* **barriers.**

bashful Shy around people. The *bashful* child hid behind the chair.
bash•ful (bash′fəl) *adjective.*

billow To rise or swell in billows. The sail of the boat *billowed* in the wind. *Verb.*—A great swelling wave of something. *Billows* of smoke poured from the smokestack. *Noun.*
bil•low (bil′ō) *verb,* **billowed, billowing;** *noun, plural* **billows.**

bison A large animal that has a big, shaggy head, short horns, and a hump on its back; buffalo. Bison are found in North America. Herds of *bison* once roamed the American prairies.
bi•son (bī′sən) *noun, plural* **bison.**

board To provide lodging and meals for pay. I *boarded* with a family in France last summer. *Verb.*—A long, flat piece of sawed wood, used in building houses and other things. The carpenters hammered nails into the *boards* on the floor. *Noun.*
board (bôrd) *verb,* **boarded, boarding;** *noun, plural* **boards.**

boon A help; benefit. The rain was a *boon* to my vegetable garden after the dry weather.
▲ **Synonym:** favor
boon (bün) *noun, plural* **boons.**

border To lie along the edge of. California *borders* Oregon. *Verb.*—A line where one country or other area ends and another begins; boundary. The tourists crossed the *border* into Mexico. *Noun.*
bor•der (bôr′dər) *verb,* **bordered, bordering;** *noun, plural* **borders.**

boulder A large, usually rounded rock. We saw many huge *boulders* at the foot of the mountain.
boul•der (bōl′dər) *noun, plural* **boulders.**

---

at; āpe; fär; câre; end; mē; it; īce; pîerce; hot; ōld; sông; fôrk; oil; out; up; ūse; rüle; púll; tûrn; chin; sing; shop; thin; this; hw in white; zh in treasure. The symbol ə stands for the unstressed vowel sound in about, taken, pencil, lemon, and circus.

---

bruise To cause a bruise on the skin of. The hard fall *bruised* my knee. *Verb.* —An injury that does not break the skin but discolors it. A *bruise* can be caused by a fall, blow, or bump. *Noun.*
bruise (brüz) *verb,* **bruised, bruising;** *noun, plural* **bruises.**

bullet A small piece of rounded or pointed metal, made to be shot from a small firearm, such as a gun or rifle. Never play with a gun that is loaded with *bullets.*
bul•let (búl′it) *noun, plural* **bullets.**

burglar A person who breaks into a house, store, or other place to steal something. The *burglar* crawled in the open window and stole the silverware.
▲ **Synonym:** thief
bur•glar (bûr′glər) *noun, plural* **burglars.**

bushel A measure for grain, fruit, vegetables, and other dry things. A *bushel* is equal to 4 pecks, or 32 quarts.
bush•el (búsh′əl) *noun, plural* **bushels.**

capture To succeed in expressing something. The story *captures* what it is like to be an only child. *Verb.* —The act of catching and holding a person, animal, or thing. The *capture* of the bank robber took place the day after the robbery. *Noun.*
cap•ture (kap′chər) *verb,* **captured, capturing;** *noun, plural* **captures.**

carelessly 1. In a manner showing a lack of attention. I *carelessly* ran down the stairs, and I tripped and fell. 2. Done without close attention or care. You will not get a good grade on your report if you *carelessly* make spelling mistakes.
care•less•ly (kâr′lis lē) *adverb.*

cemetery A place where the dead are buried. While at the *cemetery,* I put flowers on my grandmother's grave.
▲ **Synonym:** graveyard
cem•e•ter•y (sem′ə ter′ ē) *noun, plural* **cemeteries.**

Word History

Cemetery comes from the Greek word *koimeterion,* meaning "sleeping chamber."

---

characteristic A quality that belongs to and helps to identify a person or thing. Kindness and honesty are two good *characteristics* of my neighbor. *Noun.* —Belonging to and helping to identify a person or thing; typical. The *characteristic* taste of a lemon is sour. *Adjective.*
char•ac•ter•is•tic (kar′ik tə ris′tik) *noun, plural* **characteristics;** *adjective.*

charcoal A soft, black form of carbon, made by partially burning wood, used as a fuel and in pencils for drawing. The burning wood turned into *charcoal.*
char•coal (chär′kōl) *noun.*

chase The act of running and trying to catch. The *chase* ended when the police caught the criminal. *Noun.* —To run after and try to catch. The dog *chased* the bouncing ball. *Verb.*
chase (chās) *noun, plural* **chases;** *verb,* **chased, chasing.**

chemical A substance made by or used in chemistry. Ammonia is a *chemical* used in household cleaners. *Noun.* —Having to do with or made by chemistry. Rusting is a *chemical* process in which metal combines with oxygen. *Adjective.*
chem•i•cal (kem′i kəl) *noun, plural* **chemicals;** *adjective.*

chile A hot pepper. Mama puts *chiles* in the salsa to make it spicy.
chil•e (chil′ ē) *noun, plural* **chiles.**

cleft A space or opening made by splitting; crack. You can climb the cliff by holding on to the *clefts* in the rocks. *Noun.*—Divided by a crack or split. Two of my cousins have *cleft* chins. *Adjective.*
cleft (kleft) *noun, plural* **clefts;** *adjective.*

coax To persuade or influence by mild urging. I *coaxed* my parents into letting me go to camp next summer.
coax (kōks) *verb,* **coaxed, coaxing.**

cockpit The space in an airplane or a small boat where the pilot sits. The pilot showed us the airplane's control panel in the *cockpit.*
cock•pit (kok′pit′) *noun, plural* **cockpits.**

---

at; āpe; fär; câre; end; mē; it; īce; pîerce; hot; ōld; sông; fôrk; oil; out; up; ūse; rüle; púll; tûrn; chin; sing; shop; thin; this; hw in white; zh in treasure. The symbol ə stands for the unstressed vowel sound in about, taken, pencil, lemon, and circus.

Glossary

G3

collision The act of colliding; a crash. The *collision* of the two cars made a great noise.
col•li•sion (kə lizh′ən) *noun, plural* **collisions.**

commotion A noisy confusion; disorder. There was a *commotion* at the stadium as the crowd booed the referee's decision.
com•mo•tion (kə mōsh′ən) *noun, plural* **commotions.**

concentrate 1. To focus one's mind on something. *Concentrate* on your homework. 2. To bring together into one place. The population of our country is *concentrated* in the cities.
con•cen•trate (kon′sən trāt′) *verb,* **concentrated, concentrating.**

confirm 1. To show to be true or correct. The newspaper *confirmed* the reports of a flood. 2. To consent to; approve. The Senate *confirmed* the trade agreement.
con•firm (kən fûrm′) *verb,* **confirmed, confirming.**

confront To meet or face. A difficult problem *confronted* us.
▲ **Synonym:** face
con•front (kən frunt′) *verb,* **confronted, confronting.**

congratulate To give good wishes or praise for someone's success or for something nice that has happened. We *congratulated* them on doing such a good job.
con•grat•u•late (kən grach′ə lāt′) *verb,* **congratulated, congratulating.**

conquer To overcome; defeat. We *conquered* our fears.
con•quer (kong′kər) *verb,* **conquered, conquering.**

consent To give permission; agree. My parents *consented* to my going camping. *Verb.*—Permission. My parents gave me their *consent* to go camping. *Noun.*
con•sent (kən sent′) *verb,* **consented, consenting;** *noun, plural* **consents.**

convenience 1. Ease; comfort. I like the *convenience* of canned foods. 2. Something that gives ease or comfort. A washing machine is a modern *convenience.*
con•ven•ience (kən vēn′yəns) *noun, plural* **conveniences.**

cove A small, sheltered bay or inlet. The pirates hid their ship in the *cove.*
cove (kōv) *noun, plural* **coves.**

credentials Letters or documents that give the right to exercise authority. Without the proper *credentials* you cannot become president.
cre•den•tials (kri den′ shəlz) *plural noun.*

cripple 1. To injure badly. A car accident *crippled* him. 2. To disable or incapacitate; keep from working properly. The power failure *crippled* the entire city.
crip•ple (krip′əl) *verb,* **crippled, crippling.**

> **Word History**
> *Cripple* appeared in the English language before the 12th century. It comes from the Old English word *creopan,* meaning "to creep."

cycle 1. A series of events that happen one after another in the same order, over and over again: the *cycle* of the four seasons of the year. *Noun.*—To ride a bicycle, tricycle, or motorcycle. I dream of *cycling* across America. *Verb.*
cy•cle (sī′kəl) *noun, plural* **cycles;** *verb,* **cycled, cycling.**

dangle 1. To hang or swing loosely. An old kite *dangled* from a tree. 2. To tease by offering something as a treat. I *dangled* a bone in front of the dog.
dan•gle (dang′gəl) *verb,* **dangled, dangling.**

data 1. Individual facts, figures, and other items of information. These *data* from the computer don't seem to be accurate. 2. Information as a whole. Adequate *data* on that subject is sometimes difficult to find.
▲ Used with either a singular or plural verb.
da•ta (dā′tə *or* dat′ə) *plural noun.*

> at; āpe; fär; câre; end; mē; it; īce; pîerce; hot; ōld; sōng; fôrk; oil; out; up; ūse; rūle; pull; tûrn; chin; sing; shop; thin; this; hw in white; zh in treasure. The symbol ə stands for the unstressed vowel sound in about, taken, pencil, lemon, and circus.

debt 1. Something that is owed to another. I paid my *debts* when I got my allowance. 2. The condition of owing. My parents are in *debt* because they borrowed money to buy our house.
debt (det) *noun, plural* **debts.**

dedicate To set apart for a special purpose or use. Their parents *dedicated* their weekends to playing with their children.
ded•i•cate (ded′i kāt′) *verb,* **dedicated, dedicating.**

defiantly Boldly refusing to obey or respect authority. The child *defiantly* slammed the door because he didn't want to go to bed.
de•fi•ant•ly (di fī′ənt lē) *adverb.*

delivery 1. The act of taking something to the proper place or person. We get a mail *delivery* every day except Sundays and holidays. 2. A way of doing something. The pitcher's *delivery* was low and outside.
de•liv•er•y (di liv′ə rē) *noun, plural* **deliveries.**

delta An area of land at the mouth of a river. A delta is formed by deposits of mud, sand, and pebbles. It is often shaped like a triangle. The Mississippi *Delta* is the area of land at the mouth of the Mississippi River.
del•ta (del′tə) *noun, plural* **deltas.**

delta

depict To show in pictures or words; describe. The artist tried to *depict* the movement of the ocean's waves. The story *depicted* a day in the life of a typical Chinese family.
de•pict (di pikt′) *verb,* **depicted, depicting.**

despair A complete loss of hope. The family was filled with *despair* when the fire destroyed their house. *Noun.*—To give up or lose hope; be without hope. I *despaired* of ever finding my lost watch in the pond. *Verb.*
de•spair (di spâr′) *noun; verb,* **despaired, despairing.**

desperation A willingness to try anything to change a hopeless situation. They gripped the log in *desperation* as they floated toward the waterfall.
des•per•a•tion (des′pə rā′shən) *noun.*

destruction 1. The act of destroying. The *destruction* of the old building became a media event. 2. Great damage or ruin. The earthquake caused widespread *destruction.*
de•struc•tion (di struk′shən) *noun.*

detect To find out or notice; discover. I called the fire department after I *detected* smoke coming from the garage.
de•tect (di tekt′) *verb,* **detected, detecting.**

devastation The act of destruction; ruin. The hurricane left *devastation* in its wake in the small towns along the coast.
dev•as•ta•tion (dev′ə stā′ shen) *noun.*

devour 1. To eat greedily; consume. The hungry child *devoured* the sandwich. 2. To consume destructively. The flames *devoured* the house.
de•vour (di vour′) *verb,* **devoured, devouring.**

diary A written record of the things that one has done or thought each day. I keep my *diary* hidden.
di•a•ry (dī′ ə rē) *noun, plural* **diaries.**

> **Word History**
> The word *diary* appeared in its English form in the late 1500s. It comes from the Latin word *diarium,* derived from *dies,* meaning "day."

dimension 1. A measurement of length, width, or height. 2. Size or importance. Few people seem to realize the true *dimensions* of racism in this country.
di•men•sion (di men′shən) *noun, plural* **dimensions.**

discount An amount subtracted from the regular price. I bought a suit on sale at a 25 percent *discount.*
▲ **Synonym:** reduction
dis•count (dis′ kount′) *noun, plural* **discounts.**

disgrace To bring shame to. Poor losers *disgrace* their teams. *Verb.*—The loss of honor or respect; shame. The president resigned in *disgrace* when the police learned about the stolen money. *Noun.*
dis•grace (dis grās′) *verb,* **disgraced, disgracing;** *noun, plural* **disgraces.**

> at; āpe; fär; câre; end; mē; it; īce; pîerce; hot; ōld; sōng; fôrk; oil; out; up; ūse; rūle; pull; tûrn; chin; sing; shop; thin; this; hw in white; zh in treasure. The symbol ə stands for the unstressed vowel sound in about, taken, pencil, lemon, and circus.

dismay A feeling of fear or alarm. The family was filled with *dismay* when they saw the fire approaching their house. *Noun.*—To trouble or discourage. The rising flood *dismayed* the people of the town. *Verb.*
dis•may (dis mā′) *noun; verb,* **dismayed, dismaying.**

disobey To refuse or fail to obey. The driver *disobeyed* the traffic laws by not stopping at the red light.
dis•o•bey (dis′ə bā′) *verb,* **disobeyed, disobeying.**

distinguish 1. To know or show that there is a difference between certain things. The jeweler *distinguished* the real diamond from the fake one. 2. To make something special or different; set apart. The male cardinal's bright red feathers *distinguish* it from the female.
dis•tin•guish (di sting′gwish) *verb,* **distinguished, distinguishing.**

distress Great pain or sorrow; misery. My grandfather's illness was a great *distress* to me. *Noun.*—To cause pain, sorrow, or misery. The bad news *distressed* us. *Verb.*
dis•tress (di stres′) *noun; verb,* **distressed, distressing.**

division 1. One of the parts into which something is divided. Asian history is one of the *divisions* of our social studies course. 2. The act of dividing or the condition of being divided. The *division* of the house into apartments provided homes for five families.
di•vi•sion (di vizh′ən) *noun, plural* **divisions.**

divorce To legally end a marriage. Our parents have been *divorced* for one year. *Verb.*—The legal ending of a marriage. The marriage ended with a *divorce. Noun.*
di•vorce (di vôrs′) *verb,* **divorced, divorcing;** *noun, plural* **divorces.**

donate To give; contribute. The family *donated* their old clothes to people who needed them.
▲ Synonyms: present, bestow
do•nate (dō′nāt) *verb,* **donated, donating.**

driftwood Wood that floats on water or is brought to the shore by water. We walked up the beach and collected the *driftwood* the waves washed in.
drift•wood (drift′ wùd′) *noun.*

742

drought A long period of time when there is little or no rainfall at all. Our garden suffered in the *drought.*
drought (drout) *noun, plural* **droughts.**

dynamite A substance that explodes with great force. Dynamite is used to blow up old buildings and blast openings in rocks. Using *dynamite* is very dangerous. *Noun.*—To blow something up with dynamite. The builders *dynamited* the mountain so that they could put a road through. *Verb.*
dy•na•mite (dī′nə mit′) *noun; verb,* **dynamited, dynamiting.**

Ee

elementary Dealing with the simple basic parts or beginnings of something. We learned about addition and subtraction when we studied *elementary* arithmetic.
el•e•men•ta•ry (el′ə men′tə rē *or* el′ə men′trē) *adjective.*

emerge 1. To come into view. The sun *emerged* from behind a cloud. 2. To come out; become known. New facts about the case *emerged* during the trial.
e•merge (i mûrj′) *verb,* **emerged, emerging.**

emerge

enlist 1. To join or persuade to join the armed forces. Many *enlisted* in the Navy as soon as the war broke out. 2. To get the help or support of. The mayor *enlisted* the entire town in the drive to clean up the streets.
en•list (en list′) *verb,* **enlisted, enlisting.**

erosion A wearing, washing, or eating away. *Erosion* usually happens gradually, over a long period of time.
e•ro•sion (i rō′zhən) *noun.*

escort One or more ships or airplanes that travel with or protect another ship or airplane. The battleship's *escort* included three destroyers. *Noun.* —To act as an escort. The police *escorted* the mayor in the parade. *Verb.*
es•cort (es′kôrt *for noun;* e skôrt′ *or* es′kôrt *for verb*) *noun, plural* **escorts;** *verb,* **escorted, escorting.**

at; āpe; fär; câre; end; mē; it; īce; pîerce; hot; ōld; sông; fôrk; oil; out; up; ūse; rūle; pùll; tûrn; chin; sing; shop; thin; this; hw in white; zh in treasure. The symbol ə stands for the unstressed vowel sound in about, taken, pencil, lemon, and circus.

743

eventually At the end; finally. We waited and waited for our friends, but *eventually* we went to the movies without them.
e•ven•tu•al•ly (i ven′chü ə lē) *adverb.*

explosive Something that can explode or cause an explosion. The bomb squad searched the airplane for *explosives. Noun.*—Likely to explode or cause an explosion. A bomb is an *explosive* device. *Adjective.*
ex•plo•sive (ek splō′siv) *noun, plural* **explosives;** *adjective.*

Ff

fertile 1. Able to produce crops and plants easily and plentifully. *Fertile* soil is the best soil for growing vegetables. 2. Able to produce eggs, seeds, pollen, or young. An animal is *fertile* when it can give birth to young.
fer•tile (fûr′təl) *adjective.*

fireball A ball of fire. The sun was a magnificent *fireball* in the evening sky.
fire•ball (fir′bôl′) *noun, plural* **fireballs.**

flabbergast To overcome with shock or surprise. I was *flabbergasted* when I saw my low grade on the test, because I had really studied for it.
flab•ber•gast (flab′ bər gast′) *verb,* **flabbergasted, flabbergasting.**

flail To wave or move about wildly. The turtle *flailed* its legs when it was turned on its back.
▲ Synonym: thrash
flail (flāl) *verb,* **flailed, flailing.**

former 1. Belonging to or happening in the past; earlier. In *former* times, people used fireplaces to heat their houses. 2. The first of two. Greenland and Madagascar are both islands; the *former* island is in the North Atlantic Ocean, and the latter island is in the Indian Ocean.
for•mer (fôr′mər) *adjective.*

fraction 1. A part of a whole. Only a small *fraction* of the people watching the football game left before it was over. 2. A number that stands for one or more equal parts of a whole. A fraction shows the division of one number by a second number. 2/3, 3/4, and 1/16 are *fractions.*
frac•tion (frak′shən) *noun, plural* **fractions.**

744

fume To be very angry or irritated. The driver *fumed* while stuck in traffic. *Verb.*—A smoke or gas that is harmful or has a bad smell. The *fumes* from her cooking made us sick. *Noun.*
fume (fūm) *verb,* **fumed, fuming;** *noun, plural* **fumes.**

Gg

glisten To shine with reflected light. The spiderweb *glistened* in the sun.
glis•ten (glis′ən) *verb,* **glistened, glistening.**

glory 1. Great praise; honor; fame. They both did the work, but only one got the *glory.* 2. Great beauty; splendor. The sun shone in all its *glory.*
glo•ry (glôr′ē) *noun, plural* **glories.**

gorge A deep, narrow valley with steep, rocky walls. Over millions of years the river cut a *gorge* in the land. *Noun.*—To eat in a greedy way. Don't *gorge* your food. *Verb.*
gorge (gôrj) *noun, plural* **gorges;** *verb,* **gorged, gorging.**

granite A hard kind of rock used to build monuments and buildings. The builders lifted the *granite* block to its place at the top of the monument.
gran•ite (gran′it) *noun.*

gratitude A feeling of gratefulness. We are full of *gratitude* for your help.
▲ Synonym: thankfulness
grat•i•tude (grat′i tüd′ *or* grat′i tūd′) *noun.*

grit Very small bits of sand or stone. The strong winds carried *grit* through the air. *Noun.* —To press together hard; grind. I *gritted* my teeth. *Verb.*
grit (grit) *noun; verb,* **gritted, gritting.**

Hh

hail A motion or call used as a greeting or to attract attention. *Hails* from the crowd greeted the politician as he walked into the auditorium. *Noun.* —To greet or to attract the attention of by calling or shouting. We *hailed* a taxi by waving our arms. *Verb.*
hail (hāl) *noun, plural* **hails;** *verb,* **hailed, hailing.**

at; āpe; fär; câre; end; mē; it; īce; pîerce; hot; ōld; sông; fôrk; oil; out; up; ūse; rūle; pùll; tûrn; chin; sing; shop; thin; this; hw in white; zh in treasure. The symbol ə stands for the unstressed vowel sound in about, taken, pencil, lemon, and circus.

745

hasty 1. Quick; hurried. We barely had time for a *hasty* breakfast. **2.** Too quick; careless or reckless. Don't make a *hasty* decision that you'll be sorry for later.
    hast•y (hās′ tē) *adjective,* **hastier, hastiest;** *adverb,* **hastily;** *noun* **hastiness.**

herb 1. Any plant or plant part that is used for flavor in cooking, or in making medicines or perfumes and cosmetics. She used *herbs* in her cooking. **2.** Any flowering plant that does not form a woody stem, but instead dies down to the ground at the end of each growing season. Her garden of *herbs* supplies the whole neighborhood.
    herb (ûrb *or* hûrb) *noun, plural* **herbs.**

heritage Something handed down from earlier generations or from the past; tradition. The right to free speech is an important part of our American *heritage.*
    her•i•tage (her′i tij) *noun, plural* **heritages.**

heroic 1. Very brave; courageous. The firefighter's *heroic* rescue of the child from the burning house made all the newspapers. **2.** Describing the deeds of heroes. I wrote a *heroic* poem about Chief Crazy Horse.
    he•ro•ic (hi rō′ik) *adjective.*

hoist To lift or pull up. We *hoisted* the bags onto the table. *Verb.*—A device used to lift or pull up something heavy. The sailors used a *hoist* to raise the cargo. *Noun.*
    hoist (hoist) *verb,* **hoisted, hoisting;** *noun, plural* **hoists.**

host To serve as host for. I *hosted* a party for our friends. *Verb.*—A person who invites people to visit as guests. We thanked our *host* for a wonderful party. *Noun.*
    host (hōst) *verb,* **hosted, hosting;** *noun, plural* **hosts.**

hull The sides and bottom of a boat or ship. The waves crashed against the *hull* of the ship. *Noun.*—To remove the outer covering from a seed or fruit. Birds *hull* seeds before they eat them. *Verb.*
    hull (hul) *noun, plural* **hulls;** *verb,* **hulled, hulling.**

husk To take off the husk from. We cracked and *husked* the coconuts. *Verb.*—The dry outside covering of some vegetables and fruits. We took the green *husks* off the corn. *Noun.*
    husk (husk) *verb,* **husked, husking;** *noun, plural* **husks.**

Ii

immortal One who lives or is remembered forever. The ancient Greek gods were considered *immortals.*
    im•mor•tal (i môr′təl) *noun, plural* **immortals.**

incorrectly In a manner that is not right or correct. You must redo this problem because you answered it *incorrectly.*
    in•cor•rect•ly (in′kə rekt′ lē) *adverb.*

influence To have an effect on, especially by giving suggestions or by serving as an example. The older members of my family *influence* me in many ways. *Verb.*—The power of a person or thing to produce an effect on others without using force or a command. Use your *influence* to persuade your friend to study harder. *Noun.*
    in•flu•ence (in′flū əns) *verb,* **influenced, influencing;** *noun, plural* **influences.**

injure To cause harm to; damage or hurt. I *injured* myself when I fell off my bicycle.
    in•jure (in′jər) *verb,* **injured, injuring.**

inquire To ask for information. We stopped at a gas station to *inquire* the way to the park.
    in•quire (in kwir′) *verb,* **inquired, inquiring.**

insistent 1. Firm or persistent. Although we were having a good time, my cousin was *insistent* on going home. **2.** Demanding attention. The *insistent* ringing of the doorbell woke us.
    in•sis•tent (in sis′ tənt) *adjective.*

at; āpe; fär; câre; end; mē; it; īce; pîerce; hot; ōld; sông; fôrk; oil; out; up; ūse; rūle; pùll; tûrn; chin; sing; shop; thin; this; hw in white; zh in treasure. The symbol ə stands for the unstressed vowel sound in about, taken, pencil, lemon, and circus.

intense 1. Very great or strong; extreme. The heat from the iron was so *intense* that it burned a hole in the cloth. **2.** Having or showing strong feeling, purpose, or effort; concentrated. The worried parent had an *intense* look.
    in•tense (in tens′) *adjective.*

interpret 1. To explain the meaning of. The teacher *interpreted* what the author meant in the poem. **2.** To change from one language to another; translate. Since my friends couldn't speak Spanish, I *interpreted* what my cousin from Mexico was saying.
    in•ter•pret (in tûr′prit) *verb,* **interpreted, interpreting.**

isolate To place or set apart; separate from others. I was *isolated* from my sister and brother when I had the mumps so that they wouldn't get it.
    i•so•late (i′sə lāt′) *verb,* **isolated, isolating.**

Jj

journal 1. A regular record or account; diary. Each student was told to keep a *journal* during the summer. The scientist entered the results of the experiments in a *journal.* **2.** A magazine or newspaper. The medical *journal* published a report on the doctor's most recent discoveries.
    jour•nal (jûr′nəl) *noun, plural* **journals.**

Kk

keg A small metal or wooden barrel. Beer is often put in *kegs.*
    keg (keg) *noun, plural* **kegs.**

Ll

lament To express sorrow, regret, or grief. The people sang a sad song to *lament* the loss of their leader.
    ▲ **Synonym:** mourn
    la•ment (lə ment′) *verb,* **lamented, lamenting.**

landlord A person or organization that owns houses, apartments, or rooms to be rented to other people. At the end of the month I have to pay the *landlord* for my apartment.
    land•lord (land′lôrd′) *noun, plural* **landlords.**

landscape A stretch of land that can be seen from a place; view. The train passengers watched the passing *landscape. Noun.*—To make an area of land more beautiful by planting trees, shrubs, and other plants, and by designing gardens. A gardener *landscaped* the grounds around these offices. *Verb.*
    land•scape (land′skāp′) *noun, plural* **landscapes;** *verb,* **landscaped, landscaping.**

lecture To give a talk to an audience. The scientist *lectures* on the history of aviation at the college. *Verb.*—A scolding. I got a *lecture* from my parents for breaking the window. *Noun.*
    lec•ture (lek′chər) *verb,* **lectured, lecturing;** *noun, plural* **lectures.**

legislator One who makes laws, especially for a political organization. The Senator knew all of the *legislators* in the state.
    leg•is•la•tor (lej′ is lā′tər) *noun, plural* **legislators.**

livestock Animals raised on a farm or ranch for profit. Cows, horses, sheep, and pigs are livestock. We enjoy seeing the *livestock* when we go to the county fair.
    live•stock (liv′stok′) *noun.*

logger A person who logs trees; lumberjack. The *loggers* cut down the trees.
    log•ger (lô′gər) *noun, plural* **loggers.**

lush Thick, rich, and abundant. That land is covered with *lush* forests.
    ▲ **Synonym:** luxuriant
    lush (lush) *adjective,* **lusher, lushest.**

luxury 1. Something that gives much comfort and pleasure but is not necessary. Eating dinner at the fancy restaurant was a *luxury* for our family. **2.** A way of life that gives comfort and pleasure. The opera star is used to *luxury.*
    lux•u•ry (luk′shə rē *or* lug′zhə rē) *noun, plural* **luxuries.**

at; āpe; fär; câre; end; mē; it; īce; pîerce; hot; ōld; sông; fôrk; oil; out; up; ūse; rūle; pùll; tûrn; chin; sing; shop; thin; this; hw in white; zh in treasure. The symbol ə stands for the unstressed vowel sound in about, taken, pencil, lemon, and circus.

Mm

maiden A girl or young unmarried woman. The boy hoped one day to meet the *maiden* of his dreams. *Noun.*—First or earliest. The ship's *maiden* voyage was from England to New York. *Adjective.*
mai•den (mā′dən) *noun, plural* maidens; *adjective.*

masthead The top of a mast. From the shore we could see the ship's *masthead* in the distance.
mast•head (mast′hed′) *noun, plural* mastheads.

meagre Also **meager.** Very little; hardly enough. The sick child ate a *meagre* meal of tea and toast.
▲ Synonyms: small, scanty
mea•gre (mē′gər) *adjective.*

mildew A kind of fungus that looks like white powder or fuzz. It grows on plants and materials such as cloth, leather, and paper when they are left damp. *Mildew* grows in the shower if the bathroom is always damp.
mil•dew (mil′dü) *noun.*

mongoose A slender animal with a pointed face, a long tail, and rough, shaggy fur. Mongooses live in Africa and Asia, are very quick, and eat rats and mice. On television we saw the quick *mongoose* fight a snake.
mon•goose (mong′güs′) *noun, plural* mongooses.

monument 1. A building, statue, or other object made to honor a person or event. The Lincoln Memorial is a *monument* to Abraham Lincoln. **2.** An achievement of lasting importance. The discovery of a polio vaccine was a *monument* in medicine.
mon•u•ment (mon′yə mənt) *noun, plural* monuments.

murky Dark and gloomy; cloudy. We couldn't see beneath the surface of the *murky* water in the pond.
mur•ky (mûr′kē) *adjective,* murkier, murkiest.

musket A gun with a long barrel, used before modern rifles were invented. The soldiers loaded their *muskets* for battle.
mus•ket (mus′kit) *noun, plural* muskets.

mutiny An open rebellion against authority. The sailors who led the *mutiny* were punished. *Noun.*—To take part in an open rebellion. The crew *mutinied* against their captain. *Verb.*
mu•ti•ny (mū′tə nē) *noun, plural* mutinies; *verb,* mutinied, mutinying.

Nn

naturalist A person who specializes in the study of things in nature, especially animals and plants. The *naturalists* walked through the forest to study the plants and animals unique to the region.
nat•u•ral•ist (nach′ər ə list) *noun, plural* naturalists.

navigate 1. To sail, steer, or direct the course of. They *navigated* the ship through the storm. **2.** To sail on or across. Ships can *navigate* the Atlantic in under a week.
nav•i•gate (nav′i gāt′) *verb,* navigated, navigating.

> ### Word History
> The word **navigate** comes from two Latin words: *navis,* meaning "ship," and *agere,* meaning "to drive." Sailors *navigate* ships.

nestle To get very close to; snuggle; cuddle. The kittens *nestled* against their mother.
▲ Synonym: cuddle
nes•tle (nes′əl) *verb,* nestled, nestling.

nightfall The beginning of night; the end of the day. My parents told me to be sure to be home before *nightfall.*
night•fall (nit′fôl) *noun.*

normally 1. Under ordinary circumstances; regularly; usually. Heavy rain *normally* falls at this time of year. **2.** In an accepted or normal manner. Breathe *normally* while I examine you.
nor•mal•ly (nôr′mə lē) *adverb.*

nostril One of the two outer openings of the nose. In the cold air, smoke seemed to billow from the mountain climber's *nostrils.*
nos•tril (nos′trəl) *noun, plural* nostrils.

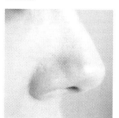

at; āpe; fär; câre; end; mē; it; īce; pîerce; hot; ōld; sông; fôrk; oil; out; up; ūse; rüle; pùll; tûrn; chin; sing; shop; thin; this; hw in white; zh in treasure. The symbol ə stands for the unstressed vowel sound in about, taken, pencil, lemon, and circus.

Oo

oblige 1. To make thankful for a service or favor. We are *obliged* to you for your help. **2.** To make a person do something by law, promise, or sense of duty. My parents were *obliged* to pay for the window I broke.
o•blige (ə blij′) *verb,* obliged, obliging.

observation 1. The act or power of noticing. The detective's careful *observation* helped solve the crime. **2.** The condition of being seen; notice. The thief escaped *observation.*
ob•ser•va•tion (ob′zər vā′shən) *noun, plural* observations.

offend To cause resentment, anger, or displeasure. Your rude remark *offended* me.
▲ Synonym: insult
of•fend (ə fend′) *verb,* offended, offending.

ominous Foretelling trouble or bad luck to come; threatening. There were *ominous* black storm clouds coming in from the sea.
om•i•nous (om′ə nəs) *adjective.*

onlooker A spectator. The *onlookers* stood on the sidewalk, watching the parade go by.
on•look•er (on′ lùk′ ər) *noun, plural* onlookers.

onlookers

orphanage A place that takes in and cares for children whose parents are dead. The children at the *orphanage* were thankful to receive attention from the volunteers.
or•phan•age (ôr′fə nij) *noun, plural* orphanages.

ozone A form of oxygen. It is formed by lightning or other electricity in the air. Ozone is used to kill germs and freshen the air. A layer of *ozone* in the atmosphere protects the Earth from some of the sun's harmful rays.
o•zone (ō′zōn) *noun.*

Pp

parallel Always the same distance apart. The road runs *parallel* to the river. *Adverb.*—Being the same distance apart at all points. If lines are parallel, they never meet or cross each other. The rails of a railroad track are *parallel*. *Adjective.*
par•al•lel (par′ə lel′) *adverb, adjective.*

paralyze 1. To take away the power to move or feel in a part of the body. After the accident, my right arm was *paralyzed.* **2.** To make helpless, powerless, or inactive. The bus strike *paralyzed* the city.
par•a•lyze (par′ə liz′) *verb,* paralyzed, paralyzing.

parapet A wall or railing built for protection. The rebels retreated to the *parapet* for safety.
par•a•pet (par′ ə pet′) *noun, plural* parapets.

peculiar 1. Not usual; strange; queer. It's *peculiar* that the sky is so dark at noon. **2.** Belonging to a certain person, group, place, or thing. The kangaroo is *peculiar* to Australia and New Guinea.
pe•cul•iar (pi kül′yər) *adjective; adverb,* peculiarly.

pelican A large bird that lives near the water and has a pouch under its long bill. The *pelican* flew overhead, carrying a fish in its pouch.
pel•i•can (pel′i kən) *noun, plural* pelicans.

pelt To strike over and over with small hard things. Hail *pelted* the roof. *Verb.*—The skin of an animal with its fur or hair still on it. Pelts are used to make clothing and rugs. The trappers traded the animal *pelts* for supplies for their camp. *Noun.*
pelt (pelt) *verb,* pelted, pelting; *noun,* pelts.

perish To be destroyed; die. Many people *perished* when the ship sank.
▲ Synonym: expire
per•ish (per′ish) *verb,* perished, perishing.

permission A consent from someone in authority. You should ask your parents for *permission* to stay overnight at my house.
per•mis•sion (pər mish′ən) *noun.*

persuade To cause to do or believe something by pleading or giving reasons; convince. They *persuaded* me to go with them.
per•suade (pər swād′) *verb,* persuaded, persuading; *noun,* persuasion.

at; āpe; fär; câre; end; mē; it; īce; pîerce; hot; ōld; sông; fôrk; oil; out; up; ūse; rüle; pùll; tûrn; chin; sing; shop; thin; this; hw in white; zh in treasure. The symbol ə stands for the unstressed vowel sound in about, taken, pencil, lemon, and circus.

Glossary

G7

petition A formal request that is made to a person in authority. All the people on our street signed a *petition* asking the city to put a stop sign on the corner. *Noun.*—To make a formal request to. The students in our school *petitioned* the principal to keep the library open on weekends. *Verb.*
pe•ti•tion (pə tish'ən) *noun, plural* **petitions;** *verb,* **petitioned, petitioning.**

pier 1. A structure built out over the water, used as a landing place for boats or ships. We walked to the end of the *pier* and watched the boats. **2.** A pillar or other support used to hold up a bridge. Modern bridges have steel *piers* to support them. Engineers design *piers* that can hold up bridges during an earthquake.
▲ Another word that sounds like this is **peer.**
pier (pîr) *noun, plural* **piers.**

pioneer A person who is among the first to explore and settle a region. *Pioneers* settled the American West. *Noun.*—To be among the first to explore or develop. American scientists *pioneered* in sending human beings to the moon. *Verb.*
pi•o•neer (pī'ə nîr') *noun, plural* **pioneers;** *verb,* **pioneered, pioneering.**

Word History
Pioneer was first used in the English language in 1523. It is based on the Old French word *peonier,* which means "foot soldier."

pneumonia A disease in which the lungs become inflamed and fill with fluid. Pneumonia is caused by a virus. A person with pneumonia might cough or have a hard time breathing. I was relieved when the doctor said I didn't have *pneumonia.*
pneu•mo•nia (nü mōn'yə *or* nū mōn'yə) *noun.*

polio A short form of the word **poliomyelitis.** Polio is a contagious disease that can cause paralysis by attacking the central nervous system. It is caused by a virus. President Franklin Delano Roosevelt was stricken with *polio* and lost the use of his legs.
po•li•o (pō'lē ō) *noun.*

754

prediction 1. The act of predicting something. The weather forecaster's job is the *prediction* of the weather. **2.** Something predicted. My *prediction* that our team would win has come true.
pre•dic•tion (pri dik'shən) *noun, plural* **predictions.**

presence 1. The fact of being in a place at a certain time. The *presence* of the growling dog at the door made me nervous. **2.** The area around or near a person. The document was signed in the *presence* of a witness.
pres•ence (prez'əns) *noun.*

prosper To be successful; do very well. The town *prospered* when several companies moved their offices there.
▲ Synonym: succeed
pros•per (pros'pər) *verb,* **prospered, prospering.**

protective Keeping from harm; protecting. We put a *protective* coating of wax on the floors.
pro•tec•tive (prə tek'tiv) *adjective.*

provision 1. A supply of food. Their ship has *provisions* for one month. **2.** The act of planning ahead for a future need. Has any *provision* been made for the party if it rains?
pro•vi•sion (prə vizh'ən) *noun, plural* **provisions.**

provoke 1. To make angry. Their rudeness *provoked* me. **2.** To stir; excite. Unfair laws *provoked* the people to riot.
pro•voke (prə vōk') *verb,* **provoked, provoking.**

prow The front part of a boat or ship; bow. The *prow* of the ship cut through the waves.
prow (prou) *noun, plural* **prows.**

publicity 1. Information given out to bring a person or thing to the attention of the public. The *publicity* about the band brought a large crowd to hear it perform. **2.** The attention of the public. Most politicians like *publicity.*
pub•lic•i•ty (pu blis'i tē) *noun.*

pulverize To reduce to very small pieces; demolish; grind; crush. We *pulverized* the corn before cooking it.
▲ Synonym: crush
pul•ver•ize (pul'və riz') *verb,* **pulverized, pulverizing.**

at; āpe; fär; câre; end; mē; it; īce; pîerce; hot; ōld; sông; fôrk; oil; out; up; ūse; rüle; pull; tûrn; chin; sing; shop; thin; this; hw in white; zh in treasure. The symbol ə stands for the unstressed vowel sound in about, taken, pencil, lemon, and circus.

755

Qq

quarry A place where stone is cut or blasted out. The crane lifted the blocks of limestone out of the *quarry.*
quar•ry (kwôr'ē) *noun, plural* **quarries.**

quench 1. To put an end to by satisfying. I *quenched* my thirst with iced tea. **2.** To make something stop burning; put out; extinguish. I *quenched* the fire.
quench (kwench) *verb,* **quenched, quenching.**

Rr

radar A device used to find and track objects such as aircraft and automobiles. It uses reflected radio waves. The Navy detected the planes with *radar* before they flew over the city.
ra•dar (rā'där) *noun.*

Word History
The word **radar** is short for *radio detecting and ranging.*

rascal 1. A mischievous character. That pup is a real *rascal.* **2.** A dishonest person; rogue. That *rascal* took off with my pocket watch.
ras•cal (ras'kəl) *noun, plural* **rascals.**

rebuild To build again. After the earthquake in California, the people *rebuilt* what had been destroyed.
re•build (rē bild') *verb,* **rebuilt, rebuilding.**

refreshment 1. Food or drink. What *refreshments* will you serve at the party? **2.** A refreshing or being refreshed. I needed *refreshment* after working all day.
re•fresh•ment (ri fresh'mənt) *noun, plural* **refreshments.**

756

register To have one's name placed on a list or record. Voters must *register* before they can vote. *Verb.*—An official list or record, or a book used for this. I signed my name in the guest *register. Noun.*
reg•is•ter (rej'ə stər) *verb,* **registered, registering;** *noun, plural* **registers.**

regulation 1. A law, rule, or order. Smoking is against school *regulations.* **2.** The act of regulating or the state of being regulated. A thermostat controls the *regulation* of heat in the building.
reg•u•la•tion (reg'yə lā'shən) *noun, plural* **regulations.**

reject To refuse to accept, allow, or approve. The voters *rejected* the tax plan.
re•ject (ri jekt') *verb,* **rejected, rejecting;** *noun,* **rejection.**

reliable Able to be depended on and trusted. We know she will do a good job because she is a *reliable* worker.
▲ Synonyms: dependable, responsible, trustworthy
re•li•a•ble (ri lī'ə bəl) *adjective; adverb,* **reliably;** *noun,* **reliability.**

reluctant Unwilling. I am *reluctant* to lend you the book because you seldom return what you borrow.
re•luc•tant (ri luk'tənt) *adjective; adverb,* **reluctantly.**

reserved 1. Set apart for a person or purpose. The only available seats in the theater are *reserved.* **2.** Keeping one's thoughts and feelings to oneself. He is a quiet and *reserved* man.
re•served (ri zûrvd') *adjective.*

reverence A feeling of deep love and respect. Everyone in the town had *reverence* for the old doctor.
rev•er•ence (rev'ər əns) *noun.*

revolt To rebel against a government or other authority. The ill-treated prisoners *revolted. Verb.*—An uprising or rebellion against a government or other authority. The citizens staged a *revolt* against the tyrant. *Noun.*
re•volt (ri vōlt') *verb,* **revolted, revolting;** *noun, plural* **revolts;** *adjective,* **revolting.**

ruddy Having a healthy redness. She has a *ruddy* complexion.
rud•dy (rud'ē) *adjective,* **ruddier, ruddiest.**

at; āpe; fär; câre; end; mē; it; īce; pîerce; hot; ōld; sông; fôrk; oil; out; up; ūse; rüle; pull; tûrn; chin; sing; shop; thin; this; hw in white; zh in treasure. The symbol ə stands for the unstressed vowel sound in about, taken, pencil, lemon, and circus.

757

Ss

sacred 1. Belonging to God or a god; having to do with religion. Our choir sings *sacred* music. 2. Regarded as deserving respect. The memory of the dead hero was *sacred* to the town.
sa•cred (sā′krid) *adjective.*

salsa A spicy sauce or relish made mostly with tomatoes and chiles. Many cooks spoon *salsa* on eggs.
sal•sa (säl′sə) *noun.*

satellite 1. A spacecraft that moves in an orbit around the Earth, the moon, or other bodies in space. *Satellites* are used to forecast the weather, to connect radio, telephone, and television communications, and to provide information about conditions in space. 2. A heavenly body that moves in an orbit around another body larger than itself. The moon is the earth's only natural satellite. All the planets in our solar system are *satellites* that orbit the sun.
sat•el•lite (sat′ə līt) *noun, plural* **satellites.**

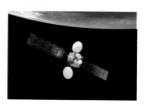

scheme A plan or plot for doing something. The crooks had a *scheme* for robbing the bank. *Noun.*—To plan or plot. The rebels *schemed* to capture the king and queen. *Verb.*
scheme (skēm) *noun, plural* **schemes;** *verb,* **schemed, scheming.**

scholarship 1. Money given to a student to help pay for his or her studies. The university awarded her a *scholarship* for her good grades. 2. Knowledge or learning. The professor is respected for her *scholarship.*
schol•ar•ship (skol′ər ship′) *noun, plural* **scholarships.**

scorch To burn slightly on the surface. I *scorched* my shirt with the iron. Verb.—A slight burn. A necktie will cover that *scorch.* Noun.
scorch (skôrch) *verb,* **scorched, scorching;** *noun, plural* **scorches.**

Word History

The word *scorch* is thought to be of Scandinavian origin, based on the Old Norse word *skorpna,* meaning "to shrivel up."

---

scratch To scrape or cut with nails, claws, or anything sharp and pointed. The cat *scratched* my arm. *Verb*
scratch (skrach) *verb,* **scratched, scratching.**

▲ **from scratch** From the beginning; with no resources. When their business failed, they had to start again *from scratch. Adverb.*

scroll A roll of paper, parchment, or other material with writing on it, often wound around a rod or rods. The official unrolled the *scroll* and read the message from the king. *Noun.*—To move the text on a computer up or down in order to read it. I *scrolled* through the document to look for words I misspelled. *Verb.*
scroll (skrōl) *noun, plural* **scrolls;** *verb,* **scrolled, scrolling.**

sculpture A figure or design that is usually done by carving stone, wood, or marble, modeling in clay, or casting in bronze or another metal. That statue is a beautiful piece of *sculpture. Noun.*—To carve, model, or cast figures or designs in such a way. The artist *sculptured* a lion. *Verb.*
sculp•ture (skulp′chər) *noun, plural* **sculptures;** *verb,* **sculptured, sculpturing.**

settler A person who settles in a new land or country. The first European *settlers* of Florida were from Spain.
set•tler (set′lər) *noun, plural* **settlers.**

severe 1. Very strict; harsh. The dictator established many *severe* laws. 2. Dangerous; serious. The soldier had a *severe* wound. 3. Causing great difficulty or suffering. A *severe* storm is expected.
se•vere (sə vîr′) *adjective.*

shabby 1. Worn-out and faded. The beggar wore a *shabby* coat. 2. Mean or unfair. It's cruel and *shabby* to make fun of other people.
shab•by (shab′ē) *adjective,* **shabbier, shabbiest.**

shoreline The line where a body of water meets the land. We took a helicopter ride up the *shoreline* and saw people swimming in the ocean.
shore•line (shôr′līn′) *noun, plural* **shorelines.**

shrivel To shrink, wrinkle, or wither. The plant *shriveled* because it was too hot in the room.
shriv•el (shriv′əl) *verb,* **shriveled, shriveling;** *adjective,* **shriveled.**

sizzle To make a hissing or sputtering sound. The bacon *sizzled* as it cooked in the frying pan.
siz•zle (siz′əl) *verb,* **sizzled, sizzling.**

---

at; āpe; fär; câre; end; mē; it; īce; pîerce; hot; ōld; sông; fôrk; oil; out; up; ūse; rūle; pull; tûrn; chin; sing; shop; thin; this; hw in white; zh in treasure. The symbol ə stands for the unstressed vowel sound in about, taken, pencil, lemon, and circus.

---

skeleton 1. A framework that supports and protects the body of an animal. Birds, fish, and humans have skeletons made up of bones or cartilage. Many different types of bones make up the human *skeleton.* 2. Any framework or structure used as a support. The workers built the steel *skeleton* of the building first.
skel•e•ton (skel′i tən) *noun, plural* **skeletons.**

skeptical Having or showing doubt or disbelief. My classmates were *skeptical* of my plan to get the governor to visit our class.
skep•ti•cal (skep′ti kəl) *adjective.*

sledgehammer A heavy hammer with a long handle that is held with both hands. The workers broke the rocks with their *sledgehammers.*
sledge•ham•mer (slej′ham′ər) *noun, plural* **sledgehammers.**

snoop One who looks or pries, especially in a sneaky manner. I caught the *snoop* looking through my personal things. *Noun.*—To look or pry in a sneaky manner. *Verb.* The detective *snooped* around the office.
snoop (snüp) *noun; verb,* **snooped, snooping.**

soot A black, greasy powder that forms when such fuels as wood, coal, and oil are burned. The chimney sweep was covered with *soot.*
soot (sut or süt) *noun.*

soothe To quiet, calm, or ease. The nurse *soothed* the crying child with a lullaby.
soothe (süth) *verb,* **soothed, soothing.**

speechless 1. Temporarily unable to speak. Hers news left me *speechless;* I didn't know what to say. 2. Not having the power of speech; mute.
speech•less (spēch′lis) *adjective; adverb,* **speechlessly;** *noun,* **speechlessness.**

spire A tall, narrow structure that tapers to a point, built on the top of a tower. The church *spire* towered above all the other buildings in the town.
spire (spīr) *noun, plural* **spires.**

spiritual A religious folk song, especially one originated by blacks in the southern United States. The group sang beautiful *spirituals. Noun.*—Of or having to do with religion. Priests, ministers, and rabbis are *spiritual* leaders. *Adjective.*
spir•i•tu•al (spir′i chü əl) *noun, plural* **spirituals;** *adjective.*

sprawl 1. To lie or sit with the body stretched out in an awkward or careless manner. I *sprawled* in the chair with one leg hooked over the arm. 2. To spread out in a way that is not regular or organized. New houses *sprawl* across the countryside.
sprawl (sprôl) *verb,* **sprawled, sprawling.**

spurt To pour out suddenly in a stream. Water *spurted* from the broken pipe. *Verb.*—A sudden pouring out or bursting forth. A *spurt* of water came out of the hose. *Noun.*
spurt (spûrt) *verb,* **spurted, spurting;** *noun, plural* **spurts.**

squirm To turn or twist the body. The child *squirmed* in her seat.
squirm (skwûrm) *verb,* **squirmed, squirming.**

stadium A structure made up of rows of seats built around an open field. The crowd filled the *stadium* to watch the soccer match.
▲ **Synonym:** arena
sta•di•um (stā′dē əm) *noun, plural* **stadiums.**

standard Anything used to set an example or serve as a model. New cars must meet strict safety *standards. Noun.*—Widely used or usual. It's our *standard* practice to send bills on the first day of the month. *Adjective.*
stand•ard (stan′dərd) *noun, plural* **standards;** *adjective.*

starvation The state of suffering from lack of nourishment. Too many people are dying of *starvation.*
star•va•tion (stär vā′shən) *noun.*

statue A likeness of a person or animal, made out of stone, bronze, or clay. The *statue* of the turtle looked so real that you couldn't tell it was made of stone.
sta•tue (stach′ü) *noun, plural* **statues.**

stern The rear part of a boat or ship. The sailor stood at the *stern* of the ship and waved good-bye. *Noun.*—Harsh or strict. Our parents were *stern* when it came to our homework. *Adjective.*
stern (stûrn) *noun, plural* **sterns;** *adjective,* **sterner, sternest;** *adverb,* **sternly.**

---

at; āpe; fär; câre; end; mē; it; īce; pîerce; hot; ōld; sông; fôrk; oil; out; up; ūse; rūle; pull; tûrn; chin; sing; shop; thin; this; hw in white; zh in treasure. The symbol ə stands for the unstressed vowel sound in about, taken, pencil, lemon, and circus.

---

stifle To smother; suffocate. The smoke was so thick I thought it would *stifle* us.
sti•fle (stī′ fəl) *verb,* **stifled, stifling.**

strict 1. Following or enforcing a rule in a careful, exact way. The teacher is *strict* about spelling. 2. To be followed in a careful, exact way; carefully enforced. That school has *strict* rules.
strict (strikt) *adjective,* **stricter, strictest;** *adverb,* **strictly;** *noun,* **strictness.**

stun 1. To shock. We were *stunned* by the news. 2. To make unconscious. The robin was *stunned* when it flew into the window.
stun (stun) *verb,* **stunned, stunning.**

submit 1. To present. *Submit* your book reports on Monday. 2. To yield to power or authority. The children *submitted* to their parents' wishes
sub•mit (səb mit′) *verb,* **submitted, submitting.**

summon 1. To ask to come. We *summoned* the police to the scene of the accident. 2. To stir up; arouse. I *summoned* my courage and dived off the high diving board.
sum•mon (sum′ən) *verb,* **summoned, summoning.**

superb Very fine; excellent. The actor gave a *superb* performance.
▲ Synonym: outstanding
su•perb (sü pûrb′) *adjective; adverb,* **superbly.**

survey To look at or study in detail. The mayor *surveyed* the damage to the city after the storm. *Verb.*—A detailed study. The company conducted a *survey* to find out who bought its products. *Noun.*
sur•vey (sər vā′ *for verb;* sûr′vā *or* sər vā′ *for noun) verb,* **surveyed, surveying;** *noun, plural* **surveys;** *noun,* **surveyor.**

survival 1. The act of surviving. The *survival* of all the bus passengers in the accident seemed a miracle. 2. A thing that survives. The custom of throwing rice at a bride and groom is a *survival* from the past.
sur•viv•al (sər vī′ vəl) *noun.*

swerve To turn aside suddenly. The driver *swerved* to avoid hitting a dog. *Verb.*—The act of swerving. The *swerve* of the car upset the driver's cup of coffee. *Noun.*
swerve (swûrv) *verb,* **swerved, swerving;** *noun, plural* **swerves.**

swollen Made larger by swelling. I can't get the ring off my *swollen* finger.
swol•len (swō′lən) *adjective.*

762

Tt

tavern A place where travelers stay overnight; inn. The weary travelers stopped to rent a room at the *tavern* for the night.
tav•ern (tav′ərn) *noun, plural* **taverns.**

teem To be full of; swarm. The creek near our house *teems* with fish.
▲ Synonym: swarm
teem (tēm) *verb,* **teemed, teeming.**

tempestuous Stormy; turbulent. The *tempestuous* seas tossed the boat around like a toy.
tem•pes•tu•ous (tem pes′chü əs) *adjective.*

tempestuous

thickness 1. The quality of having space between one side or surface and the other. The *thickness* of the walls makes the house quiet. 2. The distance between two sides or surfaces of something; the measurement other than the length or width. The *thickness* of this board is 1 inch.
thick•ness (thik′nis) *noun, plural* **thicknesses.**

thief A person who steals. The *thief* broke into the house and stole the television.
▲ Synonym: robber
thief (thēf) *noun, plural* **thieves.**

thrive To be successful; do well. This plant *thrives* in the sun.
thrive (thrīv) *verb,* **thrived** *or* **throve, thrived** *or* **thriven, thriving.**

at; āpe; fär; câre; end; mē; it; īce; pîerce; hot; ōld; sông; fôrk; oil; out; up; ūse; rüle; pull; tûrn; chin; sing; shop; thin; this; hw in white; zh in treasure. The symbol ə stands for the unstressed vowel sound in about, taken, pencil, lemon, and circus.

763

tiller A bar or handle used to turn the rudder of a boat. The pilot steadied the boat by holding the *tiller.*
till•er (til′ər) *noun, plural* **tillers.**

timber 1. A large, heavy piece of wood; beam. The strength of its *timbers* kept the building standing. 2. Wood that is used in building things; lumber. The stack of *timber* was our only clue that they were planning to build something.
tim•ber (tim′bər) *noun, plural* **timbers.**

tiresome Exhausting; tedious. It was *tiresome* writing my paper.
tire•some (tīr′səm) *adjective.*

tombstone A stone that marks a grave. Tombstones often show the dead person's name and the dates of birth and death. The *tombstones* marked the spot where the old graveyard was.
tomb•stone (tüm′stōn′) *noun, plural* **tombstones.**

tornado A powerful storm with winds that whirl in a dark cloud shaped like a funnel. It can cause great destruction. Luckily, the *tornado* touched down in a field and didn't cause much damage to the houses.
tor•na•do (tôr nā′dō) *noun, plural* **tornadoes** *or* **tornados.**

Word History
Tornado first appeared in the English language around 1556. It is a modification of the Spanish word *tronada,* which means "thunderstorm."

tortilla A thin, round, flat bread made from water and cornmeal. For lunch I ate rice and beans wrapped in a *tortilla.*
tor•til•la (tôr tē′yə) *noun, plural* **tortillas.**

track To follow the marks, path, or course of. The dogs *tracked* the fox. The scientists *tracked* the flight of the missile on their radar. *Verb.*—A mark left by a person, animal, or object as it moves over a surface. We followed the deer *tracks* in the snow. *Noun.*
track (trak) *verb,* **tracked, tracking;** *noun, plural* **tracks.**

764

treacherous 1. Full of danger; hazardous. The waters near the cape were *treacherous.* 2. Betraying one's country or friends; disloyal. The *treacherous* soldier gave secrets to the enemy.
treach•er•ous (trech′ər əs) *adjective.*

tribute Something done or given to show thanks or respect. The statue was a *tribute* to the soldiers who had died in the war.
trib•ute (trib′ūt) *noun, plural* **tributes.**

trifle To treat something in a careless way. Don't *trifle* with the camera. *Verb.*—Something that is small in amount or importance. One twin is just a *trifle* taller than the other. *Noun.*
tri•fle (trī′fəl) *verb,* **trifled, trifling;** *noun, plural* **trifles.**

tropical Relating to or found in the tropics. In the cold of winter I often wish our weather were more *tropical.*
trop•i•cal (trop′i kəl) *adjective.*

Uu

unbearable Unable to be endured or put up with. Some of us found the singer's voice *unbearable.*
▲ Synonym: intolerable
un•bear•able (un bâr′ ə bəl) *adjective.*

uneven 1. Not straight, smooth, or regular. The car bounced along the *uneven* road. 2. Being an odd number. 1, 3, and 5 are *uneven* numbers.
un•ev•en (un ē′vən) *adjective.*

unique Not having an equal; being the only one of its kind. Landing on the moon was a *unique* achievement.
u•nique (ū nēk′) *adjective.*

unpleasant Not pleasing; disagreeable. An *unpleasant* odor came from the sewer.
un•pleas•ant (un plez′ənt) *adjective.*

uproot 1. To tear or pull up by the roots. The bulldozers *uprooted* bushes and trees. 2. To cause to leave; displace. The flood *uprooted* many families from their homes.
up•root (up rüt′ *or* up rut′) *verb,* **uprooted, uprooting.**

at; āpe; fär; câre; end; mē; it; īce; pîerce; hot; ōld; sông; fôrk; oil; out; up; ūse; rüle; pull; tûrn; chin; sing; shop; thin; this; hw in white; zh in treasure. The symbol ə stands for the unstressed vowel sound in about, taken, pencil, lemon, and circus.

765

usher To act as an usher; lead. The waiter *ushered* us to a table by the window. Verb.—One who leads people to their seats in a church, theater, or other place. We showed the *usher* our ticket stubs. *Noun.*
    ush•er (ush′ər) *verb,* **ushered, ushering;** *noun, plural* **ushers.**

vague 1. Not clearly expressed or understood. The directions to the party were *vague,* so I was unsure where to go. **2.** Not having a precise meaning. To me the meaning of the poem was *vague.*
    vague (vāg) *adjective.*

variety 1. A number of different things. We bought a *variety* of foods. **2.** Change or difference; lack of sameness. A job that has no *variety* can become boring.
    va•ri•e•ty (və rī′i tē) *noun, plural* **varieties.**

violent 1. Acting with or resulting from strong physical force. The falling branch gave the gardener a *violent* blow on the head. **2.** Caused by or showing strong feeling or emotion. My friend has a *violent* temper.
    vi•o•lent (vī′ ə lent) *adjective.*

766

Ww

waterfall A natural stream of water falling from a high place. The crash of water over the *waterfall* made a thunderous noise.
    wa•ter•fall (wô′tər fôl′) *noun, plural* **waterfalls.**

width The distance from one side of something to the other side. The *width* of a football field is 52 1/3 yards.
    width (width) *noun, plural* **widths.**

wildlife Wild animals that live naturally in an area. In the forest we saw much of the local *wildlife.*
    wild•life (wild′līf′) *noun.*

woe Great sadness or suffering. The story told of the hunger, sickness, and other *woes* of the settlers of the frontier.
    ▲ **Synonym:** sorrow
    woe (wō) *noun, plural* **woes.**

wonderland A place of delicate beauty or magical charm. After the snowstorm the neighborhood looked like a winter *wonderland.*
    won•der•land (wun′ dər land′) *noun.*

writhe To twist or contort. The fish *writhed* about when we took it out of the water.
    writhe (r<u>i</u>th) *verb,* **writhed, writhing.**

Acknowledgments

Cover Illustration: Greg Newbold

The publisher gratefully acknowledges permission to reprint the following copyrighted material:

"Archimedes and the King's Gold Crown" from CRICKET, May 1989 by Linda Walvoord Girard. Reprinted by permission of the author.

"The Best Town in the World" from THE BEST TOWN IN THE WORLD by Byrd Baylor. Copyright © 1982 by Byrd Baylor. Reprinted with the permission of Charles Scribner's Sons, an imprint of Simon & Schuster Children's Publishing Division.

"The Boy Who Caught the Wind" from THE RESCUE OF THE SUN AND OTHER TALES FROM THE FAR NORTH by Edythe W. Newell. Copyright © 1970 by Edythe W. Newell. Used by permission.

"The Cleverest Son" from UNICEF BOOK OF CHILDREN'S LEGENDS by George Shannon, Used by permission of Stackpole Books.

"For old times' sake: a tree speaks" from COLLECTED SHORTER POEMS Vols. 1 and 2 by James Kirkup and the University of Salzburg Press. Reprinted by permission.

"Fox Fools Eagle" from IN A CIRCLE LONG AGO by Nancy Van Laan. Text copyright © 1995 by Nancy Van Laan. Illustrations copyright © 1995 by Lisa Desimini. Used by permission of Apple Soup Books, an imprint of Alfred A. Knopf.

"Harriet Tubman" from HONEY, I LOVE by Eloise Greenfield. Copyright © 1978 by Eloise Greenfield. Reprinted by permission of Harper Collins Publishers and Marie Brown Associates.

"How the World Got Wisdom" from THE ADVENTURES OF SPIDER by Joyce Cooper Arkhurst. Copyright © 1964 by Joyce Cooper Arkurst. Used by permission of Little, Brown and Company.

"I'd Like to Teach the World to Sing" by B. Backer, B. Davis, R. Cook, R. Greenaway. Copyright © 1971, 1972 by The Coca-Cola company.

"In Geometry Land" by Sandra Liatsos. Copyright © 1993 by Sandra Liatsos. Used by permission of Marian Reiner for the author.

"The Invisible Beast" from THE HEADLESS HORSEMAN RIDES TONIGHT by Jack Prelutsky. Used by permission of A & C Black (Publishers) Ltd.

"Jamestown, New World Adventure" by James E. Knight. Copyright © 1982 Troll Associates. Used by permission.

"The Lobster and the Crab" from FABLES by Arnold Lobel. Copyright © 1980 by Arnold Lobel. Used by permission of HarperCollins Publishers.

ACKNOWLEDGMENTS

The publisher gratefully acknowledges permission to reprint the following copyrighted material.

AMISTAD RISING by Veronica Chambers, illustrated by Paul Lee. Text copyright © 1998 by Veronica Chambers. Illustrations copyright © 1998 by Paul Lee. Used by permission of Harcourt, Brace & Company.

"Árbol de limón/Lemon Tree" by Jennifer Clement, translated by Consuelo de Aerenlund from THE TREE IS OLDER THAN YOU ARE. Text copyright © 1995 by Jennifer Clement. Used by permission of Naomi Shihab Nye.

"The Big Storm" by Bruce Hiscock. Copyright © 1993 by Bruce Hiscock. Reprinted with permission of Atheneum Books for Young Readers, Simon & Schuster Children's Publishing Division.

"Breaker's Bridge" from THE RAINBOW PEOPLE by Laurence Yep. Text copyright © 1989 by Laurence Yep. Reprinted by permission of HarperCollins Publishers.

CARLOS AND THE SKUNK by Jan Romero Stevens, illustrated by Jeanne Arnold. Text copyright © 1997 by Jan Romero Stevens. Illustrations copyright © 1997 by Jeanne Arnold. Reprinted by permission of Northland Publishing, Flagstaff, Arizona.

"Dear Mr. Henshaw" from DEAR MR. HENSHAW by Beverly Cleary. Copyright © 1983 by Beverly Cleary. Used by permission of Morrow Junior Books, a division of William Morrow & Company, Inc.

"Early Spring" from NAVAJO: VISIONS AND VOICES ACROSS THE MESA by Shonto Begay. Copyright © 1995 by Shonto Begay. Published by Scholastic, Inc. Used by permission.

"First Flight" by Frank Richards from THE PENGUIN BOOK OF LIM-ERICKS, compiled and edited by E.O. Parrott. Copyright © 1983 by E.O. Parrott.

"Frederick Douglass 1817-1895" from COLLECTED POEMS by Langston Hughes. Copyright © 1994 by the Estate of Langston Hughes. Reprinted by permission of Alfred A. Knopf, Inc.

GOING BACK HOME: AN ARTIST RETURNS TO THE SOUTH interpreted and written by Toyomi Igus, illustrated by Michele Wood. Text copyright © 1996 by Toyomi Igus. Illustrations copyright © 1994 by Michele Wood. Used by permission of Children's Book Press.

"The Gold Coin" from THE GOLD COIN by Alma Flor Ada. Copyright © 1991 by Alma Flor Ada. Illustrations copyright © 1991 by Neil Waldman. Reprinted with permission from Atheneum Books for Young Readers, an imprint of Simon & Schuster Children's Publishing Division.

"Grandma Essie's Covered Wagon" by David Williams, illustrated by Wiktor Sadowski. Text copyright © 1993 by David Williams. Illustrations copyright © 1993 by Wiktor Sadowski. Reprinted by permission.

"How to Think Like a Scientist" from HOW TO THINK LIKE A SCIENTIST: ANSWERING QUESTIONS BY THE SCIENTIFIC METHOD by Stephen P. Kramer. Copyright © 1987 by Stephen P. Kramer. Reprinted by permission of HarperCollins Publishers.

AN ISLAND SCRAPBOOK written and illustrated by Virginia Wright-Frierson. Copyright © 1998 by Virginia Wright-Frierson. Used by permission of Simon & Schuster Books for Young Readers, an imprint of Simon & Schuster Children's Publishing Division.

"It's Our World, Too!" from IT'S OUR WORLD TOO! by Phillip Hoose. Copyright © 1993 by Phillip Hoose. Used by permission of Little, Brown and Company.

JOHN HENRY by Julius Lester, illustrated by Jerry Pinkney. Text copyright © 1994 by Julius Lester. Illustrations copyright © 1994 by Jerry Pinkney. Used by permission of Dial Books.

Text of "Knoxville, Tennessee" from BLACK TALK, BLACK FEELING, BLACK JUDGMENT by Nikki Giovanni. Copyright © 1968, 1970 by Nikki Giovanni. Used by permission of William Morrow and Company, Inc.

"Life in Flatland" from FLATLAND: A Romance of Many Dimensions written and illustrated by Edwin Abbott. Copyright © 1998 by Penguin Putnam, Inc. Used by permission.

"The Marble Champ" from BASEBALL IN APRIL AND OTHER STORIES, copyright © 1990 by Gary Soto. Reprinted by permission of Harcourt Brace & Company.

THE PAPER DRAGON by Marguerite W. Davol, illustrated by Robert Sabuda. Text copyright © 1997 by Marguerite W. Davol. Illustrations copyright © 1997 by Robert Sabuda. Used by permission of Atheneum Books for Young Readers, an imprint of Simon & Schuster Children's Publishing Division.

"Paper I" from Carl Sandburg from THE COMPLETE POEMS OF CARL SANDBURG. Copyright © 1970, 1969 by Lilian Steichen Sandburg, Trustee, reprinted by permission of Harcourt, Inc.

"Philbert Phlurk" by Jack Prelutsky from THE SHERIFF OF ROTTENSHOT. Copyright © 1982 Greenwillow Books, a division of William Morrow & Company, Inc.

THE RIDDLE retold by Adele Vernon, illustrated by Robert Rayevsky and Vladimir Radunsky. Text copyright © 1987 by Adele Vernon. Illustrations copyright © 1987 by Robert Rayevsky and Vladimir Radunsky. Used by permission of Dodd, Mead & Company.

"Rip Van Winkle" by Washington Irving, adapted by Adele Thane, is reprinted by permission from Plays, Inc., the Drama Magazine for Young People. Copyright © 1966, 1977, 1983 by Plays, Inc. This play may be used for reading purposes only. For permission to produce, write to Plays, Inc., 1 Boylston St., Boston, MA 02116.

THE SEA MAIDENS OF JAPAN by Lili Bell, illustrated by Erin McGonigle Brammer. Used by permission of Ideals Children's Books, an imprint of Hambleton-Hill Publishing, Inc. Text copyright © 1996 by Lili Bell. Illustrations copyright © 1996 by Hambleton-Hill Publishing, Inc.

"The Sidewalk Racer or On the Skateboard" from THE SIDEWALK RACER AND OTHER POEMS OF SPORTS AND MOTION by Lillian Morrison. Copyright © 1977 by Lillian Morrison. Reprinted by permission of the author.

"The Silent Lobby" by Mildred Pitts Walter from THE BIG BOOK FOR PEACE edited by Ann Durrell and Marilyn Sachs. Copyright © 1990 by Mildred Pitts Walter. Used by permission.

"To Dark Eyes Dreaming" from TODAY IS SATURDAY by Zilpha Keatley Snyder. Copyright © 1969 Atheneum Books, a division of Simon & Schuster, Inc. Used by permission.

"To Make a Prairie" by Emily Dickinson from CELEBRATE AMERICA IN POETRY AND ART. Collection copyright © 1994. Published by Hyperion Books for Children, in association with the National Museum of American Art, Smithsonian Institution. Used by permission.

"Tonweya and the Eagles" from TONWEYA AND THE EAGLES by Rosebud Yellow Robe, illustrated by Jerry Pinkney. Text copyright © 1979 by Rosebud Yellow Rose Frantz. Illustrations copyright © 1979 by Jerry Pinkney. Used by permission of Viking Penguin, a division of Penguin Putnam, Inc.

"The Voyage of the Dawn Treader" from THE VOYAGE OF THE DAWN TREADER by C. S. Lewis. Reprinted by permission of HarperCollins Publishers.

WILMA UNLIMITED by Kathleen Krull, illustrated by David Diaz. Text copyright © 1996 by Kathleen Krull. Illustrations copyright © 1996 by David Diaz. Used by permission of Harcourt, Brace & Company.

"Ma Lien and the Magic Brush" copyright © 1966 by Kaisei-sha Publishing Co., Ltd. Originally published in 1966 in Japanese under the title "Maiyan To Maho No Fude" by Kaisei-sha Publishing Co., Ltd. English translation rights arranged with Kaisei-sha Publishing Co., Ltd.

"Martin Luther King" from YEAR-ROUND PROGRAMS FOR YOUNG PLAYERS by Aileen Fisher. Copyright © 1985, 1986 by Aileen Fisher. Used by permission of Plays, Inc.

"Pioneers" from PATRIOTIC PLAYS AND PROGRAMS by Aileen Fisher and Olive Rabe. Copyright © 1956 by Aileen Fisher and Olive Rabe. Used by permission of Plays, Inc.

"The Princess on the Pea" from TWELVE TALES by Hans Christian Andersen. Translation copyright © 1994 by Erik Blegvad. Reprinted with the permission of Margaret K. McElderry Books, an imprint of Simon & Schuster Children's Publishing Division.

THE WISE OLD WOMAN retold by Yoshiko Uchida, illustrated by Martin Springett. Text copyright © 1994 by The Estate of Yoshiko Uchida. Illustrations copyright © 1994 by Martin Springett. Used by permission of Margaret K. Elderry Books, a division of Simon & Schuster, Inc.

"The Wreck of the Zephyr" from THE WRECK OF THE ZEPHYR by Chris Van Allsburg. Copyright © 1983 by Chris Van Allsburg. Reprinted by permission of Houghton Mifflin Company. All rights reserved.

Cover Illustration
Greg Newbold

Illustration
Lori Lohstoeter, 16; Rose Zgodzinski, 42; Stanford Kay, 64; Stanford Kay, 92; Stanford Kay, 122; Tuko Fujisaki, 123; Cliff Faust, 134-135; Sally Vitsky, 136; Rose Zgodzinski, 164; Annie Bissett, 198; Adam Gordon, 199; Rose Zgodzinski, 220; Tuko Fujisaki, 221; Rose Zgodzinski, 240; Joe LeMonnier, 250; Rose Zgodzinski, 251; Nancy Stahl, 252-253; Selina Alko, 254; Stanford Kay, 272; Stanford Kay, 306; Stanford Kay, 338; Chuck Gonzales, 339; Annie Bissett, 370; Chris Lensch, 380; Danuta Jarecka, 382-383; Tim Jessell, 384; Rose Zgodzinski, 406; Annie Bissett, 430; Stanford Kay, 462; Rose Zgodzinski, 463; Daniel DelValle, 489; Dave Merrill, 490; Joe LeMonnier, 500; Annie Bissett, 501; Peter Fiore, 502-503; Michael Maydak, 504; Patrick Gnan, 509; Rose Zgodzinski, 530; Wallace Keller, 532-545; Annie Bissett, 552; Stanford Kay, 578; Adam Gordon, 579; Rose Zgodzinski, 600; Chuck Gonzales, 601; Rose Zgodzinski, 610; Bryan Leister, 612-613; Joan Hall, 614; Joe LeMonnier, 646; Annie Bissett, 647; Stanford Kay, 672; Annie Bissett, 696; Annie Bissett, 716; Adam Gordon, 717; Annie Bissett, 726; Chuck Gonzales, 727; John Carrozza, 735; Chuck Gonzales, 738, 741, 763; Katie Lee, 747, 753.

Photography
19: The British Library, London/The Bridgeman Art Library, London/Superstock. 44-45: National Museum of American Art, Washington, DC/Art Resource, NY. 63: b.l. Werner Forman Archive Art/Art Resource. 66-67: Corbis Images. 89: AP/Wide World Photos. 91: t.r. Archive Photos/Express Newspapers. 94-95: Collection of Mr and Mrs Paul Mellon, Upperville, VA. 124-25: Explorer, Paris/Superstock. 130: c. Timothy Marshall/Liasion International. 131: c. Howard Blustein/Photo Researchers. 138-39: The Granger Collection. 163: c.r. The Smithsonian Institute. 167: Courtesy of the Westtown School/The Brandywine River Museum. 200-01: Equitable Life Insurance Company, New York/The Bridgeman Art Library International. 219: b. David M. Grossman/Photo Researchers Inc. 222-23: David Hockney. 242-43: Wolfgang Kaehler. 248: b. Sidney E. King/MHSD. 256-57: Superstock. 271: b. Louis Glanzman/NGS Image Collection. 274-75: Barnes Foundation, Merion, PA/Superstock. 305: c.l. Arne Hodalic/Corbis. 308-09: Lady Lever Gallery, Port Sunlight, England/The Bridgeman Art Library International. 340-41: National Museum of American Art, Washington, DC/Art Resource, NY. 369: c.l. Corbis Images. 372-73: Culver Pictures. 379: b.l. The Library of Congress/Corbis. 387: Private Collection/Superstock. 409: Motion Picture and Television Photo Archive. 429: b.l. The Granger Collection. 432-33: Hermitage, St Petersburg, Russia/The Bridgeman Art Library International. 464-65: NOAA/Science Photo Library/Photo Researchers, Inc. 488-89: c. The Granger Collection. 499: b. Warren Faidley/International Stock. 492-93: Julian Baum/Science Photo Library/Photo Researchers, Inc. 499: b. The Granger Collection. 506-07: The Grand Design, Leeds, England/Superstock. 529: b. Paul Sisul/Tony Stone Images. 532-33: Milwaukee Art Museum, Gift of Mrs Harry Lynde Bradley. 554-55: Musees des Beaux-Arts de Belgique, Brussels. 580-81: Werner Forman Archive/Art Resource, NY. 602-03: Courtesy, Gilbert Elementary School, Gilbert, AZ. 617: Courtesy, Ashley Bryan. 644: b. Jacques Jangoux/Photo Researchers. 645: c.l. The Granger Collection/b.l. The Granger Collection. 648-49: Royal Ontario Museum, Toronto/The Bridgeman Art Library International. 671: t.l. North Wind Pictures. 674-75: David David Gallery, Philadelphia/Superstock. 695: t.r. Felicia Martinez/Photo Edit. 699: The Smithsonian Institute. 715 t. Matt Heron/Take Star/Black Star. 718-19: Kathleen Norris Cook. 728-29: Daniel J. Cox/Natural Exposures/. 728: b.l. The Granger Collection.

"The Sticks of Truth" from STORIES TO SOLVE by George Shannon. Text copyright © 1985 by George W. B. Shannon. Used by permission of Greenwillow Books, a division of William Morrow & Company, Inc.

"Stormalong" from AMERICAN TALL TALES by Mary Pope Osborne. Text copyright 1991 by Mary Pope Osborne. Illustrations copyright 1991 by Michael McCurdy. Used by permission of Alfred A. Knopf.

"That's What Friends Are For" by Carole Bayer Sager and Burt Bacharach. Copyright © 1985 WB Music Corp. (ASCAP), New Hidden Valley Music (ASCAP), Carole Bayer Sager Music (BMI). All Rights jointly administered by WB Music Corp. (ASCAP) & Warner-Tamerlane Publishing Corp. (BMI). All Rights Reserved. Used by permission of Warner Bros. Publications U.S. Inc.,

"There's Just So Much To Go Around" by Neil Fishman and Harvey Edelman. Copyright © 1995 Macmillan/McGraw-Hill School Publishing Company. Used by permission.

"Touch the Moon" from FANTASTIC STORIES by Terry Jones. Text copyright © Terry Jones, 1992. Illustrations copyright © Michael Foreman, 1992. Used by permission of Viking.

"A Tug of War" from IN A CIRCLE LONG AGO by Nancy Van Laan. Text copyright © 1995 by Nancy Van Laan. Illustrations copyright © 1995 by Lisa Desimini. Used by permission of Apple Soup Books, an imprint of Alfred A. Knopf.

"Turtle's Race with Beaver" from IROQUOIS STORIES by Joseph Bruchac. Text copyright © 1985 by Joseph Bruchac. Used by permission of The Crossing Press.

"Western Wagons" from SELECTED WORKS by Rosemary and Stephen Vincent Benét. Copyright 1937, renewed © 1964. Used by permission of Holt, Rinehart & Winston.

"You" from SPORTS PAGES by Arnold Adoff. Text copyright © 1986 by Arnold Adoff. Used by permission of HarperCollins Publishers.

"Sioux" from FIRST CAME THE INDIANS by M.J. Wheeler. Text copyright © 1983 by M. J. Wheeler. Reprinted with the permission of Atheneum Publishers, an imprint of Simon & Schuster Children's Publishing Division.

"Snowmaker Torments the People" from EARTHMAKER'S TALES by Gretchen Will Mayo. Copyright © 1989 by Gretchen Will Mayo. Reprinted with permission of Walker and Company.

"Souvenir" from THE SINGING GREEN by Eve Merriam. Text copyright © 1992 by the Estate of Eve Merriam by Marian Reiner, Literary Executor. Used by permission of Morrow Junior Books.

"The Steam Shovel" from STORY-TELLER POEMS by Rowena Bennett. Copyright © 1948 by Rowena Bennett.

Notes

Backmatter Contents

Harriet Tubman
by Eloise Greenfield

Harriet Tubman didn't take no stuff
Wasn't scared of nothing neither
Didn't come in this world to be no slave
And wasn't going to stay one either

"Farewell!" she sang to her friends one night
She was mighty sad to leave 'em
But she ran away that dark, hot night
Ran looking for her freedom

She ran to the woods and she ran through
    the woods
With the slave catchers right behind her
And she kept on going till she got to the North
Where those mean men couldn't find her

Nineteen times she went back South
To get three hundred others
She ran for her freedom nineteen times
To save black sisters and brothers

Harriet Tubman didn't take no stuff
Wasn't scared of nothing neither
Didn't come in this world to be no slave
And didn't stay one either

And didn't stay one either

The Princess on the Pea
by Hans Christian Andersen

Once upon a time there was a prince; he wanted a princess, but it had to be a *real* princess. So he traveled all over the world to find one, but everywhere he went something was wrong. There were princesses enough, but were they real princesses? That was the problem. There was always something not quite right. So he came home again, feeling very sad; he would so much have liked to find a real princess.

One night there was a terrible storm. There was thunder and lightning, and the rain came pouring down—it was quite dreadful! Someone was heard knocking on the city gate, and the old king went to open it.

Outside stood a princess, but goodness, what a sight she was from the rain and the cruel weather. Water was running from her hair and down her clothes. It ran in at the toes of her shoes and out at the heels, and still she said she was a real princess.

Well, we shall soon see about that! thought the old queen. She didn't say anything but went to the bedroom, took off all the bedclothes, and put a pea on the bottom of the bed. Then she took twenty mattresses and put them on top of the pea and put a further twenty eiderdown quilts on top of the mattresses. This was where the princess was to lie that night.

In the morning they asked her how she had slept.

"Oh, so dreadfully badly!" said the princess. "I hardly shut an eye the whole night long. Goodness knows what was in that bed! I was lying on something so hard that I'm black-and-blue all over! It was perfectly dreadful!"

Now they could see that she was a real princess, for she had felt the pea through twenty mattresses and twenty eiderdown quilts. Only a real princess could have such tender skin.

The prince took her as his wife, because he knew that he had a real princess; and the pea was put in a museum, where it is still to be seen, if nobody has taken it.

Now, what did you think of that for a story?

Turtle's Race with Beaver

told by Joseph Bruchac

Turtle lived in a quiet pool in the big Swamp. There were plenty of fish for him to catch and trees lined the edges of his fishing hole. One day the sun was very hot and Turtle grew sleepy. He crawled onto the mud bank at the edge of his pool, made himself comfortable and soon was fast asleep. He must have slept much longer than he intended, for when he woke up something was definitely wrong. There was water all around him and even over his head! He had to swim and swim to reach the surface and, as he poked his head up into the air, he heard a loud, earsplitting WHAP!

Turtle looked around and soon saw another animal swimming toward him. The animal had big front teeth and a large wide tail. "What are you doing in my pond?" Turtle called out to the animal.

"Your pond? This is my pond and I am Beaver! I built that dam over there and made this place."

Turtle looked. It was true, there was a big dam across the stream, and it had been made from many of Turtle's favorite trees which Beaver had cut down with his sharp teeth. Other trees, which Beaver had cut to eat their sweet bark, were lying on their sides all around the pond.

"No," Turtle said, "this was my private fishing pond before you came with your dam. I will break your dam and drive you away."

Beaver whistled loudly and slapped the water with his big tail so loudly that Turtle jumped. "Go ahead," Beaver said, "but if you break down my dam, my brothers and my cousins will come back and build it again, and they will gnaw your head off too!"

Turtle began to think. It was obvious that he could not drive Beaver away by force. He would have to use his wits. "I propose we have a contest," Turtle said. "The winner will stay and the loser will go away forever."

"Good," said Beaver. "Let us see who can stay under the water the longest. I will surely win, for I can stay under the water for a year."

Turtle was not pleased to hear that, for he had been planning to propose the same contest and it was obvious now that Beaver could beat him. "No," said Turtle, "that would be too easy a contest for me to win. I have a better idea. We will have a swimming race."

Beaver agreed to that and allowed Turtle to set the course. "We will start from this stump," Turtle said, "and see who can get to the other side of the pond the fastest. In order to make it fair, since I am such a good swimmer, I will start from behind you."

The two of them made ready, and at Turtle's signal began swimming as fast as they could. Beaver was faster than Turtle, but before he could completely outdistance his rival, Turtle stuck out his long neck and grabbed Beaver by the tail with his jaws. This made Beaver very angry, and he swam as fast as he could, hoping to make Turtle let go. When Turtle grabs something with his jaws, though, he does not let go until he is ready and Beaver could not shake him loose.

Finally, determined to shake loose his enemy, Beaver swung his tail over his head, throwing Turtle through the air like a bird. This was just what Turtle had hoped for; he landed far ahead of Beaver and easily reached the finish line first.

Thus Beaver lost the great race with Turtle and had to desert his dam, while Turtle, the crafty one, won back his private fishing hole.

Martin Luther King
by Aileen Fisher

Because he took a stand for peace
and dreamed that he would find
a way to spread equality
to all of humankind,

Because he hated violence
and fought with words, not guns,
he won a timely victory
as one of freedom's sons;

Because he died for liberty,
the bells of history ring
to honor the accomplishments
of Martin Luther King.

For old times' sake: a tree speaks
by James Kirkup

I live out my life
in these widening rings
like a thrown stone's ripples
from the centre of things.

I grew with each year
in sunshine and dark;
each ripple expanded
my long coat of bark.

How small my beginnings,
the seed of my heart—
but growing and flowing
with life from the start.

So many bird songs
are caught in my grooves,
and voices, and laughter,
and wild horses' hooves!

I once hid a king
and a highwayman bold;
I've seen thousands of seasons
but don't feel that old.

In winter I'm leafless,
my heart's in my roots.
But when spring comes, the sun
drives new life through my shoots.

I've been struck by the lightning,
been battered by gales;
but through rain, snow and tempest
my faith never fails.

It may be this ring
is the last I shall make,
but I keep the rings turning—
for old times' sake.

Practice 186

Name_____ Date_____

Judgments and Decisions

Before you can make a **decision**, you must consider your various choices and the reasons for and against the decision.

Read each situation below. List two reasons for each choice, and then make a **judgment** about what you should do. Write your final decision.

Suppose the following: You promised two friends that you would help them wash cars to raise money for your school's computer lab. Then you get an invitation to a birthday party from a boy you would like to be friends with. The party is the same day as the car wash. You really want to go to the party but you know that your two friends doing the car wash were not invited. What should you do?

Two reasons for helping with the car wash:

1. Helping with the car wash will raise money for the computer lab.

2. It's important to help good friends.

Two reasons for going to the birthday party:

3. I've always wanted to be friends with the boy who invited me to the party.

4. It'll be more fun going to a party than washing cars.

Final decision:

5. Do the car wash. I can still make friends with the boy without going to the party.

10 Book 5/Unit 6
Amistad Rising

At Home: Encourage students to write about situations where there have been more than one choice of decisions and how they made a final decision.

186

Practice 187

Name_____ Date_____

Vocabulary

Complete each sentence with a vocabulary word.

coax	escorted	navigate	nightfall	perished	ushered

1. We had to bicycle home before _____nightfall_____.

2. The city's mayor was _____escorted_____ to the fundraising ball by her husband.

3. In the olden days, every ship's captain knew how to _____navigate_____ by the stars.

4. The whole town _____perished_____ when the volcano erupted.

5. Have you ever had to _____coax_____ a frightened cat out of a tree?

6. Big celebrations _____ushered_____ in the new year.

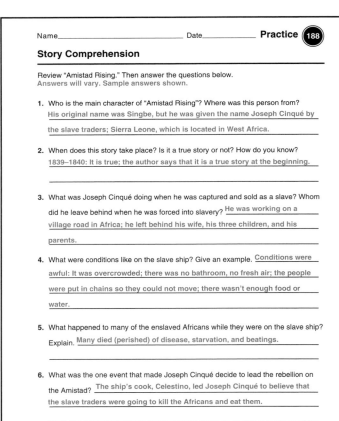

187

At Home: Have students use each of the vocabulary words in a sentence.

Book 5/Unit 6 6
Amistad Rising

Opening Night

It doesn't take much to *coax* me into attending the theater, especially on opening night. The first night of a play is the most exciting one. Almost everyone gets all dressed up. The play usually starts after *nightfall*. In the theater's lobby you may see dressed up people being *escorted* into the theater.

I'm careful as I *navigate* my way through the crowded lobby. If I'm with someone, I hold hands so we don't lose each other. As I enter the theater someone will hand me the playbill that tells me about the actors in the play. Then I will be *ushered* to the seats that are marked on my tickets. I expect I will enjoy the play, even though it's one in which all of the main characters will have *perished* by the end.

1. What is another word for *nightfall*? evening

2. What is a word that means "to persuade by urging"? to coax

3. What does the word *navigate* mean, as it is used in this story? to travel across to find your way

4. What is the difference between being *escorted* and being *ushered*?
Being escorted has a feeling of someone keeping you company; being ushered means someone is guiding you to a place as if to introduce you to it.

5. What does the writer mean when he says he will enjoy the show "even if everyone has *perished*"? The fact that it is the play's opening night should make it an enjoyable event even if the play has a sad ending.

5 Book 5/Unit 6
Amistad Rising

At Home: Have students use the vocabulary words to write a short story about an opening night.

187a

Practice 188

Name_____ Date_____

Story Comprehension

Review "Amistad Rising." Then answer the questions below.
Answers will vary. Sample answers shown.

1. Who is the main character of "Amistad Rising"? Where was this person from?
His original name was Singbe, but he was given the name Joseph Cinqué by the slave traders; Sierra Leone, which is located in West Africa.

2. When does this story take place? Is it a true story or not? How do you know?
1839–1840: It is true; the author says that it is a true story at the beginning.

3. What was Joseph Cinqué doing when he was captured and sold as a slave? Whom did he leave behind when he was forced into slavery? He was working on a village road in Africa; he left behind his wife, his three children, and his parents.

4. What were conditions like on the slave ship? Give an example. Conditions were awful: It was overcrowded; there was no bathroom, no fresh air; the people were put in chains so they could not move; there wasn't enough food or water.

5. What happened to many of the enslaved Africans while they were on the slave ship? Explain. Many died (perished) of disease, starvation, and beatings.

6. What was the one event that made Joseph Cinqué decide to lead the rebellion on the Amistad? The ship's cook, Celestino, led Joseph Cinqué to believe that the slave traders were going to kill the Africans and eat them.

188

At Home: Encourage students to write a summary for "Amistad Rising" and to share it with a family member. Students may create a visual retelling with a storyboard.

Book 5/Unit 6 6
Amistad Rising

Amistad Rising • PRACTICE

Name_____ Date_____ Practice 189

Read a Map

Study the map of Mississippi and the table giving information about the state.

Then answer each question.

```
                          MISSISSIPPI
Tennessee     Woodall Mtn.   Area      47,233 square mi. (122,324 square km.)
              806 ft.        Population              2,573,216(1995)
              Oxford         Admitted to Statehood             1817
Clarksdale    Columbus       State Bird                Mockingbird
                             Largest Cities            Jackson, Biloxi
Vicksburg     Meridian       Famous Residents          William Faulkner,
                                                       Elvis Presley, Leontyne Price
Louisiana
              N
            W   E
              S
Natchez                    Alabama
              Hattiesburg
                      Biloxi
```

1. What three major rivers of Mississippi are shown on the map? _____
   Mississippi, Yazoo, Pearl

2. In what year did Mississippi become a state? _1817_____

3. What two highways meet in Jackson, the capital city? highways 55 and 20 _____

4. Which two cities on the map are located north of Columbus, Mississippi? _____
   Clarksdale and Oxford

5. What state borders Mississippi on the east? Alabama _____

6. Which city is located on the Gulf of Mexico? Biloxi _____

7. How high is Woodall Mountain, the highest point in the state? 806 ft. _____

8. What state is located to the west of the Mississippi River? Louisiana _____

9. What is the area of Mississippi? _47,233 square miles or 122,324 square_____
   kilometers

10. What is Mississippi's largest city? Biloxi _____

Name_____ Date_____ Practice 190

Judgments & Decisions

Think about some of the **judgments and decisions** made in "Amistad Rising." Answer each question below. Explain your answers. You may look back at the story. Answers will vary. Accept all reasonable responses.

1. When Joseph Cinqué and his fellow Africans were kept on the slave ship, they were forbidden to speak, so they whispered to each other. Do you think it was wise for them to do so? Yes, because communication is important, and they could support each other; no, because they risked getting beatings.

2. What is your opinion of Celestino, the cook, who told Joseph Cinqué that he and the other Africans would be cut up and eaten like cured beef? _____
   Possible answer: I didn't like him; he was a mean person.

3. When the *Amistad* finally reached port after the uprising, the Africans onboard were sent to a prison. Do you think it was right to send them to prison? _____
   No, because they did nothing more than fight for their right to be free and so should not have been treated as criminals.

4. President Martin Van Buren did not want to upset southern slave holders by setting Joseph Cinqué free. So he made Joseph Cinqué and the other Africans face another trial. Do you think President Van Buren made the right decision? Explain. _____
   Possible answers: No, it wasn't fair or just; Yes, because as the leader of a democratic country he had to consider the opinions of different people.

5. Former President John Quincy Adams came out of retirement at the age of 72 to defend Joseph Cinqué. What does this action tell you about him? _____
   Possible answer: That he was a man who strongly believed in freedom.

Name_____ Date_____ Practice 191

Draw Conclusions

When you **draw conclusions**, you use facts from a story as well as your own knowledge and experience. Drawing conclusions as you read can help you better understand a story. Answers will vary. Accept all well-reasoned responses.

Read the selection below, and then answer each question. Describe the clues that helped you draw each conclusion. Answers will vary.

Every weekday Inga and her father walked into town together. She often had to rush to keep up with him. Inga noticed that her father always slowed down just as they got to the watchmaker's shop. There, in the front window, was a beautiful, marble chess set. Her father never said anything about it, but Inga could tell he admired it. She had seen her father's collection of faded newspaper pictures of him playing chess years ago. In them, he looked very serious as he played. Inga checked the price of the set and decided she would start saving her allowance.

Two days before her father's birthday, Inga watched closely as her father slowed down in front of the watchmaker's shop. This time he actually stopped and she heard him say, "It's gone." Inga had to hide her smile.

1. What sort of chess player was Inga's father when he was young? _____
   Probably a very good player.

2. **Story clue:** There were pictures in the newspaper of him playing chess.

3. **Experience clue:** If you are really good at something, your picture might be in the newspaper. Since there were many pictures of him, he must have won a lot of chess games.

4. What happened to the marble chess set in the watchmaker's window? _____
   Inga bought the chess set for her father's birthday.

5. **Story clue:** Inga had started saving her allowance, and she smiled when her father mentions the chess set is gone.

6. **Experience clue:** I have saved my allowance for special presents.

Name_____ Date_____ Practice 192

Context Clues

Context clues are other words in a story that help you define unfamiliar words. You can also look for familiar root words within larger words.

Read each passage below. Use context clues to help you define the underlined word. Circle the letter of the correct meaning.

1. Before the Civil War, the <u>abolitionists</u>, made up of whites and free blacks, spoke out for an end to slavery.
   An *abolitionist* must have been someone who was ___b___
   a. against the Civil War   **(b.)** against slavery   **c.** a free black

2. In a country far away, several newspaper reporters were held in <u>captivity</u> for seven years. They were sent to prison without any sort of trial, because the government claimed they were a spies.
   Being held in *captivity* is the same as being ___a___
   (a.) kept in prison   **b.** in a country far away   **c.** a spy

3. The circus trainers put heavy, iron <u>shackles</u> around each leg of the powerful and angry bear. They hoped that would keep him from moving and hurting others.
   Shackles are used to ___c___
   a. provide iron   **b.** put bears in cages   **(c.)** keep something from moving

4. My parents are <u>reluctant</u> to let me go to the movies. They are not willing to let me stay out that late on a school night.
   Another word for *reluctant* is ___a___
   (a.) unwilling   **b.** eager   **c.** careless

5. We could hear the school chorus raise its voice in <u>unison</u>. It sounded so beautiful—everyone singing all at the same time.
   Unison must mean something done ___c___
   a. in a beautiful way   **b.** for a concert   **(c.)** in one voice

Amistad Rising • RETEACH

Name_____ Date_____ **Reteach** 186

Judgments and Decisions

> Figuring out how you feel about a subject in a story can help you make **judgments** about what the author is saying. When you make judgements, you think about your reasons for and against something. When you make a **decision**, you act on your judgments.

Read the story. Then make judgments and decisions to answer the questions. Explain the reasons for your judgments and decisions.   Answers will vary. Possible answers are given.

Today was the day of the school-wide spelling bee. Gordon thought he was ready. He'd been reading his dictionary every night. He'd gotten a perfect score on the classroom spelling bee. Now he wondered whether to spend one last hour before school reviewing his list of difficult words. It would mean missing breakfast, and he would probably miss the bus as well. He'd have to walk to school and would probably be late. Still, the spelling bee was only once a year. Suddenly, Gordon remembered that he hadn't finished his math homework. Gordon sighed. He knew his math homework would take half an hour.

1. Do you think that Gordon is ready for the school wide spelling bee? Explain.
   Possible answer: Yes, he's probably ready. He had no trouble with the
   classroom spelling bee, plus he's been studying very hard.

2. How do you describe a good student? Possible answer: A good student is
   someone who studies a lot and takes school seriously.

3. Do you think Gordon is a good student? Possible answer: Yes, he is. He knows
   what he has to do and works very hard.

4. Do you think Gordon should spend the extra hour studying, or should he do his math
   homework, have breakfast, and take the bus? Explain. Possible answer: He
   should study for math; he has already studied for the spelling bee. It's
   important to eat breakfast.

Book 5/Unit 6
Amistad Rising 4

At Home: Have students put themselves in Gordon's shoes. What decisions would they make?

186

Name_____ Date_____ **Reteach** 187

Vocabulary

Write the best words from the box to complete the paragraph.

escorted	navigate	perished	ushered	nightfall	coax

Carolina worked carefully to _navigate_ the ship safely to shore through the storm. She knew she had to reach land before _nightfall_ blinded her. Once she sailed the boat into the harbor, a pilot boat _escorted_ it to the dock. At the dock, the harbor master _ushered_ in a Coast Guard officer to ask Carolina some questions. She struggled to _coax_ explanations through her chattering lips. The officer praised Carolina, saying that without her sailing skills, she might have _perished_ in the storm.

[6]

Story Comprehension   **Reteach** 188

Circle the answer to each question about "Amistad Rising."

1. Why are Joseph and the other Africans taken from their home?
   a. to be sold as slaves   b. to build a village road   c. to be killed

2. What do the captive Africans do on board the *Amistad*?
   a. buy their freedom   **b.** take over the ship   c. sink the ship

3. What were the rules about slavery at this time?
   a. Slave trading was legal.   b. Slave owning was not legal.
   c. Slave trading was not legal.

4. In what country are the Africans jailed after landing on the *Amistad*?
   a. Africa   **b.** United States   c. Cuba

5. What happens to the Africans in the United States after the trial?
   a. They are set free to return to Africa.   b. They are tried and jailed for life.
   c. They are freed to live in New London.

At Home: Think of another sentence that tells something about "Amistad Rising."

187–188

Book 5/Unit 6
Amistad Rising 5

Name_____ Date_____ **Reteach** 189

Read a Map

> To **read a map**, you first read the title and look at the map's legend or key to see how symbols are used on the map. Then study the map. A route map shows the routes, or paths, that can be used to travel from one place on the map to another.

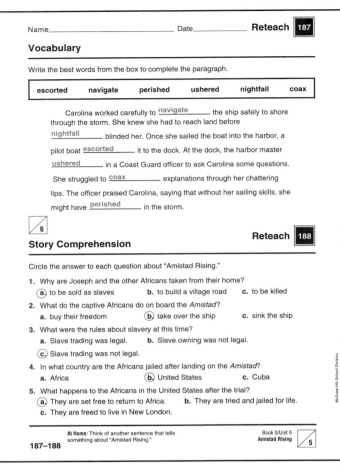

Triangular Route

Use the map to answer these questions.

1. What places are linked by each leg of the triangular route? New London,
   Connecticut, is linked to Orient Point, New York; Orient Point, New York, to
   Boston, Massachusetts; Boston, Massachusetts, to New London, Connecticut.

2. What products does New London receive from Boston? fish

3. What products does Orient Point ship to Boston? corn

4. Which routes are traveled by ship? New London to Orient Point; Orient Point to
   Boston

Book 5/Unit 6
Amistad Rising 4

At Home: Have students draw a route map for their trip to school.

189

Name_____ Date_____ **Reteach** 190

Judgments and Decisions

> You can make **judgments** about a character's actions by thinking about what you would do in the same situation. Sometimes, identifying a character's goal can help you understand the **decisions** he or she makes.

Read each story. Identify the main character's goal. Then decide which action or decision will help the main character reach his or her goal.

Phil wants to learn to sail, but he is not a very good swimmer. Before he begins sailing lessons, he has the choice of taking swimming classes or joining a computer club. Which should he do?

1. What is Phil's goal? to learn to sail

2. Which action should he take? Explain. He should take swimming lessons
   because he will be much safer when he learns how to sail.

Anastasia wants to win the Veteran's Day essay contest. At the library, she has the choice to take a book about World War II or a Nancy Drew mystery. Which book should she read?

3. What is Anastasia's goal? to win the Veteran's Day essay contest

4. Which action should she take? Explain. She should read the World War II book
   because it will help her learn about veterans' experiences.

Yolanda wants to grow tomatoes in her vegetable garden. She can spend her allowance money on gardening tools or she can go to the movies with her friend Sheila. How should she spend her money?

5. What is Yolanda's goal? to grow tomatoes

6. Which action should she take? Explain. She should spend her money on
   gardening tools as it will help her tomatoes grow.

At Home: Have students talk about the last big decision they made.

190

Book 5/Unit 6
Amistad Rising 6

Amistad Rising • RETEACH

<table>
<tr><td>

Draw Conclusions

You can use clues from your reading to **draw conclusions**, or figure out things about story characters and events. Often, you need to use clues from your own experience as well. Try to draw your conclusions by using the clues in each sentence.

Read the sentences. Circle the letter next to each correct conclusion. Then explain your answer. Use the clue from the sentences.

1. Andie plays basketball on Mondays, tennis on Tuesdays, volleyball on Thursdays, and soccer on Saturday mornings.

   a. Andie is the best athlete in school.

   (b.) Andie enjoys playing sports.

   c. Andie doesn't like schoolwork.

2. Clue: Andie plays many sports.

3. Chandra uses her books on the American West and her collection of historical movies about cowboys to write her "Ride the Range" column for the school newspaper.

   (a.) Chandra has studied the American West carefully.

   b. Chandra knows nothing about the American West.

   c. Chandra doesn't like to write.

4. Clue: Chandra owns both books and movies about the American West.

5. Ming spoke only Chinese when she entered our school last month.

   a. Ming was born in England.

   b. Ming doesn't want to speak English.

   (c.) Ming's family speaks Chinese at home.

6. Clue: Ming speaks only Chinese at school.

6 Book 5/Unit 6
Amistad Rising

At Home: Have students think about the last story they read. Have them talk about a conclusion that they were able to draw from it.

191

</td><td>

Context Clues

Some words that you read in a story will be unknown to you. **Context clues**, or the words and sentences surrounding the unfamiliar word, can help you figure out its meaning.

Read the sentences. Use context clues to determine what the underlined word or words mean. Choose the definition of the underlined word from the boxed list below.

- a shipping route between three ports whose path forms a triangle
- freedom
- when someone refuses to follow the rules
- slavery

1. Many Africans were surprised when they found themselves chained and in a state of bondage. slavery

2. Captives taken from Africa to the Americas were often part of the triangular trade route, which refers to a type of shipping route. shipping route whose path between three ports forms a triangle

3. The enslaved Africans on the *Amistad* hoped for emancipation and knew that they had the right to be free. freedom

4. The Amistad Rising was a slave rebellion. In this case the Africans attacked the slave traders and took over the ship. when someone refuses to follow the rules

At Home: Write a sentence for one of the underlined words.

192

Book 5/Unit 6
Amistad Rising 4

</td></tr>
</table>

Amistad Rising • EXTEND

Judgments and Decisions

When you make a **judgment** about something, you need to evaluate, or judge your choices. Then you can make a **decision** about the best course of action. For the situation below, decide what the best and the worst course of action would be. Give reasons for your judgments about these choices.

Situation: It is the night before a big test. You are getting ready to study and you realize you left your textbook and notes at school.

Choices:
1. You decide not to study.
2. You go to the house of a friend who is in your class and study there.
3. You call the school to see if you can get your books.
4. You decide to go to school early and study before the test.

Best course of action	**Worst course of action**
Answers will vary. Sample answer: Go to a friend's house and study there.	Answers will vary. Sample answer: Decide not to study.
Reason This is the best choice because you will get to study for the test and not be rushed to do it.	**Reason** If you do not study, you will probably do poorly on the test.

Think of a situation in which you might have several choices. Then fill out the Judgment-decision chart below. Use a separate sheet of paper if you need space. Answers will vary

Situation:	
Choices:	
Best course of action	**Worst course of action**
Reason	**Reason**

At Home: Find a favorite story and complete a judgment-decision box for the main character.

Vocabulary

coax	escorted	navigate	nightfall	perished	ushered

Sometimes it is difficult to remember the meaning of vocabulary words. You can use synonyms to help you memorize the meaning of words. For example, *escorted* means to "accompany," or "to go with." Find synonyms that can help you memorize the meaning of each word.

coax ___urge, influence___

navigate ___steer___

nightfall ___dusk, evening___

perished ___die, pass away___

ushered ___escorted, guided___

Story Comprehension

In "Amistad Rising," Joseph Cinqué makes the very important decision to rebel against the slave traders that hold him captive. Write down the reasons for his decision. Then write down the possible choices he had. Do you think he made the best choice? Explain why.

Answers will vary. Possible response: Cinqué had the choice to either remain in

slavery or to rebel against his captors. He made the right choice because he

eventually won his freedom.

_____

_____

_____

_____

At Home: Create a flow chart that shows Joseph Cinqué's decision-making process.

Read a Map

The English Colonies in America took part in the slave trade long before the events in "Amistad Rising." Ships from England and the colonies traveled in a triangular trade route across the Atlantic Ocean. The map shows the trade route of ships and what they carried.

The Triangular Trade Route

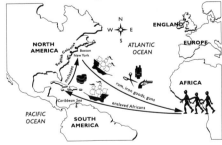

1. What trade route is shown on the map? The Triangular trade route in the 1700s— the English Colonies to Africa, Africa to the West Indies, the West Indies to the English Colonies.

2. What did the West Indies export to the English Colonies? molasses

3. What were the two major shipping cities in the English Colonies? New York and Boston

4. What did traders trade in Africa for slaves? rum, iron goods, guns

At Home: Find the trade route shown on a modern map. Use the map scale to find how many miles the traders traveled.

Judgments and Decisions

Often there are consequences to a **decision**. A consequence is the outcome, result, or after effects of the decision. In "Amistad Rising," the Supreme Court must make a **judgment** and decision regarding the future of Joseph Cinqué and the Mende with him. Use what you read in the story to fill in the judgment and decision chart below. Answers may vary, but should generally follow the answers given below.

What must the Supreme Court decide?
whether or not to free the Mende and allow them to return to Africa

3 Main Choices	**Possible Consequence of Each Choice**
1. Enslave the Africans.	They would take away the Africans' right to freedom. Abolitionist groups would be angry and protest.
2. Return the enslaved people to the Spaniards.	This was an unlikely choice because international slave trade was illegal.
3. Free the enslaved Africans.	The Mende would be free to return to Africa. Although southern slave holders might become angry.

Supreme Court's Decision
The Mende were freed and were able to return to Africa.

Did the Supreme Court make the best choice? Explain why. Answers will vary. Students will probably say that it was the right decision because slavery was wrong and illegal, and that all people should be free.

At Home: Look in the paper for a current Supreme Court decision. Tell whether or not you agree with the decision.

Amistad Rising • EXTEND

Draw Conclusions

When you read a historical story, you can often **draw conclusions** about the ideas the author is presenting. You may draw conclusions from what is written on the page and from what you already know.

1. The prisoners aboard the *Amistad* were held in the ship's hold. They had no baths, no toilets, and were chained together. Many died of disease, malnutrition, and from beatings.

   • What conclusion can you draw about the way the Africans' captors felt about their prisoners?

   Answers will vary. Possible response: The captors had no respect or regard

   for the Africans' health or welfare. They were only interested in the money they

   could get by selling them as slaves.

2. Celestino, the cook, tells Joseph Cinqué that the slave traders were going to kill the Africans, cut them up, and prepare them to be eaten, like cured beef.

   • What conclusion can you draw about the type of man Celestino is?

   Answers will vary. Possible response: Celestino is most likely a cruel person

   who has no regard for others.

3. After the uprising, the Spaniards sail the ship back towards Africa by day, but then turn the ship around and sail in the opposite direction by night. The *Amistad*, therefore, sails in circles for two months.

   • What conclusion can you draw about the Africans' knowledge of navigating ships on the Ocean?

   Answers will vary. Possible response: They were not familiar with ship

   navigation or they would have been able to tell they were going in circles.

   They did not know how to use the stars in the night sky as guides.

4. John Adams comes out of retirement to defend Cinqué and the Mende. He is worried about the responsibility he has taken on.

   • What conclusions can you draw about the way Adams felt about slavery?

   Answers will vary. Possible answer: He believed very strongly that slavery

   was wrong, or he probably would not have come out of retirement and taken

   the case.

At Home: Discuss how drawing conclusions can help you better understand what you read.

Context Clues

Write the definition of the underlined word in each sentence. Use the **context clues** in the sentence to determine the word's meaning.

1. Enslaved people brought over from Africa were often bound in shackles in the holds of the slave ships. shackles: chains

2. The captive Africans had no rights aboard the slave ships, little to eat, and were confined in tight quarters. captive: held against a person's will, prisoner

3. Abolitionists in the North fought to make slavery illegal in the United States, including in the South. abolitionists: people who were opposed to slavery

4. The Supreme Court deliberated many issues involving slavery in the nineteenth century and in United States history. deliberate: to consider facts and arguments in an issue; to make a decision

5. In Joseph Cinqué's time, the stealing of people from Africa was indisputably illegal. indisputably: without question

6. Most of the slave ships that came over from Africa had very little in the way of provisions to give to the captives. provisions: supplies such as food and other materials

7. Slave ships often carried beef that had been salted for preservation. preservation: to keep from spoiling or going bad

At Home: Find an unfamiliar word in a book you are reading. Write the meaning according to the context of the sentence.

Worksheet 161

Name _____ Date _____

Adverbs

- An **adverb** is a word that tells more about a verb, an adjective, or another adverb.
- An adverb can tell *how*, *when*, or *where* an action takes place.

Underline the adverb in each sentence. On the line, write whether the adverb describes *how*, *when*, or *where*.

1. The slave ship <u>slowly</u> left the harbor. _____ how _____
2. The ship stank <u>inside</u>. _____ where _____
3. Spanish traders treated the slaves <u>roughly</u>. _____ how _____
4. Dead slaves were thrown <u>overboard</u>. _____ where _____
5. Stormy winds tossed the ship <u>mercilessly</u>. _____ how _____
6. Cinqué <u>always</u> thought about his wife and children. _____ when _____
7. He looked <u>down</u> and started planning. _____ where _____
8. Cinqué freed himself and <u>then</u> freed other slaves. _____ when _____
9. The men fought <u>hard</u>. _____ how _____
10. <u>Later</u> a judge sat and listened to their case. _____ when _____
11. The Africans waited <u>nervously</u> for his decision. _____ how _____
12. Because they were free, they <u>gladly</u> gave thanks. _____ how _____

12 Grade 5/Unit 6
Amistad Rising

Extension: Have students write three sentences about a historical event. Ask them to tell *where*, *when*, and *how* the event happened.

161

Worksheet 162

Name _____ Date _____

Adverbs

- An adverb can describe an adjective or another adverb.

In these sentences, the adverbs describe verbs, adverbs, or adjectives.
Underline each adverb

1. The anchor sank <u>slowly</u>.
2. Cinqué decided <u>very quickly</u>.
3. The sails were <u>almost</u> full.
4. I think that Cinqué acted <u>quite bravely</u>.
5. He and the other enslaved Africans were <u>finally</u> free.

Complete each sentence with an adverb that describes the underlined word. You can choose from the adverbs in the box. Answers will vary.

almost	very	completely	terribly	quite	rather	too

6. Slave traders acted _____ very _____ selfishly.
7. The ships fought _____ quite _____ hard.
8. The skies were _____ terribly _____ black.
9. The stars were _____ completely _____ amazing.
10. The judge will decide _____ rather _____ quickly.

Extension: Ask partners to write three sentences with at least one adverb in them. Have partners try to add another adverb to each other's sentences.

162

Grade 5/Unit 6
Amistad Rising 10

Worksheet 163

Name _____ Date _____

Writing with Adverbs

- An **adverb** is a word that tells more about a verb, an adjective, or another adverb.
- An adverb can tell *how*, *when*, or *where* an action takes place.

Read the following story once. Then write adverbs in the spaces. Make sure that each adverb makes sense. Answers will vary.

Another Fight for Freedom

Abd al-Rahman Ibrahima was _____ very _____ courageous. He was the son of a West African chieftain. Because he was a prince, Ibrahima was educated _____ carefully _____. He _____ quickly _____ learned how to read and write. He studied _____ quite _____ hard to learn history, mathematics, and Moslem traditions. One day, Dr. Cox, a white man, became _____ terribly _____ lost in the jungle. He _____ earnestly _____ begged Ibrahima's people for help. They _____ immediately _____ saved his life, and Ibrahima became _____ rather _____ good friends with him.

When Ibrahima was in his twenties, he _____ suddenly _____ was captured in a war. He was sold as a slave and _____ later _____ taken to America. One day, Ibrahima was traveling _____ wearily _____ along a dirt road in Mississippi. _____ Then _____ he saw Dr. Cox. The doctor was glad to see Ibrahima. He frowned _____ angrily _____ , though, when he learned that this African prince was enslaved. Dr. Cox wrote to friends, and they _____ quickly _____ tried to help. They _____ finally _____ gained Ibrahima his liberty, and he died a free man in Africa.

15 Grade 5/Unit 6
Amistad Rising

Extension: Have small groups of students discuss the characteristics of heroism. Ask them to identify and comment upon adverbs that come up during the discussion.

163

Worksheet 164

Name _____ Date _____

Using *Good* and *Well*

- *Good* is an adjective and is used to describe nouns.
- *Well* is an adverb that tells *how* about a verb.
- Do not confuse the adjective *good* with the adverb *well*.

Read both sentences in each pair. Circle the letter of the sentence that uses *good* or *well* correctly.

1. a. The crew did not treat the captives good.
   (b.) The crew did not treat the captives well.
2. **(a.)** People on the Amistad did not eat well.
   b. People on the Amistad did not eat good.
3. **(a.)** The slaves fought well for their freedom.
   b. The slaves fought good for their freedom.
4. a. Cinqué fought for a well cause.
   (b.) Cinqué fought for a good cause.
5. **(a.)** Many good people helped abolish slavery.
   b. Many well people helped abolish slavery.

Write *well* or *good* to complete each sentence correctly. Then underline the word that *well* or *good* describes.

6. Would John Quincy Adams be a _____ good _____ <u>lawyer</u> for the Africans?
7. The former President wondered if he <u>would do</u> _____ well _____
8. When the time came, he <u>spoke</u> _____ well _____ for the Mende.
9. Adams was a _____ good _____ <u>judge</u> of character.
10. Like the American patriots, he explained, they had <u>fought</u> _____ well _____ for freedom.

Extension: Challenge students to write a poem about Cinqué's voyage home. Ask them to use the descriptive words *good* and *well* in their poems.

164

Grade 5/Unit 6
Amistad Rising 10

Amistad Rising • GRAMMAR

Adverbs

Rewrite each sentence twice. Each time, add an adverb that tells when, where, or how. Answers will vary.

1. The ship sails.

The ship sails soon.

The ship sails quickly.

2. Cinqué fought.

Cinqué fought courageously.

Then Cinqué fought.

3. Slave owners worked.

Slave owners worked quickly.

Slave owners worked there.

4. The waves are rising.

Now the waves are rising.

The waves are rising angrily.

5. The judge spoke.

The judge spoke softly.

Later, the judge spoke.

B. Write *well* or *good* to complete each sentence correctly.

6. During the storm, the ship did not travel _____ well _____.

7. A courageous leader is a _____ good _____ role model.

8. The ship's food did not taste _____ good _____.

9. John Quincy Adams argued _____ well _____ for the defense.

10. He was a _____ good _____ lawyer.

Adverbs

- An **adverb** is a word that tells more about a verb, an adjective, or another adverb.
- An adverb can tell *how*, *when*, or *where* an action takes place.

Mechanics

- *Good* is an adjective and is used to describe nouns. *Well* is a adverb that tells *how* about a verb. Do not confuse the adjective *good* with the adverb *well*.

Write *well* or *good* to complete the sentences correctly. Underline the word that each *well* or *good* describes. Then draw a picture about the sentences. Answers and pictures will vary.

1. The ship sailed _____ well _____.

2. A strong wind is _____ good _____ for sailing.

3. The Amistad sailed _____ well _____, for it was a _____ good _____ ship.

4. The Africans aboard the ship were not treated _____ well _____.

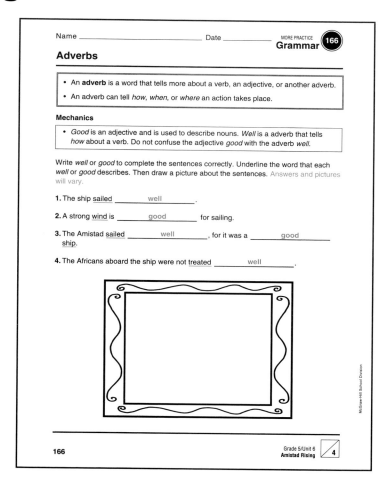

T13

Amistad Rising • SPELLING

Page 161

Homophones and Homographs

Pretest Directions

Fold back the paper along the dotted line. Use the blanks to write each word as it is read aloud. When you finish the test, unfold the paper. Use the list at the right to correct any spelling mistakes. Practice the words you missed for the Posttest.

To Parents

Here are the results of your child's weekly spelling Pretest. You can help your child study for the Posttest by following these simple steps for each word on the word list:

1. Read the word to your child.
2. Have your child write the word, saying each letter as it is written.
3. Say each letter of the word as your child checks the spelling.
4. If a mistake has been made, have your child read each letter of the correctly spelled word aloud, and then repeat steps 1–3.

1. _____	1. died
2. _____	2. stable
3. _____	3. pain
4. _____	4. wound
5. _____	5. waste
6. _____	6. bound
7. _____	7. pane
8. _____	8. waist
9. _____	9. vault
10. _____	10. dyed
11. _____	11. main
12. _____	12. sole
13. _____	13. haul
14. _____	14. current
15. _____	15. idle
16. _____	16. hall
17. _____	17. currant
18. _____	18. soul
19. _____	19. mane
20. _____	20. idol

Challenge Words

_____ coax
_____ escorted
_____ navigate
_____ perished
_____ ushered

Page 162

Homophones and Homographs

Using the Word Study Steps

1. LOOK at the word
2. SAY the word aloud.
3. STUDY the letters in the word.
4. WRITE the word.
5. CHECK the word.
   Did you spell the word right? If not, go back to step 1.

> **Spelling Tip**
> Learn the meanings of common homophones to help you use the right one in your writing.
> The belt fits nicely around my **waist**.
> If you leave the faucet on, you will **waste** the water.

Find Words That Sound the Same

Circle the word in each row that rhymes with the word on the left in dark type.

1. **hall**	(haul)	hail	hill	
2. **main**	mine	(mane)	moan	
3. **died**	did	dirt	(dyed)	
4. **waste**	(waist)	wasn't	washed	
5. **idle**	eyed	(idol)	ideal	
6. **pain**	pine	paste	(pane)	
7. **soul**	sour	(sole)	sill	
8. **currant**	hurry	courage	(current)	

Word Unscramble

Unscramble each set of letters below to make a spelling word.

9. bleast _____stable_____   11. tavul _____vault_____

10. dubon _____bound_____   12. dwonu _____wound_____

To Parents or Helpers:

Using the Word Study Steps above as your child comes across any new words will help him or her spell words effectively. Review the steps as you both go over this week's spelling words.

Go over the Spelling Tip with your child. Ask him or her to think of other words that sound the same. Help your child complete the spelling activity.

Page 163

Homophones and Homographs

died	waste	vault	haul	currant
stable	bound	dyed	current	soul
pain	pane	main	idle	mane
wound	waist	sole	hall	idol

Pair Up!

Look at the words in the box above. On the lines below, write each pair of spelling words that are spelled differently but that sound the same.

1. _died_ _dyed_   5. _sole_ _soul_

2. _pain_ _pane_   6. _haul_ _hall_

3. _waste_ _waist_   7. _current_ _currant_

4. _main_ _mane_   8. _idle_ _idol_

Double Meaning

Each of the spelling words below has two meanings. Using a dictionary, write the two meanings next to each spelling word.

9. stable _____   11. vault _____

_____   _____

10. wound _____   12. bound _____

_____   _____

Page 164

Homophones and Homographs

died	waste	vault	haul	currant
stable	bound	dyed	current	soul
pain	pane	main	idle	mane
wound	waist	sole	hall	idol

Complete each sentence below with a spelling word.

1. Wear the belt around your ___waist___ to hold the pants up.
2. My sister ___dyed___ her hair red.
3. The male lion has a ___mane___.
4. The river's ___current___ carried the boat downstream.
5. The old dog ___died___ after becoming very sick.
6. I had a ___currant___ muffin for breakfast.
7. When I hurt my arm, the ___pain___ was very bad.
8. The coat closet is in the ___hall___ next to the door.

Similar Meanings

Write the spelling word which comes closest to the word or phrase below.

9. firm ___stable___   15. chief ___main___

10. injury ___wound___   16. only ___sole___

11. useless ___waste___   17. inactive ___idle___

12. tied ___bound___   18. spirit ___soul___

13. glass ___pane___   19. carry ___haul___

14. safe ___vault___   20. image ___idol___

Challenge Extension: Imagine you went on a boat trip during your vacation. Write sentences for each of the Challenge Words describing what happened on the trip.

Amistad Rising • SPELLING

Homophones and Homographs

Proofreading Activity

There are six spelling mistakes in the letter below. Circle the misspelled words. Write the words correctly on the lines below.

To my dear wife,

My (sool) has longed for you and for Africa. The ship is ready, and I will be (bowned) for home tomorrow. Do not worry or think about the (pane) I have suffered. Every (woond) is healed. The chains that were on my ankles and around my (wayst) are gone forever. The fair wind and ocean (currint) will bring me back to you soon.

With love,

Singbe

1.	soul	3.	pain	5.	waist
2.	bound	4.	wound	6.	current

Writing Activity

In the story "Amistad Rising," the author wrote, "there is not a drop of sea water that doesn't have a secret; not a river or lake that doesn't whisper someone's name." Supposing that the water was alive, what secret might it have? Use four spelling words in your writing.

_____

_____

_____

_____

_____

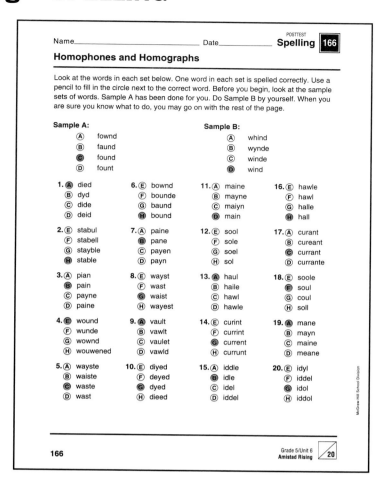

Homophones and Homographs

Look at the words in each set below. One word in each set is spelled correctly. Use a pencil to fill in the circle next to the correct word. Before you begin, look at the sample sets of words. Sample A has been done for you. Do Sample B by yourself. When you are sure you know what to do, you may go on with the rest of the page.

Sample A:
- Ⓐ fownd
- Ⓑ faund
- Ⓒ found ●
- Ⓓ fount

Sample B:
- Ⓐ whind
- Ⓑ wynde
- Ⓒ winde
- Ⓓ wind ●

1. Ⓐ died
   Ⓑ dyd
   Ⓒ dide
   Ⓓ deid

2. Ⓔ stabul
   Ⓕ stabell
   Ⓖ stayble
   Ⓗ stable

3. Ⓐ pian
   Ⓑ pain
   Ⓒ payne
   Ⓓ paine

4. Ⓔ wound
   Ⓕ wunde
   Ⓖ wownd
   Ⓗ wouwened

5. Ⓐ wayste
   Ⓑ waiste
   Ⓒ waste
   Ⓓ wast

6. Ⓔ bownd
   Ⓕ bounde
   Ⓖ baund
   Ⓗ bound

7. Ⓐ paine
   Ⓑ pane
   Ⓒ payen
   Ⓓ payn

8. Ⓔ wayst
   Ⓕ wast
   Ⓖ waist
   Ⓗ wayest

9. Ⓐ vault
   Ⓑ vawlt
   Ⓒ vaulet
   Ⓓ vawld

10. Ⓔ diyed
    Ⓕ deyed
    Ⓖ dyed
    Ⓗ dieed

11. Ⓐ maine
    Ⓑ mayne
    Ⓒ maiyn
    Ⓓ main

12. Ⓔ sool
    Ⓕ sole
    Ⓖ soel
    Ⓗ sol

13. Ⓐ haul
    Ⓑ haile
    Ⓒ hawl
    Ⓓ hawle

14. Ⓔ curint
    Ⓕ currint
    Ⓖ current
    Ⓗ currunt

15. Ⓐ iddle
    Ⓑ idle
    Ⓒ idel
    Ⓓ iddel

16. Ⓔ hawle
    Ⓕ hawl
    Ⓖ halle
    Ⓗ hall

17. Ⓐ curant
    Ⓑ cureant
    Ⓒ currant
    Ⓓ currante

18. Ⓔ soole
    Ⓕ soul
    Ⓖ coul
    Ⓗ soll

19. Ⓐ mane
    Ⓑ mayn
    Ⓒ maine
    Ⓓ meane

20. Ⓔ idyl
    Ⓕ iddel
    Ⓖ idol
    Ⓗ iddol

Page 193 — Cause and Effect

Name_____ Date_____ **Practice** 193

Cause and Effect

A **cause** is the reason why something happens. An **effect** is the result, or what happens. Many story events are connected through cause-and-effect relations.

What might happen as a result of each story event below? Write the most likely effect of each cause on the line provided.
Answers will vary. Accept all well-reseasoned responses.

1. The class planted tiny flower seeds in the ground where it was sunny. Each day the students watered their new garden. They even made a scarecrow so that the birds wouldn't eat the seeds.
   Effect: Flowers will grow where they planted the seeds.

2. Sonya was rushing to get to her friend's house. She pedaled her bike as fast as she could along a quiet street near the town dump. She was going so quickly that she didn't notice when she rode her bike over a small pile of broken glass.
   Effect: Sonya's bike is going to get a flat tire, and she is going to be late.

3. Juan is having a birthday party. His parents are sending out party invitations to everyone in Juan's class, to everyone in the school band, and to everyone on the softball team. Juan has many friends.
   Effect: There are going to be many people at Juan's birthday party.

4. Dorea really wants to play the guitar. She has an older cousin who is a very good guitar player. Dorea decides to tell him that she wants to learn to play the guitar as well as he does.
   Effect: Dorea's cousin will teach her how to play the guitar.

5. Lew and Kim are good friends. Lew has been doing poorly on his math tests lately. Kim decides to help Lew study. They have been working together solving math problems every day after school.
   Effect: Lew is going to do much better on the next test.

Page 194 — Vocabulary

Name_____ Date_____ **Practice** 194

Vocabulary

Complete each sentence with a vocabulary word.

husking	keg	landlord	oblige	rascals	sprawled

1. Those _____ rascals _____ are up to no good!

2. My father brought a _____ keg _____ of root beer to the class picnic.

3. During the summer, my cousins in Nebraska spend hours _____ husking _____ corn.

4. Everyone was _____ sprawled _____ on their beach towels and relaxing by the pool.

5. Would you do anything to _____ oblige _____ a friend?

6. Our _____ landlord _____ said he has to raise the rent on our house next year.

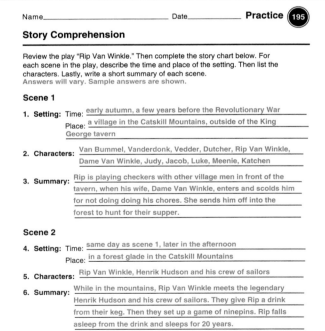

Page 194a — Husking Bee

Husking Bee

Rosa and Hank each sat on a *keg* as they worked. It was Saturday afternoon, and they were busily shredding husks from ears of corn. There was a huge pile of corn in front of them. They did this work for their *landlord*, Mr. Simpson, who owned the farm. Their work helped pay their rent on the farm.

"Those *rascals* never do their share of the work," complained Hank. He was referring to the laughing children *sprawled* on a haystack. They were the sons of Mr. Simpson.

"That's because they don't have to *oblige* anyone," commented Rosa. "They can spend their time doing as they please."

"Well, one thing's for sure," said Hank, "when I'm older, I'm going to own my own farm."

1. What is another word for *rascal*? troublemaker; lazy or dishonest

2. What is a word from the story that means "a small barrel"? keg

3. What does the word *husking* mean, as it is used in this story? removing the dry, leaf-like outer covering (husk) from an ear of corn

4. What does it mean to be "*sprawled* on a haystack"? sitting or lying on a haystack with arms and legs spread out

5. Why do you think Hank says what he does at the end? How do you think he feels about having to *oblige* the *landlord*? He is probably feeling angry that he has to work while other kids play; he doesn't want to be obliged to any landlord again.

Page 195 — Story Comprehension

Name_____ Date_____ **Practice** 195

Story Comprehension

Review the play "Rip Van Winkle." Then complete the story chart below. For each scene in the play, describe the time and place of the setting. Then list the characters. Lastly, write a short summary of each scene.
Answers will vary. Sample answers are shown.

Scene 1

1. **Setting:** Time: early autumn, a few years before the Revolutionary War
   Place: a village in the Catskill Mountains, outside of the King George tavern

2. **Characters:** Van Bummel, Vanderdonk, Vedder, Dutcher, Rip Van Winkle, Dame Van Winkle, Judy, Jacob, Luke, Meenie, Katchen

3. **Summary:** Rip is playing checkers with other village men in front of the tavern, when his wife, Dame Van Winkle, enters and scolds him for not doing doing his chores. She sends him off into the forest to hunt for their supper.

Scene 2

4. **Setting:** Time: same day as scene 1, later in the afternoon
   Place: in a forest glade in the Catskill Mountains

5. **Characters:** Rip Van Winkle, Henrik Hudson and his crew of sailors

6. **Summary:** While in the mountains, Rip Van Winkle meets the legendary Henrik Hudson and his crew of sailors. They give Rip a drink from their keg. Then they set up a game of ninepins. Rip falls asleep from the drink and sleeps for 20 years.

Rip Van Winkle • PRACTICE

Conduct an Interview

An **interview** is a way to gain information from someone. An interview follows a pattern of questions and answers. To prepare yourself to interview somebody, you need to figure out what questions you should ask.

Think about how you would conduct an interview with someone. Then answer the questions below.

Answers may vary.

1. Why is it important to know something about the person you are going to interview before you conduct the interview? It will help me to know the person's background and personality. Then I can ask more exact questions.

2. Why should you write down the questions you want to ask? So that I don't forget what I want to ask.

3. Why do you need to take notes during the interview? So that I don't forget what I hear.

4. Why is it important to be polite during the interview? I do not want to offend the person I am interviewing, because then he or she might might not want to answer all my questions.

5. What sort of information does an interview give that you might not find in a book or another reference source? I might find out more personal information or anecdotes (individual stories) that would not be in a book or reference source.

Cause and Effect

A **cause** is the reason why something happens. An **effect** is a result of the cause of what happens. Story events are often connected by a cause-and-effect relationship.

Complete the chart below to show the cause-and-effect links between events in "Rip Van Winkle." Supply the missing cause or effect in the correct column.

Cause	Effect
1. Vedder and Vanderdonk invite Rip to sit down and join them for a game of checkers.	1. Rip stops doing his chores to play a game of checkers with the men.
2. Rip stops doing his chores to play a game of checkers with the men.	2. Dame Van Winkle is angry with her husband Rip.
3. Rip forgets to mend the fence as his wife told him.	3. The cow escapes.
4. Henrick Hudson and his crew play ninepins up in the mountains.	4. Rip says the result is thunder.
5. Henrik Hudson and his sailors give Rip Van Winkle a drink from their keg.	5. Rip Van Winkle falls asleep for 20 years.
6. Rip Van Winkle has a beard and is 20 years older.	6. Judith does not recognize her father at first.

Draw Conclusions

When you **draw a conclusion**, you use facts from a story as well as your own knowledge and experiences. Drawing conclusions as you read helps you better understand a story.

Read the selection below, and then answer each question. Describe the clues that helped you draw conclusions. Answers will vary.

> When Dana got home, she closely inspected the scrape on her knee. It wasn't very deep, although she could see a bit of sand in it. She still felt a little shaky about what had happened.
>
> "That's the problem with biking on that sandy road," Dana reminded herself. "It's too slippery." Dana sighed. It would be a while before she would want to go biking again.
>
> While washing off her knee in the bathroom, Dana heard some loud seagulls outside. She looked out the bathroom window and saw a large group of seagulls that seemed to be playing in the waves. She smiled to herself. She may not want to go biking, but when her knee healed, she could still go swimming.

1. Where does Dana live? near a lake or ocean.

2. Story clue: She sees seagulls out her window; there is a sandy road.

3. Experience clue: Possible answer: I have seen pictures of beaches with seagulls and sandy roads.

4. What happened to Dana's knees? How did she scrape and bruise them? She must have fallen off her bicycle.

5. Story clue: She wouldn't want to go out biking now; there is sand ground into her scrape; she talks to herself about the problem with riding a bike on a sandy road.

6. Experience clue: Possible answer: I had an accident on my bike once, and I couldn't ride it for a while; I know how easy it is for a bicycle to slip on sand in the road.

Synonyms and Antonyms

Synonyms are words with the same or similar meaning and are used for different situations. **Antonyms** are words with the opposite or nearly opposite meaning and are used for contrast, or to show differences.

Use the words in the box to create pairs of synonyms and antonyms. Then list the pairs in the columns below.

warm	enter	hot
lazy	soft	dawdling
merry	exit	jolly
loud	cold	repair
fix	break	
village	town	

Synonyms
1. warm, hot
2. lazy, dawdling
3. merry, jolly
4. fix, repair
5. village, town

Antonyms
6. warm, cold
7. hot cold
8. enter, exit
9. soft, loud
10. fix, break

Compare the underlined words in each sentence. Write whether they are antonyms or synonyms.

11. If you keep dawdling like that, people will think you are lazy. synonyms

12. Read the poem out loud, but speak with a soft voice antonyms

Rip Van Winkle • RETEACH

Page 193

Name_____ Date_____ **Reteach** 193

Cause and Effect

Finding causes and effects will help you understand why story events happen. A **cause** is why something happens. An **effect** is what happens as a result of a cause. Notice that clue words such as *because, so, since,* and *in order to* help you link causes and effects.

Match the causes with the effects by writing the letter of the correct effect before each cause.

Causes

___b___ 1. We ran out of soap

___d___ 2. We stayed out in the sun too long yesterday.

___a___ 3. We couldn't find the car keys.

___c___ 4. We sold 16 boxes of wrapping paper.

Effects

a. We had to walk to work and school.

b. We bought soap at the store.

c. We won the first prize for selling the most wrapping paper.

d. We both got burned.

because	so	since	in order to

Fill in a word from the box to connect the causes with their effects.

1. We couldn't find the car keys _so_____ we had to walk to work.

2. _Since_____ we sold 16 boxes of wrapping paper, we won the first prize for selling the most wrapping paper.

3. We both got burned _because_____ we stayed in the sun too long yesterday.

4. We wrote soap on the list _in order to____ remember it.

8 | Book 5/Unit 6 **Rip Van Winkle** | **At Home:** Have students think of an example of a cause and an effect. | 193

Page 194

Name_____ Date_____ **Reteach** 194

Vocabulary

Read each clue. Find the correct vocabulary word in the box and write it on the line in the right-hand column next to its clue.

landlord	oblige	rascals	sprawled	husking	keg

Clues

1. jar or barrel

2. building owner

3. spread out

4. to please

5. a way of taking the husk off corn

6. mischievous people or cheaters

Vocabulary Words

keg

landlord

sprawled

oblige

husking

rascals

6

Page 195

Reteach 195

Story Comprehension

Write a ✔ next to every sentence that tells something true about "Rip Van Winkle."

___✔___ 1. "Rip Van Winkle" takes place just before the time of the Revolutionary War.

_____ 2. Rip Van Winkle thinks children are too noisy.

___✔___ 3. Rip Van Winkle would rather spend time with his friends than work.

_____ 4. Rip Van Winkle meets no one on his journey into the mountains.

___✔___ 5. Rip Van Winkle sleeps in the mountains for over 20 years.

___✔___ 6. While Rip Van Winkle is gone, the Revolutionary War is fought.

At Home: Have students write sentences using two of the vocabulary words. | 194–195 | Book 5/Unit 6 **Rip Van Winkle** | 6

Page 196

Name_____ Date_____ **Reteach** 196

Conduct an Interview

Conducting an interview is a useful way of getting information about other people's experiences. To prepare for an interview, ask yourself what you want to learn from your subject. Then think about questions to ask.

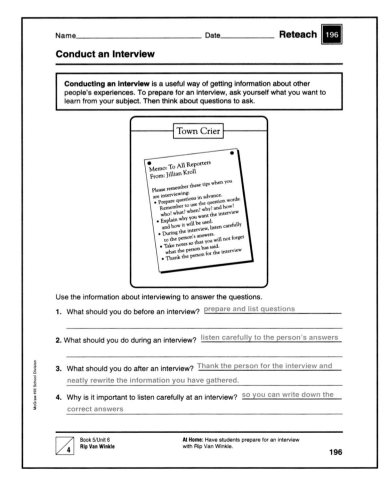

Town Crier

Memo: To All Reporters
From: Jillian Kroll

Please remember these tips when you are interviewing:
• Prepare questions in advance.
• Remember to use the question words: who! what! when! why! and how!
• Explain why you want the interview and how it will be used.
• During the interview, listen carefully to the person's answers.
• Take notes so that you will not forget what the person has said.
• Thank the person for the interview

Use the information about interviewing to answer the questions.

1. What should you do before an interview? _prepare and list questions_____

2. What should you do during an interview? _listen carefully to the person's answers_

3. What should you do after an interview? _Thank the person for the interview and neatly rewrite the information you have gathered._

4. Why is it important to listen carefully at an interview? _so you can write down the correct answers_

4 | Book 5/Unit 6 **Rip Van Winkle** | **At Home:** Have students prepare for an interview with Rip Van Winkle. | 196

Page 197

Name_____ Date_____ **Reteach** 197

Cause and Effect

A **cause** is the why something happens. An **effect** is the event, feeling, or situation that results from the cause. Clue words can help you understand the relationship between cause and effect.

Read each cause. Then circle the letter next to the effect that could most likely result from the cause.

1. Ned ate three hot dogs, two hamburgers, a plate of potato salad, and a huge slice of watermelon.
   a. Ned is still hungry.
   b. Ned might have a stomachache from being too full.
   c. Ned doesn't like picnic food.

2. Ginger left her bike out in the snow all night.
   a. She cannot use it for school today.
   b. It is bright red.
   c. Ginger's bike will stay in the garage all year.

3. Liam slammed the phone down without even saying good-bye to Sean.
   a. Liam is glad Sean called.
   b. Liam is excited about talking to Sean.
   c. Liam is angry with Sean.

4. Andrea has no money to buy a snack today.
   a. Andrea had lunch today.
   b. Andrea will not have a snack today.
   c. Andrea's friend, Hunter, will share his snack with Andrea.

5. Max broke his leg playing baseball the week before the big game.
   a. Max will hit a home run to win the big game.
   b. Max will play badly in the big game.
   c. Max will have to miss the big game.

197 | **At Home:** Have students think about something that happened in school. Have them talk about why it happened and the effects of what happened. | Book 5/Unit 6 **Rip Van Winkle** | 5

Rip Van Winkle • RETEACH

Draw Conclusions

> A **conclusion** is a decision or judgement based on information. You reach a conclusion after some thought. You can draw conclusions based on information in a story or information from your own experience.

Read each story. Then write a ✔ next to the conclusion you can draw based on the information in the story.

> When Amy entered the deli, Sarah smiled at her and started making Amy a turkey and cheese sandwich. After paying for her sandwich, Amy said, "See you tomorrow," and left.

✔ **1.** Amy often eats at Sarah's deli often and usually buys the same sandwich.

_____ **2.** Sarah makes turkey sandwiches every Monday and Wednesday.

> Tucker studied in England for several years. When he returned to the United States, many things looked different. All the shops on Main Street had changed. The tree outside his bedroom had grown past the roof of the house.

_____ **3.** Tucker does not want to be home.

✔ **4.** Tucker has been gone a long time.

> Marina stopped to chat with the children waiting for the school bus. Then she talked for a while with the man selling newspapers and coffee. During her lunch hour, Marina sat in the park and talked with the elderly lady who feeds the birds.

_____ **5.** Marina is shy and would rather read a book than be with people.

✔ **6.** Marina enjoys talking to people.

> On his way out, Abdul whistled for his dog, Skipper. When Skipper didn't come, Abdul went back into the house. When he found Skipper, he gently petted Skipper's head until the dog woke up. Then they left together.

_____ **7.** Abdul never lets Skipper sleep.

✔ **8.** Abdul loves Skipper and doesn't want to go out without him.

Book 5/Unit 6
Rip Van Winkle
8

At Home: Have students read the second and third stories. Have them identify the clues that helped them answer the questions.

198

Synonyms and Antonyms

> **Synonyms** are words with the same or similar meanings. **Antonyms** are words with opposite or nearly opposite meanings.

Read each sentence. Circle the letter of the word that is an antonym to the underlined word.

1. Mrs. Van Winkle was known throughout the town for her <u>sharp</u> tongue.

   (a.) gentle   **b.** fat   **c.** smelly

2. The children knew that Rip Van Winkle could <u>repair</u> their wooden tools perfectly.

   a. fix   **b.** mend   **(c.)** break

3. Judy often saw her mother <u>scowl</u> at her father Rip because he often forgot to do his chores.

   a. stare and frown   **(b.)** smile   **c.** shout

4. No one could believe the <u>racket</u> that Hendrik Hudson and his crew made when they played ninepins.

   (a.) silence   **b.** gloves   **c.** noise

Read each sentence. Circle the letter of the word that is a synonym to the underlined word.

5. Since he never did his chores, Rip Van Winkle thought his wife had good reason to be <u>cross</u> with him.

   (a.) angry   **b.** pleased   **c.** happy

6. Poor Jacob was so <u>terrified</u> of the thunder that he hid under the bed.

   a. glad   **(b.)** scared   **c.** tired

7. The students enjoyed themselves greatly because they did a <u>merry</u> dance.

   (a.) joyful   **b.** serious   **c.** difficult

8. At the end of a play, the curtain <u>descends</u> to show that the show is over.

   a. rises   **b.** parts   **(c.)** falls

At Home: Have students list synonyms for items 1—4 and antonyms for items 5—8.

199

Book 5/Unit 6
Rip Van Winkle
8

Rip Van Winkle • EXTEND

Cause and Effect

When you read, you often find out the reason why events in the story happen. This is known as the **cause**. What happens as a result of a cause is called the **effect**. Sometimes word clues help you see cause-and-effect relationships. Look for words like *because, so, therefore, since,* and *when* that explain why an event happened.

Read the sentences below. Then write the cause and effect on the lines provided. Underline any clue words in the sentences.

1. When John Glenn became the first United States astronaut to circle the Earth, his bravery paved the way for other space flights.

   Cause: John Glenn was the first United States astronaut to circle the Earth.

   Effect: His bravery paved the way for other space flights.

2. Because of his experience as an astronaut, Glenn was able to make a trip on the Space Shuttle as a senior citizen.

   Cause: Glenn's experience as an astronaut

   Effect: He was able to make a trip on the space shuttle.

3. Senior citizens all over the world watched Glenn's space shuttle mission with excitement.

   Cause: Glenn's space shuttle mission

   Effect: Senior citizens watched with excitement.

4. Bad weather moved into the area the day of the shuttle flight, so it was delayed for two days.

   Cause: bad weather in the area

   Effect: The shuttle flight was delayed for two days.

5. NASA experts were relieved when the shuttle flight finally took off.

   Cause: The shuttle flight took off.

   Effect: NASA experts were relieved.

Book 5/Unit 6
Rip Van Winkle

At Home: Find examples of cause-effect relationships in a newspaper article.

193

Vocabulary

husking	keg	landlord	oblige	rascals	sprawled

At the end of "Rip Van Winkle," Rip goes back to his daughter's home. Write a scene between Rip and his daughter telling what might have happened after they arrived home. Use as many vocabulary words as possible.

Answers will vary, but should include at least four vocabulary words used in the
correct context and parts of speech.

_____

_____

_____

_____

_____

Story Comprehension

At the end of the story, Judith finally believes that Rip is her father. Tell how she is able to come to this conclusion.

Rip tells her about a song he used to sing when she was a little girl. He tells her

that he had a dog named Wolf. He reminds her of the story he used to tell her

about Hendrik Hudson.

_____

_____

_____

_____

_____

At Home: Find 5 unfamiliar words in a magazine. After looking up their definition in a dictionary, discuss how you
194–195 can remember the meanings of these words.

Book 5/Unit 6
Rip Van Winkle

Conduct an Interview

In "Rip Van Winkle," Rip awakens to a world that has changed drastically during his 20-year sleep. For young people, such as his grandson, Rip Van Winkle could be an important source of information from the past.

Conduct an interview with an older person who could tell you what life was like 20 years ago, before you were born. First, create a list of at least eight questions you will ask. Write your questions below.

Answers will vary.

_____

_____

_____

_____

_____

_____

After you have finished your list, conduct your interview. Take notes as you go along. Then use your notes and what you have learned to write an article on a separate sheet of paper about the person you interviewed.

Answers will vary.

_____

_____

_____

_____

_____

_____

_____

_____

_____

Book 5/Unit 6
Rip Van Winkle

At Home: Find an example of an interview in a newspaper or magazine. What are some of the questions that were asked?

196

Cause and Effect

A **cause** is the reason why something happens. An **effect** is the result. Below are some examples of effects from the story "Rip Van Winkle." Write the cause for each effect.

1. In the beginning of the story, Van Brummel is reading that a Stamp Act Congress is being held in New York.

   Cause: You may have to remind students that this Congress, or meeting, was
   held to protest English taxation in the colonies.

2. When Rip is talking to the children, they think they hear thunder coming from the mountains. What does Rip tell them is the cause?

   Cause: Hendrik Hudson and his men are playing ninepins.

3. Dame Van Winkle is angry when she catches Rip telling stories to the children.

   Cause: Rip is supposed to be gathering wood and doing his chores.

4. Rip goes off to the mountain with his dog and his gun.

   Cause: To go hunting; maybe avoid doing chores.

5. Rip falls asleep in the mountains after visiting with Hendrik Hudson and the sailors.

   Cause: He drinks from the sailor's keg, and the drink makes him sleepy.

6. When Rip awakens, his back is stiff, his clothes are shabby, and he has grown a long white beard.

   Cause: He has been asleep for 20 years.

7. When Rip walks into town after his 20-year sleep, the townspeople think he is a spy and want to put him in jail.

   Cause: Rip says that he is loyal to King George at a time when people are
   preparing to elect the new country's first President; he does not know that the
   Revolutionary War has taken place.

197

At Home: Find an example of cause and effect in a favorite story.

Book 5/Unit 6
Rip Van Winkle

Rip Van Winkle • EXTEND

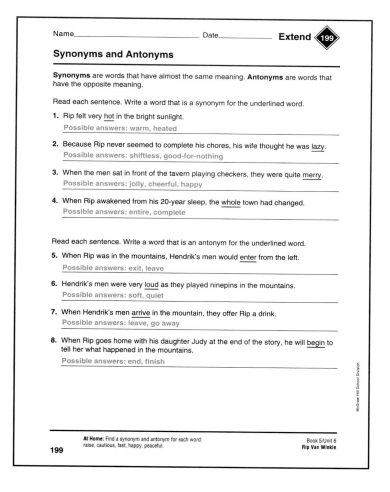

Draw Conclusions

When you **draw conclusions** about something in a story, you use the data from the text or inferences you make when reading the text. Conclusions are evaluations that you make about something you read in the story.

Draw conclusions about two situations in "Rip Van Winkle." Fill in the chart.

---

1. Question: How does Rip Van Winkle feel about his wife's scolding?

Conclusion: Possible answer: He gets tired of her scolding, even though he knows he's partially to blame.

Statements and inferences from the text: Possible answers: She yells at him constantly and threatens him with her broom, but he says he understands why she gets cross. Still, he would rather sleep outside in the mountains than in their house. At the end of the story, he remembers her as a woman who had a sharp tongue.

---

2. Question: What does Rip Van Winkle discover when he awakens from his sleep and walks into town?

Conclusion: Possible answer: He realizes that many years have passed.

Statements and inferences from the text: Possible answer: Many of his old friends have passed away. King George is no longer ruler of the colonies, and a war has been fought. George Washington is running for President, and Rip's daughter has grown up and married.

Book 5/Unit 6
Rip Van Winkle

At Home: Check the leftovers in your refrigerator and draw conclusions about who has been there before you.

198

Synonyms and Antonyms

Synonyms are words that have almost the same meaning. **Antonyms** are words that have the opposite meaning.

Read each sentence. Write a word that is a synonym for the underlined word.

1. Rip felt very <u>hot</u> in the bright sunlight.
Possible answers: warm, heated

2. Because Rip never seemed to complete his chores, his wife thought he was <u>lazy</u>.
Possible answers: shiftless, good-for-nothing

3. When the men sat in front of the tavern playing checkers, they were quite <u>merry</u>.
Possible answers: jolly, cheerful, happy

4. When Rip awakened from his 20-year sleep, the <u>whole</u> town had changed.
Possible answers: entire, complete

Read each sentence. Write a word that is an antonym for the underlined word.

5. When Rip was in the mountains, Hendrik's men would <u>enter</u> from the left.
Possible answers: exit, leave

6. Hendrik's men were very <u>loud</u> as they played ninepins in the mountains.
Possible answers: soft, quiet

7. When Hendrik's men <u>arrive</u> in the mountain, they offer Rip a drink.
Possible answers: leave, go away

8. When Rip goes home with his daughter Judy at the end of the story, he will <u>begin</u> to tell her what happened in the mountains.
Possible answers: end, finish

At Home: Find a synonym and antonym for each word: raise, cautious, fast, happy, peaceful.

199

Book 5/Unit 6
Rip Van Winkle

T21

Rip Van Winkle • GRAMMAR

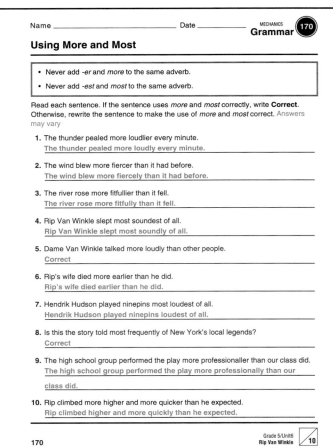

Page 167

Adverbs That Compare

- An adverb can compare two or more actions.
- Add -er to most short adverbs to compare two actions.
- Add -est to most short adverbs to compare more than two actions.

Read the sentences. Write the correct form of the adverb in parentheses.

1. (long) Of the many storms this season, this storm raged ____longest____ of all.

2. (hard) Lightning hit ____harder____ on the hill than in the valley.

3. (high) The mountains rose ____higher____ than the mesa.

4. (long) Rip slept ____longer____ than he ever had before.

5. (long) In fact, Rip slept ____longest____ of all.

6. (hard) Dame Van Winkle worked ____harder____ than Rip.

7. (fast) Rip ran ____faster____ than he walked.

8. (early) The ship's bell rang ____earlier____ the second time.

9. (early) Wolf left the mountain ____earlier____ than Rip did.

10. (late) Rip left the mountain ____latest____ of all.

11. (near) The thunder boomed ____nearer____ than a few minutes ago.

12. (soon) Rip wished that he had gotten up ____sooner____ than he did.

12 / Grade 5/Unit 6 Rip Van Winkle

Extension: Ask students to compare two actions with the following adverbs: hard, short, fast. Then ask them to compare three or more actions with the same adverbs.

167

Page 168

Adverbs That Compare

- Use more or most to form comparisons with adverbs that end in -ly or most other adverbs with two or more syllables.
- Use more to compare two actions; use most to compare more than two.
- When you use more or most, do not use the ending -er or -est.

Read the sentences. Write the correct form of the adverb in parentheses.

1. (slowly) Rip walked ____more slowly____ than Wolf.

2. (quietly) Rip spoke ____more quietly____ to children than his wife did.

3. (impatiently) Dame Van Winkle speaks the ____most impatiently____ of all.

4. (closely) Rip looked ____more closely____ around him than he had looked a minute ago.

5. (shyly) Of all the villagers, Little Rip greeted Rip ____most shyly____.

Read each sentence. If the adverb is correct, write Correct on the line. If it is not correct, rewrite the sentence so that the adverb will be correct.

6. The people shouted angrilier at Rip than they did at Wolf.

   The people shouted more angrily at Rip than they did at Wolf.

7. The whistle played more beautifully than the last one played.

   Correct

8. That man sleeps more quietly of all.

   That man sleeps most quietly of all.

9. Rip answered most soonest of all the husbands.

   Rip answered soonest of all the hundreds.

10. The thunder clapped more violenter than it had the last time.

    The thunder clapped more violently than it had the last time.

Extension: Have students write descriptions of a character in the play. Ask them to compare his or her actions to those of other villagers. Students should exchange descriptions and proofread for correct use of adverbs that compare.

168 / Grade 5/Unit 6 Rip Van Winkle / 10

Page 169

Adverbs That Compare

- An adverb can compare two or more actions.
- Add -er to most short adverbs to compare two actions. Add -est to most short adverbs to compare more than two actions.
- Add more or most to form comparisons with adverbs that end in -ly or most other adverbs with two or more syllables. Use more to compare two actions; use most to compare more than two. When you use more or most, do not use the ending -er or -est.

Circle the adverbs in these paragraphs. Then write the paragraph correctly.

Rip Van Winkle lived near the Catskill Mountains. These mountains rise highest than the land around them, and the storms rage more fiercer as you climb more higher on the slope. In the summer, thunderstorms arrive frequenter and lightning strikes most violentest in the winter.

Today, The Hudson River passes through much of New York State. It runs slowlier as it falls lowly to flat land. As it passes New York City, the river runs slower of all.

Many years ago, people worked more harder than today to ship goods upstate. Ships from New York Harbor carried cargo more efficienter than mules did. Today, trucks and trains travel more speedier and most cheaply than ships do. In the years ahead, the river will continue to be importanter to people.

Rip Van Winkle lived near the Catskill Mountains. These mountains rise higher than the land around them, and the storms rage more fiercely as you climb higher on the slope. In the summer, thunderstorms arrive more frequently and lightning strikes more violently than in the winter.

Today, The Hudson River passes through much of New York State. It runs more slowly as it falls lower to flat land. As it passes New York City, the river runs slowest of all.

Many years ago, people worked harder than today to ship goods upstate. Ships from New York Harbor carried cargo more efficiently than mules did. Today, trucks and trains travel more speedily and more cheaply than ships do. In the years ahead, the river will be more important to people.

10 / Grade 5/Unit 6 Rip Van Winkle

Extension: Invite pairs or groups of students to create and present a story about a local storm. Suggest that they include a local historical figure in their stories. Ask students to include at least five adverbs that compare.

169

Page 170

Using More and Most

- Never add -er and more to the same adverb.
- Never add -est and most to the same adverb.

Read each sentence. If the sentence uses more and most correctly, write **Correct**. Otherwise, rewrite the sentence to make the use of more and most correct. Answers may vary

1. The thunder pealed more loudlier every minute.
   The thunder pealed more loudly every minute.

2. The wind blew more fiercer than it had before.
   The wind blew more fiercely than it had before.

3. The river rose more fitfullier than it fell.
   The river rose more fitfully than it fell.

4. Rip Van Winkle slept most soundest of all.
   Rip Van Winkle slept most soundly of all.

5. Dame Van Winkle talked more loudly than other people.
   Correct

6. Rip's wife died more earlier than he did.
   Rip's wife died earlier than he did.

7. Hendrik Hudson played ninepins most loudest of all.
   Hendrik Hudson played ninepins loudest of all.

8. Is this the story told most frequently of New York's local legends?
   Correct

9. The high school group performed the play more professionaller than our class did.
   The high school group performed the play more professionally than our class did.

10. Rip climbed more higher and more quicker than he expected.
    Rip climbed higher and more quickly than he expected.

170 / Grade 5/Unit6 Rip Van Winkle / 10

Rip Van Winkle • GRAMMAR

Adverbs That Compare

Choose the sentence in each group that is written incorrectly. Circle the letter of the incorrect sentence.

1. **a.** The children work more diligently than their father does.
   (b.) The children work most diligently than their father does.
   c. The children work most diligently of all.

2. **a.** Wolf comes more readily to Rip than he does to Dame.
   (b.) Wolf comes most readily to Rip than to Dame.
   c. Wolf comes more readily to Rip than even the children do.

3. **a.** Rip works more lovingly with children than he does with his wife.
   b. Of all the men in the village, Rip works most lovingly with the children.
   (c.) Rip works most lovingly with children than he does with his wife.

4. **(a.)** Rip slept longest than he worked.
   b. Rip slept longer than he worked.
   c. Rip slept longest of all.

5. **(a.)** Judith stared hardest at Rip than Doolittle did.
   b. Of all the villagers, Judith stared hardest at Rip.
   c. Judith stared harder at Rip than Doolittle did.

B. Choose the comparing adverb that best completes the sentence. Circle the letter of your answer.

6. Hendrik Hudson plays ninepins _____ than he sings.
   a. loudest
   (b.) louder
   c. more louder

7. Hendrik Hudson dances _____ today than yesterday.
   a. most merrily
   b. more merrier
   (c.) more merrily

8. The Hudson River flows _____ in the spring than in the summer.
   a. rapidest
   b. most rapidly
   (c.) more rapidly

Adverbs That Compare

- Add -er to most short adverbs to compare two actions. Add -est to most short adverbs to compare more than two actions.
- Add more or most to form comparisons with adverbs that end in -ly or most other adverbs with two or more syllables. Use more to compare two actions; use most to compare more than two.
- Never add -er and more or -est and most to the same adverb.

With a partner, take turns reading these sentences aloud. Listen for adverb errors. Together, rewrite the sentences to correct the errors.

1. No one reads the news most entertainingly than Derrick Van Bummel does.
   No one reads the news more entertainingly than Derrick Van Bummel does.

2. Afterward, the men talked more angrilier about British taxes than before.
   Afterward, the men talked more angrily about British taxes than before.

3. Rip Van Winkle played frequenter than he worked.
   Rip Van Winkle played more frequently than he worked.

4. The children talked to Rip most easiest of all.
   The children talked to Rip most easily of all.

5. The odd sailor spoke most gruffly than Rip had expected.
   The odd sailor spoke more gruffly than Rip had expected.

6. Never had Rip slept soundest than he did that night.
   Never had Rip slept more soundly than he did that night.

7. Rip changed more dramatic of all sleepers.
   Rip changed most dramatically of all sleepers.

8. Who acted more stranglier—Rip or the people at the Union Hotel?
   Who acted more strangely—Rip or the people at the Union Hotel?

Rip Van Winkle • SPELLING

Page 167

Words with Prefixes

Pretest Directions
Fold back the paper along the dotted line. Use the blanks to write each word as it is read aloud. When you finish the test, unfold the paper. Use the list at the right to correct any spelling mistakes. Practice the words you missed for the Posttest.

To Parents
Here are the results of your child's weekly spelling Pretest. You can help your child study for the Posttest by following these simple steps for each word on the word list:

1. Read the word to your child.
2. Have your child write the word, saying each letter as it is written.
3. Say each letter of the word as your child checks the spelling.
4. If a mistake has been made, have your child read each letter of the correctly spelled word aloud, and then repeat steps 1–3.

1. _____
2. _____
3. _____
4. _____
5. _____
6. _____
7. _____
8. _____
9. _____
10. _____
11. _____
12. _____
13. _____
14. _____
15. _____
16. _____
17. _____
18. _____
19. _____
20. _____

1. preschool
2. replaced
3. unknown
4. disobey
5. invisible
6. preview
7. regain
8. unseen
9. discomfort
10. incorrect
11. precook
12. recall
13. unable
14. dishonest
15. inexpensive
16. prearrange
17. revisit
18. unaware
19. disapprove
20. incredible

Challenge Words
_____ husking
_____ landlord
_____ oblige
_____ rascals
_____ sprawled

Page 168

Words with Prefixes

Using the Word Study Steps
1. LOOK at the word
2. SAY the word aloud.
3. STUDY the letters in the word.
4. WRITE the word.
5. CHECK the word.
   Did you spell the word right? If not, go back to step 1.

Spelling Tip
Learn how to spell prefixes you use often in writing.
re-   in-   dis-

Related Words
Write the spelling word which contains the smaller word below.

1. school — preschool
2. placed — replaced
3. known — unknown
4. obey — disobey
5. visible — invisible
6. view — preview
7. gain — regain
8. seen — unseen
9. comfort — discomfort
10. correct — incorrect
11. cook — precook
12. call — recall
13. able — unable
14. honest — dishonest
15. expensive — inexpensive
16. arrange — prearrange
17. visit — revisit
18. aware — unaware
19. approve — disapprove
20. credible — incredible

To Parents or Helpers:
Using the Word Study Steps above as your child comes across any new words will help him or her spell words effectively. Review the steps as you both go over this week's spelling words.
Go over the Spelling Tip with your child. Help your child think of and spell other prefixes.
Help your child complete the spelling activity.

Page 169

Words with Prefixes

preschool	invisible	discomfort	unable	revisit
replaced	preview	incorrect	dishonest	unaware
unknown	regain	precook	inexpensive	disapprove
disobey	unseen	recall	prearrange	incredible

Sort each spelling word according to it's prefix.

re-
1. replaced
2. regain
3. recall
4. revisit

un-
5. unknown
6. unseen
7. unable
8. unaware

pre-
9. preschool
10. preview
11. precook
12. prearrange

dis-
13. disobey
14. discomfort
15. dishonest
16. disapprove

in-
17. invisible
18. incorrect
19. inexpensive
20. incredible

Page 170

Words with Prefixes

preschool	invisible	discomfort	unable	revisit
replaced	preview	incorrect	dishonest	unaware
unknown	regain	precook	inexpensive	disapprove
disobey	unseen	recall	prearrange	incredible

Complete each sentence below with a spelling word.

1. My dog ran so fast, I was unable to catch up to him.
2. I replaced my blue shirt with a white one.
3. The location of her lost glove is unknown.
4. The three-year-old boy spends each morning at preschool.
5. Do not disobey your parents.
6. The insect was so tiny it was nearly invisible.
7. If we score this goal, we will regain the lead in the game.
8. I don't recall your name, although I met you last night.

Write the spelling word that matches each meaning below.

9. to cook beforehand — precook
10. lack of comfort — discomfort
11. not correct — incorrect
12. to visit again — revisit
13. not seen — unseen
14. to view in advance — preview
15. not honest — dishonest
16. to arrange before — prearrange
17. not expensive — inexpensive
18. not aware — unaware
19. to not approve — disapprove
20. not credible — incredible

Challenge Extension: Write one fill-in sentence for each Challenge Word. Exchange your sentences with a partner and fill in the blank in each sentence.

Rip Van Winkle • SPELLING

Words with Prefixes

Proofreading Activity

There are six spelling mistakes in the paragraph below. Circle the misspelled words. Write the words correctly on the lines below.

Rip Van Winkle didn't mean to (disobay) his wife, but she continued to (disaprove) of his behavior. Dame Van Winkle wanted the wood to be fetched and the roof to be (replaiced). When Rip goes to the mountains to get wood, he hears an (unsceen) person calling his name. He meets Henrik Hudson and his crew and plays a game of ninepins and then falls asleep. When Rip Van Winkle wakes up, he is (unawear) that twenty years have passed. His daughter Judith finds it (increddible) that he has finally returned!

1. _____disobey_____   3. _____replaced_____   5. _____unaware_____

2. ____disapprove____   4. _____unseen_____   6. _____incredible_____

Writing Activity

Make believe that you have fallen asleep for twenty years. Write about what you find when you wake up. Use four spelling words in your writing.

_____

_____

_____

_____

Word with Prefixes

Look at the words in each set below. One word in each set is spelled correctly. Use a pencil to fill in the circle next to the correct word. Before you begin, look at the sample sets of words. Sample A has been done for you. Do Sample B by yourself. When you are sure you know what to do, you may go on with the rest of the page.

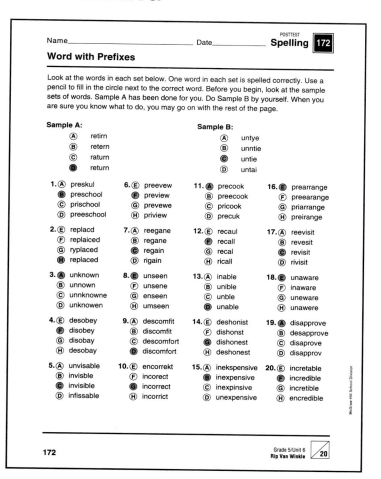

Sample A:
- (A) retirn
- (B) retern
- (C) raturn
- (D) return ●

Sample B:
- (A) untye
- (B) unntie
- (C) untie ●
- (D) untai

1. (A) preskul
   (B) preschool ●
   (C) prischool
   (D) preeschool

2. (E) replacd
   (F) replaiced
   (G) ryplaced
   (H) replaced ●

3. (A) unknown ●
   (B) unnown
   (C) unnknowne
   (D) unknowen

4. (E) desobey
   (F) disobey ●
   (G) disobay
   (H) desobay

5. (A) unvisable
   (B) invisble
   (C) invisible ●
   (D) infissable

6. (E) preevew
   (F) preview ●
   (G) prevewe
   (H) priview

7. (A) reegane
   (B) regane
   (C) regain ●
   (D) rigain

8. (E) unseen ●
   (F) unsene
   (G) ensene
   (H) umseen

9. (A) descomfit
   (B) discomfit
   (C) descomfort
   (D) discomfort ●

10. (E) encorrekt
    (F) incorret
    (G) incorrect ●
    (H) incorrict

11. (A) precook ●
    (B) preecook
    (C) pricook
    (D) precuk

12. (E) recaul
    (F) recall ●
    (G) recal
    (H) ricall

13. (A) inable
    (B) unible
    (C) unble
    (D) unable ●

14. (E) deshonist
    (F) dishonst
    (G) dishonest ●
    (H) deshonest

15. (A) inekspensive
    (B) inexpensive ●
    (C) inexpinsive
    (D) unexpensive

16. (E) prearrange ●
    (F) preearange
    (G) priarrange
    (H) preirange

17. (A) reevisit
    (B) revesit
    (C) revisit ●
    (D) rivisit

18. (E) unaware ●
    (F) inaware
    (G) uneware
    (H) unawere

19. (A) disapprove ●
    (B) desapprove
    (C) disaprove
    (D) disapprov

20. (E) incretable
    (F) incredible ●
    (G) incretible
    (H) encredible

T25

The Sea Maidens of Japan • PRACTICE

Name_____ Date_____ **Practice** 200

Sequence of Events

Events in a story happen in a certain **sequence** or order. By recognizing that sequence you can make better sense of a story.

Read the short story. The story chart below lists the story events out of order. Number each event in the correct sequence.

One sunny day, Tanika and Jamal rode their bikes to the State Fair. When they got to the fairgrounds, they discovered that there was a long line for tickets.

First they locked their bikes. Then they waited in line. While they were waiting they talked about the rides they would take. They had enough money to buy tickets for two rides and popcorn. Jamal really wanted to ride on the ponies. Since it was almost his birthday, they rode the ponies first. Tanika really wanted to go on the Ferris wheel, so that was their second ride.

While they were riding the Ferris wheel, Jamal and Tanika saw dark clouds approaching. As soon as they got off the Ferris wheel, it got windy, and started to rain. They ran for the nearest telephone booth where they called their uncle to come pick them up.

Sequence	Event
3	Tanika and Jamal wait in line to buy tickets.
6	They see dark clouds approaching.
2	Tanika and Jamal lock up their bikes.
5	They go on the Ferris wheel.
4	They ride the ponies.
8	They call their uncle to come pick them up.
1	Tanika and Jamal ride their bikes to the State Fair.
7	The wind and rain start.

8 Book 5/Unit 6
Sea Maidens of Japan

At Home: Have students identify the sequence of events of a book or movie.

200

Name_____ Date_____ **Practice** 201

Vocabulary

Complete each sentence with a vocabulary word.

cove	disgrace	driftwood	flails	host	sizzle

1. For several days after the storm, _____driftwood_____ washed up on the beach.

2. You can hear the pancake batter _____sizzle_____ as you plop it in the hot skillet.

3. The lifeguard knows a swimmer is in trouble if he or she _____flails_____ both arms in the water.

4. My dad will be the _____host_____ of the next neighborhood meeting.

5. The small ship found a safe _____cove_____ in which to anchor during the storm.

6. The team played well, so it was not a _____disgrace_____ that they lost the game.

The following vocabulary words are scrambled. Write each unscrambled word on the line.

7. iflsal _____flails_____

8. scragide _____disgrace_____

9. veco _____cove_____

10. dowordfit _____driftwood_____

201

At Home: Have students use each of the vocabulary words in a sentence.

Book 5/Unit 6
Sea Maidens of Japan 10

A Day at the Beach

My cousin Juan was the *host* of a beach party. He invited me to come. I had never been to that beach before. After we dug a barbecue pit in a sandy cove, we watched burgers and fish sizzle on the grill.

After lunch I searched for small pieces of *driftwood*, I saw my older cousin Tomás swim into the deep water beyond the cove.

"Isn't he swimming out a little too far?" I asked his sister, Marta.

"Don't worry unless he *flails* his arms," she said. "Tomás is a strong swimmer. Besides, he wouldn't do anything careless. He wouldn't want to *disgrace* himself."

1. Who is the *host* at the beach party? Cousin Juan is the host.

2. What other foods do you know that might *sizzle*? steaks, hot dogs, sausages

3. How does *driftwood* get to the beach? Where does it come from? _____
   The ocean washes it ashore.

4. What is one word that means "a small, sheltered bay"? cove

5. Why should they only be worried if Tomás *flails* his arms? Why would that be a *disgrace* for Tomás? If he flails his arms in the deep water that would mean he is in trouble. That would be a disgrace for Tomás because he is such a strong swimmer.

5 Book 5/Unit 6
Sea Maidens of Japan

At Home: Have students make a collage using pictures or symbols to represent the vocabulary words as used in this story.

201a

Name_____ Date_____ **Practice** 202

Story Comprehension

Answer the questions about "Sea Maidens of Japan." You may want to look back at the story for help. Answers will vary. Sample responses shown.

1. Whose voice is the narrator of "Sea Maidens of Japan"? Kiyomi, a little girl

2. Who is Okaasan? What does she do for a living? Okaasan is Kiyomi's mother; she is a fisherwoman, or ama, who holds her breath to dive for seafood.

3. What is Okaasan trying to teach Kiyomi? Why does Okaasan tie a rope around Kiyomi's waist? She is trying to teach Kiyomi to dive and fish along the coral reefs. She uses the rope for safety, in case she has to pull Kiyomi up to the surface quickly.

4. What do Kiyomi's two older sisters do for work? Did they choose to follow the *ama* tradition, too? No; they chose the modern life and work in a fish cannery in the city.

5. What does Kiyomi do while waiting alone on the shore as her mother dives for seafood? She pretends to host tea ceremonies (tea parties) for mermaids; she chases schools of fish from her treasure chest.

6. What does Okaasan take Kiyomi to see in the middle of one night? _____ sea turtles laying their eggs.

7. What happens when Kiyomi has to make her first deep water dive with the *ama*? She is too scared to dive into the water. She is afraid she will disgrace her mother.

8. What is so special about the sea turtle that swims with Kiyomi when she finally makes a deep water dive with the *ama*? It has the same star on the back of its shell as the baby turtle she had helped rescue.

202

At Home: Let students act out a scene from "Sea Maidens of Japan."

Book 5/Unit 6
Sea Maidens of Japan 8

The Sea Maidens of Japan • PRACTICE

Choose Reference Sources

When you want information, you can choose from a number of different **reference resources**: almanac, atlas, dictionary, encyclopedia, and thesaurus.

> An **almanac** is a book of up-to-date facts about important people, places, and events. It is published each year.
>
> An **atlas** is a book of maps. It gives information about different places in the world.
>
> A **dictionary** tells you the definition and pronunciation of words. It lists the words in alphabetical order.
>
> An **encyclopedia** is a set of books containing articles about important people, places, things, events and ideas.
>
> A **thesaurus** is a book of synonyms—words with the same, or almost the same, meaning. Sometimes it also lists antonyms—words with opposite meanings.

1. In which reference book would you look to find out how to pronounce the word _tread_? in a dictionary

2. Where would you look to find out about the feeding habits of sea turtles?
   in an encyclopedia

3. Where would you look to find synonyms for the word _pry_? in a thesaurus

4. In which book would you be able to find maps of all the world's oceans?
   in an atlas or an encyclopedia; also, some dictionaries have maps

5. Where might you look to find out the birthday of your favorite musician?
   an almanac, possibly an encyclopedia

Sequence of Events

Events in a story happen in a certain **sequence** or order. Below is a story chart listing events from "Sea Maidens of Japan." Number each event in the order in which it happened in the story.

Sequence	Event
10	Kiyomi smiles as a wave sweeps the grown sea turtle back to deeper waters.
1	Okaasan starts teaching Kiyomi to dive and fish along the coral reef.
4	Kiyomi cannot make herself jump from the boat on her first deep water dive with the _ama_.
8	Kiyomi finishes her first successful deep water dive with the _ama_.
2	Okaasan takes Kiyomi out at night to watch the sea turtles lay their eggs.
5	Kiyomi puts white cream on her face to protect it from the cold, salty water.
9	Kiyomi eats shellfish on an island beach with the other _ama_.
3	Kiyomi guides the confused baby sea turtle to the water.
7	Kiyomi recognizes the star on the grown sea turtle's back.
6	Kiyomi is afraid to jump into the deep water.

Cause and Effect

A **cause** is the reason why something happens. An **effect** is the result, or what happens. Many story events are connected through cause-and-effect relations.

What might happen as a result of each story event below? Write down the most likely effect of each cause. Answers will vary. Accept all well-reasoned responses. Possible answers are shown.

1. Sea turtles planted their eggs in the sand where the sun would keep the eggs warm. Volunteers then guarded the beach where the eggs were laid. They made sure no harm could come to the eggs.
   Effect: Sea turtles will hatch from the eggs.

2. Andrea would become forgetful after she played too many computer games. One night she decided to make a cake after she finished playing her favorite game. When she put the cake in the oven to bake, she forgot to set the timer.
   Effect: Andrea is going to forget about the cake baking in the oven; it's going to burn.

3. Julio has to quickly get to the school bus stop or he will miss the bus. On his way, he decides to stop at the newsstand for a quick look at one of his favorite magazines. He reads an entire article before he leaves.
   Effect: Julio is going to miss the school bus.

4. Jim is getting ready to run in a big race. Naturally, he is a little nervous. He even forgot to tie a double knot in his laces, the way his coach told him to. In the middle of the race, Jim suddenly feels the laces on one of his sneakers come free.
   Effect: Jim might trip over his sneaker laces if he doesn't stop to tie his shoes.

5. It is the day before the last big spelling test of the year. Amanda decides that she would much rather fly her new kite than study for a test.
   Effect: Amanda is going to do poorly on the last big spelling test.

Context Clues

Context clues are words or sentences in a story that help you define unfamiliar words.

Read each passage below. Use context clues to help define the underlined word. Circle the letter of the correct meaning.

1. Many people eat abalone. Abalone live in shells. Some people call them shellfish, but <u>abalone</u> aren't any type fish.
   An _abalone_ must be similar to a ___b___
   a. small plant   **b.** snail   c. sea shell

2. After high school, Sonny found a job at the local <u>cannery</u>. He ran one of the big noisy machines that fill cans with all sorts of food.
   A _cannery_ must be like a ___a___
   a. factory   b. can of food   c. big loud, machine

3. My great-grandparents used to harvest seaweed along the shore. They used the plant for soup. Nowadays, <u>kelp</u> is used to make all sorts of things.
   Kelp must be a kind of ___c___
   a. shell   b. fish   **c.** seaweed

4. We had to use a <u>crowbar</u> to pry open the heavy metal door.
   To _pry_ something is to ___b___
   a. hammer it into place   **b.** use force to open it   c. make a good try

5. Even though the rest of the class tried to muffle their laughter by putting their hands over their mouths, Suki could hear them laughing.
   When people _muffle_ their laughter they are trying to ___c___
   a. make it sound louder   b. make it sound silly   **c.** hide the sound of it

The Sea Maidens of Japan • RETEACH

Sequence of Events

> Determining the **sequence of events,** or the order in which events happen, will help you understand stories. Clue words such as *before, first, then, after, next, last,* and *finally* can help you understand the order in which events happen in a story.

Read the story. Underline the clue words that help you understand the sequence of events. Below the story are a number of the stories' events listed out of order. Number the listed events in the correct sequence in which they happen.

When Kenzo awoke in the morning, he <u>first</u> put on several layers of clothing. <u>Before</u> Kenzo left the house he had a bowl of sticky rice for breakfast. When he finished eating, he grabbed his mailbag. <u>Then</u> he started biking on his mail route. He stopped to drop off a letter at Mrs. Murasaki's house and <u>then</u> climbed the mountain road where he made his next stop to deliver a box to the Uchido family. <u>After</u> biking farther up the road, Kenzo made his <u>last</u> stop of the morning at Tamiko's. <u>Finally,</u> he returned home.

- 4 Kenzo delivered a box to the Uchido family.
- 3 Kenzo started biking along his mail route.
- 6 Kenzo returned home.
- 2 Kenzo had sticky rice for breakfast.
- 1 Kenzo dressed in several layers of clothing.
- 5 Kenzo stopped at Tamiko's.

6 Book 5/Unit 6
Sea Maidens of Japan

At Home: Have students think about what they did yesterday. Have them put those events in sequence.

200

Vocabulary

Choose the word that fits the clue. Then fill in the crossword puzzle.

disgrace	flails	host	sizzle	cove	driftwood

Across
3. shame, embarrass
5. flops about
6. person who invites you to a party

Down
1. bubble while cooking
2. wood brought on shore by the ocean
4. protected area along the seashore

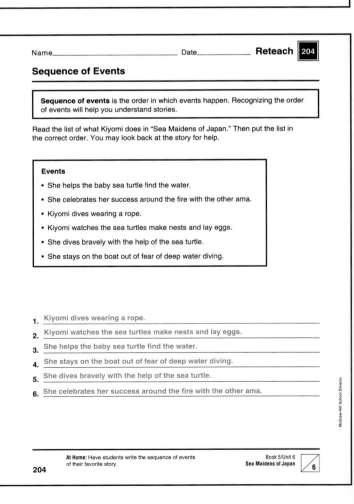

6

Story Comprehension

Write the answer to each question about "Sea Maidens of Japan."

1. What does Kiyomi want to learn from her mother? <u>She wants to learn how to become an ama, a fisherwoman who dives for seafood.</u>

2. What problem faces Kiyomi and her mother? <u>Kiyomi is afraid of swimming in the deep water.</u>

3. How does Kiyomi feel about the work she does with her mother? <u>She wants to succeed. She is afraid of disgracing the family.</u>

4. How does the sea turtle help Kiyomi on her first dive? <u>She sees the grown sea turtle as a friend. It gives her a ride up from the sea floor for air and makes her feel less alone.</u>

At Home: Have students think of something they could say to Kiyomi to calm her fears.

201–202

Book 5/Unit 6
Sea Maidens of Japan 4

Choose Reference Sources

> Choosing the correct **reference source** will help you find information. Think about exactly what it is you want to know. Then review the different types of reference sources to choose the best one for your goals.

Almanac:	Atlas:	Encyclopedia:	Thesaurus:
• gives information about important people, places, and events • published yearly so that facts and figures are up-to-date	• has different types of maps and related information about places around the world	• has articles about people, places, topics, events, ideas organized in volumes • articles are arranged in alphabetical order by subject or name • uses key words to name a topic and guide your search	• has a list of synonyms, or words with almost the same meaning • each entry word is followed by synonyms • some entries also show antonyms, or words with opposite meanings

Use the information about different reference sources to answer the questions. Circle the answer to each question.

1. In which reference source would you look for information about protecting sea turtle nests?
   a. dictionary   (b.) encyclopedia   c. thesaurus
2. In which reference source would you find a synonym for danger?
   (a.) thesaurus   b. atlas   c. almanac
3. In which book would you find information about how many sea turtles were hatched in 1997?
   a. atlas   b. thesaurus   (c.) almanac
4. Where would you look to find a synonym for the word *endangered*?
   (a.) thesaurus   b. atlas   c. encyclopedia
5. In which reference source could you find maps of Central and South America, where sea turtles live?
   (a.) atlas   b. thesaurus   c. almanac

5 Book 5/Unit 6
Sea Maidens of Japan

At Home: Have students tell you which reference source has the population of Japan.

203

Sequence of Events

> **Sequence of events** is the order in which events happen. Recognizing the order of events will help you understand stories.

Read the list of what Kiyomi does in "Sea Maidens of Japan." Then put the list in the correct order. You may look back at the story for help.

> **Events**
> • She helps the baby sea turtle find the water.
> • She celebrates her success around the fire with the other ama.
> • Kiyomi dives wearing a rope.
> • Kiyomi watches the sea turtles make nests and lay eggs.
> • She dives bravely with the help of the sea turtle.
> • She stays on the boat out of fear of deep water diving.

1. Kiyomi dives wearing a rope.
2. Kiyomi watches the sea turtles make nests and lay eggs.
3. She helps the baby sea turtle find the water.
4. She stays on the boat out of fear of deep water diving.
5. She dives bravely with the help of the sea turtle.
6. She celebrates her success around the fire with the other ama.

At Home: Have students write the sequence of events of their favorite story.

204

Book 5/Unit 6
Sea Maidens of Japan 6

The Sea Maidens of Japan • RETEACH

Cause and Effect

Causes are the reasons why something happened. **Effects** are what happens as a result of the causes. Sometimes there is more than one cause or effect.

Read the stories. Decide whether the underlined words describe a cause or an effect. Circle the letter of the correct answer.

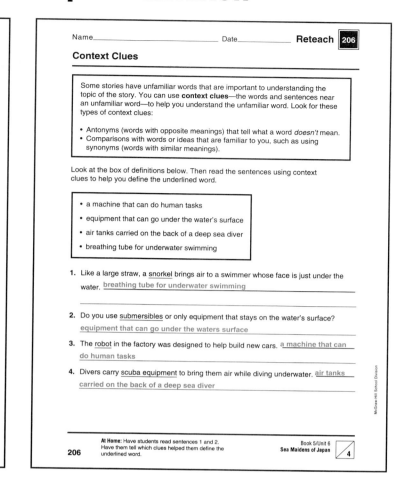

1. Since Linda was late getting to the doctor's office, the doctor took another patient in her place. Linda didn't see the doctor until an hour later than her original appointment. As a result, she didn't get to soccer practice until 6:00 P.M.

   a. cause   **b.** effect

2. Hayes went to Japan with a student group. The group leader lost all the airplane tickets. As a result, the group missed its flight home. Hayes had to wait three days to get on another flight. Hayes didn't get to his sister Julie's birthday party.

   a. cause   **b.** effect

3. Dinah wasn't allowed to swim in deep water because she had hurt her ears as a young child. At the pool each summer, she had to stay in the shallow end. Since Dinah felt left out, she usually stayed away from the pool.

   a. cause   **b.** effect

4. Many animals are in danger of extinction or dying out. One reason is that people have destroyed the natural places where these animals live.

   a. cause   **b.** effect

Book 5/Unit 6
Sea Maidens of Japan
4

At Home: Have students write one cause in "Sea Maidens of Japan" and two effects.

205

Context Clues

Some stories have unfamiliar words that are important to understanding the topic of the story. You can use **context clues**—the words and sentences near an unfamiliar word—to help you understand the unfamiliar word. Look for these types of context clues:

• Antonyms (words with opposite meanings) that tell what a word *doesn't* mean.
• Comparisons with words or ideas that are familiar to you, such as using synonyms (words with similar meanings).

Look at the box of definitions below. Then read the sentences using context clues to help you define the underlined word.

• a machine that can do human tasks
• equipment that can go under the water's surface
• air tanks carried on the back of a deep sea diver
• breathing tube for underwater swimming

1. Like a large straw, a snorkel brings air to a swimmer whose face is just under the water. breathing tube for underwater swimming

2. Do you use submersibles or only equipment that stays on the water's surface? equipment that can go under the waters surface

3. The robot in the factory was designed to help build new cars. a machine that can do human tasks

4. Divers carry scuba equipment to bring them air while diving underwater. air tanks carried on the back of a deep sea diver

At Home: Have students read sentences 1 and 2. Have them tell which clues helped them define the underlined word.

206

Book 5/Unit 6
Sea Maidens of Japan
4

T29

The Sea Maidens of Japan • EXTEND

Sequence of Events

Writers often tell about the events in a story in a certain order. This is called **sequence of events**. Words such as *first, next, finally, after, later, during,* and *while* often signal a transition from one event to another and can help you figure out the sequence of a story.

Read each of the events below. Put them in the correct sequence. Underline any signal words that help you keep the events in order.

__6__ At the check-out counter, Jan discovered she had no money.

__1__ Jan decided to make a pie for her dinner guests.

__4__ While she was shopping for the ingredients, Jan decided to get some ice cream to go with the pie.

__8__ When Jan arrived home, she was finally ready to bake the pie.

__2__ First, she chose a recipe that was her grandmother's.

__5__ Jan decided on vanilla and chocolate.

__3__ Next, Jan made a list of ingredients she would need.

__7__ The store had a cash machine, so Jan used her cash card to pay for the groceries.

Think of your favorite story. What do you remember about the sequence of the story? Write a sequence of the main events of the story from beginning to end.

Answers will vary.

_____

_____

_____

_____

_____

_____

_____

_____

_____

At Home: Cut out a cartoon strip in a newspaper. Cut apart the separate squares of the cartoon. Have a friend put the cartoon in the correct sequence.

Vocabulary

cove	disgrace	driftwood	flails	host	sizzle

Crossword puzzles are popular games that help you remember words. Below make up a crossword puzzle using the vocabulary words above and some words of your own choice. Give the puzzle to a friend to solve.

Puzzles will vary, but should include all six vocab words.

Story Comprehension

Signal, or clue words often help tell the sequence of events. Look through the story, "Sea Maidens of Japan" and find sentences with clue words that show the passage of time, or that indicate sequence. Write them in the correct order.

Answers should include sentences that indicate the passage of time.

_____

_____

_____

_____

_____

_____

_____

_____

At Home: Newspaper articles often tell news events in sequence. Find a news article and write down the main events in the correct sequence.

Choose Reference Sources

Think about the last time you needed to gather information for a report. What topic did you research? What kind of **reference sources** did you use? Knowing how to choose the proper reference materials can help you write better reports.

Read each question below the box. Then write down a reference source from the box as to where the answers can be found.

almanac	atlas	dictionary	encyclopedia	thesaurus

1. What are the meanings of the words *abalone, canneries,* and *maidens?* _____
dictionary

2. What are some synonyms for the words in question 1? thesaurus or dictionary

3. How large is a full-grown sea turtle? encyclopedia

4. What are the five longest rivers in Japan? almanac, encyclopedia, or atlas

5. What oceans surround the country of Japan? atlas, encyclopedia

Work with a partner. Choose one of the activities below. Write which of the reference materials listed above you would use to complete the activity. Then research and complete the activity. You may use a separate piece of paper.

• Draw a map of Japan. atlas

• Find out about the fishing products of Japan in 1999. almanac

• Find out about the pearl industry in Japan. encyclopedia

• Write a descriptive paragraph about what the Sea Maidens of Japan might see as they dive. dictionary, thesaurus, and encyclopedia

At Home: Make a list of the reference materials you have in your home. Remember, many references are available through the Internet.

Sequence of Events

Below are events from "Sea Maidens of Japan" that are listed out of order. Figure out the correct **sequence of events**. Then write the correct order of each event on the lines.

__2__ Kiyomi waits on the beach while her mother dives.

__12__ All day Kiyomi dives for abalone, then she sits with the sea maidens of Japan.

__4__ As Kiyomi watches, the sea turtles come out of the ocean and lay their eggs on the beach.

__7__ One baby turtle runs in the wrong direction, and Kiyomi guides it gently back to the sea.

__9__ Kiyomi is afraid to jump off the boat.

__1__ Kiyomi's mother tells her she will someday become an *ama,* a sea maiden of Japan.

__5__ Every day Kiyomi visits the nests of the sea turtles.

__3__ Okaasan wakes Kiyomi in the middle of the night to take her to the sea turtles.

__8__ After several fishing seasons pass, it is time for Kiyomi to make her first dive.

__10__ Kiyomi finally dives into the ocean.

__6__ After two full moons pass, the sea turtles hatch from their nests.

__11__ Kiyomi sees the star turtle, and it guides her back to the top of the water for air.

At Home: Write instructions on how to do something in the proper sequence such as making a sandwich or cooking spaghetti.

The Sea Maidens of Japan • EXTEND

Cause and Effect

You know that a **cause** is the reason why something happens. The **effect** is the result. Understanding cause and effect relationships helps you understand what you read.

At the end of the "Sea Maidens of Japan," Kiyomi sits for the first time among the *ama*, the sea maidens. This is an effect of her bravery in diving in the waters all day. Write a story that takes place after she sits with the *ama* on the dock. Include some examples of cause and effect in your story.

Answers will vary, but should include interesting details based on what students

have learned from the story and should also include clear cause-and-effect

relations.

_____

_____

_____

_____

_____

_____

_____

_____

_____

_____

_____

_____

_____

_____

_____

_____

_____

Book 5/Unit 6
Sea Maidens of Japan

At Home: Give examples of other cause-and-effect relationships in the story.

205

Context Clues

Read the paragraph. Write the meanings of the underlined words, using only the **context clues** from the paragraph to help you write your definitions.

There are seven species of sea turtles. They are similar in that the females lay their eggs on the beach, then return to the ocean. Most sea turtles are found in tropical and subtropical seas. An exception is the Atlantic ridley turtle, which is restricted to the Gulf of Mexico. Over thousands of years, sea turtles have evolved a streamlined carapace, or shell. They have adapted to their aquatic environments by developing special glands that remove salt from their bodies. Some sea turtles are endangered by being over-hunted by humans for their tortoise shells, hide, and oil. One sea turtle, the Indo-Pacific ridley, has been exploited for its leather and oil in such areas as the Pacific coast of Mexico.

Answers will vary, but should include an appropriate definition.

1. **species** class, breed, kind, category of animals

2. **restricted** confined to a certain area

3. **evolved** change over time

4. **carapace** the shell of a sea turtle

5. **adapting** become better suited to an environment

6. **aquatic** water, marine

7. **endangered** at risk, in danger

8. **exploited** used, taken advantage of

At Home: Choose three of the above words and use them in a sentence that shows their meaning.

206

Book 5/Unit 6
Sea Maidens of Japan

Panel 1 (Page 173)

Name _____ Date _____
LEARN
Grammar 173

Negatives

- A negative is a word that means "no," such as *not, never, nobody, nowhere,* and contractions with *n't.*
- Do not use two negatives in the same sentence.
- You can fix a sentence with two negatives by removing one.

Correct the sentences by removing one of the negatives.

1. Fresh water doesn't have no salt.
   Fresh water doesn't have salt.

2. Kiyomi's mother doesn't seem to have no fear.
   Kiyomi's mother doesn't seem to have fear.

3. Kiyomi won't use no rope.
   Kiyomi won't use rope.

4. The older girls didn't choose no diving.
   The older girls didn't choose diving.

5. The waves didn't make no trouble.
   The waves didn't make trouble.

6. Soon, working underwater won't cause no problems.
   Soon, working underwater won't cause problems.

7. Some turtle eggs don't have no chance.
   Some turtle eggs have no chance.

8. The other turtles don't have no stars.
   The other turtles don't have stars.

9. Kiyomi won't keep no turtles.
   Kiyomi won't keep turtles.

10. We can't see no clouds, today.
    We can't see clouds today.

10
Grade 5/Unit 6
Sea Maidens of Japan
Extension: Ask partners to write sentences about beaches, using two negatives in each sentence. Then ask them to correct each other's sentences by removing one negative.
173

Panel 2 (Page 174)

Name _____ Date _____
LEARN AND PRACTICE
Grammar 174

Negatives

- You can correct a sentence with two negatives by changing one negative to a positive word.

Negative	Positive
no	any
never	ever
nothing	anything
nobody	anybody
no one	anyone
nowhere	anywhere

Rewrite the sentences. Look for sentences with two negatives. Use a positive word in place of one of the negatives.

1. We never have no sea turtles where we live.
   We never have any sea turtles where we live.

2. Fish don't have lungs nowhere.
   Fish don't have lungs anywhere.

3. Flounders don't have no eyes on one side.
   Flounders don't have any eyes on one side.

4. The baby turtles didn't never hesitate.
   The baby turtles didn't ever hesitate.

5. Sharks won't eat none of these turtles.
   Sharks won't eat any of these turtles.

6. We didn't see whales nowhere.
   We didn't see whales anywhere.

7. The girl has never found no pearls.
   The girl has never found any pearls.

8. Kiyomi didn't have no problems diving.
   Kiyomi didn't have any probems diving.

174
Extension: Ask students to proofread recent writing assignments, looking for double negatives.
Grade 5/Unit 6
Sea Maidens of Japan
8

Panel 3 (Page 175)

Name _____ Date _____
PRACTICE AND REVIEW
Grammar 175

Negatives

- A negative is a word that means "no," such as *not, never, nobody, nowhere,* and contractions with *n't.*
- Do not use two negatives in the same sentence.
- You can fix a sentence with two negatives by removing one.
- You can correct a sentence with two negatives by changing one negative to a positive word.

Read each group of sentences. Cross out the sentence that is incorrect.

1. The sea is never calm in this bay.
   The sea is not ever calm in this bay.
   ~~The sea is not never calm in this bay.~~

2. ~~The girl never dove for abalone with nobody.~~
   The girl never dove for abalone with anybody.
   The girl dove for abalone with nobody.

3. ~~There weren't never so many turtles before.~~
   There were never so many turtles here before.
   There weren't ever so many turtles before.

4. I don't see any good places to dive today.
   ~~I don't see no good places to dive today.~~
   I see no good places to dive today.

Read the sentences. Rewrite each one two different ways.

5. The sun don't never shine in these caves.
   The sun doesn't ever shine in these caves.
   The sun never shines in these caves.

6. There aren't no octopuses or abalone in the bay.
   There aren't any octopuses or abalone in the bay.
   There are no octopuses or abalone in the bay.

7. We didn't catch nothing today.
   We caught nothing today.
   We didn't catch anything today.

8. The turtles aren't nowhere near here today.
   The turtles aren't anywhere near here today.
   The turtles are nowhere near here today.

8
Grade 5/Unit 6
Sea Maidens of Japan
Extension: Ask partners to write dialogues about what doesn't happen on a beach. Ask them to write at least four negative sentences, using negatives correctly.
175

Panel 4 (Page 176)

Name _____ Date _____
MECHANICS
Grammar 176

Contractions and Apostrophes

- A contraction is a shortened form of two words.
- A contraction may be formed by combining a verb with the word *not.*
- An apostrophe (') shows where one or more letters have been left out.

isn't	is not	doesn't	does not
aren't	are not	didn't	did not
wasn't	was not	couldn't	could not
can't	cannot	wouldn't	would not
don't	do not	shouldn't	should not

Rewrite each sentence correctly. Use a contraction for every underlined pair of words. Correct any double negatives.

1. I <u>do not</u> travel to Japan no more.
   I don't travel to Japan anymore.

2. There <u>are not</u> no turtle nests under those trees.
   There aren't any turtle nests under those trees.

3. Sea turtles <u>were not</u> protected until recently.
   Sea turtles weren't protected until recently.

4. You <u>should not</u> bother no turtles on the beach.
   You shouldn't bother any turtles on the beach.

5. We <u>could not</u> never swim the length of this bay.
   We couldn't ever swim the length of this bay.

6. The ama <u>is not</u> coming up for air yet.
   The ama isn't coming up for air yet.

7. <u>Does not</u> no one want to practice diving?
   Doesn't anyone want to practice diving?

8. My ancestors <u>did not</u> come from nowhere near Tokyo.
   My ancestors didn't come from anywhere near Tokyo.

176
Extension: Ask students to write a poem about the sea turtle. Ask students to use three of the above contractions in their poems. Invite students to read their poems aloud for the class.
Grade 5/Unit 6
Sea Maidens of Japan
8

The Sea Maidens of Japan • GRAMMAR

Negatives and Contractions

A. If the sentence is correct, write correct on the line. If it is not correct, rewrite it correctly. Answers may vary.

1. Please don't bother no wild sea creatures.

   Please don't bother any wild sea creatures.

2. The sea isn't never so stormy as it was yesterday.

   The sea isn't ever so stormy as it was yesterday.

3. The job of an ama is not easy.

   correct

4. The ama must not do nothing but look for abalone.

   The ama must do nothing but look for abalone.

5. My sister isn't going to work as no ama no more.

   My sister isn't going to work as an ama anymore.

B. Write contractions for the following pairs of words.

6. can not   can't

7. does not   doesn't

8. should not   shouldn't

9. are not   aren't

10. could not   couldn't

11. would not   wouldn't

12. did not   didn't

Contractions

- A contraction is a shortened form of two words.
- A contraction can be made by combining a verb with the word not.
- An apostrophe (') shows where one or more letters have been left out.

can't	cannot
don't	do not
doesn't	does not
didn't	did not
couldn't	could not
wouldn't	would not
shouldn't	should not

Look at the picture. Rewrite the paragraph on the lines below. Use contractions where possible and fix any double negatives.

The sea turtle is not a small turtle. It has a hard shell and tough flippers. The female does not stay long on land after she lays eggs. When the babies hatch, they do not hesitate at all. They know they should not stay nowhere on land. They would not want to be eaten by dogs or birds.

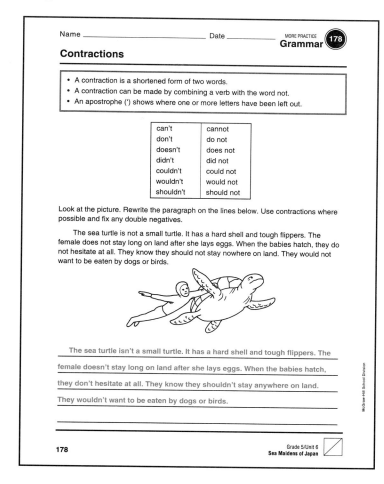

The sea turtle isn't a small turtle. It has a hard shell and tough flippers. The

female doesn't stay long on land after she lays eggs. When the babies hatch,

they don't hesitate at all. They know they shouldn't stay anywhere on land.

They wouldn't want to be eaten by dogs or birds.

The Sea Maidens of Japan • SPELLING

Words with Suffixes

Pretest Directions

Fold back the paper along the dotted line. Use the blanks to write each word as it is read aloud. When you finish the test, unfold the paper. Use the list at the right to correct any spelling mistakes. Practice the words you missed for the Posttest.

To Parents

Here are the results of your child's weekly spelling Pretest. You can help your child study for the Posttest by following these simple steps for each word on the word list:

1. Read the word to your child.
2. Have your child write the word, saying each letter as it is written.
3. Say each letter of the word as your child checks the spelling.
4. If a mistake has been made, have your child read each letter of the correctly spelled word aloud, and then repeat steps 1–3.

1. _____
2. _____
3. _____
4. _____
5. _____
6. _____
7. _____
8. _____
9. _____
10. _____
11. _____
12. _____
13. _____
14. _____
15. _____
16. _____
17. _____
18. _____
19. _____
20. _____

1. remarkable
2. peaceful
3. countless
4. foolishness
5. excitement
6. reasonable
7. graceful
8. painless
9. weakness
10. amusement
11. respectable
12. harmful
13. meaningless
14. softness
15. treatment
16. honorable
17. flavorful
18. defenseless
19. nervousness
20. announcement

Challenge Words

_____ disgrace
_____ driftwood
_____ flails
_____ host
_____ sizzle

Words with Suffixes

Using the Word Study Steps

1. LOOK at the word
2. SAY the word aloud.
3. STUDY the letters in the word.
4. WRITE the word.
5. CHECK the word.
   Did you spell the word right? If not, go back to step 1.

Spelling Tip
Learn how to spell suffixes you use often in writing.
-able   -ness

Word Scramble

Unscramble each set of letters to make a spelling word.

1. kremearlab — remarkable
2. slocenuts — countless
3. flurham — harmful
4. lamissengen — meaningless
5. swaknees — weakness
6. glafrecu — graceful
7. tetarntem — treatment
8. frouvlafl — flavorful
9. smeentaum — amusement
10. ossrenevsnur — nervousness
11. flaupece — peaceful
12. slipanes — painless
13. snooflseshi — foolishness
14. eunnanotcmen — announcement
15. horobalen — honorable
16. mextenteci — excitement
17. plebearsect — respectable
18. bronealase — reasonable
19. fonstess — softness
20. slefdensees — defenseless

To Parents or Helpers:

Using the Word Study Steps above as your child comes across any new words will help him or her spell words effectively. Review the steps as you both go over this week's spelling words.
Go over the Spelling Tip with your child. Help him or her learn to spell other suffixes.
Help your child complete the spelling activity.

Words with Suffixes

remarkable	excitement	weakness	meaningless	flavorful
peaceful	reasonable	amusement	softness	defenseless
countless	graceful	respectable	treatment	nervousness
foolishness	painless	harmful	honorable	announcement

Sort each spelling word by finding its suffix below.

-less
1. countless
2. painless
3. meaningless
4. defenseless

-ness
5. foolishness
6. weakness
7. softness
8. nervousness

-able
9. remarkable
10. reasonable
11. respectable
12. honorable

-ful
13. peaceful
14. graceful
15. harmful
16. flavorful

-ment
17. excitement
18. amusement
19. treatment
20. announcement

Words with Suffixes

remarkable	excitement	weakness	meaningless	flavorful
peaceful	reasonable	amusement	softness	defenseless
countless	graceful	respectable	treatment	nervousness
foolishness	painless	harmful	honorable	announcement

Complete each sentence below with a spelling word.

1. The president's visit caused __excitement__ among the townspeople.
2. The soldier received an __honorable__ discharge.
3. The captain will make an important __announcement__ tonight.
4. Her determination to win the medal was __remarkable__
5. The car accident caused a __weakness__ in her leg.
6. I felt quiet and __peaceful__ sitting alone by the lake.
7. The poor mouse was __defenseless__ against the hungry owl.
8. Overeating is __harmful__ to your health.

Word Meanings: Suffixes

Write the spelling word for each meaning given below.

9. the state of being foolish — foolishness
10. something that amuses — amusement
11. full of flavor — flavorful
12. the state of being nervous — nervousness
13. without pain — painless
14. the act of treating — treatment
15. without meaning — meaningless
16. full of grace — graceful
17. worthy of respect — respectable
18. the state of being soft — softness
19. too many to be counted — countless
20. showing reason — reasonable

The Sea Maidens of Japan • SPELLING

Words with Suffixes

Name_____ Date_____ PROOFREAD AND WRITE **Spelling** 177

Words with Suffixes

Proofreading Activity

There are six spelling mistakes in the letter below. Circle the misspelled words. Write the words correctly on the lines below.

Dear Sister,

As I write this to you, I am filled with (excitment) Mother took me to see the turtles hatch. It was night, and the beach was very (peacefull) Then a (remarkible) thing happened. The (countliss) turtle babies hatched! Hundreds of tiny, (defenceless) turtles crawled awkwardly across the sand. Once they started to swim in the ocean, they were very (grayceful) I made friends with one turtle. I hope to see her again next year.

See you soon,

Kiyomi

1. ___excitement___   3. ___remarkable___   5. ___defenseless___

2. ___peaceful___   4. ___countless___   6. ___graceful___

Writing Activity

Have you ever had to overcome your fear of something? Write a brief paragraph about your experience, using four spelling words.

_____

_____

_____

_____

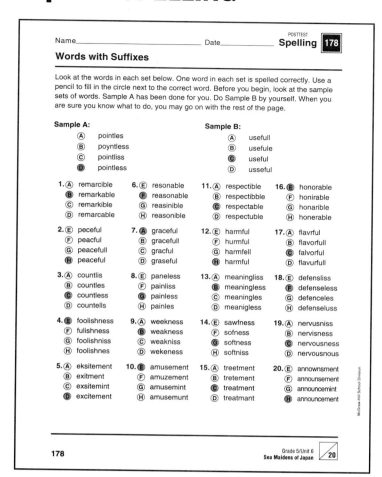

Name_____ Date_____ POSTTEST **Spelling** 178

Words with Suffixes

Look at the words in each set below. One word in each set is spelled correctly. Use a pencil to fill in the circle next to the correct word. Before you begin, look at the sample sets of words. Sample A has been done for you. Do Sample B by yourself. When you are sure you know what to do, you may go on with the rest of the page.

Sample A:
- Ⓐ pointles
- Ⓑ poyntless
- Ⓒ pointliss
- Ⓓ pointless

Sample B:
- Ⓐ usefull
- Ⓑ usefule
- Ⓒ useful
- Ⓓ usseful

1.
- Ⓐ remarcible
- Ⓑ remarkable
- Ⓒ remarkible
- Ⓓ remarcable

2.
- Ⓔ peceful
- Ⓕ peacful
- Ⓖ peacefull
- Ⓗ peaceful

3.
- Ⓐ countlis
- Ⓑ countles
- Ⓒ countless
- Ⓓ countells

4.
- Ⓔ foolishness
- Ⓕ fulishness
- Ⓖ foolishniss
- Ⓗ foolishnes

5.
- Ⓐ eksitement
- Ⓑ exitment
- Ⓒ exsitemint
- Ⓓ excitement

6.
- Ⓔ resonable
- Ⓕ reasonable
- Ⓖ reasinible
- Ⓗ reasonible

7.
- Ⓐ graceful
- Ⓑ gracefull
- Ⓒ gracful
- Ⓓ graseful

8.
- Ⓔ paneless
- Ⓕ painliss
- Ⓖ painless
- Ⓗ painles

9.
- Ⓐ weekness
- Ⓑ weakness
- Ⓒ weakniss
- Ⓓ wekeness

10.
- Ⓔ amusement
- Ⓕ amuzement
- Ⓖ amusemint
- Ⓗ amusemunt

11.
- Ⓐ respectible
- Ⓑ respectibble
- Ⓒ respectable
- Ⓓ respectuble

12.
- Ⓔ harmful
- Ⓕ hurmful
- Ⓖ harmfell
- Ⓗ harmful

13.
- Ⓐ meaningliss
- Ⓑ meaningless
- Ⓒ meaningles
- Ⓓ meanigless

14.
- Ⓔ sawfness
- Ⓕ sofness
- Ⓖ softness
- Ⓗ softniss

15.
- Ⓐ treetment
- Ⓑ tretement
- Ⓒ treatment
- Ⓓ treatmant

16.
- Ⓔ honorable
- Ⓕ honirable
- Ⓖ honarible
- Ⓗ honerable

17.
- Ⓐ flavrful
- Ⓑ flavorfull
- Ⓒ falvorful
- Ⓓ flavurfull

18.
- Ⓔ defensliss
- Ⓕ defenseless
- Ⓖ defenceles
- Ⓗ defenseluss

19.
- Ⓐ nervusniss
- Ⓑ nervisness
- Ⓒ nervousness
- Ⓓ nervousnous

20.
- Ⓔ annownsment
- Ⓕ announsement
- Ⓖ announcemint
- Ⓗ announcement

Practice 207

Name_____ Date_____

Judgments & Decisions

Before you make a **decision**, you consider the reasons for and against the decision. Read each situation below. List two reasons for or against each choice, and then make a **judgment** about what you should do. Write your final decision. Answers will vary. Possible answers are shown.

Suppose the following: You have a small collection of favorite books. One of your friends asks to borrow a book from your collection. When you notice your friend is holding a tattered magazine, you remember that last year this same friend borrowed a book, and it came back battered and worn. Although your friend apologized and even offered to replace the book, you said not to bother. Your friend has lent you his things in the past. Do you think you should lend this same friend a book this time?

Two reasons for lending your friend another book:

1. My friend has lent me things, so I will lend the book.

2. It's good to give friends second chances.

Two reasons against lending your friend another book:

3. The book my friend wants to borrow is one of my favorites.

4. My friend does not take good care of his things. The book might be ruined.

Final decision:

5. I lend my friend the book but explain that it is important to take care of the book.

_____

_____

5 Book 5/Unit 6
The Silent Lobby

At Home: Encourage students to discuss how they made their final decisions.

207

Practice 208

Name_____ Date_____

Vocabulary

Complete each sentence with the correct vocabulary word.

| interpret | pelted | persuade | register | shabby | soothing |

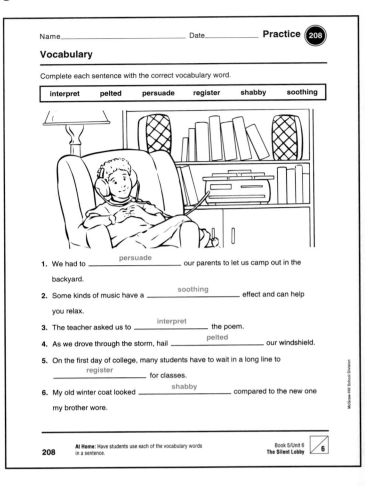

1. We had to _____persuade_____ our parents to let us camp out in the backyard.

2. Some kinds of music have a _____soothing_____ effect and can help you relax.

3. The teacher asked us to _____interpret_____ the poem.

4. As we drove through the storm, hail _____pelted_____ our windshield.

5. On the first day of college, many students have to wait in a long line to _____register_____ for classes.

6. My old winter coat looked _____shabby_____ compared to the new one my brother wore.

208

At Home: Have students use each of the vocabulary words in a sentence.

Book 5/Unit 6
The Silent Lobby 6

Batter's Up!

Every spring, our softball team has to *register* with the city league. The coach usually takes us all downtown in our uniforms to sign up.

This year we wanted to *persuade* our coach to buy us new uniforms because the old ones were looking *shabby*. My friend Alfonzo tried to tell our coach that the league rules stated uniforms "could not be torn, stained, or faded." The coach wanted to know how he managed to *interpret* that from the rule book.

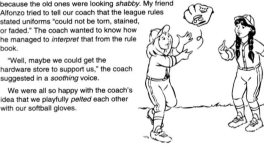

"Well, maybe we could get the hardware store to support us," the coach suggested in a *soothing* voice.

We were all so happy with the coach's idea that we playfully *pelted* each other with our softball gloves.

1. What is another word for *persuade*? convince

2. What is a word that means "one way of explain the meaning of something"? interpret

3. What does the word *soothing* mean, as it is used in this story? It means comforting or relieving.

4. What would it feel like to be *pelted* playfully with a softball glove? It wouldn't hurt; you'd just feel the thud against your body.

5. Why doesn't the team want to register in their old uniforms? What are they going to do about it? The old uniforms are too shabby; they feel embarrassed to be seen in them. They are going to ask the hardware store to help them get new ones.

5 Book 5/Unit 6
The Silent Lobby

At Home: Have students use the vocabulary words to write a short story, poem, or song lyrics.

208a

Practice 209

Name_____ Date_____

Story Comprehension

Review or reread "The Silent Lobby." Then answer the questions below. Answers will vary. Sample answers are shown.

1. Who is telling the story of "The Silent Lobby"? Explain. Craig Saunders, an 11-year-old boy from Mississippi whose father is leading a group of citizens from The Freedom Party to lobby for voting rights in Washington, D.C.

2. Why didn't Craig's mother want him to go to Washington, D.C.? She thought he was too young, and that the trip would be too dangerous.

3. What did they make Craig's father do when he tried to register to vote? Explain what happened. They made him pay a poll tax; pass a literacy test; and interpret the state constitution. They decided he didn't interpret the same state constitution correctly, so they wouldn't let him register to vote.

4. Who is Mrs. Fannie Lou Hamer? What did she do? She started the Mississippi Freedom Party and registered people to vote without charging a poll tax or making them take tests. She was also elected to be a representative to Congress, but was barred from taking office by the governor of Mississippi.

5. What happened to the 83,000 votes that the African Americans cast during Mississippi's 1964 election? What about the people they voted for? The governor of Mississippi declared the votes illegal and threw them out. Then he put the men he wanted into office instead of those the voters of the Second District wanted.

6. How would this story have been different if the doorman hadn't let the people from Mississippi take shelter from the rain in the tunnel? Explain. The ending would have been completely different because then the members of congress would not have had to face the people from Mississippi. By at least seeing the group, many members of Congress actually changed their minds.

209

At Home: Encourage students to make a storyboard to retell "The Silent Lobby."

Book 5/Unit 6
The Silent Lobby 6

The Silent Lobby • PRACTICE

Practice 210

Name_____ Date_____ **Practice** 210

Use an Outline

Using an **outline** can help you to group facts and organize information. In an outline, a Roman numeral is placed before each main idea. Beneath that, capital letters organize the important facts that support the main idea. Study this section of an outline. Then answer the questions below. **Answers may vary.**

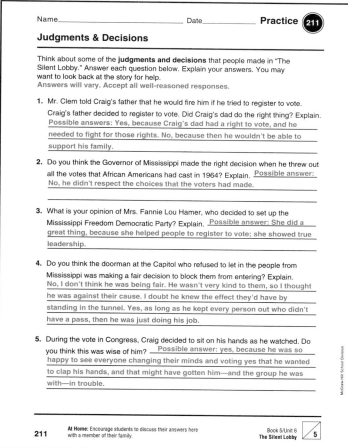

III. Women Pilots in the Thirties
  A. Beryl Markham survives crash on Cape Breton.
  B. Jean Batten sets record for South Atlantic Flight.
  C. Louise Thaden wins Bendix Trophy in 1936.
  D. Amelia Earhart makes last flight, 1937.

1. Which section of the outline is presented here? the third section

2. What is the main idea of this section? How do you know what it is about? The main idea is about women pilots in the 1930s; I can tell because it is written next to a Roman numeral.

3. What sort of information follows the capital letters? facts that support the main idea

4. If you found out about another woman pilot in the 1930s, how would you include her in the outline? Explain. I would add another capital letter (E) to this section and put the information about her there or if she was in the early 1930s, put her in the correct place chronologically and reorder the entries.

5. How could you use an outline to help you study a textbook to prepare for a test? I could make an outline of each chapter in the textbook to find the main ideas and supporting facts.

Practice 211

Name_____ Date_____ **Practice** 211

Judgments & Decisions

Think about some of the **judgments and decisions** that people made in "The Silent Lobby." Answer each question below. Explain your answers. You may want to look back at the story for help.
Answers will vary. Accept all well-reasoned responses.

1. Mr. Clem told Craig's father that he would fire him if he tried to register to vote. Craig's father decided to register to vote. Did Craig's dad do the right thing? Explain. Possible answers: Yes, because Craig's dad had a right to vote, and he needed to fight for those rights. No, because then he wouldn't be able to support his family.

2. Do you think the Governor of Mississippi made the right decision when he threw out all the votes that African Americans had cast in 1964? Explain. Possible answer: No, he didn't respect the choices that the voters had made.

3. What is your opinion of Mrs. Fannie Lou Hamer, who decided to set up the Mississippi Freedom Democratic Party? Explain. Possible answer: She did a great thing, because she helped people to register to vote; she showed true leadership.

4. Do you think the doorman at the Capitol who refused to let in the people from Mississippi was making a fair decision to block them from entering? Explain. No, I don't think he was being fair. He wasn't very kind to them, so I thought he was against their cause. I doubt he knew the effect they'd have by standing in the tunnel. Yes, as long as he kept every person out who didn't have a pass, then he was just doing his job.

5. During the vote in Congress, Craig decided to sit on his hands as he watched. Do you think this was wise of him? Possible answer: yes, because he was so happy to see everyone changing their minds and voting yes that he wanted to clap his hands, and that might have gotten him—and the group he was with—in trouble.

Practice 212

Name_____ Date_____ **Practice** 212

Draw Conclusions

To **draw a conclusion** when reading a story, you use facts from a story as well as your own knowledge and experience. Drawing conclusions as you read can help you better understand a story.

Read the selection below, and then answer each question. Describe the clues that helped you draw conclusions for question 1. **Answers will vary.**

Naseem rested his head on one arm. On the kitchen table before him was a blank sheet of paper. Crumpled papers were all over the floor under the table. Fatima pushed aside a mound of library books and sat down.

"Listen, Naseem, you just have to tell yourself, 'You can do it!' Fatima said. "Look, you've done all the research."

Naseem lifted his head and stared outside the kitchen window.

"You have until tomorrow morning," she reminded him. "If you just pick up the pen and start writing now, you'll be OK—as long as you just stop tossing away everything you write." Fatima uncrumpled one of the papers. "And I'd use this, if I were you," she suggested as she handed him the outline.

1. What is it that Naseem has to do? How can you tell? Write the clues that helped you below. He has to write a research report.

2. **Story clues:** The library books, the blank sheet of paper, the crumpled papers, the outline; Fatima refers to research and to writing.

3. **Experience clues:** When I work on a research report, I usually have a pile of library books and papers.

4. How is Naseem feeling? How can you tell? He is feeling frustrated and hopeless. I can tell by the way he has his head down on his arm, how he stares out the window, how he keeps crumpling up what he writes.

5. What kind of person is Fatima? How can you tell? She is helpful and kind. She cheers Naseem on. She gives him good advice.

Practice 213

Name_____ Date_____ **Practice** 213

Synonyms and Antonyms

Synonyms are words with the same, or nearly the same, meanings and are used for different situations.

Antonyms are words with opposite, or nearly opposite, meanings and are used for contrast or to show differences.

Divide the words in the box into pairs of synonyms and antonyms and then write each pair under the correct column below.

shabby	soothing	elect	beaten
gawked	returned	alarming	pelted
left	right	stalling	threadbare
wrong	moving	lobby	vote
awake	asleep	stared	persuade

Synonyms
1. shabby, threadbare
2. gawked, stared
3. beaten, pelted
4. elect, vote
5. lobby, persuade

Antonyms
6. soothing, alarming
7. asleep, awake
8. stalling, moving
9. wrong, right
10. left, returned OR left, right

Compare the underlined words in each sentence. Are they antonyms or synonyms.

11. While the traffic was moving quickly all around us, our car kept stalling. antonyms

12. My favorite sweater began to look shabby. Even the patches on the elbows were threadbare. synonyms

The Silent Lobby • RETEACH

Page 207

Name_____ Date_____ **Reteach** 207

Judgments and Decisions

> Making **judgments** is the process of determining how you think and feel about ideas, actions, characters, or events. After you determine how you feel, then you can make a **decision** as to whether you agree with the reasons behind the ideas, actions, character or events.

Read the paragraph. Then read the choices below the paragraph and write your decision as to which is the best choice. Explain your judgment by giving the reasons for your decisions. *Answers will vary but should be supported with reasons.*

Suppose you were on a school committee that decides what programs the school should have. When there isn't enough money to pay for every program your group decides which program to keep, and which to leave out.

- after-school classes in pottery, painting, and basket-making
- extra buses to bring students to school

1. **Decision:** Sample answer: Cut the after-school classes because they are extra. Keep the buses because students need to get to school.

- add additional desserts in the school cafeteria
- a training program to teach students how to use the Internet

2. **Decision:** Sample answer: Keep the training program for learning the Internet. Desserts aren't as important as learning how to use the Internet.

- more gym space so students can have room for other sports
- a teacher's aide so that students can have more playground time

3. **Decision:** Sample answer: Cut the additional gym space. Keep the teacher's aide so that students can get exercise both in and out of gym class.

- science program for students who like to make inventions
- program teaching students safety tips

4. **Decision:** Sample answer: Cut the science program because kids can invent on their own time. Keep the safety program because safety is important.

Book 5/Unit 6
The Silent Lobby
4

At Home: Have students think of two more sets of choices and then make a judgment about which is more important.

207

Page 208

Name_____ Date_____ **Reteach** 208

Vocabulary

Read each clue. Then find and circle the vocabulary word in the row of letters.

interpret	pelted	persuade	register	shabby	soothing

1. convince   j i k n w q (p e r s u a d e) x v d f g
2. sign up   z w i r t g s d j (r e g i s t e r) o u
3. worn out   q (s h a b b y) e i t v g s d o k j w o
4. hit hard   x z v i w o k n (p e l t e d) a e n b d
5. understand   q o i j k m d s r e (i n t e r p r e t)
6. calming   e i d s c (s o o t h i n g) m z s o k e

6

Story Comprehension

Reteach 209

Write the answer to each question about "The Silent Lobby."

1. Who is telling the story in "The Silent Lobby"? Craig, a young African American boy is telling the story.

2. When and where does the story take place? the first half of 1960s; it takes place in Mississippi and Washington, D.C.

3. What right does Craig's father think is important? He believes his right to vote is important.

4. Why is Congressman Ryan sorry that the members of the Freedom Party arrive late? He feels that they could have helped the lobby to get more votes.

5. Why is Craig surprised by his vote in Congress? There are many more votes cast in the Freedom Party's favor than he thought there would be.

208–209

At Home: Have students write and answer two questions about "The Silent Lobby."

Book 5/Unit 6
The Silent Lobby
5

Page 210

Name_____ Date_____ **Reteach** 210

Use an Outline

> An **outline** helps you organize information and plan your writing. You can use an outline for writing stories, opinion essays, or information reports. When you write an outline, make main headings for the main ideas you want to include. Then list related facts under each main heading. Label main headings with roman numerals and related facts with capital letters.

Papa loses job for trying to register.   Silent Lobby meets Congressmen in tunnel.
Governor declares votes illegal.   148 votes are cast for the Silent Lobby cause.
Silent Lobby turned away at Capitol.   Papa finds Freedom Party and votes.
Silent Lobby watches Congress vote.   Papa is not allowed to register to vote.

Organize the entries in the columns above in the outline format below. You may use information from either column for each main idea.

1. Main Idea #1 I. **History of Papa's fight to vote**
2. Related Fact: A. Papa not allowed to register to vote.
3. Related Fact: B. Papa loses job for trying to register.
4. Related Fact: C. Papa finds Freedom Party and votes.
5. Related Fact: D. Governor declares votes illegal.

6. Main Idea #2: II. **Events of Silent Lobby trip**
7. Related Fact: A. Silent Lobby turned away at Capitol
8. Related Fact: B. Silent Lobby meets Congressmen in tunnel
9. Related Fact: C. Silent Lobby watches Congress vote
10. Related Fact: D. 148 votes are cast for the Silent Lobby cause

8
Book 5/Unit 6
The Silent Lobby

At Home: Have students add one more related fact to the history of the Silent Lobby or the events of the Silent Lobby.

210

Page 211

Name_____ Date_____ **Reteach** 211

Judgments and Decisions

> To make **judgments**, you look at how you think and feel about something. To make **decisions**, you often compare two or more possibilities and choose the one that agrees with how you think or feel about the topic.

In "The Silent Lobby" many characters made judgments and decisions. Read each sentence below. Decide how you feel or think about it and write your response on the line that reads: **Judgment**. Then, write what you think should be done on the line labeled: **Decision**. *Answers will vary but should be explained.*

1. Eleven years of age is too young to be involved in political protests.
   a. **Judgment:** Possible answer: I agree.
   b. **Decision:** Possible answer: Kids can have strong beliefs, just like adults. However they are too young to be placed in dangerous situations.

2. Keeping Papa from registering to vote was wrong.
   a. **Judgment:** Possible answer: I agree.
   b. **Decision:** Possible answer: Papa had the right to vote, just like any other United States citizen.

3. The Silent Lobby should have gone home after their bus broke down.
   a. **Judgment:** Possible answer: I disagree.
   b. **Decision:** Possible answer: They should have stayed, because their presence was important to the outcome of the vote.

4. People can never change other people's ideas.
   a. **Judgment:** Possible answer: I disagree.
   b. **Decision:** Possible answer: I would try to talk to people and get them to understand my ideas.

211

At Home: Have students tell what they might do in Craig's shoes. Would they choose the same actions that he did?

Book 5/Unit 6
The Silent Lobby
8

The Silent Lobby • RETEACH

Draw Conclusions

To **draw conclusions**, first think about clues in the story and what you know from your own experiences. Then try to figure out what may happen with characters and events in a story.

Read each story. Circle the conclusion you can draw for each story.

Twana's mind kept wandering from her reading. She could picture a fresh, crispy apple. Then she thought about a warm piece of toast. Her stomach started to growl. She had to read the page over again to understand it.

1. Twana is probably
   a. bored   (b.) hungry   c. tired

Craig wants to go to with Papa to try to register to vote. When Papa doesn't come home, Craig wants to search for him. When the Silent Lobby goes to Washington, Craig wants to go too.

2. Craig probably
   (a.) wants to support Papa.
   b. wants to be alone.
   c. does not care about voting.

Jamie could hear birds chirping. The sky was bright even at breakfast time. She saw buds growing on the trees and each day was a little warmer. The ground was getting softer and water from melting snow was filling the streams.

3. Jamie can see that
   a. breakfast is great.   b. the sky is often dark.   (c.) spring is near.

Stefan wrote to the school board asking them to change the rules about skateboards. He listed facts to tell them why skateboards are safe. Stefan put up posters all around school asking other students to write the school board too.

4. It seems that
   a. Stefan loves to write letters.
   b. Stefan is not interested in skateboards.
   (c.) Stefan thinks students should be allowed to skateboard.

Book 5/Unit 6
The Silent Lobby 4

At Home: Have students identify the clues they used to help them draw the conclusion in each paragraph.

212

Synonyms and Antonyms

Synonyms are words with the same or similar meanings. **Antonyms** are words with opposite or nearly opposite meanings.

Read each sentence. Then use the clue provided to help you complete the sentence with the correct word from the box.

| dangerous | gawking | complaints | active |
| courage | alarmed | wrinkled | unfortunate |

1. The people in the Silent Lobby must have had a lot of <u>courage</u>.
   Clue: antonym for *fear*

2. During the 1960's, people sometimes got hurt during <u>dangerous</u> protests.
   Clue: antonym for *safe*

3. Mama was <u>alarmed</u> by the risks Papa was taking in registering to vote.
   Clue: synonym for *frightened*

4. The Freedom Party was very <u>active</u> in working for voting rights.
   Clue: synonym for *busy*

5. Craig felt badly when a crowd of people stood <u>gawking</u> at his bus.
   Clue: synonym for *staring*

6. The members of the Freedom Party wanted to be sure its <u>complaints</u> were heard somehow.
   Clue: synonym for *protests*

7. After standing in the rain, all our clothes were <u>wrinkled</u> and wet.
   Clue: antonym for *smooth*

8. The delay in reaching Washington was <u>unfortunate</u> as The Freedom Party missed its chance to lobby for votes.
   Clue: antonym for *lucky*

At Home: Have students write sentences for one antonym and one synonym.

213

Book 5/Unit 6
The Silent Lobby 8

T39

The Silent Lobby • EXTEND

Judgments and Decisions

When you make a **judgment** about something, you need to evaluate, or judge, your choices. Then you can decide on the best course of action. Many of our lawmakers use judgments and **decisions** everyday as they consider which bills, or laws, they want to create and enact.

Suppose that the members of your local community have gotten together and proposed some new bills for your town. Read each situation below. Make a judgment as to the best decision for each one.

1. Your local library is open from Monday through Thursday from 9 A.M. to 9 P.M. and on Fridays and Saturdays from 9 A.M. to 5 P.M. A bill has been proposed to keep the local public library open on Fridays and Saturdays until 9 P.M. and on Sundays from 9 A.M. to 4 P.M. during the school year from September through June. The reason is to allow more time for students to use the library for their school work. Some local townspeople do not want to pay for the extra cost of running the library during these additional hours.

How would you vote on this bill? Give reasons for your decision.

Answers will vary. Students should back up their judgments with reasons for

their decisions.

2. A bill has been proposed to turn the old school field into a shopping center. Some people feel that the new shopping center will bring more business into town. Others feel that the field should be used for sports events and that the new shopping center will only increase traffic problems.

How would you vote on this bill? Give reasons for your decision.

Answers will vary. Students should explain the judgments they used to arrive at

their decisions.

At Home: Look in your local paper to find an example of a bill that was passed in your community. Do you agree with the decision?

Vocabulary

interpret	pelted	persuade	register	shabby	soothing

Suppose that you are Craig in the story, "The Silent Lobby." Write a letter home describing the events of the day in Washington, D.C. Use as many vocabulary words in your letter as possible.

Answers will vary, but should include at least four vocabulary words used in

correct context and parts of speech.

Story Comprehension

Suppose you are a newspaper reporter who is covering the story of the Mississippi Freedom Democratic Party's trip to Washington, D.C. Tell in your story the events that led to the vote of 148 votes cast in favor of the party. Remember, a news story tells *who* was involved, *what* happened, *when* it happened, *where* it happened, and *how* the events happened.

Answers will vary, but should include the italicized details from instructions

---

Use an Outline

In "The Silent Lobby" you got an idea of how Congress works to pass bills. If you were asked to write a report on the three branches of our government, how would you organize your information? An outline such as the one below would help you get started.

The Government of the United States
I. Executive Branch
  A. Carries out laws
  B. Conducts public and foreign affairs
  C. Headed by the President
II. Legislative Branch
  A. Makes laws
  B. House of Representatives
    1. Elected every 2 years
    2. Number of house members based on a state's population
  C. Senate
    1. Elected every 6 years
    2. Two Senators for each state
III. Judiciary Branch
  A. Supreme Court
  B. District Courts

1. What are the main ideas of this outline? How do you know?
The main ideas are the three branches of our national government. They are

shown by roman numerals I, II, and III.

2. Where would you place this fact on the outline? One chief justice and eight justices make up the Supreme Court.
You would put in under Supreme Court and label it 1.

3. How are outlines organized?
Outlines use roman numerals and letters to show topics and subtopics.

4. Where would you place facts about the President's foreign affairs issues.
Under 1, letter B

At Home: Discuss how an outline helps you organize information.

Judgments and Decisions

In the story "The Silent Lobby" the members of the House of Representatives must make a decision as to whether or not to seat the representatives elected by the Freedom Party. Suppose you are a member of the House. As a congressperson, it is your responsibility to **judge** all sides of an issue. Then, you must make a **decision** to vote yes or no. Decide how you would vote on the issue raised by the Freedom Party. Give reasons as they are presented in the story to back up your decision. Write your argument in the space provided.

Answers will vary but should include important details form the story.

At Home: People often debate an issue. Look up the word *debate.* Write a sentence to show its meaning.

The Silent Lobby • EXTEND

Draw Conclusions

You can **draw conclusions** about a character in a story by the way the character acts, thinks, and feels. Use what you have read in "The Silent Lobby" to draw conclusions about each character below.

1. How do you think Mama feels about the bus trip Papa and Craig are going to take? Explain the reasons for your conclusion.

   Possible answer: Mama does not want Papa and Craig to go on the bus trip.

   She feels that it is too dangerous. She is afraid the bus will be bombed.

2. How do you think that Papa feels about violence?

   Possible answer: Papa does not believe that violence is the way to solve

   problems. He is opposed to violence and continues to pursue his goals by

   using peaceful ways of getting something done, such as lobbying.

3. How do you think Congressmen Ryan and Hawkins feel about the cause of the Freedom Party? Explain why you think so.

   Possible answer: They support the cause of the Freedom Party. They work late

   into the night lobbying to get votes on the side of the Freedom Party.

4. Do you think that Craig will continue to fight for causes in the same manner as his father? Explain why you think so.

   Possible answer: Craig will most likely lobby for causes rather than resort to

   violence. He has seen how lobbying can get results, and he is proud of his

   father and the Freedom Party.

Book 5/Unit 6
The Silent Lobby

At Home: Discuss how drawing conclusions can help you better understand what you read.

212

Synonyms and Antonyms

Tell whether the pair of underlined words in the following sentences are **synonyms** or **antonyms**.

1. Some members of the House were for the bill to be passed, and some members were against.

   antonyms

2. Craig's Mama was afraid for her son and her husband, but Craig and his Dad did not seem to be that scared.

   synonyms

3. The people of the Freedom party stood calmly and quietly in the tunnel as the members of the House of Representatives walked by.

   synonyms

4. To Craig, the men and women of the House seem tall and towering as they passed by him in the tunnel.

   synonyms

5. The house member to the right of Congressman Ryan voted yes, but the house member on his left voted no.

   antonyms

6. Each day, the men and women of Congress must make important decisions about laws and issues that affect people in our country.

   antonyms

7. As the Freedom Party waited outside the Capitol building, it rained and poured on them.

   synonyms

8. The people of the Freedom Party were happy and thrilled to have gotten so many votes in their favor.

   synonyms

At Home: Make a list of words that are synonyms. Then find an antonym for each.

213

Book 5/Unit 6
The Silent Lobby

T41

Page 179

Name _____ Date _____ LEARN Grammar **179**

Prepositions

- A **preposition** comes before a noun or pronoun and relates that noun or pronoun to another word in the sentence.
- Common prepositions are *about, above, across, after, at, behind, down, for, from, in, near, of, on, over, to, with*.

Read each sentence. Underline the prepositions. There may be more than one in each sentence.

1. Craig walked <u>behind</u> his father.
2. The bus traveled slowly <u>on</u> the highway.
3. The tired bus stalled <u>near</u> the Capitol.
4. Papa knew that peace came only <u>with</u> freedom.
5. <u>On</u> election day, Papa voted in town.
6. Craig waited <u>in</u> the hallway <u>with</u> his father.
7. Everyone climbed <u>off</u> the bus.
8. Papa stayed out late <u>at</u> night.
9. <u>At</u> least, we received a lot <u>of</u> votes.
10. Craig's family was worried <u>about</u> bombs.
11. <u>Across</u> the room, a congressman spoke about justice.
12. The gallery is there, <u>above</u> the main floor.
13. <u>After</u> awhile, we had seats in the gallery.
14. The congressperson spoke <u>over</u> the loudspeaker.

14 / Grade 5/Unit 6
The Silent Lobby

Extension: Invite students to write and deliver speeches on civil rights. Ask them to circle prepositions in their written copies.

179

Page 180

Name _____ Date _____ LEARN AND PRACTICE Grammar **180**

Prepositional Phrases

- A prepositional phrase is a group of words that begins with a preposition and ends with a noun or pronoun.
- The object of a preposition is the noun or pronoun that follows the preposition.

Underline the preposition in each sentence. Circle the object of the preposition.

1. We wonder who is seated <u>in</u> (Congress)
2. A congressperson spoke <u>to</u> (us)
3. Mama said good-bye <u>from</u> the (door)
4. The old bus made it all the way <u>with</u> all its (problems)
5. Congresspeople walked <u>through</u> the (tunnel)
6. Equality means one vote <u>for</u> every (adult)
7. Craig spoke up <u>above</u> the (noise)
8. Some congresspeople were <u>on</u> our (side)

Complete each sentence with a prepositional phrase. Answers will vary.

9. _____On the road_____ , it was cold and rainy.
10. Craig's family wanted to talk ___with the congresspeople___ .
11. No one would let them sit ___in the gallery___ .
12. Civil rights are important ___for everyone___ .
13. Craig was proud ___of his father___ .
14. They were sent to wait ___in the tunnel___ .
15. Craig stood ___up for freedom___ .

Extension: Ask students to rewrite sentences 9 through 15, adding at least one more prepositional phrase to each sentence.

180

Grade 5/Unit 6
The Silent Lobby / 15

Page 181

Name _____ Date _____ PRACTICE AND REVIEW Grammar **181**

Prepositions and Prepositional Phrases

- A **preposition** comes before a noun or pronoun and relates that noun or pronoun to another word in the sentence.
- Common prepositions are *about, above, across, after, at, behind, down, for, from, in, near, of, on, over, to, with*.
- A **prepositional phrase** is a group of words that begins with a preposition and ends with a noun or pronoun.
- The object of a preposition is the noun or pronoun that follows the preposition.

Underline the prepositional phrase in each sentence. Write the object of the preposition on the line.

1. Craig fought the good fight <u>for freedom</u>. _____freedom_____
2. An old bus might never make it <u>to the city</u>. _____city_____
3. Papa put his arm <u>around Craig's</u> shoulders. ___Craig's shoulders___
4. The civil rights movement was a struggle <u>in the South</u>. _____south_____
5. Today every American can vote <u>on election day</u>. ___election day___
6. <u>Across the road</u>, Craig saw the Capitol. _____road_____
7. <u>Near the Capitol</u>, a crowd gathered. _____Capitol_____

Complete the sentences with prepositional phrases. Answers will vary.

8. ___After the demonstration___ some Congresspeople changed their minds.
9. Craig learned a valuable lesson ___on that day___ .
10. ___On the way to Washington,___ the bus had engine trouble.
11. ___Before the vote,___ there seemed to be no hope.
12. Craig sat ___in the gallery___ .

12 / Grade 5/Unit 6
The Silent Lobby

Extension: Have students write ten sentences, each with at least one prepositional phrase. Have them underline the prepositional phrases.

181

Page 182

Name _____ Date _____ MECHANICS Grammar **182**

Commas and Prepositional Phrases

- A prepositional phrase may come at the beginning of a sentence.
- Put a comma after a prepositional phrase composed of four or more words that comes at the beginning of a sentence.

Read the essay. Place commas where they are needed.

Before the civil rights movement, life was hard in many black communities. In the southern states, African-Americans were turned away from many restaurants and stores. On city buses, African-Americans had to sit in the back. At many voting polls, African-Americans were forced to take unfair tests. Even in the public schools, African American students were treated unfairly.

Martin Luther King was a champion of civil rights. He knew every American should have the chance to vote. He believed all people should attend decent schools and be able to use public transportation, restrooms, and restaurants. Soon many people were marching. Over the entire United States, people spoke up for equality. With such a strong public protest, changes were bound to take place. After a long hard struggle, the Civil Rights Act was passed.

182

Grade 5/Unit 6
The Silent Lobby / 8

The Silent Lobby • GRAMMAR

Prepositions

Circle the letter of the preposition that fits best in each sentence.

1. Craig's community fought _____ civil rights.
   a. near
   b. for
   c. at
2. The Capitol is _____ Washington, D.C.
   a. in
   b. over
   c. under
3. The struggle against prejudice continues _____ America.
   a. of
   b. before
   c. across
4. People everywhere fought _____ violence.
   a. to
   b. without
   c. of
5. Please give this letter _____ the congressperson.
   a. after
   b. near
   c. to
6. Craig was a young boy _____ the south.
   a. from
   b. after
   c. with
7. Papa knew a lot _____ prejudice.
   a. across
   b. with
   c. about
8. We trust our congressperson will vote _____ our cause.
   a. over
   b. of
   c. for

Commas and Prepositional Phrases

- A preposition comes before a noun or pronoun and relates that noun or pronoun to another word in the sentence.
- Common prepositions are about, above, across, after, at, behind, down, for, from, in, near, of, on, over, to, with.
- A prepositional phrase is a group of words that begins with a preposition and ends with a noun or pronoun.
- Put a comma after a prepositional phrase composed of four or more words that comes at the beginning of a sentence.
- The object of a preposition is the noun or pronoun that follows the preposition.

Work with a partner. As one of you read the sentences aloud, the other proofreads. Look for a place in each sentence that needs a comma. Rewrite the sentences, adding the missing commas.

1. In the late afternoon the bus rolled into the city.
   In the late afternoon, the bus rolled into the city.

2. Across the crowded hall congresspeople argued.
   Across the crowded hall, congresspeople argued.

3. Below the city streets there is a tunnel.
   Below the city streets, there is a tunnel.

4. After the hard struggle voting rights were won.
   After the hard struggle, voting rights were won.

5. Through this entire experience Craig learned a lot.
   Through this entire experience, Craig learned a lot.

The Silent Lobby • SPELLING

Name_____ Date_____

Words with Suffixes

Pretest Directions

Fold back the paper along the dotted line. Use the blanks to write each word as it is read aloud. When you finish the test, unfold the paper. Use the list at the right to correct any spelling mistakes. Practice the words you missed for the Posttest.

To Parents

Here are the results of your child's weekly spelling Pretest. You can help your child study for the Posttest by following these simple steps for each word on the word list:

1. Read the word to your child.
2. Have your child write the word, saying each letter as it is written.
3. Say each letter of the word as your child checks the spelling.
4. If a mistake has been made, have your child read each letter of the correctly spelled word aloud, and then repeat steps 1–3.

1. _____	1. instruction
2. _____	2. suggestion
3. _____	3. information
4. _____	4. education
5. _____	5. imagination
6. _____	6. selection
7. _____	7. confusion
8. _____	8. invitation
9. _____	9. attraction
10. _____	10. reservation
11. _____	11. election
12. _____	12. perfection
13. _____	13. conversation
14. _____	14. location
15. _____	15. population
16. _____	16. concentration
17. _____	17. consideration
18. _____	18. demonstration
19. _____	19. constitution
20. _____	20. correction

Challenge Words

_____ interpret
_____ persuade
_____ register
_____ shabby
_____ soothing

20 Grade 5/Unit 6
The Silent Lobby

179

Name_____ Date_____

Words with Suffixes

Using the Word Study Steps

1. LOOK at the word
2. SAY the word aloud.
3. STUDY the letters in the word.
4. WRITE the word.
5. CHECK the word.
   Did you spell the word right?
   If not, go back to step 1.

Spelling Tip

Say the word to yourself one syllable at a time. Then write the word the same way.

ed + u + cate = educate
de + mon + strate = demonstrate

Word Scramble

Unscramble each set of letters to make a spelling word.

1.	niotsructin	instruction	11.	leetnioc	election
2.	gestsugnio	suggestion	12.	frenopicte	perfection
3.	frmointiaon	information	13.	vernnosactio	conversation
4.	cudaenoit	education	14.	coinatol	location
5.	gaminatiino	imagination	15.	tapulopino	population
6.	leestconi	selection	16.	trancnoceiton	concentration
7.	funcsonoi	confusion	17.	sniderinatoco	consideration
8.	vintanoiit	invitation	18.	strandtimeono	demonstration
9.	crattnaito	attraction	19.	tsiconnioutt	constitution
10.	trainvreeos	reservation	20.	rectorconi	correction

To Parents or Helpers:

Using the Word Study Steps above as your child comes across any new words will help him or her spell words effectively. Review the steps as you both go over this week's spelling words.

Go over the Spelling Tip with your child. Help him or her spell longer words by breaking them down into syllables.

Help your child unscramble the sets of letters to form the spelling words.

180

20 Grade 5/Unit 6
The Silent Lobby

Name_____ Date_____

Words with Suffixes

instruction	imagination	attraction	conversation	consideration
suggestion	selection	reservation	location	demonstration
information	confusion	election	population	constitution
education	invitation	perfection	concentration	correction

Sort each spelling word according to the suffix which it contains. Write the words which contain the following suffixes:

-ion

1. instruction
2. suggestion
3. education
4. selection
5. confusion
6. attraction
7. election
8. perfection
9. location
10. population
11. concentration
12. demonstration
13. constitution
14. correction

-ation

15. information
16. imagination
17. invitation
18. reservation
19. conversation
20. consideration

20 Grade 5/Unit 6
The Silent Lobby

181

Name_____ Date_____

Words with Suffixes

instruction	imagination	attraction	conversation	consideration
suggestion	selection	reservation	location	demonstration
information	confusion	election	population	constitution
education	invitation	perfection	concentration	correction

Complete each sentence below with a spelling word.

1. Getting a good ___education___ will help you get a good job.
2. The clothing store had a large ___selection___ of suits.
3. I sent my best friend the first ___invitation___ to my party.
4. I called the restaurant and made a ___reservation___ for dinner.
5. He ran for mayor during the November ___election___.
6. Cities have a larger ___population___ than towns.

Similar Words

Write the spelling word which is closest in meaning to each word or phrase.

7. teaching	instruction	14. display	demonstration
8. idea	suggestion	15. body of laws	constitution
9. chaos	confusion	16. revision	correction
10. appeal	attraction	17. data	information
11. excellence	perfection	18. fantasy	imagination
12. place	location	19. talk	conversation
13. close attention	concentration	20. careful thought	consideration

182 **Challenge Extension:** Write one sentence for each Challenge Word.

20 Grade 5/Unit 6
The Silent Lobby

The Silent Lobby • SPELLING

Name_____ Date_____

Words with Suffixes

Proofreading Activity

There are six spelling mistakes in the letter below. Circle the misspelled words. Write the words correctly on the lines below.

Dear Congressman Hawkins,

I want to thank you for supporting our cause during our visit to Washington. There was so much (confusin) in that tunnel before you stopped and had a (converzashun) with my father. My mother thought this kind of (demonstraton) wouldn't do any good. But thanks to you and other members of Congress, the whole American adult (populetion) can vote. I hope you win your next (elektion). Thank you again for your help and your (considderation).

Sincerely,

Craig

1. __confusion__   3. __demonstration__   5. __election__

2. __conversation__   4. __population__   6. __consideration__

Writing Activity

Think of something you would like to see the government do for you or for your community. Write a letter to your representative in Congress describing what you would like done. Use four spelling words in your writing.

_____

_____

_____

_____

Name_____ Date_____

Words with Suffixes

Look at the words in each set below. One word in each set is spelled correctly. Use a pencil to fill in the circle next to the correct word. Before you begin, look at the sample sets of words. Sample A has been done for you. Do Sample B by yourself. When you are sure you know what to do, you may go on with the rest of the page.

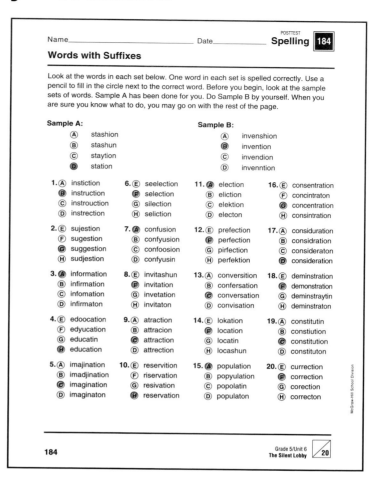

Sample A:
- (A) stashion
- (B) stashun
- (C) staytion
- (D) ● station

Sample B:
- (A) invenshion
- (B) ● invention
- (C) invendion
- (D) invenntion

1.
- (A) instiction
- (B) ● instruction
- (C) instroucion
- (D) instrection

2.
- (E) sujestion
- (F) sugestion
- (G) ● suggestion
- (H) sudjestion

3.
- (A) ● information
- (B) infirmation
- (C) infomation
- (D) infirmaton

4.
- (E) edoocation
- (F) edyucation
- (G) educatin
- (H) ● education

5.
- (A) imajination
- (B) imadjination
- (C) ● imagination
- (D) imaginaton

6.
- (E) seelection
- (F) ● selection
- (G) silection
- (H) seliction

7.
- (A) ● confusion
- (B) confyusion
- (C) confoosion
- (D) confyusin

8.
- (E) invitashun
- (F) ● invitation
- (G) invetation
- (H) invitaton

9.
- (A) atraction
- (B) attracion
- (C) ● attraction
- (D) attrection

10.
- (E) reservition
- (F) riservation
- (G) resivation
- (H) ● reservation

11.
- (A) ● election
- (B) eliction
- (C) elektion
- (D) electon

12.
- (E) prefection
- (F) ● perfection
- (G) pirfection
- (H) perfektion

13.
- (A) conversition
- (B) confersation
- (C) ● conversation
- (D) convisation

14.
- (E) lokation
- (F) ● location
- (G) locatin
- (H) locashun

15.
- (A) ● population
- (B) popyulation
- (C) popolatin
- (D) populaton

16.
- (E) consentration
- (F) concintraton
- (G) ● concentration
- (H) consintration

17.
- (A) considuration
- (B) considration
- (C) consideraton
- (D) ● consideration

18.
- (E) deministration
- (F) ● demonstration
- (G) deminstraytin
- (H) deminstraton

19.
- (A) constitutin
- (B) constiution
- (C) ● constitution
- (D) constituton

20.
- (E) currection
- (F) ● correction
- (G) corection
- (H) correcton

Name_____ Date_____ Practice **214**

Sequence of Events

Events in a story happen in a certain **sequence** or order. By recognizing that sequence you can make better sense of a story.

Read the short story. The story chart below lists story events that are out of order. Number each event in the correct sequence.

Arnie has a job delivering newspapers to his neighbors in the morning. He gets up before sunrise to start his work. It is still dark when he rides five blocks to the newspaper truck. There, Mr. Popkin loads 50 newspapers onto the red wagon attached to the back of Arnie's bike. Then Arnie spends almost two hours riding his bike up and down the streets in his neighborhood.

When he gets to Mr. Hanson's house, he finds a blueberry muffin waiting for him in the newspaper basket. Mr. Santiago greets Arnie at his fence, because he knows Arnie is scared of the Santiago's big barking dogs. Mr. Santiago hopes someday Arnie will not be afraid of the dogs. Poor Arnie always hands him the paper and rushes off.

When he arrives home, Arnie's dad has breakfast waiting for him. Arnie puts the blueberry muffin in the cupboard, deciding he'll eat it later.

Sequence	Event
8	Arnie decides to keep the muffin in the cupboard and to eat it later.
6	Arnie is scared of the Santiago's dogs, so he hands the paper to Mr. Santiago and rushes off.
3	Mr. Popkin loads Arnie's wagon with newspapers.
2	Arnie rides his bike five blocks to the newspaper truck.
4	Mr. Santiago greets Arnie at his fence.
5	Arnie finds a blueberry muffin waiting for him at Mr. Hanson's.
7	Arnie arrives home and eats breakfast.
1	Arnie gets up before sunrise.

8 | Book 5/Unit 6
Amazon Alert!

At Home: Have students identify the sequence of events of a favorite book or movie.

214

Name_____ Date_____ Practice **215**

Vocabulary

Complete each sentence with a vocabulary word.

confirmed	lush	variety	isolated	tropical	wonderland

1. The ___tropical___ storm brought warm waters into the North Atlantic.

2. For the school dance, we decorated the gym to look like a magical ___wonderland___.

3. With one phone call, the newspaper reporter ___confirmed___ that the rumor was not true.

4. After living in the desert for years, I longed for a ___lush___ green garden.

5. Who would want to live in an ___isolated___ cabin deep in the woods?

6. The bookstore downtown sells a ___variety___ of posters and postcards, as well as books.

215 | **At Home:** Have students use each of the vocabulary words in a sentence.

Book 5/Unit 6
Amazon Alert! | 6

Secret Garden

Reporters *confirmed* today that there is indeed a secret garden in the desert. Traveling to an isolated cottage on the outskirts of a small desert town, they discovered what one reporter called a *wonderland*.

"In the back of the abandoned cottage is a high stone wall that is clearly falling apart," claimed one reporter. "We were surprised to find what we did behind it."

"When we walked out of the cottage's back door and into the garden, it was like walking into a *tropical* forest," said the reporter. "I have never, in all my life, seen such a *variety* of plants and flowers. There were several kinds of palm trees and brightly colored birds flew among the trees. How could such a *lush* place survive in a desert?" Then, at the edge of the garden we saw a large well.

1. What does it mean if something is *confirmed*? It is proven true.

2. What sort of cottage is an *isolated* one? It is one set apart from the others.

3. What does the word *variety* mean as it is used in this story? a number of different kinds

4. What is one word that means "typical of the warmer regions of Earth"? tropical

5. What makes this "secret garden" a *lush wonderland*? It is lush because it has so many plants. It is a wonderland because it seems magical that such a garden could be possible in a desert.

5 | Book 5/Unit 6
Amazon Alert!

At Home: Make a collage depicting a tropical wonderland.

215a

Name_____ Date_____ Practice **216**

Story Comprehension

Answer the questions below about "Amazon Alert!" You may refer back to the story. Answers will vary. Sample responses are shown.

1. How big is the Amazon rain forest? Give the area in square miles. ___ 2.7 million square miles.

2. How much of our planet's fresh water supply does the Amazon hold? ___ one-fifth of the planet's fresh water supply.

3. What is deforestation? Who is responsible for it in the Amazon region? Deforestation is the loss of trees; loggers, miners, and farmers are responsible.

4. Why do people in Brazil burn down trees in the Amazon rain forest? to clear the land to make way for homes and farms

5. How much of the rain forest has been destroyed so far? one-eighth

6. What is the government of Brazil doing about the destruction of the Amazon rain forest? They are trying to do a better job of enforcing laws to protect the Amazon and stop people from abusing the natural resources there.

7. Why did deforestation slow down in 1996 and 1997? Heavy rainfall made it harder to burn down the trees.

8. Whose way of life in the Amazon is in danger of disappearing? the way of life of Indian groups, like the Yanomami

216 | **At Home:** Share what you have learned about the Amazon rain forest with a member of your family.

Book 5/Unit 6
Amazon Alert! | 8

Amazon Alert! • PRACTICE

Practice 217

Name_____ Date_____ **Practice** (217)

Use an Encyclopedia

An **encyclopedia** is a research tool. It is a set of books containing articles about important people, places, things, events, and ideas. The articles are arranged by alphabetical order in volumes. When you use an encyclopedia to find facts about a topic, you must have a "key word" in mind. Look at the illustration to answer the questions.

1. Why would you want to use an encyclopedia to write a report about something?
Possible answer: An encyclopedia is a research tool that can help me
quickly find out basic facts.

2. If you wanted to research information on the history of kites, what key word would
you use to find your subject? kites

3. In which volume would you look for information about *costumes*? volume 3, C–D

4. In which volume would you look for information about the history of the United
States? volume 11, T – U - V, maybe A for a general overview of the
Americas.

5. Which volumes do you think might have articles about French painters and artists?
Explain. volumes 1, 4, and 8; vol. 1 might have an article about artists,
vol. 4 F about France and French painting, and vol. 8 P–Q might list painters.
Also any of the volumes in which you would find the individual French
artists you read about.

5 Book 5/Unit 6
Amazon Alert!

At Home: Encourage students to use a key word to research information in an encyclopedia and share their findings with a family member.

217

Practice 218

Name_____ Date_____ **Practice** (218)

Cause and Effect

A **cause** is the reason why something happens. An **effect** is the result, or what happens. Many story events are connected through cause-and-effect relationships.

What might happen as a result of each story event below? Write down the most likely effect of each cause. Answers will vary. Accept all well-reasoned answers.

1. Doug woke up late and decided to skip breakfast so he could get to school on time.
Effect: Doug is going to get very hungry before lunch time.

2. It is the night before the big soccer tournament. Gerry is spending the night at Aziz's house. They stay up really late talking about how well they want to play in the game tomorrow. Their team plays early in the morning.
Effect: Gerry and Aziz are going to be tired the next morning and might not
play as well as they had hoped.

3. Lee and Sue are busy working on their tree house when they notice a beehive on one of the branches above them. Sue tells Lee that if they leave the bees alone, the bees will leave them alone. Lee decides to try to remove the beehive with a broom.
Effect: Angry bees are probably going to sting Lee.

4. Anita's sneakers no longer fit. She does not like to shop and is feeling impatient. She asks the clerk for the same style sneaker she always wears. Anita does not bother to try the new sneakers on in the store. She just buys them and leaves.
Effect: Anita might discover that the sneakers don't fit or that the laces are
missing.

5. Tanya poured twice as much milk as she should have into the muffin mix.
Effect: The muffins are not going to bake correctly.

218

At Home: Ask students to write several story events that show a cause-and-effect relationship.

Book 5/Unit 6
Amazon Alert! 5

Practice 219

Name_____ Date_____ **Practice** (219)

Synonyms and Antonyms

Synonyms are words with the same, or nearly the same, meaning. **Antonyms** are words with opposite, or nearly opposite, meaning.

Divide the words in the box into pairs of synonyms and antonyms and list them in the correct column below. You may use some words more than once.

area	preserve	save
construction	protect	shield
destruction	region	slow
lush	repair	swift
modern	rich	traditional

Synonyms
1. area, region
2. damage, destruction
3. lush, rich
4. preserve, save
5. protect, save
6. shield, protect

Antonyms
7. construction, destruction
8. modern, traditional
9. repair, damage
10. slow, swift

Compare the underlined words in each sentence. Write whether they are antonyms or synonyms.

11. There was so much damage to the house that we could not repair it.
antonyms

12. As we traveled through the southwestern region, we discovered that most of the
area was a vast desert. synonyms

12 Book 5/Unit 6
Amazon Alert!

At Home: Write several sentences using synonyms and antonyms.

219

Practice 220

Name_____ Date_____ **Practice** (220)

Context Clues

You can use **context clues** to help you define unfamiliar words.

Read each passage below. Use context clues to help you define the underlined word. Circle the letter of the correct meaning.

1. Many ecologists went to study the effects of pollution on wildlife.
An *ecologist* must be a kind of ____b____
a. firefighter   b. scientist   c. lawyer

2. During the 1980s, many rock bands made music videos. There was a huge growth in video sales during that decade.
A *decade* must last ____b____
a. a couple of years   b. ten years   c. 100 years

3. We entered the giant cave. The guide explained that this was a habitat where many bats lived.
A *habitat* must be a kind of ____c____
a. animal behavior   b. plant   c. community where animals live

4. The problem in the Amazon rain forest is that people abuse the resources there. That is what is destroying the region.
To *abuse* is to ____a____
a. use wrongly   b. treat fairly   c. be resourceful

5. The people in the village want to modernize the local water supply by putting in an electric water pump.
To *modernize* must mean to ____c____
a. keep supplying water   b. make things better   c. make things up-to-date

6. Sometime you have to sacrifice what you really want for the sake of something or someone else.
To *sacrifice* must mean to ____a____
a. give something up   b. want something   c. understand

220

At Home: Make a list of context clues you used to define any unfamiliar words you found while reading "Amazon Alert!"

Book 5/Unit 6
Amazon Alert! 6

Amazon Alert! • RETEACH

Sequence of Events

> When reading a short story following the **sequence of events**, or the order in which things occur, will help you better understand the story. Clue words such as *before, first, then, next, after, last,* and *finally* help to show a stories' sequence.

Read the story. Circle the sequence clue words. Afterwards, remember the sequence so that you can answer questions 1 to 4.

> Omar had to write a report about Brazil. (First) he located Brazil on a world map. He discovered that it is in South America. (Then) he identified three important cities in Brazil—Rio de Janeiro, São Paulo, and Brasília. (Next) he looked at many books for ideas about natural wonders in Brazil. His favorite area of Brazil was the Amazon River Basin and its rain forest. (After) outlining his report, he neatly wrote it out in long hand and handed it into his teacher. (Then) he recited his report for his class. (Finally) Omar said, "Now I'd really love to visit Brazil."

1. Did Omar identify the cities in Brazil before or after he located Brazil on the map?

   a. before   **b.** after

2. Did Omar locate key cities in Brazil before or after reading books about Brazil's natural wonders?

   a. before   b. after

3. Did Omar outline his report before or after he wrote it in long hand?

   a. before   b. after

4. Did Omar decide he wanted to visit Brazil before or after he wrote his report?

   a. before   **b.** after

Vocabulary

Use the correct word from the list to complete the sentences.

variety	lush	wonderland	tropical	confirmed	isolated

1. All around our home in Florida was a <u>lush</u> garden of plants.

2. There were bushes, trees, and a <u>variety</u> of different flowers.

3. The garden felt like my own <u>tropical</u> rain forest, complete with a small stream running through it.

4. What a <u>wonderland</u> for birds and small animals to live in.

5. The animals felt safe because the garden seemed <u>isolated</u> and protected.

6. People <u>confirmed</u> that our garden was the biggest in the city.

`6`

Story Comprehension

Write a ✔ next to each true sentence about "Amazon Alert."

___✔___ 1. The Amazon rain forest holds the world's widest variety of wildlife.

___✔___ 2. The government of Brazil wants to protect the Amazon's rain forest.

___✔___ 3. Logging, mining, and farming are dangers to the rain forest.

___✔___ 4. Brazil has begun to punish people who hurt the rain forest.

_____ 5. There are no people living in the Amazon rain forest.

___✔___ 6. The government in Brazil is now working to protect rain forest peoples and their traditional ways of life.

_____ 7. Building more roads and airports has helped protect the rain forest.

___✔___ 8. Heavy rains in some years have protected the rain forest by making it harder to burn trees.

Use an Encyclopedia

> You can use an **encyclopedia** to find information for research reports and other writing assignments. Encyclopedias contain articles and facts about people, places, things, events, and ideas. The articles are arranged alphabetically. Usually encyclopedias are arranged in a series of volumes.

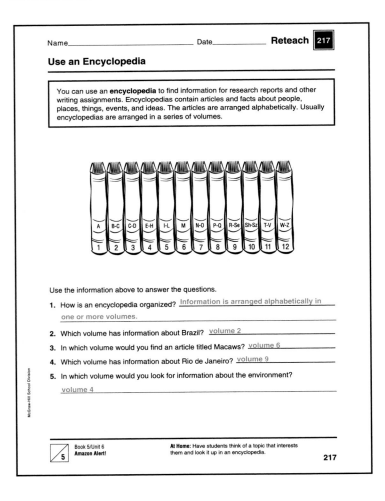

Use the information above to answer the questions.

1. How is an encyclopedia organized? <u>Information is arranged alphabetically in one or more volumes.</u>

2. Which volume has information about Brazil? <u>volume 2</u>

3. In which volume would you find an article titled Macaws? <u>volume 6</u>

4. Which volume has information about Rio de Janeiro? <u>volume 9</u>

5. In which volume would you look for information about the environment?

   <u>volume 4</u>

Cause and Effect

> When you answer the question *Why did something happen*? you are finding a **cause**. When you answer the question *What happened as a result*? you are finding an **effect**. Clue words such as *because* and *since* can help you find the relationship between cause and effect.

Read each cause. Then match it to a likely effect below. Write the number of each matching cause on the line before the effect.

1. Myron doesn't start his research project until the night before it is due.

2. No rain falls on the city of Tucson for nearly six weeks.

3. Jenna skips music practice for six straight days.

4. The Mississippi River floods its banks.

5. Pierre gets up an hour early to put on his costume for the fair.

6. Denise buys a big backpack and new hiking boots.

7. Patrick grows six inches and gains 30 pounds this year.

8. The city tears down the old apartment building on the corner.

___7___ His old clothes no longer fit him.

___1___ He doesn't finish his project in time.

___6___ She is going on vacation in the mountains.

___3___ She doesn't play well at her concert.

___8___ They replace it with a new building.

___4___ Five houses are damaged by the rising water.

___2___ Many trees and bushes die because of the lack of water.

___5___ He is on time for the fair's parade.

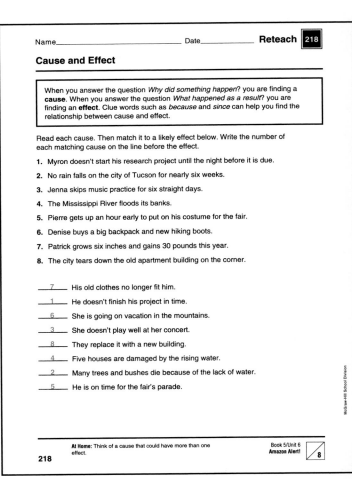

Amazon Alert! • RETEACH

Synonyms and Antonyms

> Learning new words can help you improve your reading and writing. Knowing synonyms and antonyms is one way to learn new words. **Synonyms** are words with the same or nearly the same meanings. **Antonyms** are words with opposite or nearly opposite meanings.

Circle the letter of the correct answer.

1. *Missing* is a synonym for _____.
   - (a.) absent
   - b. present
   - c. found

2. *Hunger* is a synonym for _____.
   - a. anger
   - (b.) appetite
   - c. appetite

3. *Miserable* is an antonym for _____.
   - a. sad
   - b. tired
   - (c.) happy

4. *Special* is an antonym for _____.
   - a. unusual
   - (b.) ordinary
   - c. happy

5. *Bathe* is a synonym for _____.
   - (a.) wash
   - b. bicycle
   - c. dirty

6. *Climate* is a synonym for _____.
   - a. rain
   - b. hiking
   - (c.) weather

7. *Link* is a synonym for _____.
   - (a.) connect
   - b. separate
   - c. destroy

8. *Crisp* is an antonym for _____.
   - a. crunchy
   - (b.) soggy
   - c. delicious

9. *Huge* is an antonym for _____.
   - a. big
   - b. wide
   - (c.) tiny

10. *Journey* is a synonym for _____.
    - (a.) trip
    - b. diary
    - c. home

Book 5/Unit 6
Amazon Alert! 10

At Home: Have students write one pair of synonyms and one pair of antonyms.

219

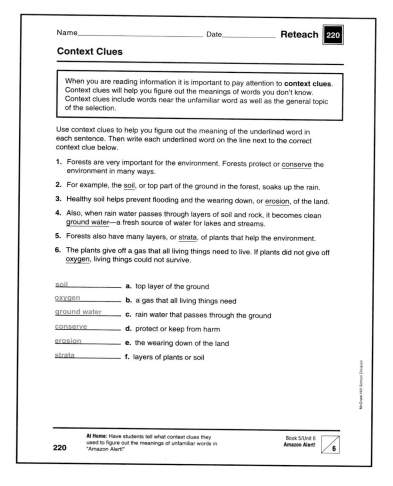

Context Clues

> When you are reading information it is important to pay attention to **context clues**. Context clues will help you figure out the meanings of words you don't know. Context clues include words near the unfamiliar word as well as the general topic of the selection.

Use context clues to help you figure out the meaning of the underlined word in each sentence. Then write each underlined word on the line next to the correct context clue below.

1. Forests are very important for the environment. Forests protect or <u>conserve</u> the environment in many ways.

2. For example, the <u>soil</u>, or top part of the ground in the forest, soaks up the rain.

3. Healthy soil helps prevent flooding and the wearing down, or <u>erosion</u>, of the land.

4. Also, when rain water passes through layers of soil and rock, it becomes clean <u>ground water</u>—a fresh source of water for lakes and streams.

5. Forests also have many layers, or <u>strata</u>, of plants that help the environment.

6. The plants give off a gas that all living things need to live. If plants did not give off <u>oxygen</u>, living things could not survive.

<u>soil</u> _____ **a.** top layer of the ground

<u>oxygen</u> _____ **b.** a gas that all living things need

<u>ground water</u> _____ **c.** rain water that passes through the ground

<u>conserve</u> _____ **d.** protect or keep from harm

<u>erosion</u> _____ **e.** the wearing down of the land

<u>strata</u> _____ **f.** layers of plants or soil

At Home: Have students tell what context clues they used to figure out the meanings of unfamiliar words in "Amazon Alert!"

220

Book 5/Unit 6
Amazon Alert! 6

Extend 214

Name_____ Date_____

Sequence of Events

In nonfiction articles, writers often use visual aides to show the **sequence of events**. Time lines show the order of events by using dates along a vertical or horizontal line. Flow charts show the order of events by using arrows and boxes to show what happened first, next, and last.

Below are examples of a time line and a flow chart. Follow the directions for each.

1. Fill in the time line below to show the sequence of the major events in your school day. Fill in the times and the events of the day as you go along.
   Answers will vary, but events should follow logical steps in a student's school day.

7:00 A.M.   Time: Time: Time: Time:

Get up. Eat breakfast.

2. Use the boxes in the flow chart to show the sequence of events on a Saturday that was special for you. Answers will vary but should include events in logical sequence.

Event 1

Event 2

Event 3

Event 4

Book 5/Unit 6
Amazon Alert!

At Home: Look for examples of time lines and flow charts in magazines and newspapers.

214

Extend 215

Name_____ Date_____

Vocabulary

confirmed	isolated	lush	tropical	variety	wonderland

Write an article that describes why it is important to protect the world's rain forests. Use as many vocabulary words as you can in your article.

Answers may vary, but should include at least four vocabulary words used in correct context and parts of speech.

_____

_____

_____

Extend 216

Story Comprehension

Work in a small group of three or four students. Turn the article "Amazon Alert!" into short informative skit. Find lines in the article that you can use in your skit, and assign each student in the group a role or character that deals with an issue discussed in "Amazon Alert!" Present your skits to the class. Then have class members answer the following questions based on the information in the skit.

1. What conclusions can you draw about the need to protect our rain forests?
   Answers will vary.

2. Why do you think the Yanomami and the other Indians of the rain forest would prefer to live in their traditional life style?
   Answers will vary. Possible answers might include: modern ways are unknown to them; they are comfortable living on their own land and following ways and customs that are meaningful to them.

215–216

At Home: Choose two of the vocabulary words shown above. Find a synonym and antonym for each.

Book 5/Unit 6
Amazon Alert!

Extend 217

Name_____ Date_____

Use an Encyclopedia

Encyclopedias include articles on a great many subjects. They are useful when you need to find basic information about a topic. Suppose you were going to write an article about rain forests. You would need to narrow down your topic. Look at the list of possible topics below, then answer the questions.

The Amazon Rain Forest	**Rain Forest Animals**
People of the Rain Forest	**Rain Forests of Africa**
Plants of the Rain Forest	**Rain Forests of New Guinea**

1. Suppose you wanted to write a report about rain forest animals. In which encyclopedia volumes would you look? You could look under R for rain; F for forests; A for animals, Africa, and Amazon; N for New Guinea. You could also look under the names of specific rain forest animals.

2. Suppose you wanted to write a report on the rain forests of New Guinea. In which encyclopedia volumes would you look? You could look under R for rain forests or under N for New Guinea.

3. Choose one of the above topics. Use encyclopedias to write an outline a short report. Look under subcategories of your topic for subject areas you could include in your report.
   Answers will vary.

_____

_____

_____

_____

_____

_____

_____

_____

_____

Book 5/Unit 6
Amazon Alert!

At Home: Research the kinds of encyclopedias that are available in your local library. Which encyclopedias would you most likely to use in a report?

217

Extend 218

Name_____ Date_____

Cause and Effect

You know that a **cause** is the reason why something happens. The **effect** is the result. Understanding cause-and-effect relationships will help you better understand what you read.

There are many examples of cause-and-effect relationships in the article "Amazon Alert!" Look through the story to find four clear cause and effect relationships. Then fill in the cause-and-effect boxes below with the information you found. Answers will vary, students answers should generally follow answers below.

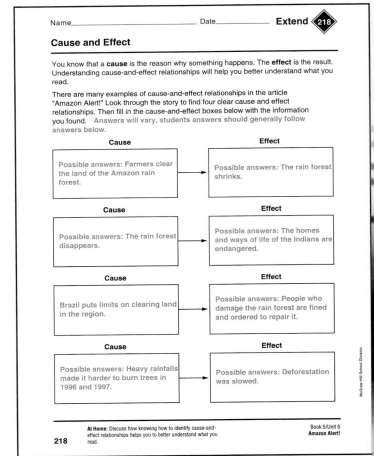

Cause	Effect
Possible answers: Farmers clear the land of the Amazon rain forest.	Possible answers: The rain forest shrinks.
Possible answers: The rain forest disappears.	Possible answers: The homes and ways of life of the Indians are endangered.
Brazil puts limits on clearing land in the region.	Possible answers: People who damage the rain forest are fined and ordered to repair it.
Possible answers: Heavy rainfalls made it harder to burn trees in 1996 and 1997.	Possible answers: Deforestation was slowed.

218

At Home: Discuss how knowing how to identify cause-and-effect relationships helps you to better understand what you read.

Book 5/Unit 6
Amazon Alert!

Amazon Alert! • EXTEND

Synonyms and Antonyms

Remember that **synonyms** are words that have similar meanings. **Antonyms** are words that have the opposite meaning.

Use the clues to find a synonym or antonym to solve the puzzle.

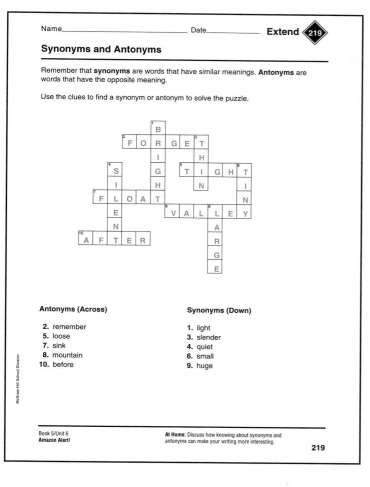

Antonyms (Across)

2. remember
5. loose
7. sink
8. mountain
10. before

Synonyms (Down)

1. light
3. slender
4. quiet
6. small
9. huge

At Home: Discuss how knowing about synonyms and antonyms can make your writing more interesting.

219

Context Clues

Read the paragraph. Use the **context clues** to write a definition of the underlined words. Answers will vary.

Today many scientists are discussing the ecology of the rain forests. Knowing about the relationships between living things and their environment has helped scientists understand more about the delicate balance of nature that exists in our world's rain forests. Even the slightest change can affect the population of an animal or plant species. To understand the rain forest, a person needs to know a little about its environment. The soil, climate, and animal life of rain forests are like no other place on Earth. Rain forests generally get a tremendous amount of rainfall each year. Large amounts of rainfall increase the growth of vegetation, causing treetops to form large canopies covering the forest floors. An abundance of plant and animal life exists in the rain forest canopies. Scientists believe there are still thousands of unknown and undiscovered species of life in the rain forests.

1. ecology __the relationship between living things and their environment__
2. relationships __connections between different things.__
3. delicate __fragile; easily unsettled or upset__
4. population __a certain number; a group of animals or plants__
5. environment __surroundings, soil, climate, vegetation, and animal life__
6. climate __general weather patterns__
7. vegetation __plant life__
8. canopies __coverings; a tree covering__
9. abundance __a large amount__
10. species __a group of similar animals or plants__

At Home: Identify the clues in the paragraph that helped you with the words.

220

Book 5/Unit 6
Amazon Alert!

T51

Amazon Alert! • GRAMMAR

Sentence Combining

> • Two sentences can be combined by adding an adjective or adverb to one sentence.

Combine each pair of sentences. Remember to leave out words that repeat or mean the same thing.

1. The Amazon is a wild forest. The Amazon is enormous.
   The Amazon is an enormous wild forest.

2. Many rivers cross this forest. The rivers are wide.
   Many wide rivers cross this forest.

3. We heard the bad news. We heard it yesterday.
   We heard the bad news yesterday.

4. People who cut trees must pay fines. The fines are huge.
   People who cut trees must pay huge fines.

5. Satellites provide information. The information is crucial.
   Satellites provide crucial information.

6. Satellites provide crucial information. They provide it quickly.
   Satellites quickly provide crucial information.

7. The Indians like their lives. Their lives are traditional.
   The Indians like their traditional lives.

8. The rainforest is a national treasure. The rainforest is important.
   The rainforest is an important national treasure.

9. Indians live in the jungle. Indians live peacefully.
   Indians live peacefully in the jungle.

10. The 1990s were destructive years. The years were terrible.
    The 1990s were terribly destructive years.

Extension: Ask partners to write short sentences about the rainforest. Than have them exchange papers and combine sentences that share a noun or verb.

10 | Grade 5/Unit 6
Amazon Alert!

185

Sentence Combining

> • Two sentences can be combined by adding a prepositional phrase to one sentence.

Read the pair of sentences. Combine each pair, using a prepositional phrase. Answers may vary.

1. The Yanomami live traditionally. The Yanomami live in the Amazon.
   The Yanomami live traditionally in the Amazon.

2. People cut trees. The trees are cut for fuel and lumber.
   People cut trees for fuel and lumber.

3. The rain hits the ground. The rain hits during the night.
   The rain hits the ground during the night.

4. Piranha eat other fish. Piranha eat in the Amazon River.
   Piranha eat other fish in the Amazon River.

5. Deforestation threatens life. Deforestation threatens around the world.
   Deforestation threatens life around the world.

6. Environmentalists protect the rainforest. They work in Brazil.
   Environmentalists in Brazil protect the rainforest.

7. Parrots live nearby. Parrots live in the canopy.
   Parrots live nearby in the canopy.

8. Farmers plant crops. Farmers plant near the rainforest.
   Farmers plant crops near the rainforest.

9. Environmentalists appreciate Possuelo. They appreciate his hard work.
   Environmentalists appreciate Possuelo for his hard work.

10. The rivers run full. The rivers run across the jungle.
    The rivers run full across the jungle.

Extension: Ask partners to give each other topics related to the rainforest. Have each student write four sentences about the topic. Then challenge partners to write as many combinations of the sentences as they can.

186

Grade 5/Unit 6
Amazon Alert! 10

Sentence Combining

> • Two sentences can be combined by adding an adjective or adverb to one sentence.
> • Two sentences can be combined by adding a prepositional phrase to one sentence.

Read each paragraph. Look for sentences that can be combined. Choose the best way to combine the sentences as you rewrite the paragraphs. Answers may vary.

The jungle has many animals and plants. The animals and plants are diverse. Scientists have not counted even half of their numbers. People study the rainforest. They study it continually. Some plants can be used for medicines. These plants are in the rainforest. Some plants can cure diseases. The diseases are serious.

The jungle has many diverse animals and plants. Scientists have not counted even half of their numbers. People study the rainforest continually. Some plants in the rainforest can be used for medicines. Some plants can cure serious diseases.

People can protect the rainforest. The rainforest is fragile. You can recycle paper and wood. You can recycle in your home. Architects can build with steel. They can build often. If you care a lot, you can also call an environmental group. You can call soon. You can save the trees. The trees are in the rainforest.

People can protect the fragile rainforest. You can recycle paper and wood in your home. Architects can often build with steel. If you care a lot, you can also call an environmental group soon. You can save the trees in the rainforest.

Extension: Ask students to write two versions of a poem about forests. Have them write one version that contains small choppy sentences and stanzas. Have them write another version by combining shorter sentences.

10 | Grade 5/Unit 6
Amazon Alert!

187

Using Punctuation Marks

> • Begin every sentence with a capital letter.
> • Use the correct end mark for each sentence.
> • Use a comma to set off a person's name when the person is spoken to directly.

Rewrite the sentences. Add capitalization, end punctuation, and commas where they are needed.

1. martin have you ever been to the rainforest
   Martin, have you ever been to the rainforest?

2. our plane landed in Sao Paulo
   Our plane landed in Sao Paulo.

3. there are so many beautiful flowers there
   There are so many beautiful flowers there!

4. this jungle is incredible
   This jungle is incredible!

5. anita can you tell me the name of that bird
   Anita, can you tell me the name of that bird?

6. the canopy is full of light
   The canopy is full of light.

7. jennifer look at the monkeys
   Jennifer, look at the monkeys.

8. kito what are you photographing
   Kito, what are you photographing?

9. dad I can't see where you are pointing
   Dad, I can't see where you are pointing.

10. i want to visit the Amazon rainforest
    I want to visit the Amazon rainforest.

Extension: Have partners write funny statements, exclamations, and questions about monkeys. Ask them to omit capitalization, end punctuation, and commas. Then have partners correct each other's writing.

188

Grade 5/Unit 6
Amazon Alert!

Amazon Alert! • GRAMMAR

Sentence Combining and Using Punctuation Marks

A. Combine each pair of sentences. Write the new sentence on the line.

1. Monkeys eat bananas. Monkeys eat in the treetops.
   Monkeys eat bananas in the treetops.

2. Monkeys play tricks. The tricks are funny.
   Monkeys play funny tricks.

3. People build houses. People build with wood.
   People build houses with wood.

4. The Amazon has trees. The trees are incredible.
   The Amazon has incredible trees.

5. Indians gather plants. Indians gather in the rainforest.
   Indians gather plants in the rainforest.

6. The Yanomami have hunted animals. The Yanomami have hunted for centuries.
   The Yanomami have hunted animals for centuries.

7. People breathe oxygen. People breathe into their lungs.
   People breathe oxygen into their lungs.

B. Rewrite each sentence. Add punctuation and capitals.

8. Fernando will you write about the rainforest
   Fernando, will you write about the rainforest?

9. these birds are amazing
   These birds are amazing!

10. amy there are orchids in this forest
    Amy, there are orchids in this forest.

11. what do the birds eat
    What do the birds eat?

12. Delia watch out for that snake
    Delia, watch out for that snake!

Sentence Combining

> • Two sentences can be combined by adding an adjective or adverb to one sentence.
> • Two sentences can be combined by adding a prepositional phrase to one sentence.

Mechanics

> • Begin every sentence with a capital letter.
> • Use the correct end mark for each sentence.
> • Use a comma to set off a person's name when the person is spoken to directly.

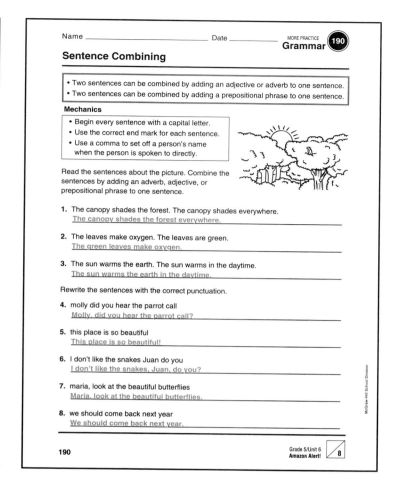

Read the sentences about the picture. Combine the sentences by adding an adverb, adjective, or prepositional phrase to one sentence.

1. The canopy shades the forest. The canopy shades everywhere.
   The canopy shades the forest everywhere.

2. The leaves make oxygen. The leaves are green.
   The green leaves make oxygen.

3. The sun warms the earth. The sun warms in the daytime.
   The sun warms the earth in the daytime.

Rewrite the sentences with the correct punctuation.

4. molly did you hear the parrot call
   Molly, did you hear the parrot call?

5. this place is so beautiful
   This place is so beautiful!

6. I don't like the snakes Juan do you
   I don't like the snakes, Juan, do you?

7. maria, look at the beautiful butterflies
   Maria, look at the beautiful butterflies.

8. we should come back next year
   We should come back next year.

Amazon Alert! • SPELLING

Name_____ Date_____

Page 185

Name_____ Date_____

Words from Math

Pretest Directions

Fold back the paper along the dotted line. Use the blanks to write each word as it is read aloud. When you finish the test, unfold the paper. Use the list at the right to correct any spelling mistakes. Practice the words you missed for the Posttest.

To Parents

Here are the results of your child's weekly spelling Pretest. You can help your child study for the Posttest by following these simple steps for each word on the word list:

1. Read the word to your child.
2. Have your child write the word, saying each letter as it is written.
3. Say each letter of the word as your child checks the spelling.
4. If a mistake has been made, have your child read each letter of the correctly spelled word aloud, and then repeat steps 1–3.

1. ___	1. ordered
2. ___	2. equal
3. ___	3. range
4. ___	4. difference
5. ___	5. volume
6. ___	6. multiply
7. ___	7. frequency
8. ___	8. mathematics
9. ___	9. centimeter
10. ___	10. formula
11. ___	11. product
12. ___	12. liter
13. ___	13. ratio
14. ___	14. bar graph
15. ___	15. millimeter
16. ___	16. estimated
17. ___	17. angle
18. ___	18. portion
19. ___	19. one-eighth
20. ___	20. quotient

Challenge Words

___	confirmed
___	isolated
___	lush
___	tropical
___	variety

Page 186

Name_____ Date_____

Words from Math

Using the Word Study Steps

1. LOOK at the word
2. SAY the word aloud.
3. STUDY the letters in the word.
4. WRITE the word.
5. CHECK the word.
   Did you spell the word right? If not, go back to step 1.

Spelling Tip

Look for smaller words or word chunks to help you remember the spelling of the word.

mathematics = **math** e **mat ics**

formula = **form** + u **la**

Word Scramble

Unscramble each set of letters to make a spelling word.

1. laque	equal	11. typillum	multiply
2. treimceent	centimeter	12. grean	range
3. proniot	portion	13. ertil	liter
4. efferdinec	difference	14. flouram	formula
5. orati	ratio	15. equitton	quotient
6. drodeer	ordered	16. ruencyfqe	frequency
7. litimmerle	millimeter	17. tammehtasic	mathematics
8. glena	angle	18. porcudt	product
9. disteamed	estimated	19. abr rahpg	bar graph
10. ovulme	volume	20. eon-tieghh	one-eighth

To Parents or Helpers:

Using the Word Study Steps above as your child comes across any new words will help him or her spell words effectively. Review the steps as you both go over this week's spelling words.

Go over the Spelling Tip with your child. Help your child find word chunks or smaller words in other spelling words.

Help your child complete the spelling activity by unscrambling the letter to form spelling words.

Page 187

Name_____ Date_____

Words from Math

ordered	volume	centimeter	ratio	angle
equal	multiply	formula	bar graph	portion
range	frequency	product	millimeter	one-eighth
difference	mathematics	liter	estimated	quotient

Say the spelling word to yourself. Then sort the word according to the vowel sound you hear in its first syllable. Write the words on the lines below.

Long vowel sound

1. equal
2. range
3. frequency
4. liter
5. ratio
6. quotient

R-controlled vowel sound

7. ordered
8. formula
9. bar graph
10. portion

Short vowel sound

11. difference
12. volume
13. multiply
14. mathematics
15. centimeter
16. product
17. millimeter
18. estimated
19. angle
20. one-eighth

Page 188

Name_____ Date_____

Words from Math

ordered	volume	centimeter	ratio	angle
equal	multiply	formula	bar graph	portion
range	frequency	product	millimeter	one-eighth
difference	mathematics	liter	estimated	quotient

Definitions

Write the spelling word that matches the definition.

1. the same as — equal
2. how often something happens — frequency
3. a chart that shows math results — bar graph
4. arithmetic — mathematics
5. 1/100 meter — centimeter
6. 1/1,000 meter — millimeter
7. proportion — ratio
8. scope — range
9. fixed rule or method — formula
10. arranged — ordered
11. remainder after subtracting — difference
12. amount of space occupied — volume
13. result of multiplication — product
14. roughly calculated — estimated
15. segment of something — portion

Challenge Extension: Write one fill-in sentence for each Challenge Word. Exchange papers with a partner and complete each fill-in sentence.

Amazon Alert! • SPELLING

Name_____ Date_____

Words from Math

Proofreading Activity

There are six spelling mistakes in the sentences below. Circle the misspelled words. Write the words correctly on the lines below.

In mathematicks, it helps to remember each formmula you learn in order to solve new problems. For example, in order to find the volume of a cube, one must multipley the length, width, and height. The resulting produckt represents the space occupied by the cube. When dealing with large numbers, an answer can be estimayted in order to first find the ranje to which the number belongs, and then locate the exact answer.

1. _____mathematics_____   3. _____mulitply_____   5. _____estimated_____

2. _____formula_____   4. _____product_____   6. _____range_____

Writing Activity

Pretend you take a trip to the Amazon rain forest. Write about what you might see or do there. Use four spelling words in your writing.

_____

_____

_____

_____

_____

Name_____ Date_____

Words from Math

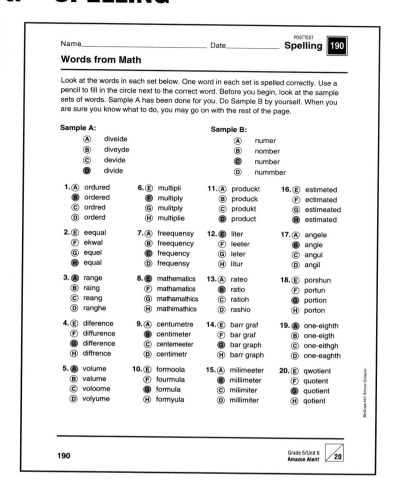

Look at the words in each set below. One word in each set is spelled correctly. Use a pencil to fill in the circle next to the correct word. Before you begin, look at the sample sets of words. Sample A has been done for you. Do Sample B by yourself. When you are sure you know what to do, you may go on with the rest of the page.

Sample A:
- (A) diveide
- (B) diveyde
- (C) devide
- (D) divide ●

Sample B:
- (A) numer
- (B) nomber
- (C) number ●
- (D) nummber

1. (A) ordured
   (B) ordered ●
   (C) ordred
   (D) orderd

2. (E) eequal
   (F) ekwal
   (G) equel
   (H) equal ●

3. (A) range ●
   (B) raing
   (C) reang
   (D) ranghe

4. (E) diference
   (F) diffurence
   (G) difference ●
   (H) diffrence

5. (A) volume ●
   (B) valume
   (C) voloome
   (D) volyume

6. (E) multipli
   (F) multiply ●
   (G) mulitply
   (H) multiplie

7. (A) freequensy
   (B) freequency
   (C) frequency ●
   (D) frequensy

8. (E) mathematics ●
   (F) mathamatics
   (G) mathamathics
   (H) mathimathics

9. (A) centumetre
   (B) centimeter ●
   (C) centemeeter
   (D) centimetr

10. (E) formoola
    (F) fourmula
    (G) formula ●
    (H) formyula

11. (A) produckt
    (B) produck
    (C) produkt
    (D) product ●

12. (E) liter ●
    (F) leeter
    (G) leter
    (H) litur

13. (A) rateo
    (B) ratio ●
    (C) ratioh
    (D) rashio

14. (E) barr graf
    (F) bar graf
    (G) bar graph ●
    (H) barr graph

15. (A) milimeeter
    (B) millimeter ●
    (C) milimiter
    (D) millimiter

16. (E) estimeted
    (F) ectimated
    (G) estimeated
    (H) estimated ●

17. (A) angele
    (B) angle ●
    (C) angul
    (D) angil

18. (E) porshun
    (F) portun
    (G) portion ●
    (H) porton

19. (A) one-eighth ●
    (B) one-eigth
    (C) one-eithgh
    (D) one-eaghth

20. (E) qwotient
    (F) quotient ●
    (G) quotiont
    (H) qotient

T55

Unit 6 Review • PRACTICE and RETEACH

Unit 6 Vocabulary Review

A. Read each word in column 1. Find its antonym, or the word most nearly **opposite** in meaning, in column 2. Then write the letter of the opposite word on the line.

	Column 1	Column 2
d	1. perished	a. made up
c	2. disgrace	b. new; in good condition
b	3. shabby	c. honor
e	4. rascals	d. survived
a	5. confirmed	e. honorable people

B. Write the correct vocabulary word on each line.

escorted	isolated	oblige	persuade	sizzle	soothing	tropical

1. How can I __persuade__ you to let me borrow your CD player?

2. To __oblige__ my parents, I do all my chores before they tell me to.

3. The old artist lived on an __isolated__ ranch about 35 miles from any town.

4. As the blizzard raged, I dreamed of visiting a __tropical__ island.

5. Sometimes a hot bath can be __soothing__.

6. Our father __escorted__ my sister to her first concert.

7. While warming butter for the sauce be careful that you don't let it __sizzle__ and burn.

Unit 6 Vocabulary Review

A. Answer each question on the line below the question.

1. Why would you have to *coax* someone? Sample answer: to convince someone to do what I wanted

2. If you were *sprawled* on a couch, how would you feel? Sample answers: relaxed

3. What does someone look like when he or she *flails*? Sample answer: His or her arms are waving about wildly in the air.

4. What does it mean to *interpret* a poem? Sample answer: To explain what you think the importance or meaning of the poem is.

B. Write the vocabulary word that means almost the same thing as the underlined word or words.

host	husking	navigate	pelted	register	variety

1. The tugboat had to <u>find its way</u> across a crowded, foggy harbor. __navigate__

2. We discovered a <u>number of different kinds</u> of butterflies in the garden. __variety__

3. We thanked the <u>person who invited us</u> for the wonderful meal. __host__

4. We <u>struck</u> each other with snowballs. __pelted__

5. The kitchen crew is out back <u>removing the husks from</u> all the corn. __husking__

6. How old do you have to be to <u>sign up</u> to vote in the United States? __register__

Unit 6 Vocabulary Review

A. Use words from the list to finish the crossword puzzle.

disgrace	coax	perished	rascals
keg	pelted	lush	escorted

Across

4. led, showed the way

6. people up to mischief

8. died, was killed

Down

1. hit again and again

2. strong embarrassment

3. barrel

5. try to convince

7. very green, with many plants

(crossword grid: ESCORTED, RASCALS, PERISHED, with DISGRACE, PELTED, KEG, COAX, LUSH)

B. Complete the sentences with the correct word from the list.

interpret	register	nightfall	persuade	ushered	confirmed

Addie was working to __register__ voters for the upcoming election. She knocked on doors and tried to __persuade__ people to sign up. Too bad it was winter and __nightfall__ came so early. Addie wasn't allowed out after dark. At her friend Sam's house, Mrs. Tabor __ushered__ Addie into the kitchen to talk. Mrs. Tabor was trying to __interpret__ the voting procedures. Addie __confirmed__ that Mrs. Tabor understood the procedures correctly.

Unit 6 Vocabulary Review

A. Read each question. Choose a word from the list to answer the question. Write your answer on the line provided.

cove	soothing	isolated	sizzle	host	husking

1. If you were the person giving your friend a birthday party, who would you be?
__host__

2. If you entered a protected area of water while sailing your boat, where would you be?
__cove__

3. If your home is 20 miles from the next nearest house, how would you describe it?
__isolated__

4. When you remove the outside leaves from an ear of corn, what are you doing?
__husking__

5. When you drop cold water into a very hot pan, what does it do?
__sizzle__

6. If you are sad and someone gives you a hug, what does that feel like?
__soothing__

B. Match each word with its definition. Write the definition on the line.

Vocabulary		Definitions
1. navigate	3	wood on the beach
2. oblige	1	to steer
3. driftwood	4	warm, from the tropics
4. tropical	2	to please
5. variety	6	spread out
6. sprawled	5	many different kinds

Unit 6 Review • EXTEND and GRAMMAR

Vocabulary

Choose the word from the box that best completes each sentence.

escorted	confirmed	oblige	persuade	register
isolated	perished	sprawled	interpret	soothing

1. The little boy tried to _persuade_ his father to let him stay up a little while longer.

2. He felt very _isolated_ sitting alone in the back of the stadium.

3. The doctor's office called and _confirmed_ her afternoon appointment.

4. The man _escorted_ his wife into the concert hall.

5. The young girl was ready to _oblige_ her parents by helping clean the house.

6. Because Margaret forgot to water the plant, it _perished_.

7. Sonny was asked to _interpret_ for a friend who did not speak English.

8. After Ben finished his daily run, he _sprawled_ out on the couch to relax.

9. Yoko went to the recreational center to _register_ for tennis lessons.

10. Shawn spoke _soothing_ words to his sister when the neighbor's dog scared her.

Write a paragraph using as many of the vocabulary words as possible.

Paragraphs will vary, but should use correct parts of speech and include the
vocabulary words.

_____

_____

_____

_____

_____

At Home: Write a sentence to show the meaning of these vocabulary words: navigate, lush, ushered, coax, and shabby.

Vocabulary Review

Unscramble the letters to form a vocabulary word. Use the letters in the boxes to make another vocabulary word. Look at the clue to help you make the word.

1. L L F A I S   FLAILS
   _ _ _ [_] _ [_]

2. E V O C   COVE
   [_] _ _ _

3. S O T H   HOST
   _ _ [_] _

4. D E L P T E   PELTED
   _ _ _ [_] _ _

5. R I S D G A E C   DISGRACE
   _ _ _ _ [_] _ [_] _

Clue: This is what we call mischievous children.   RASCALS

_ _ _ _ _ _ _

Write a poem about the vocabulary word.

Answers will vary. _____

_____

_____

_____

_____

_____

At Home: Make up riddles for new vocabulary words that you have learned and ask someone at home to guess what they are.

Sentence Parts

Read each passage and look at the underlined sentences. If the sentence is incorrect or can be written more clearly, choose the best way to rewrite it. Circle the letter of the correct answer.

> In the 1800s, many people fought fierce for African American freedom. These
> (1)
> people wanted to end slavery. They were called abolitionists. Abolitionists in the
> North and the South believed strongly in equality. Their hard struggle helped to
> (2)
> set enslaved people free.

1. A In the 1800s, many people fought fiercely for African American freedom.
   (B) In the 1800s, many people fought fiercely for African American freedom.
   C in the 1800s, many people fiercely for African American freedom.
   D No mistake.

2. F Abolitionists in the North and the South believed rightly in equality.
   G Abolitionists in the North and the South believed exactly in equality.
   H Abolitionists in the North and the South believed sometimes in equality.
   (J) No mistake.

> As Rip Van Winkle slept, the storm raged more terribly every minute. The wind
> blew most wildly than before. The thunder boomed more louder than cannons.
> (3)   (4)
> Meanwhile, Rip slept the most peacefully of anyone.

3. (A) The wind blew more wildly than before.
   B The wind blew more wilder than before.
   C The wind blew most wildest than before.
   D No mistake.

4. F The thunder boomed most louder than cannons.
   (G) The thunder boomed louder than cannons.
   H The thunder boomed loudest than cannons.
   J No mistake.

> On our vacation, my sister and I went snorkeling in Mexico. We wanted to
> see snapping turtles. We also hoped to see some dolphins. But we couldn't see
> (5)
> nothing the first day. It looked like there were none nowhere in the bay. Mom told us
> (6)
> to try again tomorrow. So we spent the afternoon looking for shells on the beach.

5. A But we couldn't see none the first day.
   B But we could see anything the first day.
   (C) But we couldn't see anything the first day.
   D No mistake.

6. F It looked like there were no nowhere in the bay.
   G It looked like there weren't none nowhere in the bay.
   (H) It looked like there were none anywhere in the bay.
   J No mistake.

> You can write a letter. You can write to your congressperson. Congresspeople
> (7)
> expect to get letters from adults and students. We wrote letters. We wrote them
> (8)
> yesterday. Our class wrote our ideas about the rainforest and equal rights.

7. A You can write a letter, you can write to your congressperson.
   B You can write a letter to your congressperson.
   (C) You can write to your congressperson.
   D No mistake.

8. (F) We wrote letters yesterday.
   G We wrote letters them yesterday.
   H We wrote letters we wrote them yesterday.
   J No mistake.

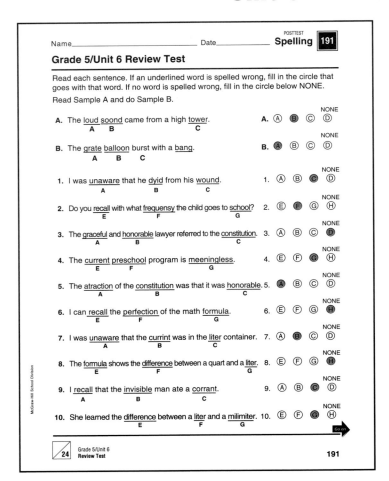

POSTTEST
Name_____ Date_____ **Spelling** 191

Grade 5/Unit 6 Review Test

Read each sentence. If an underlined word is spelled wrong, fill in the circle that goes with that word. If no word is spelled wrong, fill in the circle below NONE.

Read Sample A and do Sample B.

A. The loud soond came from a high tower. A. Ⓐ Ⓑ Ⓒ Ⓓ(NONE)
        A   B   C

B. The grate balloon burst with a bang. B. ●Ⓐ Ⓑ Ⓒ Ⓓ(NONE)
        A   B   C

1. I was unaware that he dyid from his wound. 1. Ⓐ Ⓑ ● Ⓓ(NONE)
        A   B   C

2. Do you recall with what frequensy the child goes to school? 2. Ⓔ ● Ⓖ Ⓗ(NONE)
           E   F   G

3. The graceful and honorable lawyer referred to the constitution. 3. Ⓐ Ⓑ Ⓒ ●(NONE)
       A   B   C

4. The current preschool program is meeningless. 4. Ⓔ Ⓕ ● Ⓗ(NONE)
       E   F   G

5. The atraction of the constitution was that it was honorable. 5. ● Ⓑ Ⓒ Ⓓ(NONE)
       A   B   C

6. I can recall the perfection of the math formula. 6. Ⓔ Ⓕ Ⓖ ●(NONE)
         E   F   G

7. I was unaware that the currint was in the liter container. 7. Ⓐ ● Ⓒ Ⓓ(NONE)
       A   B   C

8. The formula shows the difference between a quart and a liter. 8. Ⓔ Ⓕ Ⓖ ●(NONE)
       E   F   G

9. I recall that the invisible man ate a corrant. 9. Ⓐ Ⓑ ● Ⓓ(NONE)
      A   B   C

10. She learned the difference between a liter and a milimiter. 10. Ⓔ Ⓕ ● Ⓗ(NONE)
           E   F   G

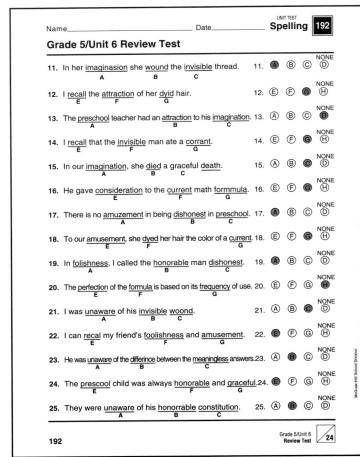

UNIT TEST
Name_____ Date_____ **Spelling** 192

Grade 5/Unit 6 Review Test

11. In her imaginasion she wound the invisible thread. 11. ● Ⓑ Ⓒ Ⓓ(NONE)
          A   B   C

12. I recall the attraction of her dyid hair. 12. Ⓔ Ⓕ ● Ⓗ(NONE)
      E   F   G

13. The preschool teacher had an attraction to his imagination. 13. Ⓐ Ⓑ Ⓒ ●(NONE)
         A   B   C

14. I recall that the invisible man ate a corrant. 14. Ⓔ Ⓕ Ⓖ ●(NONE)
      E   F   G

15. In our imagination, she died a graceful death. 15. Ⓐ Ⓑ ● Ⓓ(NONE)
         A   B   C

16. He gave consideration to the current math formmula. 16. Ⓔ Ⓕ ● Ⓗ(NONE)
        E   F   G

17. There is no amuzement in being dishonest in preschool. 17. ● Ⓑ Ⓒ Ⓓ(NONE)
         A   B   C

18. To our amusement, she dyed her hair the color of a current. 18. Ⓔ Ⓕ ● Ⓗ(NONE)
        E   F   G

19. In folishness, I called the honorable man dishonest. 19. ● Ⓑ Ⓒ Ⓓ(NONE)
       A   B   C

20. The perfection of the formula is based on its frequency of use. 20. Ⓔ Ⓕ Ⓖ ●(NONE)
       E   F   G

21. I was unaware of his invisible woond. 21. Ⓐ Ⓑ ● Ⓓ(NONE)
         A   B   C

22. I can recal my friend's foolishness and amusement. 22. ● Ⓕ Ⓖ Ⓗ(NONE)
        E   F   G

23. He was unaware of the differince between the meaningless answers. 23. Ⓐ ● Ⓒ Ⓓ(NONE)
        A   B   C

24. The prescool child was always honorable and graceful. 24. Ⓔ Ⓕ Ⓖ ●(NONE)
        E   F   G

25. They were unaware of his honorrable constitution. 25. Ⓐ ● Ⓒ Ⓓ(NONE)
        A   B   C

Judgments and Decisions

OBJECTIVES Students will evaluate decisions through designing a character graph, preparing "decision skits," and writing a group story. Students will make and analyze judgments.

Alternate Activities

Visual

CHARACTER BAR GRAPH

Materials: graph or drawing paper, markers or colored pencils

Students will demonstrate an understanding of making judgments and decisions by examining the traits and actions of literary characters.

- Have students select a character from a story they have recently read. Ask them to design a bar graph judging the character's traits or actions.

- On the bottom horizontal line, label the bar for honesty, cooperation, kindness, self-control, and so forth, as well as for actions taken by the character in the story.

- On the vertical axis, have students develop a rating scale, such as numbers from one to ten.

- Have students discuss the bar-graph profiles they created for their characters.

▶ **Intrapersonal**

Kinesthetic

DECISION SKITS

Students will create and perform skits about decisions made by familiar literary characters.

- Work with students to brainstorm a list of characters from stories they have recently read.

- Organize students into small groups. Encourage each group to select one character from the list and to review that story.

- Have students make notes about decisions the character made during the story. Prompt them to make judgments about the decisions.

- Groups will use their notes to present a skit for the class. Encourage whole-class discussion after each performance.

▶ **Bodily/Kinesthetic**

Auditory

MODERN MARVELS

Materials: history books, paper, pencils

Students will brainstorm items to include on a criteria chart, and they will make judgments about the criteria for inclusion as they write a group story.

- Brainstorm a list of inventions that have appeared in the lifetimes of students' grandparents.

- Organize students into groups of 4 or 5. Give each group a writing paper with this prompt: *Our grandparents have seen so many modern marvels in their lifetimes. They laugh about all the new things today, because they can't imagine how they ever lived without them.*

Have students pass the paper around their group, so that each student can add a sentence to the story until it is complete.

- Encourage students to discuss the finished stories and the decisions each student made when adding a sentence.

▶ **Linguistic**

See Reteach 186, 190, 207, 211

Library/Media Center

✓BJECTIVES Students will identify and use library or media center reference tools to play word games, search the library catalog, and prepare for an interview.

Alternate Activities

Visual

THESAURUS RACE

Materials: thesauruses, paper strips, index cards, pencils, paper bags

Students will participate in a team game to find synonyms and antonyms using a thesaurus.

- Prepare several sets of paper strips using the following words (one word per strip): *young, wise, complete, odd, wind, tale, tornado, danger, warm, lazy, merry, soft, exit, afraid, against,* and so on. Next to each word, write either *Antonym* or *Synonym*. Place the strips in a paper bag.

- Organize students into teams of 4 or 5 and invite them to play a game. Each team should have their own thesaurus and bag of word strips. In turn, each team member draws a paper strip from the bag and uses a thesaurus to locate either an antonym or synonym, depending on what the strip indicates.

- After locating a word, students should write it on an index card, along with the original word and a page reference. After all the paper strips have been drawn, have students exchange index cards and discuss the different words.
  ▶ **Interpersonal**

Kinesthetic

CATALOG SEARCH

Materials: library or media center, writing paper and pencils

Students will research a question or topic from the unit by locating appropriate resources.

- Have students work in pairs to brainstorm questions or topics from the unit.

- Send partners to the library or media center to locate as many sources on the question or topic as possible.

- Have students record their information sources and share them with the class. Encourage a group discussion about the variety and number of sources each pair found and listed.
  ▶ **Spatial**

Auditory

TALK SHOW

Materials: encyclopedia, library sources, pencils, paper

Students will use information from an encyclopedia or other library sources to write background information on a historical character from the unit. Students will perform in character for a class talk show interview.

- Organize students into groups of 4 or 5. Have each group select a character from the unit's nonfiction selections to research.

- Have students use library resources to write a short biographical sketch of the character.

- Encourage students to role-play a talk show skit in which they share the information they learned.
  ▶ **Linguistic**

See Reteach 189, 196, 203, 210, 217

Draw Conclusions

OBJECTIVES Students will use logical reasoning to identify different story endings, develop environmental solutions, and give auditory clues. Students will draw conclusions from two or more ideas.

Alternate Activities

Visual

ALTERNATIVE CONCLUSIONS

 Materials: children's literature film clip, drawing or writing paper, pencils

After watching the actual ending to a story, students will suggest alternative conclusions.

- Show the final 10 or 15 minutes of the film version of a familiar children's book, such as *The Wizard of Oz* or *Charlotte's Web*.

- Have students write or draw other possible endings (or continuations) for the story.

- Discuss the suggested conclusions and what ideas in the film led to the conclusions.

  ▶ **Intrapersonal**

Kinesthetic

ENVIRONMENTAL POSTERS

 Materials: poster board, crayons or markers, magazines, construction paper, paste, scissors, books on the environment

Students will create posters representing their conclusions for cleaning up the environment.

- Organize students into groups of 4 or 5. Give each group magazines and books about the environment.

- Have each group identify an environmental issue and create a poster suggesting ways to deal with that issue.

- Groups should display their posters on the bulletin board and explain what ideas led them to their conclusions concerning the issues they chose to deal with.

  ▶ **Bodily/Kinesthetic**

Auditory

I SPY WITH MY LITTLE EAR

 Students will take turns describing different environments giving only auditory clues. The rest of the class will attempt to draw conclusions about what, or where, the student is describing.

- Ask students to close their eyes and listen closely. Begin by crowing like a rooster. Wait a few seconds and then move on to the following sound effects: moo, oink, and whinny.

- Tell students to open their eyes. Encourage them to guess where they might go to hear sounds like those you just made. Ask students to discuss how your clues helped them to draw their conclusions.

- Have volunteers take turns coming to the front of the class and giving auditory clues of their own. You might suggest the following environments for describing through sounds: a traffic jam, a jungle, a birthday party, a baseball game, a crowded restaurant.

  ▶ **Linguistic/Logical/Mathematical**

See Reteach 191, 198, 212

Context Clues

Alternate Activities

Visual

CONTENT-AREA CROSSWORDS

Materials: pencils, paper, vocabulary lists, sample crossword puzzle books, content-area textbooks, dictionary (PARTNERS)

Students will create crossword puzzles whose clues require sentence completions based on context.

- On the chalkboard, create lists of vocabulary words from various content-area texts, such as social studies, science, health, and math.

Have each student use a vocabulary list from one area to create a simple crossword puzzle with word clues that require the solver to use contextual information to complete a sentence. For example, a clue for the word *endangered* might be: "The continued existence of _____ species is threatened by the careless actions of people." Use the puzzle books for writing models. (WRITING)

- Have pairs of students exchange puzzles and solve them.
  ▶ **Spatial**

Kinesthetic

CONTEXT-CLUE CHARADES

 Materials: content-area textbooks, index cards, colored markers (ONE)

In this activity, students will give oral or visual context clues for content-area words.

- Use index cards and markers to write nouns and verbs from the content-area texts that lend themselves to being acted out.

- Place the index cards face down in a pile.

- Have each student take a card in turn and give oral clues or act out clues to the word's meaning until classmates guess the word.
  ▶ **Bodily/Kinesthetic**

Auditory

FAVORITE THINGS

 Materials: content-area textbooks, writing paper, pencils (ONE)

Students will write and present an oral report using specialized vocabulary.

- Have each student select one content-area text and use it as the source for a writing topic.

 Have students write a report about the chosen topic and use five specialized vocabulary words, whose meanings will be decipherable for the reader based on clear context clues. (WRITING)

- Students will present the report orally, highlighting the five vocabulary words and the way their meanings are clarified by their context.
  ▶ **Intrapersonal**

See Reteach 192, 206, 220

Cause and Effect

Students will determine why something happened or what might happen next in cartoons, science experiments, and music. Students will use the words *because*, *in order to*, and *since* in their explanations.

Alternate Activities

Visual

BECAUSE

Materials: cartoon strips, paper, pencils

GROUP Students will select a cartoon event and determine why it happened and what will happen next.

• Organize students into groups of 4 or 5. Give each group a cartoon strip.

WRITING Have students look at an action frame in the middle of their group's cartoon. Ask them to write why this action happened and what will happen next. Encourage them to use the words *because*, *in order to*, and *since* in their written explanation.

• Have groups present their work to the class.

▶ **Spatial**

Kinesthetic

SCIENCE EXPERIMENTS

Materials: science textbooks or magazines, **PARTNERS** lab equipment, paper and pencils

Students will demonstrate and write about the cause-and-effect relationships they observed in a science experiment.

• Have students work in pairs. Invite partners to search through science texts or magazines to find an experiment they can do.

• If possible, have partners complete the experiment, either in class or as homework.

 Ask partners to write a scientific report **WRITING** explaining the experiment they chose and the cause-and-effect relationships they identified.

▶ **Logical/Mathematical**

Auditory

NAME THAT MUSIC

Materials: paper, pencil, list of types **ONE** of music, tape or CD player, various types of music

Students will identify different types of music and explain what helped them to recognize the type.

• On the chalkboard, list various types of available music, such as march, polka, rock 'n roll, rap, classical, swing, jazz, lullaby, ballad, etc. To build prior knowledge, play a little of each type of music and identify with the students features that distinguish one type of music from another.

• Play a 1-minute section of a type of music, such as a polka. Poll students to see what the majority thinks this music is.

• Identify the music type and have students orally explain how they recognized it. Encourage them to use the words *because*, *since*, and *in order to* in their explanations.

• Repeat the process randomly through the list of music types.

▶ **Musical**

See Reteach 193, 197, 205, 218

Antonyms and Synonyms

Alternate Activities

Visual

SYNONYM/ANTONYM MOBILES

Materials: construction paper, markers, string or yarn, tape or glue

Students will work together to make mobiles to display words along with their synonyms and antonyms.

- Organize students into groups. Give each group a sheet of construction paper that has a word written on it. Choose words for which there are many synonyms and antonyms, such as *huge*, *good*, *cold*, *frightened*.

- Have students cut several circle and square shapes out of construction paper.

 Invite them to write words that are synonyms for the assigned word on the circle shapes, and antonyms for it on the square shapes. Students can then tape or glue the circles and squares to pieces of yarn and attach the yarn to the construction paper showing the original word.

- Display the mobiles in the classroom. Encourage students to refer to them during independent writing assignments.

▶ Spatial

Kinesthetic

ANTONYM AND SYNONYM CHARADES

Students will pantomime pairs of words to emphasize how they are similar or opposite.

- Organize students into pairs. Have each partner brainstorm a list of synonym and antonym pairs.

- Invite students to play a game of charades with their partner by pantomiming the meanings of word pairs, such as *high-low*; *fast-slow*; *cry-weep*.

- Have students continue to take turns until both partners have exhausted their word list.

▶ Bodily/Kinesthetic

Auditory

FUNNY LANGUAGE

Materials: dictionary, thesaurus, textbook glossary, paper, pencils

Students will conduct conversations in which one partner will say a sentence using an antonym for a given word, and the other will say a sentence using a synonym for it.

- Create a list of words from the unit. Put this list on the chalkboard and have students help identify antonyms and synonyms for each word.

Have student work as partners. Ask them to write a sentence using an antonym and a different sentence using a synonym for each word on the word list.

- Call out a word. Partners will take turns reading appropriate sentences. One will read a sentence with an antonym. The other will respond with a sentence using a synonym.

- Repeat until all words have been used.

▶ Linguistic

See Reteach 199, 213, 219

Sequence of Events

OBJECTIVES Students will create a flow chart, time line, and biographical report in order to identify and use logical or time-order sequence.

Alternate Activities

Visual

STORY SEQUENCE

 Materials: drawing paper, pencils, news-papers

Students will design a flow chart to show the logical order of news events.

- Provide students with copies of current news-papers. Have them select an article to read.
- Then ask students to create a flow chart on the drawing paper, placing the events of the news article in proper sequence. They may wish to draw or write their entries for the flow chart.
- Invite students to share their flow charts with the class.

  ▶ **Spatial**

Kinesthetic

FIRST, SECOND, THIRD

 Materials: science books, large construction paper, markers or colored pencils

Students will draw a circular time line to show understanding of time order.

- Have students work as partners to locate infor-mation in science books on the life cycle of a tree or the formation of a gem stone.
- Ask them to draw a circular flow chart of the cycle. Proceeding clockwise, students will label the major stages—and include drawings, if appropriate—in the growth of a tree or the development of a gem.

- Display the charts on the bulletin board in the classroom.

  ▶ **Logical/Mathematical**

Auditory

A BIOGRAPHICAL MOMENT

 Materials: encyclopedia, biographies, paper, pencils

Students will research the life of a famous person and write a brief narrative, using logical order.

- Organize students into groups of 4 or 5. Have each group identify a famous person they would like to research.

 Students in each group will take notes on the life of the person as a child, as a young adult, and as an adult. Ask them to write a short biographical sketch, using logical order, that describes this person's life and accomplishments.

- Invite students to present their narratives orally to the class.

  ▶ **Interpersonal**

See Reteach 200, 204, 214

A Communication Tool

Although typewriters and computers are readily available, many situations continue to require handwriting. Tasks such as keeping journals, completing forms, taking notes, making shopping or organizational lists, and the ability to read hand-written manuscript or cursive writing are a few examples of practical application of this skill.

BEFORE YOU BEGIN

Before children begin to write, certain fine motor skills need to be developed. Examples of activities that can be used as warm-up activities are:

- **Simon Says** Play a game of Simon Says using just finger positions.
- **Finger Plays and Songs** Sing songs that use Signed English, American Sign Language or finger spelling.
- **Mazes** Mazes are available in a wide range of difficulty. You can also create mazes that allow children to move their writing instruments from left to right.

Determining Handedness

Keys to determining handedness in a child:

- Which hand does the child eat with? This is the hand that is likely to become the dominant hand.
- Does the child start coloring with one hand and then switch to the other? This may be due to fatigue rather than lack of hand preference.
- Does the child cross midline to pick things up or use the closest hand? Place items directly in front of the child to see if one hand is preferred.
- Does the child do better with one hand or the other?

The Mechanics of Writing

DESK AND CHAIR

- Chair height should allow for the feet to rest flat on the floor.
- Desk height should be two inches above the level of the elbows when the child is sitting.
- The chair should be pulled in allowing for an inch of space between the child's abdomen and the desk.
- Children sit erect with the elbows resting on the desk.
- Children should have models of letters on the desk or at eye level, not above their heads.

PAPER POSITION

- **Right-handed children** should turn the paper so that the lower left-hand corner of the paper points to the abdomen.
- **Left-handed children** should turn the paper so that the lower right-hand corner of the paper points to the abdomen.
- The nondominant hand should anchor the paper near the top so that the paper doesn't slide.
- The paper should be moved up as the child nears the bottom of the paper. Many children won't think of this and may let their arms hang off the desk when they reach the bottom of a page.

The Writing Instrument Grasp

For handwriting to be functional, the writing instrument must be held in a way that allows for fluid dynamic movement.

FUNCTIONAL GRASP PATTERNS

- **Tripod Grasp** With open web space, the writing instrument is held with the tip of the thumb and the index finger and rests against the side of the third finger. The thumb and index finger form a circle.
- **Quadrupod Grasp** With open web space, the writing instrument is held with the tip of the thumb and index finger and rests against the fourth finger. The thumb and index finger form a circle.

INCORRECT GRASP PATTERNS

- **Fisted Grasp** The writing instrument is held in a fisted hand.
- **Pronated Grasp** The writing instrument is held diagonally within the hand with the tips of the thumb and index finger on the writing instrument but with no support from other fingers.
- **Five-Finger Grasp** The writing instrument is held with the tips of all five fingers.

TO CORRECT WRITING INSTRUMENT GRASPS

- Have children play counting games with an eye dropper and water.
- Have children pick up small objects with a tweezer.
- Do counting games with children picking up small coins using just the thumb and index finger.

FLEXED OR HOOKED WRIST

- The writing instrument can be held in a variety of grasps with the wrist flexed or bent. This is typically seen with left-handed writers but is also present in some right-handed writers. To correct wrist position, have children check their writing posture and paper placement.

Evaluation Checklist

Functional writing is made up of two elements, legibility and functional speed.

LEGIBILITY

MANUSCRIPT

Formation and Strokes

- ☑ Does the child begin letters at the top?
- ☑ Do circles close?
- ☑ Are the horizontal lines straight?
- ☑ Do circular shapes and extender and descender lines touch?
- ☑ Are the heights of all upper-case letters equal?
- ☑ Are the heights of all lower-case letters equal?
- ☑ Are the lengths of the extenders and descenders the same for all letters?

Directionality

- ☑ Are letters and words formed from left to right?
- ☑ Are letters and words formed from top to bottom?

Spacing

- ☑ Are the spaces between letters equidistant?
- ☑ Are the spaces between words equidistant?
- ☑ Do the letters rest on the line?
- ☑ Are the top, bottom and side margins even?

CURSIVE

Formation and Strokes

- ☑ Do circular shapes close?
- ☑ Are the downstrokes parallel?
- ☑ Do circular shapes and downstroke lines touch?
- ☑ Are the heights of all upper-case letters equal?
- ☑ Are the heights of all lower-case letters equal?
- ☑ Are the lengths of the extenders and descenders the same for all letters?
- ☑ Do the letters which finish at the top join the next letter? (*l, o, v, w*)
- ☑ Do the letters which finish at the bottom join the next letter? (*a c, d h, i k l m n r, s, t u x*)
- ☑ Do letters with descenders join the next letter? (*f, g, j, p, q, y, z*)
- ☑ Do all letters touch the line?
- ☑ Is the vertical slant of all letters consistent?

Directionality

- ☑ Are letters and words formed from left to right?
- ☑ Are letters and words formed from top to bottom?

Spacing

- ☑ Are the spaces between letters equidistant?
- ☑ Are the spaces between words equidistant?
- ☑ Do the letters rest on the line?
- ☑ Are the top, bottom and side margins even?

SPEED

The prettiest handwriting is not functional for classroom work if it takes the child three times longer than the rest of the class to complete work assignments. After the children have been introduced to writing individual letters, begin to add time limitations to the completion of copying or writing assignments. Then check the child's work for legibility.

Handwriting Models—Manuscript

A B C D E F G H
I J K L M N O P
Q R S T U V W
X Y Z

a b c d e f g h
i j k l m n o p
q r s t u v w
x y z

Handwriting Models—Cursive

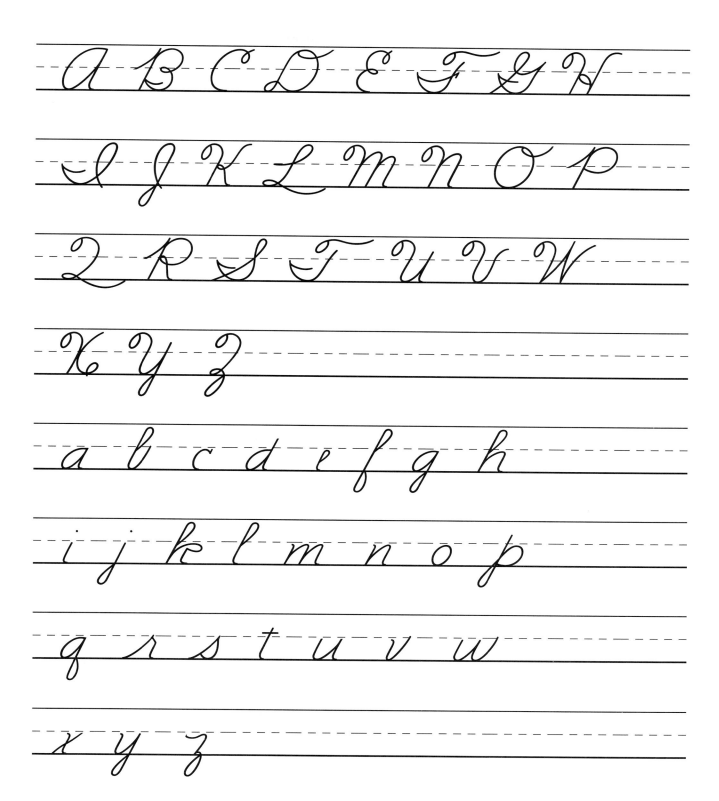

Selection Titles | Honors, Prizes, and Awards

Selection Titles	Honors, Prizes, and Awards
THE GOLD COIN Unit 2, p. 140 by *Alma Flor Ada* Illustrated by *Neil Waldman*	**Christopher Award (1992)**
JOHN HENRY Unit 2, p. 168 by *Julius Lester* Illustrated by *Jerry Pinkney*	**Center for Children's Books Blue Ribbon (1994), ALA Notable, Caldecott Medal Honor Book, Boston Globe-Horn Book Award (1995)** **Illustrator: Jerry Pinkney,** winner of Newbery Medal, Boston Globe-Horn Book Honor (1977) for *Roll of Thunder, Hear My Cry*; ALA Notable, Cadelcott Honor, Coretta Scott King Award (1989) for *Mirandy and Brother Wind*; ALA Notable, Caldecott Honor, Coretta Scott King Honor (1990) for *Talking Eggs*; ALA Notable (1991) for *Further Tales of Uncle Remus*; ALA Notable, Christopher Award, Coretta Scott King Award (1997) for *Minty*
IT'S OUR WORLD, TOO Unit 2, p. 202 by *Phillip Hoose* Illustrated by *Robert Rober*	**Christopher Award (1994)**
DEAR MR. HENSHAW Unit 2, p. 224 by *Beverly Cleary* Illustrated by *R. J. Shay*	**Newbery Medal, Christopher Award (1984), Dorothy Canfield Fisher Children's Book Award (1985)**
THE SIDEWALK RACER OR ON THE SKATEBOARD Unit 3, p. 254 by *Lillian Morrison*	**Poet: Lillian Morrison,** winner of ALA Notable (1965) for *Sprints and Distances: Sports in Poetry and the Poetry in Sports*
THE MARBLE CHAMP Unit 3, p. 258 by *Gary Soto* Illustrated by *Ken Spengler*	**Author: Gary Soto,** winner of Academy of American Poets Award (1975); California Library Association's John And Patricia Beatty Award, Best Books for Young Adults Awards (1991) for *Baseball in April and Other Stories*; Americás Book Award, Honorable Mention (1995) for *Chato's Kitchen*; Americás Book Award, Commended List (1995) for *Canto Familiar*; (1996) for *The Old Man and His Door*; (1997) for *Buried Onions*

Selection Titles | Honors, Prizes, and Awards

THE PAPER DRAGON
Unit 3, p. 276
by *Marguerite W. Davol*
Illustrated by *Robert Sabuda*

Golden Kite Award (1997), ALA Notable, Notable Children's Trade Book in the Field of Social Studies (1998)

GRANDMA ESSIE'S COVERED WAGON
Unit 3, p. 310
by *David Williams*
Illustrated by *Wiktor Sadowski*

Notable Trade Book in the Field of Social Studies (1994)

GOING BACK HOME: AN ARTIST RETURNS TO THE SOUTH
Unit 3, p. 342
by *Toyomi Igus*
Illustrated by **Michele Wood**

Center for Children's Books Blue Ribbon (1996), American Book Award Winner (1997)

TO DARK EYES DREAMING
Unit 3, p. 382
by *Zilpha Keatley Snyder*

Poet: Zilpha Keatley Snyder, winner of Newbery Medal Honor Book (1968) and George G. Stone Center for Children's Books Recognition of Merit Award (1973) for *The Egypt Game*; ALA Notable (1971) and Christopher Award (1974) for *The Headless Cupid*

VOYAGE OF THE *DAWN TREADER*
Unit 4, p. 388
by *C.S. Lewis*
Illustrated by *Amy Hill*

Author: C.S. Lewis, winner of Lewis Carroll Shelf Award (1962) for *The Lion, the Witch, and the Wardrobe;* Carnegie Medal (1956) for *The Last Battle*

AN ISLAND SCRAPBOOK
Unit 4, p. 434
by *Virginia Wright-Frierson*

Notable Children's Book in the Language Arts, Outstanding Nature Book for Children by John Burroughs Association (1998), Outstanding Science Trade Book for Children (1999)

THE RIDDLE
Unit 5, p. 510
by **Adele Vernon**
Illustrated by **Robert Rayevsky and Vladimir Radunsky**

Booklist Editor's Choice

Selection Titles	Honors, Prizes, and Awards
TONWEYA AND THE EAGLES Unit 5, p. 556 by *Rosebud Yellow Robe* Illustrated by *Richard Red Owl*	**ALA Notable (1979)**
BREAKER'S BRIDGE Unit 5, p. 582 by *Laurence Yep* Illustrated by *David Wisniewski*	**Author: Laurence Yep,** winner of Newbery Honor Book Award (1976) for *Dragonwings*; (1994) for *Dragon's Gate;* Boston Globe-Horn Book Honor (1977) for *Child of the Owl*
PHILBERT PHLURK Unit 5, p. 612 by *Jack Prelutsky*	**Poet: Jack Prelutsky,** winner of New York Times Notable Book (1980) for *The Headless Horseman Rides Tonight*; ALA Notable (1983) for *Random House Book of Poetry for Children*; (1985) for *New Kid on the Block*; (1991) for *Something Big Has Been Here*
PAPER I Unit 6, p. 614 by *Carl Sandburg*	**Poet: Carl Sandburg**, winner of Pulitzer Prize in poetry (1919) for *Corn Huskers;* (1951) for *Complete Poems;* Pulitzer Prize in history (1940) for *Abraham Lincoln: The War Years;* Poetry Society of America's Frost Medal for Distinguished Achievement (1952); ALA Notable (1982) for *Rainbows are Made: Poems of Carl Sandburg*
AMISTAD RISING Unit 6, p. 618 by *Veronica Chambers* Illustrated by **Paul Lee**	**Author: Veronica Chambers,** winner of ALA Best Book for Young Adults (1996) for *Mama's Girl*
THE SILENT LOBBY Unit 6, p. 700 by *Mildred Pitts Walter* Illustrated by *Gil Ashby*	**Author: Mildred Pitts Walter,** winner of Coretta Scott King Award for illustration (1984) for *My Mama Needs Me;* (1987) for *Justin and the Best Biscuits in the World*
FREDERICK DOUGLASS 1817–1895 Unit 6, p. 728 by *Langston Hughes*	**Poet: *Langston Hughes,*** winner of Witter Bynner Prize (1926); Harmon Foundation Literature Award (1931); American Academy of Arts and Letters Grant (1946); Spingarn Medal (1960)

Theme Bibliography

Trade Books

Additional fiction and nonfiction trade books related to each selection can be shared with students throughout the unit.

Passage to Freedom: The Sugihara Story
Ken Mochizuki, illustrated by Dom Lee (Lee & Low, 1997)

The courageous story of Chiune Sugihara, Japanese consul in Lithuania, who helped hundreds of Polish Jews escape the Nazis.

Sky Pioneer: A Photobiography of Amelia Earhart
Corrine Szabo (National Geographic Society, 1997)

Focusing on her ambition and achievement, this book captures the spirit of Amelia Earhart, with dozens of photographs and quotes from her own writings.

Run Away Home
Patricia C. McKissack (Scholastic, 1997)

In 1888, a courageous African American family gives shelter to an Apache boy who escapes from the train taking him to a reservation.

Dragon Prince: A Chinese Beauty and the Beast Tale
Laurence Yep, illustrated by Kam Mak (HarperCollins, 1997)

In this Chinese retelling of the classic story, a young girl learns that her dragon is actually a prince.

Philip Hall Likes Me, I Reckon Maybe
Bette Greene, illustrated by Charles Lilly (Bantam Doubleday Dell, 1997)

Eleven-year-old Beth Lambert is an unlikely heroine who experiences life in a thoughtful, emotional, and always heartwarming way.

Ella Enchanted
Gail Carson Levine (HarperCollins, 1997)

A new spin on an old tale introduces Ella, a fairy-cursed, ogre-embattled, spunky heroine whose courage breaks an old spell and delivers a happily-ever-after ending.

Technology

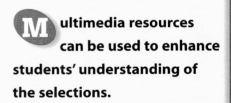

Multimedia resources can be used to enhance students' understanding of the selections.

 African American History: Heroism, Struggle, and Hope (SVE/Churchill) CD-ROM, Macintosh, Windows. A documentation of African American history that examines the achievements and struggles of African Americans.

 African Americans Tell Their Stories (SVE/Churchill) Video, 19 min. Profiles of heroic and accomplished African Americans provide insight into their lives.

 A Woman Called Moses (Zenger Media) Video, 200 min. A re-creation of the life of Harriet Tubman, from slave to spy to suffragette.

 Meet the Classic Authors Series, Washington Irving (AIMS Multimedia) Video, 18 min. A close look at the life and work of the author.

 Rip Van Winkle, American Heroes and Legends Series (Listening Library) Video, 30 min. Film version of the story, narrated by Anjelica Huston, with original music.

 Rip Van Winkle (AIMS/Pied Piper) Video, 18 min. A dramatization of the literature.

SEA MAIDENS OF JAPAN

The Sea King's Daughter: A Russian Legend
Aaron Shepard, reteller, illustrated by Gennady Spirin (Atheneum, 1997)

Sadko, a skilled musician, must make a difficult decision when called upon to play at the Sea King's underwater palace.

Off and Running
Gary Soto (Delacorte, 1996)

Miata Ramirez is determined to become fifth-grade president, but it will take some help from her opponent to get her elected.

Brian's Return
Gary Paulsen (Delacorte, 1999)

This book follows the previous adventures of the main character, Brian, from *Hatchet*, *The River*, and *Brian's Winter*. In keeping with the survival theme, Brian makes the decision to return to the woods to discover where he really belongs.

THE SILENT LOBBY

The Bus Ride
William Miller (Lee & Low, 1998)

Inspired by the Rosa Parks incident, this book tells of a young African American girl's curiosity that sparks a controversial action and causes a law to be amended.

Arrow Over the Door
Joseph Bruchac, illustrated by James Watling (Dial Books for Young Readers, 1998)

The lives of two fourteen-year-old boys, Samuel, a Quaker, and Stands Straight, an Abenaki Indian, intersect at a crucial historical moment, in 1777.

Maniac Magee
Jerry Spinelli (Little, Brown, 1990)

It takes a "maniac" to confront and resolve the racism in Two Mills, and that's just what Jeffrey Lionel Magee appears to be.

AMAZON ALERT!

Antonio's Rain Forest
Anna Lewington (Carolrhoda, 1993)

A young boy describes his life in the Amazon rain forest.

Rain Forest
Michael George (Creative Education, 1992)

A beautifully photographed book about where tropical rain forests are found and the kinds of life that inhabit them.

One Day in the Tropical Rain Forest
Jean Craighead George, illustrated by Gary Allen (HarperCollins/Crowell, 1998)

A vivid description of a rain forest, written as a log book, with observations noted over the course of a day.

 Children of Japan (GPN) Video, 30 min. This four-part series discusses the relationships of Japanese children to society, family, school, and the arts.

 The Trouble with Tuck (AIMS/Pied Piper) Video, 16 min. A young girl makes a decision that her dog's blindness will not dramatically change his life.

 Yoshiko the Papermaker (Coronet/Phoenix Learning) Video or videodisc, 25 min. Yoshiko must decide if the long and disciplined hours she spends learning the ancient art of papermaking are worth the effort.

 Eyes on the Prize II, The Civil Rights Years (Educational Software) Laserdisc CLV. The Civil Rights struggle between 1964–1985.

 Fighters for Freedom, Black Heroes Series (SVE) Filmstrip, 7 min. Video, 20 min. How black freedom fighters, cowboys, and other heroes have changed America.

 Follow the Drinking Gourd (SRA/McGraw-Hill) Video. A dramatization of how slaves used the Underground Railroad to escape slavery.

 The Environment (Decisions, Decisions) (Tom Snyder Productions) CD-ROM, Macintosh, Windows. Students make environmental decisions as they role-play political leaders.

 Kids Think About It Series: Our Disappearing World Forests (SVE/Churchill) Video, 27 min. Rainforest resources and what can be done to save them.

 Protecting Habitats, Preserving Biodiversity (Coronet/Phoenix Learning) Videodisc. Techniques and management procedures that preserve and protect the environment.

Publishers Directory

Aladdin Paperbacks
(Imprint of Simon & Schuster Children's Publishing)

Alaska Northwest Books
(Division of Graphic Arts Center Publishing Co.)
3019 NW Yeon Ave.
Box 10306
Portland, OR 97296-0306
(503) 226-2402 • (800) 452-3032
Fax (503) 223-1410
www.gacpc.com

Annick Press
(Imprint of Firefly, Ltd.)

Atheneum
(Imprint of Simon & Schuster Children's Publishing)

Avon Books
(Division of Hearst Corp.)
1350 Ave. of the Americas
New York, NY 10019
(212) 261-6800 • (800) 238-0658
Fax (800) 223-0239
www.avonbooks.com

Bantam Doubleday Dell Books for Young Readers
(Imprint of Random House)

Peter Bedrick Books
156 Fifth Ave., Suite 817
New York, NY 10010
(800) 788-3123 • Fax (212) 206-3741

Beech Tree Books
(Imprint of William Morrow & Co.)

Blackbirch Press
1 Bradley Road, Suite 205
Woodbridge, CT 06525
(203) 387-7525 • (800) 831-9183

Blue Sky Press
(Imprint of Scholastic)

Bradbury Press
(Imprint of Simon & Schuster Children's Publishing)

BridgeWater Books
(Distributed by Penguin Putnam Inc.)

Candlewick Press
2067 Massachusetts Avenue
Cambridge, MA 02140
(617) 661-3330 • Fax (617) 661-0565

Carolrhoda Books
(Division of Lerner Publications Co.)

Cartwheel Books
(Imprint of Scholastic)

Children's Book Press
246 First St., Suite 101
San Francisco, CA 94105
(415) 995-2200 • Fax (415) 995-2222

Children's Press (Division of Grolier, Inc.)
P.O. Box 1796
Danbury, CT 06813-1333
(800) 621-1115 • www.grolier.com

Chronicle Books
85 Second Street, Sixth Floor
San Francisco, CA 94105
(415) 537-3730 • (415) 537-4460
(800) 722-6657
www.chroniclebooks.com

Clarion Books
(Imprint of Houghton Mifflin, Inc.)
215 Park Avenue South
New York, NY 10003
(212) 420-5800 • (800) 726-0600
www.hmco.com/trade/childrens/
shelves.html

Crabtree Publishing Co.
350 Fifth Ave., Suite 3308
New York, NY 10118
(212) 496-5040 • (800) 387-7650
Fax (800) 355-7166
www.crabtree-pub.com

Creative Education
The Creative Co.
123 S. Broad Street
P.O. Box 227
Mankato, MN 56001
(507) 388-6273 • (800) 445-6209
Fax (507) 388-2746

Crowell (Imprint of HarperCollins)

Crown Publishing Group
(Imprint of Random House)

Delacorte
(Imprint of Random House)

Dial Books
(Imprint of Penguin Putnam Inc.)

Discovery Enterprises, Ltd.
31 Laurelwood Dr.
Carlisle, MA 01741
(978) 287-5401 • (800) 729-1720
Fax (978) 287-5402

Disney Press
(Division of Disney Book Publishing, Inc.,
A Walt Disney Co.)
114 Fifth Ave.
New York, NY 10011
(212) 633-4400 • Fax (212) 633-4833
www.disneybooks.com

Dorling Kindersley (DK Publishing)
95 Madison Avenue
New York, NY 10016
(212) 213-4800 • Fax (800) 774-6733
(888) 342-5357 • www.dk.com

Doubleday (Imprint of Random House)

E. P. Dutton Children's Books
(Imprint of Penguin Putnam Inc.)

Farrar Straus & Giroux
19 Union Square West
New York, NY 10003
(212) 741-6900 • Fax (212) 633-2427
(888) 330-8477

Firefly Books, Ltd.
PO Box 1338
Endicott Station
Buffalo, NY 14205
(416) 499-8412 • Fax (800) 565-6034
(800) 387-5085
www.firefly.com

Four Winds Press
(Imprint of Macmillan, see Simon & Schuster Children's Publishing)

Fulcrum Publishing
350 Indiana Street, Suite 350
Golden, CO 80401
(303) 277-1623 • (800) 992-2908
Fax (303) 279-7111
www.fulcrum-books.com

Greenwillow Books
(Imprint of William Morrow & Co, Inc.)

Gulliver Green Books
(Imprint of Harcourt Brace & Co.)

Harcourt Brace & Co.
525 "B" Street
San Diego, CA 92101
(619) 231-6616 • (800) 543-1918
www.harcourtbooks.com

Harper & Row (Imprint of HarperCollins)

HarperCollins Children's Books
10 East 53rd Street
New York, NY 10022
(212) 207-7000 • Fax (212) 202-7044
(800) 242-7737
www.harperchildrens.com

Harper Trophy
(Imprint of HarperCollins)

Henry Holt and Company
115 West 18th Street
New York, NY 10011
(212) 886-9200 • (212) 633-0748
(888) 330-8477 • www.henryholt.com/byr/

Holiday House
425 Madison Avenue
New York, NY 10017
(212) 688-0085 • Fax (212) 421-6134

Houghton Mifflin
222 Berkeley Street
Boston, MA 02116
(617) 351-5000 • Fax (617) 351-1125
(800) 225-3362 • www.hmco.com/trade

Hyperion Books
(Imprint of Buena Vista Publishing Co.)
114 Fifth Avenue
New York, NY 10011
(212) 633-4400 • (800) 759-0190
www.disney.com

Just Us Books
356 Glenwood Avenue
E. Orange, NJ 07017
(973) 672-0304 • Fax (973) 677-7570

Kane/Miller Book Publishers
P.O. Box 310529
Brooklyn, NY 11231-0529
(718) 624-5120 • Fax (718) 858-5452
www.kanemiller.com

Alfred A. Knopf
(Imprint of Random House)

Lee & Low Books
95 Madison Avenue
New York, NY 10016
(212) 779-4400 • Fax (212) 683-1894

Lerner Publications Co.
241 First Avenue North
Minneapolis, MN 55401
(612) 332-3344 • Fax (612) 332-7615
(800) 328-4929 • www.lernerbooks.com

Little, Brown & Co.
3 Center Plaza
Boston, MA 02108
(617) 227-0730 • Fax (617) 263-2864
(800) 343-9204 • www.littlebrown.com

Lothrop Lee & Shepard
(Imprint of William Morrow & Co.)

Macmillan
(Imprint of Simon & Schuster Children's Publishing)

Mikaya Press
(Imprint of Firefly Books, Ltd.)

Millbrook Press, Inc.
2 Old New Milford Road
Brookfield, CT 06804
(203) 740-2220 • (800) 462-4703
Fax (203) 740-2526
www.millbrookpress.com

William Morrow & Co.
1350 Avenue of the Americas
New York, NY 10019
(212) 261-6500 • Fax (212) 261-6619
(800) 843-9389
www.williammorrow.com

Morrow Junior Books
(Imprint of William Morrow & Co.)

National Geographic Society
1145 17th Street, NW
Washington, DC 20036
(202) 828-5667 • (800) 368-2728
www.nationalgeographic.com

Northland Publishing
(Division of Justin Industries)
P.O. Box 62
Flagstaff, AZ 86002
(520) 774-5251 • Fax (800) 257-9082
(800) 346-3257 • www.northlandpub.com

Orchard Books (A Grolier Company)
95 Madison Avenue
New York, NY 10016
(212) 951-2600 • Fax (212) 213-6435
(800) 621-1115 • www.grolier.com

Oxford University Press, Inc.
198 Madison Ave.
New York, NY 10016-4314
(212) 726-6000 • (800) 451-7556
www.oup-usa.org

Penguin Putnam, Inc.
345 Hudson Street
New York, NY 10014
(212) 366-2000 • Fax (212) 366-2666
(800) 631-8571
www.penguinputnam.com

Philomel Books
(Imprint of Penguin Putnam, Inc.)

Pippin Press
Gracie Station, Box 1347
229 E. 85th Street
New York, NY 10028
(212) 288-4920 • Fax (732) 225-1562

Puffin Books
(Imprint of Penguin Putnam, Inc.)

G.P. Putnam's Sons Publishing
(Imprint of Penguin Putnam, Inc.)

Random House
201 East 50th Street
New York, NY 10022
(212) 751-2600 • Fax (212) 572-2593
(800) 726-0600
www.randomhouse/kids

Rising Moon
(Imprint of Northland Publishing)

Scholastic
555 Broadway
New York, NY 10012
(212) 343-6100 • Fax (212) 343-6930
(800) SCHOLASTIC • www.scholastic.com

Sierra Club Books for Children
85 Second Street, Second Floor
San Francisco, CA 94105-3441
(415) 977-5500 • Fax (415) 977-5793
(800) 935-1056 • www.sierraclub.orgbooks

Silver Burdett Press
(Division of Pearson Education)
299 Jefferson Rd.
Parsippany, NJ 07054-0480
(973) 739-8000 • (800) 848-9500
www.sbgschool.com

Simon & Schuster Children's Books
1230 Avenue of the Americas
New York, NY 10020
(212) 698-7200 • (800) 223-2336
www.simonsays.com/kidzone

Gareth Stevens, Inc.
River Center Bldg.
1555 N. River Center Dr., Suite 201
Milwaukee, WI 53212
(414) 225-0333 • (800) 341-3569
Fax (414) 225-0377
www.gsinc.com

Sunburst
(Imprint of Farrar, Straus & Giroux)

Tricycle Press
(Division of Ten Speed Press)
P.O. Box 7123
Berkeley, CA 94707
(510) 559-1600 • (800) 841-2665
Fax (510) 559-1637
www.tenspeed.com

Viking Children's Books
(Imprint of Penguin Putnam Inc.)

Voyager
(Imprint of Harcourt Brace & Co.)

Walker & Co.
435 Hudson Street
New York, NY 10014
(212) 727-8300 • (212) 727-0984
(800) AT-WALKER

Warwick Publishing
162 John St.
Toronto, CAN M5V2E5
(416) 596-1555
www.warwickgp.com

Watts Publishing
(Imprint of Grolier Publishing;
see Children's Press)

Yearling Books
(Imprint of Random House)

Multimedia Resources

AIMS Multimedia
9710 DeSoto Avenue
Chatsworth, CA 91311-4409
(800) 367-2467
www.AIMS-multimedia.com

Ambrose Video and Publishing
28 West 44th Street, Suite 2100
New York, NY 10036
(800) 526-4663 • Fax (212) 768-9282
www.AmbroseVideo.com

BFA Educational Media
(see Phoenix Learning Group)

Boston Federal Reserve Bank
Community Affairs Dept.
P.O. Box 2076
Boston, MA 02106-2076
(617) 973-3459
www.bos.frb.org

Brittanica
310 South Michigan Avenue
Brittanica Center
Chicago, IL 60604-4293
(800) 621-3900 • Fax (800) 344-9624

Broderbund
(Parsons Technology;
also see The Learning Company)
500 Redwood Blvd.
Novato, CA 94997
(800) 521-6263 • Fax (800) 474-8840
www.broderbund.com

Carousel Film and Video
260 Fifth Avenue, Suite 705
New York, NY 10001
(212) 683-1660 • e-mail:
carousel@pipeline.com

CBS/Fox Video
1330 Avenue of the Americas
New York, NY 10019
(800) 457-0686

Cornell University Audio/Video Resource Ctr.
8 Business & Technology Park
Ithaca, NY 14850
(607) 255-2091

Coronet/MTI
(see Phoenix Learning Group)

Direct Cinema, Ltd.
P.O. Box 10003
Santa Monica, CA 90410-1003
(800) 525-0000

Encyclopaedia Britannica Educational Corp.
310 South Michigan Avenue
Chicago, IL 60604
(800) 554-9862 • www.eb.com

ESI/Educational Software
4213 S. 94th Street
Omaha, NE 68127
(800) 955-5570 • www.edsoft.com

Films for the Humanities and Sciences
P.O. Box 2053
Princeton, NJ 08543-2053
(800) 257-5126 • Fax (609) 275-3767
www.films.com

GPN/Reading Rainbow
University of Nebraska-Lincoln
P.O. Box 80669
Lincoln, NE 68501-0669
(800) 228-4630 • www.gpn.unl.edu

Journal Films and Videos
1560 Sherman Avenue, Suite 100
Evanston, IL 60201
(800) 323-9084

Kaw Valley Films
P.O. Box 3900
Shawnee, KS 66208
(800) 332-5060

Listening Library
One Park Avenue
Greenwich, CT 06870-1727
(800) 243-4504 • www.listeninglib.com

Macmillan/McGraw-Hill
(see SRA/McGraw-Hill)

Marshmedia
P.O. Box 8082
Shawnee Mission, KS 66208
(800) 821-3303 • Fax (816) 333-7421
marshmedia.com

MECC
(see The Learning Company)

National Geographic Society Educational Services
P.O. Box 10597
Des Moines, IA 50340-0597
(800) 368-2728
www.nationalgeographic.com

New Jersey Network
1573 Parkside Ave.
Trenton, NJ 08625-0777
(609) 530-5180

PBS Video
1320 Braddock Place
Alexandria, VA 22314
(800) 344-3337 • www.pbs.org

Phoenix Films
(see Phoenix Learning Group)

The Phoenix Learning Group
2348 Chaffee Drive
St. Louis, MO 63146
(800) 221-1274 • e-mail:
phoenixfilms@worldnet.att.net

Pied Piper (see AIMS Multimedia)

Rainbow Educational Video
170 Keyland Court
Bohemia, NY 11716
(800) 331-4047

Social Studies School Service
10200 Jefferson Boulevard, Room 14
P.O. Box 802
Culver City, CA 90232-0802
(800) 421-4246 • Fax (310) 839-2249
socialstudies.com

SRA/McGraw-Hill
220 Daniel Dale Road
De Soto, TX 75115
(800) 843-8855 • www.sra4kids.com

SVE/Churchill Media
6677 North Northwest Highway
Chicago, IL 60631
(800) 829-1900 • www.svemedia.com

Tom Snyder Productions (also see ESI)
80 Coolidge Hill Rd.
Watertown, MA 02472
(800) 342-0236 • www.teachtsp.com

Troll Associates
100 Corporate Drive
Mahwah, NJ 07430
(800) 929-8765 • Fax (800) 979-8765
www.troll.com

United Learning
6633 W. Howard St.
Niles, IL 60714-3389
(800) 424-0362
www.unitedlearning.com

Weston Woods
12 Oakwood Avenue
Norwalk, CT 06850
(800) 243-5020 • Fax (203) 845-0498

Zenger Media
10200 Jefferson Blvd., Room 94
P.O. Box 802
Culver City, CA 90232-0802
(800) 421-4246 • Fax (800) 944-5432
www.Zengermedia.com

	Vocabulary	Spelling

THE WISE OLD WOMAN

Vocabulary: banner, conquered, prospered, reluctantly, scroll, summoned

Words with Short Vowels

tasks	club	**wisdom**	**threatened**
rent	**son**	**solve**	slippery
weapon	grant	pump	occupy
twin	dreadful	smother	**sudden**
fond	lend	cash	blister

CARLOS AND THE SKUNK

Vocabulary: nestled, peculiar, stunned, tortillas, unbearable, unpleasant

Words with long a and long e

paste	**evening**	decorate	delay
aim	receive	indeed	heal
spray	drain	theme	concrete
leader	pace	indicate	greet
creep	flea	faith	decay

WILMA UNLIMITED

Vocabulary: astounding, athletic, bushel, concentrating, luxury, scholarship

Words with long i and long o

excite	loaf	fold	enclose
grind	obey	goal	type
notice	site	code	console
spy	**fight**	despite	notion
hose	rely	gigantic	slightly

THE WRECK OF THE ZEPHYR

Vocabulary: hull, ominous, shoreline, spire, timbers, treacherous

Words with /ū/ and /ü/

nephew	include	dispute	reunion
boom	**lose**	cruel	suitcase
truly	**view**	contribute	boost
grew	cucumber	assume	rumor
juicy	**flew**	**prove**	remove

TIME FOR KIDS: TORNADOES!

Vocabulary: destruction, detect, predictions, reliable, severe, stadium

Words from Science

twister	rainfall	**damage**	device
computers	**instruments**	horizon	energy
hurricane	front	**satellites**	sleet
strength	**warning**	surge	humid
condense	**conditions**	debris	cyclone

Boldfaced words appear in the selection.

Word List

UNIT 2

Vocabulary | Spelling

THE GOLD COIN

Vocabulary
- despair
- distressed
- insistent
- shriveled
- speechless
- stifling

Spelling — Syllable Patterns

lotion	luggage	gravy	agent
subject	**silence**	lantern	stifle
ugly	victim	active	baggage
simply	**moment**	bacon	spiral
pony	bubble	fable	blender

JOHN HENRY

Vocabulary
- acre
- commotion
- dynamite
- grit
- pulverized
- rebuild

Spelling — Words with Consonant Clusters

scramble	screech	scrape	scribble
strange	**straightest**	stray	strain
sprang	sprout	sprain	script
schoolyard	schedule	scholar	strawberry
throughout	throat	throne	strategy

IT'S OUR WORLD, TOO

Vocabulary
- auction
- dangled
- deliveries
- donate
- lecture
- publicity

Spelling — Words with /z/, /j/, and /f/

dizzy	gem	telegraph	trophy
manage	lizard	fudge	zipper
squeeze	average	represent	praise
lodge	budge	margin	postage
paragraph	**refuse**	**challenge**	physical

DEAR MR. HENSHAW

Vocabulary
- afford
- permission
- rejected
- reserved
- snoop
- submitted

Spelling — Plurals

losses	potatoes	studios	wives
stories	atlases	heroes	rodeos
reefs	difficulties	crutches	**tomatoes**
shelves	gulfs	possibilities	**thieves**
pianos	wolves	beliefs	echoes

TIME FOR KIDS: DIGGING UP THE PAST

Vocabulary
- arrowheads
- bullet
- eventually
- fraction
- starvation
- violent

Spelling — Words from Social Studies

capital	liberty	property	empire
colonists	senator	immigrant	civil
ancestor	justice	governor	**settlement**
territory	**settlers**	plantation	**historians**
congress	culture	politics	federal

Boldfaced words appear in the selection.

T81

UNIT 3

	Vocabulary	Spelling

THE MARBLE CHAMP

Vocabulary:
accurate
congratulated
division
elementary
glory
onlookers

Spelling: Words with /ou/ and /oi/

join	mount	couch	background
outfit	shower	rejoice	prowl
howl	employee	loyalty	sour
hoist	broil	doubt	turquoise
destroy	eyebrow	drowsy	trousers

THE PAPER DRAGON

Vocabulary:
billowed
devour
heroic
quench
scorched
uprooted

Spelling: Words with /u̇/ and /yu̇/

looked	understood	lure	rural
bureau	tourist	barefoot	fishhook
surely	mural	gourmet	tournament
poor	assure	bulletin	jury
cushion	childhood	textbook	purify

GRANDMA ESSIE'S COVERED WAGON

Vocabulary:
bashful
canvas
cemetery
granite
orphanage
tornado

Spelling: Words with /sh/ and /ch/

sheets	polish	vanish	publish
especially	ancient	commercial	gracious
chopped	cheap	**orchard**	arch
kitchen	clutch	latch	hitch
patient	caution	nation	function

GOING BACK HOME: AN ARTIST RETURNS TO THE SOUTH

Vocabulary:
heritage
influenced
livestock
survival
thrive
tiresome

Spelling: Adding -ed and -ing

slammed	pitied	**fascinated**	regretted
exploring	skimmed	envied	**easing**
copied	deserved	referring	qualified
jogging	applied	collapsed	forbidding
amusing	dripping	relied	complicated

TIME FOR KIDS: A MOUNTAIN OF A MONUMENT

Vocabulary:
awesome
dedicate
explosives
hail
nostril
sculpture

Spelling: Words from the Arts

carving	gallery	quality	texture
monument	portrait	technique	jewelry
memorial	impression	original	charcoal
displays	style	fabric	glaze
process	decoration	medium	creative

Boldfaced words appear in the selection.

UNIT 4

	Vocabulary	Spelling

THE VOYAGE OF THE *DAWN TREADER*

Vocabulary:
- approve
- bruised
- convenience
- offend
- presence
- vaguely

Words with /ô/ and /ôr/

forward	fawn	soar	border
course	install	chore	source
audience	**longing**	withdraw	applaud
aboard	**performing**	wallpaper	coarse
bore	astronaut	coffee	forecast

HOW TO THINK LIKE A SCIENTIST

Vocabulary:
- assignments
- automatically
- carelessly
- normally
- observations
- swerved

Words with /är/ and /âr/

cards	vary	chart	barge
carve	rare	square	beware
barely	airline	**repairman**	lair
stairway	scar	target	artistic
remark	scarce	**aquarium**	regard

AN ISLAND SCRAPBOOK

Vocabulary:
- barrier
- emerge
- fireball
- naturalist
- parallel
- teeming

Words with /îr/ and /ûr/

steer	fir	term	purse
return	**mysterious**	cashier	dreary
appear	career	squirm	alert
nerve	**surface**	experience	squirt
frontier	fearsome	eerie	material

THE BIG STORM

Vocabulary:
- atmosphere
- collision
- cycle
- data
- injured
- uneven

Compound Words

mailbox	homesick	**raindrop**	thirty-third
all right	post office	**cold front**	**snowstorms**
goldfish	twenty-five	merry-go-round	**mountaintops**
no one	somebody	teaspoon	sister-in-law
ice-skating	peanut butter	**parking lot**	**northeast**

TIME FOR KIDS: CATCHING UP WITH LEWIS AND CLARK

Vocabulary:
- bison
- diaries
- former
- glistening
- journal
- superb

Words from Social Studies

journey	**hardships**	canal	**expedition**
canoes	**trail**	**fort**	elevation
traveled	**explorer**	**native**	canyon
route	**communicate**	caravan	dwell
service	agency	agreement	**campsite**

Boldfaced words appear in the selection.

UNIT 5

	Vocabulary	**Spelling**

THE RIDDLE

Vocabulary:
- apologized
- debt
- hasty
- inquired
- lamented
- refreshment

Spelling — Words with /ər/, /əl/, and /ən/

labor	**answer**	chosen	**twinkle**
legal	regular	**castle**	central
captain	single	**clever**	sweater
fasten	camel	apron	grammar
tunnel	**pardon**	terror	**riddle**

LIFE IN FLATLAND

Vocabulary:
- dimensions
- distinguished
- landscape
- thickness
- trifle
- unique

Spelling — Spelling Unstressed Syllables

constant	distance	torrent	ransom
consult	compose	focus	**method**
neglect	dozen	purchase	emblem
patrol	collage	payment	hammock
accuse	**compass**	possess	support

TONWEYA AND THE EAGLES

Vocabulary:
- cleft
- consented
- defiantly
- gratitude
- sacred
- tribute

Spelling — Words with Silent Letters

sign	autumn	column	campaign
wrist	knuckle	knowledge	**handwriting**
knit	wring	wrench	bough
lightning	naughty	brighten	solemn
gnaw	gnat	dough	gnarled

BREAKER'S BRIDGE

Vocabulary:
- dismay
- gorge
- immortals
- murky
- piers
- scheme

Spelling — Contractions

aren't	hasn't	they're	there'll
we'd	you'd	how's	must've
would've	haven't	needn't	who'd
we'll	where'd	she's	who'll
you've	what'll	mustn't	should've

TIME FOR KIDS: CLEANING UP AMERICA'S AIR

Vocabulary:
- fumes
- protective
- regulations
- standards
- stricter
- width

Spelling — Words from Health

illness	**kidneys**	**headaches**	**smog**
breathing	safety	vitamin	artery
oxygen	organ	hazard	**ozone**
health	**lungs**	substance	symptom
heart	**reaction**	**particle**	allergy

Boldfaced words appear in the selection.

UNIT 6

Vocabulary	Spelling

AMISTAD RISING: A STORY OF FREEDOM

Vocabulary:
- coax
- escorted
- navigate
- nightfall
- perished
- ushered

Homophones and Homographs

died	**bound**	main	hall
stable	pane	sole	currant
pain	waist	haul	soul
wound	vault	current	mane
waste	**dyed**	idle	idol

RIP VAN WINKLE

Vocabulary:
- husking
- keg
- landlord
- oblige
- rascals
- sprawled

Words with Prefixes

preschool	preview	precook	prearrange
replaced	regain	recall	**revisit**
unknown	**unseen**	unable	unaware
disobey	discomfort	dishonest	disapprove
invisible	incorrect	inexpensive	incredible

THE SEA MAIDENS OF JAPAN

Vocabulary:
- cove
- disgrace
- driftwood
- flails
- host
- sizzle

Words with Suffixes

remarkable	reasonable	respectable	honorable
peaceful	**graceful**	harmful	**flavorful**
countless	painless	meaningless	defenseless
foolishness	weakness	softness	nervousness
excitement	amusement	treatment	announcement

THE SILENT LOBBY

Vocabulary:
- interpret
- pelted
- persuade
- register
- shabby
- soothing

Words with Suffixes

instruction	selection	**election**	concentration
suggestion	confusion	perfection	consideration
information	invitation	conversation	**demonstration**
education	attraction	location	**constitution**
imagination	reservation	population	correction

TIME FOR KIDS: AMAZON ALERT!

Vocabulary:
- confirmed
- isolated
- lush
- tropical
- variety
- wonderland

Words from Math

ordered	multiply	product	**estimated**
equal	frequency	liter	angle
range	mathematics	ratio	portion
difference	centimeter	bar graph	**one-eighth**
volume	formula	millimeter	quotient

Boldfaced words appear in the selection.

Listening, Speaking, Viewing, Representing

☑ Tested Skill

☐ Tinted panels show skills, strategies, and other teaching opportunities

LISTENING	K	1	2	3	4	5	6
Learn the vocabulary of school (numbers, shapes, colors, directions, and categories)							
Identify the musical elements of literary language, such as rhymes, repeated sounds, onomatopoeia							
Determine purposes for listening (get information, solve problems, enjoy and appreciate)							
Listen critically and responsively							
Ask and answer relevant questions							
Listen critically to interpret and evaluate							
Listen responsively to stories and other texts read aloud, including selections from classic and contemporary works							
Connect own experiences, ideas, and traditions with those of others							
Apply comprehension strategies in listening activities							
Understand the major ideas and supporting evidence in spoken messages							
Participate in listening activities related to reading and writing (such as discussions, group activities, conferences)							
Listen to learn by taking notes, organizing, and summarizing spoken ideas							

SPEAKING	K	1	2	3	4	5	6
Learn the vocabulary of school (numbers, shapes, colors, directions, and categories)							
Use appropriate language and vocabulary learned to describe ideas, feelings, and experiences							
Ask and answer relevant questions							
Communicate effectively in everyday situations (such as discussions, group activities, conferences)							
Demonstrate speaking skills (audience, purpose, occasion, volume, pitch, tone, rate, fluency)							
Clarify and support spoken messages and ideas with objects, charts, evidence, elaboration, examples							
Use verbal and nonverbal communication in effective ways when, for example, making announcements, giving directions, or making introductions							
Retell a spoken message by summarizing or clarifying							
Connect own experiences, ideas, and traditions with those of others							
Determine purposes for speaking (inform, entertain, give directions, persuade, express personal feelings and opinions)							
Demonstrate skills of reporting and providing information							
Demonstrate skills of interviewing, requesting and providing information							
Apply composition strategies in speaking activities							
Monitor own understanding of spoken message and seek clarification as needed							

VIEWING	K	1	2	3	4	5	6
Demonstrate viewing skills (focus attention, organize information)							
Respond to audiovisual media in a variety of ways							
Participate in viewing activities related to reading and writing							
Apply comprehension strategies in viewing activities							
Recognize artists' craft and techniques for conveying meaning							
Interpret information from various formats such as maps, charts, graphics, video segments, technology							
Evaluate purposes of various media (information, appreciation, entertainment, directions, persuasion)							
Use media to compare ideas and points of view							

REPRESENTING	K	1	2	3	4	5	6
Select, organize, or produce visuals to complement or extend meanings							
Produce communication using appropriate media to develop a class paper, multimedia or video reports							
Show how language, medium, and presentation contribute to the message							

Reading: Alphabetic Principle, Sounds/Symbols

☑ Tested Skill

☐ Tinted panels show skills, strategies, and other teaching opportunities

PRINT AWARENESS	K	1	2	3	4	5	6
Know the order of the alphabet							
Recognize that print represents spoken language and conveys meaning							
Understand directionality (tracking print from left to right; return sweep)							
Understand that written words are separated by spaces							
Know the difference between individual letters and printed words							
Understand that spoken words are represented in written language by specific sequence of letters							
Recognize that there are correct spellings for words							
Know the difference between capital and lowercase letters							
Recognize how readers use capitalization and punctuation to comprehend							
Recognize the distinguishing features of a paragraph							
Recognize that parts of a book (such as cover/title page and table of contents) offer information							

PHONOLOGICAL AWARENESS	K	1	2	3	4	5	6
Identify letters, words, sentences							
Divide spoken sentence into individual words							
Produce rhyming words and distinguish rhyming words from nonrhyming words							
Identify, segment, and combine syllables within spoken words							
Identify and isolate the initial and final sound of a spoken word							
Add, delete, or change sounds to change words (such as *cow* to *how*, *pan* to *fan*)							
Blend sounds to make spoken words							
Segment one-syllable spoken words into individual phonemes							

PHONICS AND DECODING	K	1	2	3	4	5	6
Alphabetic principle: Letter/sound correspondence	☑	☑	☑				
Blending CVC words	☑						
Segmenting CVC words	☑						
Blending CVC, CVCe, CCVC, CVCC, CVVC words	☑	☑	☑				
Segmenting CVC, CVCe, CCVC, CVCC, CVVC words	☑	☑	☑				
Initial and final consonants: /n/n, /d/d, /s/s, /m/m, /t/t, /k/c, /f/f, /r/r, /p/p, /l/l, /k/k, /g/g, /b/b, /h/h, /w/w, /v/v, /ks/x, /kw/qu, /j/j, /y/y, /z/z	☑	☑					
Initial and medial short vowels: *a, i, u, o, e*	☑	☑	☑				
Long vowels: *a-e, i-e, o-e, u-e* (vowel-consonant-e)		☑	☑				
Long vowels, including *ay, ai; e, ee, ie, ea, o, oa, oe, ow; i, y, igh*		☑	☑				
Consonant Digraphs: *sh, th, ch, wh*		☑					
Consonant Blends: continuant/continuant, including *sl, sm, sn, fl, fr, ll, ss, ff*		☑					
Consonant Blends: continuant/stop, including *st, sk, sp, ng, nt, nd, mp, ft*		☑					
Consonant Blends: stop/continuant, including *tr, pr, pl, cr, tw*		☑					
Variant vowels: including /u/oo; /ô/a, aw, au; /ü/ue, ew		☑	☑				
Diphthongs, including /ou/ou, ow; /oi/oi, oy		☑	☑				
r-controlled vowels, including /âr/are; /ôr/or, ore; /îr/ear			☑				
Soft *c* and soft *g*			☑				
nk		☑	☑				
Consonant Digraphs: *ck*	☑	☑					
Consonant Digraphs: *ph, tch, ch*			☑				
Short *e: ea*			☑				
Long *e: y, ey*			☑				
/ü/oo		☑	☑				
/är/ar; /ûr/ir, ur, er		☑	☑				
Silent letters: including *l, b, k, w, g, h, gh*			☑				
Schwa: /ər/er; /ən/en; /əl/le;			☑				
Reading/identifying multisyllabic words		☑	☑				

Reading: Vocabulary/Word Identification

WORD STRUCTURE	K	1	2	3	4	5	6
Common spelling patterns							
Syllable patterns							
Plurals							
Possessives							
Contractions							
Root, or base, words and inflectional endings (-s, -es, -ed, -ing)							
Compound Words							
Prefixes and suffixes (such as un-, re-, dis-, non-; -ly, -y, -ful, -able, -tion)							
Root words and derivational endings							
WORD MEANING							
Develop vocabulary through concrete experiences							
Develop vocabulary through selections read aloud							
Develop vocabulary through reading							
Cueing systems: syntactic, semantic, phonetic							
Context clues, including semantic clues (word meaning), syntactical clues (word order), and phonetic clues	☑	☑	☑	☑	☑	☑	☑
High-frequency words (such as the, a, an, and, said, was, where, is)							
Identify words that name persons, places, things, and actions							
Automatic reading of regular and irregular words							
Use resources and references dictionary, glossary, thesaurus, synonym finder, technology and software, and context)							
Synonyms and antonyms							
Multiple-meaning words							
Figurative language							
Decode derivatives (root words, such as like, pay, happy with affixes, such as dis-, pre-, -un)							
Systematic study of words across content areas and in current events							
Locate meanings, pronunciations, and derivations (including dictionaries, glossaries, and other sources)							
Denotation and connotation							
Word origins as aid to understanding historical influences on English word meanings							
Homophones, homographs							
Analogies							
Idioms							

Reading: Comprehension

PREREADING STRATEGIES	K	1	2	3	4	5	6
Preview and Predict							
Use prior knowledge							
Establish and adjust purposes for reading							
Build background							
MONITORING STRATEGIES							
Adjust reading rate							
Reread, search for clues, ask questions, ask for help							
Visualize							
Read a portion aloud, use reference aids							
Use decoding and vocabulary strategies							
Paraphrase							
Create story maps, diagrams, charts, story props to help comprehend, analyze, synthesize and evaluate texts							

(continued on next page)

(Reading: Comprehension continued)

| Tested Skill | ☑ |
| Tinted panels show skills, strategies, and other teaching opportunities | |

SKILLS AND STRATEGIES	K	1	2	3	4	5	6
Story details	☑						
Use illustrations	☑	☑					
Reality and fantasy	☑	☑	☑	☑			
Classify and categorize	☑						
Make predictions	☑	☑	☑	☑	☑	☑	☑
Sequence of events (tell or act out)	☑	☑	☑	☑	☑	☑	☑
Cause and effect			☑	☑	☑	☑	☑
Compare and contrast	☑	☑	☑	☑	☑	☑	☑
Summarize	☑	☑	☑	☑	☑	☑	☑
Make and explain inferences			☑	☑	☑	☑	☑
Draw conclusions			☑	☑	☑	☑	☑
Important and unimportant information					☑	☑	☑
Main idea and supporting details	☑	☑	☑	☑	☑	☑	☑
Form conclusions or generalizations and support with evidence from text			☑	☑	☑	☑	☑
Fact and opinion (including news stories and advertisements)			☑	☑	☑	☑	☑
Problem and solution			☑	☑	☑	☑	☑
Steps in a process		☑	☑	☑	☑	☑	☑
Make judgments and decisions				☑	☑	☑	☑
Fact and nonfact				☑	☑	☑	☑
Recognize techniques of persuasion and propaganda					☑	☑	☑
Evaluate evidence and sources of information					☑	☑	☑
Identify similarities and differences across texts (including topics, characters, problems, themes, treatment, scope, or organization)							
Practice various questions and tasks (test-like comprehension questions)							
Paraphrase and summarize to recall, inform, and organize							
Answer various types of questions (open-ended, literal, interpretative, test-like such as true-false, multiple choice, short-answer)							
Use study strategies to learn and recall (preview, question, reread, and record)							
LITERARY RESPONSE							
Listen to stories being read aloud							
React, speculate, join in, read along when predictable and patterned selections are read aloud							
Respond through talk, movement, music, art, drama, and writing to a variety of stories and poems							
Show understanding through writing, illustrating, developing demonstrations, and using technology							
Connect ideas and themes across texts							
Support responses by referring to relevant aspects of text and own experiences							
Offer observations, make connections, speculate, interpret, and raise questions in response to texts							
Interpret text ideas through journal writing, discussion, enactment, and media							
TEXT STRUCTURE/LITERARY CONCEPTS							
Distinguish forms of texts and the functions they serve (lists, newsletters, signs)							
Understand story structure							
Identify narrative (for entertainment) and expository (for information)							
Distinguish fiction from nonfiction, including fact and fantasy							
Understand literary forms (stories, poems, plays, and informational books)							
Understand literary terms by distinguishing between roles of author and illustrator							
Understand title, author, and illustrator across a variety of texts							
Analyze character, character's point of view, plot, setting, style, tone, mood		☑	☑	☑	☑	☑	☑
Compare communication in different forms							
Understand terms such as *title, author, illustrator, playwright, theater, stage, act, dialogue,* and *scene*							
Recognize stories, poems, myths, folktales, fables, tall tales, limericks, plays, biographies, and autobiographies							
Judge internal logic of story text							
Recognize that authors organize information in specific ways							
Identify texts to inform, influence, express, or entertain							
Describe how author's point of view affects text							
Recognize biography, historical fiction, realistic fiction, modern fantasy, informational texts, and poetry							
Analyze ways authors present ideas (cause/effect, compare/contrast, inductively, deductively, chronologically)							
Recognize flashback, foreshadowing, symbolism							

(continued on next page)

(Reading: Comprehension continued)

VARIETY OF TEXT	K	1	2	3	4	5	6
Read a variety of genres							
Use informational texts to acquire information							
Read for a variety of purposes							
Select varied sources when reading for information or pleasure							
FLUENCY							
Read regularly in independent-level and instructional-level materials							
Read orally with fluency from familiar texts							
Self-select independent-level reading							
Read silently for increasing periods of time							
Demonstrate characteristics of fluent and effective reading							
Adjust reading rate to purpose							
Read aloud in selected texts, showing understanding of text and engaging the listener							
CULTURES							
Connect own experience with culture of others							
Compare experiences of characters across cultures							
Articulate and discuss themes and connections that cross cultures							
CRITICAL THINKING							
Experiences (comprehend, apply, analyze, synthesize, evaluate)							
Make connections (comprehend, apply, analyze, synthesize, evaluate)							
Expression (comprehend, apply, analyze, synthesize, evaluate)							
Inquiry (comprehend, apply, analyze, synthesize, evaluate)							
Problem solving (comprehend, apply, analyze, synthesize, evaluate)							
Making decisions (comprehend, apply, analyze, synthesize, evaluate)							

Study Skills

INQUIRY/RESEARCH	K	1	2	3	4	5	6
Follow directions							
Use alphabetical order							
Identify/frame questions for research							
Obtain, organize, and summarize information: classify, take notes, outline							
Evaluate research and raise new questions							
Use technology to present information in various formats							
Follow accepted formats for writing research, including documenting sources							
Use test-taking strategies							
Use text organizers (book cover; title page—title, author, illustrator; contents; headings; glossary; index)		☑	☑	☑	☑	☑	☑
Use graphic aids, including maps, diagrams, charts, graphs		☑	☑	☑	☑	☑	☑
Read and interpret varied texts including environmental print, signs, lists, encyclopedia, dictionary, glossary, newspaper, advertisement, magazine, calendar, directions, floor plans		☑	☑	☑	☑	☑	☑
Use reference sources, such as glossary, dictionary, encyclopedia, telephone directory, technology resources		☑	☑	☑	☑	☑	☑
Recognize Library/Media center resources, such as computerized references; catalog search—subject, author, title; encyclopedia index		☑	☑	☑	☑	☑	☑

Writing

Tinted panels show skills, strategies, and other teaching opportunities

MODES AND FORMS	K	1	2	3	4	5	6
Interactive writing							
Personal narrative (Expressive narrative)			✓	✓	✓	✓	✓
Writing that compares (Informative classificatory)			✓	✓	✓	✓	✓
Explanatory writing (Informative narrative)		✓	✓	✓	✓	✓	✓
Persuasive writing (Persuasive descriptive)			✓	✓	✓	✓	✓
Writing a story		✓	✓	✓	✓	✓	✓
Expository writing	✓	✓	✓	✓	✓	✓	✓
Write using a variety of formats, such as advertisement, autobiography, biography, book report/report, comparison-contrast, critique/review/editorial, description, essay, how-to, interview, invitation, journal/log/notes, message/list, paragraph/multi-paragraph composition, picture book, play (scene), poem/rhyme, story, summary, note, letter							

PURPOSES/AUDIENCES	K	1	2	3	4	5	6
Dictate messages such as news and stories for others to write							
Write labels, notes, and captions for illustrations, possessions, charts, and centers							
Write to record, to discover and develop ideas, to inform, to influence, to entertain							
Exhibit an identifiable voice in personal narratives and stories							
Use literary devices (suspense, dialogue, and figurative language)							
Produce written texts by organizing ideas, using effective transitions, and choosing precise wording							

PROCESSES	K	1	2	3	4	5	6
Generate ideas for self-selected and assigned topics using prewriting strategies							
Develop drafts							
Revise drafts for varied purposes							
Edit for appropriate grammar, spelling, punctuation, and features of polished writings							
Proofread own writing and that of others							
Bring pieces to final form and "publish" them for audiences							
Use technology to compose text							
Select and use reference materials and resources for writing, revising, and editing final drafts							

SPELLING	K	1	2	3	4	5	6
Spell own name and write high-frequency words							
Words with short vowels (including CVC and one-syllable words with blends CCVC, CVCC, CCVCC)							
Words with long vowels (including CVCe)							
Words with digraphs, blends, consonant clusters, double consonants							
Words with diphthongs							
Words with variant vowels							
Words with r-controlled vowels							
Words with /ər/, /əl/, and /ən/							
Words with silent letters							
Words with soft c and soft g							
Inflectional endings (including plurals and past tense and words that drop the final e when adding -ing, -ed)							
Compound words							
Contractions							
Homonyms							
Suffixes including -able, -ly, or -less, and prefixes including dis-, re-, pre-, or un-							
Spell words ending in -tion and -sion, such as station and procession							
Accurate spelling of root or base words							
Orthographic patterns and rules such as keep/can; sack/book; out/now; oil/toy; match/speech; ledge/cage; consonant doubling, dropping e, changing y to i							
Multisyllabic words using regularly spelled phonogram patterns							
Syllable patterns (including closed, open, syllable boundary patterns)							
Synonyms and antonyms							
Words from Social Studies, Science, Math, and Physical Education							
Words derived from other languages and cultures							
Use resources to find correct spellings, synonyms, and replacement words							
Use conventional spelling of familiar words in writing assignments							
Spell accurately in final drafts							

(continued on next page)

(Writing continued)

GRAMMAR AND USAGE	K	1	2	3	4	5	6
Understand sentence concepts (word order, statements, questions, exclamations, commands)							
Recognize complete and incomplete sentences							
Nouns (common; proper; singular; plural; irregular plural; possessives)							
Verbs (action; helping; linking; irregular)							
Verb tense (present, past, future, perfect, and progressive)							
Pronouns (possessive, subject and object, pronoun-verb agreement)							
Use objective case pronouns accurately							
Adjectives							
Adverbs that tell how, when, where							
Subjects, predicates							
Subject-verb agreement							
Sentence combining							
Recognize sentence structure (simple, compound, complex)							
Synonyms and antonyms							
Contractions							
Conjunctions							
Prepositions and prepositional phrases							

PENMANSHIP	K	1	2	3	4	5	6
Write each letter of alphabet (capital and lowercase) using correct formation, appropriate size and spacing							
Write own name and other important words							
Use phonological knowledge to map sounds to letters to write messages							
Write messages that move left to right, top to bottom							
Gain increasing control of penmanship, pencil grip, paper position, beginning stroke							
Use word and letter spacing and margins to make messages readable							
Write legibly by selecting cursive or manuscript as appropriate							

MECHANICS	K	1	2	3	4	5	6
Use capitalization in sentences, proper nouns, titles, abbreviations and the pronoun *I*							
Use end marks correctly (period, question mark, exclamation point)							
Use commas (in dates, in addresses, in a series, in letters, in direct address)							
Use apostrophes in contractions and possessives							
Use quotation marks							
Use hyphens, semicolons, colons							

EVALUATION	K	1	2	3	4	5	6
Identify the most effective features of a piece of writing using class/teacher generated criteria							
Respond constructively to others' writing							
Determine how his/her own writing achieves its purpose							
Use published pieces as models for writing							
Review own written work to monitor growth as writer							

For more detailed scope and sequence including page numbers and additional phonics information, see McGraw-Hill Reading Program scope and sequence (K-6)

Daily language activities, 43M, 65M, 93M, 123M, 133M, 165M, 199M, 221M, 241M, 251M, 273M, 307M, 339M, 371M, 381M, 407M, 431M, 463M, 491M, 501M, 531M, 553M, 579M, 601M, 611M, 647M, 673M, 697M, 717M, 727M

Davol, Marguerite W., 274A

Dear Mr. Henshaw, 224–241

Decisions, making. *See* Judgments and decisions, making.

Diagrams, 68C, 117, 126C, 133A, 244C, 150, 276C, 342C, 388C, 407L, 434C, 454, 480, 491K 512, 553K, 556C, 567, 580/581, 582B, 582, 584, 586, 593, 596, 601F, 717A. *See also* Graphic organizers.

Dialogue, 25, 43A, 43L, 43P, 54, 93L, 138E, 431L, 522, 554E, 670, 673K, 702

Dickinson, Emily, 504

Dictionary, using, 103, 133O, 164, 265, 357, 624. *See also* Study skills.

Digging Up the Past, 244–251

Directions/instructions, giving and following, 272, 273K–L, 307K–L, 339K–L, 371K–L, 381K–L, 383A–F, 491K–L, Unit 6: T64

Drafting and drafting strategies, 43K, 65K, 93K, 123K, 133K, 135C, 165K, 199K, 221K, 241K, 251K, 253C, 273K, 307K, 339K, 371K, 381K, 383C, 407K, 431K, 463K, 491K, 501K, 503C, 531K, 553K, 579K, 601K, 611K, 613C, 647K, 673K, 697K, 717K, 727K, 729C
  developing a main idea, 253C
  expanding on ideas, 383C, 503C
  freewriting, 135C, 729C
  using prewriting chart, 613C

Drawing/designing, 18E, 18/19, 41, 43B, 43L, 63, 65L, 91, 121, 123L, 124E, 133L, 138/139, 166E, 166/167, 168C, 197, 222E, 241L, 242/243, 256E, 256/257, 270, 273K, 273L, 274E, 305, 307K, 307L, 308E, 371A, 371B, 371L, 372E, 379, 386/387, 405, 407L, 429, 431L, 432/433, 450, 463L, 464E, 492E, 492/493, 501H, 503F, 531L, 532E, 532/533, 539, 540, 552, 554/555, 556C, 577, 579A, 579B, 580E, 601L, 602E, 602/603, 611A, 647L, 673A, 674/675, 697B, 698E, 717L, 718E, 725, Unit 2: T63, T65, Unit 3:T67, T68, Unit 6: T66, Unit 5: T61

Early Spring, 502

Elaboration, 65K, 135D, 253D, 383D, 503D, 613D, 729D

Encyclopedias, using, 41, 63, 93B, 131, 240, 280, 369, 626, 726. *See also* Research and inquiry, Study skills.

English as a Second Language. *See* Language support.

Explanatory writing, 273K–L, 307K–L, 339K–L, 371K–L, 381K–L, 383A–F, 491K–L, Unit 6: T64

Expository writing, 407K–L, 431K–L, 463K–L, 491K–L, 501K–L, 503A–F

Extend activities. *See* Cross–curricular, Cultural perspectives, Leveled books, Meeting Individual Needs, Presentation ideas, Story activities.

Fact and nonfact, distinguishing, 166/167, 168A–B, 168–199, 199A–C, 199E–F, 221G–H, 224–241, 432/433, 434A–B, 434–463, 463A–C,

463E–F, 492/493, 494A–B, 494–501, 627, Unit 2: T64, Unit 4: T66

Features of writing, 135B, 253B, 383B, 503B, 613B, 729B

Figurative language, 29, 174, 307I–J, 339I–J, 381I–J, 383, 445, 455, Unit 3: T67

Fine arts link. *See* Visual literacy.

First Flight, 384

First person, 137, Unit 3: T68

Flashbacks, Unit 3: T66

Fluency, 28, 38, 41, 60, 88, 110, 114, 118, 128, 158, 160, 190, 194, 208, 216, 230, 236, 246, 262, 268, 302, 312, 334, 356, 366, 376, 401, 402, 426, 446, 458, 486, 496, 522, 526, 536, 548, 568, 574, 592, 596, 606, 636, 642, 666, 668, 692, 702, 712, 722
  choral reading, 110
  dramatic reading, 208, 230
  echo reading, 41, 356, 446
  reading dialogue, 54, 522
  reading with expression/intonation, 28, 76, 158, 190, 262, 294, 302, 312, 401, 414, 468, 536, 568, 592, 636, 666, 712
  repeated readings, 688
  rereading for fluency, 38, 60, 88, 118, 128, 160, 194, 216, 236, 246, 268, 334, 366, 402, 426, 458, 486, 496, 526, 548, 596, 606, 642, 668, 674, 692, 702, 722
  using rhythm in oral reading, 114

Frederick Douglass 1817–1895, 728

Free verse, 253, 505, 615

Freewriting, 135C, 729C

Generalizations, forming, 105, 165G–H, 199G–H, 202–221, 224–251, 241G–H, 251E–F, Unit 2: T62

Genre, literary. *See* Literary genre.

Gifted and talented. *See* Challenge, Meeting Individual Needs.

Giovanni, Nikki, 134

Glossary, using, 21, 43P, 47, 65P, 69, 93P, 97, 123P, 127, 133P, 141, 165P, 169, 199P, 203, 221P, 225, 241P, 245, 251P, 259, 273P, 277, 307P, 311, 339P, 343, 371P, 375, 381P, 389, 407P, 431P, 463P, 467, 491P, 495, 501P, 509, 531P, 535, 553P, 557, 579P, 583, 601P, 605, 611P, 619, 647P, 651, 673P, 677, 697P, 701, 717P, 721, 727P

Going Back Home: An Artist Returns to the South, 342–371

Gold Coin, The, 140–165

Grammar, connecting to literature, 43N, 65N, 93N, 123N, 133N, 165N, 199N, 221N, 241N, 251N, 273N, 307N, 339N, 371N, 381N, 407N, 431N, 463N, 491N, 501N, 531N, 553N, 579N, 601N, 611N, 647N, 673N, 697N, 717N, 727N

Grammar, mechanics and usage, 43M–N, 65M–N, 93M–N, 123M–N, 133M–N, 135E,165M–N, 199M–N, 221M–N, 253E, 241M–N, 251M–N, 273M–N, 307M–N, 339M–N, 371M–N, 381M–N, 383E, 407M–N, 431M–N, 463M–N, 491M–N, 501M–N, 503E, 531M–N, 553M–N, 579M–N, 601M–N, 611M–N, 613E, 647M–N, 673M–N, 697M–N, 717M–N, 727M–N, 729E
  abbreviations, 165N, 371N

adjectives, 199I–J, 221I–J, 371M–N, 407M–N, 463M–N, 491M–N, 501M–N, 503E, 613E, 647N, 727M–N
adverbs, 647M–N, 673M–N, 727M–N, 729E
apostrophes, 241M–N, 251M–N, 339M–N, 383E, 531N, 601O–P, 611M–N, 697N
articles, 431M–N, 503E
capitalization, 43M–N, 65N, 93N, 123N, 133N, 165M–N, 199L, 199N, 241N, 371N, 407N, 463N, 501N, 553N, 579N, 727N
conjunctions, 93M–N, 123M–N
contractions, 339M–N, 531N, 601O–P, 611M–N, 697N
homophones, 611M–N
hyphens, 601N
inflectional endings, 221I–J, 251I–J
italics, using, 199N
negatives and double negatives, 697M–N
nouns, 199M–N, 221M–N, 241M–N, 251M–N, 371M–N, 407M–N, 431M–N, 531N
prepositions/prepositional phrases, 717M–N, 727M–N
  sentence combining with, 727M–N
pronouns, 273M–N, 339N, 531M–N, 553M–N, 579M–N, 601M–N, 611M–N, 613E, 717M, 729E
pronoun-verb agreeement, 579M–N, 729E
punctuation, 43M–N, 65N, 93M–N, 123N, 133N, 199L, 199N, 221N, 241N, 251M–N, 273N, 339M–N, 371N, 381N, 431L, 431N, 463N, 531N, 601N, 601O–P, 611M–N, 717N, 727N
quotations, 123N, 431N
sentences, 43M–N, 65M, 93M–N, 123M–N, 133M–N, 307M–N, 339M–N, 371M–N, 381N, 727M
subject–verb agreement, 307M–N, 339M–N, 371M–N
titles, 199N
verbs, 251I–J, 273M–N, 307M–N, 339M–N, 371M–N, 381M–N, 383E, 503E, 553M–N, 579M–N, 729E

Grandma Essie's Covered Wagon, 310–339

Graphic aids/organizers
  charts, 43H, 65H, 93H, 96, 96, 102, 106, 113, 119, 123C, 123D, 123H, 126B, 126, 128, 135E, 140B, 140C, 140, 165H, 168, 177, 185, 192, 195, 199D, 199N, 202B, 202C, 202, 203, 207, 213, 221H, 221M, 224B, 225, 236, 241H, 241N, 241P, 244, 253E, 258B, 258C, 273D, 273H, 307D, 307H, 307K, 339K, 342B, 371D, 371K, 374, 381F, 381K, 383E, 388B, 388, 389, 407C, 407D, 407F, 410B, 431D, 431L, 431N, 434B, 435, 463D, 463F, 466B, 491D, 494, 496, 503E, 531N, 534, 535, 540, 545, 549, 553N, 556B, 556, 567, 570, 572, 574, 579D, 579F, 601D, 601H, 604B, 604, 611N, 613B, 613E, 618B, 673N, 676B, 697N, 700B, 700, 700C, 708, 713, 717, 717D, 720B, 720, 729E
  cluster map, 93, 123K, 407K, 491K, 531D, 618C
  diagrams, 68C, 117, 126C, 133A, 150, 244C, 276C, 342C, 388C, 407L, 434C, 454, 480, 491K 500/501, 512, 553K, 556C, 567, 582B, 582, 584, 586, 593, 596, 601F, 717A
    Venn, 68C, 117, 126C, 244C, 273L, 276C, 388C, 434C, 454, 512, 553K, 556C, 580/581, 582B, 582, 584, 586, 593, 596, 601F
  Frayer model, 401D, 501D
  graphs, 36, 171, 271, 431L, 590, Unit 6: T60

Scoring Chart

The Scoring Chart is provided for your convenience in grading your students' work.

- Find the column that shows the total number of items.
- Find the row that matches the number of items answered correctly.
- The intersection of the two rows provides the percentage score.

TOTAL NUMBER OF ITEMS

NUMBER CORRECT	1	2	3	4	5	6	7	8	9	10	11	12	13	14	15	16	17	18	19	20	21	22	23	24	25	26	27	28	29	30
1	100	50	33	25	20	17	14	13	11	10	9	8	8	7	7	6	6	6	5	5	5	5	4	4	4	4	4	4	3	3
2		100	66	50	40	33	29	25	22	20	18	17	15	14	13	13	12	11	11	10	10	9	9	8	8	8	7	7	7	7
3			100	75	60	50	43	38	33	30	27	25	23	21	20	19	18	17	16	15	14	14	13	13	12	12	11	11	10	10
4				100	80	67	57	50	44	40	36	33	31	29	27	25	24	22	21	20	19	18	17	17	16	15	15	14	14	13
5					100	83	71	63	56	50	45	42	38	36	33	31	29	28	26	25	24	23	22	21	20	19	19	18	17	17
6						100	86	75	67	60	55	50	46	43	40	38	35	33	32	30	29	27	26	25	24	23	22	21	21	20
7							100	88	78	70	64	58	54	50	47	44	41	39	37	35	33	32	30	29	28	27	26	25	24	23
8								100	89	80	73	67	62	57	53	50	47	44	42	40	38	36	35	33	32	31	30	29	28	27
9									100	90	82	75	69	64	60	56	53	50	47	45	43	41	39	38	36	35	33	32	31	30
10										100	91	83	77	71	67	63	59	56	53	50	48	45	43	42	40	38	37	36	34	33
11											100	92	85	79	73	69	65	61	58	55	52	50	48	46	44	42	41	39	38	37
12												100	92	86	80	75	71	67	63	60	57	55	52	50	48	46	44	43	41	40
13													100	93	87	81	76	72	68	65	62	59	57	54	52	50	48	46	45	43
14														100	93	88	82	78	74	70	67	64	61	58	56	54	52	50	48	47
15															100	94	88	83	79	75	71	68	65	63	60	58	56	54	52	50
16																100	94	89	84	80	76	73	70	67	64	62	59	57	55	53
17																	100	94	89	85	81	77	74	71	68	65	63	61	59	57
18																		100	95	90	86	82	78	75	72	69	67	64	62	60
19																			100	95	90	86	83	79	76	73	70	68	66	63
20																				100	95	91	87	83	80	77	74	71	69	67
21																					100	95	91	88	84	81	78	75	72	70
22																						100	96	92	88	85	81	79	76	73
23																							100	96	92	88	85	82	79	77
24																								100	96	92	89	86	83	80
25																									100	96	93	89	86	83
26																										100	96	93	90	87
27																											100	96	93	90
28																												100	97	93
29																													100	97
30																														100

Writing a Story

Scoring Rubric: 6-Trait Writing

6. Exceptional

- **Ideas & Content** crafts an unusually entertaining, richly-detailed original story about a child who overcomes an obstacle.
- **Organization** unfolds a carefully-planned narrative; sequence moves the reader smoothly through events; engaging beginning, middle and fulfilling conclusion.
- **Voice** shows unusual originality, depth, and a range of emotions that speak directly to the reader.
- **Word Choice** makes skillful, imaginative use of figurative and everyday language; exceptional vocabulary creates memorable pictures, and brings the story to life.
- **Sentence Fluency** crafts fluid simple and complex sentences; dialogue, if used, sounds natural and strengthens the story; may experiment successfully with fragments or other devices.
- **Conventions** shows strong skills in most writing conventions; proper usage enhances clarity, meaning, and narrative style; editing is largely unnecessary.

5. Excellent

- **Ideas & Content** creates a cohesive original story, with extensive details.
- **Organization** unfolds a consistent, well-planned narrative; sequence moves the reader smoothly through events from beginning to ending.
- **Voice** shows originality and a strong personal message that speaks directly to the reader.
- **Word Choice** makes thoughtful, imaginative use of new and every-day words to create clear images of the characters and events.
- **Sentence Fluency** crafts creative, effective sentences that flow with a smooth rhythm; dialogue, if used, sounds natural and enhances the story.
- **Conventions** shows strong skills in a wide range of conventions; correct usage and structure reinforce the story line.

4. Good

- **Ideas & Content** pre-sents a solidly-crafted story, with details that express the main idea.
- **Organization** shows a well-planned narrative strategy; ideas are connected; has a clear beginning and ending.
- **Voice** makes a strong effort to convey an authentic personal message to the reader.
- **Word Choice** shows an overall clarity of expression, and effective control of both new and everyday words.
- **Sentence Fluency** crafts careful, easy-to-follow sentences; may successfully use fragments and/or dialogue to strengthen the story; stronger control of simple sentences.
- **Conventions** may make some errors in spelling, capitalization, punctuation or usage, which do not interfere with under-standing the text; minor editing is needed.

3. Fair

- **Ideas & Content** has some control of crafting a story; may not elaborate clearly, or may lose control of the narrative line.
- **Organization** may not have a clear structure, or may have trouble tying ideas together; reader may be confused by placement of events or details.
- **Voice** may get a basic story across, without a sense of involvement in entertaining a reader.
- **Word Choice** may not explore words that express clear feelings or images for the reader.
- **Sentence Fluency** may have trouble with complex sentences; sentences are under-standable, but may be choppy, rambling, or awkward.
- **Conventions** makes enough noticeable mistakes to interfere with a smooth reading of the story.

2. Poor

- **Ideas & Content** does not successfully tell a story; may present images without a narrative purpose or adequate details.
- **Organization** extreme lack of structure interferes with under-standing the text; no clear story line may be evident.
- **Voice** is not involved in sharing a story with a reader; does not offer anything of personal importance or interest.
- **Word Choice** does not choose words that express clear feelings or pictures; some word choices may detract from understanding the text.
- **Sentence Fluency** constructs incomplete, rambling, or confusing sentences; may show trouble understanding how ideas, words, and sentences fit together.
- **Conventions** makes repeated errors in spelling, word choice, punctuation and usage; few explicit connections are made between ideas.

1. Unsatisfactory

- **Ideas & Content** does not tell a story; writing may go off in several directions, without a sense of purpose.
- **Organization** extreme lack of organization makes the text difficult to follow; there may be no evident structure at all.
- **Voice** does not address a reader, or has no grasp of sharing understand-able feelings and ideas.
- **Word Choice** uses words that do not relate to a story line, or are vague and confusing to the reader.
- **Sentence Fluency** constructs incomplete, rambling, or confusing sentences; text is hard to follow, and to read aloud.
- **Conventions** makes severe errors in most or all conventions, which interfere with readability; some parts of the text may be impossible to understand.

0: This piece is either blank, or fails to respond to the writing task. The topic is not addressed, or the student simply paraphrases the prompt. The response may be illegible or incoherent.

8-Point Writing Rubric

Writing a Story

Scoring Rubric: 8-Trait Writing

8	7	6	5	4	3	2	1
The writer	The writer	The writer	The writer	The writer	The writer	The writer	The writer
• has presented an entertaining story with well-developed characters, clearly described setting(s), and a well-paced plot.	• has developed an imaginative story with strong characters, setting(s), and plot.	• has developed an interesting story with believable characters, setting(s), and plot.	• has met the criteria for a story that includes clearly developed characters, setting(s), and plot.	• has written a story that includes one or two well-developed characters, a setting, and a basic plot line.	• has attempted to write a story with a setting and plot.	• has shown only some understanding of story elements, perhaps by developing one character and a simple plot, but little else.	• shows little or no understanding of story elements.
• consistently uses fluid, realistic dialogue that enhances the meaning of the story.	• often uses dialogue that adds meaning and realism to the story.	• uses expressive dialogue at various points in the story to add authenticity to the piece.	• uses some dialogue that helps to reinforce the meaning of the story.	• uses dialogue that sometimes sounds authentic.	• has created one or two characters with some important details.	• exhibits only a limited grasp of descriptive language.	• uses no descriptive language.
• maintains a tightly focused progression of story events with an inviting beginning and convincing conclusion.	• maintains a clear progression of story events with a strong beginning and conclusion.	• maintains a clear progression of story events with a good beginning and conclusion.	• maintains a logical progression of story events, with only a few minor digressions, and an adequate beginning and conclusion.	• maintains an overall structure, but may include one or two digressions that somewhat distract from understanding the story.	• does not consistently display a logical progression of events. Digressions and lack of focus may be distracting.	• often strays from the main idea, and has difficulty keeping story events in order.	• does not develop a plot or characters.
• creates vivid, well-elaborated descriptions that add clarity and authenticity to the story.	• uses engaging descriptions with meaningful elaborations throughout the story.	• uses a variety of descriptions with elaborative details throughout the story.	• uses a number of solid descriptions in the story.	• develops a good beginning, but an inadequate conclusion.	• uses descriptions that are sparse and lack elaboration.	• shows little sense of audience or narrative voice.	• shows no sense of audience.
• demonstrates an exceptionally strong narrative voice and sense of audience.	• shows a good awareness of audience and a sense of purpose throughout the piece.	• demonstrates a solid awareness of audience and purpose.	• demonstrates some sense of audience and purpose.	• does not consistently develop descriptions with elaborations.	• shows occasional awareness of audience, but a weak narrative voice.		• demonstrates problems with language, including grammar, usage, and mechanics, that seriously impair the reader's understanding.
				• displays intermittent awareness of audience.			

0: This piece is either blank, or fails to respond to the writing task. The topic is not addressed, or the student simply paraphrases the prompt. The response may be illegible or incoherent.